DISSOLUTION

DISSOLUTION

THE CRISIS OF COMMUNISM
AND THE END OF EAST GERMANY

Charles S. Maier

PRINCETON UNIVERSITY PRESS

PRINCETON, NEW JERSEY

Fourth printing, and first paperback printing, 1999

Paperback ISBN 0-691-00746-2

The Library of Congress has cataloged the cloth edition of this book as follows

Maier, Charles S.
Dissolution : The crisis of Communism and the end of
East Germany / Charles S. Maier.
p.   cm.
Includes bibliographical references and index.
ISBN 0-691-07879-3 (cloth : alk. paper)

1. Germany (East)—Politics and government—1989–1990.
2. Communism—Germany (East).   3. Sozialistische Einheitspartei Deutschlands.
4. Germany—History—Unification, 1990.   5. Opposition (Political science)—
Germany (East).   I. Title.
DD289.M34   1997   943.1087′8—dc21   96-39995

This book has been composed in Berkeley with Benguiat Display

The paper used in this publication meets the minimum requirements of
ANSI/NISO Z39.48-1992 (R1997) (*Permanence of Paper*)

http://pup.princeton.edu

Printed in the United States of America

4   6   8   10   9   7   5

FOR PAULINE

No great historical event is better calculated ... to teach political writers and statesmen to be cautious in their speculations; for never was any such event, stemming from factors so far back in the past, so inevitable yet so completely unforeseen. . . . Was the phenomenon in fact so extraordinary as contemporaries supposed? . . . What was its true significance, its real nature, and what were the permanent effects of this strange and terrifying revolution? What exactly did it destroy, and what did it create? I believe that the time has come when these questions can be answered; that today we are in a position to see this memorable event in its true perspective and pass judgment on it. For we now are far enough from the Revolution to be relatively unaffected by the frenzied enthusiasm of those who saw it through; yet near enough to be able to enter into the feelings of its promoters and to see what they were aiming at. Soon it will be difficult to do this; since when great revolutions are successful their causes cease to exist and the very fact of their success has made them incomprehensible.

—Alexis de Tocqueville, *The Old Regime and the French Revolution*

Contents

Preface

THIS book addresses one of the great transformations of our century, the sudden and unexpected fall of communism as a ruling system. As Tocqueville wrote about the French events of 1789, whose bicentennial was being celebrated even as the story told here gathered momentum, rarely was an upheaval so unforeseen. We cannot say so confidently that it was inevitable. Not because it was not, but because at best historians can circumscribe the inquiry into inevitability (What exactly was inevitable? After what date?); they cannot resolve it. Certainly in retrospect there were powerful causes militating for the radical transformation of state socialism. But to what precise degree it must dissolve, by what process it must be transformed, was not foreordained.

This indeterminacy was certainly the case for East Germany. By the late 1980s many observers held it to be a Communist "success story." That it could have remained a stalwart Marxist-Leninist state, however, once the process of perestroika was under way in the Soviet Union seems almost impossible. Still, its collapse could have been less clamorous; it might conceivably have preserved at least a temporary lease on life as a reformed constituent of a German confederation. I do not propose that this would have been a more desirable outcome, only that, as we look back at the remarkable events of 1989–90, we can at best ascribe powerful causes for the disintegration of German communism, but no ineluctable reason that predetermined today's united Germany, and certainly not so rapidly.

This book is thus the history not only of how a governing system disintegrated, but of how a particular Communist state disappeared. Like the Berlin Wall, the German Democratic Republic has now vanished. Its remains are ever more difficult to recapture. For the traveler, the concrete barrier and its graffiti, the watchtowers, lethal border strip, and crossing points that formed the frontier of the socialist world have now become just a vague winding strip of turf beneath the creaky Berlin elevated railroad or running along the curves of the Spree. Soon even that strip will be effaced by new construction. The back streets of provincial towns are still run down, industries have shut, Russian barracks are empty and desolate; the apartment blocks constructed in the past four decades remain bleak. But electronics stores and cafés now line village streets; vast merchandise outlets have been constructed near the Saxon Autobahn. The architectural legacy of past centuries—the brick cathedrals of the Altmark and Mecklenburg and the fretwork houses of Görlitz or Tangermünde, neoclassical villas, even some of the gutted synagogues—now reemerge, authentically revived, sometimes in that never-never land of expectant tourism. "The DDR: Germany's Disneyland," I have seen scrawled on one wall. The history of the interim yesterday needs to be written before preservation of the remoter past takes over.

The twin aspirations of this project—accounting for the crisis of communism and narrating the end of East Germany—have entailed different historiographical agendas. I wanted first just to convey the drama of historic transformation. The popular challenge to a regime that ruled oppressively for so long was, I felt then and still believe now, a great and heartening event. The participants who made their history in 1989 deserved an account that captured the energies, hopes, and anxieties at stake. Whether I have succeeded in this narrative task is up to the reader to decide, but it has remained an objective throughout. At the same time, to account for the collapse of communism—certainly the greatest European political development since the end of the Second World War—has required analyzing elements common to the Soviet bloc as a whole, including its systemic economic crisis, the rulers' loss of conviction, the brief heyday of "forum" democracy, and the international diplomatic framework. Although this is not a work of systematic comparison, I hope that it will encourage readers to think about the former Communist countries as a group. It may also prod some insights about how Western societies function with respect to those in Eastern Europe.

Most centrally, though, this book endeavors to describe the disappearance of a very particular society with a complicated history: small, regimented, seemingly industrious, one of two heirs to a rich, even oppressive cultural legacy. I have had to recover the vanished German Democratic Republic in an almost archaeological way. In many respects it was a repressive little state built on public self-congratulations and pervasive policing. During the years that I passed through the country, from the early 1960s on, I

found it a shabby and sad experience. There was truculence and pettifogging at the frontiers, an overweaning security apparatus within, a dismaying
love for great asphalt spaces, the inculcation of fear as a tool of governance,
the continuing celebration of mediocre achievements at home and of like-
minded authoritarian regimes abroad, the constant projection of militarist
and revanchist threats from the West. On the other hand, some people of
good conscience sought to give their East German fatherland a good-faith
effort. It incorporated for them some generous if deformed aspirations. It is
easy enough to say they were proved wrong, but the task is to understand
why they lent their efforts to the enterprise.

   For all the loyalties and life histories accumulated in forty postwar years,
there was always an elusive element to East Germany. At the very beginning
of the 1960s, the displaced writer Uwe Johnson sought to come to grips with
his foresaken homeland in a novel called *The Third Book about Achim*.
Achim, an athlete and a hero of the German Democratic Republic, turns out
to be curiously insubstantial, less his own man than a creation of his socialist society, courteous but spectral. "The persons are invented," Johnson
conceded. "The events don't relate to similar ones, but to the boundary, the
difference, the remoteness, and the attempt to describe them." The events
analyzed in this history are not invented, but my book too relates to "the
boundary, the difference, the remoteness, and the attempt to describe
them." It seeks to evoke a society whose public institutions were totally
disappearing even as all its inhabitants continued their individual lives.

German and American colleagues, familiar with the many monographs on
the end of the GDR, on Communist societies, on the economic inefficiency
of socialism, on democratic transitions, on dissident intellectuals, have
often asked what new thesis or focus would distinguish my contribution. I
felt naive confessing that I aspired to write a synthetic history rather than
advance a particular approach. My chapters, of course, do embed new argu-
mentation within their narratives: in the first I seek to cast a new light on the
difficult issues of legitimacy and consent, of the nature of private and public
spheres under late communism. In the second, I propose a reconstruction
of Communist economic difficulties that is different in part from what other
writers have provided. In the third chapter I analyze contending discourses
of protest along lines that I have not encountered elsewhere. And throughout the work, I have, in fact, emphasized one major argument. It is that the
East Germans, when they came to act collectively, had a decisive impact on
their own history. This despite the low level of prior opposition and dissent.

West German colleagues have talked of an "implosion" of East Germany as if some worn-out machine finally just broke down. Some of them, who believed that the division of their country could never be overcome, now explain why the dissolution of East Germany was so logical and even inevitable. What I hope emerges from my account is that at each critical juncture, the East Germans' collective action—no matter how hesitant at first, and how filled with doubts later—impelled decisive accommodations or allowed new initiatives. I am not claiming heroism; but I am defending agency. Before 1989, East Germans were not distinguished for their dissidence or resistance, and since unification some have shown what even sympathetic West Germans have described as a dismaying sense of inferiority: the feeling they need to be colonized. I do not want to romanticize the great demonstrations of 1989. Neither do I want to claim that episodic collective action implies a coherent collective actor. Michelet's *peuple* remain too romantic a construction to be my kind of *Volk*. But by repeatedly managing to claim public space against the will of their regime, East German protesters provoked a crisis of governance and set in motion the greater powers around them. States and organized interest groups are not the only actors that matter. Urban squares remain the site of decisive contests.

Because a seemingly authoritarian and immobile system collapsed with such rapidity throughout Eastern Europe, the events treated in this book frankly disconcerted many social scientists and historians. Some claimed that the stunning surprises of 1989 proved that all history was characterized by events and ruptures (the stuff of Braudel's *histoire événementielle*) and that sociopolitical trends or "structures" (the refractory patterns that persist over Braudel's *longue durée*) were illusory. This was a hasty conclusion. Like fractals, historical sequences reveal both recurring patterns and infinite discontinuities at every level of scrutiny. Historians who focus on discontinuity usually emphasize elements of choice, spontaneity, and, most problematically, contingency. Others feel that to make sense of events, or just the actors' perception of events, requires uncovering persisting societal pressures less affected by individual or even collective will. This account tries to combine both approaches.

Collective action, such as the mass protests in Leipzig and Berlin, can be celebrated for its spontaneity. Even more encouraging, it can be appreciated for the willingness of participants to act on beliefs and values that were long subject to state sanctions. The year 1989 helped revive the historian's faith in the importance of choice—hence the need to represent commitment, action, and event. Political action, however, must simultaneously be understood as an outcome of continuing pressures. To analyze these long-term influences—economic impasses, corruption and privilege, the loss of confidence on the part of a ruling elite—is not to deny the strategic intervention of individuals or the dramatic impact of "spontaneous" mass demonstrations. But a reading of the events of 1989 still suggests (and not just in a trivial tautological sense) that political action in its own right first beckons and then certainly succeeds only when long-term conditions permit. Conversely, the same events reveal that political activity, at least if pursued with stamina and persistence, helps shape in turn the causal environment critical to its own success. The year 1989 confirms that historical analysis must rely continuously on working out this reciprocal interaction.

The drama of 1989 awoke many of us from a weary fixation with constraint. But it did not remove the historian's need to present the web of institutions that structured choice. The *longue* or *moyenne durée* in which postwar communism was situated certainly needed a revised analysis, but as a category of historical explanation, it did not simply disappear. I have tried to organize this book to show how long-term pressures, on the one hand, and conscious choices, on the other, interacted precisely because the events of 1989 established so compelling a case for the power of both. Of course, people are always making choices. The East Germans who did not contest their condition before 1989 made choices as well. But we observers were privileged in 1989 to watch them make new and unexpected choices, to opt for self-determination and not further acquiescence. Speaking personally, since much of my work as a twentieth-century historian has involved examining the pressures that lead to choices for submission, it has been exhilarating to focus this time on choices for freedom.

When I began this project in the winter of 1989–90, I was uncertain whether a history was even possible for momentous events still unfolding. I took on the task because we historians do not often have the chance to witness the rapid transition from one regime to another and one international structure to a different one. For one who had followed the cold war, international relations, the European political economy, and the development of Germany as a professional concern for almost three decades, not to have applied the historian's craft would have been a major renunciation. Moreover, history is always being written anew. The preoccupations that dictate questions change from one generation to the next. Source bases are in constant flux. A wider range of testimony continually opens up, even as some documentation (or human memories) is extinguished. No historian ever reaches a land that is forever firm. All history is provisional.

In the meantime, however, this history was able to become somewhat less provisional. I am confident that a serious if not a final history of the transformations in Germany is possible. Above all, the state and ruling party archives—and not just the controversial Stasi records, but transcripts of policy debates in the Politbüro and Central Committee, proposals from the Planning Commission and economic agencies, and other revealing correspondence—are available until the very end of the East German regime. Because of the pressure of the *Bürgerbewegungen* or "citizens movements" (the general term for those who took the protests of 1989 in hand), the archival authorities have not imposed the normal thirty-year rule that limits access to most government holdings elsewhere, including the preunification ministries of the former West Germany.[1] (This availability does not pertain to the records of the East German Foreign Ministry, whose records have been taken over by united Germany's Foreign Office.) I have been among the early researchers, and in a few cases probably one of the very first, to work through many of these papers, which are still being reorganized.

Many sources have now been published. Members of the citizens movements and their successors (including the so-called Gauck authority for evaluating and making available the Ministry of State Security records) have published rich selections of documents. These include not merely the notorious reports on individuals but evaluations of social and economic conditions routinely submitted to the Politbüro. Hundreds of individual testimonies about the events of October and November 1989 have been collected and edited.

I have also drawn on personal observations and conversations during the period of transition. These discussions have, however, presented a particular hazard. Some inhabitants of the former GDR recalled their past socialist commitment with incisive self-criticism, some with abashed detachment, others

---

[1] Throughout this book I use GDR (German Democratic Republic) and East Germany as equivalent terms; citations to original sources often use DDR (Deutsche Demokratische Republik). "The new Bundesländer" refers to the former East Germany, now part of united Germany. I use the English abbreviation FRG, or West Germany, or Bundesrepublik, for the preunification Federal Republic of Germany, with its capital in Bonn. And I refer simply to Germany or united Germany—now sometimes called the Berlin Republic—for the postunification state, which remains officially the Federal Republic of Germany (Bundesrepublik Deutschland).

with disorientation. Many, it was evident from conversation and writing, took refuge in the melancholy that the end of East Germany bequeathed. They tended to conflate their experience of their vanished republic with the bittersweet memories they endeavored or still endeavor to maintain. They constructed a history that in some cases nurtured their nostalgia. I have sought to convey that melancholy, which is important to grasp, without being captured by it. This is doubly important since I am trying to assess the troubled aftermath of unification in which these sentiments have played a critical role. I have also sought to go beyond subjectivity by analyzing economic processes, international transformations, and political interactions that destroyed the old system and thereafter brought about unification.

From the start of this project I have benefited from strategic assistance. I am happy to acknowledge a great debt to the staff of the Goethe Institute in Boston, our local branch of the Federal Republic's major cultural centers abroad, for helping me follow a far wider range of coverage than I could do on my own during a crowded teaching year. I have been privileged to have a superb cohort of former and present students who kept intellectually abreast of the East German transformation. Anjana Shrivastava, now living in Berlin, assisted me early on in sorting through the press. Catherine Epstein has accumulated and shared a vast knowledge of who was who in the GDR. I have profited especially from continued dialogue with my former student John Connelly, now teaching at the University of California in Berkeley, who has shared his extraordinary comparative knowledge of East Germany and Eastern Europe. He regarded me as his teacher, but the relation was often reversed. Most recently, David Meskill helped me work through the final manuscript version, and Andrew Port provided invaluable scrutiny of the page proofs.

My own academic home in Cambridge, the Minda De Gunzburg Center for European Studies, has had a remarkable series of periodic seminars and reports on East European and German events and I have benefited from the stream of visitors. John Torpey, who was a James C. Conant postdoctoral fellowship holder at the Center during 1992–93, and Jeffrey Kopstein, a fellow in 1995–96, proved stimulating fellow researchers of the GDR. My long-term colleagues there—above all Abby Collins, Guido Goldman, and Stanley Hoffmann—have provided encouragement throughout. The Program for the Study of Germany and Europe, funded by the German government on the initiative of Chancellor Kohl and Werner Weidenfeld, has helped the Center to have conferences on the issues of economic reorganization, the role of women, and the reform of the university system. It also provided funding for two summer research trips. I have had opportunities to visit West and especially East Germany frequently since March 1990. In the early visits during March, July, and December 1990 and spring 1992, conversations with activists and academics were extremely useful, as were attendance at various public meetings such as the next-to-last Round Table discussions in East Berlin (facilitated by television correspondent Michael Schmitz), a church-sponsored evening with intellectuals, or meetings between church and economic leaders. Many intellectuals in East Germany who were leaders in criticizing the old system remain uneasy about what has emerged. I have not shared the depth of their misgivings, nor has the East German electorate. Nonetheless they are important as an intellectual current, and I have tried to take account of their assessments.

By 1993 the archives were beginning to open and have continued to make available more holdings, and I am grateful to the archivists at the former Deutsches Staatsarchiv in Potsdam (with special collections also dispersed elsewhere), which became a branch of the Bundesarchiv after 1990. I am also happy to acknowledge the friendly cooperation of the archivists of the Bundesarchiv Stiftung für die Parteien und Massenorganisationen der DDR, whose holdings originated with the former Institut für Marxismus-Leninismus, were then reorganized as the PDS party archive in East Berlin, and have now been moved to West Berlin quarters in Lichterfelde. Elena Danielson of the Hoover Institution facilitated my consultation by mail of some of the GDR oral history interviews that James McAdams has helped collect.

My work was immensely facilitated by collaboration with the Forschungsschwerpunkt Zeithistorische Studien in Potsdam, a research institute that includes West Germans and former members of the DDR Academy of Sciences. Jürgen Kocka, Christoph Kleßmann, and Konrad Jarausch have supervised this unique center, supported originally by the Max Planck Gesellschaft and now, as the Zentrum für Zeithistorische Forschung Potsdam, by the Deutsche Forschungsgemeinschaft and state government of Brandenburg. I have had the chance for scholarly residence, participation in some of its conferences, and have served on its board of scholarly advisers. By virtue of long and friendly colleagueship Jarausch and Kocka have provided encouragement and insight.

I am happy to acknowledge numerous discussions with political activists (Jens Reich, Bärbel Bohley, Friedrich Schorlemmer, Richard Schröder, and others) and some political leaders, including the opportunity to hear Chancellor Kohl at the Center for European Studies, Lothar de Maizière during the March 1990 electoral campaign in East Berlin, and Kurt Biedenkopf in Saxony reflect frankly on the transformations under way. Egon Krenz offered some retrospective ruminations after we both put in our day at the archives. Colleagues and fellow historians at Berlin, Leipzig, and Potsdam have provided their insights. Where appropriate, specific discussions will be cited, but I am not documenting the interviews in their own right. As a scholar venturing into new territory I have drawn gratefully on the work of those who followed the regime and society far more closely and constantly than I have. Among those with whom I've been able to exchange ideas personally over the past years: Konrad Jarausch, Christiane Lemke, Norman Naimark, Lutz Niethammer, and Hartmut Zwahr. Other authorities whom I have read with special profit include Timothy Garton Ash, who has conveyed the aspirations of all those West and East who sought to knit together the halves of their continent in liberty, and, for the diplomatic aspects of unification, Philip Zelikow and Condoleezza Rice. Mary Fulbrook's well-informed *Anatomy of a Dictatorship* appeared as I was revising my chapters; otherwise her expertise might have been acknowledged at many points. Many other helpful works are cited here. Too many friends, students, and colleagues have taken the trouble to read parts of this manuscript to name them all, but especially thoughtful comments were provided by Konrad Jarausch, Jürgen Kocka, Anne Sa'adah, professor of politics at Dartmouth and author of a forthcoming work on political justice since 1989, Philip Zelikow, and Pauline Maier. Walter Lippincott of Princeton University Press merits a final thanks, first for having proposed at the end of 1989 that I write a quick book on the upheaval under way and then for his patience as the work, I hope, deepened, but in any case slowed.

As my epilogue suggests, I think that for all its difficulties, the process of German unification has started "to take." Economic restructuring has been costly and painful and will remain incomplete for a long time; the university system might have been reorganized more innovatively; establishing legal responsibility for past abuses has been especially agonizing. With respect to the mutual alienation that is still rife, it has been fashionable to talk about the "wall in the head." But as of the mid-1990s, I believe that there is less obsessiveness about the juxtaposition of East and West; the unification agenda has evolved—Germans, to use the cliché, have moved on. Pollsters discover nostalgia for the old GDR, but no widespread desire to undo the results of 1990; and nostalgia is easy to indulge in when it is deprived of consequence. The relative success of the so-called Party of Democratic Socialism, the offspring of the Communist SED, rests on the grievances of displaced "Ossies": the PDS is a vehicle for former cadres and those annoyed by the intrusive success of West Germans; it is not an ideological vanguard.

Social scientists, I have argued elsewhere, are not at fault for failing to predict the upheaval of 1989, but they should have foreseen that the economic and spiritual difficulties of exiting from communism would be profound and persistent.[2] Throughout Eastern Europe many disappointments have followed upon the uplifting experience of 1989: the civic movements have splintered; electorates have returned in part to old, slightly refurbished Communist leaders, and, most troublingly, there has been a resurgence of ethnic conflict and prejudice. Some similar trends have gripped Western countries as well. Nonetheless I still believe that what took place at the end of the 1980s was a wonderful series of events. As a citizen of the United States, I was proud then that the values which my country has represented—at least in its best moments—proved so contagious. Discovering anew, through East German and East European courage, the attractiveness of America's own founding principles makes it appropriate to dedicate this book to my wife, Pauline, who has continually studied their emergence as well as the forms of early American political protest. It is especially fitting since through her historical research I have learned about the formation of those liberating ideas which proved so powerful in 1989 and will hopefully retain their attraction.

Cambridge, February 1996

---

[2] Charles S. Maier, "Wissenschaft und Wende. Grenze der Prognosefähigkeit," lecture to the Deutsche Vereinigung für Politische Wissenschaft, Potsdam, August 1994, now published in the volume of proceedings: *Einigung und Zerfall. Deutschland und Europa nach dem Ende des Ost-West-Konfliktes. 19. Wissenschaftlicher Kongreß der Deutschen Vereinigung für Politische Wissenschaft*, ed. Gerhard Lehmbruch (Opladen: Leske & Budrich, 1995), pp. 315–325.

DISSOLUTION

One

Losing Faith

LANCELOT: It is all very difficult, Kay. When one chases after an idea for years and years, without getting the tiniest step closer, it's very depressing. Each of us has only a brief life to dispose of, and each of us puts too many hopes in this vulnerable and all-too-quickly extinguished life. More than it can bear.

KAY: What do you mean by that, Lancelot? Do you still believe in the grail?

LANCELOT: I don't know. I can't answer the question. I can't say yes or no. . . .

ARTHUR: Lancelot, Kay: be quiet. Everything that men create suddenly comes into question, everything, every idea, every invention, every human institution. What appears sure and certain is suddenly very doubtful. But that is frightening only for an instant and in fact it will help us to get further along. It is not only an end, it's the beginning of something new; I foresaw it when I founded the realm. . . .

LANCELOT: Arthur, do you know that the people outside don't want to hear any more about the grail and the round table? Before, they respected us. . . today they only laugh if they see a knight of the round table. . . . They no longer believe in our justice and our dream. . . . For the people the knights of the round table are a pile of fools, idiots and criminals. . . .

—Christoph Hein, *The Knights of the Round Table*

BELIEVERS AND VICTIMS

Hein's play was written for production in early 1989, as the East German Politbüro buckled down to resist the winds of reform blowing through Eastern Europe. In Hein's "comedy" of disillusion, Arthur's aging knights include remaining true believers, exhausted former believers, the defector to "Merveille," that is the Federal Republic—and, outside their circle, the son and heir for whom the king's original faith was always irrelevant. Half-way through the play, the knights admit they may never find the grail. Still, Arthur endeavors to explain, it is not the grail but the quest that is essential: "If we give up on the grail, we give up on ourselves. . . . We've lost the ground under our feet and we are in danger of sinking."

When did Arthur's round table finally fall to pieces? After September 10, 1989, when the Hungarian Communist regime opened its border to Austria, thus allowing vacationing East Germans to make a detour into the West behind their own sealed frontier? On October 9, 1989, when Leipzig authorities refused to turn the factory militias and armored vehicles against the crowds? A month later, on November 9, the seventy-first anniversary of the revolution that brought down the Wilhelmian Empire, when the wall was opened, and hundreds of thousands streamed into West Berlin? In retrospect, the observer can point to earlier indications of inner transformation: mounting dependence on Western credits to prop up a vulnerable economy; an independent peace movement since the early 1980s; a growing space for careful dissent; the assurance from academics one met at conferences that they were abandoning the ritual texts of Marxism and exploring the new lines of inquiry being opened in the West; the reevaluation of a German national tradition; a radically disaffected samizdat poetry in Prenzlauer Berg, the raffish Greenwich Village quarter of East Berlin; an encroaching tone of disaffected irony in literature—all testifying to the erosion of socialist conviction, to Lancelot's weariness and Arthur's fecklessness, undermining what along with Czechoslovakia, Romania, and Albania was the last European bastion of the Marxist faith.

To whom had the grail originally beckoned? What mixture of belief and force had allowed the regime to function for four decades? Certainly it required the presence of Soviet occupiers. But the system depended on more than constraint. It was based on graduated levels of commitment or at least acceptance, which of course overlapped and were fluid: a tested, steely faith from those who formed the preexisting, "old Communist" core of the ruling party; enthusiasm and hope on the part of postwar cadres; active collaboration on the part of many others, either resigned and cynical or in good faith, within the party or in a tolerated public organization; and finally acquiescence from the rest.

First on the morrow of the Second World War, thereafter at each moment when more demanding compliance was imposed, there were always non-Communists who cooperated with those who ruled the state. Why? Some were demoralized by twelve years of National Socialist brutality and did not believe they really had a choice. Some convinced themselves that the West German alternative remained a class society riddled with social injustice and was controlled by those who had worked hand in hand with the Nazis. Some consoled themselves with the persistent illusion that from within the multiparty "block," or even within the dominant "Socialist Unity" Party (SED), they might push for reforms. The incantory reassurance of "anti-fascism" and "peace," the self-importance generated by being recruited to sign an open letter or contribute a credo, the glow of virtuous companion-ship aroused at mass meetings, the discovery that an appropriate citation from Lenin got one's articles circulated—all worked for an ambience of collaboration. Later those who thus paid their dues might point to the ac-complishments of socialism: expropriation of Junker estates, reconstruc-tion, or broader access to education. Establishing the postwar Communist world certainly required Soviet force, but until the myth lost the last shreds of its sustaining force in the 1980s, it also rested on the capacity for rational-ization. "Nothing is more inexplicable than an enthusiasm that has disap-peared," the journalist Carola Stern has written in a dual memoir of her own National Socialist adolescence and the Communist resistance activities of her later companion, Heinz Zöger:

> She too belonged to those children of the twentieth century, who, having come of age in the middle of the totalitarian movements of its first half, seduced by ideologies and ideologues, came to thirst for belief; who having been weaned from their own thinking allowed others to think and decide for them. "Chil-dren"—carried away by frightful and beautiful plans for transforming the world, aware of themselves as belonging to an elite and simultaneously fascinated by being part of a community, a member of a collectivity. Encased humans, deprived by a mesh of dogma and rigid structures, cynical or helpless and desperate. Such children of the century will need the rest of their lives to work through their "childhood."[1]

Before condemning those who in the devastated cities of East Germany wagered on making the best of a difficult situation, we should recall the Western intellectuals who convinced themselves into supporting the same politics with far fewer external pressures. Nor were opportunism and poor judgment the only persuaders in the East. Periodic purges played their part. Unless they are caught up before a judge or investigating committee, Amer-icans forget how destructive of ego, how designed to abase and unnerve, can be the inquisitorial experience. The humiliation of being dressed down and ostracized by former friends and colleagues; the demands for a cringing self-criticism of a stance that once was held with righteous passion; dismissal from jobs or honorific positions; outright prosecution as a betrayer of party and state—all the resources of political conformity were available to discipline any faltering of the faith. "Do you not realize," so the East Berlin SED secretary for culture would lash out at protesters against the expulsion of dissident Wolf Biermann, as late as 1976, "that your attitude was politically wrong and has harmed everything that you should hold dear and beloved? . . . Do you still maintain that other values are higher than party discipline?" Let the dissenter recant or exclude himself![2] The threat of denunciation by the party hack inserted into one's editorial board or faculty department or professional union, the party's control of travel opportunities or the education available for oneself or children, reinforced acquiescence, if not enthusiasm.

Occasionally a critical voice would express sardonic amazement at how repressive the whole system quickly became. Bertolt Brecht, who had chosen to return to East Germany, mocked the regime for losing confidence in its people after the uprising of June 17, 1953. (At the same time he wrote privately to his friend, Minister for Culture Johannes R. Becher, to condemn the demonstrators.) Twenty-three years later Reiner Kunze's *The Fabulous Years* conveyed the petty absurdities and search for conformity with a collection of revealing anecdotes. They resulted in his expulsion from the Writers' League.[3] The fact that those subject to such discipline could always see their kin and former compatriots, co-heirs of a common culture and language living rich and free next door, only made the system more galling. I remember an East German friend—a historian, not made for outright defiance, but never able to kow-tow sufficiently for real promotion—telling me before East Berlin's "Red City Hall" (named for its brick, not its politics) in the mid-1970s, when West German students were still contesting the supposed repressiveness of the Bonn regime: "If they had to live here, they would walk on their knees to get to West Berlin." By the end only the East German leadership persisted in affirming the ideology gone stale; and the Soviet authorities who had sustained them in power found them tiresome.

In the beginning there had been rubble and the first stirrings of scattered opponents of Nazism emerging from an enforced silence, released from concentration camps, or returning from refuges abroad. They included the religiously motivated, former trade unionists, conservative civil servants— and Communists. Even before Hitler came to power, it had required (so members saw it) unremitting discipline to persevere as a Communist. To participate at the cutting edge of history demanded subjection to the party's historically achieved insights. It required understanding that social democracy was a betrayal of class interest as retrograde as fascist thuggery; it meant realizing that Stalin's position let him see with more acute penetration than any other political leader. These tenacious beliefs had given hundreds the courage to maintain a fragmented clandestine resistance for several years after Hitler quickly outlawed their party and arrested their leaders. Some survived the brutality of concentration camps or, like the young Erich Honecker, spent oppressive years in Brandenburg, Plötzensee, and other prisons where guillotining became routine. There were émigrés returning from sojourns in New York or Mexico. Finally, there was the phalanx of German Communists suddenly flown home from their long years in Soviet exile. They had been hermetically sealed in the corridors of Moscow's Hotel Lux, had survived the lethal twists and turns of Stalin's purges, and understood the prewar and wartime agonies of the vast country he ruled only from whispers and stilted coversations. They were almost taken aback that now under Russian military supervision the moment had come to transform German society.[4]

Some local Social Democrats and Communists in East and West Germany—their feuds suspended by common persecution—exploited the brief weeks of the Nazi collapse to establish "Antifa" committees to manage factories, administer towns, and organize social services. Their wildcat local socialism offended each of the occupying powers, who quickly dissolved them.[5] Despite other differences, the Allied leaders and their proconsuls agreed on an orderly dismantling of the Reich, close supervision of the resumption of political life, and a distrust of independent initiatives as harbingers of nationalist revival. Among the non-Nazi political spokesmen acceptable to the occupying authorities (in this respect the four powers were in agreement) were Social Democrats, former Catholic Center leaders, and the Weimar liberals whose parties had collapsed so disastrously by the end of the 1920s. Communists had few indigenous roots in the United States zone of occupation, and although they might have prospered in the industrial regions assigned to the British, London's military and civilian authorities deeply distrusted them and encouraged their Social Democratic rivals. That left them under Russian sponsorship in the eastern zone and in Berlin where power was shared.

After the German surrender, Soviet policy (like that of the United States) remained in some flux through 1945, the top leadership uncertain about the rewards for interallied cooperation, unresolved about the risks of imposing outright domination over its own zone. As in the West, a welter of authorities contended for influence in German affairs: the Foreign Ministry, the Council of Ministers special committee on Germany and its plenipotentiaries in Germany, the military, and the occupation forces. Several priorities would remain central. A recovered Germany must not be able to gang up with the Western powers in any anti-Soviet alignment. There must be final, not just provisional four-power acceptance of the Oder-Neisse frontier between Germany and Poland. Economic objectives must be secured: in the short term, exploit the productive resources of Germany through factory removals, over the long run win a reparations agreement that secured continuing industrial and raw material deliveries—including the Wismut uranium ore from the Erzgebirge or Ore Mountains.[6]

How these objectives were to be attained over the long haul was subject to debate and strategic modification. Soviet policy at the Potsdam Conference envisaged the eventual reemergence of a unified but hopefully compliant Germany. Through 1947 and 1948 Soviet objectives remained complex but consistent. It was doubtful that the British and Americans would allow outright Communist control of the whole country; but a recovered Germany must never join an anti-Soviet coalition or challenge the Oder-Neisse frontier settlement. Communist Party participation in a governing coalition would guarantee this cooperation just as the Soviets hoped that party collaboration in the French and Italian postwar governments would keep these states from any anti-Soviet alignment. Indeed, if the Allies did not back down on their commitment to reestablish a united centralized government, Soviet pressure might even wrest a more preponderant role for its German Communists, much as Moscow increasingly strove for from 1945 through 1947–48 in all the countries of Eastern Europe.[7]

But there was a basic contradiction inherent in Moscow's policies. Soviet control of Eastern Germany was supposed to be the bargaining chip that secured their clients' voice in reunited Germany. Instead Soviet control became so oppressive that by 1947 it dissuaded the West from unification on terms the Russians were offering. With an eye toward a Communist leverage throughout the country as a whole, the Soviet occupying authorities worked to construct in the territory they controlled a single party front that grouped all the non-Nazi groups with a key role for the German Communists. But this very policy soon confirmed Anglo-American distrust of Russian intentions and led the Western powers to insist on a decentralized all-German government and ultimately to reject the Soviet terms for unifying a German administration.[8]

The key to Soviet formation of a single party front was absorption of the East German Social Democrats. The old SPD (Sozialdemokratische Partei Deutschlands) had resisted Hitler courageously, even though its economic policies during the Depression had remained unimaginative and its leadership preoccupied by organizational concerns. All four victorious powers recognized that the SPD had a moral right to a share of postwar leadership. But would the SPD cooperate with the Communists, who during the crisis of Weimar had bitterly denounced the reformist party? In Western Germany, where the Communists were feeble and the Allies distrusted them as well, the Social Democratic answer was clearly no. But in the Soviet zone, as elsewhere in Eastern Europe, where all organizational rights depended on the approval of Russian military authorities, the balance of power was reversed.

By February 1946, Berlin SPD leader Otto Grotewohl decided that he had to accede to the pressure from Soviets and Communists and take his rank and file into a new unified Marxist coalition, the Sozialistische Einheitspartei or SED, which was to become the ruling party until the end of 1989. An "iron curtain" had descended for good over the Soviet zone, Grotewohl explained to British officials in Berlin; there were no choices left.[9] Was his distress genuine? His speeches in the aftermath of fusion were devoid of any distance: he became an enthusiastic spokesman for Marxist reunification, celebrated Soviet policy, and was elevated as head of government when the GDR was granted national status in 1949. The new SED grouped the ideologically determined Communists and those Social Democrats who either cynically accepted their subordination or hoped at least to preserve some freedom of action and keep options open from within. After all, Hitler had come to power—so the European Left believed after 1933 through the early postwar years—precisely because the two great currents of Marxism had quarreled between themselves. The political unity of the working class imposed itself as a commandment.[10]

For Russian officials, who had survived first the cruel and capricious tests of Stalinist purges and then participated in a massive war effort, security in Germany could only mean control. If Communists were a minority, then their political resources must be leveraged. The new SED was a marvelous instrument for this end, and it in turn dominated a "unity front of anti-fascist-democratic parties"—Liberal Democrats, Christian Democrats, Peasants' League, and the National Democratic Party of Germany—whose cooperation with the SED as the so-called block parties would endure until December 1989. The original goal of the SED and its Soviet sponsors, however, was not merely to rule a separate German state. They aspired at least to parity if not preponderance within a unified Germany. By 1947, however, the impetus of the cold war conflict (in good part arising out of the very policies of communization in Poland, Romania, and Hungary!) made agreement on a single German state ever more remote. Mutual recriminations over the progressive breakdown of the complicated reparations arrangements also seemed unbridgeable. Neither side was willing finally to make the accommodations demanded by the other at the Moscow Foreign Ministers Conference in April 1947. With the announcement of the Marshall Plan six weeks later, and the exclusion of the Communists from postwar coalitions in Belgium, France, and Italy during these very months, jockeying over the German future also became intense.

In Western Germany a British-American bizonal economic organization placed Germans in administrative positions and provided for an embryonic parliament. Reconstruction of government within nine western federal states enlarged the role of the postwar parties: the independent SPD of the Western zones, the Christian Democratic Union (CDU), the smaller Liberal Democrats (who in the West became the Free Democratic Party), and other political fragments, some nationalist, some refugee oriented. In the Soviet zone, consolidation of the ruling party and construction of a new East German regime would procede in tandem. Within the SED, the Communist nuclei, led by Moscow trainees and reinforced by the factory cells that had struggled to continue clandestine work during the Third Reich, quickly subordinated the Social Democrats who had been persuaded to join. The wider "block" of collaborating parties was also brought to heel, as they were pressured to oust conservative and nationalist members who urged more independence from the Soviet Union or who objected to final recognition of the Oder-Neisse border. As late as October 1989, however, representatives of the smaller parties still defended their long collaboration with the SED, for reasons of history, as the Liberal Democratic leader said, "and from knowledge of the general laws of development of human society."[11]

Despite their subjection of independent political currents in the late 1940s, the Soviets' goals seem to have remained unresolved through most of 1947. Major differences still existed within the Moscow leadership over how to respond to increasing anticommunism in the West. During 1947, German representatives in all the occupied zones still had to learn that unification was not to take place. West German and East German CDU organizations worked together and hoped for a "national representation" but found their proposals vetoed by the Allied Control Council. In October,

West European Communist leaders were instructed by the Soviets that in light of the recent Marshall Plan initiatives and the exclusion of Communists from Western coalitions, a new era of confrontation with capitalism was at hand. The Soviets established a new Cominform to coordinate Communist parties East and West and to replace the earlier Comintern, which had been dissolved to facilitate the wartime coalition.

Moscow, however, did not immediately foreclose all alternative policies for Germany: a new Foreign Ministers Conference was to convene on Germany at London in late 1947; the SED was not yet enrolled as a Cominform party. Ostensibly to petition the four powers, the SED organized a massive "Volkskongress" in early December on behalf of unity and a "just peace." More than a quarter of the two thousand delegates traveled from the West, only to return disillusioned by the blatant pressure to endorse the "block" policies of the East. For Jacob Kaiser, Berlin trade-union leader of the Christian Democrats, the Congress was rigged, and it signaled the end of any autonomous CDU in the East. The staged convention called for national unity even as the London Foreign Ministers Conference confirmed the rupture among the four allies over the German issue. The Western powers prohibited the movement on behalf of the People's Congress from continuing in their zones, but as a would-be national forum and a propaganda device in the East, the institution served Soviet purposes. Developments in the Soviet zone might in fact preclude interallied agreement, but the Congress meanwhile claimed to be a popular movement that wanted with Soviet sponsorship to recreate national unity from the base up. A second People's Congress in March 1948 revealed an even more dominant SED presence, and now moved to elect a German People's Council, of whom one-third still claimed to represent the West.

This new Volksrat again urged German unification even as the Western allies were preparing the currency reform of June 1948, and the hitherto recalcitrant French joined their zone with the British and Americans. In response to the Western initiatives, the Soviet delegate had walked out of the Allied Control Commission in March: there was to be no further effort at unified administration. Currency reform in June, the Russians' blockade of land routes to West Berlin, and the drafting of a constitution for the Western zones under the auspices of the British, French, and Americans followed in rapid succession.

As Allied authorities and *Land* representatives moved to establish a provisional West German state, the East German SED continued to impose the Cominform model of Communist control. The emerging pattern included central economic planning, a "people's democracy" with its suppression of effective opposition, and, by 1950, the molding of adherents in factories or ministries or faculties into "a party of a new type." Stalin's ideological bulldog, Andrei Zhdanov, had laid down the law in September 1947, and in February 1948, the Communists took control of the Czech government from a tolerant, alas at times ingenuous coalition regime. The seizure of power in Prague and Washington's now decisive responses in terms of foreign aid and West German rehabilitation effectively consolidated the division of Europe into two spheres. Still, it was Marshall Tito's rejection of Soviet control over his undoubtedly Communist state later in 1948 that catalyzed an even more ruthless repression throughout Eastern Europe. Dissent among Communists always represented the most devious conspiratorial challenge in Stalin's eyes. His dark suspicions could only be echoed by henchmen such as Zhdanov, Molotov, and Beria, who had achieved their prominence by faithful loyalty during the frightful purges and wartime reverses. Tito's challenge unleashed a convulsive series of denunciations, party purges, and rigged trials. Although the SED was not yet a Cominform party, German Communists responded to the encroaching demands for conformity. At the SED executive's session of September 1948, convened as the Yugoslav insurrection was intensifying, SED leaders shelved their earlier concept of a specific German road to socialism. The Leninist and Stalinist model of Communist transformation was henceforth to dictate the policies and organization of the Socialist Unity Party. Grotewohl himself demanded so "unambiguous and unreserved an orientation to the East" that Stalin allegedly told him to slow down: "you German communists, like your ancestors, are Teutons."[12] Nonetheless, Teutonic discipline tightened further. As a "party of the new type" the SED was to be controlled by its cadres; Stalin's *Short History of the CPSU* and his interpretation of Leninism became the holy texts; the emphasis of organizational work switched to the factory where the Communists, not former Social Democrats, were strong. In subsequent meetings of the party executive (Vorstand), a Politbüro and a Zentralkomitee (ZK) were established to consolidate control. Wilhelm Pieck and Otto Grotewohl remained joint chairmen, but the dour organizational adept, Walter Ulbricht, took over as general secretary of the ZK.[13]

For an interval in 1990, the former ZK building—drab and gray labyrinth originally constructed for the Reichsbank—served as the "Parliamentarians' House." It provided office space for the transitional, freely elected Volkskammer of the vanishing GDR, and is slated now to house the Foreign

Ministry. Its facade faces obliquely across the vast Marx-Engels-Platz (for whose inspiring asphalt acreage the East Germans razed the baroque royal palace), to one of the most glorious remaining architectural legacies of Berlin: Schinkel's neoclassical "Old Museum." Even closer is Schinkel's sober neo-Gothic Friedrichswerdersche Church, a testimonial to the loving restoration work that the regime found congenial for its historical claims by the 1970s and 1980s. Within the ZK's parallel wings, long drab corridors with office after office testify (even after the portraits of Honecker were unceremoniously removed) to the mass of bureaucratic control that the apparatus eventually took in hand. Even from more compact quarters at the beginning of its long domination, the ZK supervised the transition to a satellite.

A satellite, but no longer merely a zone. With the establishment of a West German state in 1949, the Russians adopted the counterstrategy of giving statehood to their own area of control. The People's Council, emanating from the Second People's Congress, worked out a constitution. Soviet-style constitutions were always formally democratic, and the new East German charter incorporated many of the innovations that the West German Basic Law also featured, including limitations on no-confidence motions and restrictions on the office of president. But the electoral system ensured that the people's choice would be safely controlled. Open, competitive elections for state and local offices had registered embarrassing results in the first postwar balloting in October 1946. Although the SED won 47.5 percent of the votes in the five safely controlled *Länder* of the Soviet zone, in the all-Berlin elections—held under interallied ground rules and featuring an independent SPD list—the Unity Party attracted only about a fifth of the votes. The system was amended for the Third People's Congress in 1949, when a single list grouping the block parties and professional organizations was presented to the East German electorate. As in the other countries of East Europe, elections henceforth were to involve not a contest among party alternatives, but plebiscitary approval or rejection of a unified slate and perhaps an innocuous policy aspiration. It still required considerable effort for the SED in 1949 to convince two-thirds of the eligible voters to vote yes for peace and for the list of candidates presented. The electorate must have been delighted with the progress made when it voted again, in the fall of 1950, for the first regular Volkskammer elected under the new constitution. Allegedly 98.5 percent of the voters participated, and 99.7 percent of them voted for the single list. In theory the SED claimed only one-quarter of the Chamber for its own delegation. In fact it also controlled the 30 percent of the seats granted to its subservient "mass organizations," including the

Federation of German Trade Unions and the youth federation, and it dominated two new satellite parties (the National Democratic Party of Germany, NDPD, and the Democratic Peasants' Party of Germany, DBD), who were given shares of the list. Finally, the Liberal Democrats and Christian Democrats in the block found it increasingly difficult by 1950 to pursue any sort of independent course.[14]

Behind all the orchestrated enthusiasm, the unremitting pressure on the remaining enfeebled party organizations to cooperate with the hegemonic claims of the SED, and the inflated election figures, remained the police. Opponents disappeared. Consolidation of the satellite regimes rested on political sanctions. By 1947, those resisting communization in Albania, Romania, Poland, Hungary, and Bulgaria were being intimidated, arrested and tried, sent to prison, on to Moscow, or occasionally shot and hanged. Tito's own regime, claiming the most ardent communism as its own legacy, had already liquidated many of its political opponents in rival Resistance groups as a prolongation of its guerrilla against the Germans. Non-Communist political leaders disappeared in Soviet-occupied Poland. Once he took decisive control in 1947, the Hungarian Communist Mátyás Rákosi sent the non-Communists who had prevailed at the elections a year earlier to prison or the firing squad. The Bulgarian Agrarian Party leader Nikola Petkov met the same dismal fate. Jan Masaryk, son of the founder of independent Czechoslovakia and foreign minister even through the 1948 coup, went to his death from the window of the Foreign Ministry. Within the SED, thousands of East German Social Democrats were imprisoned or purged. Almost 600 Christian Democratic Union members are known to have been arrested, some of whom died in prison, a few in Soviet labor camps.

The party dismissals and criminal trials came in waves. The first cycle targeted the non-Communists and accompanied the establishment of the satellites. Within a year or two, the new Communist masters fell upon each other and liquidated their own real or imagined rivals as Titoist conspirators. In the most spectacular of these ritual humiliations, the Communist leader László Rajk, former Hungarian foreign minister and minister of the interior, and seven other defendants went to the gallows in September 1949.

The search for spies continued through the next few years, until the gathering momentum of the rumored Doctors Plot in the Soviet Union and the "Slansky trials" in Czechoslovakia at the end of 1952 threatened to unleash an even more profound wave of terror, now profoundly anti-Jewish. This last great convulsion of Stalinism, which emerged in part from murky factional rivalries, generated a wave of accusations against alleged Zionists, Jewish doctors, and loyal Communists who had been foolish enough to think that loyalty was an objective category. Only the dictator's death in March 1953 seemed to forestall another hecatomb within the Soviet Union. Soviet advisers, however, had already compelled their Czech wards to take up the dark accusations of Zionist counterrevolutionary treason in brutal trials that resorted to drugs as well as psychological degradation to extract confessions from former loyal Communists. Twelve defendants, including Rudolf Slansky, who had been himself so cocksure of his role in the triumph of the working class, were formally sentenced to death, their ashes scattered on the icy highways outside Prague to help prevent skidding. Czechoslovakia usually won praise as the exceptional country in Eastern Europe, industrialized early on, liberal during the dismal 1930s, and the last to fall to the Communists. In fact its recurring and arbitrary purges testify as well to less attractive attributes of political culture: the pervasive recourse to concealment and role playing, disavowal and betrayal. The toll throughout this small country of 14 million may have reached many thousands.[15]

The death of Stalin would bring some abatement of the satellites' obedient terrorism. East Germany and Poland, moreover, refrained from the most slavish compliance in bloodletting during the early 1950s. Nonetheless, political disgrace and noncapital trials shook up the cadres in these countries as well. Walter Ulbricht, whose policies initially appeared discredited by the workers uprising of June 17, 1953, managed to deflect possible blame for this first open anti-Communist revolt behind the Iron Curtain and to purge close party colleagues. June 17 came as a shock. What began as a march of construction workers through Berlin became a widespread series of strikes and angry confrontations, ending only when Soviet tanks overwhelmed defiant rock throwers. Perhaps half a million workers struck and demonstrated in East Berlin, the industrial centers of Saxony, and up to several hundred localities all told. Despite the SED's effort to depict the upheaval as a fascist putsch or the work of West German provocateurs, the movement revealed how alien and dependent on a continuing Soviet presence the regime remained. Until the disappearance of the GDR, the uprising remained an anxious memory; as their authority evaporated in 1989, Politbüro members repeatedly asked whether unrest had become as serious as it had been in 1953.

The explosion in the streets culminated two years of intraparty disagreement over the pace and rigor of communization. Workers had been brought to the threshold of revolt by the accelerated "construction of socialism" that

Ulbricht had announced at the Second Party Conference of the SED in July 1952. This formula promised further pressure on East Germany's non-Communists, including church members, a new wave of collectivization of land, and an increase in the so-called work norms—that is, what Western labor would call a speedup. In fact, the "construction of socialism"—now to be reiterated in countless harangues and editorials as the lofty road to progress—meant in fact more expropriation of family farms and trades, more ideological bullying, harassment of non-Communists, sniping at the church, and denunciation of doubters.

The "construction of socialism" was a slogan that resonated in East Germany with more overtones than elsewhere. No other satellite had to confront the national issue; East Germany's claim to statehood was always in question, whether in 1949, 1953, or 1989. For the ruling party, perfecting socialism reasserted the national legitimacy of the GDR. Each further step toward collectivism was a further bulwark against dissolving into the Federal Republic. For the real enthusiasts, true socialism might even lead the working classes and intelligentsia living in West Germany to break with their "vassal policy" vis-à-vis the Western capitalist powers. In mid-1952, the chance to accelerate the march toward socialism appeared especially welcome because earlier that spring the Soviets had appeared to waver in their support for the three-year-old republic. The so-called Stalin note of March 1952, which had proposed reunification of a neutralized Germany on the basis of free elections, may well just have been a negotiating ploy and thus unlikely to alarm the Eastern Communists.[16] Even so, just having on the table a Soviet offer to trade away their new state must have tested the SED's self-assurance. Whether the offer was meant as a sham to undercut progress toward West German rearmament and consolidation as a state has remained subject to politicized debate ever since. Recent treatments argue from the lack of supporting evidence in Moscow archives that the note was most likely a negotiating ploy.[17] At the time, American policy makers and Chancellor Adenauer presented it as a Soviet tactic designed to demoralize the Bonn Republic's political consensus and arrest its progress toward integration with the West and rearmament. The long-term negotiations that just exploring the offer would involve would also unravel all the progress toward integrating the Federal Republic in the West, including its rearmament. After the West posed its own counter-conditions, in turn unacceptable to Moscow, the East German leadership had to feel relief; the interim of ambiguity lay behind them. Not only did the East Germans welcome the intensification of socialism that Stalin seemed to sanction once again, but they typically applied the new line with uncompromising zeal.

Not for the last time would they outrun their patrons' wishes. Kremlin leaders had misgivings about the ham-handed fervor with which the East Germans forged ahead. When Stalin died in early March 1953, his heirs nervously jockeyed for position within the framework of "collective leadership." Now they wanted to lower the ideological tensions and the pressure on living standards that heavy postwar investment imposed. And even the most menacing possible successor, Lavrenty Beria, who controlled the secret police, proposed exploring a deal on German reunification with the West. The Soviet Politburo seemed divided and irresolute; the representatives in Berlin were also unclear as to how to proceeed. East German colleagues once again seemed clumsy and out of step. Forced-draft socialization led to increasing numbers of East German refugees to the West, up to 100,000 by March 1953, and an East German plea for Soviet aid. By May the new Soviet leaders summoned Ulbricht and Grotewohl to Moscow to criticize the East German insistence on the introduction of collective farms, and they pressed for a "new course" that would relax the tempo of socialization.

Reversing course could not be easy. Switching from heavy to light industry promised massive unemployment; collective farms could not be left in the lurch. The party faithful would be mystified, and those workers angered by the prior months of demands and austerity would be encouraged to protest. Those within the Politbüro who dissented from Ulbricht's increasing authoritarianism—among them Anton Ackermann, Fritz Dahlem, Rudolf Herrnstadt (editor of the paper *Neues Deutschland*), and Wilhelm Zaisser—had not publicly opposed the construction of socialism. After an uneasy Politbüro meeting on June 9, in which the long-standing dissenters denounced "the Secretariat," Soviet High Commissioner Vladimir Semenov demanded immediate publication of the rollback measures. Herrnstadt feared such a rapid disavowal of party policies and pleaded for a fortnight to prepare the faithful to accept the change of course, only to be told by Semenov, "In two weeks it's possible you'll no longer have a state."[18]

Publication of the communiqué of June 9, designed to mollify workers, in fact helped to undermine what control remained. On June 16, the SED meeting dissolved in dispute; on the next day massive demonstrations broke out in Berlin, Chemnitz, Gera, Halle, and elsewhere. The Russians in Berlin, Semenov and Marshall Sokolowski, were preoccupied by possible clashes with Western units as well as the demonstrations in their half of the city and, despite their use of force, still toned down the excited messages from Moscow that urged massive use of firepower and exemplary executions. Although Moscow's chief of staff, who came to Berlin in the crisis, suspected a counterrevolutionary conspiracy, the Russians were also unhappy with the clumsy East German policies that had required their intervention. Sokolowsky and Semenov urged Ulbricht's dismissal after the uprising; but for the new rulers in the Kremlin, uncertain of their own control after Stalin's death a few months earlier and wary of each other's ambitions, it was an unfavorable moment to remove Ulbricht and retroactively justify the East German demonstrations. They were preoccupied with preparation for the arrest and trial of Beria in late June; the task in East Germany was to pacify discontent gradually. There was no desire in Moscow to force a major shakeup within Berlin ranks. After submitting to a cursory self-criticism, Ulbricht stayed. Some responsibility had to be meted out, however, for what became officially designated as a fascist putsch. Although a criminal trial was avoided in favor of an internal party inquest, Herrnstadt and Zaisser were removed from their offices and vilified as alleged "capitulators" to imperialism, and as members of a pro-Beria faction.[19]

A renewed wave of persecution followed the far more serious Hungarian Revolution of 1956 and its supression. The bloodiest reprisals claimed the Budapest rebels, preeminently the Communist leader Imre Nagy, who had sought to respond to the ebullience and navigate Hungary toward autonomy without provoking Moscow's intervention. He was executed for his failure. The crackdown also struck East German writers and intellectuals who had been in touch with the leading intellectual in the Nagy government, Georgy Lukács. Lukács found it necessary to submit to an abject self-criticism; his German contacts were delivered to the mercies of Hilde Benjamin, the zealously partisan SED jurist who took over as minister of justice once she helped oust her less ideologically oriented predecessor after June 17, 1953. The regime enforced orthodoxy on the forums for mild reformist ideas, the journal *Sonntag* and the Aufbau publishing house—a circle of reformist intellectuals inspired by the post-Stalinist thaw in East European Marxism. The literary figures were linked to Wolfgang Harich, a young Humboldt University philosopher and advocate of workers councils and of ties to the West German Social Democrats, who was sentenced to ten years' imprisonment in March 1957 for formation of a conspiratorial group hostile to the state. Two of the more seasoned editors at Aufbau, Walter Janka, who had

paid his dues since the Spanish Civil War, and Gustav Just, recruited to the
SED in his late twenties after wartime service, were also put on trial. Their
elderly guru, Ernst Bloch, was forced into retirement, silence, and eventual
exile. Another eminent intellectual who would not endorse the Writers
Union condemnation of the counterrevolutionary Budapest coup, Alfred
Kantorowicz, departed for the West in 1957.[20]

These recurrent paroxysms—each attended by denunciations, extracted
confessions, betrayal of friends, and harsh sentences—must themselves be
set in a longer context. From the mid-1930s, with the opening of the Soviet
purges, until the early 1960s, political trials testified to the ideological confrontations of the century. On the surface, they were manifestly absurd: men
and women who had devoted their lives to socialism or the revolution were
led to confess they had been wreckers or spies. Others had to acknowledge
how mistaken and misguided they had been. Some were persuaded or constrained to denounce those who had been their political friends. At the least
they remained silent as their comrades were abased and imprisoned. Show
trials, moreover, were just the tip of the iceberg; even as the defendants
suffered in public, thousands of others were dismissed or disgraced or imprisoned. The Soviet purges of the 1930s swallowed up millions of victims.
In Germany, the National Socialist People's Court would denounce those
compatriots who doubted the outcome of the war and, when real conspirators were delivered to its mercies, would decree their brutal execution, including hanging by piano wire. In France, the Vichy regime decided to try
Léon Blum as the symbol of all the evils democracy had allegedly inflicted
on France. Only the evident absurdity of the accusation that he was responsible in 1936 for the 1940 defeat (which had brought his accusers to
power!) led them to suspend the procedings. Mussolini, reestablished as
puppet dictator of the north of Italy by his German rescuers in late 1943,
was compelled to try and execute those who had voted for his removal and
had not fled in time (including his own son-in-law). In the gloomy aftermath of the Spanish Civil War Franco's courts consigned thousands of defeated opponents to prison and firing squads.

Political trials did not come to an end with the defeat of fascism. The
Resistance forces, too, united in the demand that postwar purges must
cleanse their land of collaborators. The victorious allies agreed that National
Socialist leaders must be publicly tried. And if we are to understand this
wave of political justice in its entirety, we must also take account of the

quasi-judicial investigations unleashed in the United States by Joseph McCarthy, the purge of the U.S. State Department, and the trials of Smith Act attorneys. Of course, there were crucial differences in the nature of the charges, the judicial procedures resorted to, and the punishments meted out. Nonetheless, as the cold war moved toward its climax during the period of the Korean War, McCarthyism and the final years of Stalin's rule, all these exercises shared some parallel objectives. They were intended to inhibit dissent, to narrow the limits of political discussion, and, by ritualized confrontations under oath and confession, to dramatize the conflict between the faction ruling in the name of public virtue and its ubiquitous enemies.[21] Not since the French Revolution had the courtroom been so exploited to demonstrate who should rule. There were some atavistic postscripts in the 1960s. A Spanish military tribunal imposed a death sentence on a Communist organizer in April 1963 for the invented crime of "continuing rebellion." The Greek junta that seized power during 1967 mobilized the courts against its foes. Czechoslovak Communists would imprison or rusticate those who had been active in the Prague Spring. By and large, however, a great cycle of judicial violence in Europe was ending. When capital sentences resumed they were imposed by the clandestine terrorists of the 1970s.

East German judges contributed a continually shabby but relatively unsanguinary chapter to the history of twentieth-century political justice. After 1951 the Politbüro required that all GDR judges sacrifice their judicial "chastity" and sit on criminal as well as civil cases. Even before she succeeded to the Ministry of Justice, Benjamin utilized her control of its personnel division to appoint SED members as judges and, above all, as prosecutors. The worst of the East German trials took place in the 1950s, echoing the moves against Zionists, and sweeping up Communists who had spent the Hitler years outside Russia. Except for the executions in the aftermath of June 17 (of which the Soviets imposed eighteen within a few days and the East Germans later carried out two), capital punishment was largely avoided. Still, for a while, over 50,000 political prisoners, or about 1 of every 200 adults, must have been in prison or internment camps. Criminal procedures were used widely to suppress peasant resistance to collectivization. In October 1956, Grotewohl claimed to have released over 21,000 political prisoners (many of whom went West), but admitted 26,000 were still detained.[22] The aftermath of the Hungarian Revolution at the end of October 1956 had important ramifications in the GDR. Khrushchev might have denounced Stalin at the Twentieth Congress of the Soviet Communist Party in July; but he had also sent tanks and soldiers to restore orthodoxy in Budapest. Ulbricht was anxious to exploit the opportunity to cut short the percolating ideas for "national" communism that had motivated Polish and Hungarian reformers. Such concepts might help Warsaw and Budapest Communists stand up to Moscow, but East Germany was a precarious national entity. Its reform-minded Marxists wanted more intensive relations with West German Social Democrats and thus appeared to threaten the regime. Wolfgang Harich's "crime" consisted preeminently of arguing for an all-German socialist initiative. He and his friends had to confront trumped-up accusations, the studied silence of friends, and the hardship of arduous imprisonment. "Put simply," one of those persecuted, Walter Janka, has written, "it might be said that we argued about the forms of socialist democracy in order to free it from the concept of 'proletarian dictatorship,'" which had become a burden.[23]

The 1950s, so these intellectuals learned, was not a favorable moment for discussion of socialist theory or workers councils or any alternatives to Stalinist orthodoxy. The fact that Janka's one-time patron, Johannes R. Becher, the regime's poet laureate, author of its national anthem, and minister of culture, joined in the denunciation of Janka's alleged counterrevolutionary conspiracies came as a bitter lesson: "his love of truth as a politician causes me difficulties," Janka has written with studied understatement.[24]

The following two decades were also not to be terribly favorable for intellectuals. If freezing jail cells and isolation no longer formed part of the repertory of suppression, denunciation of skeptics and dissenters, and attacks by Ulbricht or his rising lieutenant, Erich Honecker, remained withering. Modern literature, with its implicit abandonment of a socially constructive view of collective progress, aroused unrelenting suspicion despite repeated pleas for its assimilation. Joyce, Proust, and Kafka were formalist and decadent, narcissistic exponents of a late bourgeois civilization. Through the 1960s the GDR leadership resisted as socialists elsewhere began coming to terms with modernism. After a decade of ostracism following the Prague Spring, Kafka was republished in the late 1970s and became a staple after his 1983 centennial.[25] Nonetheless, affirmation remained the order of the day. The skepticism of Wolf Biermann, Christa Wolf, and other intellectuals who retreated from bouyant affirmation drew dark warnings, ostracism, prison, or expulsion. After all Germany had "real existing socialism."

REAL EXISTING SOCIALISM

Postwar Germans—whether under Honecker in the 1970s or under Kohl since unification—have taken satisfaction in having a "normal" country. Normalcy in the East was expressed by the smug formula of "real existing socialism." Achieving or enforcing real existing socialism in turn required the Wall, but it took the GDR a dozen years to complete its frontier by closing off East Berlin. This brutal but effective step—so crucial to stabilizing the regime—required Soviet support, and Moscow did not quickly resolve on so conclusive an approach to the GDR's continuing vulnerability. What brought the Soviets to accept the Wall?

Soviet German policy was a high stake in the Kremlin's own intraparty politics. Although control of East Germany became in effect the Soviets' prize from World War II, Russian policy makers recognized how dependent the GDR was upon their support. At times they asked whether more might be gained by trading the entity than by propping it up. Up to 1948, Moscow policy makers probably hoped to arrange reunification on terms that would give German Communists major if not exclusive voice in the politics of a united Germany. Even a neutral Germany would preclude the rapid emergence under Marshall Plan auspices of a solidly anti-Communist Western Europe. The Moscow and London Foreign Ministers Conferences, however, seemed to foreclose the possibility: America and Britain were unwilling to accept the degree of Communist influence unification would require. Of course, once the superpowers had encouraged the native German forces that could govern their respective affiliated states, it was hard to cut the ground from under their clients' feet. When responding to Soviet notes, the Western powers could hardly simply disavow Adenauer and the Germans who wanted a staunchly Western-oriented democracy. If it suited their purposes, the Soviets would probably have written off their SED clients, but Moscow too was reluctant simply to do away with them: East, as well as West, the weaker party could exert leverage over its stronger patron. Such is the dynamic of alliance structures.

For a while Soviet policy seemed to hover between a final choice, perhaps a result of interagency dispute in Moscow. In 1947, the military government (SMAD) encouraged the SED to spearhead a movement for all German unity—calculating perhaps that West German opinion would be won over even if the nascent parties were reluctant. At the same time SMAD encouraged the SED to consolidate decisive authority within the Russian zone through a series of repressive crackdowns that were hardly likely to win sympathy from Western onlookers.[26] In 1952 came the Stalin note proposing a demilitarized but unified Germany. Rebuffed by the West, however (probably as they really expected), the Soviets and SED went on to emphasize the consolidation of socialism in the German Democratic Republic.

Developments throughout the 1950s locked the Russians into reinforcing East Germany's national status. Beria's proposals to negotiate for German unity served as a means of discrediting the feared NKVD leader after Stalin's death. Nonetheless, once Beria was safely buried, the Soviet leadership seemed prepared to play a new German card, if only to forestall West German entry into NATO. In 1954 and 1955, however, the Soviets and the Western powers could not overcome what became their fundamental and repeated disagreement: Moscow argued that progress on unification required West German negotiations with the East German state; the Western powers countered that unification would require free all-German elections that would presumably sweep the East German state away. Confederation of the two Germanies, or dissolution of the East? The two approaches contended as late as early 1990 when unification was imminent. The difference could certainly not be overcome during the cold war, and by 1955 each Germany was locked into an alliance system. Following final French veto of the European Defense Community, West Germany was admitted to NATO, while East Germany became part of the new Warsaw Pact. With Bonn's adhesion to NATO in 1955 and the threatening Polish and Hungarian uprisings in 1956, Soviet policy renounced its interim experimentalism.

Paradoxically, uncertainties within the Soviet bloc strengthened the Soviet commitment to the East German state. Any notion of trading it for neutralization of a united Germany became far too adventurous for even the reformist Khrushchev, once the Polish and Hungarian upheavals shook Eastern Europe in 1956, especially as he sought to cement relations with his military establishment. Khrushchev wanted to stabilize the Eastern bloc, reinforce its East German bulwark, and confirm Western acceptance of the status quo. Treated by the West as a pariah regime, denied any legitimacy by the Bonn government, the GDR must gain a recognized status as a real state. As Anastas Mikoyan argued in June 1957, "If we do not strengthen the regime inside East Germany then our army will be surrounded by fire. And we maintain half a million troops there. And what does the loss of East Germany mean? We know what it means."[27]

Frustration at the failure to prod the Western allies, including the Federal Republic, to negotiate cold war issues directly with East Germany, likewise preoccupation with the spread of NATO nuclear weapons to West German territory, led Khrushchev to open a protracted crisis in 1958 by threatening to turn over access to Berlin to the East Germans. Soviet control over access rights was part of the four-power structure left by World War II; the Western powers did not accept that it might be unilaterally renounced. A decade before the Soviets had blocked the land routes to Berlin; now they threatened to allow the East Germans to repeat this blackmail at will. Khrushchev's threat initiated a continuing challenge to the Western presence in Berlin, which was not fully to be superseded until the inter-German agreements and Four Power Treaty on Berlin over a decade later.[28]

The Soviet diplomatic offensive, however, could not change the fact that the East German economy was foundering and ever greater numbers of its residents emigrating to the West. Almost 200,000 had fled in 1960, another 103,000 through June 1961. Many were highly qualified professionals, such as physicians, who might enjoy high salaries but found their children's life chances stigmatized because of their "privileged" class background.[29] Khrushchev was willing to sanction an international confrontation over Allied rights in Berlin, and he was also prepared to let the East Germans stanch this open wound. On August 13, 1961, the East Germans rolled barbed wire across the open frontier in their capital city. Imperialism, they explained to the citizens they penned up, could no longer exploit the gap in the border to extend its domain eastward.[30] In effect the erection of the Wall represented the second founding of the regime. Brutal though the action was, it did not lack nerve. It seemed to promise an economic respite; it won the East Germans grudging recognition of the status quo. Hitherto their capital had been referred to slightingly as Pankow, the government quarter in northern East Berlin. Henceforth it would be simply Berlin. At home, the party cadres were mobilized for guided discussions; labor "norms" were raised—a move that eight years earlier had brought the explosion of June 17. This time, however, the Republic buckled down.

Policy in the Khrushchev era from 1956 to 1964 followed sharply conflicting impulses. The mercurial first secretary evidently wanted to dismantle Stalinist repression; he denounced his overshadowing predecessor's earlier repression at the Twentieth Congress of the CPSU, and encouraged freer expression and discussion of economic alternatives to central planning. Nonetheless, he could wager on liberalization within the bloc only if he firmed up the frontiers of the Communist world. The changes in East Germany reflected this double thrust. Indeed Khrushchev envisaged rapid gains at Western expense: he would demoralize the West Berliners, support a Communist base off Florida, and overtake capitalist technology. American resistance set a limit to Soviet ambitions. But although the Kennedy administration reaffirmed the commitment to West Berlin and compelled Khrushchev to withdraw his missiles from Cuba, Havana and East Berlin still emerged with stronger guarantees for their Communist regimes.

Khrushchev's colleagues tired of his volatile politics and removed him from office in 1964. By the end of the decade Leonid Brezhnev was established as his durable successor and in effect sought a new comprehensive set of agreements with a Nixon-Kissinger team that responded to Realpolitik. He hankered after a recognized condominium with the West. The Communist reform movements that Khrushchev had encouraged had finally escaped control in Czechoslovakia during 1968. In the ensuing crisis, which culminated in the Warsaw Pact's intervention—urged, above all, by an uneasy Ulbricht[31]—Brezhnev insisted that orthodox Communist states would not shrink from forcibly imposing orthodoxy and upholding the Warsaw Pact. Economic decentralization, factory councils, vigorous party debate, and the other alternative concepts of "humanistic" communism that flourished in the 1960s were soon stifled. In terms of international relations, the objective was to secure recognition as a military power on a parity with the United States. Brezhnev strove for orthodoxy behind a facade of great-power bonhomie: he curbed dissenters and unleashed his military-industrial complex even as he treated important foreign guests to wild boar hunts in the Urals. Between Nixon and Brezhnev there was a reciprocal need for compulsive self-basking in recognition that would help to disguise the economic and international pressures threatening their joint primacy.

The end of the 1960s in the West introduced a decade of social and economic turmoil marked by antiwar demonstrations and racial conflict in the United States, by endemic strikes and militant demonstrations on the part of students and women in Western Europe. Social and political unrest also shook Czechoslovakia in 1968 and Poland in 1970, but did not penetrate the Soviet heartland sufficiently to permit any systemic reform. Accompanying the domestic turmoil was a new flux in the international arena marked by Willy Brandt and Egon Bahr's Ostpolitik and the superpowers' experiment with détente, as Brezhnev, Nixon, and Mao sought new and decisive negotiations. Ostpolitik and détente required each other, but they responded to different political motivations: the former strived for liberalization, the latter for stabilization. The East German regime coveted the latter and was prepared to purchase it with small concessions in terms of the former. Normalizing German-German relations, of course, had to be a central stake in both Brandt's Ostpolitik and the superpowers' aspirations for détente.

Within the context of Ostpolitik and détente East German politics "normalized" further. Between 1969, when Willy Brandt's Social-Liberal coalition came to power, and 1973, when both German states entered the United Nations after signing the "Basic Treaty" that stipulated mutual recognition, the DDR advanced toward international acceptance. Brandt wagered that his negotiations with the GDR must ease the political restrictions on the East German population. In the Basic Treaty, moreover, he insisted on retaining the Federal Republic's claim to speak for all Germans. Nonetheless, the West German recognition of the SED's republic could not guarantee its significant liberalization.

The German treaties composed part of what was intended as a general cold war settlement, including a West German treaty with Poland, the German-German accords over Berlin, the Quadripartite Treaty of the former victors anchoring the new German-German agreements, and the ongoing work of the Conference on Security and Cooperation in Europe (CSCE, or KSZE in German).[32] The latter, popularly noted as the Helsinki process, had long been demanded by the Soviets: Brezhnev set great store by it. The thrust of Helsinki—disciplined détente—also fit in with the Kissinger-Nixon notion that the world should be run for the sake of international "order" by the great powers: the United States, the Soviet Union, and perhaps now China. Washington distrusted local independent dissidents almost as much as Moscow: they were troublesome. More than any other event in the intervening three decades, the signing of the accords at Helsinki recapitulated the settlement reached at Yalta: it sought to trade assurances of territorial control for a promise of good behavior (and with all the same vulnerability). The attitudes of Brezhnev and Nixon were not so different from Stalin, Churchill, and Roosevelt: leaders of great powers who remained convinced that great powers must keep the peace, that small claimants to local rights were troublesome, parochial, and needed curbs for the sake of a higher destiny. So FDR had regarded de Gaulle; Churchill, the Italian left; Stalin, Tito and even Mao Tsetung. Hence Helsinki—following on all the overlapping treaty architecture of the previous five years—reaffirmed the sanctity of borders in Europe. Implicitly it confirmed socialism in the East; effectively it meant that the West would no longer fret about the 1968 Soviet intervention in Czechoslovakia and seemed to seal the Yalta partition.[33]

As a counterweight, the West gained the East Europeans' signature to guarantees of human rights that governments and private agents would now systematically monitor. American critics would later dismiss the Helsinki accords as a few worthless promises from the East in return for a new confirmation of the Communist status quo. But aside from protests, there was little challenge that the West was prepared to mount against Communist repression; and East European dissidents found the Helsinki process important during the next decade and a half. Helsinki meant that at least there was a standard of free expression that they could hold up to their regimes; there was a group of committed Western activists devoted to monitoring their work. These were thin reeds, but preferable to being totally written off. In effect Helsinki completed Brandt's vision of negotiating with the East German regime to allow its citizens more day-to-day liberty and travel rights. It also provided a basis in international law for President Jimmy Carter's emphasis on human rights. Granted, Helsinki was an ambiguous initiative: the critic must nonetheless ask what the realistic alternative was after the Soviets had crushed Prague.

This international evolution of the 1970s had profound effects within the GDR, for it encouraged a redefinition of national identity. Brandt's Ostpolitik advanced the idea of two states within one German nation. This decisively amended the original claim of the Federal Republic to be the only legitimate political representation for the German people. But across the Wall the idea of a single nation still seemed unacceptable and destabilizing. The East Germans' ideological commentators developed the thesis that socialism was a fundamental component of national identity. As one of their poets wrote, "Two nations lie where once Germany was." It would be wearying to follow in detail the steps by which these concepts were worked out by social theorists and political leaders: Honecker's inaugural Eighth Party Congress of 1971 separated the East German socialist nation and the West German bourgeois capitalist nation; the constitutional amendments of 1974 eliminated all references to German unity; from a socialist state of the German nation, the GDR became a socialist state of workers and peasants. If two German nations now existed, then East Germany might safely claim part of the cultural patrimony. The new SED party program of 1976 sanctioned "German" as an adjective once again, but for a German land that had securely emerged from the chrysalis of the bourgeois-socialist transformation. The regime felt established enough so that "German" was not a threatening concept.[34] GDR intellectuals and ideologues grew confident enough to pull some of the old national artifacts out of the closet without feeling overwhelmed or threatened.

East German historians, for example, could supposedly begin to reevaluate their national past without forcing it into the stilted progression of feudal and bourgeois eras, culminating in monopoly capitalism and fascism, before final redemption by the Soviet Union. They were allowed now to come to terms with the complex legacies of major figures from the German past, such as Frederick II and Bismarck. "Prussian rulers were not always reactionary," Frederick's East German biographer wrote. Bismarck's realism allowed him to seek good relations with Russia. The idea of "tradition and heritage" justified departure from a caricatured unilinear Marxist concept of progress; tradition was that part of the heritage that one might carry on.[35]

Historians also contributed to a new emphasis on regional particularism. As Walter Schmidt, the head of the Institute for History, argued, the task of the GDR historian was to convey the specifically territorial struggles of progress and reaction. Emphasizing the legacies of Thuringia or Saxony or Mecklenburg—and, increasingly, a vanished Prussia—allowed the GDR to overcome its handicap of occupying only a fragment of former German territory. With their rich local traditions, each region in the GDR enjoyed a historical legitimacy in its own right. A West German writer explained the renewed appeal of localism as she reflected on her trip through ancestral Mecklenburg before it became apparent that there would be again one Germany:

> It isn't any easier for the Germans in the GDR to be German than it is for us. We are all descendants of that so-called Great German Reich which committed so many terrible crimes. German nationalism must be painful, either here or there. But in the long run one can't do without some sort of identification. One way out is the connection to smaller territories, to landscapes and regions. The GDR government has realized in the meanwhile that a new GDR nationalism, as it imagined it, doesn't exist. It will be hindered by the covetous glance at the glittering German neighbors in the West, also by the relationship to real existing GDR-socialism. Therefore a new dedication to the regional is not only permitted but encouraged.[36]

On the thirtieth anniversary of the founding in 1979, a widely distributed poster showed a happy family living in a house drawn as if by a child and reading "Here we're at home."[37]

The turn to localism served the regime, but also limited its ideological pretensions. It hovered between socialism and *Gemütlichkeit*. The state might want "Love of the Fatherland" to emerge strengthened by regional loyalties and modest consumerism and local activity, but it also encouraged a tendency toward cozy fossilization. Intellectuals talked of "our Republic"; the notion had a built-in diminutive quality, as if in the local milieu, whether the sleepy towns of provincial Brandenburg or the pubs of Prenzlauer Berg, the demands of ideology and Marxist self-righteousness could be evaded. In the small towns and villages of the GDR, its resorts on the Baltic, its Thuringian or Mecklenburg villages, the quality of private landscape seemed frozen as in the late 1930s. The transformation of the environment through neon, markets, and the spread of suburbia had not kept pace in the East. A certain German Rip van Winkle quality persisted: the "breath of memory," as Günter Gaus termed it.[38] Gaus, who served as the first permanent representative of the Federal Republic in the GDR from 1974 through 1981, popularized the idea of a society of niches, or private refuges, in which GDR residents increasingly lived their real lives. "What is a niche in the society of the GDR? It is the preferred place for people over there, the place in which the politicians, planners, propagandists, the collective, the great goal, the cultural legacy—in which all of these depart so that a good man, with his family and among friends, can water his potted flowers, wash his car, play Skat, have conversations, celebrate holidays."[39] Gaus did not mean that the East Germans deviated from Western norms in their retreat into the private sphere. Rather, he suggested that despite the total claims of the socialist state, the GDR could not annex its citizens' personal lives. Germans in the East cultivated their *Schrebergärten* with the same assiduousness as did those in the West: these allotments alongside the railroad tracks, with their miniature dachas, allowed evenings of chatting and card playing as well as tending to tomatoes and carrots and dahlias. The regime itself seemed to conspire in the growing preoccupation with private life. Newspaper columns revealed that young readers, concerned in the 1960s with their public obligations as youthful socialists, were more worried in the 1980s by issues of personal friendship and loyalties.[40] "Freedom, unity, and socialism," according to an aging woman pilot who had been given a job as a guard in the Dresden military history museum, "meant progress, love for the German fatherland, and a content life with my little white miniature poodle."[41]

"Real existing socialism" was the regime's own self-description of this Biedermeier collectivism. Of course, it was not the dissenters'. They believed it threatened to disarm outside critics, especially those in the West who wanted to believe Ostpolitik had made life less repressive for the East

Germans. They were not willing to accept the society of "niches" as a modus vivendi because they understood that in fact it continued to mask continued repression. "Every observer or interested party from abroad," the dissident Wolfgang Templin burst out later, "who did not do what was possible [to encourage resistance] and wanted to trivialize the GDR, with its paltry offerings, which is all that they were, as basically a niche society or a leisure society, essentially reinforced people's political immaturity and dependence."[42]

Ulbricht, too, might still have mocked such a smug self-designation as "real existing socialism," but the Soviets finally signaled that he must be removed in 1971. He had insisted on the fraternal suppression of Prague Spring in August 1968; he was not respectful to Brezhnev; his own economic experimentation came to grief in 1970. As he aged, he responded angrily to beat and rock and, above all, girls with ponytails. Stubborn, curmudgeonly, old, and tiresome, Ulbricht was directed to stand down in favor of the energetic former youth leader, Erich Honecker, who would himself end as stubborn, curmudgeonly, old, and tiresome in October 1989.[43] Honecker did not have Ulbricht's personal experience of debating with, chastising, but nonetheless feeling some obligation to listen to the founding generation of GDR intellectuals such as Brecht, Bloch, Kantorowicz, and Mayer. By the 1970s these ancient Marxists and their oeuvre seemed anachronistic. They were heirs to a Hegelian tradition in which "real" signified rational, not just existing. They stood for a continuing "utopian" scrutiny of institutions, even Communist ones: a perpetual self-interrogation on the part of Marxism, perhaps best represented during the 1960s by the reimplantation of Theodor Adorno and his ideas at the University of Frankfurt.

If the new generation of East German dissenters were less massively erudite than the philosophers who had returned from exile, they were witty and persistent. The poet and balladeer Wolf Biermann, then in his thirties, had the most pungent wit on the left since Tucholsky and would not stop carping about the suppression of Prague Spring. "Enraged" by his mockery during a Cologne performance in 1976, the regime took advantage of his tour to strip him of his citizenship and refuse him readmission.[44] Sixty-year-old Robert Havemann was to become the spiritual guide for Biermann's generation. A physicist by training, Havemann had served time with Honecker in Brandenburg prison and narrowly escaped execution so he might continue scientific work. Although shaken by Khrushchev's "secret speech," he still sought to remain a loyal GDR intellectual and supported the closing of the frontier in 1961. Nonetheless, his continuing insistence that natural science must be liberated from political premises brought down the strictures of ideologists whom he did not shrink from labeling ignorant and contemptible.[45] Having recourse to publication in the West led to expulsion from the party and the Academy of Sciences, but he never disavowed a democratic socialism; indeed, he became a fervent advocate for the Czech experiment of 1968, which he saw as the necessary complement to 1917. Havemann carried on through the 1970s as a nonperson, unwilling to flee to the West so long as his essays might make their periodic escape, and at the end of life in the early 1980s he became a cosigner of the Berlin Appeal for Peace. (See chapter 4.) His posthumous reinstatement in the Academy of Sciences served as one of the great ceremonies of civic reconstitution in the fall of 1989.

Despite their great differences from each other, Havemann and Biermann were key symbols of the 1970s opposition. The older was cool, refined, and made his critics sound boorish; the younger was ironic, funny, and made his critics look oafish. In effect both were present on both sides of the Wall at the same time, with full access to an eager Western literary market that would flash their messages back to the East. It was difficult to arrest opponents who knew how to use the resources of the Western media. Increasingly by the end of the 1980s, the regime would seek to expel its malcontents; the GDR had learned to wall people in, but it was harder to keep information out. Nonetheless, the dissenters' critiques were far from disabling. East German society still endeavored to educate its new generations to be good socialist functionaries. Its bureaucrats labored at economic development; they worked at being progressive and constructive. For all the fastidious complaints or easy jokes on the part of disillusioned intellectuals who might pile up their Western royalties at the cost of mocking the steady achievements of their hardworking countrymen, the East Germans—so it was insisted by regime spokesmen—had built the best socialist state possible. They were industrious; their economy was the powerhouse of the Eastern bloc; they were "antifascist." This was the fruit of socialism in the here and now, maintained against counsels of perfection and in opposition to the seductive wealth of the West. Even more collectivization came in the 1970s and renewed orthodoxy. By the mid 1980s Western observers even described the GDR as a success story. The regime was represented in the UN, with embassies in the United States and West Germany. The country had trained one of the world's most formidable athletic establishments; statistics suggested they were the tenth or eleventh largest industrial producer in the world. They had exploited the 750th anniversary of Berlin and Luther's quincentennial to advance their claim to historical legitimacy. West Germans seemed almost disconcerted by this hijacking of historical patrimony. In the spring of 1987 the SPD was willing to negotiate a charter of shared principles with the SED. It was still possible to find many in the West who detested the German socialist state and many who believed that its ties with the West would force a slow liberalization—but few who believed it might simply collapse, as its Soviet guardian had warned as early as June 1953.

PRIVILEGE, SECRECY, AND COMPLICITY

The East German intellectuals who came of age at the time remember the end of the seventies or the early eighties as a turning point. The emergence of Charter 77 in Czechoslovakia and the organization of the Polish Workers Defense Committee (KOR) with intellectuals who would be active in Solidarity restored a sense of international protest. In June 1979, the Writers Union expelled nine leading East German authors, preeminent among them Stefan Heym, and provoked the protest of other major novelists. When protest failed, detachment and withdrawal took over. Christa Wolf's heroine juxtaposed the suppressed memories of a childhood under Hitler with the amnesiac qualities of East German existence. Günter de Bruyn depicted the foibles of the petted intellectual classes, their writer colonies or their institutes, with a delicate irony. Christoph Hein disturbed the public with a portrait of a woman with anesthetized moral connections. A quality of removed self-observation characterizes the narrator in late East German fiction.[46]

For younger intellectuals protest would find expression less in a tradition of high mandarin texts than in an underbrush of film, readings, graffiti, music, church-affiliated peace movements, or ecology actions.[47] It was less explicitly political, more keyed to rock and poetry and cultural alternatives, the expression of a third or even fourth "generation" of GDR dissenters: Biermann's successors. Protesters did not believe in negotiated settlements with the state. They felt quite despairing and wanted either to get out or just carve out a sort of permanently subversive sphere. The dilemmas of rock and roll in the mid 1980s offer a revealing window on developments. Free German Youth (FDJ) organizations had gone from stalwartly trying to resist the appeal of rock to sponsoring discos so they did not lose touch with local adolescents. Official efforts to offer enough rock would culminate with a Bruce Springsteen concert in summer 1988.[48] But could state sponsorship control the apolitical and thus potentially subversive thrust of the music?

When a West Berlin journalist published a well-informed account of the GDR rock scene in 1983 and charged that, despite the many bands, the regime tended to stifle the music, his allegations provoked consternation among the cultural guardians of the republic. Ursula Ragwitz, a former piano teacher and still earnest didact, who served as one of the SED's chief censors, sent the work out for an evaluation from the General Directory of the Entertainment Arts Committee. They detailed its dangers: "The book appeared at that very moment in which the FRG approved of stationing U.S. rockets and a certain disappointment and resignation appeared among the GDR rock musicians." For all the author's apparent objectivity, so the in-house review emphasized, despite his supposed commitment to the socialist ideal and his detailed knowledge (perhaps furnished by secret-service sources), his work actually sought to undermine "real" socialism by falsely construing an antagonism between the regime and rock and arguing that GDR rock was inauthentic because it was caught up in state institutions. In fact, as the General Directory of the Entertainment Arts Committee implicitly conceded in its confidential "position paper on the development of rock music in the GDR," rock was political. Sponsorship of the "rock for peace" concerts served the campaign against NATO's intermediate missile upgrading and allegedly helped counter the influence of the West German stations (the Neue Deutsche Welle) "that had been conceived by the ruling circles of the FRG as a response to DDR rock development." Unfortunately, despite the emergence of more than eighty professional rock groups, a certain insecurity emerged in 1983; artists were defecting because of supposed Western subversion and contradictions in their "material" milieu. Despite the success of "rock for peace" performances, by 1986 party authorities decreed that non-GDR bands were not to be invited to the popular New Year's concert. The Entertainment Arts Committee (Rock Section) protested this heavy-handed intervention all the way up to the cultural arbiter of the Politbüro, Kurt Hager. The SED censors were themselves embarrassed but would not take responsibility for reversing the measure. Hager sat on the request for almost half a year, then, a month after the date for which the concert had originally been scheduled, finally approved the participation of a Cuban and a Canadian group.[49]

The simplicities of the Ulbricht days had given way to a sense of social complexity and private claims that was hard to reconcile with "real existing socialism." Privilege as well as irony suggested the waning moral hold of the regime. More Western goods had to be admitted: citizens brought back computers and Levis from the West. The regime resorted to rationing consumer goodies from abroad through Intershops where Scotch and perfumes and clothes were available for Western currencies.[50]

The academic disciplines revealed a growing sophistication and openness to complexity that could no longer be encompassed by simplistic appeals to Marxism-Leninism. Historiography, as already noted, had been allowed to be more liberal, annexing regionalism, seeking to explain political setbacks as well as alleged progress.[51] Psychological models also evolved. In the 1960s "cybernetic" sociology, which focused on information processing in individuals and organizations, suggested some convergence of Eastern and Western psychological research in the relatively reformist atmosphere that prevailed. It was choked off in the 1970s, but by the early 1980s concepts of individuality were being presented that were hard to square with earlier calls for a psychology that recognized the priority of social formation. Earlier a taboo, Freud's teachings were being assimilated, and a conference debated his contributions on the occasion of the 125th anniversary of his birth in 1981.[52] These remained timid and halting revaluations, but signaled at least some challenge to the earlier stifling orthodoxy.

These trends in fact were long in the making. Societies in the West had entered a new era of fluidity once the urgent tasks of postwar reconstruction were under way and the political discipline of the cold war had become routine. Societies in the East remained more stagnant, less set in motion by affluence, still subjected to ideological control, but some of the same pressures gradually accumulated. Reassuring senses of identity, familiar loyalties etched so sharply during the war and its aftermath of austerity and ideological struggle, were blurred by the transformations that gathered speed and scope from the late 1950s through the succeeding decades: the diffusion of vacation travel, of consumer goods and choices; the partial transfer of care of young children and aging parents to public agencies; the lengthening of study before work and parenthood; the advent of television with its continuous messages of societal interconnectedness and its montage of image and event; the emancipation from heavy state agendas promised by rock and jeans. Such changes undercut ideological allegiances based on the simpler and more exclusive identities of prior decades, such as employer or worker, antifascist or anti-Communist. "By virtue of its complexity, modern industrial society," wrote the leading East German reformer Ulrike Poppe, "is increasingly hard to envision as a whole and makes it hard to find one's identity."[53]

The new personal or collective orientations had an unsettling enough impact on political routines in France, West Germany, Italy, and the United

States. Marxist governments were even less prepared to integrate the increasingly complex interests of civil society. The class conflicts that Marx
and his followers had discerned as the basis of their ideology were always
oversimplified: at the turn of the century European society remained fractured by ethnic and religious conflict as well as class cleavages. And when
economic issues were at stake, opposing material interests divided city and
country dwellers, craftsmen and industrial workers, shopkeepers, tenants
and landlords. Still, class seemed to generate the most pervasive lines of
division within Western society through the First World War or even the
1930s. Class had become an intrusive presence: bourgeois society felt the
encroaching shadow of proletarian parties and socialist aspirations. Class
cleavages did not go away; they seemed to shape the geography of cities and
the functioning of public services. After World War II, moreover, it hardly
mattered whether Marxist sociology was accurate. The military outcome
allowed Communists to impose their rule in the wake of the Red Armies, no
matter how appropriate or irrelevant their political analysis. For a quarter
century after 1945, by virtue of totalitarian control and the extent of the
Russian military presence, they could impose an agenda built upon the
model of Soviet central planning in the 1930s.

But how was the successor generation to rule when issues of gender,
environment, cultural identification, and personal fulfillment cut across the
simplified concepts of class that had nurtured the movement fifty years earlier? By what principles of social arbitration could Communist parties resolve contending claims for work and leisure, environmental protection or
hydrocarbon production, investment in infrastructure or consumer welfare,
if they excluded the legislative bargaining that Western regimes relied
upon? Different ministries and intraparty offices might speak for segments
of an increasingly complex society, but who would then represent the supposedly overriding interests of the party itself?

Liberal regimes, moreover, did not claim to control the matrix of private
social relations. Communist parties sought a more ambitious tutelage: they
conceived of all relationships and roles as potentially public. They could
attempt such a demanding task of societal management only by monopolizing the organization of sport, seeking to channel young people's multivalent
loyalties into inauthentic youth organizations, or suppressing cultural dissent outright. Coercion remained an ultimate recourse that was always
available; but if it might silence overt dissent it could not renew allegiances.

As in the case of economic reform the late 1960s marked a decisive watershed for both Communist and non-Communist societies. "Sixty-eight" in

the West involved a great deal of romantic posturing, outright intolerance, and shabby intellectualizing. At the same time, the turmoil of the period testified to genuine dissatisfaction. Students and militant factory workers claimed to feel that they were being processed like punch cards by mass institutions that were managed without reference to their personal needs. Coming to terms with the expressive politics of student revolts, frequent strikes, and public demonstrations by women or peace marchers was obviously difficult in the West. Despite control of the streets, Communist regimes ultimately found the new issues just as troublesome.

"Against the will of the SED, society since the beginning of the sixties had attained a certain autonomy. It had emancipated itself from the Party."[54] This drift toward the autonomy of society is crucial for understanding the quality of politics under real existing socialism. Marxist theorists between the two world wars had developed the concept of Bonapartism to help analyze the rise of fascism and Nazism. Bonapartism suggested that when class antagonisms tended toward stalemate, state officials might liberate themselves from the pressures of class interests and, thus emancipated, could become far more authoritarian and efficient at repression. What seems to have happened by the 1960s and 1970s was the reverse. Society—that is, the matrix of professional and personal roles that absorbed people's energies— became too complex for the state or party to control. Instead of the self-assertion of the state (*Verselbstständigung des Staates*) that Bonapartist theory had discerned in the 1930s and 1940s, the 1960s brought a tendency toward the self-assertion of society. This trend played a crucial role in establishing the particular texture of public life in Communist Germany.

Günter Gaus had coined the idea of a niche society—but that term suggested primarily an opting out of civic participation on the part of families and individuals and a flight into the sanctuaries of private life. Contemporary historians of East Germany have applied the concept of *Eigen-Sinn* (a sense of one's own interests) to describe a trend less toward private life than toward maintenance of one's own "space" or sphere of autonomous action within public institutions, the workplace above all. Such behavior was possible less for individuals than groups of workers: team activity might reassert meaningful public participation. Indeed, as one historian has noted with respect to the early years of the GDR, pride in work, all the more so when challenged by shortages or demanding "norms" for performance, facilitated not a socialist industrial utopia, but a group bonding that kept its own independence from the regime's agenda.[55] A concept such as *Eigen-Sinn* thus allows historical research to explore how citizens constructed

daily life without succumbing to oppression or despair. It can thus counter-
balance the tales of manipulation, collaboration, and coercion that this
chapter has emphasized. But if used too facilely, the notion can also obscure
the inequality of power between rulers and ruled—a dilemma that is all too
familiar from earlier efforts to write the social history of dictatorships.

Why, so the question naturally arises, did the growing "emancipation of
society from the party" not lead to a broader and more open opposition?
The very growth of social complexity—the increasing diversity of job structures, the intrusion of issues of gender, the opportunities for (and frustrations with) consumption—undermined the regime's efforts at pervasive
control. These very trends, however, may also have undercut group solidar-
ities and resources for autonomy. In any case, resistance did not simply
increase apace. Insofar as political concepts were discussed, it was by tiny
groups under church roofs. But church leaders were often cautious and
caught up in the networks of informing or at least consulting with the police. Only a few insisted on absolute independence; others, including high
church officials, might encourage limited dissent but simultaneously negotiated with the Ministry of State Security, modulating their flock's opposition to win it partial tolerance.[56] Opposition did not take place within a
mass movement that had already emerged politically, as in Poland. It did
not take place within the party itself, as in Hungary. It did not take place
by testing the regime's patience with petitions and demonstrations, as in
Prague. At best there were fragmented partial publics—dissenting writers,
young intellectuals, church enclaves, timid faculties—but no general civic
public until the very end. Looking back at the "group" activity that had
gained a foothold under church roofs in the 1980s, Ulrike Poppe found a
line going back to the pacifists of the 1950s, and the "circles" of the 1960s
and 1970s that met in apartments to draft reformist left-wing programs. "In
small groups anonymity can be given up in favor of shelter and collective
meaning. They allow us to confirm our individuality whereas institutions
are experienced as dominating."[57]

To be sure, there were particular difficulties to overcome in the case of
East Germany. First of all, many GDR intellectuals still sought to cling to a
vision of their Germany as the better state because it was socialist and not
capitalist. Rudolf Bahro's *Alternative* envisaged a new, reorganized Communist left, not a pluralist competition of parties.[58] Through the elections of
March 1990, many East German dissenters felt the Federal Republic remained morally inferior by virtue of its private economy. Had the national
basis of their own state not been so precarious, it might have been easier to

mobilize protest earlier. Second, the issue of emigration remained troubling. By far the major civil rights abuse felt by the population as a whole was its confinement to barracks. Freedom of publication remained abstract for most GDR residents, but not the chance to vacation in the West, much less to seek one's fortune abroad. But many of the dissenters at home distrusted the would-be *Ausreisende*. Until it became clear that the deep yearnings of those who wished to flee strengthened the effectiveness of those demonstrating for reform at home, a gulf persisted between the groups.[59]

Looking at the closing decades of the twentieth century, historians who have any taste for irony will take note that all the social phenomena that so alarmed Western conservatives about their own societies in the 1970s in fact subverted the rival Communist regimes far more effectively during the subsequent decade. But these regimes proved so vulnerable because they undermined their own capacities for governance. Late socialist governments could offer no convincing alternative to the countercultural tendencies that encroached in the East as well as the West. The fascinating question in this case, as in all instances of "decline and fall" from Rome to Russia, must be why. How does the determination to rule falter among the ruling elite of an imperial system? Why do the rulers feel overwhelmed by social complexity? The ultimate wellsprings of decay may remain mysterious. But the historian can demonstrate how the principles of governance that were supposed officially to prevail became distorted enough such that they eroded from within. Late socialism in fact suffered from its own progressive and characteristic degenerative disease.

Critics and party members alike envisaged the task of Communist governance—even at the moment it broke down (see chapter 3)—as a problem of properly meshing state and society. How did the regime seek to control a complex, and even elusive, if not rebellious society in this last decade of its existence? Repression increasingly became an unserviceable option for the Communist states. It might temporarily silence opponents, but it drew down foreign opprobrium. As General Jaruzelski learned in Poland, it did not gain the cooperation of the aggrieved social groups, nor did it fulfill urgent economic needs. And by the late 1980s it was perhaps not even feasible in Russia after the Soviet disillusion with their own military role in Afghanistan. In any case Moscow leadership did not wish to try. In August 1988 the Soviets tried to explain their reform course to a rather uncomprehending Honecker. Vadim Medvedev, secretary of the Soviet Party's Central Committee told the East German leader that Soviet society had to liberate its own energies and allow the expression of diverse opinions. Honecker was courteous but just did not understand. The Germans, he confessed, had not expected the Soviet developments to the degree they were taking place. Westerners were using glasnost and perestroika as slogans to intervene in GDR internal affairs.[60] A few months later, Jan Foitik, secretary of the Czech Central Committee, fretted to Honecker about perestroika and the influence of Western media on Czech youth but implied that repression would be fruitless. "The overall situation in Czechoslovakia was not simple. There was a certain nervousness among the active functionaries of the Communist Party after demonstrations on the Wenceslaus Square. The 1968 syndrome still had an effect. It was too simple just to speak about 'antisocialist elements.'" Honecker assured him that in the GDR, "socialism is unshakable since it has something to offer mankind."[61]

What did it have left to offer? Late socialism relied in effect on an increasing effort to corrupt its own public. Ostensibly socialism existed to enhance solidarity, and visitors to East Germany often claimed to perceive a sense of community they lacked in the West. Loyal East Germans claimed social cohesion as a major virtue of their state. In fact, however, the regime survived precisely by undermining solidarity with differential rewards such as travel and education, even by dividing up its supposedly loyal proletarian supporters into competitive work brigades, and by rewarding snooping. The authorities were willing to live with thousands of small complaints precisely because these impeded efforts to rally a broad oppositional coalition. How was social and political peace secured after 1953, during the long decades that the regime endured with hardly a noticeable opposition movement? Not overtly by force, although the potential for force conditioned every political transaction, but by the systematic disaggregation of a united and potentially oppositional public.

By the late 1970s and 1980s, the state socialist regimes emerged as a very particular historical formation. The principles by which they functioned (with considerable variation) deserve sustained reflection because they were not readily assimilable to earlier models. Vaclav Havel resorted to the term "post totalitarian" to convey the general pressure for conformity that the regimes elicited from their own subjects.[62] The term seems problematic, however; and it might be simpler just to refer to "late socialist" or "late communist" regimes, as Western analysts tended to refer to late or advanced capitalist states. No matter what designation political analysts may finally choose, the quality that rendered these regimes distinctive was no longer just the use of political coercion (although the possibility of repression underlay all efforts to renegotiate consensus). Rather it was the systematic manipulation of supposedly public relationships between citizens and the authorities. Late socialism functioned by infiltrating what it claimed was an authentic public or civic domain but in fact became an arena for clientelism and privilege. Even as Communist rulers criticized the economic power of capital for reducing Western democracy to a sham formality, they resorted to a regime of privilege, propaganda, and constraint that undermined their own claim to represent society in general.[63]

Late socialism, in effect, sought to govern by concluding private bargains with each citizen or potential dissenter. It felt threatened by emerging collective identities—women, professionals, ecology or peace activists. Hence it sought by the pervasive manipulation of privilege and complicity to transform supposed citizens into clients—and clients in both the ancient and modern senses. That is, late socialism encouraged a traditional clientelism in its encouragement of needy and cowering subordinates who craved the protection of a powerful mediator; and it simultaneously created clients in the newer sense of dependents who were subsidized and counseled by the case workers of a modern welfare (and secret-police) bureaucracy. Instead of reconstructing its own public sphere according to socialist norms (i.e., by rewarding public service or achievement or even folkloric background), late socialism relied increasingly on offering Western consumer goods, publication, educational and professional chances, even preferential health care to its corporate elites.

By the late 1980s the adversaries of late communism praised "civil society" as the format in which autonomous collective loyalties might challenge state socialism. "Civil society" proved a superbly infectious slogan. (See chapter 4 for a more extensive discussion.) But the concept of civil society remained underspecified as a precise description of what had actually been taking place in the socialist public or civic sphere. To reclaim civil society sometimes implied that Communist states had simply suppressed collective activity group by group. In fact, group activity proliferated.[64] Honecker told the Soviets in 1988 that two-thirds of the adult population in the GDR exercised some official function in an organization. "That reflects the diversity of social life and is simultaneously an expression of the developed socialist democracy of the GDR."[65] The point was, however, that this sort of organizational proliferation—teams, choruses, hobbyists, beekeepers, etc.—did not make claims on the civic sphere. Certainly Stalinist practices through the 1950s had sought to crush the independent organizations that might claim political or spiritual allegiance and contest the party. Still, late socialism did not deny that the organized activities of everyday life might continue to flourish, especially when based on popular culture.

Contrast briefly the strategies for governance on the part of late communism with the political recourses of contemporary market liberalism, which was also under stress. Only the outright collapse of communism, after all, diverted attention from some of the disquieting tendencies in Western regimes. The comparison is not meant to suggest any equivalence; for a liberal, the coercion that a late socialist system always had in reserve and the reliance on a pervasive secret police must weaken all analogies with the non-Communist countries. Nonetheless, it can still be useful to examine the overarching political and cultural pressures that both systems faced and to compare the often unavowed adaptations they resorted to. Western democracies also underwent dismaying changes in the 1980s: the growing role of private wealth for political participation, the replacement of debate with simplified slogans and images of personality, and in the wider society, the fraying of urban public services and safety, and increasing income disparities. Democratic preferences were aggregated less through legislatures, no longer even through "corporatist" special interests, but through the interaction of television audiences and interpretors of public opinion. Western television-democracy tended to merge the idea of the public with the advance of publicity. The media and the process of selecting elites focused obsessively on individual distinction, whether meretricious or authentic. No historian can yet say whether these changes were irreversible or ultimately insidious. Western institutions did not collapse; they did not provoke mass defection and revolt. Still publicity in the West played somewhat the same subversive role as did privilege in the East. Publicity and privilege proved to be characteristic symptoms of institutional decay—publicity, reflecting the strength of the media in late capitalism, privilege revealing the continuing domination of a single ruling party. Lest the argument be misunderstood, I am not claiming that the distortions of the public sphere were as insidious in the West, or that the media rendered the freedom of communication meaningless, or that communism and liberalism were equivalently manipulative. I am proposing that each system evolved its own characteristic response to the strains of social complexity that beset it.

Privilege under late communism did not mean merely access to Western goods, scarce cars or apartments, and visas for travel to the West for those who were loyal (the so-called *Reisekader*). Privilege became a pervasive way of rationing valued aspects of life, access to which was less political in the West, so that the regime could get the credit for doling them out. Travel and publication were transformed from generalized rights to negotiated favors: the party expected gratitude for its watchful care of those in its charge. Favor had to be curried at the state publications office or the police presidium the way it might have been sought by a resident of Palermo or Chicago fifty years earlier. Moreover, as every Western visitor to East Berlin who watched his passport disappear for a half hour at Check-Point Charlie could testify, every favor finally granted was a reminder of how easily another might be withheld. For those who lived inside the frontiers, the smothering favoritism of the regime had far greater consequences. The right to travel might be denied; poems might remain unpublished for years; one's colleagues could gang up in a withering critique; children could find their advance in school endangered; Stasi operatives could establish their chilling presence. Privilege finally involved less the nature of what was given than the process of political grace by which it was bestowed or denied; any effort to carry on a scientific or professional or artistic career required entering a fabric of negotiations to win the permissions that allowed professional survival. Writers and artists associations existed to nurture acceptable expression and to allocate travel opportunities, scientists or faculty department heads were expected to report on their colleagues' contacts, the Stasi encouraged the undermining of solidaristic relations and friendship. The real objective was less information than control, the subordination of any collective activity to party tutelage.

As was to be expected, the degradation of a public sphere brought the simultaneous corrosion of any complementary private sphere. Late socialism rested on the systematic distortion of key categories for public-private interaction that had been nurtured over two centuries of liberalism. It worked to transform the category of public to that of privileged and of civic to complicit. While liberal society emphasized a domain for privacy, late socialism tended to replace privacy with secrecy. Instead of civic participation, its agents solicited denunciation. It systematically sought to degrade the domains of social and individual autonomy, no longer through terror but pervasive manipulation and unavowed clientelism.

I do not intend to suggest by virtue of this argument that public and private spheres can remain hermetically sealed domains of activity, whether under liberal or socialist regimes. When GDR citizens needed help, so a recent sociological inquiry suggests, workplace colleagues remained alongside family partners an important resource for personal assistance. The office, the factory, the faculty offered support between the private and the political.[66] Careful biographical reconstruction demonstrates that themes of power and affection, betrayal and sanction, connect the private and the political. Gaus's niche society was an arresting first formulation but remained an oversimplification. As the historian Alexander von Plato suggested at the end of an intense 1987 interview with an elderly East German citizen, family violence, the loss of a satisfying public service job (not subject to party control), and a child's flight across the German-German border all formed part of a single tangled narrative: "The complicated gray zone between political and private spheres . . . shows that these categories can only help us to a limited degree in the description of a world that blurs such boundaries." Insensitivity to the ramifications of personal loss "was perhaps one reason that this so sharply controlled and apparently so transparent East German society still remained so opaque for its 'authorities,' while 'its people' were or became so strange and incomprehensible."[67]

Still, even if private and political spheres are never neatly separable, liberal and socialist regimes each sought to maintain concepts of separate domains. They each structured a legal and administrative order according to the respective limits set upon the political. The point here is that late socialism increasingly violated its own norms of public and private. In the modern era, it has been French writers, above all Montesquieu, Rousseau, Constant, and Tocqueville, who have reflected most shrewdly on how particular regimes depend upon and inculcate particular collective mentalities. They have been preoccupied with the impact of public rewards on private behavior, with civic spirit and authenticity under benign institutions, or with bad faith and posturing when institutions decay. Their reflections help us understand what happened under late German socialism. For Montesquieu, who wrote almost half a century before the Americans wagered otherwise, republics seemed capable only of governing small territories. The commitment they required from adult males for civic participation rested upon "virtue" or an unselfish devotion to the public good. Opposed in spirit and method, despotisms manipulated fear to instill servility. Between these extremes of governance, aristocratic monarchies offered the most stable and liberal institutional compromise. They did not demand selfless service, but the proven incentives of privilege and honors, the striving for distinction of wealth and rank, and the support of an established church. Under the aristocratic monarchies of the eighteenth-century Enlightenment, intellectuals fretted continually about abuses and superstition, extremes of wealth and power, tax evasion, and the artificiality of court culture. Still, moderates such as Montesquieu or Hume understood that monarchical or aristocratic systems rested on the unequal distribution of goods, the manipulation of rewards for the sake of engendering loyalty and obedience. By the twentieth century, however, privilege had ostensibly long since been undermined as a principle of governance; every revolution and suffrage reform had chipped away at differential political rewards. Privilege was allegedly incompatible with the equality ostensibly underlying democracy and socialism. For this reason, the resumption of privilege as a principle of governance under late socialism requires explanation.

Certainly capitalism generates privilege; but capitalist privilege has come to be expected as a principle of economic distribution and motivation. It inheres in markets, and sometimes it rewards not just inherited capital but pluck and innovation. What was remarkable about late socialism—the East European regimes of the last two decades of their existence—was how they too relied on privilege although their official ideology was exactly at odds with the concept. Privilege means the granting by an act of apparent grace the permission or enjoyment that might under a regime of law and liberalism come automatically. Since the GDR's economy could not provide vast rewards, it functioned by making access to small rewards arbitrary.

Censorship thus became, for example, the reverse side of privilege; it made every producer of literature dependent upon opaque decisions by supposed mentors, editors, and friends. In theory censorship did not exist. In the first decade after the war many of the older generation felt useful and wanted to help in socialist reconstruction. A certain upbeat tone came naturally. In the decades to come, self-censorship came into play: authors knew the limits and applied them in advance. By the 1960s censorship was a taboo term (in the summer of 1968 Ulbricht expressed his astonishment to learn that censorship existed in Czechoslovakia since it did not in the GDR; Honecker likewise denied that there was censorship). For a regime without censorship, there was a great deal of guidance! Party and government authorities worked with authors to ready socially constructive literature for state publication.[68] Within the Ministry of Culture the Administration for Publishing and the Book Trade under Deputy Minister Klaus Höpcke ("minister for books" he liked to be called) had the job of planning the output of socialist literature. Increasingly envisaging his role as an advocate of authors, he took the projected lists over to Ursula Ragwitz at the Central Committee's cultural division and returned with a list of sanctioned projects and their planned print runs. For the authors, approval opened a process of tutelage: first the publishing house assigned the author a

"Lektor," an editor and quasi tutor who went over the aspiring author's poems or prose, sometimes winning his or her confidence by accepting what the author might believe was daring, sometimes arguing for a less provocative locution. How many of the testimonials of the process suggest the writer's surprise at their editor's tolerance! The perfect censorship was self-imposed; the willingness to pull punches in advance, the gratitude for the editor's own understanding; it created a web of complicity between the grateful and instructed author and his mentor.[69] From the publishing company, the book went to one of Höpcke's censors, who had, as one later explained, developed an intuitive feel for the "sensitive" points to be modified or avoided, such as the Wall or the environment. "Actually we always wanted to have the book printed. . . . In the last analysis we were mediators between publisher/author and Party/State Security. . . . It was really just a question of working with the authors so that criticism of 'real existing socialism' was kept out."[70]

The system could guide writers directly and not just their books. Ragwitz also conscientiously transmitted guidelines to the leadership of the Writers Union (Schriftstellerverband) headed by Hermann Kant after 1978. Stasi agents continually sniffed at Höpcke's office and monitored writers. Even if the party allowed words into print, colleagues might subsequently pull the leash short, as did Max Walter Schulz, a vice-president of the Writers Union when he admonished Christa Wolf in 1969—"Remember your roots, Christa,"—when *The Quest for Christa T.* threatened to veer into dangerous subjectivity.[71] The union could make life easy for loyal or talented authors who would get their trips to the West approved or be allowed to collect foreign royalties. Conversely, the copyright office of the GDR could cut off returns and the union could impose discipline, as it did under Hermann Kant's chairmanship in May and June 1979, when loyal authors orchestrated a servile defamation campaign against Stefan Heym, who, with eight other writers, was expelled from the union. "What is the issue?" Heym protested. "Not foreign currency or something similar. The issue is literature. The Writers Union should really exist to support those who strive to show our world in its contradictory nature and to make it understandable. Instead it prints resolutions that confirm to the apparatus how right it is to suppress precisely this aspect of literature."[72]

Socialism corrupted the public sphere through privilege; it corrupted the private sphere through secrecy. A rich, well-functioning public sphere requires an authentic sphere of private relationships as a counterpart. Perhaps because the state has historically had a weighty presence in Germany, intellectuals have long stressed the claims of private life and intimacy. Families and individuals have worked (the term is purposely chosen) diligently at the construction of affection—often to fail and become overwhelmed by its dark counterpart of loneliness. The literature of German romanticism and the novels of the GDR testify alike to this heroic construction of private sensibility. The guardians of German socialist culture were wary about this tradition. They distrusted its subjectivism and potential melancholy. Marxist theory, moreover, tended to believe that the private-public dichotomy "reified" an archaic bourgeois ideology and amounted to a sophisticated defense of privilege; socialism should overcome the outworn distinction. On the other hand, East German leaders wanted to compete with the West in terms of a consumer culture oriented toward private satisfactions. They insisted on encouraging national traditions and were ill-prepared simply to accept second place in nurturing such a rich domain of German culture as the private sphere. Still, as their debates on Kafka and then Freud, modernism and subjectivity revealed, intellectuals and party leaders alike remained deeply wary about the claims of the private and public spheres.

For Günter Gaus, the private enclaves (he wrote, admittedly, more of card games and garden allotments than intimacy) made the regime bearable and served as a safety valve. For anyone with intellectual or political pretensions, however, the allegedly benign refuge of the private sphere offered less shelter than it seemed to. It was discouraging enough that Marxist Mandarins were leery about recognizing any sort of autonomous private domain. More debilitating was the party's effort to undermine privacy with secrecy. Increasingly, secrecy—as exemplified by the pervasive presence of the state security agents, the Stasi—corrupted private relationships and undermined trust among individuals. To a degree such spying and manipulation could be accepted as part of a cat-and-mouse game; but often it was unsuspected and understandably taken as betrayal. Beyond spying came interventions designed to demoralize adversaries. Stasi directives instructed their agents to seek "disintegration" of opponents by means of "systematic discrediting of reputation . . . systematic organization of professional and social failure to undermine self-confidence . . . creation of doubts . . . sowing of mistrust and mutual suspicion . . . determined exploitation of personal weaknesses."[73]

The Stasi, of course, became the most notorious creation of the regime, emerging as an object of obsessive fascination during the two years after its fall. This was a consequence of the agency's size, of the feelings of betrayal it left behind,[74] and the smug reactions of West Germans who could exploit the theme to nurture a certain political self-righteousness (see chapter 6). East Germans were genuinely shocked by the extent of its recruitment. Perhaps 85,000 paid agents, and perhaps 180,000 "unofficial collaborators," or Inoffizielle Mitarbeiter (IM), fed its ravenous hunger for information.[75] Its sanctions were lighter than the cruelties meted out by the Gestapo; they included imprisonment, the aborting of one's career, the prejudicing of educational opportunity, the denial of travel. But its intrusiveness was just as great. Its presence led some intellectuals to a moral cynicism: the writer Sascha Anderson encouraged dissenters among his circles of young East Berlin writers, only to report on them. The brilliant Prenzlauer Berg poet Rainer Schedlinski wrote that only he who is with the Stasi is really not with them and became a willing informant. Schedlinski's "excuse" was that East German reality in the 1980s had become no more valid or compelling than a TV program, and his simultaneous dialogues with his intellectual friends and with the state secret police meant little more than switching the channels on the television. Such cynical reasoning gained force in a society, where the government sought to control information, but its "audience" went home to watch Western television.[76]

What impact did all the spying have? Ostensibly it gathered information, kilometers of reports, often of the most trivial and self-evident kind conveyed in the jargon that secret police everywhere use to describe "subversives" or elements hostile to the state. But ultimately, the information was not what was important. What really counted, I would argue, was first the opaqueness that the institution created for the regime or, more precisely, the distorting translucence. The Stasi provided the regime with its *arcana imperii*, the power of mystification and secrecy on which its capacity to corrupt independent action, stifle dissent, and preclude the emergence of a public realm depended. Second, it wove large numbers of East Germans, over 1 percent of the whole population, probably over 10 percent of the adult "intellectual" population, into a network of corrupting complicity. By the end many intellectuals did not really know how deeply complicit they had been: Christa Wolf admitted that she had repressed memories of her "unofficial cooperation"; Günter de Bruyn confessed to forgotten conversations in the 1970s; the opposition leader Wolfgang Templin had also reported on friends.[77] Those who discovered they were reported on and, to an even greater degree, those who reported (no matter how harmless they depicted their friends' views and conversations), were unlikely to rely on the supposed shelter of a private sphere and even personal relations. Secrecy and complicity undermined the potential not only for outright opposition, but autonomy and authenticity.

The Stasi made complicity a key principle of governance. The emphasis differed from the Third Reich, which relied far more on terror and acclamation. Stasi officials themselves—we shall return to this theme in chapter 3—envisaged their roles as much as social workers as policemen; they were the heirs to eighteenth-century *Poliezeywissenschaft* and cameralism. Their efforts to praise stressed informants' quiet demeanor and their constructive behavior; their criticisms noted egocentrism, curiosity, and self-esteem.[78] Stasi agents seemed to believe that the objects of investigation should be grateful for the tutelage provided. The good Stasi officer upheld the social order without being a fanatic. He was a quiet but steadfast supporter of socialism: "For me the 'harmony of indvidual and social interests in socialism,'" one of them recalled later, "was an actual reality." He could take in stride a bit of criticism and nonconformity:

> I found a general condemnation of long hair or jeans inappropriate. Naturally I did not welcome or defend them. But long hair in my opinion was only an external matter that had nothing to do with the internal attitudes of people. I was personally against long hair, but more from reasons of fashion because one had been brought up conservatively. . . . We did not want to suppress the opposition "outwardly." In our view of "political underground activity" we always proceeded from the idea that the majority of people were "led astray". . . . Only a few "salient representatives" had taken up a "hostile attitude," as we called it, and they wanted to overturn the socialist order in general. The majority were always "led astray" or "fellow travelers [Mitläufer]."[79]

Stasi collaborators obeyed any number of motives: the writers, at least, have discussed them extensively since 1989, although with an artfulness that warns against reading them as simple confessions.[80] For some over fifty, there was a desire to help the state; others acted out of fear or Stasi intimidation. Younger authors, such as Sascha Anderson, argued they might create a space for modern writers. For a few, collaboration just complemented their natural cynicism; Heiner Müller felt that a writer of his intelligence had the right to have dialogues with whom he wanted; and Stasi officers were more informed than ordinary party members. In the churches or the "block parties" allied to the SED, political mediators such as Manfred Stolpe or Lothar de Maizière believed they could more usefully negotiate within the system in order to win some freedom of movement than refuse to cooperate. Real existing socialism thus rested on a double distortion. It transformed the public sphere into one of negotiated bargains, while it twisted the idea of a private sphere into a domain of complicity and secrecy.

Now, Western societies are not immune from analogous degeneration. The importance of access to the mass media in a plebiscitary democracy— that is, the crucial role of television—also undermines the public and private domains that earlier liberalism presupposed. On the one side, the media undermine the distinction between publicity and public. On the other side, the preoccupation with publicity often tends to reduce the meaning of the private sphere to issues of erotic behavior. What saved the Western democracies from crisis, however, was the decentralized nature of this process: no ruling party was identified with the erosion of political boundaries; indeed each sought to benefit. Governance in the West did not require a secret police and did not rest on sustained complicity. It sometimes entailed pervasive corruption, the uncovering of which, as in Italy during 1992–93, deeply shook the regime. But it did not claim to suppress dissent by prison and exile. Thus the undermining of public and private spheres exerted a more gradual subversion in the West. Whatever West European or North and South American crises might yet mature were thus still relatively remote as of 1989.

Should the crisis of regime have seemed less remote in East Germany by 1989? Any observer predicting trouble for the GDR would certainly have had to take account not just of opponents but of *Aussteiger*, those opting out. The independent intellectual life of the late 1980s, as one participant has noted, was not precisely an underground, but a tolerated unofficialness. "The Stasi is no longer a theme," some of the younger writers were explaining by the latter 1980s.[81] But in fact the slogan suggested just how effective the network of secrecy had become. The literary scene became one of gifted dropouts: a proliferation of poets and short-lived little magazines, a search for a new audience, not political transformation. The political alternative, so the avant-garde generation envisaged, was emigration, not change. Certainly political organizers were also active, still largely within church forums, on behalf of issues that the regime found threatening, such as peace, human rights, and ecology. Nonetheless the dissenters were fragmented and harassed, a few hundred activists, all under police surveillance. Indeed, outsiders could interpret their semi-subversive protests as a testimony to regime flexibility. Western observers argued that the GDR was no longer monolithic, was keenly aware of modern social and gender tensions, and, in some respects (e.g., child care), offered models for the West. If dissent became bolder, as when the ballad singer Stephan Krawczyk openly criticized GDR cultural policy in November 1987, Westerners argued that the regime was allowing more toleration. In fact, Stasi preoccupations with censoring the church and dissent were growing more obsessive.[82]

The fact that the regime persisted even when reform was under way in the Soviet Union, going so far as to block distribution of the German-language Soviet magazine *Sputnik* in 1988, made it harder to avert a crisis. Under Honecker, there was no possibility of abandoning the party's claim to remain the privileged political force. Neo-Stalinist formulas were invoked for a last time: Everything with the people, everything through the people, everything for the people. But *Volk* was a concept that had a Stalinist (and earlier a National Socialist) history. It suggested a monolithic popular will that could be delegated to a ruling party put in charge of arranging all of public and private life. Not "people" but "society" was emerging as the key reformist political idea.

In retrospect, it seems fair to state that Western social scientists should have been more sensitive to the besetting contradictions of late socialism. Our fault was not the failure actually to predict the great collapse, but the reluctance to entertain contradictory and contingent possibilities. Historical outcomes are complicated and subject to multiple causal chains. Surprise is always possible. Social scientists err when they forget how precarious their insights are or how many variables they might be slighting. By the end of the 1970s, the Helsinki process of rapprochement, the economic difficulties evident in capitalist regimes, the academic pressure to be safe and judicious, all discouraged entertaining the idea of Communist instability. It took percipient courage to write, as did Robert Havemann in 1978, "I have no thought of leaving the GDR, where one can really observe how step by step the regime is losing, or has already lost, all credibility, and how it would only take a few external impulses or events to send the Politbüro to the devil."[83]

Conversely, once the regime fell, the temptation of some social scientists was to explain how from the beginning "real existing socialism" was unstable. Such retrospective reasoning was no more honest or useful than the earlier insistence on late Communist stability. The problem is not that retrospective analysis plays no useful role; societies have always put a lot of effort into historical reconstruction. But historians and social scientists should not be devoting their effort to making large-scale outcomes seem inevitable. Their craft should involve making remarkable events seem plausible, not foreordained. Explanation of an outcome does not require excluding other possible denouements, but demonstrating how it rested on sufficient prior circumstances. Even had the GDR endured, social scientists who emphasized its stability would have been deficient in not signaling the possibilities of crisis.

Social scientists find it difficult to envisage that tendencies toward breakdown continually coexist with pressures for stability. They also find it difficult to accept that coercive regimes may rest on general acceptance and sometimes enthusiasm. The issue is inherent in the thorny concept of legitimacy. Legitimacy tends to imply that a regime enjoys normative support; its rule does not rest on the threat of force alone. Do regimes that persist without the continued use of force thereby demonstrate their legitimacy? Does their collapse mean that they lost legitimacy or were just overwhelmed by circumstance?

In testing legitimacy we inquire about one or several criteria: (1) a lawful or at least majority-ratified process by which a regime comes to power; (2) its ability to maintain itself in power without resort to coercion alone; (3) finally its use of power for ends acceptable to a broader international public opinion. Political analysts with a stringent sense of what legitimacy entails may insist that all three criteria be satisfied. Less demanding or more "realistic" commentators may impose fewer tests, say the first or the second. To take the first criterion: can ruling cliques that rely on the weapons of powerful foreign sponsors ever overcome the stigma of their collaboration? Did the circumstances of 1940 render Vichy illegitimate, or was the Kadar regime of 1956 illegitimate because it was imposed by Soviet armed force? If so, did it gradually assume legitimacy as Hungarian participation in public activities resumed and the government actually endeavored to overcome repression and move toward reform? The same questions dogged the Franco regime and that of Augusto Pinochet.

The second issue becomes difficult because a regime that relies on the secret police may still enjoy consensus. Did the Stasi, or at other times and places, the Gestapo, the NKVD, or Iran's Savak, preclude legitimacy? Some commentators would accept that even an authoritarian regime can be legitimate if it wins some voluntary consensus or acceptance. They would credit mass participation in state-sponsored public (but not policy-making) activity, such as education, sports, vacation excursions. Other writers focus on the willingness of elites to carry out instructions. The allegiance of the cadres, more than the tranquillity of the masses, provides the test. Until they desert, legitimacy remains.[84] But if we pose the third test about the uses of power, it becomes debatable whether loyalty alone creates legitimacy. Could the acclamation of German and Austrian crowds in 1938 legitimate a National Socialist regime that wantonly terrorized its opponents and Jewish residents? These issues will always remain open. Debates over legitimacy will always end up hinging on definitions. If the possibility of force is never renounced and organized opposition is never sanctioned, the concept of "legitimacy," I believe, will not serve any historical or social science analysis. The question must be reformulated: what quality of acceptance was at stake under communism?[85]

A TETHERED CONSCIOUSNESS

From its formation until Mikhail Gorbachev's visit to Berlin in October 1989, the fate of the GDR depended on the perceived requirements of the Soviet leadership. As early as 1951, the British analyst J. P. Nettl wrote that by the summer of 1947 "it was clear that Communism in Germany must be based on Russian power and could never have the strength of popular support sufficient to enable it to stand on its democratic feet. . . . Since Communism had been brought in by Russian bayonets, and served exclusively Russian purposes, it was entirely dependent on their continued presence, until sufficient German bayonets could be found to take their place."[86] During the crisis of 1953 the Soviet authorities in Berlin were the arbiters of East German policy. In the fall of 1989, the Soviets decided they would not intervene to suppress any upheaval. From the first to the last, Soviet power was critical for the regime.

Did this dependence mean that the East German state (and by extension other Communist regimes in Eastern Europe) engendered no loyalties, had no vital principle of its own? Did dependence preclude striking down real roots? The question is difficult. Day-to-day acquiescence cannot in any case provide much guidance to loyalties when the police can always be unleashed. Soviet tanks in East Berlin on July 17, 1953, in Budapest during November 1956, and in Prague in summer 1968, and the imposition of martial law in Poland in late 1981 demonstrated that the Communist states of Eastern Europe repeatedly had to resort to repression. Even in the Soviet Union, where the instrumentalized memory of the revolution and World War II was continually invoked by the regime, once the party embarked on glasnost, it could no longer stabilize its rule.

The power of coercion, moreover, does not disappear if the police are smiling, any more than deterrence evaporates if missiles remain unfired. True, over a long period, political usages may durably change and force may disappear as a plausible option. Nonetheless, coercion hardly has to be continually applied to discourage opposition. One exemplary trial, the periodic breaking up of a public meeting, rustication of a Prague economic historian, say, to an agricultural school in rural Slovakia, the presence of a known party stalwart among a traveling delegation of intellectuals, the firing of a worker who can't take the ideological pressure anymore and applies for an exit visa—all serve as ideological booster shots to keep immunization at an adequate level. The potential for repression makes it impossible to judge the quality of consent. It is safe to say that without the potential for Soviet intervention, none of the satellite regimes would have endured. And once Soviet leaders made it clear they would not intervene, these regimes collapsed. Probably we should abandon the concept of legitimacy altogether and talk about civic postures that range from resistance to acquiescence, and acceptance to enthusiasm.

Part of the difficulty is the level of aggregation that such judgments involve. In most modern dictatorships, and certainly under the East European regimes, elements of allegiance and submission were present simultaneously. It did not always require the level of cognitive dissonance that Brecht demonstrated on and after June 17, 1953, when he both criticized the East German regime and abjectly wrote Walter Ulbricht and Otto Grotewohl to express his loyalty to the SED.[87] There were always projects worthy of support: peace campaigns, mobilization against revanchism, educational reforms. Totalitarian societies are societies involved in continual projects: they are always "constructing" something, whether a factory, dam, or socialism. Thinkers of consequence, as well as those hack functionaries certified as writers or intellectuals, enrolled in this constructive effort, often with genuine commitment. It would be incorrect to conclude that these regimes generated no loyalties outside of the party apparatuses and nomenklatura that had a direct interest in the system. East European communism was repression tempered by enthusiasms.

From day to day the citizens of Eastern Europe could help create a regime of normalization. They could enter a series of transactions with the authorities to live within the limits of the possible: Christa Wolf confessed that she never thought she was living "in the truth," as Havel described the stance of noncooperation. She and others who came of age in the 1950s certainly accepted that the realm of the possible was durably circumscribed. They confronted regimes already in place, and spent their careers building socialism over three decades.[88] Western intellectuals who visited the regimes participated in the process of normalization. Naturally we do not like to visit before the bloodstains fade on the asphalt; musicians canceled concerts after Dubček fell; writers no longer craved invitations to Beijing after Tiananmen Square. But after a decent interval we returned. I would not have visited Warsaw directly after martial law was proclaimed in 1981, but I could justify attending a conference two years later. My colleagues and I briefed our hosts on the most recent scholarship; we learned about the texture of opposition (a curious coexistence where dissenters might languish in prison and then enjoy trips to the West or have their ideas discussed by the moderates of the regime in pseudonymous reviews). We arranged for needed journal issues to be sent to colleagues. We could always persuade ourselves that the victims of the repression should not be penalized by quarantine; they needed the contacts. We historians, for example, also met with our counterparts in East German academic life. They were not heroes, but they were, so we felt, working at the limits the system allowed. We encouraged their edging away from stilted determinist paradigms, appreciated their work on Frederick the Great or regional economic development, and were grateful when at last they began to confront German anti-semitism. Did our collaboration reenforce these twilight authoritarian regimes or encourage their citizens to contest them further?

Socialism generated some loyalties, some hopes for the future, and the conviction that it kept reaction at bay. When the novelist and head of the East German Writers Association, Hermann Kant, was asked what had been the accomplishments of the regime as he watched it collapse, he said that antifascism was a major justification. (Having blessed the last purge of the group in 1979, he was himself removed in 1990.) And indeed antifascism was often used as an ideological rallying point.[89] That such a negative cry could function for so long was noteworthy. Was there a fascist threat in East Germany or even in the Federal Republic? How long would a mission of eradicating "fascism" (forget the problem of whether the Nazi past was appropriately labeled fascist!) serve to justify the socialism of the GDR? The concept of antifascism was problematic in the extreme. First of all, the GDR took far fewer active steps to discuss and examine its responsibility for the Nazi past than the Federal Republic. Just establishing the regime had allegedly made the past irrelevant, the product of an earlier social system. Socialism was antifascist in its essence. So too, its supporters suggested that it was a bulwark for peace. But how did it intervene for peace? By training its goose-stepping soldiers to fight with the Warsaw Pact forces? Did it just deter West German revanchism? The justifications became increasingly formulaic. Perhaps socialist loyalty was generated most elementally in the early decades of the republic by the sense of communal concern that its citizens experienced. Strangers shared tables in restaurants, they were asked to sign ubiquitous, homey guestbooks in offices, hotels, even police stations. East Germans who crossed to the West allegedly felt the anomie created by its wealth and capitalism. At home they claimed somehow to cultivate a fraternal consciousness, if only that of scarcity.

Whatever this quality of socialist consensus, or acquiescence, it blew away virtually overnight. The novelist Christa Wolf and the writer Stefan Heym tried to rally intellectuals to the remnants of an ethical socialism, but their appeal seemed desperate, their "socialism" without substantive content: the fading memory of the grail. The options that had been impossible were now possible, indeed urgent. The dimensions of the feasible had expanded enormously. Philosophers have recently discussed the dilemmas of changing mental states and preferences. We know that under some circumstances our desires will change fundamentally and thus we seek to bind ourselves according to a set of "higher" preferences that represent our most future-oriented sense of self. Odysseus is canny enough to know the sirens will destroy him if he is not bound to the mast.[90] If we are prone to temptation, we may put liquor out of reach. We rank-order our priorities. Unfortunately, authoritarian political systems impose constrictions on our higher, not our lower selves. There is a logic of optimizing under politically constricted circumstances. Those who accept it sacrifice some degree of moral autonomy for measured doses of conditional freedom. The apparent consent that communism garnered in Eastern Europe depended on this sort of behavior.[91] It rested on what might be usefully called a tethered consciousness. Unless one chose emigration or silence, this involved working within, indeed internalizing, a set of apparently permanent and irremovable constraints, thanking the censors, as it were. Why were there not more protestors, especially since repression was less severe than in the 1950s and 1960s? The question has continually challenged those scrutinizing the last stages of the regime. To be sure, real sanctions persisted. Punishments were meted out. Individuals and families seeking exit visas were called in by their employers, given a week to think it over, and, if they persisted, fired because they were unworthy of their job in the public sphere.

Still, the dialectic of threat and reward, as Wolfgang Templin has sought to describe it, remained complicated. By the 1970s and 1980s the strategies of repression were not designed to imprison the would-be dissenter, but just to establish within what boundaries dissent had to be confined. The Wall not only established the limits of travel; it was the paradigm for a regime of confined space, within which privilege might be granted but beyond which no political challenge was allowed. "A calculated critical intellectual who stayed within a determined boundary but possessed some room for maneuver on account of his personal situation or biography . . . was far more valuable for this mixed system of control, repression, and, simultaneously, attraction that one sought to organize until the very end."[92]

What occurred in autumn 1989—first when the Hungarians allowed border crossings in September, irrevocably when the Berlin Wall opened on November 9—was that the permanent constraints suddenly disappeared. The Wall at the frontier had made possible all the walls within; the GDR had been a regime of walls, the most effective being those within its citizens' heads. It was as if animals who had spent their lives within a zoo—say, the Leipzig zoo with its well-fed lions that was a source of pride to its city and its country—suddenly found the ditches filled and the cages open. Before it would have been irrational to spend one's force trying to jump the moats; now life's most basic political parameter had been radically changed. Citizens of the GDR after November 9 had the opportunity to transform their rational preferences. Their earlier behavior was not just an expression of duress, but it had never been the expression of autonomous collective choice. Now the incentives for socialist efficiency, prosperity, and purposeful activity suddenly dissipated. The moral premise of the regime did not extend beyond its sponsors' willingness to use force for its support.

The future historian will ask why authoritarian governments, East and West, left and right, jointly lost the political and administrative resources required to manage the pressures emanating from civil society. Military dictators ceded control in Greece and Portugal and Spain during the 1970s, in Brazil and Argentina, Chile and Paraguay in the 1980s. In some cases, notably Greece and Argentina, military rulers discredited themselves in disastrous military campaigns. Elsewhere they seemed foiled by more fundamental political divisions and intractable contradictions, as in Brazil. The Communist regimes hardly fought to retain control in Hungary or Czechoslovakia—or East Germany. Certainly there was some early resistance, but what was striking was the quick demoralization of the rulers and their efforts at self-transformation. Where possible, as in Budapest or Belgrade or

Bucharest, ex-Communist rulers sought to pose as ministers of national salvation or transition. But in other capitals they accepted, even initiated political changes that they understood must destroy their political power. When the Czech Communists allowed East Germans to exit indirectly across their frontier in October 1989, they must have foreseen that this signaled the abandonment of their own mechanisms of control. How do we explain the virtual abdication of authority?[93]

Perhaps the most effective solvent of power by the end of the 1980s was the accumulated force of international public opinion. The concept resonates with echoes of nineteenth-century British liberalism—Mill, Bright, and Bagehot each believed in its civilizing influence. Before 1989 it might have sounded totally archaic. Nonetheless, political values diffuse across frontiers. In the 1930s the authoritarian party and regime seemed the wave of the future. Disciplined collective man was apparently on the march. Liberalism appeared the effete indulgence of a beleaguered Anglo-American elite or some aging West European philosophers. By the 1970s and 1980s the opposite was becoming true; not to be democratic was to be benighted and obsolete. International public opinion, however, does not function as a disembodied spirit; it requires an institutional setting. In the 1930s the spokesmen for democracy were divided and apparently demoralized. The League of Nations seemed powerless before aggression. By the 1970s and 1980s the European Community beckoned as a club of wealthy and liberal societies; the Social Democratic parties of Europe were prepared to subsidize their colleagues in fledgling democracies; NATO had not lost its resolve; and the Conference on Security and Cooperation in Europe (the so-called Helsinki process) in theory committed even the Communist states to take account of human rights. These were not organizations designed to roll back the Iron Curtain but they created an evident infrastructure for democratic values. Democratization emerged as the only acceptable political agenda in Europe and the Americas.

To put it slightly differently, by the end of the 1980s, most authoritarian rulers no longer believed in their own original political vision. In East Berlin or Prague, they shared their critics' sense that the economic and social stalemate could not continue, but they did not know how to extricate themselves or devise decisive reforms. Modern authoritarian regimes had been governments based on projects.[94] They would build hydroelectric works, then steel mills, remake "man," or achieve national salvation. Whatever the blueprint, they proposed an activist summons to some new physical or political construction. By the end of the eighties, however, no credible secular projects remained. (Religious projects, especially in Islamic societies, regained vitality.) Only the echo of earlier crusades might be invoked to enthuse a narrowing circle of party faithful.

World history offers no recent parallel for such a peaceful ideological rout. Fascism and Nazism suddenly collapsed in 1945, but only after Allied victory in the largest war ever waged. Communism self-destructed. More precisely, in the face of social and economic transformations that strained West as well as East, its guardians discarded it. Nonetheless, self-destruction or so-called implosion will explain only so much. Historical upheavals require agents as well as trends. Trends are large aggregated results over which individuals sense no personal influence. They are macro-outcomes obeying a logic of social interaction independent of intentionality. (In the next chapter we shall examine such decisive "trends.") Still, for all the ineluctable momentum of trends, ultimately individuals, groups, and crowds attempt purposeful political action in the belief that they can change history. Ironically enough, the aggregate developments to which they have contributed without any sense of autonomy may bring them to the point at which they can act, with intentionality, as protagonists. So they hesitantly but courageously came to believe (and so we shall follow them in chapters 3 and 4) in Leipzig and Berlin by the fall of 1989.

Two

The Economic Collapse

I am for trade with the nonsocialist economies, but not for dependence. We have come to a point where our room for maneuver has continually shrunk. . . . Increasing foreign trade means we increasingly confront the principles of the world market. We have to be careful about that in a country like ours, which can only live by value-added production. Increased indebtedness to the nonsocialist world is not possible. We've gone as far as we can politically. Otherwise we'll get into a situation that is politically dangerous, and in that case our comrades in the Volkspolizei and the Ministry for State Security won't be any help at all. These are issues that have piled up for years, where we've chosen the path of least resistance, and the GDR will have to pay.

—Alfred Neumann in the Council of Ministers, October 19, 1989.[1]

THE DEBT CRISIS AND THE CONTRADICTIONS OF COMECON

"Ali" Neumann was a Politbüro old-timer and hardly one of its leading thinkers, but when the Council of Ministers convened for a session of collective breast-beating a day after Honecker agreed to retire, he put his finger on the economic dilemma of the GDR. Only as Communist rule was disintegrating could party leaders openly address the country's precarious situation. It was not foreordained that East German socialism had to collapse, but the financial pressures were becoming unrelenting. At the end, they culminated in a debt crisis, the extent of which astonished and demoralized party delegates. The GDR, so Gerhard Schürer, head of the Planning Commission, reported to Honecker's successor, Egon Krenz, at the end of October 1989, had accumulated a foreign debt of 49 billion "valuta marks" ($26.5 billion), the currency unit used for foreign trade accounting and pegged at roughly the value of the West German deutsche mark. The deficit on current account would amount to over $12 billion for 1989, and debt service alone cost $4.5 billion or over 60 percent of yearly export earnings. Just to stabilize the debt by an austerity program would require a drop in living standards of 25 to 30 percent, and even such a sacrifice could not assure that the GDR would be able to sell the needed exports.[2] As in all national credit crises, the looming East German disaster had its origins in the persistent failures to resolve contending claims on national income. In this case the defects arose from ideological commitments. To understand the terminal crisis that overtook the regime, one has to work back to the long-term disabilities imposed by socialist production.

How far back, however? Was socialism doomed from the outset, or were there later fateful turning points? The SED Central Committee's chief finance expert, Günter Ehrensperger, dated the difficulties from November 1973, when Honecker responded to his projections that foreign debt would rise from its still modest 2 billion valuta marks total to 20 billion by 1980. "I was summoned to him on the same evening and he told me I was immediately to cease working on such calculations and studies. I was to receive no further material and I was to have all the statistical bases in the department destroyed. That was the beginning. That was the beginning."[3] When Schürer confessed to the Central Committee the extent of foreign indebtedness, he claimed that the difficulties originated with the Eighth Party Congress in 1971, which resolved that German communism must support a generous consumer society and welfare state. This decision enshrined what became known as "the unity of social and economic policy," which Günter Mittag stubbornly defended as party orthodoxy for the next decade and a half. In practice it meant subsidizing consumer prices, vacations, and social services so that the gap with West Germany did not undermine acceptance of the regime. But it also limited the investment that East Germany required to produce goods that might be internationally competitive. As Schürer told the Central Committee, "It was hardly visible then, but that was when the switches were set. From then on the train traveled millimeter by millimeter in the wrong direction. It traveled away from the realities of the GDR."[4]

Most Western commentators would have countered that the switches were set wrong from the moment central planning was imposed in postwar Eastern Europe. Was socialism ever viable? Or was it viable only as a closed system? This is a crucial historical and economic issue, to which this chapter must return. To its shaken supporters in 1989, what seemed so intractable about the denouement of German socialism was its international dimension. No matter how workable or unworkable socialism might originally have appeared within each country, by the 1980s Communist societies were exposed to the world market, that is, to their increasing need for goods originating outside the socialist bloc. That involvement magnified every vulnerability. The technologies needed for modernization or the consumer items that their populations coveted—whether PCs and telecommunication systems or jeans or Walkmen—came from the West, but collectively they could generate few of the exports needed to purchase them. They were condemned to trade for each other's less desirable products or else had to borrow from the nonsocialist world. In effect the policy makers of the major socialist economies felt that they were locked into a club of poor relations, the so-called Council for Mutual Economic Assistance, abbreviated as either CMEA or Comecon. Each participating country was growing impatient with this community of relative backwardness. Each increasingly wanted its partners to pay in convertible currencies that they might spend elsewhere. Protocapitalist restlessness began to afflict the industrialized economies of the socialist world. By 1989 the Comecon was confining but difficult to renounce.

East Germany in the 1980s faced increasing pressure to import Western goods and technology. Although the country aspired to increase its export earnings in convertible currencies, in fact it had financed imports through a rapid rise in debt. The total was not so great as Poland's, but it was still preoccupying and the per capita burden was just as heavy. Publication of the total had become impossible, Schürer had to admit in October 1989, because of the danger that capitalist banks would limit or cancel their credits. "Preservation of the GDR's creditworthiness, however, is a basic assumption for the continued functioning of our economy on a socialist basis." Only the party faithful were deceived, however. Economic policy makers understood that East Germany's welfare provisions and relatively high personal consumption rested not on its own earnings but on growing indebtedness. Revealing the fact, however, "would have seemed to contradict the general depiction of GDR economic strength, fulfillment of the plan, and international position (tenth industrial country)."[5]

Although East German export earnings increased, they could not grow fast enough to meet import requirements. The GDR forced West German and foreign visitors to change a daily quota of their respective currencies into East German marks, thus earning about 1.5 million valuta marks per week as of 1989; but this provided the regime with little more than petty cash.[6] At home, consumption climbed and savings dropped as a share of national income. According to Schürer's report to Hans Modrow at the end of 1989, the rate of "productive investment" had fallen from 16.1 percent in 1970 to 9.9 percent in 1988.[7] West German credits above all had become crucial for the GDR; and no matter how anti-Communist they might be, the political leaders of the Federal Republic effectively competed to provide them. After the Kohl government replaced the Social Democrats, the chancellor and his finance minister, Franz Josef Strauß, vied with each other in effect to normalize contacts with the GDR regime and extended a first credit of a billion marks in late June 1983. A second "*Milliardenkredit*" (DM 950 million, to be exact) followed in summer 1984.[8] West German credits were still East German debts. The service charges were fast outrunning any corresponding export earnings. Schürer reported to his dismayed colleagues that Western banks felt that a country's yearly debt service charges should amount to no more than one-quarter of its export earnings. The GDR's yearly charges on its debts to the capitalist world, however, had mounted to one and a half times the receipts from exports sent West. When calculated in terms of domestic currency units, the debt represented the equivalent of two-thirds of the yearly national income.[9]

As indebtedness to the West increased, (see Table 2-1) tensions grew within the international socialist trading community. The periodic conferences of Comecon economic ministers revealed the centrifugal pressures. So did the important bilateral East German-Soviet trade negotiations. Comecon had been designed as a supposed counterpart to the West's Organization for European Economic Cooperation (the OEEC, subsequently reorganized as the Organization for Economic Cooperation and Development or OECD), in part to implant and nurture central planning throughout the satellites and in part to coordinate barter arrangements among Communist economies that had no significant reserves of convertible currencies. Unlike the West European efforts at "integration," Comecon's planners did not originally aspire to intraregional specialization. Its organizers sought to clone Stalinist-type economies, not to integrate them. To be sure, comparative advantages arose: Bulgarian fruits and wine, Soviet petroleum, Czech vehicles, East German machine tools. And by the 1960s and 1970s the Soviets sought to assign different contributions to each national economy. Their respective leaders, however, resisted accepting low-technology assignments; they instinctively aspired to develop their own heavy industry as the sign of socialist maturity. They certainly did not want to sell commodities and raw materials that had hard-currency potential within the bloc. By the late 1980s those economies ambitious to sell to the nonsocialist world rebuffed most efforts to take part in common planning.[10]

Table 2-1. Convertible Currency Indebtedness of CMEA
and Selected Members (in million U.S. dollars)

	1975	1980	1985	1989
East Germany				
Gross	5,188	13,896	13,234	20,600
Net[a]	3,548	11,750	6,707	11,045
Poland				
Gross	8,388	24,128	29,300	41,400
Net[a]	7,725	23,482	27,705	37,953
Soviet Union				
Gross	10,577	23,512	25,177	52,392
Net[a]	7,450	14,940	12,115	37,621
CMEA				
Gross	34,778	88,588	96,931	53,425
Net[a]	26,290	73,505	69,999	119,866

Source: Vienna Institute for Comparative Economic Studies, ed., *COMECON Data, 1989* (London:Macmillan, 1990), p. 379.

[a] Net debt subtracts assets held in convertible currencies by the borrowing country from its gross debt. Note that these totals for the GDR differ from the estimate of $26.5 billion provided in October 1989 by Gerhard Schürer.

Comecon sheltered the Communist economies at the cost of perpetuating their relative backwardness. By the 1980s its constraints became glaring, but Soviet subsidies as well as the overall political pressures imposed by the confrontation of East and West precluded easy reforms. Moscow was willing to pay for its hegemonic position. During the 1970s, Soviet oil exports, priced according to a moving five-year average of world market costs, at least ensured that their CMEA partners enjoyed subsidized energy as the prices set by the Organization of Petroleum Exporting Countries (OPEC) soared. The Russians also furnished other raw materials, such as iron ore, at prices lower than prevailed in the West. Estimates of the Soviet subsidy from 1970 to the mid-1980s have ranged from about $30 to $118 billion. As world market prices for oil slid by the mid-1980s, Soviet oil, however, became relatively more expensive and the Comecon countries became restive. Nonetheless, they still benefited from the fact that the Soviets were also willing to purchase the second-rate manufactures that CMEA partners needed to sell for their oil imports, and to pay relatively high prices.[11] How large a subsidy these intrabloc exchanges involved remains uncertain. Prices remained politically determined inside the bloc, many manufactures had no Western markets, and Eastern bloc currencies were nonconvertible. (Of course, Western oil prices both before and after the OPEC price hikes of early 1974 were also politically determined.)

No matter how substantial the advantages the East European economies might draw from Soviet subsidies, the incapacity to generate convertible currencies within Comecon was increasingly disabling. The nonsocialist world promised access to modernization and consumerism, but its sophisticated scientific equipment, its electronics, Mercedes, rock performers and the like could be purchased only through Western credits, or limited exports of East European goods: Soviet oil and gas for resale in the case of East Germany, handicrafts such as Czech and Polish crystal, or inexpensive versions of Western goods, such as Romanian and Polish suits. Occasionally there was the special art sale or East European performing artist that generated the Western currency windfalls that Alexander Schalck-Golodkowski had charge of arranging and distributing inside the GDR. But these remained slender recourses. No matter how important it remained as a market for their second-rate manufactures, CMEA disadvantages became ever more constraining.

CMEA trading relationships remained based on direct bilateral contracts and on five-year collective agreements in which the goods traded were priced in so-called valuta or transferable rubles. This unit of account served for intrabloc clearances, but did not represent a convertible currency and could not be used for purchases from what the East Germans called the NSW or Nichtsozialistisches Wirtschaftsgebiet, the nonsocialist economies. The Soviet Union itself wanted to change the system so that it would have more freedom to buy quality goods from the West. Soviet economic experts signaled in November 1985 that their exports of commodities and raw materials to CMEA partners had reached a plateau and that "the present model of cooperation in fact has no future."[12] Whereas the less industrialized socialist economies—Vietnam and Cuba—were fundamentally hostile to any evolution of market relationships, by the mid-1980s Hungary and Poland and, soon thereafter, Bulgaria, Czechoslovakia, and Gorbachev's Soviet Union urged far more liberalization. Hungary was particularly interested in switching to trade in convertible currencies, for it ran a current-account surplus with the Soviets.[13] No wonder that by the time Hungary opened its border with Austria in September 1989, the East Germans were long convinced that it had degenerated into a de facto capitalist state. The East Germans resisted this trend, as they resisted liberalization more generally. Clashing with the Hungarian delegate in June 1987, Günther Kleiber told the CMEA Executive Committee that demands for freer exchange of goods and services were "incompatible with the necessity of strengthening the planlike cooperation of our countries."[14] East Germans felt increasingly beleaguered by the new enthusiasm for market reforms, just as they did by the growing pressure for political liberalization.

By early 1987, Moscow was proposing significant CMEA trade reforms, which East German experts anxiously interpreted as just another step in the long effort to avoid agreeing to padded prices for East German industrial exports. In a long internal analysis of early 1987, East German foreign-trade authorities warned that Soviet proposals involved moving toward market prices from 1988 on and abandoning the transferable or valuta ruble within eight to ten years. "The convergence of internal prices and the [CMEA] mechanism for price formation envisaged by the Soviet experts—so they argued—fundamentally contradicts GDR economic and social policy as agreed on at the SED Eleventh Party Congress, especially with regard to preserving price stability for basic commodities and payments for services." Since the CMEA-negotiated prices for machine tools were higher than GDR supply costs, Soviet proposals for direct contracts between Soviet and East German Kombinate based on immediate payment would cost the GDR's machine-tool industry dearly. Moscow further wanted to repeal Comecon automatic credit facilities, to eliminate long-term negotiated prices and coordination of economic planning—in short, to move from subsidized trade toward genuine market conditions, developments that would all mean "incalculable economic disadvantages for the GDR."[15]

But even as they resisted Soviet proposals for CMEA reform, East German planners also insisted on the right to strike their own special deals with the capitalist world. Conversely Russian planners could invoke traditional appeals to socialist bloc solidarity at the cost of market relations. As negotiations in May 1987 between the chair of the Soviet Council of Ministers, Nikolai Ryzhkov, and his East German counterpart, Willi Stoph, indicated, Soviet-East German trade agreements were in some jeopardy. The East Germans sought to purchase a Japanese rolling mill rather than the Soviet plant for which they had contracted almost two years earlier. The Russians were not appeased by East Berlin's promise to buy supplementary equipment instead and threatened to withhold the iron ore the new plant would process. Claiming that the quality of the Russian equipment was as high as any in the capitalist world (except, admittedly, Siemens control systems), Ryzhkov argued that contracts with the nonsocialist world "bring us no advantages, but from the political point of view are a step toward the West." Soviet leaders also felt that the East Germans were delaying their promised cooperation in the modernization of the Ukrainian iron ore mines of Krivoi Rog.

On their side, the East Germans were concerned about the availability of Soviet petroleum. The Russians and East Germans had negotiated their trade for the five-year period 1986–90 as a total package priced at 82 billion transferable rubles (calculated as 380 billion internal marks). But the decline in Soviet oil prices (keyed in turn to world market moving averages) meant that the value of Russian exports would fall 4 to 5 billion rubles (18–24 billion internal marks). GDR planners wanted to compensate for the intervening fall in the world price of oil by having the Soviets raise their annual deliveries from 17 million back to the 19 million tons they had supplied until the five-year trade package negotiated in 1981, not by having them reduce their own imports from East Germany. Since the Russians were supplying 85 percent of East German petroleum, the 1981 reduction had proved a heavy blow. It had not been eased when an allegedly tearful Brezhnev rejected Honecker's personal appeal and argued that East Germany must help the Soviets bear the burden of their then grave economic difficulties. Once again, in 1987, any increase in oil deliveries, the Soviets responded, was simply impossible.[16] The oil dispute proved contentious for almost two years. The Russians offered to supply more natural gas instead of oil, but as Schürer explained in July 1988 to his Soviet counterpart, substituting gas for oil was unsatisfactory. The need was not just fuel—to ease this constraint the East Germans had expanded their lignite mining—but foreign currency. The East Germans actually refined and "cracked" 75 percent of their oil imports for chemical products, some of which, in turn, they exported to the West. In 1985 they had earned about 2.5 billion valuta marks from the nonsocialist world from exports of refined gasoline, diesel, and heating oil, but this had declined to about 1 billion in 1986 and 900 million in 1987. Schürer was not exaggerating when he pleaded that "lower deliveries of petroleum from the Soviet Union would have catastrophic consequences for the GDR."[17]

The records of the ongoing Soviet-GDR trade negotiations cast a penetrating light through the murky dusk of socialism. For both partners the long-term economic relationship was simply too valuable to surrender to acrimony. It had to be preserved. The GDR was caught between its need for Western goods and its dependence on the assured demand for its exports to the Soviet Union. The Soviets purchased its machine tools, its agricultural implements, its Baltic Sea vessels. East Germany was certainly the most robust export power in the Eastern bloc. In 1988, when Soviet exports totaled

$108 billion by official reckoning, the GDR with about one-fifteenth the population exported just under $48 billion, while the Czechs followed with $26 billion, the Poles with about $13 billion, and the Hungarians about $10 billion.[18] Thirty-nine percent of East German goods went to the Soviets, including 65 percent of East German machine tools;[19] Soviet oil was crucial for East German industry, and for East Germany's precarious capacity to earn Western currencies.

In fact the extensive Soviet–East German interdependence was as much a sign of weakness as strength. More of East Germany's trade remained confined to the CMEA countries than did that of Hungary and Poland, and in dollar terms the percentage of its exports going West stagnated in the second half of the 1980s (from 30.1 percent in 1985 to 26.6 percent in 1988). Indeed overall GDR performance, East as well as West, flagged after 1985, as planners were well aware.[20] At the meeting of Comecon delegates in Prague in July 1988, Ryzhkov warned that the Comecon was bound to fall even further behind the West with respect to technology and labor productivity. The structures of Soviet foreign trade were "archaic." Since 1985 the overall volume of CMEA trade had climbed only 4 percent. Willi Stoph might declare that the Complex Program for technological cooperation was yielding tangible results; the Soviets, however, argued that it had contributed only a feeble impulse to modernization of production. "The historic division of labor among our countries," Ryzhkov warned, "has exhausted its possibilities."[21]

The oil discussions continued into 1989. A high-powered East German trade delegation led by Mittag and Schürer traveled to Moscow in late January and again for follow-up talks in early February. By this time the East Germans recognized that they could not increase their 17 million ton oil allocation; the question was whether they might retain it without further cutbacks. "We've said openly, we East Germans originally wanted an extra 2 million tons of oil imports per year; the Soviets threatened to fall below the 17 million stipulated."[22] Both sides faced the harsh trade-off that every ton of fuel consumed within Russia, or inside East Germany, meant a ton less for export. The chief Soviet negotiatior, Nikolai Slyunkov acknowledged East Germany's requirements and its dependence on Soviet crude oil. Nonetheless, he pleaded, the GDR must understand Soviet difficulties. Every ton of oil extracted was increasingly expensive. Yields were low, fields more dispersed, the equipment needed had tripled or quadrupled in price. The Soviet Union used to be able to develop its energy resources to meet the needs of the socialist bloc as a whole. No longer: "The process of developing our economic structures has become a tedious process. Not to mention the resources required." Slyunkov recalled the energy crisis at the end of the 1970s, when 4,500 kilometers of pipeline and 31 million kilowatts of compressor/condensor capacity had to be constructed in five years, at the price of social services, education, and higher wages. "We don't want to dwell on this. We are working for the goals of socialism. We have to carry out economic reform and we have to prioritize social development. Therefore we have neither the possibility nor the right to force further investment in energy." Economic plans required cutting energy consumption yearly by 3.5 per cent per year. Nevertheless, the proposed 2 million ton cut in petroleum exports, Slynkov conceded, would be tough on the GDR economy, since the issue for East Germany was not just fuel but petroleum for its important petrochemical cracking industry. Consequently, he reported, the Soviet Union was prepared to maintain the oil quota and cut back on natural gas if it could agree on a broader inventory of GDR products that would replace imports otherwise needed from the nonsocialist countries.

The point, Slyunkov summarized, was to minimize each other's needs for imports from the nonsocialist bloc. Each country's balance of payments was tied up with its oil needs. If the Soviets used their oil to help develop a backward countryside—Slyunkov cited abysmal village conditions in Russia—they could not sell it abroad. If they provided it to the GDR, the East Germans must replace what the Soviets must otherwise import from the West. If the East Germans did not get Soviet oil, Mittag pointed out in his response, they could not export petrochemicals to the West and they would have to sell machinery otherwise destined for the Soviet Union. Schürer argued even more brutally that the GDR was not just another socialist trading partner; it alone had a cracking industry that would require oil to be obtained from one source or another. "I have to state openly that every million tons we don't get is a million tons imported from the nonsocialist world. The GDR has no further room for maneuver, because we have to exhaust every possibility for our cracking industry."

Out of mutual necessity came the lineaments of a deal. "East Germany is a machine-building country and must remain a machine-building country," the Soviets conceded. It had no other choice. Russia was prepared to allocate more of its ever more expensive oil and accept East German rather than Western goods, so that the GDR could maintain its chemical and machine-tool industries without having to seek Western buyers. Mutual dependence must be confirmed, indeed even deepened. The East Germans were to present a list of high-quality machine tools and chemical exports in early February, which the Soviets would otherwise have to purchase with hard currency from the nonsocialist economies. (In fact it was topped up with clothes and consumer goods.) The Russians would maintain their 17 million tons of oil exports and cut back instead on natural gas deliveries, which presumably could be diverted to satisfy other Comecon partners. Meanwhile the Soviets pleaded that the special agreement be kept secret from the other CMEA partners: "Under no conditions can we take this route with all of the socialist countries. That's totally unrealistic." Moscow had already denied to the Czechs that the East Germans would be given special treatment.[23] East German-Soviet interdependence thus came at the expense of a wider Comecon solidarity; for both sides, the direct relationship was more crucial. Reporting back to the Politbüro, Schürer was congratulated by Honecker: "You've done a good job, Gerhard."[24]

In fact, East Germany still set more store by Comecon solidarity than many of the other CMEA partners. By March 1989, the Soviets were envisioning substantial but not complete convertibility for CMEA currencies by 1995.[25] When in early June 1989, the Communist Party economic secretaries assembled in East Berlin, the Bulgarians announced that they were adopting a so-called plan-market economy and insisted that the socialist world should not underestimate the possibilities for technology cooperation with the leading capitalist countries and firms. The Hungarian delegate agreed and stressed the need to raise competitiveness on the world market. The CMEA, he urged, should not impose binding policies; and it must work toward achieving realistic prices and peg the convertible ruble to Western currencies. The Soviet representative tried to bridge the divergent viewpoints: "It seems to me that the diversity of opinion here is not accidental. It arises from the particularities of the national mechanisms and the transitional character of the present. . . . Two qualitatively different spheres of integration coexist among us, although not cooperatively enough: one based on the state and the other on economic calculation." The Soviet Union wanted to work toward the latter, toward the use of convertible currencies and world market prices among the socialist partners—but this would take time.[26]

The structure of padded prices, sheltered barter, and "soft budget constraints" collapsed sooner rather than later. Barely twelve months later, amid the wreckage of their East European empire, the Soviets announced that after the end of 1990 they would accept only hard currencies for their exports at world market prices. The Comecon had lingered half a decade in its debilitated condition. In effect, it was capitalist credits that postponed its disintegration. Western bank and government loans allowed the socialist economies to find a mutual market for their low-productivity and energy-wasteful manufactures and still finance their demand for Western technology and consumer goods. By the late 1980s world market constraints caught up with the Comecon, and with the GDR and Poland in particular. Of course, the denouement did not arrive without warning; figures for indebtedness had long been mounting. What were the options that East German policy makers considered while this latent crisis grew more acute?

Two strategies were in competition, although there were dissenters from both. Schürer, sometimes supported by Willi Stoph, longtime chairman of the Council of Ministers, was the insistent champion of high-tech development in microelectronics. He envisaged that ultimately the GDR would become a major developer of computer-assisted (CAD/CAM) production of numerically controlled machine tools. His policy required imports of capital goods, long-term modernization, and the cutting of consumer-price subsidies at home. It also meant curtailing the ambitious building projects in East Berlin, "Capital of the GDR" and showplace of socialist achievement for Honecker and Mittag. Mittag, Honecker's close economic advisor for two decades and Schürer's principal adversary, remained bitterly opposed to curtailing the development of the consumer welfare that had marked the 1980s. Communism must and could secure both consumption and investment in line with the "unity of economic and social policy" that the 1971 Eighth Party Congress had inscribed as the foundation of socialist development. The minister of trade, Werner Jarowinski, similarly criticized Schürer's effort to develop a computer industry, which, he argued, entailed a hopeless misallocation of resources. Nonetheless, he certainly agreed on the need to cut back the subsidies that had climbed from 8 billion marks in 1970 to 58 billion in 1989, outpacing by almost two to one the growth in national product.[27]

No observer of United States public finance during the Reagan, Bush, and Clinton administrations should be surprised that East German policy makers avoided a clean decision among these contending prescriptions. Within the cadres of a Communist state, where an aging dictator still had to endorse major decisions and party discipline prevented public dissent, the full consequences of the dispute remained muffled. Honecker's interventions were fitful. He contented himself with homey examples that suggested the large implications of issues might be beyond his grasp, and he avoided any resolute course of action. Even within the semiconstitutional structures the GDR did feature, Honecker generally avoided open cabinet or Politbüro debate over the issue by consigning economic debates to a special "small circle," or "Circle of Politbüro members with special responsiblity for the economy."[28] Only as the regime crumbled did the dissenting advisers get to disclose their story of long-term policy errors to supposedly shocked Central Committee members. Schürer reported that Honecker had supported some efforts to confront the debt situation between 1976 and 1978, but the pressure to purchase abroad soon nullified the hopeful results. In May 1978, renewed reform efforts came to naught when the Council of Ministers insisted that the State Planning Commission's effort to orient policies so that the balance of payments did not further deteriorate would undermine the unity of economic and social policy. Honecker endorsed the line and reproved Schürer. Further consultations followed in October 1978, February 1979, and June 1980. By June 1982, Stoph was also supporting "decisive measures" on behalf of austerity, only to be told in the Politbüro by Honecker that "we don't want to hear the slogan of decisive measures again." Nonetheless, the ominous deficits continued to mount, and in 1986 the Planning Commission was charged with developing a way to halve the cumulative total.[29]

By November 1987, however, the accumulated deficit with the nonsocialist world had risen to 38.5 billion valuta marks. The finance minister was rebuked in the Politbüro (presumably by Mittag, though he did not specify) for his pessimism. He had supposedly argued that the deficit was no longer controllable. "But if that were the case we would have to call it quits."[30] In late April and May 1988, Schürer made his "most massive personal thrust" to push his ideas through the Politbüro. Honecker's support was critical but uncertain. Schürer pleaded with the general secretary for a special meeting to clarify the situation. "It is hard for me to estimate how far you are able to support my 'Reflections.'"[31] A few days later Mittag responded with a sharp attack. To accept Schürer's concepts, he argued, would be to place in question the decisions of the Eighth and Eleventh Party Congresses. The price rises that his program entailed were unacceptable; his complaints about the extensive construction program in Berlin focused too exclusively on the costs.[32] Although the president of the Council of Ministers, Willi Stoph, carried Schürer's proposals to the council level by early May, they were aborted in the Central Committee, which retained the more extensive decision-making power.

This dispute had major ramifications within the economic agencies of the regime. Schürer himself later confessed that he had not dared break party discipline. "For several years I have lived with the conflict," so he told the Central Committee, "how far could I press the opinion I recognized as correct even if it did not correspond to the official party line?" Until the upheaval of 1989, however, he opted for fidelity to the SED.[33] In any case he was always a "candidate" member of the Politbüro, an expert in its service, and never fully credentialled in the SED ruling elite. The Stasi's own economic watchdog unit, Hauptabteilung XVIII, warned how demoralizing an effect Mittag's attack was exerting on economic debate within party ranks: "The reproach that Comrade Schürer's ideas contradict the base lines of the Resolutions of the Eighth and Eleventh Party Congresses of the SED is just not understood. . . . In this connection the opinion is expressed that in the future no leading functionary is likely to summon the courage to prepare proposals that aim at bringing production and distribution into a more favorable relation. If such 'taboos' persist, it will be impossible to solve the problem of presenting a real, challenging plan for 1989."[34]

Honecker seemed to understand the fatefulness of these choices, but he apparently hoped to muddle through. In a major policy review in September 1988, he admitted that assuring the international solvency of the GDR would be decisive; "it was a basic issue for our further development." But Honecker attributed the major problem to Soviet incomprehension for the GDR plight, as manifested by cutbacks in oil supplies and disadantageous pricing. He recalled that when he had complained to Brezhnev about oil cuts in 1981, "We received the laconic answer that the GDR must solve the problem on its own. I discussed this also with Comrade Gorbachev and he said that he thought the answer was absolutely correct."[35] Despite Honecker's professed awareness of the debt crisis, he could not bring himself to change course. When two weeks earlier Vadim Medvedev, secretary of the Soviet Central Committee, had explained the need for perestroika and glasnost, Honecker insisted that the East Germans were trying to evaluate these new and unexpected developments in the Soviet Union, which had far exceeded expectations, and "to connect these with the further implemation of the resolutions of the Eleventh Party Congress and not just to copy the experiences."[36]As Schürer saw it, Mittag exerted a major and pernicious influence on the general secretary. "Erich Honecker himself did not understand the signs of the time."[37] By the time Schürer spoke out, neither Mittag nor Honecker was in power.

THE COSTS OF COMPUTERIZATION

The constraints and trade-offs were stark enough for planners to debate implicit input-output models of East German difficulties, above all of the pressures that were accumulating in the late 1980s. For all the deficiencies in the domestic economy the immediate crisis manifested itself in the country's fragile international position, dependent on the one side for its raw materials, including energy sources, from the Soviet Union, and on the other, for Western credits to import consumer goods and sophisticated inputs for its exigent computer development program. More than any other sector, it was the computer program that incorporated the conflicting strategies for East German development. Crudely put, the East German economy was in a race between computers and collapse.

The East German microelectronics sector involved several major product lines. First, there was an effort to develop high-capacity chips. Schürer understood that the GDR lagged behind the Western and Japanese competition. The chip itself was developed from Western models. But he calculated that East Germany might "marry" the considerable level of sophistication it was developing with its traditional skill in machine-tool manufacture.[38] East German machine tools dominated the CMEA markets. On the other hand, by the 1980s demand was highly specific; mass production of standardized items was becoming obsolete and, in any case, taken over by lower-cost suppliers, such as the Bulgarians. East Germany had to wager on the application of microelectronics to computer-assisted development (CAD) for the rapid production of specialized machine tools, themselves computer controlled (CNC).[39]

CAD development, according to the Planning Commission concepts, would allow East German industry to become more productive. Despite the huge investments required, it was important as a key technology at home. But the strategy was not merely autarkic. East German CAD and CNC output, Schürer predicted, would also achieve a monopoly status in the Eastern bloc. Although East German computers were more expensive than the Western versions, given the scarcity of convertible currencies, the CMEA countries must continue to buy from East Germany. What convertible earnings were earned would be used to defray the needed inputs from the West.[40] Ultimately, Schürer hoped, if the East Germans could insist on world market prices for their exports within Comecon, they would thereby secure better terms of trade for the raw materials they required to sell more manufacture or petrochemicals to the West. The resources of a closed trading bloc would thus allow the GDR to ratchet itself up to a viable position with respect to the nonsocialist economies. Indeed, Schürer hoped, the East German marriage of computers and machine tools would also secure a direct bridgehead in Western markets.

Did such a strategy make sense? Schürer remained convinced that computers were "the key industry that permeated all other branches." Unless it wagered on modernization, East Germany would slip into a second-rate position. The country had important productive resources that would otherwise dissipate: centers of research and development at the Kombinat Mikroelektronik in Erfurt, Robotron in Dresden, Zeiss in Jena, and affiliated university faculties. During the very weeks that the regime was coming apart, state planners put together an extensive survey of the key CAD sector. Written, probably, to justify continuing investment in such a costly activity, it may well have been far too optimistic about creating a viable industry. Nonetheless, it testified to significant progress and a serious commitment:

> With respect to the qualitative level of scientific-technical results attained within the parameters of the state's mandate, our estimate is that when 16- and 32- bit chip technology is available, the CAD solutions that have been introduced can hold their own against the very best international achievements. . . . On the other hand, these results are unattainable when this computer technology is only partially available. A lack of, or a shortage of peripherals, such as large external memory and monitors with graphics capacity, has a specially deleterious effect on our scientific and technological level. So too does our lower work-station capacity as compared with the leading capitalist industrial countries, as well as our insufficient development of software for computer-supported technology. Above all, our future capacity to quickly introduce high-quality complex solutions will depend decisively on further progress in making available efficient machine technology.[41]

The report argued that the small state had made significant progress in endeavoring to keep up with world standards in its advanced machine-tool sector. On the other hand, important components remained scarce or unavailable. High officials within the Ministry for Electrotechnology and Electronics as well as Kombinate directors, so the Stasi reported, did not believe that the 1989 export targets were realistic.[42] And by Schürer's own admission, the industry seriously lagged. The GDR aspired to produce 500,000 256-kilobyte memories (already outmoded abroad) and had turned out only

90,000 even after importing Western equipment. ("Little Austria," the critical trade minister, Werner Jarowinski reminded him, turned out 50 million,
and world production was 800 million.) Pilot production of the one mega-
byte systems was also behind. In terms of comparative advantage, the East
German industry also seemed woefully inefficient. To lower the cost of computer components, large-scale output was crucial. Herein lay the technological "catch-22." CAD development was necessary precisely because domestic users and foreign purchasers demanded specialized equipment. But for
the GDR to equip itself at home for such customized production, it would
have to manufacture chips and memory boards on a vastly more massive
scale than it was capable of doing. A similar contradiction beset the labor
situation. Skilled labor remained a bottleneck, according to Schürer. On the
other hand, so Jarowinski reminded him, to employ a worker who had ten
years of education on a production line that in Hong Kong was serviced by
an assembler with three years of schooling represented a "waste of 'intellectual capital,' as the capitalist would say."[43] Could the GDR ever become
"Fordist" enough to emerge as a "post-Fordist" competitor?

Jarowinsky believed that the effort had represented a serious misallocation of resources. The microelectronic program had cost 12 to 14 billion
marks; the result was that the country had developed a 40-kilobit memory
chip that cost 40 marks at home, while the world market price was 1 to 1.5
valuta marks, or about one-tenth as much. So too, the 256k memory cost
GDR consumers 534 marks instead of 4–5 valuta marks—a subsidy of 517
marks for each unit produced. "These are supposedly the plow horses," he
waxed ironic, "that will develop the rest of our economy!"[44]

It is not easy to sort out the merits of these opposed viewpoints. Had the
East Germans been integrated into the world market, they could not have
sustained their fledgling industry. The rapid deindustrialization of East Germany since unification demonstrates how devastating the competition has
been for the former country's industrial structure. Schürer's strategy, however, depended on continued development, not the given distribution of
capacity and advantages. In this respect it followed many earlier examples
of state-supported catch-up industrial development, which for a generation
or more sacrificed comparative advantage for the sake of future manufacturing capacity. But in the East German case, the contradictions involved may
have been even more problematic. For Schürer proposed in effect to mediate
between two markets, that is, to exploit the monopoly position within the
Eastern bloc in order gradually to develop the expertise and resources to
participate more successfully with the nonsocialist economies. In effect

Schürer's insistence on computer development presupposed the continuation of a socialist bloc, even as he sought to make the East German economy more capable of participation in the nonsocialist world. Even into the spring of 1990, the Plan Commission envisaged that East Germany would continue to offset higher Soviet oil prices, which would now rise to world market levels, by marketing "top-of-the-line machine and finishing tools that the GDR's monopoly in the socialist lands lets us count on; offering attractive consumption goods, for which the Soviet Union has an extraordinary need; and a strong market position in machine construction and electronics, which have led to close relations between GDR suppliers and Soviet consumers."[45] Unless the socialist economy remained a protected enclave, East German investment costs would never be recovered. The more that the socialist economies pried themselves loose from the constraints of Comecon, the less viable the East German position would have remained.

As always, the penury of convertible currencies remained the overwhelming motive for home production. When Soviet oil became more expensive, the GDR expanded its own lignite production, devoting one-quarter of its industrial investments to the energy sector and accepting frightful ecological costs. It was not that East German planners merely aspired to autarky in microelectronics. They envisaged conquering an East European market greater than their own small country provided. But was it rational to negotiate all the steep learning curves that American and Japanese producers, with their far vaster sales and far greater number of qualified engineers, could negotiate far more rapidly?[46] It made no sense, claimed Günther Kleiber, GDR delegate to the Comecon, to develop 4- and 16-megabyte chips, when one couldn't master the output of 256-kilobyte chips. The planners, he pointed out, had finally developed their own "Walkman," so essential for meeting the taste of youth. But it cost the kids who wanted one 399 marks, about the equivalent of $400 under American conditions; and it cost the government more to import from Japan those parts it could not produce than it would have to purchase complete units.[47]

In this respect, Mittag and Jarowinski (from opposed perspectives) had an important point. The cost of the electronics strategy was enormous. The investments in producing chips and other equipment came at the cost of many other sectors. Whatever success could be achieved in striving for high-tech competitiveness came at the cost of deterioration in other sectors. As late as the Council of Ministers session on October 19, 1989, Willy Stoph repeated that the computer was not everything: "no matter how important microelectronics remains, it can't modernize our national economy on its own. Let me repeat: It's no panacea."[48] Other sectors of the economy were in terrible shape. The Ministry of State Security, which maintained an economic intelligence unit, reported on the aging of chemical, coal, and energy plants. Despite massive expenditure on repairs, wear and tear had reached dangerous proportions at many important sites. In 1985 in ten plants—above all in the Buna works in central Saxony—fires and accidents had been responsible for almost 2,400 interruptions of production and a loss of output of 600 million marks. Electrical generation for the chemical plants was particularly susceptible to breakdown.[49] The report on the building industry in the fall of 1989 was especially devastating: steam shovels and construction vehicles were in short supply, overused, and breaking down. Only 30 percent were usable at any time; 70 to 90 percent were too old; twice as much money had to be spent on repairs than was allotted for amortization; imported repair parts were scarce; every third worker had to take on heavy physical labor to compensate for the machines.[50] As anyone who turned off the main boulevards in the large cities could report, the building stock of the GDR was run down and dilapidated. The economy chronically suffered from a lack of Western currencies to finance the imports needed for modernization and consumption. It was short of skilled professionals and workers. (Revealingly, the report on computers calculated the labor savings that automation had brought to different sectors—a manpower budget that spotlighted skilled labor as a major constraint.) Consumer dissatisfaction was rife as shortages mounted for men's and women's clothing, domestic electronics, shoes, and, above all, spare parts for cars and motorcycles. In small towns fruit and vegetables were lacking. By the fall of 1987, the Stasi monitors of public opinion reported, many citizens were complaining that provisioning had not been so meager in years."[51]

Most devastating for future balance-of-payments viability, industrial productivity had continued to decline with respect to that of West Germany—from about 70 percent in the 1950s to less than 50 percent by the 1980s.[52] In September 1989 Schürer had to rebuke the minister for heavy equipment construction for the deterioration of productivity within this crucial and prized industrial sector.[53] Within two months, the reform government of Hans Modrow estimated that it would have to reduce domestic consumption in 1990 to 95 percent of 1989's level to balance its accounts with the nonsocialist economies.[54] A vicious cycle of aging capital, equipment failures, falling productivity with respect to the nonsocialist economies, and inadequate hard-currency earnings seemed to run counter to any rosy prospects for CAD exports. Schürer's concepts were far more oriented toward world market production than Mittag's; they presupposed a painful perestroika. But it is doubtful that they would have promised swift enough success to avert a complete breakdown.[55]

RETREAT FROM REFORM: STATE SOCIALISM IN RETROSPECT

Indebtedness to the West and the conflicting interests within the CMEA economies arose out of deeper dilemmas of socialist production. To overcome these would have meant disavowing the ideological imperatives of the Communist regimes and prevailing over entrenched political interests. Reformers in each Communist society, including Mikhail Gorbachev himself, believed that partial introduction of market principles might allow a relatively painless modernization. Between the mid 1980s and the early 1990s this proved an illusory hope. Yet for all its troubles, East Germany was still the most advanced and efficient producer of the socialist countries, and it was not disabled. It remained the tenth or eleventh largest industrial producer of the world and, like the advanced capitalist societies, relied on imported labor. It was making arrangements to bring 6,000 workers from Mozambique when the Wall fell. It attempted to satisfy modern consumer demands: 1.2 million jeans were being imported from Hong Kong; 5,000 judo jackets and pants would follow in 1990.[56] Did the system have to fail?

It would certainly have had to change radically. For all the frustrations and consumer dissatisfaction, disposable income was increasing faster than national output: "In terms of distribution, we're champs," Willi Stoph observed with a rare flash of irony.[57] But family income was bestowed at the cost of domestic investment and further foreign indebtedness. Even then consumers were frustrated by the recurrent shortages. Had there not been a political crisis and an opening of the frontiers in 1989, we can only speculate what would have been the economic trajectory of East Germany. Environmental degradation (to which the regime was belatedly beginning to respond, if only because it appreciated the political discontent ecological concerns might mobilize), consumer longings, and the need for technological modernization would have slowly undermined its heavy-handed "socialism." Reformers inspired by Gorbachev would have contended with the orthodox Marxists who despised him; indeed, the conflict was already apparent by the late 1980s. Although the reformers were frustrated before 1989, generational change would have eventually made their voice decisive.

Time was on the side of perestroika. The regime would have gradually eased its authoritarian controls at home as it sought more Western credits. Cultural and economic exchanges with the Federal Republic would have intensified in their osmotic flow. Traffic across the Wall would have increased. The Wall might eventually have been bargained away for more credits, higher subsidies, joint ventures, and technology transfers. The question is what degree of central planning such an infiltrated socialism might have retained. As it turned out, the political upheaval of 1989 precluded any such trajectory of gradual reform. On the other hand, political turmoil had many of its roots in economic dissatisfaction. As President Gorbachev told the Lithuanian Communist Party in mid-January 1990, "It is politics that follows economics and not vice versa."[58]

But why were the planned economies in such deep trouble by the 1980s? Most Western economic analysts have maintained that the final crisis of communism merely culminated its insoluble long-term contradictions. The economic difficulties that finally overtook socialism, in this view, were inherent from the outset. Long-term liabilities, however, need not be fatal. All economies have bottlenecks and stagnant sectors. This chapter proposes an alternative scenario, namely that socialist policy makers might have evolved toward more flexible production in the 1960s, but then put off reforms for a fateful decade or more. Ultimately it was a political crisis and not an economic one that led to the upheaval of 1989.

Admittedly central planning was unwieldy and often absurd. Feedback had to take place through continued monitoring since prices were set administratively. To supplement the work of the planning authorities, the state established a "Worker and Peasant Inspection," or ABI, which employed an army of investigators to check out abuses. Worried about unauthorized investments by Kombinate leaders in late 1988, the Council of Ministers ordered an inspection. The ABI, the State Bank, the Planning Commission, and State Construction Board (Staatliche Bauaufsicht) sent 16,700 agents into 5,013 firms to check on investments over 100,000 marks. By the end of 1989 they had unearthed 970 violations amounting to 589 million marks—most of which they admitted had gone to construction to improve productivity or living conditions in the factories and territories.[59] Retail establishments, another ABI crew reported in the summer of 1988, were not providing what the plan stipulated, and there were significant failures of management. In happy contrast, though—so ABI teams could report in August 1989—the majority of restaurants were working diligently and offering a wider choice of food and drink at a higher "gastronomic niveau."[60] By this time, however, enhanced menu options could not deter the mass exodus through Hungary!

What the East Germans called "the thousand little things" were usually in short supply. Legions of planners up to cabinet level had to estimate in advance the actually tens of thousands or more production decisions that a decentralized market can signal cybernetically. As Honecker's lieutenants pointed out on the very morrow of his fall, contradictions abounded: there were many deep-freezes but not enough foil wraps and containers. Wholesale houses produced nineteen models of anoraks for children, but retail stores wouldn't buy them because they were penalized for having inventories in stock. Consumers always preferred the same few fragrances of room sprays (the popularity of which probably testified to the attrition of plumbing expertise after artisanal and small-scale firms were progressively nationalized in the early 1970s); but the factory continually had to change the assortment offered to attain its prescribed innovation ratio of 30 percent.[61]

Large-scale projects likewise stumbled over their internal cumbersomeness. The GDR had a powerful enough industrial plant to win a 1984 contract from the Spanish state energy authority to build two mammoth paddle-wheel excavators designed for open-pit mining operations. The TAKRAF Kombinat, which specialized in heavy earth-moving machinery, deliberately underbid the West German firms that dominated this sector precisely to gain a market foothold. From one perspective this was a bold entrepreneurial move, but the enterprise soon ran into all sorts of difficulties. As the state inspectors reported, TAKRAF promised unrealistic delivery times; it had to put together a huge consortium, including many Spanish subcontractors, which was subject to all sorts of delays and required far higher up-front payments in Western currency than envisaged; it allowed the clients to impose more demanding technical specifications, and finally it had to compensate for defective parts and the consequences of industrial accident. The promising initiative in a Western market dissipated in a dismaying series of setbacks.[62]

But was the problem that of state socialism or the facile expectations that underlie so many unwieldy large-scale ventures, whether the Stealth bomber, the Concorde, or the Channel Tunnel? The most recent treatise on state socialism in practice exhaustively documents its systemic failure to eliminate unproductive employment, its inability to meet consumer aspirations, and what might be called its vocation for scarcity.[63] True enough; the market and a functioning price system usually—certainly not always, however—allow a more efficient use of resources and satisfaction of wants. They encourage innovation. But Western economies have not always functioned so smoothly and certainly not always equitably. And socialist economics did not always fail so clamorously. They served to organize postwar reconstruction in Eastern Europe. As will be detailed, growth rates from the 1950s through the 1960s and into the 1970s were comparable with those in the West, even if the baselines of the societies were far lower.

The disabling failures, this author believes, came later. Schürer was right when he looked to the early 1970s as the watershed for the Communist economy.[64] Errors accumulated throughout that decade and emerged spectacularly during the 1980s. Moreover, they became disabling at the very moment Western capitalist economies were also widely perceived to be undergoing grave systemic difficulties. The difficulties of the 1970s, it is important to recall, had an impact across economic systems. The breakdown of the Bretton Woods system, the oil price shocks, labor militance, and the emergence of persistent unemployment in the West also produced abundant diagnoses of crisis: inflationary crises, crises of leadership, crises of legitimation, crises of capitalism.[65] Granted: crisis is the most overused trope of social analysis. Despite the deathbed alerts, capitalism survived to become feted as the "enterprise culture" of Margaret Thatcher or the glitzy prosperity of Reagan's America. Communism collapsed instead a decade later. Nonetheless, many of the difficulties of communism also assailed the West, where they produced real, if less paralyzing difficulties. Although the decomposition of communism certainly was a function of its own rigidities and injustices, it resulted as well from strains and stresses that afflicted capitalist as well as socialist economies. Each system saw energy costs rise; each system confronted the limits of large-scale "Fordist" mass production; each system felt it had to devote more resources to satisfying labor demands, either in direct wages or social welfare institutions. Capitalism and communism together left behind the period of rapid and relatively easy capital accumulation that marked the quarter century after World War II to enter a far more troubled era of harder productivity gains, harsher distributive struggles, and more unsettled relations with the so-called Third World. This was an epochal transformation that challenged all industrialized societies. But the capitalist and socialist economies responded in different ways, and they paid a different price. Market flexibility allowed the Western economies to restructure and reorient their priorities, above all to modify their postwar commitment to full employment. The Communist regimes, however, shrank from the logic of reform and sought to reaffirm the principles that had guided the Soviet Union since the 1930s. The effort to cast loose from the system in the latter 1980s came too late to forestall political upheaval.

How did the state socialist systems arrive at this impasse? Until late 1989, the GDR was counted a relative success story even by Western analysts; a small country of 17 million, its per capita industrial product was among the highest in the world, even if its productivity per worker lagged. Its machine tool, optical, and "robotron" computer factories supplied apparently quality instruments for Eastern Europe. By 1990 its economic residue was perceived in terms of second-rate machines, crumbling housing, cardboard cars, and an atmosphere choked by chemical fumes and lignite dust. Nonetheless, through the 1950s and 1960s, Eastern and Western European societies enjoyed roughly comparable rates of growth. Socialism and capitalism alike responded to the demands of recovery from the ravages of the war. The West remained ahead of the East, but it had started from a more advanced position. It also benefited from the impulse provided by the undamaged United States economy. East Germany had to serve as the major source of Soviet reparations until 1950; thereafter it had to make a major military contribution to what would become the Warsaw Pact. And for perhaps another decade thereafter, the Russians exploited their hegemony to draw industrial goods from their satellites by means of favorable trading agreements imposed through Comecon. Thereafter, the Soviets began in effect to subsidize their satellites by the provision of cheap energy and raw materials.[66]

The statistics available are hardly firm numbers. Estimates of output varied widely, and they measured different quantities in the East because services were often not included. Official "net material product" (NMP) statistics significantly overstated the performance that Western estimates of constant-dollar GDP would have suggested. To find a common basis with Western data required estimating services by reference to the shares they occupy in comparable Western economies. Once GNP estimates were made in local currencies, there was the thorny problem of expressing them in a common monetary unit. Since East European currencies were not convertible and governments imposed unrealistic conversion ratios, exchange rates provided little basis for a common numerand. This left estimates of purchasing power parity as the most serviceable approach, but these comparisons, too, were often difficult because East Europeans hardly had access to

Table 2-2. Average Annual Growth Rates (%)[a]

	1950/52–67/69	1967/69–79
West Germany	6.2	3.6
Austria	5.0	4.4
Italy	5.4	3.5
Spain	6.1	4.5
Greece	6.0	5.6
Portugal	5.1	5.0
East Germany	5.7	4.9 (NMP)
Czechoslovakia	5.2	5.1 (NMP)
Hungary	4.8	5.4 (NMP)
Poland	6.1	6.3 (NMP)
Bulgaria	6.9	7.3 (NMP)
Romania	7.2	9.3 (NMP)

Source: Nita Watts, "Eastern and Western Europe," in Andrea Boltho, ed., *The European Economy: Growth and Crisis* (Oxford: Oxford University Press, 1982), p. 262, table 9.3

[a] Estimated in terms of gross domestic product or, where indicated, net material product (NMP).

the same market basket of goods. Nonetheless, increasingly sophisticated approaches were established.[67]

UN agencies and the World Bank sources were the most faithful monitors of the centrally planned economies as a whole. Sources suggest that the centrally planned economies' indices considerably overstated their own performance, but the overall trends were still relatively hopeful (see Table 2-2).[68] The East European performance consistently remained behind the West, but registered significant growth through the 1960s.

Given its initial backwardness and the devastation of the war, the performance of Eastern Europe was certainly creditable in terms of percentage growth.[69] Such measurements suggested that Eastern European economies might progress rapidly. But conventional statistics could not capture the inferior quality of socialist economic output so long as the blocs remained separate. For this reason the drastic collapse of demand for East German industrial products came as an unpleasant surprise after unification. Quantitative measures had never reflected the fact that building tiles soon fell off the facades of Frankfurter Allee apartment buildings in the 1950s, that the masses of shoes produced in the Soviet Union quickly fell apart, and that many nuclear generators and not just Chernobyl operated close to catastrophe. Nor did the statistics count hours spent shopping for scarce goods as a labor input. As of the late 1970s it was estimated that queuing in the GDR—the bloc's most prosperous society—effectively reduced real wages by 13 percent.[70] The statistics did not allow for the disappointment when the purchases that consumers had to settle for were not those they had waited in line to buy.[71] The data suggested that workers under communism were supported by extensive capital equipment, but they did not reveal that it was far older than machinery in the West and was not depreciated.[72]

Nor did the indices readily indicate that huge amounts of production went to interfirm purchases that yielded fewer end products for consumers. Capitalism sought to cheapen or improve goods even at the price of eliminating jobs. Socialism tended to freeze jobs at the cost of technical progress. Socialist managers kept each others' firms afloat, employing workers, seeking to hoard the factors of production and producing low-quality tools for their fellow directors. It was precisely the continued exchange of occult inventories that prolonged the twilight existence of Soviet state industry during the early 1990s. Unification precluded this expedient in the former East Germany. Nevertheless the Federal Republic had to acquiesce in concealed boondoggling (*Kurzarbeit-Null*: shortened work weeks with zero tasks) so that East German workers might be kept on payrolls even for fictitious labor.

Political constraints within the socialist bloc as a whole also produced characteristic anomalies of development. After the economic and political division of Europe in the late 1940s, Communist leaders sought to organize a more intense exchange that would compensate for the rupture of East-West commerce. At the same time, however, Stalinist politics imposed a pattern of forced-draft centralization and collectivization that dictated replication and not complementarity.[73] A common model of heavy industry beckoned all Communist planners no matter how diverse the starting point of their respective economies and their respective comparative advantages. Dominating all was the huge plant of the Soviet Union, which had passed through a wrenching transformation in the 1930s—idealized in the postwar decade as the shining path to socialism—and had then incurred tremendous material destruction and human losses in the war.[74] East Germany and Czechoslovakia were relatively mature, developed economies, although the former had suffered considerable destruction and remained prey to extensive dismantling thereafter. Hungary and Poland had begun the path to development but remained a stage behind. Yugoslavia, Romania, and Bulgaria were comparable with the southern Mediterranean peripheries of Europe; they were susceptible to the highest percentage growth rates and qualitative transformations as they took off from backwardness into the process of industrialization.[75] On the basis of their overall performance into the 1960s, serious-minded economists could still argue that central planning might serve developing countries better as a model than Western capitalism. Socialism—in the stringent sense of national planning, state ownership of key sectors, and firm control of the national accumulation process—appealed to intellectuals in India, Egypt, sub-Saharan Africa, and elsewhere in the developing world for two decades after the war. No matter how fervid its rhetoric of internationalism, it attracted adherents because it promised to overcome their societies' subaltern role in the world economy. It beckoned as socialism in one country,[76] and by the 1980s it beckoned only the most sectarian.

How did state socialist policies evolve? The tightening of Soviet control after 1947–48 brought with it rapid nationalization, collectivization of agriculture (outside Poland), and central planning, essentially imposing on the economies of East Central Europe the Soviet apparatus of the 1930s.[77] The results in terms of investment and rearmament were impressive, as were the costs in terms of deferred consumption. The discrepancy between overall growth performance and improving living standards may have been highest in East Germany, where the reparations exacted seem to have totaled about 20 percent of production. In 1946, perhaps over a quarter of zonal income went to the Soviets—over twice the extraction rate of the Western powers at the same time. Improvement in performance by 1949 rested on a Soviet decision to ease up on dismantling.[78] By then the Russians in effect had decided that in light of the European division, their influence would be confined to the eastern part of Germany. As the most meticulous early study suggests, growth from 1950 to 1955 was rapid because the 1950 level was so low.[79] Given the rate of Soviet extraction from the East German economy until 1950 and, conversely, the fact that West Germany enjoyed considerable subsidies from the British and American occupiers and thereafter Marshall Plan aid, it is not clear that the differing performances can be attributed to differences in the economic system.

Stalin's death led to a less draconian approach to development. Workers who were pushed too hard could revolt, as the East German uprising of 1953 demonstrated. In fact the Eastern bloc as a whole yearned for a respite. The East European regimes moved to relax their rates of investment after the advent of Khrushchev and the discrediting of Stalin in 1956. Real wages were allowed to rise in the mid-1950s after their compression from 1950 to 1953. With the advent of Władysław Gomułka in 1956, the Poles outlined a tentative plan that was slated to grant autonomy to firms, restore criteria of profitability, and liberate prices. Despite condemnation by the East Germans (still cracking down on dissent after the Hungarian uprising) and the Communist International in 1957, such concepts spread, and the Czech leadership advanced similar projects a year later. Such plans might have remained mere trial balloons because the tentative decentralization during 1956–57 failed to yield the promised results. Nonetheless, the neo-Stalinist planning and investment that was resumed at the end of the decade also ran into trouble. Communist systems were apparently suffering from their own stop-go business cycle in the early 1960s, as managers of firms and central planners encountered bottlenecks and shortfalls.[80]

But the very setbacks of the early 1960s gave the reformers a second chance. *Pravda*'s publication in October 1962 of "Plan, Profit, and Bonus" by the Kharkov economist Yevsei Liberman opened extensive debate throughout the bloc. *Khozraschet*, or firm accountability, became the new mantra of communism. Developing ideas of the Polish economists Oskar Lange and Włodimierz Brus, Ota Šik in Czechoslovakia urged further de-centralization, enhanced firm accountability, increased labor incentives, and more resolute liberation of prices. Šik's works pointed to the market as the decisive arena for reconciling the interests of consumers and producers. Between 1965 and 1968 the Czechs restored some autonomy to enterprises; they expanded the scope for wage differentiation; they reformed taxes on firms to encourage performance, and they gradually began to free wholesale prices. Such an economic program could not be introduced without politi-cal ramifications. The role of state and party planning was necesssarily cir-cumscribed, as administrative prerogatives were devolved on firms and their workers councils.[81] The Hungarians simultaneously moved toward reform while engaged in anguished debates about the petty bourgeois inclinations encouraged by "refrigerator socialism" (the predecessor of "goulash com-munism"). By 1968 they cut back the scope of planning, allowed more play for price mechanisms, encouraged agricultural cooperatives, and sanctioned company profit-sharing and investment funds.[82]

It seems paradoxical in retrospect that Ulbricht himself, so hostile to po-litical liberalization and critical of Gomułka's earlier reformist concepts, should introduce a significant package of economic changes from 1963 to 1970. Ulbricht's tactical adaptibility vis-à-vis the new currents of commu-nism unleashed by Khrushchev contrasted with the rigidity that proved so tiresome for the Soviets a decade later. (And it certainly differed from the stubborn fronde that his successor Honecker conducted against glasnost in the late 1980s!) East German vulnerability left Ulbricht little choice, how-ever. In 1958 Khrushchev had warned the West that the GDR was to be given control of access to East Berlin, and a year later the East German Party formally boasted that its state would catch up to West German living standards by 1961 (a claim, however, that was never taken seriously by the GDR's own planning agencies). Adenauer's cancellation of the inner-German trade arrangements in 1960 and the renewed waves of "Flight from the Republic"—200,000 left in 1960 for West Germany—exposed the hollowness of these pretensions. Ulbricht responded on August 13, 1961, by rolling barbed wire across the hitherto open Berlin sector boundaries and rapidly erecting the Wall that became the most notorious feature of the republic during the next three decades. The new barrier tourniqueted the flow of skilled labor and stabilized the political situation, but it did not prevent further economic difficulties in 1962.

How should the party use the respite for stabilization bestowed by the Wall and Khrushchev's patronage? East German republication of Liberman's proposals unleashed a major series of economic debates, reassessments, and self-criticism. Between December 1962 and early 1963, the SED thrashed out major proposals for economic decentralization along the lines envisaged by the Soviet and Czech reformers. By mid-1963 the reform concepts were ready to be introduced and refined over the next few years, with apparently good results until 1968. As the structures were refined, the Economic Council of the GDR delegated decision-making powers not only to the socialized enterprises (the Volkseigene Betriebe or VEB), but also to eighty supervisory units established to oversee different branches of production (the Vereinigungen Volkseigener Betriebe or VVB). The reliance on sectoral supervision remained a fixture of East German economic approaches, first under decentralization and then as a basis for renewed central planning through the new "Kombinate" of the 1970s and 1980s.[83] As did similar reforms elsewhere, the New Economic System (NÖS) deemphasized central planning and placed more power in the associations (VVB) of socialized industries (VEB). Profits were to serve as measurements of firm performance and could be retained to cover reinvestment and finance. Banks were to exercise a supervisory role in the extension of credit; prices of energy and raw materials were raised to reflect real input costs. By the third stage of the reform in 1968–70—the so-called Economic System of Socialism (ÖSS)—the introduction of "structure-concrete planning" directed state investment into "progressive" or high-tech sectors, namely petroleum products, high-quality metallurgy, and electronic data processing.[84]

Clearly there were inconsistencies: state planning for key sectors was to be combined with greater reliance on market mechanisms, while socialism

Table 2-3. East Germany: Average Annual
Growth Rates (%)

	Official NMP	Western Estimates GDP-GNP
1960–65	3.4	3.0–3.5
1965–70	5.2	3.1–5.1
1970–75	5.4	3.5–5.1

Source: Irwin L. Collier, *The Estimation of Gross
Domestic Product and Its Growth Rate for the German
Democratic Republic*, World Bank Staff Working Pa-
pers, No. 773 (Washington, DC: World Bank, 1985).

was stated to be so far along that the private sector, reduced as it was by
1959, might maintain its share of national activity. By 1967 the regime decided that the VVB were not up to their assigned role and began the process
of building horizontal combinations or Kombinate. For all the inherent tensions between market and plan, however, the New Economic System delivered encouraging results until 1970: the period 1968 to 1971 brought a
spurt in annual growth rates to 5.2, 6.1, and 5.9 percent, respectively—not
quite the performance of West Germany, Japan, or Italy, but still rapid and
substantial (see Table 2-3).[85]

Looking back from the early 1990s it is easy to minimize the implications
of the reform programs of the 1960s. In comparison with the dismantling of
state socialism after 1989, the East European reforms remained fragmentary
and limited. At their hardiest they envisaged decentralized management,
and not privatization.[86] Most advocates were unwilling to give up the role of
party and state in setting overall economic targets. All shuddered at the idea
of reintroducing capitalism. The logic of reform in the late 1960s was to free
prices, which alone might reliably communicate social preferences, allow
supply and demand to converge, and reconcile the needs of the present with
ambitions for the future. Property relations seemed less pressing an issue;
the reformers never claimed, as did those who took the reins in 1989, that
private ownership was needed to encourage entrepreneurial vigor. As elabo-
rated most fully by Šik, who effectively carried on the prescriptions of the
socialist theorist Karl Korsch in the early 1920s, each firm was supposed to
sustain a collective motivation. The reformers never aspired to challenge the
hegemonic role of the Communist Party.

For all their limits, however, the reforms were potentially explosive: the
logic of decentralization, incentives, and free prices was inherently expan-

sive. Had the reform measures remained on the agenda, they must have eventually unleashed forces for pluralism. The environment conducive for change, after all, powerfully gripped both blocs. After the intense energy devoted in the 1950s to establishing Communist and anti-Communist orthodoxy, reconstructing their war-devastated economies, and shoring up rival alliance systems, capitalist and socialist societies alike shifted their priorities. Western publics aspired to less confrontational political agendas. Examination of national-income distribution (not to say the changing electoral results) reveals that the non-Communist countries shifted their collective priorities from investment to welfare, education, and household consumption. The return of the Democratic Party in the United States, the "Opening to the Left" in Italy (facilitated by the advent of a reformist pope in 1958), election of a Labour government in Britain in 1964, and, by 1966, the inauguration of a Great Coalition in Germany that accepted Keynesian countercyclical public spending, all brought a wind of change to the Western world, which culminated in the effort at détente. In the looking-glass symmetry that has so marked postwar history, East and West together relaxed the orthodoxies that had been so zealously enforced in the previous decade. Their respective reformers were encouraged by their counterparts' efforts. Theorists interpreted the objectives and achievements of both systems in terms of "industrial society," "modernization," and occasionally "convergence."[87]

Socialist reform, however, fell victim to the logic of imperial control. By August 1968, Moscow—urgently prodded by the Ulbricht regime—decided that unless constrained by force, the Czechoslovak reformers were destined to liquidate the party's hold and break out of the socialist bloc and Warsaw Pact. Soviet intervention in Prague in 1968 followed a course that the imperial organization of the Russian and Soviet state had made depressingly familiar since at least the Polish uprising of 1863. Reforms undertaken both at the center and periphery aroused strivings for independence that threatened disintegration of empire, and the centrifugal forces unleashed provided those resisting liberalization inside Russia with the decisive arguments needed to throttle reform. In 1968 the emancipatory currents in Prague impelled Brezhnev to insist on centralized control and forced all the reformers throughout Eastern Europe on the defensive.[88] In Russia's recurrent cycles of foreign challenge, reform, loss of control, and repression, Mikhail Gorbachev was the first leader to resist the logic of rollback, although, as he confronted the Lithuanians in January 1990, the issue hung in the balance. And just as hard-liners so often warned, the price would be at least the temporary territorial and political disintegration of Moscow's power. For Gorbachev, however, the risk of reversing reform appeared more disabling than pressing ahead. It was, in fact, the rejection of market-based modernization after 1968, precisely the fifteen-year reaffirmation of an anachronistic neo-Stalinist model with its incapacity to guide Russia toward a postindustrial economy, that impelled Gorbachev to accept the risk of socialist and imperial dismantling Brezhnev had believed he might still reject.

East and West, the crises of the 1970s had both political and economic origins. The political shocks of the late 1960s—Prague Spring in Eastern Europe, the student upheavals and the rise of labor militance in the West—presented a profound challenge to the "modernizing" or reformist trajectory of the 1960s. In Eastern Europe the Communist parties tended to react, though not immediately, by aborting their experiments with decentralized decision making. But politics aside, they also retreated from reform as they found that partial liberalization produced bottlenecks and shortages. In Western Europe the resurgence of class militance disrupted the ease of macroeconomic management. By the early 1970s deepening economic difficulties added to the political shocks of 1968. United States reluctance to impose fiscal austerity to balance its domestic budgets and international accounts contributed to the dislocation of the Western international monetary system. The oil-producing nations organized a successful cartel to revolt against the inexpensive provision of energy supplies that had helped make earlier Western growth so robust. Faced with a slowdown in economic expansion Western entrepreneurs and unions sought to protect their relative shares of national income. The result of the revived distributive conflict was wage and profit spirals, increased demands on welfare budgets, heavy inflationary pressures, and an accompanying slowdown of productivity gains.

Looking back on the half century of postwar history now concluding, the 1970s emerge as a decade of wrenching reorientation for politics and economics. The Keynesian tools of macroeconomic reflation, which seemed finally to have won general acceptance under social democratic governments in the 1960s, were hardly in place when they apparently failed. Inflation increased without significantly denting unemployment. Part of the reason was that highly sophisticated producers and workers anticipated inflationary pressure in a self-fulfilling prophecy. Governments, moreover, had to divert more national output to sustain the unemployed as well as pay for the social services expanded in the prior decade. Most unsettling, societies were trying to contend with an imperious long-term change in industrial structure as if they were facing only a series of short-term cyclical disturbances. European and North American markets for "upstream" industrial inputs such as basic steel grew more saturated, even as Japanese and Korean producers now competed for shares. Opportunities for new services and the data-processing industry increased; so too did the demand for differentiated products requiring high inputs of skilled labor (so too the need for low-skilled physical labor, which migrants were required to fill). But to get laboring men who had acquired one set of skills into upgraded positions elsewhere would have been difficult in the best of times. The task was agonizing enough in the Ruhr or Lorraine or the Great Lakes when monetary disturbances, higher energy prices, and labor disputes preoccupied economic decision makers. Its solution seemed to defy imagination in much of Eastern Europe.[89]

Neither capitalism nor socialism could remain immune from such major pressures. But beset by social conflict and confusion over policy, Western leaders eventually opted for the discipline of the world market. While the West adjusted, the East unsuccessfully sought to resist. For all the difficulties inherent in a centrally planned economy, the Communist collapse came about as a reaction to forces for transformation that gripped West and East alike, but which Western Europeans (and North Americans) had responded to earlier and with less cataclysmic an upheaval. In their divergent responses to the seismic pressures of the 1970s lay the subsequent history of the 1980s. The use of force in Communist Europe to halt the reformist trajectory after 1968 had momentous consequences. The reforms were not immediately abolished, but centralization was inexorably reestablished. Despite Dubček's capitulation to most of Moscow's demands, by the next spring his orthodox opponents were firmly in power and punishing the enthusiasts of the previous spring. The economic reforms fell victim to the socialist counterrevoltion as the works councils, so central to Šik's concepts, were abolished and central controls reimposed. As early as October 1968 in the GDR, Günter Mittag, secretary for economic affairs of the Central Committee and the leader most identified with the New Economic System, criticized those who wanted to introduce a "socialist market economy."[90]

The East German economic reforms did not fall immediate victim to political reaction, but they were unlikely to survive for long. The serious 1970 worker protests in Poland added to the pressure to end experimentation. For different reasons the Romanians, Hungarians, and Poles might carve out semi-independent courses during the 1970s, but the GDR had been instrumental in calling for the Soviets to stifle political dissent in Czechoslovakia.

The New Economic System had not been the work of dissenters but of the politically orthodox, but this sponsorship did not save the program. It was ironic that Ulbricht, whose troops helped enforce the suppression in the neighboring state, would himself be brought down in the aftermath. He himself was too identified with the NÖS and despite or perhaps because of his ideological posturing, too uncongenial to Brezhnev to survive for long. Moreover, the reforms were vulnerable in their own right; East German economic performance was flagging in 1969–70, and it was easy to blame the difficulties inherent in organizing an economy simultaneously based on planning and market impulses. As an experienced Western visitor observed during 1970, the New Economic System stipulated more market coordination on paper than it allowed in reality.[91] The halfway innovations led to bottlenecks and stagnation of consumer goods. State investment funds were being sunk into automation efforts, while the country underwent energy crises in 1966 and the winter of 1969–70. The year 1970 also brought shortages in basic consumer goods and an unavowed inflation. Mittag found himself under attack in the fall and had to confess to errors and difficulties. By December 1970, the SED decided to abandon the seven-year reform effort. The cantankerous Ulbricht was forced to step down in May 1971. Without a serious analysis of economic policy, the party reintroduced central decision making and controls at the Eighth Party Congress of June 1971.[92] "The trauma of the NÖS collapse," Mittag claimed later, "was in my view a major reason that no comprehensive reform effort was ever again attempted. . . . The reform proposals and the effort at a real cooperation with the West failed for the same reason: throughout all the years to 1989 there was always a group of concrete dogmatists in the leadership."[93] But Mittag, too, had done his bit for dogmatism.

The nationalization of the remaining mixed private and public enterprises, especially prevalent in crafts and small industries, followed in 1972. Centralization intensified: the 546 firms that produced building material in 1970 were reduced to 132 by 1988; 876 chemical enterprises were down to 236; 2,589 machine and transport production enterprises had been more than halved to 1,157 (while the employee number had risen by about an eighth). In total 11,564 industrial enterprises in 1970 employing 2,818,000 workers had shrunk to 3,408 employing 3,219,000—or from an average 243 to 945 employed per unit.[94] Efforts at encouraging managerial initiative were not fully abandoned. But Mittag and other policy makers turned to the new Kombinate or production associations rather than to individual enterprises. Like some socialist equivalent of the contemporary Western enthusiasm for conglomerates, they seemed to reconcile coordination with initiative. But they also created a new powerful lobby of director generals with an interest in postponing more painful restructuring.[95]

East German developments reflected wider systemic difficulties. The Soviets followed the East Germans by a year in trying to group individual factories into production associations. The Brezhnev years, now roundly (if not fairly) condemned for their "stagnation," brought a final ambitious effort to resuscitate the old formulas—central control, large projects, mobilization of cheap energy and cheap labor, mass output—even as the regime carried out a significant rearmament effort and sought to avoid cutting back into household consumption. Socialist Fordism might be the most appropriate term for the revived industrial development of the 1970s, applicable also to Poland, where the new prime minister, Edward Gierek, enlisted Western capital for massive investments in new steel mills and shipyards, prolonging inefficient production, and postponing for about a decade major price increases, such as had sparked the uprisings of 1970 and the fall of his predecessor. The resulting program of often inappropriate investment would lead to the debt crisis of 1980 and economic bottlenecks that forced wage hikes and helped trigger the emergence of Solidarność in 1980.

Czech reformers ended up stoking coal and washing windows. Opponents of the Hungarian reform also mobilized to criticize the innovations and remove their major architects from power during the mid-1970s. They did not succeed, however, in reestablishing compulsory planning. As the toll of the oil crises and world economic turmoil became evident, Hungary continued to develop a more decentralized and incentive-based economy—a curious hybrid of state socialism and private production, often in the same plants.[96] Elsewhere, too, in Eastern Europe, the clock was not simply set back; some of the reform initiatives were preserved. Nonetheless, the reflex of centralization, the retreat back to the safe ideological priorities of central planning, came at a moment when world economic forces made the recipe especially inappropriate. The 1970s, with its rise in the price of energy, pressures for stagflation (that manifested themselves in Eastern as well as in Western economies), and the acceleration of electronic technologies, provided the worst moment to reinstitute even a modified centralization. But the Soviet Union's subsidization of oil prices helped postpone sharp declines in growth until the mid-1970s. So too did the Western credits that grew massively during the 1970s and then the 1980s, most lavishly extended to Poland and the Soviet Union.[97] Western loans also postponed the need to confront structural reform. Socialist planners preserved their raison d'être as conduits for Western capital. Even where centralized planning was minimized, as in Hungary, extensive nonmarket supervision of economic processes persisted. Halfway reform generated a miasma of stunted adjustments, but decisive efforts to liberate prices or allow bankruptcies were postponed until the very end of the 1980s.[98]

The 1970s proved a decade of misdirected priorities for the socialist economies. The renewed wager on orthodoxy, impelled by political fears as well as economic contradictions, forestalled the modernization that world market trends imposed elsewhere. The most disastrous consequences were concealed because Western policy makers, intellectuals, and businessmen decided that their interest lay in stabilizing the Eastern bloc. Hegel's cunning of history rarely acted so deviously as during the Brezhnev era. By subsidizing socialist Fordism, Western banks and states allowed it a new lease on life, but ultimately helped to undermine the bloc, which believed it was the path to stabilization. Détente and Ostpolitik meant attempting to improve the lot of ordinary citizens in Eastern Europe by dealing with their single-party regimes. The rapid growth of investment was the financial side of the policies that led to the Helsinki agreements. Accelerating inflation and the glut of dollar reserves in Europe that accumulated during the early seventies made it easy for Western banks to extend credits, whether in Latin America on the part of North American banks or in Poland and East Germany on the part of West Germany. By exporting inflation the United States helped conceal the weakness of socialism.

Conceal, but not eliminate. By 1980 all the countries of Eastern Europe still seriously lagged behind Western standards. Of the lot East Germany turned in the best performance. Per capita GNP (calculated in terms of purchasing power) as of 1980 ranged in Eastern Europe from a quarter to a half that of the United States. East Germany's GNP was reckoned at 52 percent of the American figure, Czechoslovakia at 42, Hungary 39, the Soviet Union 37, Poland 33, and Romania 24.[99] No matter what their relative prosperity, however, the 1970s deepened the difficulties of each CEMA economy. A fundamental contradiction ensured their vulnerability. In each case party leaders embarked on a staunch effort to save or resurrect as much centralized planning as possible. But this was a strategy that could work only in isolation from the West. Yet, at the same time, each society became more involved in world markets, if only by virtue of the Western loans they contracted to give central planning a new lease on life.

When questioned in 1989–90, critics of the then expiring GDR traced the difficulties of the economic system back to the reimposition of orthodoxy in the early 1970s. One word served during the unification period as the most prevalent description of East Germany's physical aspect: *verkommen*, or delapidated and run down. *Verkommenheit* was the legacy of the renewed nationalizations of the 1970s. Socialization of mixed enterprises during the early 1970s meant the effective destruction of the small-scale handicrafts that had remained so crucial a component of both German economies. Craftsmen disappeared. Those left were overtaxed or undertrained. Plumbers took shortcuts, roofers became scarce, buildings leaked and decayed. Residential construction eventually lagged. New apartments and individual homes did increase each year until 1980 from 66,000 to 103,000, then declined to 83,000 in 1988.[100]

The crises became overt in much of the bloc by the 1980s. One can look within at the heavy legacy of the late Brezhnev era, when détente collapsed and the Soviet economy snarled in failed planning targets, shortfalls of grain, steel, and petroleum, even an increase in mortality statistics.[101] The decade opened with a serious collapse of Soviet growth: three consecutive bad harvests, an aging leader, serious absenteeism, and social degeneration. Poland suffered an even graver decline of national output (13 percent in 1981, 8 percent in 1982) and its own credit crisis as the conflict between Solidarity and the regime resorted to martial law.[102] To be sure, inherent Communist difficulties were aggravated as the OECD countries slipped into recession and the sharp rise of American interest rates made the foreign debt burden for Eastern Europe far heavier in real terms.[103] Harvest yields might rise again and Yuri Andropov sought to reinfuse discipline through the railroads and the ministries. Recovery seemed under way by mid decade.[104] But even had Andropov survived, underlying difficulties were not easy to overcome. Productivity per worker hardly grew, nor did machines become more efficient. Soviet technological progress declined after the interval of reforms in the sixties. Prototypes of machines and instruments came on stream rapidly during the 1950s and 1960s and slowed during the 1970s and 1980s.[105] Total factor productivity may have declined.

The system depended on more muscle and more people to bend more metal—not on ingenious breakthroughs. Socialist economic gains in the Soviet Union had resulted from "extensive" development; that is, growth depended upon increased amounts of labor, capital, and land, not on the heightened efficiency of production. Extensive development, however, means declining returns to scale. The marginal yield of capital falls, so that for growth to continue at a constant rate, the share of investment has to grow continuously, a condition as impossible to sustain as the indefinite growth of the labor force.[106] Labor utilization by 1980 was higher in the Soviet Union than anywhere else; demographic resources were near their limit. The 1970s brought 24 million new workers into the labor force; the 1980s promised only about 6 million.[107] Even as the supply diminished, enterprises hoarded workers since they came with no marginal cost; managers had to worry about plan fulfillment rather than net revenues. Perhaps this stacking up of excess labor power represented part of the residual humanity of socialism, but it set severe limits on restructuring. Farmland, oil, and other inputs had also reached their limits. The growth of Soviet per capita consumption slowed from about 4 percent per annum between 1950 and 1970 to about 2.4 percent during the 1970s and under 1 percent in the 1980s. Social organization seemed to be fraying; health care was apparently declining.[108]

To a degree, East Germany seemed to escape Soviet difficulties. Through the 1980s, culminating in the 750th anniversary of Berlin in 1987, the GDR projected its favored image as the successful heir of Prussian bureaucratic efficiency. But, as we have seen, by the second half of the decade productivity and investment were stagnating.[109] Bureaucratic planning seemed excessive and needed to be simplified. What the Germans called *Eigenwirtschaftung* or firm autonomy, Schürer argued, was crucial to the most dynamic Kombinate and had to be carried further.[110] Unfortunately for every state official who possessed what in the West might be called a corporate strategy, there were many who wanted merely to control. The general director of Carl Zeiss asked Mittag whether it would not be better simply to abolish the Ministry for Science and Technology, which merely imposed bureaucratic reporting requirements and encouraged "no strategic impulse whatsoever from the Kombinate."[111]

The question was whether the incremental process of reform could reverse the tendencies toward sclerosis quickly enough. Political considerations at the top of the Politbüro militated against decentralization. The economic reform movements in Hungary (which Honecker told Gorbachev was already lost for socialism), General Jaruzelski's resumption of negotiations with Solidarność in Poland, and, of course, Soviet glasnost seemed increasingly threatening. How could the economic reformers, whether Schürer or the heads of the leading Kombinate, consistently advance an East German version of perestroika when the political leadership steadfastly resisted glasnost? The aging Politbüro ideologues hunkered down to resist the wave of reform emanating from Moscow. No longer was the motto: "To learn from the Soviet Union is to learn victory." Now, declared Honecker, "Among the socialist nations there are no longer teachers and pupils, masters and apprentices as it once was. We are learning together."[112] In fact, only some East German rulers were learning, and all were overtaken by political upheaval.

THE ARCHAEOLOGY OF COAL AND STEEL

Let us look back at the system of central planning as a long-term historical phenomenon, and not just in the GDR, but in Eastern Europe and the Soviet Union as a whole. Where had communism performed relatively well? Its economic success, it becomes apparent in retrospect, depended on a particular stage of industrial development. Central planning and development appeared viable from 1930 to 1960 because the preponderant technology of the era seemed to be based on large productive units and heavy industry. Communism idealized the factories and their mass work force. East German leaders praised their massive chemical capacity in Saxony, the steel complex of Eisenhüttenstadt, and their premier machine-tool industry. From Ulbricht's New Economic Plan on, some of its leaders understood the urgency of developing electronics and computers. Still, for the ideologically committed, economic progress, it appeared (the reality was more complicated), depended on mass production. Efficiency was symbolized by the assembly line, the mechanized output of standardized products. Communist planners indulged in the mystique of Fordism as enthusiastically as Western economic leaders.[113] Assembly line methods, mechanization, intensive labor on the part of workers assigned repeating tasks: these were accepted as the components of a productive process that could be nurtured under socialism or capitalism. East and West, the 1930s and 1940s had bequeathed an imagery of the gigantic industrial site: TVA and the Dnieper dams, the Donbass, River Rouge, the Kaiser shipyards. By 1950 the industrial status symbol par excellence was the steel mill or auto assembly line, and the most modern steel plants were continuous rolling mills. Each country in the West sought such mills in the 1940s and 1950s as the centerpiece of its postwar growth. Jean Monnet pressed French steel firms to organize USINOR as a holding company for a new continuous rolling mill. The reconstruction proposal for the Thyssen nucleus at Duisburg-Hamborn, the Sinigaglia Plan for Italy, the expansion of Hoogvens all envisaged modern steel plants as the keystone of industrial development.

The Communist societies subscribed even more ardently to the romance of steel and to standardized output based on steel. Bolshevism, Lenin had said, equaled the Soviets plus electrification. Stalinism, it might have been updated, consisted of steel mills and the secret police. The Communist states certainly could build steel plants, and observers testified to their increasing sophistication as the 1950s and 1960s progressed. In developing the coal and steel infrastructure of the late industrial era—the apogee of smokestack industry—central planning remained appropriate, as the need for state leadership in some of the West European economies demonstrated. Captivated by coal and steel output as the indices of basic industrial prowess, the East European economies continued, in effect, to pump iron. In Poland, after the 1970 confrontations at the Lenin shipyard, Prime Minister Gierek sought massive infusions of Western capital to expand heavy industry and mining without curtailing living standards. The steel complex of Nova Huta produced unconsumable iron and steel while its black smoke covered the medieval carvings of neighboring Kraków. The East Germans also pressed ahead, and by the 1970s, the Soviets became the world's largest steel producer (see Table 2-4).

But did basic steel production testify to economic advance? By the 1970s, the great era of postwar steel expansion was over. Japanese (and later South Korean) foundries were replacing higher-cost producers in the United States and Western Europe. Comparative advantage in iron and steel production shifted to Asia. Western countries had to close down their foundries or stabilize production with fewer workers. It made more sense for Western societies with their increasingly high-cost labor to switch to services, to products that required less labor per unit (chemicals), or to the manufacture of value-added items in which the costs of highly qualified labor were more easily recouped, such as specialized steels, machine tools, or electronic assembly.

The same situation pertained to coal production. The economic task of the 1970s was to shut down the coal mines and reduce the work force in basic industries. The mines that remained open had to be rendered more efficient. (The United States ran counter to the Western trend; it chose to expand coal extraction as a substitute for imported oil.) This too was a painful transformation. The unemployment in Northumberland, around the Ruhr, or in Lorraine testified to the economic difficulty. The unemploy-

Table 2-4. Crude Steel Production (1,000 tonnes)

	1950	1971	1980	1988
Belgium	3,789	12,444	12,321	11,280
France	8,652	22,859	23,176	18,598
West Germany	14,019	40,313	43,838	41,023
Italy	2,362	17,452	26,501	23,760
United Kingdom	16,554	24,175	11,278	19,008
United States	87,848	109,055	101,698	90,012
East Germany	995	5,350	7,308	8,133
Poland	2,515	12,688	19,485	16,872
Soviet Union	27,329	120,637	147,931	163,037
Japan	4,839	88,557	111,395	105,681

Source: United Nations Economic Commission for Europe, *Quarterly Bulletin of Steel Statistics for Europe* 61 (Geneva, 1955), pp. 12–13; idem, *Annual Bulletin of Steel Statistics for Europe* 16, 1988 (New York, 1990): 8–9, and 8, 1980 (New York, 1981): 10–11.

ment that continues in Asturias or the Midlands or Charleroi reveals that the transition was not made easily. One does not simply move workers from hewing coal or rolling plate to assembling microchips. But just expanding output and digging ever more coal could not protect the socialist economies. If they were to rejoin a world market, they would find themselves with uncompetitive mines and industries. When they finally had to confront ecological concerns, they would find some of the worst environmental degradation on the planet. For decades socialism had pursued the romance of coal and steel without calculating the opportunities forgone in other activities. By the end of the 1980s they awoke to find their old loves aging, demanding, wasteful, and slovenly. As a French journalist rightly emphasized, "Communism and coal. Coal and communism. United from the beginning by productivist ideology, the defense of national resources, a taste for heavy industry, and working-class struggle. From *Germinal* to . . . Bucharest, where the muscular intervention of the 'black faces,'" so she wrote as the miners rampaged in Romania, "once again spectacularly illustrates this natural alliance anchored in conservatism."[114]

The mystique of coal mining was central to the projects of industrialization and the hopes for socialism East and West. No accident that Stakhanov had been a miner: superhuman effort would exceed all the norms. British Labour's belief in collectivism, Jaurès's advocacy for Carmaux, SPD schemes for socialization after the two world wars—all were sustained by the energizing vision of mining communities and a coal-based industrial order. "All of us," Orwell had written, "*really* owe the comparative decency of our lives to poor drudges underground, blackened to the eyes, with their throats full of coal dust, drawing their shovels forward with arms and belly muscles of steel."[115]

By the sixties and seventies, however, the Western economies were furloughing their miners. In the Ruhr, for example, the number of mine workers fell from almost 500,000 in the mid 1950s to 128,000 in 1977.[116] Miners were to be demobilized from their heroic struggle as decisively as the armies of the world wars had been discharged in the preceding generation. Rising productivity would have required fewer miners in any case; declining output and enhanced mechanization together portended a double blow. The link between models of industrial development, visions of socialism, and the mystique of coal mining was severed—reluctantly in Britain or Germany, but unflinchingly (see Table 2-5).

In effect, the CMEA countries faced up to the problem of restructuring only by the mid 1980s. Few state financial officials were willing to stand up to aggrieved managers or threatened workers and let a firm go under. For all the talk of *khozraschet* or firm accountability—concepts that survived their original identification with the reforms—firms could plead for help. "Soft budget" constraints or the possibility of financial support prevailed in the East.[117] (Of course, through the 1970s "bailouts" in the West offered similar extensions of credit. They merely imposed a public dramaturgy of managerial supplication to absolve the new bosses for sackings that afflicted post-Keynesian consciences.) Not until recent years was the painful task of shedding workers finally confronted in Poland and Czechoslovkia: as the general director of the Polish coal mines explained, the problem was closing the pits in a humane way. The situation, he felt, was similar to the Departments of the Nord and Pas de Calais. "Charbonnages de France is a model for us," the Czech mine director also told the reporter from *Le Monde*—the French national coal agency that halved its employees in four years and was the target of French Communist Party wrath.[118]

In part the pressure to shut down derived from the threat of ecological disaster: sulfur spewing forth above the Saxon plain or the Sudeten hills, chemicals dumped into lakes and rivers. For Czechoslovakia nuclear energy and imports of natural gas might eventually promise a cleaner future; unfortunately for the East Germans the nuclear plants were Soviet models, some of them time bombs waiting to go off like Chernobyl. Less dramatic a danger, but more costly on the environment, was the East German de-

Table 2-5. Coal Production and Productivity (1,000 tonnes)

	1980 output	Tons/man-hour[a]	1988 output	Tons/man-hour[a]
United Kingdom	130,096	385 (1985)	101,386	633
West Germany	94,492	539	79,319	630
France	18,136	399	12,139	498
Belgium	6,321	na	2,487	na
United States	714,472	976	783,492	na
Poland	193,171	534 (1985)	193,015	512
	(+36,866 lignite)[b]		(+73,849 lignite)	
Soviet Union	552,952	na	599,486	na
	(+163,417 lignite)		(+172,395 lignite)	
East Germany	307,720	na	360,014	na
	(lignite only)		(lignite only)	

Source: United Nations Economic Commission for Europe, *Annual Bulletin of Coal Statistics* 23, 1988 (New York, 1989).

[a] Underground workers. The high productivity figures for the United States may suggest the large component of output from surface, open-pit mines.

[b] Lignite has two-sevenths the energy capacity of hard coal per unit of weight. For the GDR, I have summed tonnage of raw lignite and pressed briquettes.

pendence on lignite. The GDR was as dependent on this fuel as the Poles were on coal, because indirectly it augmented export earnings to the West. Subsidized Soviet oil was too valuable to burn as fuel within the republic; as discussed above, it could be refined and resold to the West for hard currency or transformed into chemical products. The GDR would get through winter or generate its power by scratching its own brown coal from the vast open pits near Leipzig. West German electric utilities also exploited huge lignite deposits outside Jülich and Aachen, but they were constrained to follow after the monstrous shovels with extensive replanting, whereas the flat plains near Leipzig remained barren and scarred. Within the same region, the air and water were fouled by the effluvia of the great cracking plants. Dust, sulfur dioxide, nitrous oxide, sulfuric acid, and other contaminants hovered above Bitterfeld and its surroundings; acids, chlorides, phenol, and heavy metals ran off into the Mulde River and thence to the Elbe; industrial waste and ash as well as domestic garbage were stored in exhausted surface mines.[119] Comparable wastes, of course, might pollute Cleveland or Tourcoing or the Potteries. But, again, cleanup in the West could begin a decade earlier. So long as East Germany and the CMEA economies remained locked in their mutual dependence, they could not afford to extricate themselves from the equivalent of "slash and burn" industrial processes.

Insofar as Western economies could not shift labor from the old industrial base to the new competitive industries, long-term unemployment became a painful affliction. Even where restructuring succeeded, joblessness accompanied the process. (Only Japan, in effect, could expand steel output and develop an electronic industry simultaneously, in both cases as a supplier of its own and Western industries. By the 1980s steel production was moving offshore from Japan as well, to Korea and Taiwan.) The transition was a painful one (see Table 2-6).

The centrally planned economies sought in effect to resist this trend. Just as Eastern Europe kept a far higher proportion of its workers in agriculture, so it persisted in expanding its coal and steel sector. To be sure, the socialist economies avoided the bleak closings of smelters in Gary, Indiana, or Oberhausen that preoccupied local unions and politicians in the West. The socialist economies found work, of a sort, for everybody: from excess factory labor to bathroom attendants. In effect, the socialist bloc ran an industrial Speenhamland, a subsidized system of "outdoor relief" or job subsidies.

Through the 1960s, of course, the insistence on maximizing employment was a legacy of the Great Depression and the postwar welfare state in Western Europe. Certainly this author and doubtless many readers came of age believing that unemployment was a social scourge. But Western managers faced market constraints. In an era in which technological innovation lept ahead, and agricultural nations were industrializing rapidly, it seemed beyond the imagination of policy makers both to guarantee employment and to develop new value-added industries and services.[120] As recently as the late 1970s West European policy makers remained sensitive about abandoning the Depression-bred idea that double-digit unemployment was a scandal. Econometric studies have suggested that the reluctance to sack workers in Western Europe in the 1970s had made its adjustment to the oil crisis more cumbersome than in the United States, where the right to lay off workers was hardly contested.[121] But by the early 1980s West European economists and policy intellectuals had overcome their ideological aversion to unemployment. They had decided it was more profitable to pay former jobholders not to work than to keep obsolete factories open as workhouses. Not many officials embraced the monetarist idea that being out of work was a quasi-voluntary choice or reflected a finicky attitude toward the jobs being offered. But they did come to accept that having a tenth of one's national

Table 2-6. Annual Unemployment Rates (percentage of total labor force)

	France	West Germany	Italy	United Kingdom	United States
1970	2.5	0.8	5.3	3.0	4.8
1975	4.0	3.6	5.8	4.3	8.3
1980	6.3	3.0	7.5	6.4	7.0
1981	7.4	4.4	7.8	9.8	7.5
1982	8.1	6.1	8.4	11.3	9.5
1983	8.3	8.0	8.8	12.4	9.5
1984	9.7	7.1	9.3	11.7	7.4
1985	10.2	7.2	9.6	11.2	7.1
1986	10.4	6.4	10.5	11.2	6.9
1987	10.5	6.2	11.2	10.2	6.1
1988	10.0	6.1	11.2	8.3	5.4
1989	9.5	5.6	11.4	6.4	5.2

Source: United Nations Economic Commission for Europe, *Economic Survey of Europe in 1989–1990* (New York, 1990), appendix, table A. 12, p. 385.

labor force out of work for a period of several years was a condition of industrial modernization.

Even formerly diehard Keynesians now came to concede that much unemployment was "structural," the result of changing industrial technologies and evolving comparative advantages. Seeking to lower this supposedly noninflationary stable rate (what the monetarists had once called "natural" but was later redefined as the rate that did not accelerate inflation) only led to spiraling prices, current-account deficits, and perpetuation of obsolete jobs. The new wisdom thus provided a theodicy of unemployment, justifying the economy's way to man, or at least the man who did not himself get the sack. A decade of stagflation, that is, of high unemployment coupled with inflationary pressures from oil and labor, pounded the Western economies from the early 1970s to the early 1980s. The distress effectively ended the support for social democratic political leadership in West Germany, the United States, and Great Britain. It forced the governing socialists in France and Spain to become as orthodox as their conservative (or neoliberal) opposition.[122] Emerging from the 1970s, some of the Western industrial cities might be industrial wastelands, but offices were computerized, and services had expanded. Therapists, travel agents, and insurance clerks replaced printers and puddlers. This painful decade of restructuring was hardly attempted in most of Eastern Europe. Nonetheless, the Communists could not postpone the task once they perceived the need to join the world economy.

With this observation our analysis must return to the starting point of this chapter: the encroaching world market. Why could not socialism have continued, it might be asked, to remain an enclave of heavy industry, Fordist assembly lines, a continuing living monument to the economic technology of the 1950s? The problem was that the Communist world could no longer remain an enclave. It had set its ideological validation first on the competition with the West, and then on at least providing some of the goods Westerners enjoyed, and it was falling further behind.[123] CMEA trade figures reflected the continuing ghettoization of its trade, which opened to the West very slowly. In 1970, 63.5 percent of the CMEA countries' exports stayed within their own bloc, and despite the growth of their exports to trade with the West in absolute terms (from $6.374 to $39.415 billion), 56 percent remained intrabloc trade as of 1982. (Imports from outside the bloc amounted to 63 and 57 percent in the respective years.)[124] Remaining a closed system meant growing backwardness and sacrifice—for the power that maintained the bloc as well ultimately for its subject economies.[125] The Comecon had tended to function somewhat like the down-at-heels district of a modern city, where usorious moneylenders, sweatshop industries, and merchants of shoddy goods work out their own neighborhood equilibrium of self-subsidized poverty. But the residents were no longer satisfied with such a mediocre prospect.

The East Germans were in a relatively advantageous position to escape the constraints of the CMEA because they could turn to the Federal Republic. German-German trade was growing, from a total import-export exchange of 2 billion deutsche marks in 1961 to almost 5 in 1970, 11 in 1980 and 14 to 15 in the second half of the 1980s. Soviet imports climbed (albeit to a modest 5 percent of GNP) by the early 1980s and the OECD share increased.[126] The Gierek regime in Poland had effectively borrowed stability through Western loans. But by the 1980s, with default threatening in Latin America, financial institutions demanded the prospect of returns. The nexus of international pressures logically enough first undermined the Polish regime, which finally resorted to military repression in 1981 to suppress the challenge of Solidarity. The Communist economies were being drawn into an interbloc network of commodity and capital flows. They would have to conform to Western rules of the game, and by 1986 four of them had taken the step of joining the IMF to prove they were safe for renewed Western investment.[127] Meanwhile the East Germans ceased publishing their foreign debt figures lest their Western creditors become alarmed and turn off the spigot.[128]

The thirst for Western credits was one major incentive to modernize; Soviet military aspirations were another. If the Soviets no longer believed they would close the gap in economic performance, they knew that their arsenals still commanded awe. But Brezhnev's military ambitions were no longer compatible with the economic resources available. Huge armies, monstrous missiles, and a national quotient of defense spending that was twice that of the United States were still insufficient to assure parity. The Soviet General Staff understood that computerized guidance systems and optics were increasingly important. Arab-Israeli conflict or occasional aerial shoot-outs confirmed the superiority of "smart" weapons over less smart ones. One constituency for perestroika emerged from the Soviet defense and intelligence establishment and had believed that former KGB chief Andropov would recognize the urgency of economic reorganization.[129] Pressure for reform came late, however. The model of industrial prowess relevant for the generation from 1940 to 1970 continued to mesmerize the socialist countries for a decade after their Western competitors had begun the process of restructuring.

That decade of delay, in effect, cost the nomenklatura their system. By the end of the 1980s the Communist Party claim to political and societal leadership could no longer be sustained in view of the developmental deficit that had to be remedied.[130] Still, the historian would be wrong to forget that restructuring in the West also imposed its own wrenching transformations, which many observers perceived as significant sacrifices. These included the loss of confidence in macroeconomic management for at least a decade; the end of the commitment to full employment—which from 1945 to 1975 had seemed such an unshakable article of faith; an increasing stratification of skilled and unskilled workers in the postindustrial economy; growing income inequality even within industrial sectors; the running down of physical infrastructure and perhaps social capital as well—not to cite such hard-to-quantify indices of social pathology as renewed mendicancy, addiction, and violence. For some West Europeans and Americans, this decay appeared as an acceptable or at least necessary trade-off. What mattered in the 1980s was the modernization of activities, the revival of market liberalism, the chance for new fortunes and the creation of new jobs. No matter how great the costs of capitalist stagflation in the 1970s, no matter how pessimistic the predictions, the system had survived. By 1989 capitalism seemed trumps.

By the time of the American presidential campaign of 1992, and of the concurrent Western recessions, the tones of "triumphalism" had faded. Western economies had to face severe contractionary forces as they confronted the transnational legacy of the prior decade's intoxicated credit binges. The global financial system had to lower cascading claims on vastly overvalued assets in Eastern Europe, Latin America, the American West, and elsewhere. Even when recovery came in the mid-1990s, European unemployment, West as well as East, remained preoccupyingly high. Success for firms was accompanied by downsizing and shedding workers.

The "victory" of market capitalism consisted of its capacity to advance technological change and generate wealth and welfare for many despite these casualties. The casualties created by communism had been more widely diffused, less segregated and less marginalized. They were deprived more by universal shortages rather than selective joblessness. Finally, of course, all East Europeans continued to suffer from restrictions on politics, movement, and free expression—all the more a stimulus for rebellion once the socialist governments lost their will to enforce silence. The economic failures undermined any partial legitimation by virtue of efficiency that the Communist regimes might have claimed. The dissatisfactions of the 1980s could be laid at their doorstep because they had refused to let economic development succeed or fall short as an activity independent of political control.

By September 1987, the Stasi reported, economic discontents were discrediting the East German regime. In light of the continuing shortages they encountered, citizens "openly expressed doubts about the objectivity and credibility of the balance sheets and economic results periodically published by the mass media of the GDR." The population was no longer prepared to acquiesce in that party tutelage which had so long served as the real system of governance. "Frequently workers are demanding to be kept informed about emerging problems and their solutions. In part this is tied to the question of whether the party and state leadership actually knows the real situation." When they got the chance to talk with West German visitors, East Germans deprecated the productive capacity of their own economy and condemned the wasteful expenses on Berlin. "To an increasing extent manifestations of indifference and even resignation are evident." Progressive citizens were dismayed about growing corruption and bribery, especially rife in the western used-car market. Comparisons between the level of consumption in the GDR and the FRG drawn by East German citizens returning from allowed family visits "glorified" the West: the returnees were "doubting the productive capacity of the GDR economy in general, or deriving conclusions about the superiority of the capitalist mode of production."[131] Ultimately transformation would require focusing not just on the glum realities of economics but on the recourses of politics. What would it take to move this discouraged population from apathy, resignation, and grumbling dissatisfaction to the belief that mass protest might force a transformation? The chance to leave? The discovery that many others shared their discontents? The willingness to claim public space? Getting to that point, overcoming passivity, always requires some catalytic events. By late summer 1989 they were at hand.

Three

The Autumn Upheaval

PROLOGUE: A REVOLUTION IN GERMANY

What happened? News of the startling changes in foreign capitals spread with great rapidity; the authorities in Berlin failed to comprehend the challenge, then reluctantly agreed to shuffle ministers; mass demonstrations forced the pace and extent of concessions; authority irreversibly evaporated from a state apparatus earlier renowned for its efficiency and capacity to use force; repeated changes of government were attempted to accommodate the pressure from the streets; the old spokesmen had to apologize for attempting to control earlier demonstrations with police. There was negotiation of a new constitution, countless discussions of national unity, and a season of collective euphoria: all in all, an apparently stunning and inspiring revolution from below. This was Germany in autumn 1989. It was also Germany in spring 1848. Indeed it was Central Europe in the fall of 1989, and Central Europe in the spring of 1848.

Why cite these earlier events? Because they illuminate recurring patterns of German upheaval, relevant across a century and a half. At first glance, the societies were strikingly different: mid-nineteenth-century Central Europe was largely rural and poor, with rudimentary industry localized in a few towns or dispersed among household textile producers. Word of mouth and shared newsletters provided its network of public communication. Families with hereditary titles and manorial estates dominated the county administrations and village economies east of the Elbe River. Protestant pastors in the north, school teachers, tutors, professors in the university towns, and public officials comprised the civic elite that might discuss and participate in administrative and local affairs or read about international events. In some towns the local regiment furnished a pool for society life; in Berlin and Potsdam and other administrative centers soldiery was far more conspicuous. Society was provincial and bounded, yet not without dense networks of associations: gilds, churches, agricultural or commercial betterment societies, gymnastic and shooting clubs. Protestant regions at least were quite literate; and while Germans spoke their highly structured language with wide ranges of intonation and accent, an almost obsessive print culture was standardized and pervasive enough to establish a broad sphere of public discourse. Catholic towns were occasionally populist, often conservative, hostile to the encroaching Protestant secularism of the state. Society was highly stratified and redolent with the differential privileges inherited from the ancien regime. But shared work relationships among participants in common economic activity on the land or in the workshop could cut across the status divide, while access to the written culture and to professional qualifications allowed alternative principles for defining a would-be elite. The members of this potential elite would provide the revolutionaries of 1848. More precisely they would comprise those who sought to take the revolutionary upheaval in hand and institutionalize its popular force. Nevertheless, they never really organized as a coherent force before the revolutionary crisis, and they soon fragmented during the revolution itself.[1]

The Western European observer before 1848 might have been easily misled. The lack of social glitter and absence of a metropolis, the presence of uniforms and preoccupation with official rank, the persistence of censorship and distrust of intellectuals conveyed the impression of backwardness. Exiles like Heine might become homesick but could not accept the stultifying enforced provincialism. At the same time, leading German thinkers were fully versed in the ideas from abroad: they studied British science, Scottish political economy, American economic ventures, French constitutional ideas; they pushed poetic lyrics and philosophical reasoning to as brilliant a level as did their more socially sophisticated neighbors. And for all their narrow-minded suspicion of public discussion and debate, government officials encouraged railroads, the training of engineers, trade treaties, and national development.

It is startling, at least at first glance, how many of these organizational patterns still characterized the East Germany of 1989. The Federal Republic had become a modern European society where international business firms, mass consumption, youth culture, and travel had helped to dissolve the old state's supervision of the private sphere. But while the West apparently dissolved into the flux of modernity, the East nurtured its provincial Prussian orderliness. Despite the successive impacts of industrialization, world wars, mass politics, and dictatorship, eastern Germany preserved the artifacts of an earlier era. Of course, many regions were now densely urban with a workforce organized in large collective units. Nonetheless, outside the gray mass of Berlin or the industrial landscape of Saxony, provincial and small-town remoteness belied the compactness of the territory. Even in large cities, many families devoted loving attention to their garden allotments and miniplots. Before 1848 family formation and the relations between husbands and wives, parents and children had been regulated by religious authority or village custom. After 1949, the East German state was determined to organize production and to encourage women's labor force participation, aspirations that required a national politics of family formation and provision for public child care. Both eras required an active *polizei*, to borrow the cameralist term for the authorities' tutelage of the supposedly private sphere.

"Police, in the broad understanding of the term," to cite a standard handbook of the eighteenth century, "refers to all those measures in the internal affairs of a nation through which the wealth of state may be more permanently established and multiplied. . . . Police, in the narrow sense of the term, refers to all that which is required for the proper condition of civil life, and in particular for the maintenance of good order and discipline amongst subjects . . . the police have therefore to attend to (1) the moral condition of subjects, (2) civil order and (3) internal security and the control of evil and injustice."[2] The cameralist author would have been reassured over two centuries later when an East German recalled, "The GDR citizen was educated to remain nice and orderly and go along with everything. Our self-consciousness was really taken away. In principle we always had someone to speak on our behalf."[3] It should not be surprising that the texture of political life thus revealed striking continuities. State authorities in the late 1980s still believed censorship indispensable. They extruded their dissenting intellectuals no longer to Paris but to West Germany, where they responded with a mockery similar to that of earlier exiles.

German authorities, in fact, pursued two approaches to governance. For the generation after the Napoleonic Wars the officials really sought only to guarantee obedience and good order. In the century and a half thereafter, successive, newer ideologies—nationalist, National Socialist, and finally, Marxist-Leninist—motivated the political leaders to orchestrate well-organized public affirmation, as well as mere obedience. Official politics in the GDR thus strived for rituals of enthusiasm and consensus. At the same time, state authorities in the late twentieth as well as the early nineteenth century sought everyday compliance, acquiescence, and acceptance of bureaucratic order. In the earlier era officials had tried to adopt the French Napoleonic mix of civic mobilization and bureaucratic reform; in the later years of the GDR, they borrowed the Soviets' reliance on a self-perpetuating party apparatus to mobilize, but simultaneously to discipline society at large.

If day-to-day politics discloses suggestive continuities, so too does the pattern of revolution. The revolutions of 1848, certainly outside of France, and the second round of uprisings in 1849 were perceived as a failure, their original enthusiasts either thrust toward reaction or bitterly disillusioned. Significant changes in the legal order did result—the liberation of serfs in Austria, the end of ghettos, the granting of a Prussian constitution—but the revolutionaries' agenda was largely reversed. The monarchs and their armies recovered their power, pushed through reforms to reinforce their authority, frustrated the hopes for German national unity. They overran barricades, dispersed protesters, dissolved assemblies, imprisoned and executed those revolutionary leaders who did not flee to London or Paris or New York. In terms of institutional change, the 1848 uprisings (like 1968) proved most significant in discrediting radical paths to reform and thus pointing the way, fifteen to twenty years further on, toward more gradualist compromises with state leaders and social elites. But reformists and revolutionaries could not accomplish their agenda on their own terms. In contrast, 1989 seems to have ushered in a new democratic era, and German reunification quickly became a fact.

Many reasons can be cited to account for the different outcomes. One was geostrategic: Russia remained impervious to revolution in 1848 except for some ferment in aristocratic salons. The waves of change rolled eastward only to smash without effect against the tsarist breakwater. The Russian autocrat could assist the Habsburgs to reimpose military order on their unruly lands and then pressure the Prussian monarch to eschew any effort at organizing a federal structure in northern Germany. In contrast, the transformations already under way within the Soviet Union by the end of the 1980s meant that Russia no longer acted as a bulwark of stability in Central Europe. Indeed glasnost and partial perestroika provided the impetus for upheaval within the Communist system as a whole.

The precedent of 1848 alerts us to further lessons. In light of 1989, 1848 proves most revealing by virtue of its drama of crowds and power. In both instances German states, renowned for efficiency, authority, the efficacious transmission of directives from above, and the loyalty of their administra-

tive elites, simply ceased to command. Like some marionette released by
its guiding hand, the German state fell in a heap of unsinewed limbs. A
similar collapse characterized the revolution of November 1918, when
imminent, engulfing defeat in World War I suddenly severed, as it were,
the networks of authority. The imposing German Empire, which for four
years had conducted a vast two-front war, and had indeed come close to
victory in the previous spring, simply lost its power of command. Once the
army leaders disavowed countless prior assurances and confessed that Germany faced defeat, administration unraveled. Soldiers began streaming
home from the front. Sailors mutinied in the North Sea ports. Crowds
surged into central Berlin, the kaiser fled, and a reluctant Social Democratic
party leadership took power for want of any alternative. What authority
persisted was generated on the local level by councils of soldiers, workers,
or local notables.

These three upheavals at seventy-year intervals suggest a characteristic
model of political breakdown, which we can contrast, for example, with the
classic scenario of French revolutions. It was tempting in the fall of 1989 to
chart the course of East German turmoil against the canonical progress of
revolution in Paris during 1789. Crowds assembled, the Wall was breached,
just as the Bastille had fallen two hundred years earlier. A stage of further
radicalization seemed at hand when angry mobs invaded the State Security
Police Headquarters on the Normannenstrasse in January 1990. The tempo
was quicker, but the paradigmatic slide toward a radical republic seemed
visible for the historically conscious. Indeed historians and observers tend
to chart every revolution against the stylized drama of Paris from 1789 to
1794. They may witness an accelerated sequence but they usually find a
process that lurches from popular grievances and mass demonstrations, to
substantial liberal reforms, to radical seizure of power, to Thermidor.[4]

Fixation on the French paradigm, however, obscures important elements
of German revolutions. It was not just that the moment of spontaneous
crowd action was brief in 1989, whereas in revolutionary France it could be
remobilized periodically for almost a decade.[5] More important, revolutions
in France (and elsewhere in the West) involved the passage of power to an
opposition anxious to exercise control. As authority bled away from the
French monarchy in May and June 1789, reformist aristocrats, intellectuals,
spokesmen for the Third Estate were avidly reaching for it. The deputies of
the Third Estate reconstituted themselves as the National Assembly and
collectively pledged that they would continue their struggle for rights and
power. In England a century and a half earlier, the parliamentary opposition

had pressed Charles to disavow his ministers and relinquish his claims to sovereignty. When his soldiers came to arrest their leaders, they felt confirmed as a countervailing source of legitimacy and authority.

But the revolutions in Germany had no equivalent opposition, anxious to take control. Before 1848 the participants in print culture, the consumers of newspapers, had never united as an "intelligentsia," much less a political party. Observers in the summer of 1989 argued that the government had fragmented the opposition in its "niches," sent its spokesmen into West German exile, confined its critics to the churches, even as many of these critics overestimated their oppositional role. Most important, they believed, the chance to go West had undermined the formation of a cohesive adversarial power at home. As one would-be leader wrote, "The opposition in the GDR today is just as pallid as the party."[6] But the same impotence and atomization had characterized opposition earlier. Liberal grouplets challenged the German regimes before 1848, but without building a cohesive alternative regime. Before the collapse of the Wilhelmine Empire, the opposition had indeed voted as a bloc in the Reichstag and vociferously demanded changes. But it had never been able to offer a convincing shadow government. When in fact revolutionary crowds and councils crystallized in defeated Germany, the major oppositional forces were endeavoring to support a newly installed reformist government. What power they possessed was thrust upon them. The formation of an opposition that is prepared to take power from those in charge—a counterelite—before authority disintegrates in the streets has never characterized revolution in Germany.

Periods of crisis in Russia, it is relevant to note, reveal some analogous patterns. The observer of 1905, of early 1917, and the period of turmoil during 1990 and early 1991, is struck by the growing incapacity of government. Not the ambition of a compact counterelite or the coherent force of the liberal or working-class opposition, but the continuing breakdown of authority and economic exchange is most striking. Developments in the Soviet Union during 1989 were most reminiscent of the political breakdown from spring to autumn 1905. Can we generalize? On the one side, revolutions in seventeenth-century Britain, eighteenth-century North America, and then, most spectacularly, France culminate a period of growing tension in which the development of a coherent opposition emerges step by step with the growing crisis of the regime. The Western revolution is an adversarial trial, the upshot of a struggle between a regime fearful of further devolution, and a phalanx of reformers determined to secure it. In Germany in 1848, 1918, and 1989, the opposition hardly advances beyond a loose network of dissenters before the streets explode; it organizes only after the previous bureaucratic state has lost control. Indeed, throughout the once authoritarian states of Central and Eastern Europe (Poland excepted), revolution has historically involved more a process of bureaucratic decomposition than coherent challenge.

Can we account for the persistent difference? Critics often mocked the timidity of revolutionaries in Germany: the tired joke had it that the police would not let the Germans hold a revolution. Chancellor Bülow believed that it was not German to conduct politics in the street.[7] Excessive veneration of authority supposedly precluded direct political action. But Germans, in fact, have taken to the streets even if infrequently. Leaving aside the revolutions, Berliners demonstrated in 1910 (unsuccessfully) for direct universal male suffrage in Prussia. Working-class crowds protested the assassination of Walther Rathenau in 1922 and the depredations of Storm Troopers during the crisis of Weimar. Students and antinuclear marchers have confronted the police during recent decades. Moreover, what has characterized German upheaval has been less a reluctance to begin revolution than a capacity to carry it through. German regimes break down, lose their capacity overnight to enforce obedience as angry crowds finally take to the streets. But the revolutions in Germany and Central Europe have had, in a metaphoric sense, no tomorrow. No leadership emerges to harness popular protest into a decisive democratization of institutions. In 1848, the old regimes recovered their nerve and recaptured political momentum. In 1989, West Germany's political leaders, preeminently Chancellor Helmut Kohl, stood ready to exploit the momentary victory of the crowd. But in both cases the moment of revolutionary autonomy was relatively fleeting, as if the aperture of historical spontaneity opened briefly, admitted a ray of piercing light, then closed.

It is not just wise restraint or collective gentleness that has limited the scope of German revolution. Vaclav Havel called the Czech upheaval in November 1989 the "velvet revolution," and it followed the course of Czech politics more generally. Except for the obscene self-consuming abasement and murderous persecutions of the Communist regime after 1948, a certain self-limiting habit has tempered political passion in Prague: restraint, tolerance, unwillingness to push a political victory to penalize the opposition. But earlier German revolutions have hardly been gentle. The denunciation of political adversaries has been harsh and bitter. In 1848 and 1918–19 confrontation and physical violence attended the mobilization of crowds. Those who enlisted for counterrevolutionary repression enjoyed a license to kill. Revolutionary sequences have been less "velvet" than confused and short-term civil wars.

Sometimes overlapping geographical loyalties have played an important limiting role. In 1848 the rivalry among centers of revolution in Central Europe—the new ministers in Berlin hostile to the claims of the liberals in Frankfurt, the radicals of Vienna distrustful of the aspirations of Budapest—undermined the fledgling regimes. In 1989, access to West Germany cut short some of the revolutionary momentum: it was perhaps unfortunate, Lothar de Maizière—the transitional prime minister of the GDR in its last months of existence—admitted privately, that "our people went traveling" in November 1989. Still, when revolutionaries in France or Britain or America claimed power, they were prepared to exercise it, sometimes harshly, sometimes inefficiently, but without diffidence. They understood that government must serve as an instrument for like-minded political friends, who had grievances and a common transformative agenda. German elites governed cities and might debate national affairs. Germans of all social strata organized a rich fabric of associations to limit economic competition, train and regulate their craftsmen, run their towns, assure their music, encourage their gardening, sports, and riflery. They nurtured an active periodical literature to debate and criticize the ideas of the day. In short they had established the institutions so important for "civil society."[8]

Civic assertiveness did not necessarily follow however. Neither in 1848, nor in 1918, nor originally in 1989 did German leaders possess an intuitive sense how to organize coalitions to consolidate their own authority and secure their own political agenda. Power had been entrusted to a bureaucratic leadership. After 1933, of course, any opposition had to be clandestine at best and was brutally repressed. The means of repression became less sadistic after 1945, but control remained stifling. East Germans after 1945 hardly had the chance to take a catch-up course in Western traditions of political participation. (In fact the East German regime increasingly looked to the model of the Prussian bureaucratic state as a model for its own style of government. Fossil-like it retained a respect for orderly obedience and a patronizing attitude toward its citizen-subjects.)

But why, it must be asked, had the long-term tradition of German political contention been relatively weak? We know how it differed from patterns elsewhere; the challenge is to find causes that are not just tautological. Weak liberalism cannot simply be ascribed to a weak liberal tradition. Many reasons have been offered; every big generalization in history usually has too many possible causes that might serve as explanation.[9] I think it makes most sense to start with national patterns set in the seventeenth century, which is not to argue that they were inevitably engraved into national history. (History often affords chances to catch up and switch back; few options are foreclosed irrevocably even if they are foreclosed repeatedly.) In Europe modern political ambitions emanated originally from the landed magnates and the urban traders and lawyer-intellectuals they admitted to their circles. British aristocrats conducted two seventeenth-century revolutions to demonstrate that their monarchs must accept their active collaboration expressed in Parliament to raise money and rule. The more diffuse French aristocracy did not collectively claim that their representatives must share in national government, but leading spokesmen did insist that their status was privileged. They claimed tax exemptions and argued that the courts of the realm, which they staffed, must be allowed, if not to draft, at least to take official cognizance of royal legislation. Their members might serve the court and claim the great offices of the realm, as they wished.

The relationship of magnates to crown was different in Central and Eastern Europe. The landed aristocracy and the educated civil servants did not prevail against their monarchs or manage to negotiate a compromise role for their provincial diets. Instead the monarchs of Prussia and Russia and Austria curbed the claims to political autonomy on the part of their nobility, even as they conscripted them to administer their military apparatus and civilian administration. Educated to administer as servants of their monarch, they found it unfamiliar work to contest their rulers, much less to substitute for them. Not every noble accepted this subordination and the great crisis provoked by the Napoleonic conquests in Germany allowed for some renegotiation of responsibilities. Parliamentary government, however, did not take root; the landed classes remained civil servants or agrarian estate managers, identifying with king and fatherland. Emerging professional and industrial leaders were too small a segment of the population to prevail in 1848. They too became enthusiasts of the national idea and accepted the constitutional compromise with which Bismarck restricted their parliamentary influence in the new Germany. The rapid industrialization of united Germany and the emergence of a militant and well-organized working class made the older elites, whether landed or commercial, bureaucratic or professional, hesitant to press too hard for suffrage reform or the right to control the national ministries. By the mid-nineteenth century, Germany teemed with vigorous businessmen, proud city councillors; it supported an advanced academic establishment and broad elementary education. Its urban elites often pressed for imperialist expansion, they shared the Darwinian convictions, and envisaged conflicts among nations far more fatalistic and militarized than their counterparts elsewhere. They supported ideologically argumentative parties and continuing debate. But the passion to govern—to control the major offices of the state, distribute positions to one's trusted colleagues, impose a legislative vision—was less developed than in Western governments based on representation. No German Gladstone or Lincoln understood how to accumulate majorities or had the institutions that rewarded such democratic passions. Numbers were the fundamental resource of politics in Western Europe by the late nineteenth century; but appealing to numbers loomed as a fearful debasement for many of the Germans, who otherwise had a strong commitment to acting in the civic sphere.[10] The sociologist Max Weber caught the distinction between the British and German regimes. His critique of the German monarchy could have been applied to the GDR: "A merely passive democratization would amount to a totally pure form of a bureaucracy free of control."[11] Only democratic politics, the struggle over policy and leadership carried out through parliament and parties (not meaningless plebiscites) would allow responsible harnessing of national energies.

Germany did not lack the potential for such political maturation to take place. Its broad male suffrage since 1871 was as advanced as any other regime. Electoral participation rates were high, and elections were vigorously contested. The 350-year-old religious rivalries nurtured tenacious Protestant and Catholic political cultures. These were overlaid in turn by strong social and economic cleavages. Despite their active contests at the polls, Reichstag deputies could not force the resignation of a government or exercise much leverage over military and foreign policy. Bismarck viewed parliamentary politicians with increasing contempt. Nonetheless, his successors no longer possessed his prestige and found it harder to hold majorities. Still, had World War I not interrupted political struggle, it is likely that Germany might have become a more liberal state. To be sure, the German legacy of policing the populace was more intense than in Britain, and more pervasive than Italy and France. The cameralist approach to the well-ordered *Polizeystaat* had made snooping a bureaucratic virtue (a tradition that the GDR, of course, would continue). In short, German institutions offered footholds to expand the sway of liberal representative government despite clear handicaps. But German political habits continued to encourage passivity. Democratization was not precluded; it would require perseverance.

The bankruptcy of the militarized imperial regime at the end of World War I briefly discredited the bureaucrats and the generals. It allowed the intrusion of mass passions and rewarded democratic entrepreneurship. Germany's democratic experiment, however, was overburdened by conditions of near civil war, nationalist resentments about the lost war, and highly doctrinaire politics. In 1945 the Allied armies arrived before a similar populist reaction might have taken root, and they brought an agenda of orderly reform. West Germans learned to be good liberal democrats; East Germans had to accept the inauthentic claims of popular democracy, which quickly meant domination by a Marxist, even Stalinist single party. Finally in 1989, in East Germany, the opportunity came again, as it had in 1848 and 1918, decisively to wrest political control from trustees that had become remote and sclerotic. Unlike 1848, a nation did not have to be constructed; indeed, the difficulty might be that the West German national destiny might dampen the process of East German renewal. Or so the intellectual leaders of the upheaval believed. For most of those involved, absorption in West Germany was precisely the guarantee of liberty and welfare they craved. Unlike 1918, there was no bitterness about a lost war, no feeling of betrayal on the part of returning soldiers, no plausible radical ideological alternatives on the left or right. (Indeed 1989 was a revolution against the Marxism that had beckoned part of the working class in 1918, but had been imposed from outside in 1945.) The year 1989 was thus an upheaval far less doctrinaire, less polarized, more tolerant and civil than the 1918 revolution. At last Germans might apparently claim a revolution that did not degenerate into civil war or succumb to armed reaction.

But from the outset, commentators contested applying the term revolution to the transformations under way.[12] They were supposedly too easy and too brief, beginning with the exodus of GDR visitors from Budapest and Prague to the West, and culminating in the great but peaceful demonstrations of October and November 1989. These reached a climax with the great manifestation in Leipzig on October 9 and the opening of the Berlin Wall a month later. Thereafter the crowds just confirmed and accelerated the dismantling of the Communist states. Compared with the upheavals in France in the summer of 1789, 1792, and after, the conflicts in Petrograd, or the Chinese Civil War, this easy victory hardly seems a revolution.

Some analysts have found the analogue of decolonization (with the Soviet Union playing a role parallel to that of Great Britain after 1945) more persuasive. Decolonization, of course, need not exclude revolution. Both descriptions of historical process can be applied simultaneously. The geostrategic retreat of the Soviet Union, and ultimately its own decomposition, can be envisaged as a renewed and final wave of decolonization. But this international perspective leaves unspecified the degree of penetration that was attempted and the nature of transformation within the newly decolonized regions. When colonizers depart willingly, well-groomed successors can sometimes claim office. But when departure follows a long independence struggle, the colonized society is often convulsed. Even when evacuated peacefully, the newly independent countries have often fallen into turbulent regional or ideological struggles. In any case, despite the "imperial" analogues of Soviet control, decolonization will hardly describe the failing loyalties, the crowd passions, and the scope for autonomous decision–making on the part of the East German authorities. As a summary of events, it bypasses too much history.

Nevertheless, within a few months many Germans themselves shied from using the term revolution. Their hesitations require a hearing and, if appropriate, a response. East Germans who were active in the democratic protest movements of the late 1980s, but then became disappointed that their state so quickly merged with the West, suggested that their countrymen had not desired real revolutionary change. They were disappointed by the electoral majorities for the CDU and rapid unification. But the changes that demonstrators in Leipzig and Berlin and elsewhere initially wanted amounted to a radical liberalization of the East German political order. And when in March 1990 citizens voted for reunification, they did not envisage it as a choice for Thermidor or mere stabilization. They wanted a consolidation of conditions that had already been transformed politically, although not yet in terms of material welfare.

Some West German political analysts also argued that no revolution had occurred. Instead, they claimed that the GDR had collapsed as a result of its inner difficulties; it had suffered "systems failure" or "imploded." Indeed, they explained, such an outcome had been inevitable. These judgments were occasionally condescending. To a degree, the East German popular movement seemed actually embarrassing to some West German social scientists, especially those fifty or older who had been trained in the structural-functional sociology that had characterized the first generation of postwar renewal. They were used to thinking in terms of abstract processes, and the powerful intrusion of crowds and demonstrations seemed vaguely threatening even when directed against the GDR, not the Bundesrepublik. The East German protesters were like obstreperous children at an adults' dinner party. A popular movement was an explosion of mass passion that the Federal Republic had never really experienced except perhaps for the student demonstrations of the late 1960s. It appeared inchoate. Perhaps it also seemed a rebuke to the orderliness of politics at home and the acquiescence in division. Thus the months of upheaval generated the curious result of a mass upheaval that social scientists and political commentators never anticipated and then explained away as perfectly obvious and predictable.

But the fact that the regime revealed elements of "systems failure" does not diminish the role of the popular movement. Every regime that succumbs to revolution passes first through a period of institutional stress and even breakdown. Direct action emerges because fiscal crisis and administrative sclerosis have already set in. Nor does the avoidance of violence—a further objection to the idea of a 1989 revolution—undermine the authenticity of a revolutionary upheaval. Dying regimes often draw back from wagering on forcible suppression. Popular mobilization, not bloodshed, is the criterion. Members of the Politbüro wavered and disagreed about the use of force. At a decisive moment in the history of Communist regimes, the leadership divided and backed away from the escalation of violence. Power passed to the streets as demonstrators gathered in continuing protest. As in the few prior revolutionary moments of German history—March 1848, or November 1918—force was exercised by the massed public, not by the administration in being. The swiftness of the victory does not disqualify the achievement. Revolutions are built out of *grandes journées*.

Of course, it is easy to deprecate the popular movement. To judge from photographs and protesters, young people played a disproportionate role: adolescents provided a mass base. Moreover, unless we count the uprising of 1953, the Germans did not initiate the long chain of protest that undermined Communist rule; Poles and Hungarians had been pressing for democratization; Czechs had tried twenty-one years earlier. Still, at a critical instant, the crowds of Leipzig and Berlin pushed the process of Communist concession and erosion beyond the point of return. How did these events gather force and momentum?

DECOMPOSITION AND FLIGHT

"At the end we were just too tired to make jokes about the regime. Everything had been said. . . . We discovered that we were in a position to overthrow a regime. . . . It was easy because this government was moribund and rickety to its marrow, but not because we were organized. Any organization would have been chicken-feed for the secret police."[13] Any revolution involves a double transformation of sentiments: a profound change both among ordinary citizens and at the summit of political power. Anger and mobilization among the mass of the population, then perhaps a heady sense of fraternity—"in reality (let's not forget) it was just nice to be in this crowd of people, to laugh under the common strain, to sense one's neighbor and be at one with him"—but, at the same time, dissent and recrimination within a formerly cohesive elite.

These two changes interact, each acceleration of the one hastening further change in the other. A history of a revolution is thus at least a two-tier story. Of course, it is more complicated. No society is simply bifurcated. Between elite and the wider political public mediate key social groups. Their members share both situations: potential members of the elite by education or social origin or qualification are still outside, still angered, and prepared to articulate the grievances of the wider public. Their increasing alienation undermines the remaining moral basis for consensus and obedience. Intellectuals, journalists, and university students have played this double role in European societies. Dissenting writers gave visibility to the discontent in the GDR as they were extruded to West Germany—Rainer Kunze in 1977, Wolf Biermann in 1976—or simply pushed literature to the limits of tolerated critique. The university role in East Germany was more ambiguous. University teachers and students played a catalytic role in voicing German radical aspirations in the early nineteenth century. And in recent decades universities have become instrumental in challenging established governance, West and East: prepared to articulate the grievances of the wider society, positioned to play a role within the governing elite, they have been the stormy petrels of civic discontent. In East Germany, however, faculties and students were locked into the SED. Advancement and even enrollment in the humanities or social sciences—except for theological studies—usually required party membership. Those who could not make their peace with the authorities never entered academic institutions. Those who became quarrelsome later were sometimes ousted or steered into academic byways. Troublesome students could be expelled, as occurred at the Humboldt University in the 1970s.[14] What tended to develop inside the universities during the last years of the regime was a percolating generational split or disgruntled accommodation. Younger researchers increasingly angered at their own teachers' prevarication (if not outright collaboration) tried to make their way under the supervision of a cautious middle-aged professorate. Disagreements were muted, innovation was incremental.

The regime, however, undermined this acquiescence in January 1988 when it attempted to censor news about the progress of Soviet glasnost by removing the magazine *Sputnik* from kiosks. "The discrepancy between the views of Gorbachev and those of the SED leadership really opened up people's eyes."[15] The Sputnik-Verbot was a sign that the GDR Politbüro could not or would not follow Gorbachev's lead: the prohibition sent a new shock even through SED ranks; there were protests and disillusion. It was certainly not the first protest within the SED, but the first in which the Russians might serve as the standard of reform. Each year on the anniversary of Rosa Luxemburg's death at the hands of the Free Corps in the disastrous Spartacist Week of January 1919, the SED held party-inspired festivities, parades, and speeches. Honecker liked to sing the old songs. Now, on the 1988 anniversary, protesters paraded with Rosa's slogan: Freedom means freedom for those who think differently. The party was hanging on, forcing its critics into West German exile, torn between a rising generation who felt that the old-timers were frozen into disastrous conservatism, and the hardliners who felt that to give way would unleash disaster.

In this last year or two of the SED, observers could sense that the old party was in conflict. Those members allowed to travel—a privilege granted only to the reliable—suggested that they were distancing themselves from repression. If academics, they were undertaking new inquiries: for the historians, social history, the Prussian monarchy and Frederick II, and at last catching up on the history of the Holocaust. If writers, they were voicing new dissent, forcing a conflict within the writers gild. Christoph Hein told his parable of King Arthur's feckless court. Even within the party the old dissenters, preeminently Havemann, now came to be read as underground classics—a silenced generation of "good" Communists repressed by Ulbricht apparatchiks. Factory workers, whom Westerners did not meet, were also in disarray. "It wasn't as if we comrades of the rank and file had not had problems," one engineer recalled after the Leipzig demonstrations. ". . . we demanded a clear position on perestroika in the Soviet Union and spoke out against the attitude of leading comrades."[16] How was consent to be manipulated within an atmosphere riddled by such inner conflict? On May 7 the party manufactured the electoral results for the local voting, allegedly giving the SED 97 percent of the vote. All but the most steadfast supporters believed the results were fraudulent.

The party leadership was divided. In February, Gerhard Schürer, preoccupied by the impending debt crisis, had suggested to Krenz that they move to impeach Honecker at the Politbüro: "Egon, I'll make you a proposal. I'll make a motion. . . . I'm an old man in any case, I'm close to retirement, have to leave sometime soon, and I'll demand that Honecker and Mittag be removed. . . . You can't intervene and say, I want to become general secretary, but I can propose you. I'll provoke the issue because otherwise the GDR will go kaput." After a three-hour talk, Krenz said he was not prepared to unseat Honecker, his "foster father, his political teacher."[17] The second rank of the Politbüro might read the signs of the time, but the old guard, Honecker, Mielke, Hager, and others, saw only a lamentable failure of nerve.

The relationship with the Soviet Union remained special for Honecker; he could never disavow it, but he did regret the new course. In a long conversation on February 1, 1988, Soviet Ambassador Kochemasov had told Honecker that the fate of the Soviet Union and the GDR were "inseparably tied together," but gravely insisted that there was no alternative to the transformation of Soviet communism and better relations with the United States and West Germany. We don't mix in the internal affairs of our friends, Honecker had responded, but "the ambassador will not have the illusion that the transformation evokes only optimism in the world." Then he listed some of his griefs. "There are matters we can't agree with. One can't say that Stalin was the same as Hitler." For this reason he had suppressed the translation of *New Times*, a Soviet review that was a voice for reform; it required so much additional ideological and political labor to explain to people why that sort of material appears in the Soviet Union. Honecker reaffirmed his deep feelings for the Soviets—his own speech at the Soviets' Twenty-seventh Party Congress had been no mere ritual. "But the Soviet comrades had to understand that the developments in the Soviet Union had to be digested by us, and that's no simple matter at present."[18]

For Honecker, Mielke, Hager, and Mittag other Warsaw Pact regimes might be defecting, but not their own East Germany. In early May 1989, Honecker told the Czech leader Miloš Jakeš that the West German government had lost its own base of popular support and was not ready to give up its old goals of subverting the GDR. It was all very well to talk about a "general humanitarian atmosphere" in the world, but "we know that the history of mankind is a history of class struggle."[19] Honecker went to the Communist summit at Havana in June 6, where, so he reported back to the Politbüro, Sheverdnadze allegedly told him that the Polish situation was disquieting and where he expressed his own fear that Hungary was almost lost to socialism.[20] The discussions at the Warsaw Pact meeting in Bucharest in late July were even more disturbing. Gorbachev expressed his concern over the Chinese repression at Tiananmen Square. The Hungarian delegate, Nyers, argued that the internal development of the socialist countries was "at the threshold of a new epoch and the requirements of the New Thinking played an ever more determining role." Even Jakeš referred to the "break-through" character of the present age and argued that a complex transformation of Czech society that required extensive democratization had now begun. And Jaruzelski justified his government's round-table negotiations with Solidarity by tracing the repeated cycles of working-class protest. In 1981, he emphasized, Solidarity had burst over our life like a typhoon, like a tornado. But the Poles were attempting to solve the current crisis "without the application of violence, without bloodshed. We can't forever take a path that brings us into conflict with the working class, that tears open a rift that can be overcome only with difficulty if at all." The party was the guarantor of the stability and strength of socialism. "But the party is no absolute monarchy. I can only speak about Poland. But I have to admit that we have behaved like an absolute monarch who was always right, who gives commands and orders, so to speak a superbureaucrat, who certainly commands the military apparatus, but has suffered a political defeat."[21] Some of the Politbüro members sensed their growing precariousness. On August 1, they met with embattled Nicaraguan leaders, who vented their own concern about flagging Soviet aid and the general trends within the Soviet Union, Poland, and Hungary.[22] The Nicaraguans wanted more fraternal aid and they echoed the view that the GDR stalwarts already shared: Hungary in effect had gone capitalist, Poland was on the way, and the Soviet Union was in the throes of some risky experimentation. The Politbüro members could draw two conclusions: tough it out at home, or follow the new trend. For the moment the former line still prevailed.

The fissuring within the party alone would not have ended the regime. Intellectuals alone could not provide the mass force; they could articulate demands, but finally numbers had to prevail. How did one form a political public when hitherto garden allotments, the month at the down-at-heels Baltic resorts, or sports had absorbed citizens' energies? From the private to the political is the key transition: masses must be energized; intellectuals can channel the process and accelerate it—but not provide the energy alone. By summer 1989, however, decisive impetus came from outside the vulnerable frontiers of the German Democratic Republic. Within a few weeks the issue of travel rights plunged the regime into its own crisis.

If there was one mass grievance it was the inability to go abroad. Permission to travel was the currency of the regime, conferred for good behavior.[23] The Berlin Wall and subsequent enforcement of the frontier not only stopped the hemorrhaging of emigrants; they provided the all-purpose incentive to reform and they conferred on professional associations (who in effect retailed travel permits) the means to enforce subordination. But they also made the absence of freedom an almost tangible condition, no longer abstract and of interest to intellectuals alone. Freedom was the freedom to think differently, Rosa Luxemburg had said. Freedom would be the freedom to travel West, most East Germans believed.

The upheaval began because, thanks to liberalization in Hungary, the chance to travel suddenly beckoned. GDR residents were allowed to vacation in once reliable Eastern bloc countries: but how often gazing at the posters for the Bulgarian riviera might they have dreamt of Italy! Communist states had pledged themselves not to allow travelers from fellow regimes to exit to third countries. A protocol of June 20, 1969, provided that Hungary and East Germany would honor each other's travel restrictions. On May 2, 1989, however, the Budapest reformers, gradually moving their system toward Western alignments, opened the barbed wire that had closed the Hungarian frontier. Budapest authorities did not originally plan to allow non-Hungarians through the official frontier crossings (this action would follow on September 10), nor did they envisage the volume of East German vacationers who would cut through open country. But GDR travelers took their little Trabants—the two-cycle boxy cars—into Hungary, abandoned them, and crossed through the woods. "It was clear to me that a lot would happen when the Hungarians cut the barbed wire. Naturally everyone had to think about whether he should go or not. . . . It had its pros and cons. But had there not been those people [ready to go], then we would still be sitting here and getting ready for the forty-first anniversary."[24]

If caught in the woods, the East Germans would normally be turned back, and their passports marked with a stamp that could bring punishment at home. But as of early August the East Germans learned that the Hungarians, allegedly under West German pressure, would no longer stamp the passports of those intercepted on the way into Austria; this meant that no sanction would be possible.[25] Hopeful East Germans could use their summer holidays to set out for Hungary via Czechoslovakia, many now just waiting for further developments or seeking asylum in the West German embassy. By August 7, two hundred crowded Bonn's embassy in Budapest—camping out, overcrowding toilets and beds, finally winning permission to leave from the Hungarians. By late August Budapest was planning to disavow its travel protocol with East Berlin and remove restrictions on all frontier crossings. As angry Politbüro members complained, Hungary had really stuck it to them.[26] Party members are asking, Horst Dohlus reported, "How can we allow ourselves to be kicked around? We have to guard against being discouraged—also because of developments in the Soviet Union, Poland, and Hungary. More and more people are asking: how is socialism going to survive at all?"[27]

Despite East German assurances that there would be no punishment for those returning home, when GDR Foreign Minister Oskar Fischer met with his Hungarian counterpart, Gyula Horn, on August 31, he was told that the East Germans in Hungary, now reaching a total of 150,000, did not believe their government. East German citizens were clashing with Hungarian border police, Deputy Foreign Minister Ferenc Pallazi told Fischer; the refugee camp growing in Budapest had been set up spontaneously by the East Germans, not the Hungarians. Horn likewise told Günter Mittag that Hungary did not want to trouble relations with the GDR but it "excluded inhumane solutions." The refugees piling up in the West German embassy were a special challenge. Hungary would not infringe on East German sovereignty by allowing the West Germans simply to give them FRG passports, but they had to act according to humanitarian considerations. If the Austrians would stamp the East German passports with visas, as of September 11 they would be allowed to cross the frontier.[28] On the first day 8,100 poured over the border, and within three days, 18,000.

The Russians were not going to be much help. While refraining from direct pressure on the GDR, they found the recriminations among Warsaw Pact countries an embarrassment. When Fischer proposed to summon the committee of foreign ministers of the Warsaw Pact to lean on the Hungarians, the Soviets were reluctant, even though they agreed that Budapest was yielding to West German pressure. Mittag claimed the West Germans were rewarding the Hungarians' recent liberalism with a credit of DM 3 billion. In the Politbüro session of September 5, Heinz Keßler went so far as to recognize that young people saw real opportunities in the West, and even in Hungary where the shops were full; but his colleagues were angry. Stoph fumed that the Hungarian position contradicted all their treaties and sprang from a long-term West German plan for subversion; Horst Sindermann saw "a general attack against socialism. We are the first target." "Hungary is betraying socialism," Mielke added. "It's a question of the power relations in socialism in general."[29] "What Hungary has done," he insisted again a week later, "is to violate its agreements with the GDR under the pretext of humanism." Reszö Nyers, the reformist chair of the Hungarian Communist Party, insists that they fell into a trap. "That's pure *Schwindel*."[30] As Krenz noted privately by September 17: "The situation is as tense as I've ever experienced it." Reagan and Bush had set the agenda, and Reagan's 1987 rhetorical appeal in Berlin, "Open the Wall," "*Die Mauer muß weg*," Krenz felt, had become a general NATO campaign—one, moreover, that was far more effective among the East German populace than earlier.[31]

How would the West Germans play this turn of events? Through July at least they were unprepared to depart from the guidelines of Ostpolitik, which stipulated an implicit partnership with the East German government on behalf of liberalization. Rudolf Seiters, head of the Kanzleramt, met with Honecker on July 4 to argue that if the GDR wanted West German opinion to persevere in Ostpolitik, the Helsinki accords had to be pursued. Progress on travel liberalization was promising but could be improved. Honecker's interpretation of Helsinki emphasized recognition, not human rights: it was illusory to expect new travel laws.[32] When midlevel officials conferred five weeks later on August 11, 131 East German citizens had taken refuge inside the permanent West German mission in East Berlin. The West Germans would not expel them, the representative of the Chancellor's Office said, but might advise them to vacate if the East Germans were prepared to let them leave the GDR. Was it really true, as the representative of the Kanzleramt said, "The chancellor has no interest at all in exercising any sort of pressure on the GDR"? The West Germans were prepared to turn again to Dr. Wolfgang Vogel, the East German lawyer who had negotiated so many individual releases across the frontier; but they also urged the East Germans to enter high-level political discussions. The East German negotiator was angry: the West Germans had admitted the East Germans to their legation grounds and let them stay illegally. East Germany was prepared to promise privately that no punishment would be inflicted on them, but it was not prepared to guarantee they would be given emigration visas.[33]

A week later Deputy Foreign Minister Herbert Krolikowski met with Seiters in the East German Foreign Ministry and asked what Bonn would do to get the squatters out of their legation. Seiters as usual was restrained: he had come to resolve "a difficult political and humanitarian problem." But he insisted crucially that although East Germany had the right to set its own travel regulations, Bonn was still constitutionally obligated to negotiate on behalf of all Germans. This was a position that Willy Brandt had insisted on preserving as a reserve clause to the German-German treaty of 1972, but of course it had never been accepted in East Berlin. Now it remained a legal lever the West Germans might exploit—indeed, would have to in light of their own public opinion—in August 1989. To persuade the East Germans to leave the embassies in East Berlin, Budapest, and Prague, Seiters stated further, GDR authorities would have to promise more than immunity from punishment. Krolikowski argued that their petitions to emigrate would get the review provided by law for all such applicants, but could not receive special treatment. "Giving special advantage to citizens who are staying illegally in the embassies of the Federal Republic is not possible."[34] Honecker unsurprisingly remained even firmer in tone when he wrote Kohl on August 30 that West German harboring of GDR citizens "denies the fact that according to international law, the Federal Republic can take on no authority for citizens of the German Democratic Republic."[35]

The sudden emergence of the travel issue radically undermined the status quo so laboriously crafted since the Berlin and German treaties of the early 1970s. The East Germans had to worry not only about the precedents for those seeking to leave, but soon the general unraveling of authority even over those who wanted to stay. They had in fact allowed a considerable expansion of travel and emigration in the last few years—it was, after all, a major source of deutsche marks. In 1987, 2,475,804 East Germans had traveled to West Germany, in 1988, 2,790,582 had gone over.[36] From January 1 to September 1, 1989, 2.2 million private trips to nonsocialist countries had been approved, 10 percent more than the corresponding 1988 period. Liberalization seemed to bring little credit either at home or abroad. East German citizens resented the guidelines that had to be met. From November 30, 1988, to September 30, 1989, 86,150 of 160,785 requests for permanent emigration had also been approved—several times the number allowed the previous year, but deemed "urgently necessary" to deter foreign policy difficulties.[37]

The difficulties that their border restrictions created, so embittered East German leaders were learning, no longer just involved the West. Hungary's reform Communists won decisive positions in both the government and the party in spring 1989. They had accepted the wager of free elections, sought to co-opt the rituals of national reawakening (most lavishly demonstrated in the mid-June reburial of Imre Nagy), and were seeking overall to stay in control of an accelerating process of democratization. They were also trying for an economic soft landing in the nonsocialist world, hoping for credits from the Western countries discussing aid packets for Eastern Europe. The Federal Republic would be crucial in facilitating these developments. The Budapest authorities, moreover, had to resolve the status of Romanian fugitives, whom they would certainly not consent to turn back to the Ceausescu government. A leisured decision no longer seemed possible as the East Germans thronged into the country; refugees were clashing with Hungarian border guards, who were still directed not to let them exit. On August 25, Minister-President Miklos Németh and Foreign Minister Horn flew secretly to confer with Foreign Minister Genscher, the chancellor's advisor, Horst Teltschik, and then Kohl himself at Castle Gymnich near Bonn. East Germans complained to each other that Bonn promised the Hungarians half a billion deutsche marks to let the East Germans exit. (Mittag in fact claimed a payment of DM 3 billion.) Németh later reported that the West Germans did ask what Budapest wanted, but that his delegation urged FRG officials to wait before making any formal offer. Loan credits of DM 1 billion were announced on October 1, half from the federal government, half from Bavaria and Baden-Württemberg. The loans naturally might have been proferred without the change in policy. Hungary in any case was in the process of long-term realignment; its leaders must have realized that no other gesture could so demonstrate its new commitment to Western values. On September 10, the Hungarian government announced that it would no longer keep East Germans from crossing the national frontier. The minister of the interior asked Horn if he understood that this meant that of the two German states they were choosing the West German one. Horn claims to have responded that he was choosing Europe.[38]

Choosing Europe, in effect, meant opening the terminal crisis of the GDR. The Soviets acted as if they still supported the East Germans. Schevardnadze wrote sympathetically to Fischer that he felt the root of the problem was Bonn's claim to represent all Germans.[39] But while the Russian nominally supported the DDR position, he underlined that travel restrictions were damaging for the status of socialism and he warned that Bonn could continually heat up the conflict.

For Bonn, in fact, the commitment to Ostpolitik might now begin to waver. Why stabilize the GDR? Did the refugee issue not allow the possibility of undermining the East German regime? Might the Kohl government not appear complicit if it did not act decisively on behalf of those thronging its embassy courtyards? There were risks on both sides, as became clear when East Germans thronged into Czechoslovakia, not merely to transit to Hungary, but to seek shelter at the West German embassy in Prague. Czechoslovakia would normally have been the most stalwart supporter of East Germany's hang-tough approach to maintaining communism. Unlike the Hungarians, the Czechs were not about to cut the barbed wire across their frontier and undermine control of their own repressed citizenry. But the

Czech leadership was embarrassed by the growing crowds of East German refugees who were besieging the West German legation, gracefully set among the baroque palaces and gardens of the normally tranquil Prague embassy district. By the beginning of September, 3,500 would-be refugees were packed into the embassy grounds, sharing beds, queuing for water or the bathroom, while other GDR "tourists" swarmed outside and, defying the inhibited Czech police, sought to climb the embassy wall. The Czechs did not appreciate serving as border enforcers for the East Germans before the world's television cameras. On the other hand, they were not prepared to disavow the East German regime and offer GDR citizens a direct exit from Czech national territory. On September 25, the Prague regime informed the GDR that they could no longer intervene to keep the East Germans from scaling the walls of the FRG's embassy and they beseeched Honecker to find some sort of solution. But neither could the West German embassy accommodate the refugees indefinitely; they wired Bonn that sanitation was degenerating, East Germans were continuing to enter, cholera and other diseases threatened. How could they refuse the most elementary search for refuge on the part of a people they always claimed to represent![40] The federal government needed the cooperation of at least the Czechs, and preferably the GDR's permission as well, to convey the migrants to the West.

Hans-Dietrich Genscher used the opportunity provided by the UN General Assembly session in New York to negotiate with the East Germans.[41] Faced with pressure from Czech ideological comrades as well as the West Germans, unwilling to have the televised refugees mar the upcoming fortieth anniversary of the state, Honecker sought a face-saving way out. He took advantage of an opera gala for the celebration of the fortieth anniversary of the People's Republic of China to convoke his Politbüro and inform its members that the wayward refugees in Prague might exit, but only by special trains returning through GDR territory. Among the faithful, the decision caused consternation; others saw it as a "declaration of bankruptcy" on the part of the regime.[42] Supposedly to announce that they were expellees from the republic's own land would preserve East German dignity and demonstrate that Prague was no escape hatch! On September 30 the West German authorities announced they would grant the embassy crowd asylum, and the East Germans allowed special trains—locked while traversing GDR territory to keep others from climbing on—to ferry those whom Honecker declared expelled. On October 3, the East Germans denied their citizens further access to Czechoslovakia, and in the next two days another 7,000 East Germans, who had meantime stormed the Prague embassy, were shipped across GDR territory to Hof in Bavaria. This time the route was known and large crowds stormed the Dresden station. By the time the Wall opened 10,000 East Germans had gotten to the West through the FRG embassy in Budapest, 17,000 via Prague, almost 5,000 via Warsaw.[43]

How could a regime restrict access to the Soviet journals supporting glasnost and prepare to welcome Mikhail Gorbachev for the fortieth anniversary of its founding? How could a state that enforced its writ by controlling exits (over 200 would-be fugitives had died at the frontiers since 1961) maintain its norms while it allowed the trains to take its refugees from Prague to West Germany? Two decades ago the economist Albert Hirschman wrote an influential essay that analyzed the role of consumers or organization members in terms of "exit, voice, and loyalty." Scholars, as well as Hirchman himself, have sought to apply this spectrum of responses to the expiring GDR.[44] In the case of the GDR, in fact, options for "exit" also meant raising the level of "voice." For a regime that allowed only a minimum of emigration, and often punished requests to leave, exiting amounted to an act of resistance. It encouraged those staying behind to raise their own alternative protests so that their slogan, "We are staying here," became as peremptory a challenge to the state. For the official spokesmen of the regime, it was the old story: the West was tempting its citizens with the promises of a meretricious consumerism. In fact those responsible for government security conceded widespread demoralization. People no longer believed in the goals of the party and regime, no longer expected personal improvement. As the Stasi itself recognized, "Such attitudes are especially evident among those who hitherto were socially active, but because of the aforementioned reasons have become 'tired,' resigned and have finally given up."[45]

TWO LANGUAGES OF REVOLUTION

"The exodus is only a sign of social problems that have clogged up all spheres of society," critics wrote in October.[46] Linger for a moment on the phrasing. The language was indicative: less about politics per se than the needs of a society. But the regime's own analysts resorted to the same idiom: which forces, then, were on the side of "social" development? Opposition and defenders of the status quo shared a concept of underlying social needs that each claimed to represent. Even in the moment of political confrontation, there was a tendency to reify (as the Marxian idiom of a generation ago might have articulated the notion) underlying social forces. Marxist sociologists, borrowing Western concepts as well as their own jargon, in effect scripted the discourse of the East German upheaval in terms of "social needs," "praxis" (i.e., real life), "learning processes" or "knowledge processes," and "the achievement society" (*Leistungsgesellschaft*). Of course personal needs were acute, but their manifestation arose because of societal failings. Even the ubiquitous shapers and monitors of state security perceived their task as a type of social tutelage, their deficiencies in terms of inadequate provisioning of social needs. Why, for example, were East German citizens seeking to emigrate West, the East German intelligence apparatus asked itself two months before the Wall was opened. "Essentially it's about a whole bundle of complexly interacting factors." They might be exaggerated by the Western mass media, but real enough in their own right. "The overwhelming number of these persons evaluate problems and deficiencies in the social development, above all in their own personal ambit."[47]

In the spirit of social tutelage, the municipal elections of May 7, 1989, were to be orchestrated as a reaffirmation of social solidarity—"a significant political high point in the social life of the GDR with which the confidence of the citizen in the policies of party and government can be strengthened anew." But the ritual of solidarity was threatened by the growing dissatisfaction expressed even among still loyal cadres about "the level of consumption," water and sewage, "emerging environmental degradation," and "issues of the social control of citizens."[48] As hostile behavior during the elections, security forces cited the abstentionism of Protestant and Catholic churchmen, and the fact that more voters were taking advantage of the optional voting booths to cast their ballots unobserved, or even voting against the government slate! At the School of Fine Arts in Berlin 105 students voted against the list and only 102 for, whereas the vote in 1986 had been marred by only one nonvoter! Pastors and others had added protests against environmental pollution to their ballots. Nonvoting was up among all ages of qualified voters as well as workers and employees. This antisocial behavior did not prevent an alleged 98.5 percent vote of approval for the government slates. Since officials never conceived of the election as a contest, those who questioned the results were just plain subversive, conspiring to discredit the state internationally and at home, to force a pluralism "of a western stamp," and to open room "for uncontrolled social political movements, and thus for a destabilization of the political power relationships in the GDR."[49] In fact, however, the results were fraudulent. According to Günter

Schabowski, Berlin district secretary of the SED, the government had actually expected perhaps 5 to 7 percent dissent (thus only 93 or 95 percent approval!) and had instructed local mayors in Berlin to hold a clean vote. The district mayors remained convinced, however, that the party wanted better results. No matter at what level the tally was doctored, as Schabowski sought to explain, the officials who connived accepted the policy "right or wrong, as their task in life and set about it . . . they did it out of habit and discipline and believing that it was willed and blessed from on high."[50]

A society breaking down, a regime out of touch with its society: The founding manifesto of the opposition's New Forum began, "In our country, the communication between state and society is clearly impaired."[51] Groping to understand the upheaval with an adequate conceptual language, participants on both sides viewed the breakdown through sociological lenses. The synod of the Evangelischer Kirchenbund, the Federation of the East German Lutheran Churches, convening at Erfurt on September 19, cited the consequences of the accelerating emigration: "Families and friendships are torn apart, old people feel themselves abandoned, the ill are losing their caretakers and doctors, workers' collectives are decimated. . . . Today we find ourselves facing the challenge of preserving what has proved its worth while we search for new ways to advance a society of greater justice and participation. . . . We need an open and public confrontation of our social problems, we need everybody for responsible cooperation in our society."[52]

Such declarations echoed the party's wooden paeans of collective progress. As a critical East Berlin sociologist noted, SED declarations were characterized by a style "dripping with harmony: . . . 'classes coming together,' 'reduction of differences between physical and mental labor or between city and country.'"[53] Nonetheless, the polarization of autumn 1989 could also endow jargon with a liberating force that transcended its stilted sociological formulation. The breakdown of acquiescence transformed sociology into politics, just as the regime had long since endeavored to transform politics into sociology.

In fact, the listener could overhear two discourses in the fall of 1989. One was the language of social functionalism shared by the Stasi and the protesters, the regime and the new reform groups. It was the language of Durkheimian sociology, of interacting roles and collective needs. It articulated, on one side, the paternalism of the security forces and, on the other, the earnest protests of the citizens' groups. It was the modern language of social complexity.

But alongside this shared discourse of complexity reemerged a more venerable rhetoric of simplicity. It began with the language of Christian nonviolence in the peace sermons: Christof Wonneberger told worshipers at the Nikolaikirche on September 25 that Stasi violence would not prevail: "In the words of Jesus: 'Do not be afraid, unto me is given all power in heaven and earth.' . . . Against such power Stasi apparatus, dogs, and police phalanxes are but paper tigers. . . . We can renounce violence." Pastor Hans-Jürgen Sievers of the Reformed Church cited Martin Luther King, Jr., and the worshipers sang "We shall Overcome."[54] Outside the churches language took on older German tonalities of political mobilization, the discourse of the militant Reformation, intimating both liberation and vengeance. As the mass demonstrations gained momentum during the fall, Luther's language held its own as well: "We are the people" alongside "societal" progress and needs. The regime's counterpart to this primeval discourse would have been the language of simple repression and power. The head of the Ministry of State Security spoke in these terms within the government. But no spokesman for the state dared invoke this language in public. In effect, the rhetoric of simplicity and emancipation found no official response.

Thus one might write the history of the revolution in terms of two rhetorical traditions. On the one hand, the discourse of flawed functionalism—the vocabulary of social needs, interests, roles, groups—was invoked both by the regime and by the intellectuals who would transform it. On the other hand, a rhetoric of primeval popular assembly—the language of "antistructure,"[55] of shoulder-to-shoulder community—arose anonymously from the crowd. This second language was the more potent; like Joshua's trumpets it brought down the Wall. It often relied on music, whether church hymns or, as a continuing subversive alternative, the rock bands that were the nexus of solidarity for the young. But it would have been too much to expect that it might become a durable hegemonic discourse. The vocabulary of social differentiation, or articulated parts rather than holistic community, always reoccupied the linguistic terrain. Four and a half centuries earlier, Luther's wrathful words had yielded to the legalistic formulas of synods, estates, and princely orders. In postrevolutionary France the exalted language of fraternity (already exploited to justify political terror) ebbed before the ideological invocation of society. These kindling tongues never entirely disappear; they remain potentially utterable and serve as occasional ritual invocations, paraded like aging veterans: but they cannot verbally structure a new political order. Nonetheless, their potential force can for a brief moment or a longer decade still infuse a reformist potential into the reencroaching discourse of social structure. Sociology could not be ousted, but it could be made the transient language of reform. Indeed, by virtue of this linguistic contention and outcome—so we shall return to the issue in the next chapter—arose the central reformist ideological concept of 1989 throughout Central and Eastern Europe: the claim of "civil society."

MONDAY NIGHTS IN LEIPZIG

Language, of course, does not speak itself. Often a durable vocabulary emerges in which participants describe their demands and depict their longings. Sometimes the logic of political argument virtually imposes a belief in conspiratorial opponents or compels radical resistance. Discourse seems to take on a life of its own; it can be analyzed as an autonomous product. Germans since Hegel and Dilthey conceived of text and artifact as a realm of objective spirit long before modern French theorists proposed language as an opaque prison built by the powerful. Still, the historian mystifies his subject if he forgets the speakers. Who were they in autumn 1989? At the risk of oversimplifying, the historian can point to three major groups that converged to generate (and limit) conflict in Leipzig: earnest prayer participants motivated by human rights, peace, and other public issues; the old working classes of the metropolitan area, distressed by the region's declining industrial base, decaying housing, and inadequate transportation; and the regime's police, hovering uncertainly between wary caution and tough repressive tactics.

These collective actors knew that they were periodically on stage. Fair time put Leipzig ("Open to the World") under the gaze of television cameras in March and September. On the first Monday evening in March as the spring fair opened, several hundred demonstrators carried posters for travel rights. The police closed in right before the cameras, were filmed making their arrests and roughing up demonstrators as others fled into the church. On March 13 again a crowd of 850 protesters was broken up by police before Western cameras.[56] The next Monday the church prayers were far more crowded, and the Nikolaikirche authorities refused state blandishments to discontinue the Monday peace vespers. With the end of the fair, Western witnesses departed, but the prayer meetings remained active, especially after the protested elections of May 7. Demonstrators seeking the right to emigrate henceforth pressed their case as worshipers entered and left the peace prayer services. From May 8 (after election-fraud protests) the police, too, regularly made a show of strength outside the prayer meetings. They brought dogs, made arrests, and set up a video camera above the church portal to film those entering.[57]

The end of August and early September brought the fair and its visitors back to Leipzig. East Germans were already leaving Hungary through the woods, and on September 10, Budapest allowed them to cross the Austrian frontier legally. Many who remained felt impelled to justify their decision by exerting pressure for reform at home. Advocates of emigration competed with advocates of reform. On August 28, four pastors and a representative of the group "Peace and Human Rights" met at the Golgotha Church in Leipzig to call for a social democratic party aspiring to parliamentary democracy and a market economy. A week later on September 4, the Nikolai- kirche prayer meetings resumed after summer break, although state officials sought unsuccessfully to postpone the services until after the fair closed. Church Superintendent Friedrich Magirus (a superintendent is an ordained minister serving as administrative assistant to the provincial bishop) told 1,200 participants that the regime was at fault for refusing to face up to the reasons for the emigration. But the ensuing protest march dispersed when demonstrators calling for civil liberties at home and chanting "We are stay- ing!" broke with those demanding the right to emigrate ("We want out!").[58] Ironically enough it was precisely the opportunity to leave that crystallized the formation of opposition groups among those determined to stay. The growing flight compelled those unprepared to uproot themselves to demand reforms that might justify their remaining.

On September 9, opposition leaders announced the founding of New Forum—endorsed soon after by several dozen pop and rock performers. Its manifesto deplored the gulf between state and society, denounced the in- formers, the violence, of the state. Avoiding inflammatory rhetoric, al- though its very call for a broad-based political association was a challenge, it called for a broad-based democratic dialogue.[59] In familiar terms, the SED condemned protesters—now gathering momentum in church meet- ings, manifestos, and the citizens movements (Bürgerbewegungen)—as ac- complices of the foreign effort to defame socialism and the GDR. At the Nikolaikirche prayer meeting of September 11—by now the fair had ended and Westerners had left—the police arrested worshipers leaving the ser- vice, contributing to further polarization.[60] "From September 19, [univer- sity] studies resumed and in the introductory courses there was a lot of discussion in the seminar groups and a main question was, Why isn't New Forum legalized?"[61]

Nikolaikirche prayer participants had attempted a public march after the resumption of peace prayers on September 4. The first major demonstrations took place on Monday evening September 25. Leipzig's geography allowed focused dramatic confrontations. The city of 600,000, second largest in the GDR, was big enough to muster crowds, but less inchoate than sprawling East Berlin. The old center of Leipzig has an inner city perhaps a kilometer wide enclosed by a broad ring street following the site of old walls. Inside the ring, as of 1989, were the desolate squares with which straitened socialist planners had coped with World War II destruction, but also a mix of a few restored buildings—the sixteenth-century city hall, the churches—and modern structures. (See map on p. 141.) Since unification the pace of refurbishment has increased as banks and government agencies have taken to spiffing up neoclassical edifices and other legacies of nineteenth-century opulence. On the ring at the southeast stand the monuments of 1960s and 1970s GDR modernism: the successfully designed Gewandhaus or concert hall, the opera theater, and a seventeen-story tower for the university alongside a lower structure with a large bas relief of Marx and Engels. On the outside of the ring, too, is the Main Station, the largest "sack" terminal (i.e., trains have to back out) in Europe: a broad, handsome turn-of-the century structure. In front of the station lies the wide northern segment of the ring called the Platz der Republik, perhaps two hundred meters long, where the masses assembled. And finally inside the old city on different sides of the tourist Rathskellar, where Goethe's Faust and Mephistopheles confronted the students, are the two major late Gothic churches. St. Thomas's, Bach's home church, under the conservative pastor Hans-Wilhelm Ebeling, played no role in the growing protests. Closer to the eastern Ring, St. Nicholas's or the Nikolaikirche, gussied up during the rococo with side balconies and carved palm leaves to cover its stone columns, all repainted in white, apple green, and mauve, became the center for the dissidents, its reformist pastor sheltering peaceniks and environmentalists.[62]

These sites became the amphitheater of protest, as on September 25, spilling out from the Nikolaikirche to the Karl Marx Platz on the Ring, between Gewandhaus and Opera at a point equivalent to four o'clock, thence counterclockwise to the Platz der Republik (one o'clock) to the Tröndlinring (at eleven o'clock) tens of thousands of demonstrators assembled. The next day's *Leipziger Volkszeitung* condemned the demonstrations as "unapproved, illegal conspiracies" with clear antisocialist tendencies that had been restrained by the reserved and careful behavior of the police.

Leipzig did not have to be first; the upheaval might have begun in Berlin or in Dresden. In February the Politbüro had been just as preoccupied by Dresden, the Saxon capital that was almost as large as Leipzig. Housing conditions were as strained; it had the highest concentration of applicants for emigration, and Honecker noted that "if we let out all doctors who want to leave, public health would collapse in Dresden."[63] In the critical days of early fall, Dresden lay on the rail route that brought fleeing East Germans from Prague to the Federal Republic, and there were violent clashes with the police at the station. On the other hand, it did have a leadership trying to cope with local problems. There was, moreover, no televised trade fair to be an incentive for street demonstrations. And Dresden was not a foyer for the church prayer assemblies that proved so catalytic.

The Leipzig university had been intellectual home to the older, critical Marxian thinkers, among them Hans Mayer, Ernst Bloch, and the historian Walter Markov, who had fled or been muzzled in the 1950s. But the university was not a major source of protest in 1989. Its faculties remained too riddled with a younger generation of SED members, often frustrated by their unyielding geriatric national leadership, but too hobbled by their party affiliation to organize public protests or sing in prayer meetings. Demonstrations grew from a more heterogenous segment of earnest middle-class citizens, young people, and angry workers who added their agenda of grievances. Christoph Hein, who addressed the massive Berlin crowds on November 4, in the largest demonstration of them all, termed Leipzig the city of heroes. But why not Berlin? To a degree the answer must be contingency or the momentum of events. In 1953, after all, the workers' demonstrations that shook the regime originated in the capital. Then, however, they had begun at construction sites. The protests of 1989 were no longer proletarian, and the capital had more state and party employees, willing perhaps to join a movement under way, but less likely to emerge from the shadow of the hard-liners and take part in early demonstrations. Leipzig may have been more congenial for protesters. Its administration allowed dissenting authors or painters to find a voice; its writers declined to purge their critical members.[64]

Economic and ecological factors also played a role. Berlin benefited from the construction projects that Honecker and Mittag lavished on the capital; Leipzig remained run down. It was easy to become resentful at the rulers in the favored metropolis. Even more of an incitement, according to the Leipzig district SED secretary, Kurt Meyer, one of the signatories of the appeal that forestalled violence on October 9, was the discrepancy between the semiannual fair and everyday decrepitude. For years the infrastructure of the city had been neglected even as the regime displayed whatever glittering wares it could muster to impress foreigners. "In Leipzig the contradictions were displayed more drastically and tangibly . . . for the citizen they could be grasped, experienced and were really concrete."[65] The region's lignite and chemical industries also played a role. While they operated at full tilt, they contributed to the fearsome pollution of the region—Leipzig's air was laden with twelve times the concentration of sulfur dioxide as the GDR average, three times as heavy a concentration as the Ruhr's. But when in the late 1980s the regime began to shut down the most noxious plants in the area, the workers threatened with unemployment joined the protesters.[66]

The church assemblies were critical, first in Saxony, then in Berlin. In Leipzig, Deacon Günter Johannsen had initiated Monday, five o'clock prayer meetings in the Nikolaikirche as early as 1982. The long-standing weekly prayers for peace provided a preexistent nucleus of disaffiliation. The regime had left the church its alternative political space and voice— provided that it remain enclosed and not directly oppositional. But as crowds thronged to the churches in the late 1980s they had to listen from the steps and from the surrounding grass or street: the enclosure no longer contained, and the masses of candles that flickered symbolically brought the dissenting message from within and established a stark contrast to the security apparatus with helmets and water cannon. When demonstrators gathered elsewhere, as at the Dresden railway terminal, the church quickly provided the resources of countervailing legitimacy as crowds prayed for peace and then joined the brass choir in the Reformation hymn: "Wake up, wake up, O German land, you have slumbered long enough."[67]

In effect the fate of the East German regime was decided on the Leipzig Ring on four successive Monday evenings between September 25 and October 16, then confirmed in Berlin between Saturday, November 4, and Thursday, November 9. In the Leipzig confrontations two views of the crowd were contested: the regime's and the New Forum's. For the loyal trade unionists or party functionaries cited by the *Leipziger Volkszeitung*, the movement was conspiratorial, a defamation of socialism, or—the all-purpose explanation—the product of rowdyism. "It is high time in my opinion that all currents of opinion, associations, and organizations take a stand on the events of the day, especially in Leipzig, so that the ambiguity of word and deed is ended. The comrades of the party and the Ministry of the Interior deserve my full support and thanks for the restoration of peace and order."[68] "We don't understand how representatives of the church can permit such action, when every citizen is guaranteed freedom of belief in our socialist state."[69] FDJ (Free German Youth) collectives during 1988–89—so it was reported in connection with the fortieth anniversary commemoration—had inspired 80,212 young workers to labor overtime to deliver 871,561 tons of scrap and 227,241 tons of old paper, and had reconstituted 102,397 hectares of agricultural land for irrigation.[70]

For the demonstrators, solidarity overcame fear. Many who came did so at first out of curiosity. Many were young; others who could not leave the GDR made their demand a pendant to those fleeing through the embassies: "We're staying here" (Wir bleiben hier), the shout rang outside the Nikolai- kirche at the September 11 demonstration, thereafter to become a rallying cry.[71] One young couple recalled an old man, who despite the warm weather wore a Russian fur hat with a photo of Gorbachev pinned on it, as if some protective ikon: "And in my delight at this 'worker's monument' was inter- mingled the sudden awareness that this was the revolution, so sweet, so long desired, and for so long deemed impossible. We learned that we were in a position to overthrow a government, and I determined never to forget it again."[72]

On October 2, demonstrators before the Nikolaikirche shouted again to Stasi observers, "We are staying." Then with the churchgoers exiting from the Monday evening peace prayer, they surged to the nearby Karl Marx Platz to call for reforms and legalization of the New Forum.[73] The police—many of whom were young and frightened—sought to close off the Platz der Re- publik, but demonstrators surged past, and they could do no more than keep the marchers from crowding back into the center city from the Ring. SED youth leaders were mobilized against so-called Chaoten—the East Ger- man specter of youth gang anarchists—only to find that they never came, and then to read the next day that they had protected the city against row- dies. Two sixteen-year-olds recalled the politeness of the crowd and a fan- tastic solidarity: "It was clear when we stood next to the men and women, they were simple workers, they were the people."[74] Still, there were arrests and violence: the individual accounts in newspapers or recorded before citi- zens committees investigating the police in Leipzig and Berlin became a minor literary genre in the days after the "Wende."[75] By October 5, the Ministry for State Security had issued orders to get tough. From October 5

LEIPZIG CITY CENTER

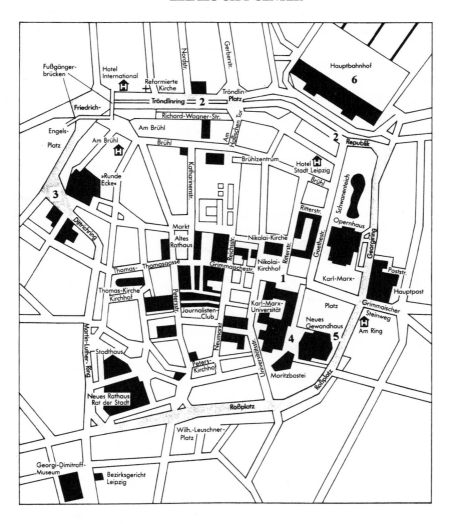

1. **Nikolai Church and square: site of Monday prayer meetings**
2. **Platz der Republik - Trondlinring: sites of main crowd assembly**
3. **"Runde Ecke": "Round Corner," or Stasi HQ**
4. **University   5. Concert Hall   6. Railroad Station**

to 8, Erich Mielke sent instructions to mobilize factory militia units (Kampfgruppen) and reinforce the police with party reservists. "Enemy-negative activities are to be resolutely prevented by all possible means"; "members who usually carry weapons are to carry their weapons continuously in line with the usual requirements."[76] In fact, lethal force was avoided and there were fewer heavy casualties than in American racial insurrections or campus riots in the 1960s—but the uniforms, nightsticks, occasional machine guns were frightening. Witnesses felt the police just wanted a provocation to start beating. Kids were rounded up in police trucks, taken into mass custody, held in crowded conditions at least through the night and sometimes for several days. A protest or effort to reason with the officer twisting the detainee's wrist usually brought another blow with the night-stick. For the younger East German generation, the behavior recalled what they had learned of storm troopers and Gestapo. "In school we were taught how the Nazis were. In peacetime, praxis showed me, because these police acted the same toward us."[77] In fact, the police were divided; young draftees were used to enlarge militia (Bereitschaft or Bepo) units. But some were clearly unreliable; unwilling to carry nightsticks, debating events in the barracks. One aimed his water cannon above demonstrators heads.[78]

October 9, the third mass march, proved decisive. There had been clashes again on the previous Saturday, as police broke up a crowd of 10,000;[79] demonstrators were injured; now the regime assembled tanks and water cannon and apparently prepared hospital beds and blood plasma. Tiananmen Square was still fresh in the minds of both sides, when the SED leaders announced in the most widely sold paper, the *Leipziger Volkszeitung*, on October 6, that "law and order would be restored once and for all," if necessary with force.[80] On the "prayer wall" in the Thomaskirche where visitors could tack up their written intentions, many expressed their anxiety: "I am afraid that 10/9/89 will be a day like Tiananmen Square in China. And that the rest of the young people will shed their blood for this senseless state. I, we, are frightened."[81] By one o'clock that afternoon, the Nikolai-kirche was already full—and surrounded by the police, this time experienced units. Tension was high: from outside there were shouts of, "Gorbi, Gorbi," "We are staying here," "No violence," and "We are the people." Inside there was fear of a violent clash and being arrested.

At five o'clock, however, the balconies were opened for regular worshipers and Pastor Peter Zimmermann—"exhausted and unnerved"—had a statement read, in which Kurt Masur, the conductor of the Leipzig Gewand-haus orchestra, cabaret performer Bernd-Lutz Lange, three district SED secretaries, and he himself pleaded for dialogue. The crowd poured out into the streets: "And now my fear became so great," Susanne Rummel recalled, "that I thought—I have to counteract it somehow. So I went over to the people in the Kampfgruppen. . . . We talked with them, asked them whether we looked like *Chaoten* or enemies of the state and whether they would really beat us." Gudrun Fischer overcame her husband's reluctance to participate—"I knew that only the largest possible crowd could prevent something bad"—and they flocked to the inner city, listened to the Masur statement ("the first public participation by public leaders in the events that were moving us"), and joined the march. "We are still proud," recalled Sybille Freitag, pensioner, "to have been present on the 9th of October."[82]

"As the police opened the barriers on the ring that surrounded the inner city and the parade of demonstrators passed the ring unhindered with an astonishing and almost frightening discipline . . . it was clear that there could be no return to the old GDR."[83] Leipzig had no SED leaders of stature. The party could not retain a controlling voice, as in Dresden where Mayor Wolfgang Berghofer and local Secretary Hans Modrow would manage to calm angry demonstrators with a process of controlled dialogue. Leipzig's demonstrators remained sovereign and did not yield, although by mid November—when the demonstrations were climbing from the 70,000–80,000 of October 9 to 300,000—the slogans changed again, from "We are the people" to "We are one people."[84]

In fact by October 9 the party in Berlin as well as the provinces was in disarray. Within the Politbüro Krenz, Schabowski, and others were convinced that Honecker's stubbornness was heading them toward disaster. Honecker's imminent successor, Egon Krenz, later claimed that he had helped to firm up Berlin's decision not to use force in Leipzig—so long as the demonstrators did not resort to force.[85] In the heated atmosphere, that conditional restraint guaranteed little. Party members, we know from the Stasi's own reports, were divided between those who wanted firmness and others who believed their leaders were hopelessly unresponsive.[86] SED loyalists at the university from the Marxist-Leninist social sciences faculty were instructed to infiltrate the Nikolaikirche. But the party had its own troubles. A meeting of SED cadres at the Rathaus dissolved into recriminations against the leadership and the distorted press accounts of the demonstrations published by the official press. Those sent by the party to infiltrate the church meeting were hissed at and asked to leave and had to return to a university lecture hall, in theory to be held ready if needed (or perhaps to be protected). Meanwhile Kampfgruppen were mobilized from the factories against the demonstrators, resolute and brave, but some at least were as frightened as their adversaries by the specter of impending violence—and obviously demoralized by their treatment as pariahs. They ended up in debates with New Forum marchers and agreeing with many of their points. "Many comrades began to acquire a new awareness, even if only out of fear."[87] How would they have behaved if it had come to a confrontation? "That is hard to say. We knew we wouldn't attack first." Both sides were fearful. The upshot of the demonstration was that those who were mobilized felt ill-used: there would be no further drafting of Kampfgruppe alongside the police. A week later, the university teacher joined the demonstration: "But I had the feeling that I really had no right to go along. This was the solution of the others. I agreed with a great deal. But I had nothing to bring to it."[88]

The plea signed by Masur and the others of the Leipzig Six was critical in defusing the momentum toward violence on October 9. Masur and his orchestra had been close observers of the Nikolaikirche crowds over the prior weeks as they crossed to their concert hall where, with growing preoccupation, they were recording Beethoven's *Eroica*. The tape was made, but Masur feared that outside events precluded the artistic concentration needed. On October 2 Masur admitted to West German interviewers that he felt ashamed; on the next day the orchestra resolved to take part in the public discussions. News of the Berlin clashes on October 7 and 8 was frightening. As Leipzig threatened to head toward its own battle on Monday night, the conductor (in what he later described as a "humanitarian act of the moment") telephoned District Secretary Meyer about a joint declaration. They met on Monday afternoon to draft their appeal. Looking back two months later, Masur agreed that the political message about reforming socialism was already overtaken—"I think that there are a whole series of words that have undergone an enormous change of meaning." His commitment was to New Forum's call for dialogue, not unification or even multiparty competition. What was crucial was the demonstrative effect, not the ideological subtleties.[89] In effect, Masur got the local SED secretaries to promise that they would not resort to violence if the demonstrations remained peaceful.[90] Cosigner Peter Zimmermann felt that the appeal was effective thanks to the "moral authority" of the conductor; it was a "security partnership" between three SED officials, Masur, and a theologian: "This combined offer made it acceptable, for the demonstrators, for the security forces."[91] On the other hand he and the churchman who signed were also pledging that the SED was prepared to embark on that now talismanic course of "dialogue," which

New Forum and others had made so central. A trade-off: minimal trust for the authorities and disciplined crowds in return finally for real talks on opening up the system.

Could events have culminated in violent repression? Certainly in an attempt at repression. The authorities had prepared for clashes and readied the hospitals. Berlin authorities, however, did not apparently agree to order the forcible halting of the marchers. Krenz allegedly told Kochemasov that he had been asked by Honecker to take charge in Leipzig, but he seemed primarily interested in getting the Soviet ambassador to warn him that violence must be avoided. On the other hand, Honecker, Mielke and other old stalwarts were prepared to countenance the use of force, including firearms, if a clash erupted. The orders transmitted seemed to have left discretion to units in Leipzig. With such scope delegated to local security personnel, bloodshed and firing were not determined but remained a real possibility. Even those police who did not wish to fire might have yielded to fear and panic. Those who were ideologically inculcated believed they faced fascists, brawlers, and rowdies. Others, often including the auxiliary units, were just plain scared, unused to making mass arrests.[92] Demonstrations were getting larger by the day. At the Dresden station, where the sealed trains carrying East Germans from the Prague embassy to the Federal Republic had passed through, 10,000 assembled on October 4. Police used billy clubs and water cannon and tear gas; demonstrators responded with cobblestones. The clashes were repeated the next day, and on October 7 police broke apart a crowd of 30,000.[93] On the same day in the small city of Plauen, also on the route of the emigrants, 10,000 demonstrators took to the streets and barricaded the mayor in his city hall; violence seemed close at hand.[94] Three thousand took to the streets in normally tranquil Potsdam. On October 8, demonstrators reassembled in Dresden and police seemed prepared to use force, when news spread that Mayor Wolfgang Berghofer had met with churchmen and then a citizens delegation. His willingness to release those arrested earlier and to open a continuing "dialogue"—the first major government figure to seem responsive—transformed the confrontation into a festival. On the night of October 9, 22,000 exuberant citizens swelled the "information" meetings at the Dresden cathedral and three other city churches.[95] Similarly, when 4,100 participants, mostly young people, crowded the Magdeburg cathedral's Monday prayer meeting, it was the pastor's promise of dialogue—so the Stasi reported—that kept the gathering peaceful: "'Now we are waiting to see the results of dialogue; patience should not be stretched too thin.'"[96]

The more challenging question is not whether repression might have been attempted, but whether under prevailing conditions it could have brought more than a momentary respite. This is doubtful. East Germany did not possess the huge autonomy that China does; its leadership could not emerge from the shadow of the larger Communist movement that Gorbachev had been pushing toward reform. A glance at what we know of Berlin developments suggests that the momentum was irreversible: violence would have only delayed the denouement or made the upheaval more radical. The smaller northern cities had not yet exploded into mass demonstrations; they had fewer concentrations of intellectuals and factory workers. Nonetheless, the churches were filling in Mecklenburg and Brandenburg; marches would have followed. Perhaps most crucial is that the Politbüro was deeply divided: It takes resolution to carry through with force and only a few of the old guard still had it. Ultimately the leadership no longer possessed the coherence or conviction to impose force successfully.

BERLIN: RULERS AND RULED

Following the Leipzig demonstration of October 2 and the Dresden clashes of October 4, Berlin was swept into the movement. There were two epicenters to the agitation. In the modern center of East Berlin, another monument to pavement and modern hotel construction about two kilometers east of the Brandenburg Gate, crowds and police would confront each other in a quarter circle of urban space bound by the curve of the S-Bahn from the Marx-Engels Platz stop at its north to "Alex," or the Alexanderplatz at its east, and by the Red City Hall at its south. Alex is the crossroads of the city, lively by day, but then bleak at night. If only for its S-Bahn and U-Bahn transfer stations, it was the logical place for crowds to find each other and for the police to control the train exits.

The other epicenter lay a couple of kilometers to the north in Prenzlauer Berg, the locus of East Germany's would-be avant garde, some of whose leading members turned out to be Stasi informers. It was filled with once substantial but long decaying tenements whose peeling facades still revealed the pretentious pediments and window caryatids of bourgeois *Gründerzeit* prosperity. In the neighborhood of Käthe Kollwitz square, a congenial small park where a seated bronze sculpture of the weepy-looking artist is surrounded by dozens of playing children, lively, refurbished cafés testified to some slow gentrification. Another kilometer to the north the 1890s red-

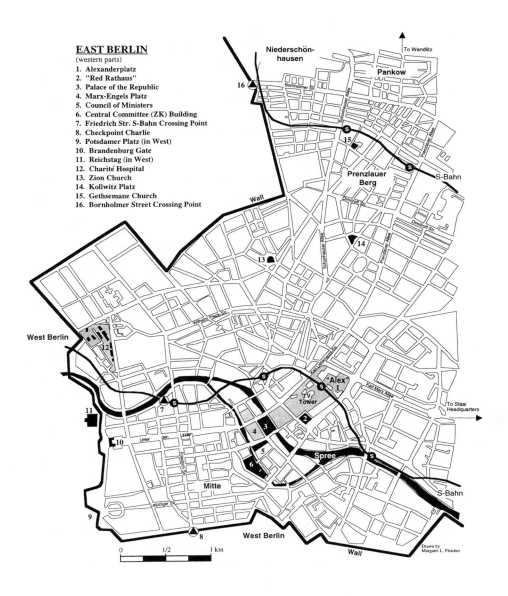

EAST BERLIN

(western parts)

1. Alexanderplatz
2. "Red Rathaus"
3. Palace of the Republic
4. Marx-Engels Platz
5. Council of Ministers
6. Central Committee (ZK) Building
7. Friedrich Str. S-Bahn Crossing Point
8. Checkpoint Charlie
9. Potsdamer Platz (in West)
10. Brandenburg Gate
11. Reichstag (in West)
12. Charité Hospital
13. Zion Church
14. Kollwitz Platz
15. Gethsemane Church
16. Bornholmer Street Crossing Point

brick, neo-Gothic Gethsemane Church, accessed by the Schönhauser Allee
S-Bahn stop, served as sanctuary for peace prayers and vigils. Its narrow
portal opened into a surprisingly capacious interior designed like a broad
Franciscan preachers' church, but with wide curving side balconies, which
could accommodate about 2,000 worshipers. On October 5, crowds gathered, their candles flickering in the evening dark. Since the Wall ran close by
to the east, western televison camera stands were constructed in an effort to
follow the demonstrations.

The party enforced its claim to the central city one last time the next
night, as it mustered 100,000 Free German Youth for a torchlight parade
past Honecker and Gorbachev. But the next two nights, October 7 and 8,
thousands of protesters sought to pour into central Berlin and gathered
again in the streets around the Gethsemane Church. Many were young,
still evidently in their teens, generally good humored and restrained, but
peace was not to last. High-school student Martin M. left his house at 8:15
P.M. on October 7 to confirm firsthand the activity the newscasts were reporting and found the church and steps full, "The candles were burning; it
looked fantastic." Police were closing one street after another; the crowd
sought to break through. The police began to hit. "I never knew how hard
a rubber billy club was. And in that moment I thought, 'It's right for me to
be here.' And it was clear at that moment that I would participate to the
end."[97] The police took hundreds in custody for long nights of abuse, waiting in smelly and overcrowded cells with minimal sanitation. Martin M.
spent a frightened week in his mass cell as one of the "brawlers," who,
according to official GDR news agency reports in *Neues Deutschland*, sought
to disturb the fortieth anniversary festivities. When finally released he
found that his parents had burned his poems and letters because they feared
being searched.

The impact of the provisional arrests or "Zuführungen" was noteworthy
in several respects. On the one hand the confrontations of October 7 and 8
in Berlin appeared traumatic. The regime deployed 16,000 police and in the
two nights arrested 1,047 demonstrators. Those seized testified to their
being struck with nightsticks, hauled off to jail in paddywagons, crowded
into garages, threatened if not beaten, held for days with limited access to
toilets, their occasional and ineffective appeals to the constitution of the
GDR rebuffed. Young detainees might be released into the custody of their
parents. But this last crackdown only infuriated the citizenry. After the regime crumbled and the Wall opened, increasing numbers of civic groups,
artists, academics and the like were to demand an investigation of these

events. The Berlin city government established a commission to look into the arrests, a third of its membership drawn from urban and judicial officials, two-thirds independent. This official committee soon agreed to cooperate with an unofficial investigation commission set up on November 3 by the Academy of Arts, democratic citizens groups, and churchmen. By late November they had taken a lot of testimonies—a selection of which were mimeographed for public distribution.[98] With the fall of the SED the police became cooperative; some police were removed; charges were dropped against the demonstrators. During the next months, however, the investigation did not really advance. Participants in the demonstration who still angrily remembered the police action felt disappointed that no sanctions followed. When he spoke about the work of the commission, Hans-Dietrich Schmidt, professor of psychology at the university, expressed a certain resignation.[99] It was becoming clear that the police leadership would not be punished. By this time, however, the conduct of the police seemed a secondary problem compared with the earlier, more insidious role of the Stasi. Dispensing justice was even harder when so many had cooperated in a structure of informing and denunciation. Striking in retrospect, however, is the fact that the arrests, while frequently accompanied by gratuitous clubbing and certainly humiliating, were not followed, no longer could be followed, by long imprisonment. A week in an overcrowded cell was not the Gulag. Police detention, without arraignment and trial, was the last and ineffective response of the regime.

Recall that crescendo of popular mobilization. Trainloads of young citizens gladly going into exile. On October 2, mass demonstrations in Leipzig; on October 5, crowds spilling out of the Gethsemane Church in Berlin; on October 7 and 8, with the Soviet president barely off the tarmac, massive clashes again in the capital, while in Dresden SED city officials agreed to formal talks with citizen representatives after the clashes around the railroad station; on October 9, the triumph of the masses in Leipzig anew. What shards of legitimacy could the regime claim, what credibility might it retain when it blamed rowdies or Western capitalist conspiracies?

What in fact did the leaders of the regime really believe was taking place? Thanks to the storming of the Stasi headquarters, the effort to entrust State Security files to citizens committees established to assess the repressive efforts, and the early publications of the insurgent East German historians, we can follow the Politbüro's perspectives on the decomposition of authority. Local informants sent their reports about "negative and enemy forces" to

Berlin, where the Central Evaluation and Information Group (ZAIG) culled them and passed them up to the minister, Erich Mielke, who shared some with the Politbüro and Honecker himself. The files also included transcripts of some of the critical meetings that addressed the growing unrest. Additionally, we have some of the prompt memoirs of key players: transcripts of tape recordings with a somewhat dazed Erich Honecker, reduced from once decisive if deluded leader to deposed prisoner; the quick book of Egon Krenz, written in the earnest if banal prose of those who rose for years through the youth organization of the party; the acount of the least prejudiced political observer within the ranks of the old regime, Günter Schabowski. Together they afford the beginnings of insight into the inner working of the regime.

Thanks to its informants the regime could peer into almost every effort at organized dissent. Granted, its leaders' sense of vulnerability, their growing awareness of isolation, their need to blame the decomposition of loyalty on outside agitation conditioned the reports they received. In any organization subordinates tend to be evasive about bad news. And after years of snooping and enforcing orthodoxy, the top ranks of the Ministry of State Security were hardly prepared to face up to the potential for disaffection. Counting the manifestations of discontent was not difficult; believing there were homegrown causes was the obstacle. The ministry accumulated its reports on ecology groups, kept track of the sympathy extended by the pastor of St. Luke's in Leipzig or Superintendent Magirus in Leipzig or the Lutheran bishop of Dresden.[100] The report of June 1 provided a detailed inventory of would-be subversive groups, which had arisen since the 1980s, largely harbored in the Protestant churches, supposedly nurtured by the embassies of the Federal Republic, Britain, and the United States, assisted in their communication by sympathetic television correspondents from the West German channels.[101] There were about 160 such groups and ten coordinating committees, ostensibly agitating for ecology, peace, and the like.[102] Their informants reported on the "hardly religious" gathering of 1,500 participants in the Sophienkirche on June 7 and the Gethsemane Church the next night, when in the presence of Western correspondents and a member of the American embassy staff, the electoral fraud of the previous month was discussed. The Stasi reports show how closely briefed they remained about the discussions among Lutheran Church officials, who counseled against any ensuing public demonstration outside the church.[103] The 1991–92 controversy over the conversations of the lay manager of the Brandenburg church (and later minister-president) Manfred Stolpe with the Stasi likewise revealed how important Protestant leaders sought to expand the circumscribed autonomy for their church by reassuring the regime their dissent was limited. Stolpe in Brandenburg, Pastor Zimmermann, who signed the "no-violence" appeal in Leipzig, and others were caught up in the web of reporting and collaboration. Unless one opted to leave the GDR or quit public activity, the price appeared to be some degree of collaboration: briefings on meetings abroad, conversations about one's own activity, defensive efforts to reassure the ministry about collaborators' good intentions, or sometimes outright denunciation. Once across the table from an interrogator it was hard to limit the scope of one's revelations. The regime entrapped even its adversaries in a web of pervasive informing.[104]

A month later a detailed report on those leaving the country recorded an alarming increase vis-à-vis the same six-month period a year earlier, even if those fleeing were supposedly deceived about the standard of living in the West or just had to resolve some deep personal problem. Despite the regime's best efforts, it was becoming harder to suppress the emigration requests.[105] Those wanting to leave came overwhelmingly from the actively employed, including highly skilled professionals. Party activists sought to talk those applying for exit permits out of their plans, but, despite the pressure, few withdrew their applications.[106]

The reports talked about subversion, provocations, hostile and negative forces. Nonetheless, informants clearly testified to pervasive social dissatisfaction and grievances, including the flagging of spirit within the ranks of party loyalists. On August 31, the regional commanders of the Ministry for State Security gathered to discuss the possibility of demonstrations disturbing the upcoming "World Peace Day." It was an inconclusive but revealing report from throughout the south of the republic. The Berlin commander, Major General Hähnel reported that timely countermeasures had suppressed the electoral protests scheduled in June and July; they could control the open demonstrations, but the Protestant leaders were actively forming new associations. (Pastor Hilsberg of the Golgotha Church had agreed to inform the ministry on the progress of the initiative.) Erich Mielke wanted party loyalists mobilized and asked what was the mood in the factories. Hähnel responded, "That is a very complicated question at the moment, Herr Minister." "It is a very simple question," Mielke retorted. "It is a question of power—nothing more." His military adviser was less certain. The population watched Western television; party loyalists were dismayed by the sanction given to those fleeing via the embassies; all that the regime had achieved counted for little. As Mielke himself said, "they recognize the advantages of socialism . . . but still want to get out because they take the party's work for granted. . . . We want to find something here to aspire to, and something we can improve." But for the skeptical military adviser, there was little upbeat to propose. The flight of young people was especially demoralizing. It reflected "the whole problematic of the provisioning problem, that is the palette of fulfilling the principles of the meritocratic society, i.e., that everyone should get what, but only what he deserved."[107] Stasi evaluators also reported why GDR citizens were weary. Their complaints included "dissatisfaction with the supply of goods, anger over insufficient services, impatience with deficiencies in medical services, limited travel possibilities within the GDR and abroad, unsatisfactory working conditions and discontinuity of the production process, insufficiency or inconsistency in applying or carrying out meritocratic principles, as well as dissatisfaction about the development of wages and salaries; anger about the bureaucratic attitude of directors and members of state organs, enterprises, and institutions as well as about heartlessness in their interaction with citizens, impatience with mass media policies of the GDR."[108]

Stasi agents were clearly dismayed by this loss of support. To judge from the protocols left behind, they did not really envisage their role as primarily police agents. To be sure they were a huge agency for collecting intelligence, for snooping, for trying to sow doubt among would-be enemies of the regime. Inside their large headquarters on the Normannenstrasse in Berlin or at the "Round Corner" in Leipzig, they accumulated kilometers of dossiers. Agents steamed open and then reshut thousands upon thousands of letters. They developed false stomachs in which cameras could be concealed. They wiped the chairs on which they had seated suspects called in for questioning and then put the small rags into glass jars as a smell collection ("Geruchskonserven") in case they ever needed dogs to track them down. They interrogated the family and seized the notebook of a high-school student whose compositions compared the Trabi unfavorably with the Volkswagen Golf. They endeavored to monitor every current of possibly independent thinking within their republic. Motivating this occasionally absurd zeal lay the Central European tradition of state tutelage and *Polizei*. The more citizens they could entice into "unofficial collaboration," the more they might preserve their subjects from deviant thought and deed. "I was convinced that the goal of the SED to build a socialist state and a socialist community was feasible and good for everyone," recalled a Stasi officer in 1990.[109] In effect the Ministry of State Security defined its collective role not as cops but as social workers. And at the end agents became mystified that their clients so resented their paternalist supervision.

At the August 31 meeting, Minister Mielke recalled the 1953 uprising and put the hard question to Colonel Dangrieß from Gera: have things gone so far that tomorrow there could be a 17th of June? "Tomorrow, no, it won't take place; that's why we're there."[110] But one district commander after another referred to demoralization and dissatisfaction—the failure to appreciate the achievements of socialism, the complaints about the economy. Lieutenant General Gehlert reported on the alienation of doctors in Karl Marx Stadt, where since 1980 the hospital roof had gone unrepaired and twelve cancer patients had to share one room and basin.[111] And from Leipzig: "The situation is lousy [mies]. There are major discussions about all justified and unjustified problems we have, and what is especially relevant, these lousy currents exist within the party organization. . . . Otherwise, as to the question of power, Comrade Minister, we have the situation strongly in hand, it is stable. We don't have a situation like we had in the past [1953]. But extraordinarily high attentiveness is required. . . . It is a fact that from a situation arising accidentally here or there just a spark would suffice to bring something into motion."[112] Mielke would be ready. Demonstrations, especially with visual elements such as candles, would be suppressed. Churchmen were observing restraint, but Berlin, Leipzig, and Dresden were dangerous. Still, the churches had the right to conduct religious exercises, and intervention would only provoke more anger. Overall one had to stay observant; incidents could always arise: "But let's always be tuned in, that is our most important task of all in the GDR. All the rage and hatred on the part of the enemy lie in the fact that they would like to see a major event."[113]

The regime, however, was no longer united. Krenz and Schabowski, who had led official friendship delegations to China, supposedly returned convinced that the use of force against demonstrators was inadmissable.[114] The growing number of emigrants after the Hungarian border had opened revealed a clear crisis despite "every effort at pseudostability."[115] Informants of the Ministry of State Security minced no words. In a memo that testified to the disintegration of the regime's authority, the central evaluation group (ZAIG) wrote that SED members themselves believed that the "socialist state and social order were in serious danger . . . many party members and functionaries are quite open about saying that the party and state leadership are no longer capable of really sizing up the situation and taking the appropriate measures for urgently required changes." They were too old to react constructively.[116] Nonetheless, despite the helplessness of the regime, the idea of abandoning the system was not yet up for debate. The later critics, Krenz and Schabowski, claimed to be increasingly at odds with the regime's rigidness, but did not challenge the hard-liners. At the Politbüro session of early September—the chairing of which an ill Honecker entrusted to the self-assured defender of the party line, Günter Mittag—former deputy minister-president Werner Krolikowski asked whether the government did not need to make some announcement about the Hungarian situation, if perhaps only to blame all the difficulties on the usual occult capitalist suborning. Schabowski claims to have asked what such a statement would propose positively: were they prepared to confront the travel restrictions and the economic shortages that were so alienating? His tone was supported by the district secretaries from Chemnitz, Cottbus, and Halle. Kurt Hager, the ideological palladin of the party, asked that the incipient debate be postponed until Honecker was back as chairman. Looking back, Schabowski saw the postponement as fatal; at the time the proposal relieved the situation inside the ruling circle. To carry such a debate to the point of an attack on the Chairman—absent or present—still seemed hopeless.[117]

No general policy debate was possible in this situation without opening a debate on personalities. To change course could only mean to change personnel. Was there a possible successor? As chairman of the Council of Ministers, Willi Stoph was head of state and, according to the KGB chief in East Berlin, had been seeking Soviet support to unseat Mittag and Honecker since at least 1986.[118] Stoph, who had supported Schürer against Mittag in the late 1980s, told the Soviets that at least a third of the Politbüro wanted Honecker out, but he himself was too identified as an old party warhorse to head a reform effort. Neither could Schabowski, who, if less unorthodox than he presented himself in his subsequent memoir, was still too marginal an apparatchik in his rapid climb to the Berlin leadership. Nor yet Modrow, also too recent a player outside Saxony and insufficiently trusted. Perhaps Krenz, who like Honecker before him, directed the youth corps and whom Schürer had already approached. It seemed unlikely that a departing Honecker could impose Mittag, by now roundly distrusted in view of the simmering economic crisis as well as his conceit. In any case, Gorbachev was coming to help celebrate the fortieth anniversary: Honecker wanted no unseemly disturbances; and those who were growing discontented hoped that the Soviet chairman might exert renewed pressure. The East German leader, perhaps sensing his physical frailty, seemed to entrust more functions to Mittag. Indeed, the other Politbüro members thought (erroneously it turned out) that Honecker had favored Mittag by including him in the private meeting with Gorbachev on the morning of October 7 and passing over the head-of-state, Willi Stoph.

Was Gorbachev prepared to intervene in the German situation? Subsequent reports made a great deal of the alleged warning he delivered on his state visit: history punishes those who come too late. But in fact the Soviet leader took a reserved stance. He would not use a fraternal celebration to undermine the leader of his most sensitive and economically powerful ally. Through 1989 both countries were deeply involved in prolonging and intensifying their economic relations: as we have seen in chapter 2, the Soviets needed German machine tools and computer expertise; the Germans depended on Russian oil. In the fall of 1988 the two leaders had initialed plans for continued close cooperation. As for ideological divergences, in effect they had agreed to disagree. Nonetheless, the bathetic reaffirmations of Communist faith by Honecker or the sentimental invocation of his 1931 studies in Moscow could not disguise his stubborn resistance to glasnost and perestroika. He did not really want to listen when, from the fall of 1986 on, Gorbachev emphasized the theme of a common European house. In fact, Kurt Hager asked about perestroika in April 1987, just because the neighbors put up new wallpaper did one have to repaper at home. Nor did Honecker really absorb the message when in early 1988 the Soviet ambassador, making explicit Moscow's evaluation of the international situation, emphasized the new critical importance that the Soviets assigned to their cooperation with the German Federal Republic.[119] At Warsaw Pact meetings, the East Germans insisted on the dangers that still emanated from NATO and West German circles, while Russians, Hungarians, and Poles stressed the possibilities for cooperation. If Honecker was occasionally alarmed at the risky behavior of the Soviets, he still believed he could count on his own sturdy bastion of socialism. This self-confidence rested on a misapprehension of the domestic situation. Until the end he never sensed how alienated was the population as a whole and, just as serious, how disoriented party cadres had become.

Nonetheless, Gorbachev was not prepared to force a change in leadership. During his visit on October 7, he met first with Honecker and Stoph and listened as the GDR leader complained about Hungary's treachery, reported that everything was in order at home, and smugly said "Your problems are significantly worse than ours." When the Soviet leader then met with the GDR Politbüro as a whole, he did not question its leader's self-assured evaluation, but talked instead about the difficulties that his own reforms encountered in the Soviet Union. At this meeting he supposedly let fall the famous phrase, history punishes those who come too late. Krenz and others took it as a warning for themselves, although Gorbachev later told Krenz that he had been reflecting on his own experience.[120] Whatever differences existed were composed for the public appearances of Soviet and East German leaders. Gorbachev flew off, supposedly (but we have no confirmation) urging some of the Politbüro dissenters, as he climbed into the limousine for the airport, to act before it was too late; but more plausibly enjoining his own ambassador—who repeated the caution to his embassy staff—not to put pressure on their German comrades, who had to decide their own policies. "Give no advice! Listen but don't comment!" Stay out, then? But how did this square with his reported insistence that "We cannot accept the destabilization of the GDR and the dismantling of socialism in the Republic. . . . Under no circumstances can we lose the GDR."[121]

Contradictory pronouncements, in fact, often characterize grave political crises: the Soviets were prepared neither to force Honecker out, nor to back the regime with force. When Krenz sounded out Kochemasov on the eve of the October 9 demonstration, the ambassador gave his "categorical advice" (despite the injunction against doing so): "under no conditions resort to repressive measures, certainly not by the army." Krenz agreed; the purpose of the call was to communicate that he stood for a different policy from Honecker. But Honecker himself, it became clear, was no longer resolute enough to insist on a military response and Berlin waited upon local decisions. Apparently the party leaders in Leipzig were left to their own judgment, and they responded to the "no violence" appeal that emerged from the local notables. We have more detail about the party's weighing of a possible military recourse in the hours after the Wall was breached a month later. The SED never asked for Soviet military assistance, and Kochemasov instructed the Soviet military commander to ensure that Russian troops remained in their barracks, an order that Moscow authorities reiterated directly in the hours before the crowds surged across the Wall.[122]

Schabowski and Krenz were convinced that Honecker must depart. While the two attended a planning meeting for security measures at the Stasi headquarters on the morning of October 8, Krenz passed Schabowski a draft communiqué for *Neues Deutschland* that would serve to summarize the next Politbüro meeting. Despite its cautious wording, the document was intended both to initiate a debate on the leadership and then to signal to party members that the Politbüro was taking stock of the dissatisfaction emanating from the economic situation and signaled by the mass emigration. After Krenz and Schabowski edited the communiqué, it was sent to Honecker himself. Honecker was angry, called Krenz back that very day in an effort to dissuade him, and allegedly hinted that the challenger was slated to be named imminent successor, despite the fact that hitherto he had always seemed to favor Mittag. "Do what you want," he finally warned; "you'll see what results." The conspirators called up the members they calculated might be sympathetic or at least not bitterly opposed to prepare them for a debate; on their side were Siegfried Lorenz, Harry Tisch, the leader of the Communist Trade Union Federation (FDGB), and various district leaders: Mittag, Krolikowski, Mielke, and Joachim Herrmann were clearly going to be opposed. At the meeting itself on the next day, Honecker aimed most of his indignation at a report that disillusioned party youth believed the leadership too old for their task. The debate on the Krenz paper seemed anticlimactic: most discussants, Schabowski believed, might have assumed that the statement had been agreed to as a basis for discussion by Honecker. Nonetheless, resentments began to spill out, first directed at Mittag's role but soon becoming a general litany of complaints. Werner Jarowinski, responsible for trade, jumped in with a critique of the GDR's effort to achieve autarky in such common goods as microchips. Alfred Neumann, eighty years old and himself a preeminent example of the paternalist old guard, vented his spleen at Mittag, who, he felt, had kept him from being named successor to Ulbricht. In fact, all speakers including Mielke agreed that the situation was serious indeed; only Heinz Kessler, the defense minister, warned against disunity in the ranks. Honecker gave way; he summarized the consensus that there were grave problems. There was no choice but to issue a public communiqué; he urged, however, that it be assigned to a drafting committee composed of Krenz and two of his own stalwarts, Mittag and Herrmann. At Krenz's urging he added Schabowski, but insisted that the upbeat conclusions of his own fortieth anniversary report be harmonized with Krenz's warnings. In fact the four editors let the critical version largely stand: the world would be given to understand that some knowledge of the GDR's precarious situation had penetrated the inner sanctum. Hardly a basis for restoring faith overnight in a bankrupt system![123]

During the next week the chairman's power continued to evaporate. He left the October 9 meeting effectively isolated. District party chiefs summoned to Berlin, especially Hans Modrow from Dresden, complained that the national leaders had provided no assistance in overcoming the crisis raised by the demonstrations during the previous ten days. Discussions in

Berlin factories sharply criticized the economic difficulties fostered by the regime; Schabowski told Honecker that tempers were too aroused for him to make a personal appearance and rally loyal workers. Krenz and Schabowski spoke with ten or eleven potential allies over the weekend about the procedure for the next Politbüro session on Tuesday, October 17; they informed the Russian ambassador. The first to plunge the dagger was Willi Stoph, who interrupted Honecker's opening remarks in effect to move his master's removal. Perhaps he thereby hoped to rescue his own position as head of state. In any case, no speaker spared the general secretary; even Mittag placed the blame at his doorstep. Mielke raged that his boss had compelled him to enforce the policies that were so unpopular. The meeting unanimously agreed to recommend the dismissal of Honecker, Mittag, and Herrmann—responsible for "propaganda"—to the Central Committee (ZK) on October 19. Honecker capitulated. At a further Politbüro session on October 18, he presented a draft resignation statement to lay before the ZK, now summoned for the same day. When he actually came to read his text, he recommended, with what Schabowski felt was a Machiavellian twist, that the ZK confirm Krenz as his successor: this "Curse of the Pharaoh" blemished Krenz's reformist credentials from the outset.[124]

Krenz's was a brief interregnum. He debuted before the Central Committee with a speech flawed by its lack of plans and promising only what became the byword for the whole reform process: the so-called *Wende* or change, a term that seven years earlier had served to describe Chancellor Kohl's rejection of Social Democratic policies in West Germany. "A party such as ours," Krenz insisted, "has no other interest than that of the people. . . . Our historical optimism results from the knowledge of the ineluctability of the victory of socialism founded by Marx, Engels, and Lenin." Hans Modrow gently chided "that we have to recognize that we might elaborate a bit further the declaration Egon gave us today."[125] The Volkskammer dutifully confirmed Krenz as chairman of the Council of State six days later, but for the first time in that legislature there were votes opposed.

The new leader—ripe for caricature as a caped "Krenzman" or the wolf masquerading as grandmother in Red Riding Hood with his mouthful of huge teeth—never really came to grips with the growing wave of unrest. He promised elections on the basis of the constitution, which guaranteed the "leading role" of the SED, and he invoked a "market-oriented socialist planned economy." Dialogue remained the word of the day, but the outcome of dialogue still seemed likely to be constrained.[126] The Monday meetings remained gigantic—less tense, more civic celebrations, at which soon the theme of unification would be heard. In Leipzig, on October 22, the first of the "Sunday Conversations" was held in which SED leaders joined New Forum protesters to discuss needed reforms. On November 4, half a million demonstrators listened to writers and artists call for more reform—above all, the right to travel—at the Alexanderplatz. The huge rally at "Alex" culminated the mass demonstrations, but the event amounted to more a confirmation of the transformation under way than a revolutionary challenge. Organizers sought to include the broadest spectrum of participants from New Forum spokesmen, leading writers such as Christoph Hein and Christa Wolf, all the way to the director of East German counterintelligence, Markus Wolf. Demonstrators made it clear that for the government to demonstrate goodwill it must introduce the unhindered right to travel abroad.

As events soon revealed, moreover, halfway liberalization was impractical in the changed East European Communist landscape. The Krenz team had initiated consideration of liberalized travel and emigration legislation on October 20, and reopened the border to Czechoslovakia on November 1. The new regulations they announced on November 6 appeared a timid bureaucratic compromise: travel abroad after approval by the authorities and for only up to a month per year. The proposed legislation, moreover, was to be discussed for a further month before implementation. Even as this reform was announced, a mass demonstration in Leipzig—only two days after the giant assembly at the Alexanderplatz—demanded travel without visas or legislation, an end to the Wall and even to SED rule.[127] Reports from Prague meanwhile indicated that the West German embassy had again been besieged since November 1. This time the Czechoslovak Party Secretary Jakeš urgently pressed Krenz to allow GDR citizens crowding Prague to cross directly into the Federal Republic. On November 3, the Politbüro felt it must authorize the GDR embassy to distribute exit permits immediately, each to include an explicit right to retain citizenship and return home without sanction. A total of 23,000 GDR citizens crossed into Bavaria from Czechoslovakia over the November 4–6 weekend, but the surge of would-be emigrants through the Czech escape hatch led the Prague leaders to threaten closing the East German border. GDR Minister for Foreign Affairs Oskar Fischer summoned delegates from the Ministry for State Security and from the Ministry of the Interior to work out jointly a new travel and visa regulation. On November 7 they proposed a decree that would open a single border crossing point to the Federal Republic near the Czech frontier but inside GDR territory. Krenz, as usual, wanted Soviet approval. This was not an obstacle; but it was soon realized that it would be counterproductive just to grant travel possibilities to declared emigrants and not to those East Germans who merely wanted to visit the West and then return.

Events of the two following days have been the subject of confused and sometimes conflicting reconstructions. The partial travel reforms announced on November 6 did not open the Berlin frontier. On November 7, the Volkskammer, feeling its independence, rejected the new provisions as pettifogging. In the face of this unprecedented disavowal, Willi Stoph and the Council of Ministers resigned, retaining only caretaker status until appointment of a new council. In the course of a tumultuous Central Committee meeting over the next three days, the entire Politbüro would submit its resignation. Most members were promptly replaced (with Modrow now added and Mielke removed), and the renewed Politbüro instructed Krenz to propose a less restrictive travel ordinance. On the morning of November 9, two officials from the Ministry of the Interior and two from the Ministry of State Security worked out new draft legislation that declared all citizens with a passport were entitled to an exit visa over any border crossing, including East Berlin. This regime still promised some regulation of the flow. Only four million East Germans had passports and it would take up to a month or more for applicants to secure one. Again the Soviets were urgently consulted, now because opening the Berlin frontier involved Soviet rights and the Four Power Treaty of 1971. Approval again granted—but apparently from Gorbachev unofficially and not via the Foreign Ministry.

On November 9, Krenz brought the revised decree before the Central Committee, which was in the middle of its agonizing review of the chaotic political situation. This time the Central Committee approved the changes "henceforth" (*ab sofort*) although "henceforth" was envisaged as beginning the next day, November 10. Krenz did not bring the revised draft back to the Volkskammer, or to the Soviets (although there are contradictory reports). Schabowski was charged with announcing the amendments to the press on the evening of November 9. He had not sat through the Central Committee discussion, seemed to be surprised by the inclusion of Berlin as a frontier crossing point, and when questioned when the regulations would take effect, announced, "Immediately, without delay." When and under what conditions, if any, remained unspecified.[128]

By 9:30 P.M. a crowd was assembling at the Bornholmer crossing point north of the Brandenburg Gate. The border guards did not know that those leaving were entitled to come back, and stamped their identification cards as those of permanent emigrants. Soon short-term visitors who had not noticed their cards had been stamped as those of permanent emigrants were thronging to return, sometimes to the children they had left at home; others were thronging to go east. By 11 P.M. perhaps 20,000 East Berliners were shouting for the crossing gate to be opened; the local guards decided on their own authority that they must simply allow free passage, and crowds poured across the frontier that had been so deadly up to a few hours earlier. Within an hour and a half the other Berlin crossing points were also opened and crowds of young people were dancing on the Wall. Western crowds gathered as well. Hearing that the border was to be opened, East Berliners flocked to the Wall. The guards and officials expected the worst: an aneurism of East Germans that would mean the immediate liquidation of all remaining GDR authority. To their astonishment, East German citizens produced their identity papers for official stamping. The border did not disappear; it became normalized.[129] Not without danger of a violent clash, however. Although neither political nor military leaders were contemplating a "Chinese solution" by this date, troops were put on a status of high alert, which gave local officers the possibility to resort to force. Throughout the next day disorder and uncertainty beset the regime. Soviet ambassador Kochemasov called three times on the morning of November 10 to express concern about the improvised way in which the border had been opened.[130] The GDR could have expired in a bloody confrontation, not in the aftermath of a popular festival.

Seventy-one years earlier to the day, on November 9, 1918, in an effort to appease the giant throngs around the Reichstag, the Social Democratic leader Philip Scheidemann had announced the kaiser's abdication and the proclamation of a republic—a declaration unplanned, uncoordinated with his party comrades, but bowing to the crowd's demand for some fundamental recognition of their power and aspirations. So too, dismantling the Wall was a last desperate effort to ride the tiger, control the anger and the ebullience that had challenged the government. Reform communists and the peaceful opposition—the churchmen, the proliferating citizens committees, the massive adhesions to New Forum—had called for dialogue. Over the next months the local and national "round tables" would be dialogue in action. But the bounds of dialogue had spilled way beyond the controlled process of reform.

The revolutionary interval was brief, but it was genuine. As Otto Reinhold, chairman of the party's think-tank, the Academy for Social Sciences, told the Central Committee in its most agitated session to date, on November 9, a social as well as political crisis prevailed. The leadership had lost confidence among the party's rank and file; the party as a whole had sacrificed its authority among the population. He accused Kurt Hager, the venerable guardian of ideological orthodoxy, of preventing publication of reformist diagnoses of the social crisis by his Academy of Social Sciences.[131] Dismayed delegates listened to Gerhard Schürer and Günter Ehrensperger disclose the extent of the financial crisis. And sharp debate ensued over the responsibility of the police for the clashes in Berlin in early October. Many of the interventions were to be omitted from the published summary lest, as one delegate threatened, "We pour oil onto the fire. The working class is so angry that they're going to the barricades. They're howling: get the party out of the factories. They want to cut out the unions, get rid of the party secretaries."[132] When discussion resumed the next day, November 10, East Berliners were pouring unimpeded through the Wall. Krenz also reported growing turmoil, and not just inside the factories. "The situation has grown more acute in the capital, in Suhl and in other cities." He cited strikes and runs on the banks in Schwerin and Dresden. Within the ranks of the ruling party, the demand for resignations testified to panic and disintegration. The old guard had to face up to the anger of the SED's younger activists. Frank Fichte, an outspoken factory delegate, reported that local members were reproaching the party with halfway measures of renewal. Discredited Politbüro members who had been replaced should also withdraw from the larger Central Committee. Hager resisted. Rather unbelievably he now confessed that the party had underestimated the potential for democracy. It had slighted "the cooperation and collaborative influence of the masses on the working out of our ideas." The situation, Hager admitted, was even graver than that of 1953, when the party had almost surrendered its authority and dissolved the regime. For now the government had to turn to the public and make it clear: "Jetzt ist Ruhe die erste Bürgerpflicht" (peace and order were now the highest civic duty).[133]

In fact, the majority of delegates felt that ridding themselves of the old guard was the most urgent priority. Two days earlier they had replaced the old Politbüro. Now they voted to expel Günter Mittag and party propagandist Joachim Herrmann from the Central Committee, but not without provoking some embittered objections: "I find this catastrophic," announced the seventy-five-year-old director of the Leipzig Theater, Karl Kayser, who declared he would voluntarily resign, but only for reasons of age and out of disgust with the proceedings. "I have tried to live my whole life with this party," another unidentified speaker similarly objected. "But what I have experienced here is so depressing, so shocking, that I can't get over it. And now when we're told that we have to get back to work, how can we get back to work? The party is basically kaput. . . . It's an avalanche."[134]

This limited sacrificial offering was not sufficient, however. When the Central Committee reconvened on Monday, November 13, Moritz Mebel reported that the party secretaries in the factories were being "slaughtered" one after another. So too, the current Volkskammer debates, he complained, lacked any of the humane spirit that might indicate civilized men were still taking part. Kurt Hager again pleaded that no further resignations should be required until the new Central Committee was summoned. Demanding or accepting individual resignations—he was clearly next in line— would unleash a process of dissolution. Hager, who had so insistently served as watchdog of orthodoxy, now was "gradually getting a feeling as if we were in the medieval inquisition." "I just don't understand," Fichte rejoined, "I just don't understand a few who won't resign. The rank and file demands it. . . . At the level of the rank and file, believe me, the comrades are kaput."[135]

Krenz rather forlornly called for discipline—"We are not just a mere heap"—but did not cut off the painful debate. When Hager again asked whether the party had to yield to the demand for scapegoats, Schabowski told him he was harboring illusions. Modrow soothingly claimed that the party did not want a massive purge. The newly chosen Politbüro commanded respect, but members of the old one (in addition to Honecker, Mittag, and Herrmann, who had already departed) should retire now from the Central Committee, where they still held their seats. An hour's adjournment allowed the group to finesse a painful vote of explusion: when its members reconvened at 10:15 P.M. they could listen to a collective letter of resignation from Hager and the old guard.

Recrimination, feelings of mutual betrayal, anger quickly spread to all the institutions of the GDR once dominated by the SED. Harry Tisch, head of the FDGB, found himself forced to resign despite his vote against Honecker.[136] Those who came under attack in the next months (to recall examples I encountered) referred to pogroms or ostracism. Communist cells in factories or faculties went through an authentic upheaval. Longtime party members felt betrayed by their leaders, demoralized by their co-workers' rejection, sometimes unworthy to claim further moral authority. Resignations would reach floodtide during the months to come. During the winter, anger surged at the representatives of the old order, symbolized above all by the Stasi and the nomenklatura's suburb of official residences at Wandlitz, north of Berlin. By most standards the privileges were modest: well-stocked food stores, well-tended lawns, a comfortable enclave of houses—but hardly great luxury. Corruption there certainly was in the system—pervasive even. Later it would be charged, for example, that officials got health care and blood transfusions and transplants at the Berlin Charité while elsewhere modern medicine was scarce and rationed.[137] The party was not to overcome these taints, and bitterness would grow. Anger peaked with the storming of the Stasi headquarters on the Normannenstraße on January 15: the huge crowd was no longer ebullient and celebratory but ugly and on a rampage. But the turbulence crested after Minister-President Modrow decided to move up the date of elections from May to March. Elections would allow a referendum on unification, which meant that an autonomous trajectory of events in Eastern Germany could not really develop. No sooner out of the force field of the SED, the country drifted into the gravitational pull of the Federal Republic. The moment of dialogue—dialogue on the eastern side of the Wall and not across it—was to be brief indeed.

Nonetheless, the momentum of liberalization was intense. The Czechs, who had not wanted to open their own borders to the West, were now convulsed by a similar popular movement. The end of 1989 was one of peaceful exhilaration: a mature revolutionary change. Many would later be disillusioned—especially some of those who wanted some reformed socialism to persist. Still, October and November were an achievement: the sustained mobilization of crowd action, of new participants in politics, of masses without violence and with a high degree of civic responsibility. Such moments had been rare in Germany and had usually had disappointing institutional results. For a long time the East Germans had lived in their "niches," their masses less defiant than the Poles, their intellectuals less defiant than the Czechs. In the autumn of 1989, they redeemed that passivity.

By the March elections, Robert Darnton, an American historian of the French Revolution and a resident in Berlin at the time, discerned the possibility of a Thermidorian reaction.[138] In the aftermath some intellectuals grew cynical. Those who wanted to reform the old GDR and not dissolve it beheld the opening of the Wall almost as a Machiavellian trick. They grew almost resentful that their citizenry could and would vote to liquidate the whole republic and join the crass materialist West. They grew bitter about the German national spirit that soon proved so contagious. Those of us who talked with GDR reformers and intellectuals during the early months of 1990 encountered occasionally elitist resentment at the gratifications of travel—as if the Wall had been breached only for the famous bananas of West Berlin. It is easy to see the limits of the action and the quick channeling of it into unification. But unlike 1871 German unity did not come at the cost of liberalism. In retrospect it seems unlikely from reading the Stasi's own feckless memos that force would have been applied with sufficient resolution to curb the rising protests. But this conclusion does not mean that demonstrators could have reckoned on reason prevailing. They faced police clubs and harsh arrests and perhaps more. West Germans, moreover, had never had to brave that risk to construct their democracy. Their quasi countrymen across the Wall—they were uncertain what national status to bestow on them—deserved full credit. In the months to come—as East Germans grew increasingly abject over their delapidated economy and environment, as West Germans grew more astonished at the institutional detritus they uncovered across the Wall—inferiority on the one side, smugness on the other, grew apace. Few emphasized that insofar as national constitution rests upon the intervention of direct popular will, only the East Germans had demonstrated that courage, once sporadically in 1953, again more massively, generously, tolerantly, but decisively in 1989.

The demonstrations of autumn 1989 compel us to ask whether national and democratic governments may be strengthened by a founding moment of direct popular intervention, at least a sacramental instant of collective unmediated affirmation so that later representative institutions rest upon some primeval expression of popular will. Such a constitutive moment need not be long; but, if need be, it must incur a risk: it must demonstrate a willingness to face repressive force. Now the sober political analyst or the historian troubled by the slippery slope from *grande journée* to the unleashing of manipulated mob terror may ask whether such a founding crowd is really necessary or beneficial. A few months prior to sharing the excitement and joy of the 1989 transformations behind the former Iron Curtain, Europeans and Americans were purposefully disavowing or at least diluting the legacy of 1789. Despite the festivities of the official French commemorations, the bloody aftermath of that earlier revolutionary moment seemed dark enough to discredit the contribution of collective, extralegal action. For all its wonderful partying, the *bicentenaire* was designed more to celebrate the safe distance from the French Revolution than to confront its problematic history. In the optic of the bicentennial, the crowd of 1789 became menacing, although just a few months later the crowd of 1989 appeared liberating. Could these perspectives be reconciled? Was one more justified than the other?

Part of the discrepancy was overcome as the German crowd of 1989 evolved from a political to a festive gathering. The participant or spectator during late 1989 could intuitively grasp what was meant by the most elusive element of the revolutionary trilogy: fraternity. As Darnton summarized the New Year's Eve of outgoing 1990: it was "neither Apollonian nor Dionysian but videogenic: crowd bathing in folk-rock."[139] Dancing on the Wall, on November 9, December 22, and December 31, 1989, brought the crowd to the flushed and reassuring enthusiasm of the street balls in Paris the previous July 13 and 14. By the time of the Pink Floyd concert at the edge of West Berlin on July 21, 1990, the crowd had become merely one of partygoers and the organizers had to re-evoke segments of the now dismantled Wall in styrofoam. Yet the young people taking part reported that they felt the rock concert was itself historical. For these groupies of history, the psychic distance between the event and its celebration simply collapsed.[140]

Nonetheless, it would be too easy to let the crowd dissolve into unproblematic historical memory as just a *moment musical* of Folk communitas. The more instructive lesson to be drawn was that crowds and crowd action were not all of a piece. They were certainly not to be understood simply as monolithic actors possessed of a single intolerant will. The political crowd could be disciplined; it could act as restrained proto-association. Still, the concept of association may connote too instrumental a gathering. The crowds in Leipzig were restrained, but not just a pressure group that took to the streets. They were bonded by a vision of an alternative public sphere; they shared a fraternal identity for their month of protest; they demonstrated the exaltation of will that social theorists such as Durkheim and Victor Turner have emphasized; they helped bring down a regime, and, in this sense they were revolutionary.

As commentators on the American "riots" of the late 1960s had argued—and so, too, historians of the eighteenth-century crowd—not all mass demonstrations were mobs.[141] (Perhaps, despite the impression created by conservative penitents at the French bicentennial, not even those of 1789 had been just mobs!) Certainly during 1989, the candles flickering outside the Gethsemane Church, the self-policing in Leipzig, and the earnest appeals for dialogue suggested that crowds might still embody a special emancipatory potential. They could open a window for history or create a constitutive moment that served to orient later institutional development. Resistance uprisings and Allied liberation in 1944–45 had opened such a constitutive moment in Western Europe. Similarly, the Civil Rights and antiwar movement in the United States had renewed the earlier constitutive moments of the eighteenth century. It remains an open question whether democratic achievements require such a founding moment of popular mobilization. Scandinavia has enjoyed stable liberties without a legacy of revolution. Closer examination of Northern Europe may confirm that decisive broad general strikes or decisive and dramaturgic electoral campaigns could serve as sufficient moments of constitutional mobilization. In West Germany, too, representative government had emerged without that moment of constitutive crowd intervention—it was created from troubled memory and through allied midwifery. It had functioned very well. In 1989 many West Germans would feel uncomfortable about the force potentially inherent in the crowds; Willy Brandt was a salient exception. Chancellor Kohl would soon seek to graft the GDR onto the ongoing Federal Republic as seamlessly as possible. Even good Social Democrats in West Germany would agree in the spring of 1990 that it was not worth risking their achieved constitutional stability for some demagogic and possibly dangerous celebration of national reconstitution. Nonetheless, the West Germans too at the end of 1989 became beneficiaries of the popular movement across the Wall. At the threshold of democracy lies a moment of public civic assertion, of collective insistence against arbitrary repressive power.[142] The crowds in Leipzig, Berlin, and throughout the streets of the little bastion of paternalistic control that was the GDR gave their renewed larger nation that founding gift.

Four

Protagonists of the Transition

INTERVIEWER: Everyone is talking about the NEW FORUM: What is it?

SCHULT: . . . On the 9th of September thirty people from eleven districts of the GDR met in Grünheide, had discussions for a day and a half, and decided finally to found an association with the name NEW FORUM and to request its legalization. We were agreed we did not want to found, nor could we found a party. . . .

INTERVIEWER: Fine. You were thirty people. Meanwhile more than 150,000 have signed up for the NEW FORUM. Demonstrations throughout the country are demanding that it be legalized. Had you reckoned with that?

SCHULT: No . . . and it overwhelmed us a bit. We have no office, no telephones. Only our apartments and private telephones. And most of us must still put in their eight and three-quarter hours at the plant or the institute. And every day dozens of letters arrive. People are coming from the whole country. Occasionally we are just simply overloaded.

> —Interview with Reinhard Schult, one of the founders of
> New Forum, in photocopied ten-page newsletter,
> *Neues Forum* 1/1989 [c. November 1]

Information: Schult, Reinhard (36, born 23.9.1951) . . . skilled building-trades worker . . . active since the end of the 1970s in diverse hostile-negative groups, and as leader of the church-affiliated "Peace Circle of Berlin-Friedrichsfelde" is one of the leading organizers of numerous underground political oppositional groups (organization of the so-called East-West seminar, "Bicycle Path" and other "environmental action groups," organization of interregional "human rights seminars," coproducer of "Blues Fairs," and "Peace Workshops," drafting and signing of numerous politically provocative manifestos, etc.) . . . Member of the editorial group of the illegally produced and distributed newsletter, "Friedrichsfelde Fire Alarm." Functions as informant and contact man for Western journalists active in the GDR and other hostile-negative forces in the FRG and West Berlin.

—Stasi Information No. 454/87, Berlin 30.11.87.[1]

NEW FORUMS AND ROUND TABLES

"For us it's clear. Now is the time of the citizens committees."[2] New Forum did not want to be a party. In this goal it succeeded. By the time of the elections for a renewed East German legislature in March 1990, New Forum's electoral organization won approximately 2 percent of the electorate. For some the result was a reproach; for others, consistent with the attitude taken since its organization the previous autumn. Reinhard Schult, the heating and plumbing worker who gave the interview on behalf of the New Forum and had been such an object of Stasi research two years before, was typical of the early activists. So too was his network of overlapping opposition grouplets during the late 1980s—jazz and peace, earnest seminars, ecology initiatives, many loosely encouraged under Lutheran Church auspices (one of the pastors turned out to be a Stasi informant!) and viewed as subversive by the state security apparatus. Typical too was his feeling overwhelmed by mass politics. Perhaps it was finally fitting that he and a dozen supporters walked out of the New Forum's convention at the end of January 1990, when the movement constituted itself as a political association in view of the upcoming elections.[3]

During the last meeting of the East German Volkskammer in July 1990, a temporarily discouraged and distracted Jens Reich, cofounder of New Forum, looked back on the heroic weeks of the previous autumn and reaffirmed that New Forum had never wanted to rule. "The question of power never was discussed. We believed in the will of the people in smashing the secret police. But no group was prepared to take power." "Did we miss our opportunity?" he reflected again in November 1990. "We never wanted power. It would have conflicted with our commitment to legality. It simply never occurred to us to seize power; if we had we would have been pulverized to dust."[4] For some this abnegation seemed admirable, for others naive.

In either case the degree to which this massive reform movement failed to awake an electoral following was remarkable.

It is not the first time that great spontaneous movements fail to institutionalize their energies for ongoing politics. Loyalties born of collective enthusiasm are hard to sustain. Not so differently, the non-Communist parties emanating from the French and Italian resistance in 1944 and 1945, who seemed so assured of their moral claim on the future, had also seen their votes dwindle by 1945–46 to only a few percent of the electorate. It is difficult to make the transition from moral ebullience to electoral machine. And New Forum members did not think that the priority was especially high.

New Forum was not the only organization to emerge in opposition, but it was the initiative that overcame the fragmentation of earlier dissenting groups. "From the beginning of the 1980s the hostile efforts at misuse of the churches and religious communities took on a new quality," the Ministry of State Security recognized as it sedulously combed through the underbrush of peace agitators and ecology activists.[5] "From the beginning of the 1980s," it warned again in its gumshoe jargon a few weeks later, "continuing efforts at assembling and forming of such persons whose goal is the fomentation, disintegration, and political destabilization up to and including the transformation of social relationships in the GDR led to the construction of corresponding groupings and groups."[6]

How had the church gotten into the peace movement? Much of the history of German Protantism in the twentieth century has been a debate over how to resolve the agonizing ambiguities inherent in Romans 13: "Everyone must submit himself to the governing authorities for there is no authority except that which God has established." Had God established the GDR? Unlikely. Might it evolve so that obedience was justified? Perhaps. Unlike the situation of Roman Catholicism after the papacy of John XXIII, the 1960s had not been a propitious decade for Lutheran radicalism. The regime made overtures to the East German clergy at the same time that it cut off easy access to the West and pressured parents to withdraw their children from the church.

In these circumstances East German Protestant leaders sought accommodation. Many of them found the uncompromising opposition of the crusty bishop of Berlin-Brandenburg, Otto Dibelius, tiresome and inconvenient. They found it awkward to persevere in the theology of noncooperation or resistance developed by the anti-Nazi "confessional church" and later Dietrich Bonhöffer, which had insisted on a fundamental disjuncture between Christian life and state demands. Instead, over the course of the late

1960s and 1970s they reorganized an East German Protestant Church Federation (Evangelischer Kirchenbund) and worked out a modus vivendi as
the "Church within Socialism." The process was never smooth nor univer-
sally supported. Post-Helsinki human-rights activism and concern with
peace issues continued to percolate within the Kirchenbund. The regime
gave with one hand and took with the other: in March 1978 it received the
Protestant leadership in an unprecedented formal summit but shortly thereafter introduced military instruction in ninth and tenth grade. Church authorities protested in vain, and jarred by the general acceptance of the new
curriculum, they introduced a new parish program, Educating for Peace.
The degree of militarization of society thus remained a battleground of
choice between church and state.[7]

The local contest between Caesar and God soon became enmeshed with
the European-wide peace movement that was mobilized by NATO's "double
track decision" in response to Soviet intermediate missile deployment and
Moscow's intervention in Afghanistan. A less defensive regime might have
deflected some of the peace agitation. Church activists were mobilizing their
parishes less against their own regime than as part of an international Christian protest against the arms race.[8] But the state's hostility and suspicion
ensured that it too became a target of protest. Dresden church protesters
unsuccessfully demanded social service work as an alternative to the national draft. The Berlin Appeal of February 9, 1982 (signed by the guru of
dissident communism, Robert Havemann, who had earlier applauded Prague Spring, and organized by pastor Rainer Eppelmann) called for removal
of nuclear weapons and foreign troops from both Germanies; in 1981–82
sympathizers sported "Swords into Plowshares" badges until the Church
grew wary. The annual "Peace Seminars" with their ongoing committees,
"Concrete for Peace," "Doctors for Peace," and the "Working Circle of
Christian Doctors," emerged in Halle in 1983 along the lines of experiments
a decade earlier.[9] In February 1986, 170 delegates from fifty-eight church-
affiliated peace circles convened to discuss their movement, without much
result, according to the government. In May 1987, Schult and Vera Wollenberger organized the Church from Below. (The East Germans were not the
only authorities to judge these activities as subversive: many advocates of
NATO missile upgrading condemned the Western peace movements of the
early 1980s as destabilizing and a product of the same Germanic political
romanticism that had earlier led to National Socialism. But these critics
could not arrest demonstrators, deny them passports, or expel them from
universities.)[10]

After the peace movement, so the Stasi reported, came the effort in 1983–84 by the same malcontents to exploit ecological initiatives. Under the impact of a Western press that "hysterically exaggerated" forest die-offs (*Waldsterben*), troublemakers took to organizing collective bicycle trips or demonstrative tree plantings to discredit the regime. They got pollution-measuring apparatuses from the West and produced an underground video, "Bitterness from Bitterfeld," allegedly the most polluted city of the GDR. The police only assured the political thrust of these activities by descending on the Berlin Zion Church's "Environmental Library" in November 1987, arresting editors, and confiscating journals and printing equipment.[11] A few months later they confronted a new church-affiliated "Green-Ecological Network, Ark."[12]

After mobilizing for environmental protection, the dissenters focused on the central issue of human rights. In the summer and fall of 1985, the physicist Gerd Poppe, influenced by Havemann and consigned to menial jobs since his support for the exiled balladeer Wolf Biermann, helped organize the "Initiative Frieden und Menschenrechte" (IFM; Initiative for Peace and Human Rights) with his wife Ulrike, who had also founded "Frauen für den Frieden." IFM organizers went on the next year to distribute *Grenzfall*, a mimeographed paper with a punning title (Fall of the Border or Limiting Case). As in the Church from Below, *Grenzfall*'s contributors ventured beyond a still-cautious Church sponsorship; they were young and already discriminated against in terms of professional advance. If that did not suffice, the security apparatus was prepared to exert further pressure. A couple of months after the raid on the Environmental Library the police pressured the Wollenbergers into British exile, by providing them with passports and threatening family reprisals or prison if they remained. Other troublemakers were thrust into the FRG.[13]

Those who stayed attended fugitive discussions and poetry readings in Prenzlauerberg cafés and friends' apartments, circulated underground magazines and essays, and slowly built a subculture of dissent. Still, for all the discontent and ferment, as the regime's secret police recognized, the opposition remained fragmented until late into the decade. Church-oriented sociologists greeted the proliferation of groups "under the roof of the church" as a rebuff to the received wisdom of irreversible secularization.[14] But while some groups were religiously church oriented—as was "End to Exclusion in Theory and Principle" (Absage an Theorie und Prinzip der Abgrenzung), from which Democracy Now later sprang—others just took advantage of the shelter available. They also quarreled and fissioned. The Rosa Luxemburg demonstration of mid-January 1988, which provoked party ire for brandishing Luxemburg's motto that freedom had to be freedom for those who think differently, also revealed some persisting disagreements. Not all organizers wanted to allow advocates of the right to emigrate to march alongside those demanding rights for citizens who stayed.[15]

The Protestant churches, moreover, were hardly unanimous in the sanctuary they provided. Many ministers and theologians were too uneasy about dissent to support the activists. They expressed sympathy with the ideals of a socialist alternative to capitalism; they insisted that any "groups" within their own churches remain strictly religious in nature.[16] Some of the Lutheran bishops felt they had to distance themselves from peace declarations in order to keep the degree of church autonomy they had earlier negotiated, or to be able to extricate their pastors from arrest. Like university faculties, the official church had been snared in a web of negotiations and reporting to preserve its institutional role. Even sympathetic leaders such as Bishop Forck or Manfred Stolpe doubtless felt that they were not in a position to indulge in the outright declarations, say, of Rainer Eppelmann. Perhaps at times they felt that the peaceniks or environmentalists were irresponsible poseurs. The bishops and superintendents had to live with a regime of precarious and partial negotiated autonomy. The result, therefore, as the Stasi recognized, was meager: "Not least as a result of state and societal influences, every effort so far to organize these church peace and environmental circles, to give them a common platform, and thus overcome their stark differentiation has been unsuccessful. Interregional meetings, gatherings, seminars, etc. which still continue, have remained nonbinding so far and have revealed the incapacity of the organizers to develop viable political concepts."[17]

The crises of 1988–89 changed this situation. The ill-concealed displeasure with perestroika and censorship of Soviet periodicals isolated the regime from its external prop. "Ideas such as glasnost, democratization, dialogue, civil rights, freedom for 'dissenters' [Andersdenkende], or pluralism of opinions are misused in order to conceal particular political concepts and goals."[18] By the spring of 1989 there were about 160 locally based dissident groups and 10 umbrella organizations, but the Stasi believed only 2,500 individuals were steady activists and only 60 "hard core."[19] Their names appeared over and over again: among others, pastors Marcus Meckel and Rainer Eppelmann, Bärbel Bohley and her husband, Michael Bohley, one of the physicians for peace, Sebastian Pflugbeil, Ulrike Poppe, Reinhard Schult, Wolfgang Templin, Pastor Hans-Jochen Tschiche, Vera

Wollenberger. Berlin was their favored ground: under a sympathetic Berlin-Brandenburg diocesan leadership, many Protestant parishes (*Kirchengemeinde*)—Bartholemew's, Confessing, Gethsemane, Golgotha, Old Pankow, Redeemer, Resurrection, Samaritan, Zion—might each shelter a "basis group." In the vastness of East Berlin they might meet sympathetic West German journalists and organize effective telephone networks, weave connections with Charter 77 or Hungarian environmental activists, have access to illegally imported photocopiers, VCRs, and personal computers, and turn out about twenty-five underground bulletins. Outside Berlin, Leipzig, Karl-Marx-Stadt (Chemnitz), Dresden, Gera, and Erfurt were the major centers—the cities of the southern half of the GDR where demonstrations would be most massive in the fall of 1989. But dissenters had outposts elsewhere: a few youth in northern Mecklenburg, groups in Halle, Pastor Friedrich Schorlemmer who tended Luther's house and pulpit in Wittenberg.

The rigged voting of May 1989 and the refugee hemorrhage during the summer of 1989 swelled the ranks of those willing to sign manifestos and join marches. At a meeting in the East Berlin Confessing Church (Bekenntniskirche) on August 13, the physicist Hans-Jürgen Fischbeck, just one of a number of speakers and later a member of Democracy Now, called for a nationwide opposition movement. The founding of New Forum provided the unifying structure independent of the churches that the regime knew had been lacking. In "Aufruf 89," its founding "summons" of September 12–13 (three days after the meeting Schult attended), the new group called for "dialogue" and social restructuring. The document asked for an end to violence and secret policing and freedom for private economic initiative, but without antisocial competition ("no elbowing") or unlimited growth. The group declared it would register as a political association on the basis of article 129 of the GDR constitution and the ordinance of November 6, 1975, regulating the formation and activity of associations.[20] Even as the authorities temporized, New Forum sponsored an almost spontaneous wave of local, regional, and professionally based discussions and organization. It enjoyed the charisma of opposition and quickly became the umbrella for the other quasi-collaborative, quasi-competitive associations.[21] "New Forum finally awoke us out of a frightful lethargy," declared a neurologist in the provincial town of Quedlinburg.[22] On September 18, rock musicians and singers welcomed New Forum and called for democratically organized groups to take the solution of outstanding problems into their own hands. On September 19 as New Forum adherents registered with the authorities in districts throughout the GDR, the synod of the united Lutheran Churches met at Eisenach, cited the wave of emigrants, and called for fundamental reforms.[23]

Whether from principle or ambition, opposition leaders began to differentiate their platforms. Dissident SED members and FDGB trade unionists who viewed New Forum with distrust announced a "United Left," which tapped perhaps 300 to 500 adherents and hoped to reinvigorate long dormant factory councils.[24] "Citizens Movement: Democracy Now" (Bürgerbewegung: Demokratie Jetzt) stressed a more socialistic and ecological set of reforms. It too included a group of ministers, and its leader, Wolfgang Ullmann, born in 1929, was a church historian.[25] Pastors Eppelmann, Richter, and Schorlemmer sought a more structured organization than New Forum when they launched Demokratischer Aufbruch (DA, or Democratic Awakening on October 1. Eppelmann (although the Stasi had identified him as a fervent opposition leader two years earlier) viewed the mass demonstrations in Leipzig with some uneasiness and called for their end once representatives of the regime were willing to talk. Moving beyond the reluctance of most new protesters to declare they wanted to compete for power, Ibrahim Böhme and Angelike Barbe announced the formation of an East German Social Democratic Party by the end of September, stressing, however, their independence from the West German SPD. The autumn ferment mobilized one constituency after another. When Dresden became the scene of clashes, actors of the State Theater declared they had a right to dialogue and stepped out of their roles to call for reforms. Berlin homosexuals did not lag: "As left lesbians, gays, and human beings . . . we unite the striving for an inclusive human emancipation with the struggle for a liberated sexuality and love," and called for a Pink-Purple (Rose-Lilac) Forum.[26] As the *Tageszeitung* (*taz*) reported, "Within a few weeks the social and political situation in the DDR has dramatically changed. Until then the regime presented itself as without ideas, politically paralyzed, all-powerful—and unassailable. The opposition owed its almost total social isolation to an intense provincialism and fragmentation, to an omnipresent state apparatus and a population whose choices for the future were limited either to resignation at home or emigration into the Federal Republic."[27]

The word of the hour for all these groups was dialogue. New Forum called for dialogue; the demonstrators called for dialogue; Democratic Awakening asked for dialogue. As they confronted the crowds, party officials took up the appeal as their own, first in Dresden, where Mayor Wolfgang Berghofer sought to defuse two days of clashes by meeting with demonstrators on October 10,[28] and then in a Politbüro statement on October 11, two days after the march in Leipzig: "We have all the necessary forms and forums for socialist democracy. We call for their even more encompassing utilization."[29] Of course, the party's statement added, "socialism on German territory is not up for discussion."

Such a limitation was illusory. The implications of dialogue cut two ways. Most immediately the police would have to refrain from swinging their billy clubs and arresting demonstrators. In the days and weeks to come the regime would have to concede that more than one interpretation of truth and policy was legitimate. The party would have to do what it had always resisted—listen seriously to voices from outside its ranks and respond with more than a paternalist dismissal. Whether such pluralism could be contained within a single party was doubtful. The SED would be in for a rough ride at best. Although New Forum had not begun with goals that outside any repressive system would be deemed revolutionary, the call for dialogue was inherently expansionist. It required opening ever wider realms of public affairs and the historical past for scrutiny and debate.

On the other hand, "dialogue" set limits on the protesters. Although the presence of tens of thousands of demonstrators on the streets made the situation volatile, to appeal for dialogue was to accept for the short-term a self-limiting role for the crowd and to renounce any seizure of the state. For both sides dialogue thus postponed violent confrontation in exchange for ambiguity and openness. But in the long run, dialogue was bound either to burst through the constraints that the SED hoped to impose—or (and here was the consolation of the hard-liners) finally to let the crowds grow weary enough to acquiesce in some minor touch-ups of the status quo.

How could dialogue be institutionalized? The rulers hoped for controlled and private parleys; the crowds demanded public exchanges. On the night of October 16, demonstrators left a prayer meeting at the Dresden Kreuzkirche to join the crowds outside the Rathaus. The mayor was inside in a "dialogue with citizens" concerning the environment, travel, and elections, and even the difficulties of commuting. The demonstrators outside demanded that a microphone connection be wired to the square so they could stay in touch with the delegates within.[30] The structure in which dialogue took place at the national level was the Round Table, borrowed from the Polish example on the advice of the churchmen who were now emerging as go-betweens. Round Tables were quickly formed at the local level, but the principal Round Table became a quasi parliament that held sixteen meetings between December 7, 1989 and March 12, 1990, first at the church hall of the Herrnhüter Brethren, then at the pleasant villa of Niederschönhausen in the suburban northern quarter of East Berlin.

In contrast to the Polish Round Table, where Solidarity delegates sat as a united force opposite the government, or the Czech variant, where the Civic Forum dominated, the East German Round Table remained fragmented among the diverse citizens movements and the new SPD, the formerly collaborationist block parties, and the SED itself. While it was understood in Prague and Warsaw that the Round Tables could serve as protoconstitutional conventions, in Berlin the importance of the institution was less certain given the growing possibility of reunification. Nonetheless, far more than the Volkskammer elected in the last rigged elections, the Round Table became the repository of whatever legitimacy existed. The table in fact was not actually round, but an open rectangle arranged as if for an international negotiation. At the head were chairs for up to seven government representatives (the most eminent and respected being Wolfgang Ullmann, himself drawn from the ranks of Democracy Now) and three moderators drawn from the Church leadership. Around the other sides were two delegates each from the official, badly compromised trade union federation (FDGB) and the United Left (the alternative union grouping), the new SPD, and the various civic movements—Democracy Now, and Democratic Breakthrough, the Green Party, the Green League, the Independent Women's Movement, the Initiative for Peace and Human Rights (IFM), and the New Forum, which was allocated a third representative. These enthusiasts for reform, fresh from their mobilization in the streets, sat across from the older block parties, each with three delegates and now seeking themselves to emerge from their conformist past—the SED (soon to be the PDS), the CDU, the Liberal Democrats (LDPD), the National Deomcrats (NDPD), the Peasant League—and finally a representative of the small Sorbian ethnic minority.[31]

Round Table delegates and fledgling government ministers alike had to learn a new game whose rules were still fluid. The old ruling party and its state were rapidly decomposing. A new dualism of legislature and Round Table was emerging by fits and starts. "Dual power," however, quickly became no power. With the elections of March 18 and the negotiations for the Economic and Social Union, it was clear that only the fine print of merger remained to be negotiated. That outcome was uncertain during the intervening winter, however, and neither of the two successive SED ministerpresidents was in a position to impose an orderly transition. Egon Krenz, who had replaced Honecker as general secretary of the SED on October 17, was elected by the Volkskammer a week later to take over Honecker's former role as chair of the Council of State and the National Defense Council. Willi Stoph soldiered on as chair of the Council of Ministers until November 7, the eve of the traumatic rendering of accounts at the tenth meeting of the Central Committee. Along with rushing through travel legislation and purging the old guard, the tenth ZK confirmed the nomination of Modrow as Stoph's successor and declared that new, democratic elections would be held to renew the national legislature. Hitherto the Volkskammer had served only as a supine parliament, its SED and block party members ratifying the nominations and measures proposed by the SED party organs or the council of ministers. Not all were prepared to change and some of the old leaders still sought to cling to the assembly's decorative role. Other deputies, however, now sought to exercise the legislative power that the old GDR constitution nominally assigned them. The Volkskammer confirmed the party's selection of Modrow as minister-president on November 13, and set up a committee to draft a new electoral law. On December 1, the legislature removed the SED's constitutionally enshrined "guiding" role as the state party.

The unraveling of the party state had just begun. Anger at the grass roots compelled the tenth Central Committee meeting to convene a special party conference, then within two days forced the Politbüro and a newly summoned ZK meeting to call for an emergency party congress, whose date was to be moved up to December 7 and 8. On December 3, Krenz, who had remained as party secretary after surrendering the minister-presidency, resigned, along with the entire Politbüro. (On December 6, Krenz relinquished his last posts as head of the Council of State and Defense Council, and the long-serving chair of the Liberal Democratic block party, Manfred Gerlach, was chosen as acting head of state.) The emergency SED congress listened to an emotional appeal by Modrow—now minister-president—to purify the party and selected Gregor Gysi as their new chairman. SED travails remained evident throughout the recrimination-filled conferences that debated dissolution and party name during the winter of 1989–90. At the December emergency congress, the SED indecisively added the label Party of Democratic Socialism (PDS) to its old name; in late January they flirted with dissolving altogether; and finally on February 24–25, they summoned up resolve enough to drop the old designation entirely and enter the electoral campaign simply as the PDS.[32]

Despite a hopeful beginning and the passage of key measures for democratization, Modrow's position as chief of government quickly deteriorated.

Attractive politician though he might seem, he was caught between incompatible forces. He was not prepared to wager on quick privatization, and his economics minister, Christa Luft, offered no decisive concepts for an economic reform program. To whom, moreover, was he legally responsible: to the Volkskammer, which despite its reviving energies was still composed only of the SED and block parties, or to the Round Table, half of which represented the citizens movements and whose preeminent force, the New Forum, he found tainted with arrogance and opportunism? And what responsibilities did he feel toward the SED, now convulsed by division and recrimination, but which had nominated him and whose members still staffed the ministries?

The most sensitive issue Modrow had to face was the fate of the former Ministry for State Security, the old Stasi, transformed (or just renamed) by mid-December into an Office for National Security and assigned the future role of protecting the constitution. Members of the Round Table pressed to eliminate what they perceived as a conspiratorial redoubt of the old order; SED-PDS members claimed that the authority was required to protect against a rising tide of neo-Nazi provocation and possible violence: the Soviet war memorial in Berlin-Treptow was defaced with graffiti at the turn of the year, alarmist rumors circulated about impending putsch efforts—did not every state need an internal security agency to protect itself against extremists? Modrow vacillated. At the January 8 meeting of the Round Table, the cabinet's unwillingness to promise a definitive dissolution provoked unanimous criticism from the opposition groups, who demanded that Modrow appear within two hours to discuss the issue. Modrow, it turned out, was in Sofia at the final meeting of the Comecon. Faced with the threatened secession of the block parties (CDU and Liberals) from his coalition, Modrow withdrew the proposed Office for the Protection of the Constitution on January 13, and agreed to appear before the Round Table two days later. Despite the belated concession his government emerged badly shaken: on the very day he first went before the Round Table, the New Forum summoned a protest demonstration at the Stasi headquarters on the Normannenstraße. The crowds turned ugly, invaded the barracks-like compound, and sacked some offices. Modrow had to rush down with New Forum and other delegates to appeal for calm. Was there to be a second major upheaval? Was the GDR really governable as an independent state? Would Modrow have any standing when he traveled to meet Kohl in a few weeks time? And what degree of influence did the opposition parties want to assume?[33] "The situation in the GDR is becoming more and more obscure and contradictory," the *Zeit* reported.[34] Faced with the opposition not only of the citizens movements, but of the former block parties, a population still streaming west, a demoralized SED-PDS quickly shedding longtime comrades (including his own Dresden colleague, Mayor Berghofer), Modrow realized that he needed to widen his political base. Only the Round Table support promised some democratic legitimation, and at the session of January 22, he called for the new parties to nominate candidates for a broad-based government of democratic reconstruction.

Modrow's invitation posed political dilemmas. Although SPD leaders proposed that they be summoned to the government, with elections ahead they were wary of having to cooperate with SED-PDS and CDU ministers. As of the first round of negotiations on January 24, no agreement was reached. In the next few days it was the turn of the East German CDU to waver. Lothar de Maizière, serving as deputy minister-president, now seemed the principal obstacle and briefly pulled the CDU members out of the government. Did he object, as he alleged, to Modrow's high-handed style? Was he trying to show his West German CDU patrons (most notably Volker Ruhe, who was demanding the break) that his party was not too cozy with the PDS? Or was he exerting pressure on the SPD to come to terms such that both major parties would have to share responsibility in the run-up to elections? The CDU maneuver, however, antagonized the other block parties and de Maizière retreated. In a weekend flurry of meetings Modrow and the parties approved a reorganized cabinet. Reeling under their defections and their diminished government role, SED-PDS district delegates also convened. They considered dissolving the party but, rallied by the new chair, Gregor Gysi, decided to persevere. Between January 28 and February 5, Modrow succeeded in constructing a "government of national responsibility," including SPD as well as former block party delegates.[35]

Supporters of the Round Table tasted victory. They had ended the continuing SED-PDS domination of office and, they felt, displaced the pseudo-democratic Volkskammer. In fact the upshot suggested that the East German government had little remaining authority whatsoever. Volkskammer elections were moved forward from May 6 to March 18; both SPD and PDS leaders thought that they would fare better, the former because they now seemed to be the logical heir to power, the latter because they were continuing to disintegrate. The closer date confirmed to most onlookers that the old regime did not have vitality enough to limp through a further four months; it also made the stakes of East German politics even more urgent for Modrow and Gorbachev, who at this point shared a common interest in precluding a CDU electoral victory and with it Kohl's domination of the unification agenda. Even while Modrow was constructing his government of national responsibility at the end of January, he flew to Moscow to secure Soviet endorsement for a plan for gradual federation that would strengthen him at home and at the talks scheduled for mid-February in Bonn (see chapter 5). He returned with Gorbachev's nominal blessing, but in doubt about his real degree of commitment. Lingering hopes for prolonging the existence of an autonomous, democratic socialist GDR were likely to give way to unification, economic aid, and the dominant role of the West Germans.[36] Ten days later Modrow's concepts would evoke an even more dismissive reaction from Chancellor Kohl in Bonn.

The full Round Table convened for the fifteenth time on March 5, 1990. I accompanied Michael Schmitz, the television journalist from the ZDF network already identified by the Stasi a year earlier as a provocateur, to attend this next-to-last session. By this date the procedure was quite formalized; the atmosphere of confrontation had dissipated, elections were two weeks away. The proposals under discussion concerned the elaboration of social rights that were the particular concern of the constituencies represented. Above all, in that next-to-last session, participants were concerned with the problem of how to anchor the generous East German provisions for family support and child care into the constitutional order so they might be preserved in the coming negotiations with the Federal Republic. The Independent Women's Union proposed establishing a ministry for the equalization of men and women. The ex-Communist trade union federation and the Greens pressed the government to adopt an extensive social charter, including a constitutionally protected right to employment.

Certainly in retrospect, and probably to many sober observers at the time, the elaboration of social welfare wish lists had a frivolous aspect. Nonetheless, it was useful to incorporate diverse constituencies and their agendas into the process of negotiation. Civil society now posed its demands not on the streets but in the mimeographed legislative proposals passed out during Round Table sessions. One striking aspect about the Round Table process was the fact that it telescoped classical liberal procedures and postmodern social demands. The German Democratic Republic provided advanced welfare and family guarantees while it suppressed free speech and assembly. The Round Table sought to preserve the former and reclaim the latter. New Forum's constitutional draft, which the Round

Table pressed upon the incoming de Maizière cabinet, exemplified this dual thrust. In effect the Round Table bridged two gaps: between SED rule and reunification, and between authoritarian and social democratic legislative orders.

In the winter of 1989–90, round tables proliferated locally and at the national level in the GDR and later Czechoslovakia and Hungary. As institutions they hovered between legality and revolution. For the enfeebled regimes that sanctioned them, they represented a final effort to maintain authority by negotiating directly with delegates who could control the protests. For the movements represented, they provided a revolutionary but legitimate expression of society's autonomous needs. The German representatives, however, emerged out of disparate and fragmented circles of dissent. Only the demonstrations compelled the party to give them a hearing. The Polish Round Table arose out of a long standoff between Solidarity and the regime of General Jaruzelski. Martial law since December 1981 had not been able to reverse the decline of the Polish economy in the mid-1980s or establish the government's legitimacy. Throughout the 1980s some government members understood how isolated they remained. The regime had played a cat-and-mouse game with dissenters, jailing some at times, debating with them at other moments, but to no avail.

Such vacillation between repression and liberalization has often characterized the last stages of authoritarian regimes. Certainly not always: the Third Reich under siege resorted to ever crueler repression rather than contemplate defeat, while Stalin's last years brought preparations for a renewed wave of judicial (and anti-Semitic) terrorism. But these two dictatorships were exceptional; their leaders conceded no slackening. Others have sensed that time was running out. Napoleon III in the late 1860s, Italy's fascist hierarchs from 1940 to 1943, Spain's rulers in the late 1960s and 1970s, and Brazil's military regime in the early 1980s all attempted to prepare a transition. Declining despotisms watch fitfully as their own authoritarian structures become infiltrated with dissidents and experimenters. If no potent ideological myth still motivates an aging cadre of rulers, the usual response is to try gradual concessions. There seems to be no alternative but to negotiate with a hitherto illegal opposition. These situations are fluid and precarious, hostage both to impatient opposition forces and contemptuous government hard-liners. Violence remains a potential recourse, and both sides seek to define the terms of the contest in terms of ideology and their diagnosis of the crisis.

In Poland both sides acknowledged an economic crisis by 1986–87. The government went so far as to frame, and thus endeavor to control, its own dialogue with the opposition in the journal *Konfrontacje*. In a published *Konfrontacje* interview in late 1987, Solidarność spokesman Bronisław Geremek suggested that in view of the difficulties that both sides recognized, Solidarity might negotiate with the regime on behalf of the public. This was an implicitly dualist notion: Solidarity—legitimated by its heroic leadership of the working-class movement in 1980–81—would represent the components of society; the state still could claim political hegemony; together they would work out an anticrisis pact. Following renewed strikes in May and August 1988, the government saw little choice and General Kiszczak, the minister of the interior, proposed what became the Round Table negotiations, accepted by Lech Wałesa on August 31. They would lead not merely to economic measures but a provisional constitutional settlement. A proportionally elected upper house would coexist with a lower house in which the party was guaranteed 65 percent of the seats. The momentum of democratization and continuing economic tribulations revealed this compromise to be untenable during the next year, and Poland finally adopted a freely elected parliament alongside a president with strong but rather ill-defined powers.[37]

The East German recourse to a round table borrowed from the Warsaw precedent. To be sure, no preexisting movement in the GDR could claim the established role that Solidarity had earned during the 1980s. Members of the New Forum (and two months later "Civic Forum" in Prague) acquired their authority only as the protests and emigration gathered momentum. In fact they had their advocacy role virtually thrust upon them. "Anyone who claims to be from the New Forum has listeners." "The people are calling for New Forum."[38] Solidarity's leadership had undergone a long apprenticeship including prison; Geremek and Adam Michnik and Jacek Kuron had all done their time in jail and they had spent many years developing sophisticated arguments about the relationship of society and regime. East German dissenters had not worked out elaborate analyses of authoritarianism or social claims. Nevertheless, some had also served prison sentences. As in Poland (and Czechoslovakia), these earlier incarcerations bestowed on them representative legitimacy. At the same time the round tables forced their jailers to confirm that their old adversaries had been courageous and their demands justified. This was a sacramental function that subsequent parliaments could no longer fulfill.

While earlier persecution provided legitimacy, it also taught prudence. Just as Solidarity was prepared to bargain in 1988 on the basis of a social pact, New Forum settled for dialogue. The leaders of Solidarity in 1987–88 and the leaders of New Forum in 1989 understood that their respective adversaries still controlled decisive police power. Even if economic logic argued for compromise, the cornered Communists might choose to strike out in anger or desperation. The dissenters realized further that the regimes they confronted were divided between conciliators and hard-liners; there was no guarantee that the forces of compromise could prevail. Such considerations helped to channel popular mobilization into a provisional dualist settlement, an armistice between protesters and state, for which the round tables provided the transitional format. This was the aspect of the upheaval that Czechs and Poles called self-limiting.[39] This self-limitation would also influence the subsequent treatment of former party officials when the issue of retroactive sanctions and purges arose in 1991–92.

Erich Honecker did not seem initially inclined to make the compromises that General Jaruzelski reluctantly accepted and the Czech leader Milos Jakeš would swallow when the wave of upheaval swept over Prague at the end of the year. Jaruzelski was keenly aware of the Soviet factor, or lack thereof, in the force he might invoke. He claimed to have acted to forestall a Soviet invasion in 1981, but he understood equally well that Gorbachev was not about to back him up in any confrontation in 1988. The moderates in the Warsaw government also realized that bayonets and tanks did not assure production, and Poland was in heavy debt to Western banks. If Solidarity and the Catholic Church provided powerful reservoirs of social power within Poland's borders, the dependence on foreign creditors, private banks and governments, exposed the government to an important source of pressure from without. What the East Europeans were to term "civil society" emerged, in the case of Poland, as a transnational as well as domestic force. In the case of East Germany, once the frontier was open, the cross-border pressure of wages replaced the cross-border pressure of investment. East German labor had become almost as mobile as Western capital, and its accelerating flight proved a decisive force for compromise.

The round tables served only a brief period, but they played a special role in at least three respects. They provided an institutional bridge from the Communist claim to incorporate all legitimate social forces to the opposition's claim that authentic civil society existed only outside the party. They further provided a surrogate for the constituent assemblies that the transition process never convoked in full solemnity, and which certainly were to be lacking in the case of an East Germany that would ultimately just join the Federal Republic as a congeries of separate provinces. They retained a mystique of consent that the subsequent parliaments would no longer benefit from. Finally the round tables set limits on the political purges and anathemas that might subsequently take place. Despite the many old scores to settle, the process of negotiating within an institutionalized arena required each side to accept the other as an interlocutor, not as an unconditional adversary or outlaw. Wolfgang Ullmann sought to capture the historical uniqueness of the institution a few months after it had finished its work: the perspective of the Round Table, he noted for a public speech, would not simply disappear. It differed from the "linear" arrangement of left-center-right parties in the usual parliaments. Rather it forced participants to orient themselves on an invisible center, "which [is] not to be reached by force or competition, but only in a common discourse and common resolution for a realizable future. The Round Table teaches us this circular perspective. It does so through its enduring pressure for consensus, through discussion freed from ideology, and through the continual obligation to demonstrate its capacity for decision."[40] Ullmann's confidence that the Round Table could become an enduring institution for posttransformative politics was misplaced. Nonetheless, political philosophers will revisit the round tables in years to come as a unique moment of renewing a social contract.

REDEEMING "CIVIL SOCIETY"

In any standoff between an authoritarian regime and its adversaries, both sides claim legitimacy, that is, the moral right to represent the civic public. In Poland the Jaruzelski government had endeavored to pose as national saviors above party, evoking memories of Piłsudski. The old East German leadership took it for granted that the Socialist Unity Party had a historical legitimacy because it represented the most historically advanced social classes. During the 1980s, moreover, they became bolder about claiming German national and even Prussian traditions. But for whom did the protesters speak? East Germans addressed the issue largely in passing: they signaled the new importance of "groups" within the church; they protested the deformation of "society"; they spoke on behalf of the environment and "human rights," for the cause of "peace," for the "citizens movement." They found it difficult to define the appropriate alternative collective subject; even the "Church in Socialism" had concluded its uneasy armistice with the regime. Finally, by the time of the mass protests in fall 1989, the slogan "We are the people" suggested a national uprising.

It is crucial to underline the communitarian dimension of the protests that brought down communism. Collective participation merged with individual rights in the ideology of liberation. The Helsinki accords and the Carter administration's later pressure for human rights emphasized individual liberties; so too did the protests of such courageous Soviet dissidents as Andrei Sakharov. But as the seventies progressed the role of the movement became more prominent. It required individual decisions, as Vaclav Havel put it, to "live in truth"—to refuse to submit to the state's claims that it acted on behalf of society by declining to go along with even the most innocuous professions of faith. But living in truth soon became a "citizen's initiative" and collective demonstration. Society counted as an independent force. It could and must act through what Adam Michnik would call its "self-organization." When it did so, it emerged as civil society.[41]

In its oppositional sense, the term apparently first appeared in the writings of Jaček Kuron as the Workers' Defense Committee (KOR) emerged in 1976. The Slavic word translated into English as "civil" (as distinguished from its German counterpart) meant "social" in the broad sense; it did not overlap with "bourgeois" as did the German *bürgerliche Gesellschaft* from which the concept had originally descended. In the context of the Eastern European and East German upheavals, "civil society" referred specifically to the reenergized networks of protesters or political and religious constituencies. Ideals of participatory democracy from the late 1960s still infused these circles. Their advocates in the 1970s and early 1980s sometimes criticized Western parliamentarism as bureaucratic or mechanistic: "It would appear that the traditional parliamentary democracies can offer no fundamental opposition to the automatism of technological civilization and the industrial-consumer society," Havel argued a decade before he helped Czechoslovakia return to parliamentary democracy.[42]

Religious communion remained a significant impulse, even for secular dissenters. Not suprisingly Protestant and Catholic traditions (and differences within national Catholic churches) produced diverse emphases. East German writers had absorbed the sociology of alienation and *Angst*; they emphasized "groups" as a response to marginalization and fragmentation, and suggested they might well be "critical of ideology, querulous [*protestlerisch*], and unfriendly to every institution."[43] The church as an institution needed groups to unsettle it.[44] They could teach members how to cope with discord even as they nurtured authentic communication in an urban society that produced "depression through anonymity and the devitalization of relationships."[45] The Czechs were less preoccupied by loneliness, more tuned to the promise of Vatican II. "Are not these informal, nonbureaucratic, dynamic and open communities that comprise the 'parallel *polis*,'" Havel asked, "a kind of rudimentary prefiguration, a symbolic model of those more meaningful 'postdemocratic' political structures that might become the foundation of a better society?"[46] He confessed his debt to his younger comilitant, the Czech Catholic philosopher Vaclav Benda, who called for the mobilization of "parallel structures," as if for every controlled organization set up by the Communist Party, an authentic counterpart had to be established in latent opposition.[47] Through the 1970s, Czech "Chartism" revealed the influence of conciliar Catholicism and 1960s socialism.

By the mid-1980s, the idea of civil society came with fewer religious overtones but even more expansive political claims. Intellectuals applied it to all the pulsing underground forces claiming autonomy from state and party. They certainly referred to more than just the teams and associations that were compatible with what Gaus strikingly described as the niche society. Garden or cycling clubs would not suffice even if they had retained their independence—which was doubtful since the party strove to control associational space.[48] Civil society bridged what liberals tended to separate as public (or political) and private spheres. Private networks—that is, associational ties that the state had not sanctioned—formed the matrix or humus for the political effort. But as components of civil society these associations no longer spoke just for what benefited their own restricted objectives. They were implicitly constitutive; they claimed a voice over citizenship, legislation, and political authority. The idea of civil society thus implied that there existed a potential national public opinion. It played a role akin to what "the rights of man" had played in the late eighteenth century, but now for an era when social movements had become the agents of political transformation.

It was not self-evident that "civil society" should emerge to claim so catalytic a role. Earlier uses did not always imply such a progressive idea. In medieval thought civil society had simply meant the state and government, that is, the sphere of politics. British political writers later focused the notion to describe a regime in which king and parliament coexisted. Parliament after all represented the nation's underlying interests and estates: the episcopacy and peerage, landlords, trading monopolies, and ancient towns. From the late seventeenth century British Whigs emphasized the capacities of society's interests to organize markets and governance; the state merely

provided the common defense and a legal framework for enterprise.[49] Civil
society was a historical acquisition according to the Scottish philosophers
Adam Ferguson, John Millar, David Hume, and Adam Smith. It developed
as commerce, culture, and urban society replaced a harsher rural feudalism.

For Hegel, who wove the Scottish ideas into the fabric of German ideal-
ism, civil society mediated between the family and the state. Natural kinship
formed the underlying layer of community that composed the private realm.
Businesses and corporations, gilds, cultural associations, and universities
comprised the fabric of civil society, while the state bureaucracy, freed from
economic interest, discerned and acted upon a more universal public good.
The cohesive forces binding together civil society included interest and a
sort of self-interested ethics; the state called upon law, constraint, and a
higher patriotic morality. For Hegel, as for Adam Smith (and even John
Locke), civil society involved an extraordinary proliferation of interests, associations, and common endeavors. It comprised more than just economic
enterprises and market rationality; civil society was also the domain of public discussion and journalism, cultural activity, universities, civil law, and
concerted philanthropy. It had really come into its own with Protestantism
and mass literacy and the Enlightenment. Still, the German philosopher did
not believe that civil society alone could secure the lofty and encompassing
public rationality that the state provided.[50] People acting in civil society
operated from the restricted motives of self-interest or utilitarian morality.
The state was needed to guarantee a higher degree of ethical and public-
spirited behavior. The bureaucratic state would culminate the dialectical
self-construction of the legal order.

Marx took over Hegel's analysis of a restless, ever more inclusive and
rational unfolding of social relationships, although he focused on relations
of production and exchange as the motive force. He construed *bürgerliche
Gesellschaft* as a nakedly bourgeois society rather than a universal civic
society: corrosively liberal and meritocratic, destructive of feudal privilege,
subject to rules of market rationality in which the devil took the hind-
most—but not to the higher rationality and humane outcomes socialism
would provide. Whereas Hegel had assigned the bureaucratic monarchy
the task of elevating civil society, Marx explained that the proletariat must
serve as the agent to overcome bourgeois society. For his twentieth-century
disciples, Lenin most eminently, the Communist Party would fulfill the
collective mission of the proletariat. It would interpret and transform the
stages of history, demand individual sacrifice when necessary, hammer and
forge civil society on the anvil of proletarian dictatorship. Dismayed by

Leninism, the European left in the 1960s warmed to the theoretical contributions of the Italian Communist leader Antonio Gramsci, who, imprisoned by the Fascists for a decade before his death in 1936, wrestled explicitly with the nature of civil society and the role of intellectuals in rooting it in national culture. Nonetheless, if Gramsci refocused the left's attention on civil society, as a would-be revolutionary he remained uneasy about its role. Certainly he pointed out that in a Catholic country like Italy—and here was a relevant parallel for the Poles—civil society comprised not just economic but cultural forces. It included the role of traditional intellectuals, the church and its clergy, and legal culture. In a country like Italy, where a democratic revolution had failed to take place and the Fascists might build upon retrograde survivals of the old regime, above all in the south, civil society was regressive. It provided, so Gramsci proposed in a striking metaphor, a fortified glacis that allowed the hegemonic classes to resist the forces of reform.[51]

It was probably because Communist ideology so stressed overcoming, dominating, and remolding civil society that the Polish opposition of the mid-1970s returned to its virtues. Like some knotty oak, civil society resisted the totalitarian project. Ideas are retrieved selectively and often out of context. Intellectuals in the West turned to Gramsci in the 1960s for his emphasis on culture and intellectuals, his rejection of mechanistic laws of development, and the pathos of his personal situation. He was remembered as a victim of totalitarianism, not as a potential abettor. Interpreters tended to divest his concept of civil society of its reactionary potential and celebrated its value as a resource for resistance. "Civil Society," moreover, promised a shelter from state or party oppression that "society" as a concept did not. In Communist Poland, Michnik, Kuron, and Geremek might plausibly appeal to "society" because the church and the working-class movement persisted independent of the regime. In most Communist milieus, however, the idea of society had become hopelessly tainted by the regime. In fact, the term society has generally had an ambiguous career since the Enlightenment. As often as not it served pseudoemancipatory ends, evoking a heavy collective presence to limit individual rights. Revolutionaries invoked society to justify repression in the name of the future. Reactionaries appealed to society to silence critics of the injustices left from the past. These repressive overtones had also to be overcome. "Civil society" avoided their portentous hypocrisy. Indeed, it helped to rally precisely those who were claiming the rights of the present against the oppressive loyalties demanded on behalf of past and future.

The champions of civil society in Poland and Czechoslovakia claimed to be revolutionary and self-limiting at the same time.[52] But what was to be limited? Violence, as in the case of Havel's notion of a "velvet revolution"? Or the claim on governance? Solidarity leaders, for instance, disagreed on how much power they sought as the authority of the Polish regime dissipated in the mid and late 1980s. Recalling the 1968 Czech suppression and the 1981 imposition of martial law, Adam Michnik argued that the reformers must accept continued Polish membership in the Warsaw Pact as a limit on their aspirations. Interviewed in *Konfrontacje* in late 1987, Geremek seemed prepared to settle for a negotiated equilibrium between the party's political leadership and freely organized social forces to be led by Solidarity.[53] Another Solidarity leader, Aleksander Hall, rejected Geremek's dualist architecture and argued that Solidarity must claim decisive political power. To be sure, Solidarity's leadership might be contested by other nonparty groups; young workers who had come of age after martial law felt they had moved beyond the union and its intellectuals. Hall's general claim still held: representatives of civil society could not durably concede the state a domain of reserved power.[54]

The Polish debate echoed West European controversies in the eighteenth and nineteenth centuries. Liberals then insisted that the representation of socioeconomic interests was a crucial political task and that legislatures were the appropriate agents. Conservatives maintained that monarchs and their civil servants were better able to reconcile and integrate contending social claims. Within their brief apprenticeships, the civic movements and round tables had to relearn and reclaim the legislative vocation originally staked out by classical liberal theory. East European intellectuals had to renew arguments eloquently worked out by Montesquieu, Madison and Mill, Constant and Tocqueville. Measured in terms of formal theory, they were often going back over old ground.

But the older writers and statesmen never had to confront totalitarian claims or institutions. They understood "despotism" from histories of antiquity, stylized notions of Eastern empires, or the brief Jacobin experiments. In the case of Tocqueville the Second Empire provided a model, but one that was relatively benevolent compared with the Communist regimes. In contrast, the activists of the 1980s had grown up in an enduring milieu of repression. Where their analyses excelled was in diagnosing the systemic distortion of truth that privilege and favoritism, as well as fear and coercion produced. To borrow from American slang, the East Europeans described their rulers and jailers in terms of a refined "good cop–bad cop" routine rather than in terms of unremitting despotism. And they stressed how insidiously and easily complicit participation was extracted. There was always the temptation to assure the police that oneself or one's friends were not actively disloyal. Whether Havel or Jens Reich, or earlier Leszek Kolakowski and Czesław Miłosz, exiles and dissenters communicated the corrupting nature of their dictatorships.

As they outlined institutional reform, the East European reformers did enjoy one advantage in a posttotalitarian (Havel's term) or, more precisely, a post-Stalinist environment that earlier liberal theorists lacked. Post-Stalinist regimes inherited most of the interests that authoritarian governments had bundled together in subservient organizations: labor unions, peasant associations, intellectuals and writers, women, sportsmen. Communist governments had never really sought to destroy these groups; they used them precisely to keep control of society. In the post-Stalinist moment, civil society existed "in itself," if not yet "for itself."

On the other hand, post-Stalinist dissidents suffered from a grave disadvantage as compared with their earlier liberal ancestors. Communist society had suppressed markets. Markets provided a framework for association; they taught organizational skills and the calculation of costs and benefits. Intellectuals in the West had earlier felt that too great a role for markets might undermine civic spirit. From Adam Ferguson in the eighteenth century to Charles Lindblom in the 1970s many asked whether the economic interests of civil society might not encroach upon the public domain and impose a sort of private tyranny. Tocqueville, however, had suggested that the problem was misconceived; without private associations men would never learn how to associate for public ends and vice versa.[55] By the 1980s intellectuals West and East tended to agree.

Certainly without markets the economic basis for civil society was far more precarious. In all the transitions to democracy during the past two decades, a crucial issue has been what societal interests and emerging groups might become the strategic claimants for civil society. Entrepreneurs, labor unions, intellectuals and churchmen, enlightened minorities within the ruling bureaucracy, foreign investors? In the transition from authoritarianism in Spain, the role of foreign investment and economic development was crucial. It sanctioned a more technocratic political style from the late 1950s on, allowed the infiltration of independent syndicalism within the official labor movement, and encouraged the cautious search for independence on the part of intellectuals. In effect, economic development had allowed liberalism to metastasize underneath the country's au-

thoritarian carapace. But market forces had been eradicated or weakened
in Eastern Europe. Even where a union preserved its strength and was not
just a phoney front organization, such as in Poland, markets were underdeveloped. (Strong unions and underdeveloped markets tended to produce
strong corporatist and correspondingly weaker parliamentary settlements.)[56] In Eastern Europe churches and cultural forums had to provide
the networks for a reemerging civil society. Were they robust enough for
this purpose? On the one hand, journalists and intellectuals had always
formed the nuclei of dissent and liberalism in the nineteenth century. Pietist
ministers, university professors, had organized against the claims of absolute monarchs and had sought to infuse the German estates with parliamentary capacities. On the other hand, they had been weak and isolated in
their efforts.

East Europeans had to wager that civil society could first win its political
rights and then create its own market infrastructure. In contrast to the
reformers of the 1960s, they now accepted that this would require privatization and not just freeing up prices. The literary intellectuals of Eastern
Europe lands were not particularly enamored of materialism. But they understood that communism had meant perpetual privation and they believed
that citizens should enjoy the rights of enterprise, pluck, and labor. A market economy, they were persuaded, in good part by enthusiastic Western
advisers now flocking to their capitals, provided the most robust support for
a vibrant civil society.

East Germans remained the most reluctant converts to the civic mission
of capitalism. Geremek, the most refined emissary of the Polish transition
and author of a history in French of the dispossessed of fourteenth-century
Paris, could courteously second the American multimillionaire who boasted
to a distinguished East-West audience about the attainments of capitalism.
The writer-president Havel was willing to stick with the rigors that his self-
assured monetarist finance minister and then premier, Vaclav Klaus, imposed on his country. But East German intellectuals remained reticent. In
the winter of 1989–90, many still supported Minister-President Modrow
and the new economics minister Christa Luft, who hoped to stabilize a market-oriented mixed economy based on the *Kombinate*. Their support for a
"third way" between socialism and capitalism reflected their national pre-
dicament as much as their economic preference. By the winter of 1990 the
mood of nostalgia for a vanishing East Germany suffused many of the citizens movements. They hoped to preserve the cozy autonomy of their familiar republic and to resist the pressures for merger with an overwhelmingly

more populous and wealthy West Germany. Some clear-eyed intellectuals such as Jens Reich or the plain-speaking Helga Schubert understood that civic aspirations might be satisfied in a reunited national state. But more often the lament, so often expressed during conversations I had with activists of 1989, was that the West Germans would not allow the East Germans to retain even a little bit of their former "national" identity.

In this respect the East Germans' malaise prefigured the more encompassing issue of nationalist revival in the disintegrating Communist bloc.[57] Could democratic transformation and nationalism remain in harmony? *Bürgerbewegung* activists had watched the surge of German national feeling with unease; they regretted the transition from *Wir sind das Volk* to *Wir sind ein Volk*. Christa Wolf told Hans Modrow that the flag-waving masses were not her people. West German liberals and conservatives contested this view. So did many of the new SPD and CDU members in the East, who resolutely accepted that unification was a long-held aspiration, which must advance democratic self-determination. But the possible tension between democratic reform and national emergence threatened to isolate the intellectuals. The electoral returns of March 18 would reveal that New Forum (to campaign as a component of Bündnis 90) had no vocation as a mass political party. Solidarność might function effectively for a longer period, but by 1991 it would fragment into more populist and more parliamentary-oriented factions. For at least a brief period, it appeared that Jews—no matter how depleted their numbers in the populations of Eastern Europe—might again serve national populists in Hungary, Poland, and elsewhere as a symbol of destructive cosmopolitanism. Was it not the Catholic masses with their healthy religious and national instincts or the Gdansk shipyard workers who had triumphed over the martial law regime, rather than the intellectuals?[58] In Czechoslovakia representatives of neither national group were prepared to bridge the opposition between the Catholic and ex-Communist Slovaks, convinced of their victimization, and the agile Czechs, wedded to market modernization and intellectual leadership.

In part the appeal of populist nationalism was a reaction to the moral stance of the earlier dissidents. The mass of their compatriots, after all, did not incur jail sentences or stage dangerous protests or sign defiant petitions. Charter 77 intellectuals in Czechoslovakia, like the early organizers of the "Initiative for Human Rights" in the GDR, had been a tiny minority. Those who stayed on the sidelines do not like to be reminded of their passivity; it is easy to resent the presumed moral superiority of those who led the struggle.[59] The same phenomenon emerged after 1945, when French, Italian, and

Belgian voters rebuffed Resistance party organizations in early postwar elections. The name of the Italian movement that mobilized electoral resentment against Resistance moralism during 1946 is evocative: Uomo Qualunque, or Everyman. *Qualunquismo* combined neofascist nostalgia, backwater conservatism, and the manipulation of resentment. Its adherents were fed up with what they heard as the Resistance's claim to moral superiority. *Qualunquismo* lurked in East Central Europe after 1989 as national populism and anti-intellectualism, and, from time to time, anti-Semitism.[60]

So too in Germany the far smaller Resistance circles that had survived Hitler's ferocious reprisals after July 20, 1944, had to confront two decades of public uneasiness. None of the parties except the Communists made anti-Nazi Resistance the basis of its postwar appeals. Even the Communists downplayed the comrades left underground or in concentration camps within Hitler's Germany lest they rival the Moscow-based cadres that established the GDR. And in West Germany, just three years before the 1989 upheaval, the so-called historians' controversy or *Historikerstreit* tapped some of the same resentments that appeared in Eastern Europe after 1989. Was it not time, asked West German conservatives, including some major historians, to cease harping on Nazi crimes?[61] Pressure to reinstate German patriotism as an acceptable political loyalty existed in both German Republics before the uprising of 1989.

Even when it does not overtly permeate post-1989 politics, the supposed division between intellectuals on the one side and the groups who seized the public squares on the other (not even to speak of the mass of bystanders) is waged as a contest over historical interpretation. Did the strikers "lead" the intellectuals in Poland? Or did KOR elevate a movement that aimed at higher wages into a political struggle? Was New Forum an ineffectual protest movement ultimately to be rejected by the masses who brought the regime to its knees in 1989? Or did New Forum leadership transform a crowd that aspired to travel rights into one that might remake an oppressive regime? Ultimately, if the concept of civil society is to have any lasting resonance—if it is to outlive the discourse of 1989—it must serve precisely to bridge these polarized interpretations. Only the demands of contemporary party politics require insisting on a one-sided story. History can record that political intellectuals and trade unionists or even adolescent protesters needed each other's contribution—ideas and political mass—to topple the Communist regimes. The concept of civil society renders credit to the combined impact of all collective actors. This is its potential historiographical as well as its political contribution. It would be sad if either contribution turned out to be ephemeral. Nonetheless, by the mid 1990s, the moment of "civil society" had passed. Organized parties, including the parties organized by former Communists that seemed increasingly popular in Eastern Europe, had recaptured the political arena from civic movements. Civil society in the sense of interest groups and associations remained important and happily liberated from the heavy hand of an authoritarian state, though subject to all the factionalism and contentiousness social groups always are. But they were no longer envisioned as directly constitutive of a democratic politics. Political parties had reclaimed the function of representation. For all its appeal, the concept of civil society had remained somewhat vague and totemic; it was not surprising that its political force dissipated so quickly.

POLITICAL PARTIES AND THE ELECTIONS OF MARCH 18, 1990

The fall of the Communist regimes constituted a magical or "liminal" moment in which public rallies, round tables, and the emotional rehabilitation of earlier victims initiated the revival of democratic participation.[62] As in many revolutionary moments, politics became liturgical. Where prior heroes had paid a heavy price, it was advantageous to claim their legacy, whether that of Gdansk Shipyard workers or the martyred Imre Nagy. After the French elections of 1981, the new Socialist government reburied the Resistance leader Jean Moulin in the Pantheon, much as the Popular Front had reburied the Socialist Jean Jaures, assassinated in July 1914. The East Germans had no repertory they might draw upon: June 17, 1953, had not left a clear pantheon. But the early acts of reform had to involve ritual and real rehabilitation. In October 1989, Walter Janka told a theater audience of his ordeal in 1957; at the Academy of Sciences in November, Ernst Bloch and Robert Havemann were posthumously restored to membership.

Still, liturgical politics was bound to be brief. No matter how precious the rituals of participation, there comes a moment of postrevolutionary melancholy in which structures and partisan division assert themselves once again.[63] There was more postrevolutionary melancholy in Germany than elsewhere. The reason was the quick conversion of the radical movement into a movement for unification. By late November and December, the Monday demonstrations in Leipzig were attracting more national slogans and occasional skinheads. The new motto "We are one people" did not, of course, signal any moral decline or coarsening of aspirations. Reunification was a venerable goal even if an entire generation had tacitly abandoned it as unfeasible. West Germany was a robust democracy; it was not asked to suspend constitutional government for the sake of unity as Bismarck had demanded in the 1860s. Rather national consciousness seemed in 1989 to be a renewed manifestation of democratic will in Eastern Europe, where, as in 1918, it went hand in hand with the progress of self-determination. A wave of spontaneous fraternity followed the breach of the Wall. "What belongs together will grow together," as Willy Brandt expressed it on November 10. The longing for national unity should not in its own right have undercut the new groups speaking for civil society.

Nonetheless, the intrusion of the national agenda did deal a major blow. As the East German writer Rolf Schneider argued in *Der Spiegel* in late November, "It's striking that all talk about the state unity of the Germans is currently an exercise exclusively on the part of West German conservatives. The Left, SPD, and Greens have fallen so in love with the status quo that they have been totally overwhelmed by events and are standing there now with open mouths, empty hands, and empty brains. . . . The East German opposition has only one taboo left: German unity." Unfortunately for the intelligentsia, Schneider recognized, the GDR working class, underrepresented in the civic movement, was voting with its feet. "Their *volonté générale* is all-German."[64]

It was Chancellor Kohl's merit to understand this reality, and he exploited the opportunity with unexpected alacrity. While the SPD wavered and foreign commentators envisaged a long step-by-step process of working gradually toward confederal union at best, Kohl quickly worked out a rapid ten-point program. He seized the high ground on the national unification issue; and his policies from December 1989 through October 1990 rightfully earned him a profile as statesman that prior tactical skill had not bestowed. The chancellor acted decisively both because he recognized a national historic moment and because it was good politics. Had the SPD rushed to embrace the East German developments with the fervor of Willy Brandt, it might have posed alongside the chancellor as a joint patron. Indeed, unification might possibly have been undertaken by a Great Coalition in West Germany as a special national duty during which party politics was temporarily suspended. Of course, it was preferable from the perspective of partisan advantage for the CDU not to have to share the limelight; and the SPD obliged by hanging back on the issue, grumbling about financial costs (in this respect it was more accurate than Kohl, who woefully underestimated). Its leader Oskar Lafontaine, intelligent but arrogant, demonstrated no enthusiasm. A political party retreats from participation in a great national test and transformation at its peril. The SPD was left in disarray, for the elections of 1990 and 1994. Perhaps unfairly in light of CDU collaboration, the Social Democrats had to justify their earlier negotiations with the East German ruling party to enlarge the scope for dissent and travel rights within the GDR. SPD and SED delegations had issued a joint position paper in summer 1987; it adumbrated more open cultural contacts but also confirmed that the rival ideological systems must not contest each other's underlying security and values.[65] As their SED interlocutors lost control, the Social Democratic policy tended to appear as a collaboration that had only legitimated the East German Communists' grip on its society.

No matter how one judged SPD policy, the fact that the chancellor put unification on the table while the GDR regime was in disarray meant that any upcoming elections must test the unification question. No matter how agilely it might reform, the East German government now faced the menace of rapid liquidation. Modrow hoped to sell Kohl his plan for a Treaty Community that would secure West German aid, but preserve at least transitional East German autonomy. But the chancellor (as explained in chapter 5) was rapidly moving to a more exigent stance.

Modrow was in many ways the most attractive creation of the forty-year long regime, not one of its founding ideologists or Third Reich exiles, but a bright working-class youth nurtured for his talent, rising as a provincial abbot might have made his way in eighteenth-century Austria or Bavaria. Born in 1928, he had trained as a mechanic, served briefly at the end of the war in an anti-aircraft battery, then been held as a prisoner of war by the Soviets for over four years, returning to a new GDR. As a promising young SED leader he spent 1953 in Moscow; he embodied that long institution-building generation for whom, as Lutz Niethammer points out, the GDR was a means to social mobility and advance. He also represented Dresden, and it was essential in 1989, if the party were to survive, to step beyond the hunkered down bureaucrats of Wandlitz.[66] But Modrow embarked with perhaps excessive caution. He wished to bring the old block parties with him, preserve the state, secure Western aid, and prevent a total collapse of the SED. His early economic statements urged an opening of the system to private entrepreneurs and foreign investment; he recognized the need to end the pervasive subsidies, but was cautious about promising any dramatic end of socialism.[67] West German economic experts said they expected more.

In any case, how viable was any SED leader in the winter of 1989–90? Kohl's initiative quickly found an echo, if not among the intellectuals, then at least the ordinary folk of the GDR. The proposals also bled the Modrow government of its remaining partial authority; the locus of decision would be in Bonn, Moscow, and Washington. As noted above, Modrow had to advance the polling date rather than spin out the somewhat unreal interim stage of superficial autonomy. New Forum and the citizens movements objected, but the new East German SPD, organized as an explicit political alternative for the contests ahead, supported the acceleration. Impending elections gave rival East Germans an incentive to transplant the West German party alternatives into the GDR or to refurbish the East German analogues they already possessed. Small and hitherto compliant block parties had existed in the GDR to serve the fiction of party pluralism since 1949. An East German CDU existed; the FDP found its Liberal Democratic counterpart in the East (the LDPD). Now even these block parties began to show signs of new vigor, housecleaning, and autonomy. The possibility of unification put a premium on preparing for realignment with the corresponding West German party organizations.

Nonetheless, the citizens movements, New Forum in the lead, might still have contested the emerging political space. The movement enjoyed great respect. The fact was that in the critical months after November 1989, New Forum leaders felt ambivalent about what was emerging. Bärbel Bohley, cofounder of New Forum, had labeled the opening of the Wall a misfortune, because it had skewed the incentives for reform; she feared that free elections would be scheduled before the East German electorate was civically educated. Her New Forum colleagues persuaded her not to go public with this assessment; it took two days for the leaders, Reich, Pflugbeil, Bohley, Schult, and Eberhard and Jutta Seidel to resolve on a joint statement: "We have waited almost thirty years for this day. Sick of the Wall, we rattled the bars of our cage. Youth grew up with the dream one day to be free and experience the world. This dream is now fulfillable. This a festival day for all of us." Nonetheless, New Forum still revealed a tinge of apprehension and suspicion. The new East Germany might succumb to a crass managerialist capitalism or consumerism: "Don't be diverted from demanding a political reconstruction of society. . . . Be aware of who will benefit from the now entering enterprises and businesses and how high the social costs are to be. . . . We will be poor for a long time, but we don't want to have a society in which profiteers and sharpies elbow ahead."[68] The elbowers and the elbow society, as obviously incorporated in the Federal Republic, quickly emerged as the shadow side of the democratic future for GDR reformers.

Friedrich Schorlemmer, the Wittenberg pastor now active in Democratic Awakening, claimed not to care about power and suggested that what remained of the Wall should "exist a bit longer."[69] Free elections, demanded one of the spokeswomen for New Forum in Leipzig, but not too soon.[70] As the New Forum delegate from Magdeburg said, "No one calculated that it would go so quickly. We envisaged discussion of a new electoral law, local elections in the summer or fall of 1990, and new GDR parliamentary elections only in 1991. For now the citizens committees should remain dominant." The New Forum was divided and disconcerted: "Yes, at the moment there is tension over what we really want. Takeover of political responsibilty say some. Others want to continue as sort of an extraparliamentary opposition. Still others are opting for a party."[71] By mid-February three New Forum district leaders from the south of the GDR even proposed that the movement disavow Bohley as an official spokesperson; following Reinhard Schult's earlier protest, she withdrew as chair of the citizens movement she had been instrumental in founding half a year earlier.[72]

The prospect of political party competition and a crass capitalist takeover obviously disconcerted New Forum. Its delegates continued to propose important reforms within the Round Table, including by March 1990 a full-blown constitutional draft. New Forum's constitution, adapted by the constitutional working group of the Round Table, included a long catalog of human rights, both individual and collective minority guarantees for women, the aged, the handicapped, homosexuals.[73] Increasingly, however, a tinge of utopianism hovered about their discussions. It had also characterized the November 28 appeal "For Our Land," drafted by Stefan Heym, Christa Wolf, and the other intellectuals who urged saving the achievements of socialism and the separate existence of the GDR.

What in fact was worth saving? Relative East German affluence, which had been a source of pride for many, was an artifact of the second-rate performance of the centrally planned economies. In any case, the frame of reference was changing rapidly. The economic situation appeared increasingly disconsolate, while next door the larger German republic promised abundance and a vigorous economic future. Any retention of independence or "third way" socialism meant living with relative poverty. As Heym recognized, however, if East Germany was not to remain socialist, why should it survive at all? "Let's talk about unity. The fact is that two capitalist German states are unnecessary. The raison d'être of the German Democratic Republic is to offer socialism, whatever form it takes, as an alternative to the freebooter state with the harmless name of Federal Republic. There's no other reason for the existence of a separate East German state."[74]

If in the first month after the breaching of the Wall, the citizens movement felt that Modrow might still rescue a reformed social-democratic state, prospects seemed bleaker by midwinter. New Forum delegates responded to the changing moods, albeit reluctantly. On the weekend of January 27–28, the group met in East Berlin to revise its program draft, dropping the original call for two German states and an alternative to capitalism. Insisting it wished to remain a citizens movement, the group nonetheless constituted itself as a political association. The assembly was divided over unification. The final effort to bridge the differences argued that German unity should be achieved as part of the dynamic toward a broader European unification. The original draft, which warned that the dictatorship of planning might be replaced only by dictatorship of the market, was replaced by an appeal to the social market economy; a call for councils was finally vetoed.[75]

Renewal of the Volkskammer confronted New Forum and Democratic Breakthrough with the unwelcome necessity of behaving like political parties, having to seek support no longer in a great movement on the streets against a repressive regime, but in an open competition. Conversely it gave the former block parties—and perhaps even the PDS—a chance to regroup in electoral competition. Such an open rivalry was obviously novel, but nonetheless certainly preferable for their future to the waves of movement politics that had presented them merely as time servers. Even the SED was determined to cut as good a figure as possible. Egon Krenz had not lasted long as head of government. He was not trusted; his huge toothy smile could not erase the fact that he had been an up-and-coming functionary, the boy-scout leader in effect of the old regime. Immediately after the opening of the Wall, popular anger mobilized against what seemed the two most abusive fiefs of the party: its privileged residential enclave in Wandlitz and the role of the Stasi. The Stasi continued to grow as a major issue because it involved the whole question of how a former dictatorship would deal with its past, and as such will be considered in chapter 6. The ramifications of Wandlitz were also important but did not cast so long a shadow.

Wandlitz was hardly big-time corruption by any Western standard, much less in comparison with some of the personal enrichment of dictators elsewhere. But it typified the accretion of privileges to the party elite, while ordinary citizens had to wait years for an apartment or a small auto. The corruption issue was made more prominent by the focus on Alexander Schalck-Golodkowski, a state secretary in the Ministry for Foreign Trade, who had been entrusted with securing foreign currencies and had made his own tidy fortune by monopolizing the marketing of scarce Western goods in foreign-currency shops.[76] Only a few shabby exemplars were needed to discredit the nomenklatura. Schalch and Wandlitz provided the corruption. Later would come new revelations or even rumors, such as the alleged funneling of scarce high-tech medical care to the party functionaries at Berlin's Charité hospital while provincial medicine languished. The SED regime revealed itself prone to the corruption that afflicted one-party rule everywhere. And it was only typical of the wider society in which privilege was allocated by ideological toadying and party membership.

In fact, the 1980s had proved to be a decade of accumulation of wealth and privilege throughout the industrialized world. One of the great historical trends of the decade had been the apparent progress of economic inequality, or at least the amassing of income and property that critics of earlier and more sensitive eras would have subjected to harsh scrutiny. Huge transfers of at least relative purchasing power flowed within developing societies and even some of the advanced welfare states from the poor and disadvantaged to the thin upper crust of those well-off. The fallout from these regressive trends might yet prove as corrosive to democracy as the fall of communism was beneficial. Such a dispersion of fortune was probably less remarkable than the worldwide absence of serious analysis and critique. When indignation flared, there were few if any public critics able to focus it on "structural" or systemic trends in the West. Instead it was easier to focus on "corruption" or the flotsam and jetsam of outright dishonesty rather than the deep tides and currents beneath. And East as well as West, Schalck and Boesky, Wandlitz and the Japanese Recruit scandal could be discerned and denounced more easily than the societal mechanisms that advanced plutocracy in the West and privilege in the East. Professional journalists too often renounced systemic analysis; their newspaper or television employers believed in the picturesque scandal. Academic critics seemed cranky radical fossils.

To a degree the collective anesthesia resulted from the fact that earlier reforms had bred their own disillusion. After a decade of inflation and economic vicissitudes in the 1970s, few public voices found it worthwhile critiquing the inequality that accompanied an apparent revival of productive energy in the West. Moreover, market societies provided a mixture of outcomes. To be sure, what Susan Strange called the "casino capitalism" of the West rewarded speculation and luck, the manipulation of combinatorial finance, massive litigation, political lobbying, and crowd psychology. But market economies also rewarded technological intelligence and real organizational capacity (including financial organization). And even when their seamy operators rode high, markets provided an alternative hierarchy of rewards to political office or cultural prestige. In the communist countries, the rewards all seemed to be allocated by one set of authorities. Moreover, market participants, their enthusiastic onlookers, and their hired wordsmiths had always been frank about their rewards: they offered wealth, hopefully to the public at large, but certainly to the successful players. Socialist parties had become based on privilege even as they steadfastly claimed to be abolishing it. The disillusion rebounded on their reputation in autumn 1989.

Was it hopeless then for the SED to try and retrieve its fortunes at the end of 1989? Like the communist parties in the other East European states, it could change its name and baptize itself as social democratic. Only in Romania because of Ceausescu's resistance and in Russia after the abortive August 1991 countercoup was the party prohibited from all activity outright. In Hungary, Czechoslovakia, Eastern Germany, and elsewhere, Communists went through a quick cocoon-like retreat, to emerge at least as hairy large-bodied moths if not irridescent butterflies. In East Germany there were forces for reform within the SED, now PDS. Rank-and-file members had come of age as loyal Communists, internalizing and defending decades of restrictions, trumped-up achievements, denigration of the Bonn Republic, only to see their countrymen mobilize their anger in the streets against all this spurious achievement. Now they experienced the betrayal of a life-long fool's errand. They too demanded reforms. Several thousand members demonstrated before the Central Committee headquarters in early November; they were fed up with Stalinism, felt left out as the crowds took to the streets—"Where were we when the people took to the streets?" They still believed that there was a chance to make their party viable and to correct its "deformations." While most blamed their collapse on the leaders' abuse of power—"Through how much corruption, misuse of power, and arbitrariness did the SED leadership bring about this crisis of socialism?"—some were ready to renounce the party's constitutionally prescribed leading role in the state. "No one," as one member said, "has a monopoly on truth."[77]

Once Modrow became minister-president, chances for renewal seemed more promising. Another encouraging development was the emergence of the new party secretary, Gregor Gysi, who had served as lawyer for dissidents and possessed a certain Berlin sass and humor. Provincial officials began to catch on to the new order; the council chairman in Quedlinburg advocated "True democracy" and assured the public he would not lag in carrying out what Krenz had declared to be the "*Wende*."[78] In the first fortnight of November all 15 district leaders of the SED were changed: 4, including Modrow, were brought into the reshuffled cabinet or Central Committee, while 11 were voted out. Of those sent into retirement 5 had come to power during Ulbricht's leadership; the average age of the district leaders dropped from 62 to 47. The new leaders were certainly not outsiders; they had been active in their organizations and 6 had even studied at the party university in Moscow. But their arrival seemed an omen of change; the new Leipzig chief, Roland Wötzel, had been one of the signators of the "No violence appeal" along with Kurt Masur.[79] We have a precious report of the grass-roots debates in the Thuringian district of Bad Salzungen where the reformist first secretary superintended the volatile reform process. Disillusioned delegates angrily confronted orthodox SED veterans who asked for discipline; lifelong communists complained they could not cast off their Marxist-Leninist convictions like old clothes. The party, it was decided at the extraordinary Berlin conference in late December, would have to dissolve the professional political bureaus it kept in the factories. The district branch had employed 119 secretaries in factories and border villages; 100 would have to be let go. Workers wanted these paper pushers out of their factory sinecures. The party would have to move its district headquarters into a far more modest building. One-third of the 12,000 district members had already resigned. None of these measures kept the struggling local leaders from getting angry anonymous letters or facing demonstrations at their homes.[80]

Could the apparent opening of the SED really save the party in an open campaign? Who was still likely to support its refurbished cadres in the winter of 1990? The state and public functionaries concentrated in the Berlin area, communists by conviction, perhaps some repelled by what they felt to be the egregious moralism of the opposition, those inured to trusting authority, or those still believing and wanting to believe in the reformist capacity of the party. Nonetheless, during the first fortnight of January the SED appeared to be recovering its fortunes. West German promises of economic assistance were helping to stabilize its position. The party, charged one columnist in the conservative *Frankfurter Allgemeine Zeitung*, was surviving much better than its comrades in the other ex-communist countries.[81] Unhappy West Germans wanted Kohl to call off his planned meeting with Modrow. But despite pressure from Free Democratic (FDP) coalition partners, the chancellor refused to renounce the chance to begin exerting economic leverage on his vulnerable counterpart. He saw no other way to keep East Germans from fleeing West; moreover, promises of assistance would guarantee that the East German government did not interfere with Western support for the new parties fighting their first real election in the East.[82] And in fact, despite hasty prognoses, the SED was hardly recovering. Demonstrators continued to denounce the party at the Leipzig Monday night rallies and in the provinces. "Liars grow a longer nose; Gregor Gysi's certainly shows." "SED and Stasi power are still active at this hour."[83] In late January the party was shaken by the resignation of Dresden's mayor Wolfgang Berghofer and thirty-nine other Saxon Communist officials. After the violent clashes at the Dresden railway station on October 6 and 7, Berghofer had been the first SED official to announce a policy of "dialogue." Now he and his colleagues announced that they did not believe the party had the strength to transform itself.[84]

For the other parties the task might be easier. They had West German partners and promised the rewards of Western affiliation. After Kohl's ten-point plan, the CDU appeared as the party of quick and painless reunification. As one provincial physician who now entered politics declared, "No matter how lousy it was in the past, the CDU has structures in being and is technically superior."[85] The Christian Social Union, the conservative Bavarian affiliate of the CDU, offered support to any viable conservative movement. Hans-Wilhelm Ebeling, the conservative pastor of the Leipzig Thomaskirche, who had kept his church off limits to the protestors of the Nikolaikirche, became chair of a new Christian Social Party of Germany (CSPD), seconded by Peter-Michael Diestel, a youthful lawyer given in his public appearances to Italianate double-breasted suits with exaggerated shoulders. When he became interior minister in the Modrow government, Diestel was charged with the difficult problem of mastering the Stasi legacy but, whether because of youth, naiveté, or a liking for order, found it difficult really to uproot the secret police. Other conservatives founded an East German Christian Social Union (CSU); it took a while but gradually under the inducement of the Bavarians these splinter organizations agreed to merge as a German Social Union (DSU). Some CDU members in the West preferred to support this new DSU for its conservatism because their East German CDU colleagues seemed too connected to the Modrow government.[86] The East German CDU in short appeared as the advocate of the quickest unification, the most painless path to the wealth and security of the West; the CSU promised a similar outcome but with a greater stress on quiet and order. Increasingly, New Forum and its related citizens groups seemed committed to an unclear program of rescuing a reformed socialism in a confederally linked GDR. Their Western interlocutors seemed to be the marginal Greens.

The formation that logically appeared as the most promising was the new East German SPD, officially founded as the Social Democratic Party (SDP) in the GDR after several months of preliminary discussion on October 7, 1989, but then reclaiming the official historical designation of SPD (Social Democratic Party of Germany) at its Delegates Conference on January 13, 1990.[87] Eastern Germany, especially the industrial heartland of Saxony, had traditionally been a redoubt of the working-class parties before Hitler. Since mining, chemical works, and factories continued to dominate its economy, that affiliation still seemed to make sense. Social Democracy in 1990 offered a powerful electoral alternative; it promised reforms, reclaimed an indigenous historical legacy, and was connected to a major Western party. If some SPD intellectuals and candidates had come to the East German cause belatedly, this was clearly not true of the party patriarch, Willy Brandt, who had received enthusiastic welcomes in his pioneering 1970 visit to Erfurt, and was a staunch and emotional spectator of the events of the fall. In some ways, once the moment of the New Forum had passed and the Wall had opened, the SPD in the East seemed the logical heir to the reform impulses and a practical vehicle as well. By mid January the party members craved the now frequent visits from the West German SPD leadership, just as they wanted the faxes, copiers, computers, and typewriters that their Western comrades were trucking in. They also were committed to unification with the West, both for their party and their country. Emerging from their founding congress, they were determined to combat not only the former SED or current PDS (Stefan Reiche told the party to dissolve), but also, it was becoming clear, the New Forum and the allies of November.[88]

Nonetheless, the SPD began as a curious implant in 1989 Eastern Germany. In the West the Social Democrats, while no longer confined to the working class, still drew on a strong social base in affiliated or sympathetic trade unions. The DGB, or national trade union federation, was formally unaffiliated with the party, but provided, in effect, an electoral reservoir, as did its powerful component unions such as the metalworkers (I. G. Metall). But no equivalent organized proletarian bedrock was at hand in the East. The trade-union federation in the GDR, the FDGB, had long been a creature of the regime and until the fall of 1989 had precluded any real representational activity on behalf of labor.[89] No unions were yet in place. The working-class population of Saxony and elsewhere seemed preeminently concerned about achieving a better economic break. For this goal, the CDU with its ties to Kohl might well appear the most promising alternative. And most strikingly, the East German SPD had emerged as a pastors party, but churchmen with a political calling who were seeking a more disciplined and electorally competitive vehicle than New Forum.

Several shared the same formative educational experience. As Richard Schröder, one of their most thoughtful and appealing founding members explained, they had entered theological studies, moved less from profound calling than because theology was the only university course of study outside the hard sciences that did not demand SED membership. Key SPD members, moreover, were graduates of the Sprachenkonvikt, originally the Lutheran language-institute in East Berlin that became the Protestant seminary after erection of the Wall in 1961 precluded East Berliners from studying at the Kirchliche Hochschule of Berlin-Zehlendorf in the West. This institute, which enrolled about twenty-five to thirty new students each year, had itself emerged from the anti-Nazi Protestant "confessional church," whose leaders, persecuted or in exile, disavowed the easy acceptance of state authority that had made German Lutheranism such a prop for authoritarian government. Confessional-church theology combined an insistence on keeping a skeptical distance from power with the sense that political resistance and activity retained an ethical dimension.

Schröder taught philosophy and theology at the Sprachenkonvikt. Out of the Arbeitskreis Philosophie und Theologie emerged Markus Meckel and— as an outside participant—Ibrahim Böhme, one of the founders of the SPD. But where Meckel was stolid, Böhme was volatile, unanchored, indeed ultimately a fantasist. No theologian, he had struck up friendships with the pastors of the SPD and with Rainer Eppelmann through the peace seminars. He remained something of an outsider—claiming partial Jewish parentage, changing the spelling of his name to sympathize with the Palestinian cause, and moving from job to job and one circle of dissent to another. He had joined and then quit the SED, worked as a mason, librarian, postal employee, sawmill worker, cemetery worker, theater director, contributor to the illegal *Grenzfall*. He charmed acquaintances who supported his ventures, was complaisant, conveyed a sense of activity, and, implausibly enough in the winter of 1990, was the odds-on favorite to become the first elected minister-president of East Germany.[90] It turned out that he had also had conversations with the Stasi and had to withdraw from politics into an unexpected obscurity. This did not prove a crippling blow for his party. Despite his networking, Böhme proved less essential for the emerging SPD than the others of the Sprachenkonvikt nucleus who provided the early cadres before merger into the all-German SPD. (Graduates also were active elsewhere, notably Wolfgang Ullmann in Democracy Now.) No stellar intellectuals emerged from this milieu: no Barth, Bonhöffer, or Bultmann, such as had distinguished the confessional church three and four decades earlier. What promised success was their early claim to the vacant Social-Democratic political label for their party initiative.

In conversations I found these SPD churchmen more political than the pastors who had gotten swept up in the peace prayer evenings and manifestations of the previous fall. The Social Democratic pastors found no conflict, such as Max Weber had insisted on, between the ethic of the gospels and political action. As Markus Meckel, the student of Hegel, declared, "We want power."[91] Similarly, as the young pastor and party activist Martin Gutzeit, Meckel's friend from student days and Richard Schröder's teaching assistant at the Sprachenkonvikt, explained to me, Genesis commanded, *Macht Euch die Welt untertan*: "Subdue the earth." The same equanimity attended his belief in economic improvement. He was skeptical about any third way for reformed socialism. Citizens, he suggested, could be concerned about their economic future in good conscience; to be paid honest wages for honest work was not just a materialist pursuit but a recognition of dignity and dignified labor. Schröder was clearly the most wide-ranging and sensitive of these ministers. But in general they felt justified and rightfully satisfied by having nurtured their political colleagueship over the previous years, first clandestinely, then in the electoral arena. The young Michael Moeller in March 1990 returned from teaching at a small Lutheran College in South Dakota in order to vote in the Volkskammer elections. He too was a laureate of the Sprachenkonvikt and was recruited by his teachers and friends to serve for a brief couple of months in the East German Foreign Office—even, so he stated, being briefly groomed as the final designated ambassador in Washington to wind down the embassy, before the West German Foreign Office cut off the operation. Indeed, of the final ambassador designates to Paris, London, and Washington, two, according to Moeller, were Sprachenkonvikt laureates.

Generalization is difficult, but Sprachenkonvikt Protestantism, I think, was informed by a less acute sense of eschatological confrontation than was that of the Saxon church officials active in October and November 1989. If only because it emerged most prominently after the great demonstrations, it was less oriented toward earnest prayers for peace and less preoccupied with the pleas for nonviolence. The SPD ministers certainly had a sense of mission but not the exhilaration or dread of Armageddon. Like Dürer's famous knight, they were riding forth imperturbable, sometimes a bit ingenuous about the demands of politics, but not without shrewd tactical savvy. By the spring of 1990, their New Forum allies of the fall now found the Social Democrats somewhat opportunistic. "They could come to terms more easily with party hierarchy," as one New Forum activist explained to me. But fresh enthusiasm seemed the real motivation. To cite Meckel again: "We are seeking power. We want it because we see no one better suited to exercise it than us."[92] Rainer Eppelmann, who was also a pastor with a long pedigree of protest, had felt similarly. While he had not joined the SPD, he had organized Demokratischer Aufbruch because New Forum seemed too unstructured. He, too, conveyed the Protestant enthusiasm for capturing the state: in the 1970s he had felt "like one who plows and sows and if he is fortunate will see the shoots emerge. And now with great satisfaction I am certain that I will be among those who reap. I can only say, like Ulrich von Hutten, it is a joy to be alive."[93]

The spring of 1990 was a season of ebullient amateurism for Central European party politicians.[94] The weather was mild—a warm winter had saved Berlin from economic catastrophe, Lothar de Maizière believed—and patches of early yellow forsythia cheered the otherwise gray pavements of the capital. The Round Table was finishing its effort to secure an advanced agenda of social entitlements. The SPD had moved into the uninviting offices of a former SED office building near the Jannowitz Bridge and filled the corridors with new photocopying machines. Citizens groups and fledgling parties had been allocated space in the Haus der Demokratie, a rechristened office building on the Friedrichstraße a block south of Unter den Linden, that gave the impression of a down-at-heels American urban high school soon to elect a student council. Rooms were allocated for the Civic Alliance, the Democratic Breakthrough, the Independent Women's League, and the block parties, with shared space for news conferences downstairs. Mimeographed party platforms on the coarse gray paper of the GDR were piled next to new faxes and photocopy machines and distributed with the glossy bumper stickers sent by West German affiliates. Czechoslovakia's Civic Forum distributed leaflets and happy-face buttons out of similar improvised offices at Jochmann Square in downtown Prague. The parties have long since decamped from these hectic bivouacs. But they served for the first, still unpredictable campaigns

After the elections of March 18, the deputies to the Volkskammer would have caucus offices and a parliamentary chamber in the Palace of the Republic: erected in the boxy international style of the 1960s where the old royal castle had been razed. Today the traditionalists have scheduled its removal in turn, although its architecture, if banal, is in fact no worse than many public structures in the United States. Individual deputies and parties had their offices in the "House of Parliamentarians" (described in chapter 3), the utilitarian block of long parallel corridors constructed by the Reichsbank, which had thereafter served as Central Committee headquarters.

Did joyless buildings make for joyless politics? What was remarkable outside the corridors of the candidates and parties was the sense of unease that accompanied the electoral process. How different from the euphoria of the previous November, or the hopefulness that would characterize spring and summer 1990 in Prague as the Civic Forum geared up for an electoral contest and Vaclav Havel prepared to become president. Some form of unification was in the air. The Modrow government was a lame-duck regime. Kohl had put unification on the agenda, and none of the non-German powers seemed disposed to slow down the momentum—not even the Soviet Union. But the dominant mood of the country seemed to be anxiety that the upcoming negotiations would undermine their modest but secure standard of living. Would not the East German currency be sharply devalued with respect to the deutsche mark? Would not rents, held at a low level, be allowed to rise without limit? What trumps might their depleted fragment of country bring to the process of merger?

The campaign turned out to be a referendum on unification. By mid-February Kohl seemed on the way to securing the Soviets' assent to German unity. The procedure for parallel negotiations between the Germans and then between them and the four World War II allies was emerging in rushed conferences (see chapter 5). Modrow sought to behave with the dignity of a visiting head of government when he met with Kohl on February 13, but rumors circulated that the GDR might collapse as a state even before the March 18 elections. Modrow asked for immediate help; Kohl responded by envisaging a treaty for economic union: the deutsche mark would steady the outgoing GDR during the months to unity.[95] Modrow reportedly felt that the chancellor had backed off from the support he had tendered when he came to Dresden in mid-December. In the interim, of course, the GDR seemed to have moved close to collapse: 26,000 East Germans had gone West in the first half of February alone. Kohl had no need to bolster Modrow's domestic situation, except to prevent a backlash of sympathy. Even assuming Kohl had no hostile intentions, he saw himself as the soon-to-be chancellor of a united Germany. Reality was bound to be bitter for the delegates from the East, who came as supplicants but believing in parity.[96]

The question for East German voters was which party could arrange the best terms for this upcoming merger. The New Forum/Bündnis 90 slate was hampered by its standoffish view on unification. Its intellectual leadership regretted the rush toward unity—"Zu schnell, viel zu schnell, furchtbar!" one of the Berlin activists lamented in July. The other citizens movement, Democratic Awakening, was no longer a vital force. It had always thought itself more of a party than New Forum and its major leader, Rainer Eppelmann, deemed himself a political pragmatist.[97] But for the campaign it joined the East German CDU and conservative DSU in the Alliance for Germany, whose second major candidate behind de Maizière was soon identified as a Stasi agent.

The major puzzle became the future division of votes among the PDS or the ex-Communists (could they preserve a significant core of support?), the Social Democrats, and the Christian Democrats. As Eppelmann said, to have expected to build an independent political structure was an illusion. "I overestimated the effect of forty years of the GDR and underestimated the effect of the Western media. Most GDR citizens had already joined the Federal Republic in the evening and thought and lived in categories of SPD, CDU, and FDP."[98] Despite the rapid cloning of West German parties, the PDS managed to put its most modern face forward. Its campaign task was to convince an angry electorate that it had completely abandoned the methods of the past forty years. Although Modrow apparently weighed withdrawing from the race, the rank and file persuaded him to stand for election.[99] At a dramatic party congress he spoke of his being burdened by his thirty-year service on the Central Committee and by his current role of representing the people and not a party. Nonetheless, he finally announced, he would run. Modrow enjoyed stature and sympathy outside party ranks; East Germans felt that Kohl had treated him patronizingly during the February visit. Did his persistence not suggest that honestly owning up to his earlier role, but trying to renovate from within, was a more admirable stance than just re-

signing? Gysi was a more cultivated taste with an edge of humor and intel-
lect (including "Take it Gysi" buttons). None of the party faithful believed
that they would have a future government role since they would be coalition
pariahs after the voting. Their task was just to remain a viable minority
alternative and keep from disappearing into historical oblivion.[100]

In contrast to the PDS, campaigning in effect to survive, the Social Democrats felt they were well placed to become a dominant force. They abjured
socialist experiments and embraced the market, albeit an "ecologically oriented social market."[101] The leader of the Christian Democratic campaign
was the diminutive Lothar de Maizière, a cultivated attorney and former
professional violist, who would appear physically overpowered when he
visited Chancellor Kohl. De Maizière was convinced that rapid unification
was the only way to keep the GDR from spiraling downward into depression
and depopulation. He had defended dissenters but operated within the system. The last time he had played in a string quartet, he told me, was when
friends arranged a musical evening for his fiftieth birthday a few months
earlier. The Christian Democrats had to overcome the impediment of being
scorned for their forty-year collaboration as a domesticated "block" party.
"Can someone who has played 'block-flute' [the German term for a re-
corder] be first violinist?" de Maizière's critics jibed. But his modesty was
attractive. Unfortunately, he too would be politically destroyed by revelations that he had served the state security forces as an unofficial collaborator. Perhaps he might have weathered this charge, which by late 1990 and
1991 could be leveled against so many of those who had paid for their efforts to negotiate within the system by reporting on the dissenters they dealt
with. But he denied charges of impropriety, and revelations that he actually
had a code name in Stasi records undercut his credibility.

East Germans took seriously this first chance at meaningful elections since
1933, with 93.2 percent of elegible voters casting ballots. Throughout the
republic as a whole, the CDU received 40.9 percent of the votes and 184
seats in the new Volkskammer. The SPD won 21.8 percent and 87 seats. The
PDS, thanks to its strength in East Berlin, returned with 16.3 percent and 65
seats. The conservative DSU won 6.3 percent and 25 seats; the Liberals or
FDP analogue was close behind with 5.3 percent and 21 seats. But where the
West German FDP, with its somewhat higher long-term performance as
third-largest party, long played the decisive role in making and breaking
coalitions, its GDR counterpart was in no position to do so. The PDS won
about three times as many votes—even if no party would work with it as a

coalition partner. Bündnis 90, the electoral vehicle of the New Forum, received only 2.9 percent and 12 seats, just 1 percent more than the East German Greens (2.0 percent, 8 seats) and with even less of a margin over the East German Peasant League (2.2 percent and 9 seats).

These results included some major surprises. Polls had suggested an SPD victory was likely. With its low Catholic population and pre-Hitler traditions of Social Democratic strength, it had long been presumed that East Germany would reemerge as an SPD bulwark. This expectation, it had been said, was one reason that Konrad Adenauer had never been an ardent supporter of reunification. The other major surprise was the regional and class support for the parties. In the West SPD strength rested on the traditional working class and their trade unions. In East Germany, so the exit polling of 12,000 voters revealed, the CDU and the Alliance for Germany (CDU plus DSU plus Democratic Awakening) captured the majority of working-class and white-collar employee votes. Social groups traditionally deemed as intellectuals (functionaries included) divided their vote almost equally among the PDS (26 percent), CDU (24 percent), and SPD (23 percent). The social class differentiation corresponded to the regional differences, which were also surprising. The Saxon industrial region, with Dresden, Leipzig, and Karl-Marx-Stadt (Chemnitz), was expected to reemerge as a bastion for the SPD. Instead the Alliance for Germany won almost 58 percent and in Thuringia (Erfurt, Gera, Jena, Weimar) slightly over 60. It won almost 50 percent in Saxon-Anhalt (Magedeburg, Halle, and the chemical districts around Merseburg and Leuna). The respective CDU components of these hefty Alliance totals were 44 percent, 53 percent, and 45 percent. The DSU component scored relatively well in Saxony (13.2 percent), eked out 5.6 percent in Thuringia, and elsewhere remained marginal. The third Alliance party, the Democratic Awakening, won about 2 percent: it never really made the transition from "citizens movement" and was badly discredited by the Stasi connections of its campaign leader, Wolfgang Schnurr.

The electoral districts of the North—where the population had entered the demonstrations of the previous fall far more hesitantly than in Saxony and Berlin—turned in different results. The CDU results in Mecklenburg and Brandenburg fell under 40 percent. All in all, the electoral geography of East Germany emerged strikingly reversed from the Weimar and even imperial eras: the northern districts, once rural backwaters of reaction, divided their parties fairly equally among Social Democrats, Christian Democrats, and even PDS. The industrial Saxon and central regions strongly endorsed

Chancellor Kohl's CDU. The mass forces that had taken to the streets voted essentially for quick unification. Only Berlin remained contrary to the general patterns. In the capital, where the former Communists had been a major employer and organizer of benefits, the PDS vote remained strong (30.0 percent), and the Social Democrats scored best with 35 percent, the Bündnis 90 won over 6 percent, and the Alliance for Germany won less than 22 percent. Berlin's electorate was clearly ambivalent: it believed more strongly in the transformation of the PDS and in any case was reluctant to underwrite unification and Kohl's local allies.

Other factors for differentiation worked less powerfully than in the Federal Republic. The discrepancy between young and old was less pronounced so far as the CDU profile went; but it did affect the SPD-PDS split. Older voters turned to the SPD if they stayed "left"; younger ones stayed with Gysi and Modrow, but the plurality of all age groups went CDU. SPD and PDS both did slightly better in urban areas with populations above 50,000, while the Alliance benefited more in the smaller towns. Religious differences played analogous roles as in the West, but the proportions of churchgoers were far lower. Of the 6.5 percent registered Catholics in the East, the CDU alone took 66.3 percent; among the 35 percent Protestants, the CDU won 55 percent, and even among the nonchurched, the CDU took 30 percent (for the Alliance as a whole, the respective figures were 73, 62, and 37 percent).[102]

In effect the March 18 vote ended the East German revolution. It showed a strong preference for unification and a quick end to the economic and political halflife of the "Rest-DDR" (or German Democratic Republic remnant). The protesters who had filled the streets of Leipzig and Dresden in October had moved beyond claiming reform and liberty to demanding unification. These were not incompatible; but the unification path meant that there would be no longings for some vague middle way between Marxism and Western markets. The Berlin electorate was less workaday, clung more persistently to a vision of a reformed independent state. Whether because they believed that Modrow and Gysi would reconstruct a viable democratic socialism or because the old "Seilschaften" or patronage networks might still be relied on, East Berlin voters clung more persistently to the PDS, or at least trusted the SPD with its ties to Willy Brandt and the West German opposition. The SPD in East Germany was no longer just a pastors party, and it had managed to weather the charges raised against Böhme and his moody withdrawal. Still, it was not yet a firmly rooted working-class or professionals party.

Indeed it was not clear that this vote represented how the East German electoral scene might finally shake out. The vote in the first all-German elections for the national Bundestag in December 1990 would register comparable votes—a CDU plurality, especially marked in Saxony, and a hesitant Berlin. But both elections were in effect referendums on the unification process. The SPD was hurt by its belated enthusiasm for unity. That hesitancy on a supreme national issue may well have cost it votes in the 1994 election as well. As of 1990, most East Germans wanted to be part of West Germany's success. Kohl's party promised that with more decisiveness and skill than the opposition. Voting for Kohl represented the equivalent of going West the previous fall. It was an option for what seemed a more solid future—perhaps less autonomous, less socially experimental, less likely to keep the cozy welfare and family support systems; but more promising in the long run because it hitched East Germany to Europe's premier economy. At the time they voted, the electors had little expectation how quickly their own economic structure would be exposed to the merciless scrutiny of competition and a market. They beheld the deutsche mark as a sufficient rescue vessel. Now the interim liminal moment of political solidarity, of danger and living democratic resistance was over; the months of trying to prop up the economy and negotiate what was to be a fire sale were at hand. Would the East Germans enter the new Germany as a junior partner, as Modrow had proposed and de Maizière might hope to succeed in? Or would they come in as a rather down-at-heels province, feted but patronized or even displaced? The vote alone could not determine which outcome was likely. It would be the negotiations for unification now under way that would be crucial.

Five

Unification

Because it was politically undesirable, the text of the national anthem has remained unsung for more than two decades. The GDR is thus the only country in which the national anthem is performed without words. The main reason is because the text expresses the idea of a united Germany. Written in 1949, conceived even earlier in the years of emigration, the text should now be rehabilitated. . . . Its connection to the national and cultural identity of the German people can no longer simply be excluded.

—Motion from the Committee for Cultural Affairs of the Volkskammer to the Council of Ministers, January 4, 1990[1]

IT WAS typical of the German Democratic Republic that it dared not play the lyrics to its own national anthem. As such songs go, Hans Eisler and Johannes Becher's *Einig Deutsches Vaterland* was not a bad effort: "Reemerging from the ruins, face toward future now we stand, let us serve you for the better, united German Fatherland." Among the many reforms enacted in his four-month tenure, Hans Modrow did agree to "rehabilitate" the text: "GDR Radio and Television are to be informed that at the end of broadcasting, the national anthem of the GDR will be transmitted with the text of Johannes R. Becher."[2]

For a few days short of nine months, the GDR could play its national hymn complete with words. Then the country disappeared and, with it, the song. West German newspapers ran polls in the interim as to what national anthem should be chosen after the impending unification. Some readers thought the Eisler-Becher hymn would still be appropriate; some nominated Brecht's unsuccessful effort of 1949; most proposed continuing the West German hymn: "Unity, Law and Freedom," the nineteenth-century patriotic lyric sung to Haydn's familiar music, which after 1945 had been shorn of its offensive first verse, "Deutschland über Alles." Both Germanies had had problems with their national anthems, but the Federal Republic's inoffensive alternative finally prevailed, as it did for most other contested issues.

STILL MASTERS OF THE GAME?

SOVIET POLICY SHIFTS ON GERMANY

Why did the GDR disappear so quickly? Its total, rapid liquidation was not inevitable. Indeed, it was surprising. As throughout its forty-year history, East German outcomes were shaped in the final account by the interplay of a restive, cowed, or acquiescent population on the one side and the Soviet occupiers on the other. The East Berlin regime itself played an important role, to be sure, because it could convince the Soviets at key points to help it maintain its shaky hold on the province. But ultimately the SED state was poised between the Russians above and its own people below, whether these acted as a remarkably diligent labor force or as impatient clients of a modern welfare state—or, finally as individuals trying to break out, to the West, or to break through, to political rights and participation.

But without a change in the Soviets' calculations, the populace alone could not have determined the swift final dissolution into the Federal Republic. Had Moscow's leadership insisted, a reformed GDR might well have survived within a confederal German structure for at least several years, and perhaps far longer. Such a solution would have pleased many in West European capitals. It had indeed been mooted by some East Germans in the last couple of years before the upheavals of 1989.[3] It was excluded neither by Chancellor Kohl's appraisal of future developments in November 1989, nor by American preferences after the Wall opened. Western observers had little reason to expect that Mikhail Gorbachev's government should relinquish East Germany so completely. What sense did it make? The division of Germany, and the Russians' perch in the GDR, after all was the major trophy of the Soviet national epic, the Great Patriotic War. It had been the keystone in the arch of Soviet influence in Central Europe and might remain such. The industrial output and technological expertise of the East Germans remained integral to Soviet economic plans deep into 1989; economic partnership was taken for granted even while political relations had become querulous. Granted, in the early 1950s Lavrenty Beria had proposed—and perhaps even Stalin had seriously weighed—giving up the GDR in return for prizing loose

West Germany from its emerging institutional commitments with the West, especially with the Western military alliance.[4] In the decades since, however, the interlocking of protector and ostensible dependent had grown ever more mutually compelling. What advantage did the Russians envisage from such a change of the postwar status quo?

To date we have partial, although well-informed reconstructions of Soviet decision making. Gorbachev and some key advisers have now published their memoirs. For their richly documented study of U.S. policy and international negotiations from the opening of the Wall to unification, Philip Zelikow and Condoleezza Rice could draw on some Soviet memos, interviews with key diplomatic personnel of the major powers involved, and, above all, U.S. diplomatic correspondence and minutes. Every scholar will remain indebted to their account, and I have utilized it extensively here. The protocols of East German–Soviet conversations in the former SED archives allow some additional perspectives, all the more important since from the Washington vantage point East German policy makers seemed marginal actors. What, then, do we know about the Soviets? Even when they grew frustrated with Honecker's stubbornness, Moscow's professional diplomats tended to advocate caution, among them Aleksandr Bondarenko, one of the *Germanisty* who staffed the Third European Department of the Ministry of Foreign Affairs; Igor Maximychev, who served as diplomat in Leipzig and Bonn, and then as second in command of the embassy in East Berlin; Yuly Kvitsinsky, embassy councillor successively in East Berlin and Bonn, and thereafter ambassador in the FRG from late 1986 to 1990; or Valentin Falin, negotiator for the 1970–71 German treaties that anchored Ostpolitik, then ambassador to Bonn until 1978, when he returned to Moscow to take on various party functions and culminated his career as head of the consolidated International Department. Their traditional expertise and bureaucratic orthodoxy prompted distrust of the new impulses that emanated from Gorbachev's own circle, including Edward Shevardnadze, the foreign minister; Aleksandr Yakolev, who had headed the Institute for World Economies and International Relations and from the Politburo oversaw the party's International Department; and Anatoly Chernyaev, the new leader's major foreign policy adviser. They have granted interviews and, in some cases, left memoirs. Of course, their negotiating partners have also published their versions, and although the GDR Foreign Ministry archives have been taken over by the Foreign Office of United Germany, to remain off limits for thirty years, historians have revealing traces within the other East German archives that are now available.[5]

For all their expertise, the Soviets, like almost everyone else, were caught by suprise by the upheavals of autumn 1989.[6] They had not expected such a rapid discrediting of the East Berlin leadership. Prior discussions of possible German policy gave them no blueprints. What the historian must account for is the unexpected flexibility of the Soviets: was it conviction or confusion, or lack of perceived alternatives that allowed Gorbachev and his advisers to remain so acquiescent as this crucial component of the Soviet international position was dismantled? For all the difficulties that the Russians might later pose during the course of 1990, for all the partial second thoughts to which a disconcerted Gorbachev periodically reverted, the essential historical fact was his acceptance of unification and of continued NATO adherence on the part of united Germany. For all the gnats he strained at, he swallowed a very large camel. He did not have to do so. Even without any egregious denial of German self-determination, he could have insisted on a longer confederal transition. On the other hand, would such an artificial prolongation of the GDR have brought the Soviet Union any significant advantages?[7] Probably not. Not, in any case, in the perspective of 1989–90, by which time Gorbachev and Shevardnadze had come to envisage good relations with Bonn as the most valuable component of their overall European policy.

Until the mid 1980s, the Soviets resented any GDR bilateral coziness with the Federal Republic, all the more so once the Federal Republic ratified the stationing of NATO middle-range Cruise and Pershing missiles on its territory.[8] Moscow remained wary of the two "billion-credits," the first extended in July 1983, and the second, under Franz Josef Strauß's initiative, a year later. At a special Moscow summit in August 1984, the then Soviet party leader, Konstanin Chernenko, chastised Honecker for concessions on inter-German visits and his growing financial dependence on the West.[9] Even more directly the Russian leadership, including Gorbachev, pressured Honecker to renounce an official visit to Chancellor Kohl that had been long prepared and would have let the GDR leader bask in an important public demonstration of CDU commitment to East German legitimacy. Until 1987 only Soviet mortality had allowed the two German leaders to meet directly: first on the occasion of Andropov's funeral in February 1984 and then at Chernenko's burial in March 1985. At this second occasion, at Honecker's suggestion they issued a joint declaration reaffirming the sovereignty and current boundaries of all European nations and pledged commitment that German soil must never again become a source of war. Kohl was clearly following, and Honecker clearly enjoying the trend of collaboration that the Social Democrats had initiated fifteen years earlier. German-German talks continued on a lower level, conducted primarily by Wolfgang Schäuble at the Federal Chancellery (Bundeskanzleramt) and motivated in large part by the West German hope that the GDR would help staunch the flow of non-European asylum seekers who got transit visas through East Germany. After continued conversations, Kohl's successful electoral campaign of 1986, and Genscher's important visit to Moscow in September 1986, Honecker could finally make his long-desired state visit in September 1987. This time he did not seek permission from his Soviet comrades, and they resented the slight.[10]

By this date, too, the Soviets' assessment of world politics had significantly changed. Even as Honecker congratulated himself on the GDR's new international respectability—a state visit to Paris followed the reception in Bonn, the SPD and the SED issued their joint position paper, both German republics feted the 500th anniversary of Luther's birth and the 750th anniversary of Berlin's founding as major national commemorations—Gorbachev's views were evolving. Honecker may have sensed the wind of change at the Twenty-seventh Party Congress of the CPSU in April 1986, for when Gorbachev reciprocated by attending the Eleventh Congress of the SED a few weeks later, he noted to his older East German counterpart that "Comrade Honecker is irritated by something."[11] When Honecker arrived in Moscow ten days after Genscher in October 1986, to help dedicate a monument to the pre-1933 German Communist leader Ernst Thälmann, the Russian leader emphasized the importance of the USSR, GDR, and FRG "triangle" for world peace. Honecker took the remark as approval for going ahead with his own visit to Bonn, not as the harbinger of a Soviet reorientation. He grew overtly disenchanted with the progress of perestroika, and declined to transmit the full discussion protocols with Gorbachev to his own Politbüro, allegedly telling the Soviet leader that they would appear naive. He decided to prohibit the German language editions of *Sputnik* and *New Times* and received Alexander Yakolev icily at his country retreat in late summer 1987. When the Soviet emissary said Moscow did not wish to export Russia's inner transformation but did seek understanding for its policies, a smug Honecker wished him well but stressed the stability of East Germany. At the 1988 New Year's hunt—the annual rite in which the rulers of the workers' and peasants' republic and their guests were chauffered into the German forest to blast the deer that had been rounded up to facilitate their bonding—Honecker informed the Soviet ambassador that the term "perestroika" would henceforth be removed from official Soviet documents distributed in

East Germany. "We are against the practice of the purest slander of the CPSU history and socialist construction in the USSR. We are surprised by doubtful economic experiments, not to speak of the information sphere. For years we educated GDR citizens about the example of the CPSU and the heroic struggle of the Soviet people. Now we learn, however, that it was all a string of failures."[12]

Gorbachev resented the signs of disapproval as he mooted a transformed socialism.[13] Why must Honecker, now in his mid-seventies, call him to account and pose as the preeminent guardian of orthodoxy?[14] Still, vexation with the pedantic and disapproving East German leader could not alone determine so fundamental a policy shift as abandoning the GDR. Moscow foreign policy circles discussed various concepts, with conflicting emphases and implications, during 1987 and 1988. Economically the East German contribution was still critical. Apparently impressed at his visit to the SED's Eleventh Party Congress in April 1986, Gorbachev told his ambassador to East Germany to prepare a program to raise Soviet-GDR relations to a qualitatively new level.[15] When Richard von Weizsäcker visited Moscow in July 1987, in part to repair Kohl's insulting comparison of Gorbachev with Goebbels, the Soviet chief answered Weizsäcker's allusion to a common German national sentiment by observing that history would resolve the future of Germany. Perhaps in a century (accelerated, on Weizsäcker's urging, to possibly fifty years) unity might emerge. Meanwhile the two states had learned to make their respective contributions to peace; anything further would arouse justified concerns among their neighbors.[16] On the occasion of Honecker's participation at the seventieth anniversary ceremonies of the Bolshevik Revolution, the two leaders initialed a program of enhanced cooperation designed to authorize closer planning efforts. Nonetheless, in the very same months between late 1986 and early 1988, Gorbachev and Shevardnadze fundamentally downgraded the maintenance of a divided Germany as a Soviet priority. Instead they increasingly defined Soviet interests as lying in a web of East-West accords that transcended the division of Europe. A "common European house" might have been a somewhat vague formula, but it was no empty phrase. It implied a program for overcoming the rival blocs and diminishing the burden of armaments on the Soviet economy. Two days after Margaret Thatcher concluded a visit to Moscow on April 1, 1987, Gorbachev told his advisers that no question was resolvable without Europe, not even Russia's own internal ones: as if to emphasize the point, he added that no sooner did the Japanese seem to leave everyone behind than the FRG made another technological leap forward.[17] Even as he made clear to Weizsäcker the constraints on German unity, he offered the West Germans enhanced and warmer cooperation.

It is difficult to specify when the unthinkable on the German question became conceivable or, more to the point, conceivable within a finite, if still extended time frame. Shevardnadze would later claim 1986 as the time in which he decided the division of Germany must be overcome within the framework of "new thinking." Nikolai Portugalov, a German expert in the Central Committee, noted in a January 1987 *Moscow News* comment that citizens of the GDR belonged to the same nation as those of the FRG—a low-key but significant challenge to East German claims. Vyacheslav Dashichev, a forceful young enthusiast of West German pluralism and economic prowess, claims a catalytic role in prodding the Central Committee. When Anatoly Chernayev was appointed as special foreign policy adviser by Gorbachev in February 1986, he allegedly wrote to his new chief that German unification was inevitable in one form or another if the Soviets wished to develop a long-range strategic concept. The progress of relations with European leaders during 1987–88, he believed, made it easier to win Gorbachev's approval for reunification, and in December 1988 he cautioned Gorbachev that the traditional fraternal visits of "demonstrative friendship" to old-style despotic Communists, such as Castro, Ceausescu, Kim Il Sung—and Honecker—would set back relations with the West.[18] The Communist leaders admitted to themselves that the 1970s doctrine of two separate German nations—one defined by its socialism—was the artificial construct of Brezhnev and Gromyko in collaboration with the ideologists of the GDR.[19]

By early 1988, West Germany's strategic role was assuming ever more crucial importance for the Soviets. The ceremonial exchanges with Weizsäcker, Genscher's second visit, Franz Josef Strauß's arrival, both in December 1987, and the mission of Lothar Späth, minister-president of Baden Württemberg, to prepare a summit with Kohl, convinced Gorbachev that now the Germans wanted closer relations. To judge from the message that Moscow's ambassador to East Germany conveyed to Honecker, the Soviet foreign-policy establishment believed that a fundamental shift in influence was under way. Washington's influence among the Western allies was diminishing, whereas Bonn's was increasing. The "common European house" could not be constructed without the Federal Republic, ambassador Kochemasov explained. West Germany was taking realistic positions on a whole group of issues. Its industrial potential had grown massively and had overtaken that of the United States in certain products and was approaching

Japan's. "It would no longer be content with the role of a junior partner to the United States. It is against this background that the contradictions are growing within NATO. The differences in military and strategic questions are of great significance in this connection, but so too are the conflicts of interest in the economic sphere. These processes are growing. Therefore the policies with respect to the FRG are an important question for the Soviet Union." Even Franco-German military cooperation, although it had its undesirable aspects, was "the expression of discontent of the West European countries with the United States." Although Kochemasov stressed that the "German Treaty" of 1970 remained the basis for future relations and envisaged that the East Germans would play a positive role in the new developments, the focus on Bonn implicitly downgraded the importance of the GDR.[20] When Gorbachev visited Bonn in June 1989, Kohl interpreted their discussions and the warm personal encounter as a decisive milestone toward unification. Gorbachev intended to remain more cautious; nevertheless, his chief adviser noted: "Even in the GDR it was understood at all levels that the FRG would now have priority in Soviet German policy. It would become the most important partner in the construction of a new Europe. The bottom line for the East Germans was clear: the Soviet Union would no longer prevent unification and the GDR could negotiate—which the East Germans quickly did."[21] Not, however, without a prior revolution!

The task of future relations in the Soviet view was less to firm up their own bloc than to overcome the division with the West and work harmoniously with the preeminent European power. Kochemasov conveyed to the East Germans Moscow's belief that Reagan wanted a major settlement to conclude his presidency; if so, fine, and all the greater incentive to work with the Europeans and most critically the FRG. When the political advisory committee of the Warsaw Pact allies met in Bucharest on July 7 and 8, Gorbachev declared that the positive trend in international relations was no longer reversible, although Western circles had not yet decided whether to accept the changes or revert to a model of confrontation. The transformation of international relations, so the recently selected Hungarian party chairman Rezsö Nyers underlined, entailed the internal evolution of the socialist countries as well as their external relations. The East Germans remained silent as Hungarians, Poles, Russians, and others testified to a world in flux.[22] Nonetheless, the East German regime still existed; the Hungarian border had not yet been breached. Even as he pressed for a more dynamic and realistic relationship during Chancellor Kohl's October 1988 visit, Gorbachev remained cautious about undercutting the GDR, a reticence he

continued to observe during his own trip to Bonn in June 1989.[23] He continued to envisage desirable German-Russian relations as a "triangle" that
linked Bonn, Berlin, and Moscow in mutual commitments. Even on the
famous visit on the fortieth anniversary—as we have observed in chapter
3—Gorbachev behaved correctly. He did not want to intervene directly, and
his famous remark that history punishes those who come too late was probably a reflection on the choices he had made in reorienting Soviet policy.
When he urged the Politbüro to act decisively, he thought in terms of policy, not personnel.[24]

Gorbachev could hardly have been surprised at the removal of Honecker.
Given the demonstrations under way during the very day of his visit—even
more telling, hearing the cries to the reviewing stand from the official parad-
ers, "Gorbachev, rescue us," or so his Polish colleague translated them for
him—he believed that younger and more flexible leaders were needed to
infuse East Germany with the spirit of glasnost. Despite the warning of his
ambassador in Bonn, Kvitsinski, that East German collapse was only a matter of time, Gorbachev hoped that an East German acceptance of perestroika
would stabilize the situation.[25] The opening of the Wall on November 9 did
not immediately change this; East Germans would satisfy their curiosity
about the West and then—precisely because they could henceforth depart
at any time—return to their homes and workplaces. Nonetheless, the West
Germans might exploit the days of ebullience and demonstrations. It was
necessary to set a limit to what Moscow might sanction, and Gorbachev
immediately warned Bush on November 10 that he feared FRG currents
would work to reject "the postwar realities, that is, the existence of two
German states." He may now have recognized that German unity was inevitable, but counted on a certain transitional period.

Although he probably preferred a more decisive reformer than Egon
Krenz, who seemed so compromised with the Honecker regime and had
made a weak impression with his original speech to the Central Committee,
Gorbachev received the new man warmly in Moscow at the beginning of
November and assured him of Soviet support for a reformed East German
regime. The lengthy minutes of their conversation reveal the fluidity of Soviet policy and the ill-founded hopes of the East Germans that, despite the
economic difficulties and mass mobilization, they might still stabilize the
state.[26] Gorbachev warned that from Soviet experience, reform would not be
easy: in Russia "the horse had been saddled but the ride not completed. One
could still be thrown off." On his side, Krenz confessed to major faults on
the part of the old regime: above all economic self-deception and callous-

ness about the emigration of young people. Honecker, Gorbachev noted, had repeatedly rejected his bid to discuss the GDR's debt crisis. Krenz confessed that East Germany's five-year plan had not succeeded, that the rates of accumulation (capital formation) and overall growth had both slipped. Although he insisted, along the same lines as Gerhard Schürer, that the GDR must persevere with "key technologies," to sustain the microelectronics industry required more than 3 billion marks per year. Doubtless Krenz was hoping for more concrete assistance than Gorbachev was willing or able to promise when he divulged that the GDR owed foreign creditors 49 billion valuta marks or $26.5 billion, and that the 1989 deficit on current account would amount to over $12 billion, a figure that his Soviet partner found astonishing. Debt service alone cost $4.5 billion or 62 percent of annual export earnings. Krenz promised rapid introduction of an economic reform, but he offered no details and insisted the basis of the economy must still be socialist. Gorbachev could offer little support—indeed, he was wrestling with similar ambiguous programs. He emphasized that the Soviet Union would continue its deliveries of raw materials, but he also emphasized that the GDR would have to negotiate with West Germany—without, however, surrendering control to Bonn.

The relationship with West Germany, in fact, was the underlying issue, but both partners were constrained to approach it warily. Only the Federal Republic, the Soviets admitted, might sustain East Germany economically, but at what cost? Krenz urged, in effect, that Gorbachev prop up the international position of the GDR by emphasizing that both Germanies had an important role to play in the "common European house." The GDR in a certain sense was the child of the Soviet Union and the father had to recognize its child. Gorbachev assured Krenz that recent talks with Thatcher, Mitterrand, Jaruzelski, and Andreotti had revealed that they all presupposed the continuing existence of two German states. Even the Americans and Willy Brandt did not want the disappearance of the GDR. For the socialist countries it was best to emphasize that the present situation was a result of historical development, but not to cut off relations between the two Germanies. In response Gorbachev alluded to the importance of the triangular relationship among the Soviet Union and the two Germanies. The GDR must continue to develop its relations with the FRG. To sum up, Gorbachev noted, there was no reason to unleash speculation about how the German problem might someday be solved. In the future, cooperation might advance such that possibilities appeared different: "But this was not a problem for politics today. In present-day politics the previous line must be carried on." Gorbachev asked Krenz to communicate this recommendation to the Politbüro—advice that might have seemed superfluous had he not recalled Honecker's earlier refusals to transmit the Soviet viewpoint.

Krenz seemed relieved that Gorbachev was apparently ruling reunification off limits, but did he really absorb the subtext that the GDR would have to seek its economic salvation to the West? Even more intriguing, did Gorbachev really understand how feebly he was counteracting any quick rush to unification? Krenz evidently did not comprehend how precarious his position might yet become; nor would his successor, Hans Modrow. "De-ideologization of the FRG-GDR relationship," Krenz pleaded to Gorbachev, was a very complicated question. The intra-German relationship was different from the connection with other states. De-ideologization would mean renouncing the defense of socialism. The issue of the Wall and the border regime would be placed in question again. "The GDR found itself in the complicated situation of defending these things that were no longer appropriate but were still necessary." Gorbachev warned that if the GDR could not find a formula that let men and women visit their relatives, the result would be highly unsatisfactory. Krenz discussed his phone conversations with a voluble Helmut Kohl; Gorbachev estimated that although "Kohl was no intellectual beacon . . . he was a skillful and persistent politican. Reagan had made himself popular and stayed in power relatively long. That was the case for Kohl as well."

For both political leaders, the prerequisite of major reform remained "cadre politics," the renewal of the Central Committee and Politbüro with political allies. When informed which old Communists were to be removed, Gorbachev intervened on behalf of Willi Stoph (who was in fact not mentioned by Krenz). "One could not place all old comrades into one pot." It was no doubt reassuring that reform might be conceived primarily in terms of replacing outworn cadres: personalities seemed easier to manipulate than the intractable economic realities. In this sense both Gorbachev and Krenz were victims of their own political formation. Gorbachev believed that the crowd enthusiasm that greeted him in foreign capitals—most recently in East Berlin itself—must ensure the success of his reforms. Krenz believed that by removing the old hard-liners he could ride out the great popular mobilization. He told Gorbachev about the great impending demonstration scheduled for November 4 in Berlin, and admitted that he was not sure how or whether to deal with New Forum, lest it develop as had Polish Solidarność. Gorbachev emphasized that perestroika involved "a genuine revolution"; but he would not let the divisions within the Soviet Union develop into civil-war–like conditions. Still the Soviet situation, he admitted, was very tense and involved a real political struggle. He insisted on his commitment to socialism. A flaw of socialism had been in the difficulty of replacing leaders; the people had to be brought into decision making, and society had to be consolidated and its creative strength mobilized. Despite the vast superiority of Gorbachev to Krenz in terms of conceptual imagination, both leaders underestimated the difficulties of their task. Both believed that renewal of party cadres would enable the Communists to remain in power as the legitimate vanguard of reform. Both retained an allegiance to "socialism," that is, to a residual political control of productive forces, at least to partial state ownership of capital assets, and to continued state intervention to soften the impact of economic change.

Most critics of the 1990s transition in Eastern Europe charged that any such halfway house on the way to market economies would have been doomed to fail. "The Third Way"—so the spokesman for West German industry expressed it trenchantly—"was the way to the Third World."[27] If Gorbachev believed too easily in the robustness of reformed socialism or of a multinational socialist state, his great historical merit was to resist imposing it by force. He also had become convinced of the epochal importance of the German Federal Republic and aware of the fragility, if not artificiality, of the small German client state whose future he had to weigh. The Russian president would certainly become angry and threaten to halt the unification process when he felt that the Western powers were seeking to steamroller him; in the upcoming negotiations he needed to be treated with suaveness and dignity. But the substantive outcome was not to be an insuperable obstacle.

The Soviets had indeed once been masters in East Germany. As of late 1990, however, they were abandoning initiatives and control over the rapidly evolving situation to the power that Gorbachev had come to believe held the key to Europe and to his overall international politics: the Federal Republic. For the Soviet leadership, West Germany was the key mediator to Western financial support; in terms of economic vitality or military potential in Central Europe, it ranked almost alongside the United States. It was the indispensable center of the common European house, the logical claimant to a common German nationhood. Its new economic and political presence reduced the significance of East Germany in the calculation of security or even of economic promise. A cooperative Federal Republic even promised, in effect, to help redeem perestroika at home in Russia. The pallid

German Democratic Republic—all the feebler for its resistance to reform—did not really matter much after November 1989. Its national claims seemed increasingly artificial although its economic output was still important. But if a united Germany could replace the GDR's industrial contribution, there was little need to nurture the former. What leverage on history might its rulers or its people still maintain?

2 = 1 OR 1 = 1? THE ECONOMICS OF UNIFICATION

As for the Federal Republic, the leverage it could most powerfully exert was economic. In this domain, Helmut Kohl acted with full awareness of his superiority. After three months of fraternal reassurances to the East Germans, Helmut Kohl made his own evaluation of the two Germanys' position starkly clear to Hans Modrow in mid-February 1990. Any hopes for a confederal union of the two states had slipped by, the bulky, confident chancellor informed his subdued and preoccupied East German counterpart. (Modrow, recall, had barely limped through a debilitating crisis with the parties of the Round Table. His hesitations on dissolving the Stasi had triggered angry demonstrations.) Continuing emigration, running almost 50,000 per month, revealed that the GDR was disintegrating economically. Kohl was prepared to deploy the deutsche mark as a sort of life raft to keep East Germany afloat in an economic and currency union; but in return he envisioned rapid movement toward a federal state (*Bundesstaat*)—although, so he claimed, he did not mean to impose a simple annexation.[28]

These were far from the terms that the reform-minded Dresden party leader had imagined after he succeeded Egon Krenz's ineffective interim government in mid-November. Modrow wanted to preserve as much GDR identity as possible in any new German structure. Through his first two months in office, he hung on to his hope that East Germany would enter a confederally structured "Treaty Community." The GDR, he believed, would bring an enhanced status into the unification talks by virtue of its own reforms. He also counted on the previous CDU commitment to Ostpolitik and retained the illusion that the Soviet Union would insist on some continuing institutional role for their loyal clients.

Kohl's ten-point plan of November 28, with its scenario of a phased progress through confederation, might also have plausibly encouraged the East German leaders to believe that they would enter talks as equal partners.

That hope was evaporating through the winter months as the vulnerability of the GDR regime became increasingly exposed. For the German negotiations on unity, monetary questions proved crucial. The deutsche mark was king. When they collected the visa fees and per diem conversions required of Western visitors, the East German government claimed officially that the currencies were on a par. In fact, they reckoned from their own internal calculations that on the basis of what comparable export goods cost to produce at home, the value of the East mark hovered at about one-quarter that of the deutsche mark. Western currency dealers who exchanged the currencies for travelers discounted the GDR's mark even more drastically. It had fallen from 2.5 to the deutsche mark in 1980 to almost 10:1 at the end of 1988 and about 20:1 in the weeks after the Wall had opened. The decade-long decline of the East German currency, the ministers were told in early 1990, reflected the fact that the economy consumed more than it produced. Despite that fact, East German families had not been able to consume all they would have desired; instead they had taken home high nominal salaries that exceeded their collective real output. From 1986 to 1988 especially, GDR citizens had accumulated a monetary "overhang" of perhaps 30 billion marks due to their relatively high nominal income and a long "unsatisfied demand for automobiles, home furnishings, modern consumer electronics, and foreign tourism."

The remedies needed, so the authorities recognized, were precisely those which would have been proposed by orthodox treasury officials anywhere: reduction of state expenditures, assignment of more autonomy to the Kombinate, moves toward convertiblity of the currency.[29] The report of November 10, 1989, had showed that of 1989's planned net export profits of 1.3 billion marks only 0.3 had actually been realized.[30] In his first Volkskammer speech on November 17, Modrow called for a creative alliance to carry forward democratization and promised to "do everything such that we achieve the stabilization of our economy so urgently needed and our national product resumes its real growth." The Council of Ministers resolved on November 23 to develop a "Basic Concept for the Stabilization of the Economy of the GDR."[31] And it still grasped at straws. Demands for permanent visas and permission to emigrate, so the reformers cheered themselves, had plummeted in the fortnight since the Wall was opened.[32] (By January, however, the numbers were way up again.) The basic challenge was the balance of trade with the nonsocialist world: the DDR had to achieve in 1990 a net surplus of 2 billion valuta marks, which meant lowering domestic consumption to 95 percent of 1989—austerity measures that were far more demanding than Schürer's projections of what was likely.[33] What would the new economic policy look like? Greater reliance on the principle of productivity; greater openness to foreign investment.

The Modrow government did not really have a well-thought-out policy in the face of the impending transformation. Its strategy was first to "stabilize" production and only then to reform. The Planning Commission, industrial ministries, and Institute for Applied Economics bent their efforts to keeping up production in the face of emigration and a general crisis of socialist confidence, not to restructuring. The new economics minister, Christa Luft, had no better concept. She enjoyed meeting West German economic leaders but pushed through no urgent changes.[34] At the end of April, Lothar de Maizière told Gorbachev that the task of the Modrow government in which he had served had been to keep the people from freezing or starving. "The whole activity of the government was really a reaction to these real fears of the time. We succeeded in averting them."[35]

These preoccupations were understandable, but hardly went far enough. As Harry Maier, the expert on the GDR economy who had fled in 1987, argued, the effort to stabilize rather than abandon the system "testifies to a very confused plan."[36] In fact, many economic diagnoses of winter 1990 were confused in both the East and the West. It dawned only slowly on East Germans (and on many West Germans as well) that the East German industrial plant, viable among the decrepit economies of the East, would be catastrophically obsolete in a Western context. The press during the winter months was slowly moving away from the autumn's still somewhat optimistic estimates of the reforms and assistance needed to make what one GDR manager hoped might, admittedly over the course of a decade, turn out to be an East German Switzerland.[37] The most urgent problem seemed the disparity of incomes and consumption. This "take" emerged naturally from the pictures of East Berliners surging across the newly opened Wall in their boxy Trabants to purchase the fresh fruit or other goods of the West. What seemed to loom ahead during the interim between November 1989 and the elections of March 1990 was less a collapse of production than a preemptive consumer revolution. Even in late January 1990, East German publication of its third-quarter 1989 statistics suggested merely that the GDR economy had grown only 2 percent instead of the predicted 4 percent—hardly a catastrophic downturn.[38] Industrial production and the supply of repair parts for agricultural machinery were in short supply—but repair parts had always been a weak point. Meanwhile enterprises were departing from planning guidelines and making private deals to secure what they needed for their own production: in effect going over unofficially to market principles. Pay increases were being conceded faster than productivity increased; families sought consumer goods. In effect the pressure of popular mobilization was dissipating in a pay hike—a phenomenon common enough in twentieth-century Europe, whether Germany after 1919, France and Italy in 1968–69, or Poland in 1970 and 1980. In most all those situations, employers and the state paid workers to return to their factories and offices and then usually depended on inflation to annul what they had conceded.

Germans, however, were not about to use inflation to take back what they could not afford to concede. Instead they tended to minimize the cost estimates, and quickly agreed that the West should cover many of them. Most West Germans did not realize in the winter of 1990 that the bill would be far higher than it initially appeared, since ultimately it included more than a decade of nonrenewed capital. The Social Democratic leadership would challenge Chancellor Kohl on the projected costs of taking over East German salary and welfare obligations and renewing its productive base. The political stakes of the dispute in light of the impending elections, first in the East, then later in the West, did not encourage sober analyses. Social Democratic leader Oskar Lafontaine was correct when he argued through 1990 that the chancellor's estimates were far too low; but what the SPD did not grasp as it later campaigned on the issue of the true cost of unification, and what the chancellor understood but refused to declare outright, was that for such a great national achievement as democratic reunification, no financial exertion should have been too high.

Analysis of the East German economy as of early 1990 reveals a paradoxical situation. In the months before unification West German policy makers and commentators focused more on the relative deprivation of East German consumers than the deficiencies of production. In their countless interviews, many of the Western business leaders suggested that with a relatively brief and inexpensive investment, the East German economy would surge forward quickly, so long as it was set on market principles. Consumer disparaties seemed more preoccupying, for they threatened to unleash continued and increasing migration of young and vigorous workers to the West. In fact, raising real incomes in the East was probably less urgent than it seemed. East Germans remained relatively prosperous with a per capita national income about half of the West's, comparable with that of the poorer countries in the European Community. This degree of prosperity rested in part on Western credits, and in part on refining and selling underpriced Soviet oil to the West. In any case, the only comparison that counted in the winter of 1990 was with West Germany. In a late February report, one of the government's major economic institutes summarized the economic situation for Modrow. The East German mark commanded almost as many domestic goods as did the Federal Republic's, but real income of FRG households was twice as high. And this disparity, reflecting the almost-twice-as-high Western labor productivity, existed despite an estimated net 28 billion marks of East German price subsidies, not even counting artificially low rents.[39]

Nonetheless, despite the income disparities, the preoccupation with the plight of consumers was misplaced. East Germans faced no catastrophic shortages in early 1990. The mild winter weather meant that power supplies were not overstretched. The trouble was that what consumers wished to buy, often with their accumulated salaries, was marginally less available: apartment construction had slipped, there were fewer swine going to market. The decline was not catastrophic, but it set in at the very moment East German consumers raised their expectations. In late January the ministers were told of increasing consumer dissatisfaction; there was a monetary "overhang" and insufficient goods.[40] Yet conditions were not disastrous; basic provisioning continued through February; groceries and meat were available; the population wanted more meat, children's clothes, chocolate, and consumer electronics. Groceries and fancy foods (Genußmittel) climbed in February 1990, 5 percent over the previous February and almost 7 percent over the prior month, as West Berlin and FRG food concerns offered high-priced vegetables and fruits on the Eastern market. By this time most East Germans had crossed to the West or gotten complete reports on the consumer goods it offered: 600,000 to 900,000 residents of East and West were crossing their border daily; and over a million on Saturdays and Sundays. The pathologies of consumerism were also emerging. Drugs were appearing in greater supply: from the opening of the Wall to March 1, 300 border crossers were caught with diverse narcotics. Traffic accidents were increasing: in the first two months of 1990 there were almost 8,500 accidents with 284 deaths, almost 50 percent more than the corresponding period in 1989. In short, decades of Communist austerity were dissolving as fast as the decadent and dangerous offerings of Western consumer capitalism allowed.[41] A consumer revolution of rising expectations was taking place.

Preoccupied by the income gradient, observers were only beginning to understand how costly would be the renewal of decayed infrastructure and the industrial restructuring of an economy that had thrived in the socialist world, but would prove unviable in the capitalist context.[42] By focusing in early 1990 on public deprivation, FRG experts underplayed the deficiencies of capital. Most GDR projections were no better; they envisaged a relatively small shortfall of planned output. There were some exceptions. The Institute for Applied Economies signaled the potential catastrophe ahead. Its economists estimated that a three- to five-year adjustment period would be needed in the transition to a market economy to avoid mass unemployment.[43] Most frightening: up to 80 percent of the country's enterprises were noncompetitive and threatened because of technological backwardness, worn-out capital, and poor quality output.[44] This report had the virtue of at least estimating a capital requirement from the FRG of 700 to 720 billion marks, which proved to be far closer to reality than some of the lighthearted West German estimates ranging from 60 to 100 billion.

Whether Germans fretted about consumption or focused on investment, the East, it was clear, must become ever more dependent on the West. The Federal Republic would have to underwrite the East German currency, in effect peg the Ostmark at a high level and pay for East German imports from the West. As his price for such support, Kohl would press for a rapid and total unification. Could the GDR leadership have resisted the chancellor's deutsche mark blandishments? Only insofar as East Germans were willing to reduce the purchasing power of their own cosseted currency by accepting further devaluation and increasing exports might they aspire to a convertible Ostmark and set limits to their dependency on the FRG. Such an austerity program, however, would, it was feared, accelerate the flow of impatient migrants to the wealthier Federal Republic next door. The potential for mass migration alarmed both sides: it frightened East German leaders whose precarious economy had traditionally required the young and skilled labor and professionals who could now freely depart. On the other hand, the prospect of a massive immigration likewise disquieted the West Germans and thus remained one of the few remaining trumps GDR negotiators still retained in their negotiations with Bonn.

The specter of unabating migration thus tended to make both sides focus on the vulnerability of East German purchasing power. It militated for a currency rescue plan, the substitution of the East German currency by the West German deutsche mark. It would pressure the East Germans to accept subsidies and dependency rather than attempt the consumer austerity that alone might prop up the GDR as an independent country. It would persuade Kohl and his compatriots to rescue the purchasing power and the savings of the East German citizenry by proposing a vast substitution of deutsche mark for East marks at a level far higher than the free market would ever have warranted. In effect Modrow's republic was too dependent on hand-outs to insist on its own independence; only the unwelcome prospect of a mass flight of East Germans to the West provided the GDR with any lever-age. When Modrow met with Rudolf Seiters, head of the Federal Chancel-lery, on January 25, Seiters expressed concern that 42,500 had already moved to the West since the turn of the year. Modrow was happy to sum-mon up the specter that developments could careen out of control to argue against West German insistence on rapid unification. In fact, Modrow was more fundamentally hostage to East German impatience than was Kohl. Modrow had a state to lose, Kohl had only a deficit to risk. "If developments are provoked in an all-German direction, as in Leipzig," so Modrow com-plained to Seiters about the prounification slogans the Monday night dem-onstrators now routinely shouted, "there's a danger of escalation."

Both Modrow and Kohl appealed to "Europe": Modrow to slow the pres-sure for unity, Kohl to demonstrate that unification would enhance, not endanger the European project. Since "Europe" as such was an aspiration and not an actuality, the invocation was more likely to help Kohl. From the 1860s on, appeals to "Europe" have never effectively impeded German na-tional aspirations. (On the other hand, they need not always be at odds.)[45]

Rescuing East German purchasing power attracted many supporters in West Germany. It seemed the right gesture to make toward their long-de-prived compatriots. Citizens of the Federal Republic were long aware that while their former co-citizens in the East had paid heavy postwar repara-tions to the Soviets, they instead had benefited from Marshall Plan aid. The SPD senator from West Berlin, Heide Pfarr, and the maverick CDU leader, Kurt Biedenkopf (later to become minister-president of Saxony), both pro-posed FRG reparations to the GDR in late 1989. Indeed Chancellor Kohl dangled the notion of a "solidarity contribution" of DM 15 billion when he visited Dresden on December 19—an offer the government withdrew, how-ever, in early February in favor of the currency union proposal that was gathering support.[46] The idea of supplanting the GDR mark by means of a so-called currency unit was first proposed publicly by the SPD finance spokesperson in the Bundestag, Ingrid Matthäus Maier, in mid-January. It had the advantage of not appearing just as compensation for the FRG's prior good fortune, but was nonetheless rejected by members of the CDU-FDP coalition who preferred the East Germans to get their own house in order; the Council of Economic Advisers (Sachverständigenrat) did not even men-tion a currency union in its January 20 report on the state of the economies. Two and half weeks later, it responded to the emerging concepts with a gradualist plan. Most West German commentators and organizations urged only a phased monetary merger. FDP Economics Minister Haussmann rejected the idea of an immediate currency union as a panacea that might undermine the deutsche mark. It should come in early 1993, along with the completion of the European Community's 1992 project, after the GDR had reformed its economy from within. Similarly the president of the Federation of German Industry, Tyll Necker, suggested on January 23 a five-stage plan culminating in a currency union only at the end of 1992. Advocates of a gradual currency union envisaged that economic restructuring and convertibility of the Ostmark must precede monetary unification. A price reform (i.e., increase) that dismantled the implicit subsidies so pervasive in socialist economies was also necesssary.

Such a long prospect no longer fit in with Kohl's thinking; as Modrow's late January talks with Seiters revealed, the chancellor was pressing for a rapid and thoroughgoing unification. On February 6, the same day that Economics Minister Haussmann was expounding his gradualist three-stage concept to FDP parliamentarians, the coalition party leaders, Kohl, Otto Graf Lambsdorff of Haussmann's own FDP, and Theodor Waigel of the CSU, resolved instead to propose an immediate negotiation on an economic and currency union to Modrow, a plan they announced and extracted cabinet approval for the very next day. The economic and currency union, the government claimed, would staunch the flow of East German migration, would encourage Western investment in the GDR, and would accelerate political unification as well. In fact the tempo of the decision suggests that Kohl and his advisers were rushing to stay ahead of an economic and political momentum that might otherwise overwhelm their own control of events. "We have to take into account," said Waigel, "that things there [in the GDR] are accelerating extraordinarily, that almost all forces desire and demand political unity, and also a common currency, that is the introduction of the deutsche mark."[47] The sudden decision disconcerted Bundesbank President Karl Otto Pöhl, who on February 6 was being briefed by his GDR counterparts on their dismaying situation, and had told the press that the financial experts on both sides regarded a currency union as "rather premature and rather fantastic." Nonetheless, the bank, he announced with discomfort, would accept the plan as a political decision: in return it must retain freedom of action in fulfilling its mission in the East German territory. In other words, Frankfurt would swallow the currency union provided it was guaranteed its policy autonomy with respect to East as well as West Germany: there could be no special pleading by Bonn or the new

Länder. And in fact, when the government resorted to deficit financing to cover the costs of unification after 1990, the bank responded with sharp rises in interest rates. Having secured Pöhl's reluctant support, the Kohl government formally proposed the union when Modrow arrived in Bonn on February 13. Other bank directors and members of the Council of Economic Advisers, who were not officially consulted, reacted skeptically and did not conceal their opposition. They envisaged huge costs and massive unemployment unless the East German currency was devalued and made convertible. The bond market also reacted badly as interest rates rose as purchasers anticipated inflationary pressures. "To provide the GDR with hard Western marks," so *Der Spiegel* explained,[48] "the Bundesbank would have to resort to the printing press" and risk that German bogey, inflation.

The currency union proposal aroused enthusiasm within the GDR. The political elements friendly to the CDU were natural supporters, and the chance to have savings accounts and wages converted at par seemed a bonanza. Rainer Eppelmann's Demokratischer Aufbruch was the first organization to call for an immediate introduction of the deutsche mark into the GDR, and with a one-to-one exchange for East German savings accounts. By March and April introduction of the deutsche mark had a 90 percent approval ratio, despite the expectations that a reduction of social welfare provisions and an increase in unemployment would follow. Economically sophisticated commentators feared that, if East German firms were weighted down with deutsche mark debts and had to pay deutsche mark salaries, recession and unemployment might strike hard. The Modrow government understood, too, that a currency union must effectively wipe out any freedom of action for the GDR regime; it was tantamount to de facto unification. Nonetheless, by the eve of the elections, the East German leader had been amply warned that he had precious little room for maneuver.[49]

When Modrow met with Gorbachev and Nikolai Ryzhkov, president of the Soviet Council of Ministers, in Moscow on March 5 and 6, he may have been cheered by Gorbachev's somewhat rambling fulmination against Kohl's rapid moves toward unification. But the Soviet leader promised little concrete assistance, and someone so mercurial might easily change. In terms of economic development, Modrow told Ryzhkov that their two countries should preserve all the advantages of cooperation they could. Nonetheless, he cautioned, we must not succumb to any wishful thinking: There were three realities: (1) Both countries were on the way to a market economy. The GDR had recently taken the needed legislative steps; foreign capital would be entering the country. That would bring in the next months completely new conditions for the cooperation of enterprises and institutions of both lands. (2) Completely new conditions were intervening on the world market; not a few enterprises faced going out of business. And not only from the world market but from the agreement that after 1991 Soviet-GDR trade would be factored in world market prices and eventually convertible currencies. (3) "The currency union of the GDR with the FRG and thus the takeover of DM as the means of payment on the territory of GDR could not be resisted for long." Modrow would endeavor, he said, to use the combined German economic assets to work for Soviet as well as GDR advantage. Kohl had offered to help the GDR fulfill its delivery commitments to the Soviets, on the one hand to buy Moscow's acquiescence in unity, on the other to ease the GDR burden.

Modrow found the proposal had some difficulties but was not simply to be rejected. Triangular relationships were to be developed. A particularly sensitive point was the evidently huge East German uranium mining firm, Wismut-AG, which had been a cynosure of the Soviets since the days of the occupation zone. But uranium needs were dropping and 40,000 workers were threatened. The Soviets were also unilaterally cutting oil deliveries. No solutions were promised.[50] At home the GDR public was focusing on the chancellor and the rescue of purchasing power that he stood for. When East Germans took to the streets, they did so as part of the electoral campaign. While the Monday night demonstrations in Leipzig now drew only 5,000 participants, apparently composed prevailingly of West German demonstrators (including the right-wing populist Republikaner), 100,000 had gathered in Chemnitz to hear Chancellor Kohl on March 1.[51] The vote for the CDU on March 18 was a vote for rapid unfication and a vote for Kohl to deploy the deutsche mark in a currency union. In early April FRG finance bureaucrats prepared a paper outlining the conditions for an economic union. Modrow's efforts to legislate conditions for joint ventures and other economic frameworks were effectively disregarded; the new terms provided that initiatives for finance legislation would remain with Bonn.[52]

After the election, an alarmed Jürgen Habermas, the preeminent left intellectual of postwar Germany, condemned deutsche mark nationalism and the premature foreclosure of choice for the GDR. "What will become of German identity? Are economic problems steering the unification process down a sober path? Or has the deutsche mark been invested with libido, and thus emotionally bid up such that a sort of economic nationalism is overwhelming republican consciousness?" All German interests were being weighed in terms of the deutsche mark. "Granted, the whine of the Stukas was worse than this coda. But the view of German muscle flexing is obscene nonetheless."[53] Habermas was certainly not alone in March to worry about the intoxicating mood of impending nationalism, especially given Kohl's apparent reluctance in these very weeks to acknowledge the finality of the Polish border. Nonetheless, unless the majority of March 18 was to be condemned for voting under conditions of false consciousness, it was hard to criticize the popular result. Moreover, even at the level of Habermas's philosophical arguments, it would have been possible to respond that monetary unification should be construed not as the alarming wedge of an atavistic nationalism, but as acceptance of the fact that the transactions comprising modern national life took place preeminently at the level of business, commerce, credit, and savings, and not of sovereign power. The East Germans in effect were voting for a unified civil society, not any exalted authority. But if civil society in Eastern Europe meant the reemergence of an automous press and church and unions, it also meant revitalization of autonomous economic organizations: a chance for capitalism. Actually the East German voter was voting for his security as a consumer more than his freedom as an entrepreneur, and public opinion was ill prepared for the rude awakening to East German economic decrepitude that would follow in the next few years. Monetary union beckoned in March 1990 in effect as a rainbow bridge to an economic Valhalla; not to a resurgence of German nationalism. In fact, it ended up bringing about neither.

Now the decision for a currency union did not specify at which rate the conversion would be made; this became the major social and economic choice confronting the Kohl government in the period after the March 18 elections. The issue was lurking from the first mention of a currency union. Would East German savings accounts be credited at one deutsche mark for each East mark or would they receive only a fractional sum consonant with the depleted exchange rate of the GDR currency? Kohl had promised "small savers" a one-to-one rate shortly before the election. But a few days afterward, on March 22, the president of the Bundesbank, Karl Otto Pöhl, urged the chancellor to choose a lower ratio. He stressed the burden of debt that would also be converted into deutsche marks: a net 34 billion marks owed by the GDR to foreign creditors and 260 billion East marks owed by Kombinate and enterprises to the East German State Bank, slated to be absorbed by the Bundesbank. Pöhl pointed out to Kohl that the Bundesbank was legally precluded from taking over the foreign debt; that would have to become the liability of the federal budget, to be covered by deutsche mark borrowing or taxes. As for the Kombinate debt, if it was to be converted into deutsche marks at one to one, the annual interest charges of about DM 20 billion would simply bankrupt a large number of East German enterprises. The ministers thus agreed that the debts of the state firms must be halved by revaluing them at a ratio of 2 East marks to 1 deutsche mark.

But Kombinate debt was a central bank asset. The 50 percent cut would reduce Bundesbank holdings by DM 130 billion. If Frankfurt could not correspondingly write down GDR savings accounts (which were listed as a central bank liability), the difference would have to be covered by credit creation on the part of the Bundesbank. Even if these credits were sold as bonds to West German or foreign purchasers, the economy would have to come up with about DM 10 billion per year in interest payments. Thus the higher the conversion rate for savings accounts, the greater the transfer needed from West to East. As it turned out the Bundesbank would end up expanding the all-German monetary base (M3, which included savings accounts and bank credits as well as cash and ready money) by DM 180 billion in 1990. This amounted to expanding the previous West German M3 by about 15 percent. But this initial injection was only the beginning of a stream of transfers and credits whose extent few were able or willing to imagine.[54] Certainly few among the government spokesmen who would face an all-German electorate in December.

Finding the appropriate ratio for converting East German wages into deutsche marks was also a vexing issue. Nonetheless, GDR wages in East mark figures were already significantly lower than West German wages; they could not be further cut in the conversion since East Germans would soon pay higher social and medical insurance premiums and most likely face higher rents. In any case, wage levels would progressively be renegotiated after the union. Wages also had an impact on social insurance premiums and retirement benefits, keyed as a percentage of pay. Even if East German pension rights were not vested as in the West, they would have to be met at some ratio of preretirement wages. Norbert Blüm, Kohl's social welfare minister and a long-term proponent of active social intervention, urged a one-to-one conversion for pensions as well as wages to make the private social contributions possible. The finance minister, Theodor Waigel, preferred a less generous ratio in order to lighten the new social contributions he feared the state must take over.[55] With such major approaches in contention it was not surprising that the debates were leaked to the public. At the very end of March, the Bundesbank leadership proposed a savings account conversion ratio of two to one, fifty pfennigs for every East German mark. When their recommendation was leaked to the press, it provoked massive street demonstrations in East Berlin and Dresden as marchers and speakers protested against the "betrayal" on April 3: "Unless it's one to one, we won't be one."[56]

Faced with these claims on the West German economy, Kohl seemed to waver in his preelection assurance that a mark would be a mark. Accepting too high a claim from East Germans might risk inflation and endanger his prospects for the 1990 all-German elections. Backing away from his one-to-one promise exposed him to Lafontaine's repeated charges that his electoral promise had been deceitful. Otto Graf Lambsdorff, the leader of his coalition partner, the FDP, called him to order: GDR savings accounts must not be sacrificed. The newly elected Volkskammer convened on April 5, poised to elect CDU delegate Lothar de Maizière as minister-president of a Great Coalition supported by all parties but the ex-Communist PDS. De Maizière added his normally restrained voice to the clamor: "One to one is our goal." Walter Romberg, the SPD minister of finance in the GDR Great Coalition, likewise supported the generous conversion ratio.

What conversion might have been suggested by the inherent comparative value of the two currencies? Certainly not one to one. The unofficial exchange rate had fallen first to eight to one just before the opening of the Wall and then to twenty to one by late November 1989, but that rate was far too speculative to establish a standard. Before the crisis of the regime threw the GDR currency into free fall, economic analysts calculated that it required 3.73 East marks of labor and material to earn 1 deutsche mark from the West. Nonetheless, the regime had calculated that its unit of account, the valuta mark (set at 1 deutsche mark) should equal 4.4 East German marks. This would give East German exporters a premium for turning in their earnings to the State Bank for local currency. In any case, without a system of market-determined prices these exchange rate calculations had to remain estimates.[57]

Indeed a one-to-one conversion of marks—indeed, any rate that might be chosen—had to be a problematic concept. In theory the GDR tried to keep wages and prices for its own citizens in some rough parity to what West German citizens paid or received in deutsche marks across the frontier. At the same time, however, the regime reckoned that the deutsche mark bought about four times the output of East German goods or services than its own mark did. Establishing a one-to-one conversion for monetary balances would allow East Germans to feel that their savings would still command the same domestic purchasing power after unification; at the same time, it would also give them a far greater claim on Western goods than their savings might have commanded before (if they could have taken them into the West). From a West German perspective providing parity meant giving East Germans a windfall; from the East German vantage it was merely avoiding expropriation. The value to assign had to be an arbitrary decision.

For the Bundesbank and many in the West German industrial community such a windfall would be perilous; the new exchange rate should confirm the significant amputation of real monetary assets that East German policies had brought about during previous years, but which a nonconvertible currency had concealed. The bank's option would incorporate, in effect, a "monetary reform," or an amputation of paper claims on the economy, similar to that imposed by the Allies in 1948, when old Reichsmark accounts were replaced by new deutsche marks at a ratio of one to ten. Even earlier, at the end of the great post–World War I hyperinflation, the Weimar Republic had replaced the old mark with new currencies, first the Rentenmark, then the Reichsmark, at a rate amounting to one to a trillion! Such a write-off of paper claims effectively wipes out savings accounts and mortgages and preserves the value only of real assets such as houses and factories. Pension accumulations and insurance policies have to be adjusted if they are to retain any continuing value. In effect replacing the old money finally takes account of the fact, so long disguised, that the society has squandered its productive power in a war, or used it to invest in obsolescent plants. It hurts those who have most virtuously deferred from consumption and reveals to angry savers or pensioners that their parsimony has been in vain. Nonetheless, such a write-off has the advantage of freeing firms from old debt, thus allowing new business expansion. Since, too, there is no overvalued currency to defend, central bank officials can keep domestic interest rates relatively low, thereby facilitating domestic investment and expansion. It can rescue employment at the cost of savings. It may favor the future at the expense of the past, the young at the cost of the old.

Preserving the value of the old currency (or even raising it far beyond its effective purchasing power) produces the opposite effect. This is what a one-for-one exchange implied: East marks currently trading at anywhere from ten to one to twenty to one, would in this scenario be replaced at a one-to-one ratio. Such a conversion would grant savings account holders the value of their monetary claims now in deutsche marks, thus rendering real the fiction that the GDR had long sought unsuccessfully to claim. This policy would preserve the full value of East German savings accounts and pension plans in the new all-German economic union. In fact it would multiply their effective purchasing power in the West by about four to one, and for some big-ticket items such as autos and appliances even more. The West German industrial worker had to labor 83.5 hours for a color television; the East German needed 739 hours.[58] But, as explained already, a one-to-one conversion would require more credit creation, higher transfers West to East, and greater inflationary pressure. Given the Bundesbank's priority of price stability, these pressures would have ultimately to be contained by tax hikes or higher interest rates, lest foreigners otherwise shun a deutsche mark they now believed overvalued. Higher rates would weigh down the indebted Kombinate and impede modernization. As the international monetary crisis of Black September 1992 finally revealed, high rates did off-load some of the real costs of recapitalizing Germany on to foreigners in the European Monetary System. But the "higher" the conversion ratio in terms of old East marks to new deutsche marks (i.e., the lower the value attributed to the East mark), the less need for the higher interest rates that would burden the indebted Kombinate and discourage new investment.

The stakes involved in the dispute thus involved not only the accumulated savings of the East German population, but the level of employment as well. And not only because prevailing interest rates would rise, but because wages seemed likely to climb significantly. Labor productivity was so much lower in East Germany that any campaign for wage equality with the West must also undermine firms and endanger jobs. Despite this danger, however, the West German trade-union federation (DGB) soon supported a rapid equalization of wages to protect salaries in the FRG. So, too, the East German labor federation, the FDGB, finally speaking with some independence after forty years of domination by the party, also wanted to make wage catch-up an issue. Conversion of savings at one to one promised a useful precedent for wage equalization. The DGB and FDGB were not yet persuaded by the argument that they might be pricing their jobs out of existence.

In effect, the 1990 currency union turned out to be the third major German monetary reform of the twentieth century. The Germans avoided the term "monetary reform" because it implied a drastic reduction of outstanding monetary claims, whereas 1990's operation was the only one that revalued money-denominated assets, and thereby gave priority to the claims of savings over job security. In 1924 and in 1948, bank account holders effectively sacrificed their accumulated savings, but the cancellation of debt allowed the economy to rebound quickly and new savings to be generated. The opposite course was chosen in 1990: with the encouragement of the unions, savings were privileged over jobs. It was ironic that the unions endorsed this approach. Still, it made sense from another perspective; for the monetary reform of 1990 also involved trade-offs that were fundamentally different from the earlier currency operations. The adjustments, after all, were to take place within a relatively small part of the country. Whereas the monetary replacements of 1923–24 and 1948 involved transfering claims on wealth within the whole national economic community (by and large despoliating bank account holders for the benefit of those with real estate or enerprises), the Economic and Monetary Union required a transfer of resources from West to East. All East German elements—savers and wage earners—and many West Germans, too, thought this transfer should be as large as necessary to reach parity of living conditions as soon as possible.

In 1990 the full extent of these transfers was still unsuspected. Germany had not squandered productive assets in a major lost war; the powerful West German economy seemed large and robust enough to support the smaller GDR; the massive infusions of capital that would be required to make East German industry competitive were only slowly dawning on the experts. Harry Maier, the rather savvy former East German economist, argued that there was really no need to write down the East German bank accounts. Despite the fact that GDR wages had outpaced the goods its citizens might purchase, the currency "overhang" was moderate: savings accounts per capita averaged 9,000 local marks, versus an average of 11,600 in the Federal Republic. Gerhard Fels of the Cologne Institut der deutschen Wirtschaft agreed: "Ten thousand marks savings per head is nothing exceptional." As long as the central bank of the GDR remained independent, a one-to-one rate could be defended; after all the Austrians effectively pegged the Schilling to the deutsche mark and the East Germans could do the same if they didn't strive for a catch-up of wages.[59]

The internal debate on the terms of the Economic and Currency Union lasted approximately a month after the elections of March 18. Increasingly the chancellor found himself at odds with the members of his own CDU and the allied CSU, who took up the hesitations of the Bundesbank. An unconditional exchange of savings accounts, wages, and pensions at one to one, CSU spokesmen Michael Glos charged in the Bundestag, brought with it the danger of inflation, as the bank would create the money to meet these new claims.[60] The Bundesbank and the minister of finance won a compromise on the bank account conversion: one-to-one conversion was granted for savings accounts up to 4,000 marks for savers between fourteen and fifty-nine. Children under fourteen received a one-to-one conversion up to 2,000 marks; citizens over fifty-nine got the benefit extended up to 6,000 East marks. Above these respective maximums, conversion came at 50 pfennig to the East mark or one to two. Blum prevailed in his effort to protect wages and pensions, both to be converted at one to one, although even a full deutsche mark conversion still had East German wages significantly lower than those in the West. In his official government declaration before the Volkskammer on April 19, de Maizière provided the outlines of the impending compromise, along the lines of the Bundesbank's scheme, and the West German government published its proposals on April 23.[61] The East Germans accepted the terms on May 2 and the State Treaty establishing a Currency, Economic, and Social Union was signed in Bonn on May 18, to come into force six weeks later, on July 1.[62] It was ratified by the respective parliaments on June 21 and 22, after each had passed a resolution recognizing the Oder-Neisse line as the permanent border between the unified state and Poland.

The "State Treaty" was the first of two intra-German compacts to merge East and West (for the second or "Unification Treaty" signed on August 31, see the subsequent discussion): this first agreement expressed formally the two countries' aspiration for unification, now on the basis of article 23 of the 1949 Basic Law (entry as a whole or as individual Länder into the existing Federal Republic), not article 146 (which envisaged the alternative of a new constitutional convention). The "social market economy" was sanctioned as the basis of the common economic order of the two treaty partners and East German rules that stipulated "socialist" legality or the supremacy of socialist parties or concepts were abrogated. FRG legal principles and provisions, including the existing West German role of the Bundesbank, were extended to East Germany. The thorny questions of property rights were regulated: restitution of private property was granted to all those whose holdings had been expropriated after the foundation of the DDR (but not to those whose property was taken over during the Soviet occupation period between 1945 and 1949). On July 1, branches of the Deutsche Bank opened in East Berlin; Burger King brought in a mobile hamburger outlet into Dresden; the massive Bertelsmann Verlag sent bookmobiles. This writer took a train from Prague to Dresden two days later. Calculated in dollars but purchased in depreciated crowns, the first-class Czech rail ticket cost less than the German taxi, its meter now ticking away in deutsche marks, from the Dresden train station to the hotel a kilometer away. East Germans had landed in the capacious monetary arms of their once and future countrymen—but their economic difficulties had hardly ended. The now expensive Dresden taxi driver would not face competition from the cabbie in Stuttgart or London, but the Leipzig computer firm or the Rostock shipyard was no longer shielded.

2 + 4 = 1: THE DIPLOMACY OF UNIFICATION

East Germans had rarely made their own history, but they had often had a larger role in its construction than Western onlookers imagined. What role, though, could they play in the final euthanasia of their republic? The East German government had far less influence than it hoped. The new officials of the GDR initially expected that their reform course would guarantee their status vis-à-vis their West German counterparts. In fact the leadership continued to be marginalized between November 1989 and the summer of 1990. The opening of the Wall immediately reduced one resource for bargaining that the GDR regime still held. After all, its major asset vis-à-vis the Federal Republic had been the capacity to open and close the spigot of movement and human rights more generally. But if the East German regime faded into fecklessness, the GDR's populace as a whole, if mobilized in the streets, as again in January, or at the polls in mid-March, could still retain a major collective influence.

Two issues proved critical between autumn 1989 and summer 1990. The first was substantive and involved the final lodging of a united Germany within the North Atlantic alliance; if the West and the West Germans insisted on continued German adherence to NATO, the Soviets might still choose to exert a veto. The second issue was procedural and involved the very pace of the fusion. Hesitations about German unification that might be harbored by GDR residents, or by non-Germans, were expressed coyly in terms of tempo. Reluctant participants or onlookers could not decently deny German self-determination outright—it had been inscribed as a goal in Western declarations ever since the war—but they might contest the speed of the process. Unable to say "stop," they might plead "slow down." Would not a rush to unification upset the delicate European order and destabilize the relations on a continent where both sides had made a fetish of stability? Between a stately andante of gradual confederation and an impetuous allegro, so the reluctant observers argued, the stake was the continued prospect for European security. *Takt* and tact, tempo and prudence must hang together. The very preoccupation with tempo, however, provided the East German crowds with a capacity for collective agency that their fading regime was losing. Mass migration to the West or further demonstrations in the East would signal to Kohl and to the non-German powers that progress must continue. Demonstrations could force the process of negotiations until elections confirmed popular aspirations. The unwillingness of any outside power to deny ultimate unification allowed popular mobilization to render the flow of history less viscous. As Chancellor Kohl was to tell CDU delegates convening in West Berlin in mid-December, "The developments in the GDR will be shaped by the people there; they can't be planned at the green baize table or according to a date book."[63]

As early as November 20, the Leipzig demonstrators had chanted: "We are one people," not just "We are the people." Despite the suspicion of intellectuals affiliated with the civic movements, the slogan did not emanate from opportunistic late-comers to the popular upheaval or nationalists crossing from the West. Surveys of 2,000 demonstrators revealed by mid-December that a third were strongly for unity, another third more for it than against. Of the demonstrators on December 11, half had participated seven times, that is at least since late October; indeed 30 percent claimed to have been at the church prayers for peace before October 9. About 85 percent were Leipzig residents, and most were workers or white-collar employees. A third were women. Although Leipzig was a university town, student participation ranged only from 4 to 17 percent in December: the SED, whose members tended to remain at home, effectively constrained protest from student ranks. Those on the streets, in short, were committed and mature members of the local workforce. Until the emerging political parties took up campaigning at the marches in early 1990, the crowds and their slogans expressed generally held aspirations—and these became increasingly oriented toward unification. For the Leipzig historian Hartmut Zwahr, this aspiration was neither surprising nor undesirable: the crowd's national aspiration emerged naturally, almost archaically, and to many intellectuals, West as well as East, even embarrassingly from the deprivation of national and democratic rights that this stolid citizenry had hitherto endured. "Before them hovered a vision of the nation-state that Europe, perhaps no longer needed and which, despite the division of Germany, the normal change of generations seemed to have removed from view in West Germany."[64] "Germany: united fatherland": the shout thus had its logic—but also its echoes. "German unity will come, earlier than anyone presumed," wrote Rolf Schneider in *Der Spiegel*, now accessible, like all the West German media, to the East German intelligentsia, "It will come and many Germans are themselves uncomfortable, justifiably and for good historical reasons."[65]

Indeed each of the major nations concerned with the upheaval in Central Europe saw the potential for unification immediately even if their leaders talked in terms of continuity and reform. After the opening of the Wall, West Germans hastened to a public meeting before West Berlin's Schöneberg City Hall, summoned by Mayor Walter Momper, who, ten days earlier, had predicted along with so many others, a separate and democratic GDR. Willy Brandt heralded the end of the "unnatural division" of Germany and promised that "what belongs together will grow together." Chancellor Kohl cut short his visit in Warsaw and hopped an American plane in Hamburg to get to a Berlin that was not yet accessible to German carriers. Germans were moved, the Soviets cautious. Gorbachev urged Kohl to avoid precipitating events and to help avert "chaos." The chancellor thanked Gorbachev in his remarks and praised their personal relationship, demanded the right of self-determination for all Europeans and Germans, and argued for "thoughtful step-by-step" advance.[66] Before a larger spontaneous crowd at the Gedächtniskirche, he responded more freely to the cheers: "A free German fatherland lives. A free, united Europe lives." To the press conference in Bonn the next day he insisted that the East Germans must decide what they wanted, but "I have no doubt what they want. There can be no doubt that the Germans want the unity of their nation." His remarks reconfirmed the linkage between united Germany and a European commitment that he had already emphasized to the Bundestag as the premise of his diplomacy on the day before the Wall opened: "We are no wanderers between East and West, and we have learned from the history of this century. Reunification and integration with the West, German policy and European policy, are like two sides of the same medal."[67]

Of the non-German powers the United States was most prepared to welcome unification. Certainly the Bush administration reacted to the dramatic events in Berlin with proper caution. Secretary of State James Baker told Genscher that unrestricted travel was not unification; and the president said that he did not want to gloat to the Russians—he was not an emotional kind of guy, he told reporters.[68] Still, the American government would see unification as the reward for steadfast resolution, and not just as a frightening development to be delayed as long as possible. Indeed Americans had continued to believe in eventual unification in a way that even Germans had largely ceased to do: as State Department official Rozanne Ridgway commented in March 1989, unification was "the subject that all Americans are interested in and no German cares about."[69] The Republican Party in the postwar era had traditionally been more moved by the need to draw upon German strength and solidity in the NATO framework than it had over any lingering memories of Germany's prior aggressions. If one asked "middle-American" travelers on a flight back from European vacation, they thought of Germans as the non–English-speaking Europeans most similar to themselves. No overtones of Henry Jamesian complexity shadowed the German experience most Americans had enjoyed. U.S. visitors liked the sociability of beer drinking; the Germans were friendly to students; they would not overcharge tourists as Latin peoples allegedly might; they were clean; they did not have the French hang-ups about insisting on their language; the cities were physically spiffy and not so large as to feel threatening. To be sure, the left of the Democratic Party, intellectuals, academics, and most adults of Jewish background had not mentally transmuted Auschwitz into Colonel Klink's layabout Stalag. They had longer historical memories and some, though certainly not all, might fret about the potential danger of a reunified Germany; nonetheless, the American political class generally felt that Germany was a tried and true democracy.[70] They had been reassured by Helmut Schmidt and Chancellor Kohl's successful fight for upgraded missile deployment in the early 1980s against the significant left opposition within the Federal Republic. In the months of late 1989 and early 1990 American policy circles would support unification with frank enthusiasm, as if the child that they had helped to nurture to such robust stature was finally to make his own way in the world. Bush especially supported unification, in private and public. "Let Europe be whole and free," he told a German audience on June 1. "We seek self-determination for all of Germany and for Eastern Europe." "There is in some quarters a feeling," he recognized in a Montana press conference on September 18, "—well, a reunified Germany would be detrimental to the peace of Europe, of Western Europe some way; and I don't accept that at all, simply don't." Five weeks later he told R. W. Apple of the *New York Times*, "I don't share the concern that other countries have about a reunified Germany."[71]

An Agenda Emerges

Members of the National Security Council (NSC), including Robert Black-will and his young staff who monitored European developments, shared President Bush's straightforward stance, which was so unencumbered by the shadows of the Third Reich. State Department advisers were more oriented toward signals from the European foreign offices, and contextualized German policy in a larger matrix of unavowed hesitations. When younger NSC staff members had suggested in early 1989 that in light of the rapidly disappearing sense of confrontation, it was time for the United States to raise again the issue of German and of continental division, State Department advisors threw cold water on the idea: "There is no more inflammatory and divisive issue, and it serves no U.S. interest for us to take the initiative to raise it."[72] In the spring of 1989, from Moscow to Washington, there was a heightened expectancy that the fundamental issues of German and European division might soon emerge again: indicatively the London *Economist* raised the unification issue directly in its June 17 issue. "A common thread ran through every wish [for unification]: the wishers did not mean it. Or rather, they did not need to wonder whether they meant it; for it couldn't happen. This comfortable hypocrisy is no longer available."[73] Still, the *Economist* recognized that the outcome was up to the Russians. American policy makers were not prepared to make any serious effort to put unification on the agenda before the crisis of the GDR. Why should they, so long as Germans seemed to have adjourned the possibility with customary pieties?

Americans would support unification, of course, so long as the price was not an enforced German neutrality. Such a condition would mean that the Russians won as much as they lost and, cold war score cards aside, might also result in an unmoored and unpredictable giant. Unification within the NATO framework, however, would amount to a tremendous shift in the balance of power—unless the Soviet Union were no longer thinking in terms of a fundamental rivalry. Would the Soviets be willing to surrender a separate and friendly East Germany, this major acquisition of World War II? Would they be willing to do so if the new united Germany did not leave NATO? Even if Gorbachev believed, as he told the UN in December 1988, that the countries of East Europe had "freedom of choice," would his military establishment and more conservative Communists really accept a renunciation of the prize that had been so costly to attain four decades earlier?

And did freedom of choice really go so far as to encompass unification? This seemed to strain all credulity. After the event, various Soviet foreign-policy experts said that from early on during Gorbachev's tenure they began thinking about overcoming the "unnatural" division of Germany (see p. 221). But entertaining long-term prospects and overcoming the inertia of a massive and complex policy bureaucracy were different matters. When Kohl visited Moscow in October 1988 Gorbachev had not actively discouraged, but did not respond to Kohl's comment that all Germans had maintained an underlying community persisting despite the boundaries. In February 1989, the then head of the chancellery, Wolfgang Schäuble had declared that Bonn's policy must content itself with the safeguarding of communication between the peoples East and West. Still, Gorbachev could and would eventually wrench Soviet policy along with tremendous alacrity. The question was when and under what form he would allow unification to be put on the table. The East German protesters had demonstrated that they might determine the nature of rule within their country. Only the Soviet Union—as a signator of the still valid 1945 agreement and the 1971 Quadripartite Agreement, and as the possessor of decisive military force in East Germany—could finally determine whether the country stayed in being or ceased to exist. But it would not do so without weighing the transformation that had taken place, the dissolution of the East German frontier, and the evident shakiness of its government.

The clearest protests against unification emanated from London. Margaret Thatcher had cautioned against emotional reactions in a public speech on November 13 and told Bush that the West must make plain that "German reunification is not a matter to be addressed at present." Thatcher repeatedly argued in late fall that consolidation of democracy in the DDR and Eastern Europe was the top priority and that premature talk about reunification would endanger this possibility. Indeed it might undermine Gorbachev and his reforms. This reluctance would remain the continuing theme of British policy through the coming winter and even led—it was charged—to covert appeals to Gorbachev to stand firmer against the rush to unity.[74]

Unless British foot-dragging had support in Paris, however, it would remain ineffective, as had every British effort to slow down the fate of Franco-German convergence since 1950. And the French were unwilling to come out openly against the momentum of events. Mitterrand would doubtless have been happy to have the process move far more slowly; although he publicly stated on November 3 that he did not fear unification, he warned against making Gorbachev insecure and stressed the priority of the European Community. Through early 1990, he would coyly encourage the Soviets to take the lead in opposing Germany in NATO. Still, the Elysée and French diplomacy were not prepared openly to block West German aspirations unless Gorbachev took a harsher line. Although French commentators occasionally fretted about the emergence of a Germany that would dominate their long-term partnership, the only alternative for Paris was to pretend to benevolent sponsorship of the emerging unified Germany, while reassuring the Soviets of their special concern. The result was a pattern of velleity, not a policy of veto. The Germans easily sensed Mitterrand's ambivalence, but Kohl, as an admirer of Adenauer, understood how critical it was for Germany's international status to have a supportive France at his flank. France and President Mitterrand in particular would require a reaffirmed commitment to the European Community, ultimately, as an implicit quid pro quo, support for the negotiations that yielded the Maastricht Treaty.[75]

As Bonn statesmen understood, however, a general benevolent attitude toward unification could quickly sour if the Federal Republic appeared too brusque or clumsy. Suaveness was crucial; declarations of support for "Europe" must be heartfelt and constant. "Europe" would be the mantra—whether the Community for the West or the CSCE for the East—even while Germany was the goal. Kohl's task was to keep the Western allies from becoming upset at too quick a move toward unification. He must also respect East German wishes; indeed, what would finally emerge must have been unclear. Unification, after all, did not preclude a whole spectrum of intermediate confederal type agreements that a still existing East Germany could enter into. Most important for Kohl, though, was to reassure the Soviets that a new united Germany would not constitute a threat. All this meant that the Americans would welcome, the French would not veto, and the British could not veto unification: only Moscow could still impose a halfway solution. For that reason on November 16 the chancellor returned to a cautious line: the East Germans would decide their future for themselves. Visiting Washington, Foreign Minister Genscher even cut short President Bush's speculative question about the possibility of German reunification, which he declared was being talked about more outside his country than within it.[76]

As of late November, then, different strategies were emerging: the British stressing East German liberalization as a goal to set against unification and the four powers as the framework to decide the issue; the Americans emphasizing that the future of Germany was a matter for the Germans to decide;

the West Germans flagging the new institutions to emerge from Ostpolitik and the Helsinki accords as the appropriate frame of reference; the French and Soviets waiting. Could opponents of a quick unification have mobilized a more effective opposition? The politics of memory was perhaps on their side; misgivings were vaporous and diffuse: editorials in the *Washington Post* and the *New York Times* said there was no pressure for unification. At the Christmas reception held by the Council on Foreign Relations, George Kennan pleaded to an audience of members, and to the children (my own included) they had brought to hear the legendary diplomat, against political unification: let there be cultural unity instead.

Against the backdrop of these multiple and confused voices, Chancellor Kohl moved to capture the initiative lest the hesitancies of the Europeans enmesh him in a two-Germanies policy. As his policy adviser Horst Teltschik noted, the discussion at home and abroad was becoming more intense but also more diffuse. Even the friendly Americans' stress on self-determination and their assurance that they would accept unification (the message Genscher heard from Baker) remained nonspecific. But there was an encouraging intimation from the Soviets. Teltschik was informed by Nikolai Portugalov of the international department of the Soviet Central Committee that Moscow was speculating about all sorts of alternatives—"even the almost unthinkable"—though for the midterm it would prefer a possible confederation. Encouraged by this conversation, Teltschik urged Kohl to propose a scenario for unification. If he did not claim the lead, then the FDP or SPD might preempt the issue. (For domestic politics, the fact that the former was the CDU coalition partner made little difference: the chancellor and his own party needed to set the agenda.) On November 24 and 25 Teltschik's staff worked intensively on a draft statement that Kohl would present before the Bundestag in connection with the budget debate.[77] Three days later the chancellor set out a ten-point program that might encompass a treaty community and move toward a federal system within a unified Germany, while embedding any new framework within the European community and in an all-European framework. Along with the unprecedented length of his tenure—as of 1996, the most enduring since Bismarck's—the November 28 speech establishes Kohl's claim to historic achievement. It overshadowed the proposals of the enfeebled GDR regime without seeming overtly hostile; it established reunification as a goal toward which an uncertain public in the West, and a possibly yearning one in the East, might repair; it wrapped up these objectives in European Community and East-West rhetoric so no suspicion could exist that Kohl wanted to rupture Ostpolitik. It accredited the Christian Democrats with a clear initiative in light of the following year's elections, placing the SPD in the position of having to support the speech or risk seeming antinational. And it captured the foreign policy momentum from his own FDP foreign minister, who, nonetheless, graciously told the chancellor: "That was a great speech, Helmut."[78]

Kohl's speech had its risks. He felt that there could be no consultation with allies before announcing the ten-point program. Opinion abroad wavered. Mitterrand was angered—"Mais, il ne m'a rien dit! Rien dit!"—but ostensibly deferred to German self-determination.[79] The Socialist Party defense minister, Chévènement, more resolutely opposed, alluded to lack of Soviet and American sympathy. In fact Bush was nonchalant. And the Russians? Gorbachev came to his Malta shipboard meetings with Bush with no well-articulated plan for Germany, asking only that the movement of history not be rushed. Throughout the next weeks and months, foreign malaise would be signaled by complaints of haste and pleas for gradualism. No one supposedly wished to oppose the historical transformation outright, but they felt uneasy with the pace. But which tempo, the American policy architects asked themselves, would better guarantee a stable outcome? A gradual unification, or a rush to seize the moment before the onset of possible East German disillusion or West German concern about costs or rising resistance to Gorbachev in Moscow? Might not haste avert waste?

When the president and chancellor conversed at Brussels on December 3, Kohl told Bush that he did not want to press, but that time was working for federation (i.e., a degree of unity beyond mere confederation), although it might take five years. The United States, so Bush emphasized in his own address at Brussels, welcomed German unity if it were compatible with four points (which in fact were closer to seven): respect for self-determination; a continuing German commitment to NATO and the European Community and the remaining treaty rights of the Allied powers; a gradual pace; and confirmation of the European borders according to the Helsinki Final Act. The chancellor must have been pleased with the president's support: unification would become in effect an American and German project that would have to bypass the British and not make life difficult for the Soviets, who were welcome as partners "as all the countries of Europe to become part of a commonwealth of free nations." The Italians and British demurred indirectly from this endorsement, but the Dutch joined the American affirmation.[80]

Momentum Stalls

The NATO powers might apparently close ranks, but Gorbachev was having second thoughts about the West German initiative. When Genscher came to Moscow in early December, the Soviet president criticized Kohl's ten-point plan and the chancellor's failure to inform Moscow about the initiative; "the talk was unpleasant for us both," he recalls. The Soviet president insisted that Modrow's state must remain independent and allegedly pledged to the Central Committee on December 9 that the Soviet Union would not abandon the DDR. Modrow, barely a week in power and just concluding the traumatized SED party congress of December 8 and 9, claimed to welcome Kohl's idea of a confederal "treaty community," but pleaded that all outside forces resist "offering up [East Germany] on the altar of reunification." Kohl himself sought to reassure the Soviet leader and wrote him on December 14 that the real source of instability in the GDR was not the West German agenda but the East German refusal to reform. Bonn, he promised, did not wish to take advantage of the present weakness and confusion of the East German state.[81]

Without a resolute signal from Gorbachev, those Soviet advisers hostile to unification could slow down the thrust toward unification. Preparing an address for the political committee of the European Parliament on December 19, Shevardnadze retreated from a forthright approval of unification in the face of resistance from Bondarenko at the European Department of the Foreign Ministry, Falin at the Central Committee, and then, just before his presentation, from Kvitsinsky at the Bonn embassy. German self-determination, Shevardnadze ended up declaring, was not to be the only consideration in the process ahead; any new "national formation" would have to be squared with the Helsinki process and the CSCE, which guaranteed the stability of existing states.[82]

The uneasy reaction to events and the murky alternatives that Shevardnadze proposed did not fundamentally differ from the prevailing mood at year's end in Western Europe (indeed even briefly afflicting White House and State Department policy advisers). Each NATO ally of the Federal Republic had questions as to what outcome was desirable. Mitterrand, too, probed the feasibility of alternatives even if ultimately prepared to let the Germans prevail. In early December Thatcher perceived the French president to be as inwardly reluctant about unification as she was. He and his

foreign minister, Roland Dumas, would stress the inviolability of the German-Polish border as if to use the issue (so at least the chancellor's assistant
felt) to retard unification. Let us go slow, Mitterrand pleaded to Bush when
they walked the beach together at St. Martin. Strengthen the CSCE and the
Helsinki process; enclose any emerging German federation in European
structures.[83] These ideas were widely shared. Some association of East and
West Germany certainly lay ahead, but might not confederation be less destabilizing than an outright fusion? Would not a long period of transition be
desirable? Should not the Germans solicit the goodwill of all interested
powers, West and East? Should the Germans not be respectful of or perhaps
defer to "Europe" even in a matter of great concern for themselves?

Such hesitation, whether voiced explicitly by intellectuals and journalists
or pondered *sotto voce* by public officials, could not be deemed surprising.
The forty-five year framework of bipolar stability in Europe had after all
kept the peace despite both side's dissatisfaction with its limits. A united
Germany possessed a potential for dynamic disturbance, no matter how
sincerely it professed peace and democracy. German division had turned
out to be a major feature of the international order in which, after all, a wary
peace had survived. Did continued peace require continued division? No
issue in Europe could have been more suffused by memories or clouded by
the aura of the past. Might "Europe" in fact emerge as an inertial force
conjured up to frustrate the Germans?

Europe, as represented by the CSCE, was not the only recourse for
those seeking to slow events; in January 1990 the Soviets appealed to the
four powers, signers of the Yalta and Potsdam accords and the Quadripartite Agreement of 1971, as the custodians of Germany's international
status. What the Germans did not want was any revival of residual claims
on the part of the victors. For this reason the notion that any "peace conference" might ultimately seal the process of unification remained anathema
in the months to come. After one embarrassing lapse, the Americans backed
them up. In December Baker had reluctantly agreed to a Soviet request
for the four powers' ambassadors to confer in Berlin for the first time
since 1971. Despite the innocuous agenda, the conspicuous meeting at the
site of the old Control Council piqued Genscher, who resented the evoca-
tion of the occupation status.[84] Still, there was no way around involving
the four: they would have to be mobilized to avoid the more cumbersome
process of giving every other possible player in East and West Europe a
voice. No one quite saw the way ahead, however, at the end of the remarkable year, 1989.

The Process Resumed

It was the sudden erosion of credibility for the East German government in mid-January that impelled the major actors to overcome their hesitation. Once again, as in October and November, the crowds in East Germany exerted a decisive push on events. This time the demonstrators were angry and no longer waiting upon churchmen and intellectuals to articulate demands for "dialogue." Fury at the Modrow government's apparent reluctance to shut down internal security policing brought Berlin crowds rampaging at Stasi headquarters. As explained in chapter 4, Lothar de Maizière pulled the East German CDU out of the coalition, and the subsequent crisis ended only with the ministry further hobbled and elections moved up to March 18. Kohl had no interest in resuscitation. By late February he told Bush that the Modrow collapse had impelled him to accelerate the careful ten-point plan of just two months earlier.

American policy makers adjusted their assessments according to the process of decomposition they were watching in Central Europe. The NSC staff in late January became convinced anew that the time had come to move quickly toward unification—delay would encourage deals to neutralize Germany, whereas the Soviets, so the NSC urged, would now accept a rapid outcome. Baker's closest State Department advisers, Robert Zoellick and Dennis Ross—who served as head of the policy planning staff—were arriving at the same conviction: "we need to shift to a 'fast-track' unification sequence," they advised the secretary. Germans, however, would resent a four-power negotiation so long as the Soviets might veto a settlement between the Germans; hence their proposal to combine four-power negotiations with direct German-German talks once the March elections were held—a two-plus-four framework. Not all their colleagues thought this scenario feasible; the European bureau argued that four-power tutelage might alienate the Germans but, as Zoellick countered, exclusively intra-German negotiations might allow Moscow to pressure Bonn into accepting some degree of neutrality in return for unification. Moscow and the GDR were both proposing the removal of foreign forces from Germany; Bush remained convinced that it was in the United States' interest to maintain a substantial (if reduced) American military presence in Europe. (The potential dissolution of the Warsaw Pact did not change that incentive; indeed, it meant that the United States might maintain European forces without facing the same countervailing power it had for the past forty years.) The key was that Moscow could play the spoiler, whether engaged in four-power negotiations or excluded. Bush decided that the simultaneous negotiations allowed for the more predictable outcomes for both force reduction and the continued viability of NATO.[85]

Only the Soviets could have insisted on a different outcome—and they were not prepared to do so. In the very weeks when the Russian leader had to decide whether to use force in Lithuania, he had to review the German options as well. In fact, the Soviets made a fundamental decision against holding up events in late January, when Gorbachev bypassed conventional Politburo channels and convened his close advisers on Germany: his chief policy aide Chernyaev, Shevardnadze, Prime Minister Ryzhkov, Yakolev and Falin, the two men responsible for the party's International Department, and several others. For four hours they debated Russian options. Chernyaev was most ruthless about the situation; there was no choice but to deal with Kohl. Modrow and the SED possessed no authority, Gysi's PDS did not really exist and had no future; the West German SPD was playing politics with the issue; only the chancellor was reliable and wanted to preserve a European dimension to his policies. Falin and his deputy, Fyodorev, supported by the reformer Yakolev, looked to an SPD option. Gorbachev summarized the upshot: to establish a group of six to negotiate (the four occupation powers and the two Germanies) rather than convene a massive conference, to deal principally with Kohl but invite Modrow and Gysi to Moscow and keep lines open to the SPD.[86]

When Modrow visited Moscow on January 30, Gorbachev nominally endorsed his concept for step-by-step unification, entitled, in the words of the GDR's national anthem, *Deutschland—einig Vaterland*. The East German premier announced it two days later, without bringing it to the Round Table and even before his government of national responsibility was formally confirmed by the Volkskammer. Inside East Germany, speakers from the civic movements and the Volkskammer criticized Modrow for pressing ahead with a plan for unity. In fact, he felt he had no choice: by late January he had time to experience the GDR's economic vulnerability and domestic political disintegration; his state could not retain its autonomy even within a larger confederation. Moreover, even Soviet support was in question. In view of the mass demonstrations against the Stasi, the continued exit of citizens, and the coalition crises of the previous weeks, staunch Soviet support would be crucial for lending Modrow sufficient credibility to negotiate as an equal in his upcoming talks with Chancellor Kohl. The Soviet "Germanists" likewise supported a firm Moscow stand on behalf of the GDR. But although Gorbachev formally endorsed Modrow's initiative, Modrow took away the impression of a flagging commitment to the GDR. Kochemasov, tending the Russian embassy in East Berlin, chafed at his government's passivity and Gorbachev's vacillation: Modrow, he claimed, was inwardly disappointed and Moscow's lukewarm support would provide no buttress for the dissolving GDR. When the East German leader met the chancellor unofficially at the Davos conclave of economic leaders on February 3, Kohl was personally solicitous but did not develop or repeat earlier assurances of economic aid. For Kochemasov and Modrow, Gorbachev missed an important opportunity to slow down the rush toward unification in early February. On the other hand, Gorbachev, like Kohl, must have understood that the domestic basis of the East German regime had virtually evaporated. Even Modrow had admitted to the Soviet leader in his January 30 visit that the majority of the GDR population no longer supported the idea of the existence of two German states. "The arguments that we have used to date are just no longer effective." Not merely gradual confederation, but rapid merger loomed ahead.[87]

Falin and Kochemasov offered no positive alternative, but their dismay with Gorbachev was not irrational, for he remained inconstant in a situation where only the Soviets could have propped up the continued existence of the DDR. "I am in complete despair," Chernyaev confided to his diary on March 3. "The state is falling apart and there is no new beginning in sight."[88] Where could the East Germans find support? The East German leadership received aid from Bonn, but largely to dissuade East Germans from migrating westward en masse, not to make the fading East German regime viable. The British and the French might have hesitations about a rush to unity, but they had no real leverage unless they convinced Washington that hesitation was justified. Margaret Thatcher was clearly opposed to the rapid pace, and her adviser Lord Ridley probably voiced her opinions (although he had to be removed for the price of his frankness) when he said Germany would dominate Europe and the French were acting as Kohl's lapdog. Thatcher's meeting with Mitterrand on January 20 yielded no concrete result. Only the Soviets might have put a stick in the spokes. Later in the spring Thatcher and Mitterrand would come close to encouraging their doing so.

The most obvious spokes to poke at were those concerning NATO. Was it plausible that Moscow would permit a confederal or unified Germany to adhere as a whole in NATO? Would a new unified Germany or even a continuing West Germany inside an all-German confederation be allowed to keep nuclear weapons on its soil? Might not the Soviets give way on unity in order to extract neutralization and removal of foreign troops? Foreign Minister Genscher sought to address the issue of the alliance in his repeatedly reworked speech at the Protestant Academy of Tutzing on January 31: "German Unity in the European Framework." The site was auspicious, for Egon Bahr had defined the thrust of Ostpolitik at Tutzing as "change through rapprochement" two decades earlier. The speech was also important for Genscher's own delicate personal role in the unification process. Although he was continually in negotiations, stressing Germany's collaboration with its allies, he and his small Free Democratic Party ran the risk of being marginalized by the chancellor's initiatives in the progress of events. Loyal to Kohl, Genscher still fretted that the chancellor might miscalculate, whether through insensitivity about the Polish border, or supposedly by proposing a confederal alternative he believed already bypassed by events. Genscher was particularly sensitive if the four powers made any gesture of settling the German issue on their own. On the other hand, any effort at a revived peace conference or even a major CSCE gathering to negotiate unification would become a cumbersome source of delay and open up such issues as reparation. His own East German origins, moreover, made him respond to the momentum of events with genuine emotion, as was evident when he had the chance to return to Halle after thirty-seven years and speak in the market church that his family had sometimes attended and tell his East German audience that unity must be their decision.

Tutzing involved a more substantial address since it took up the NATO issue, but with some of the same ambiguities that had sometimes characterized his earlier policy. Bush's NSC staff read the speech as a proposal to run Europe's security frontier down the middle of a united Germany, which would remain nominally in NATO but unable to base NATO defense units in its eastern or ex-GDR region. Whatever German units would ultimately be garrisoned in the ex-GDR would then, presumabley, have to be detached from the NATO command. Genscher himself—perhaps responding precisely to this interpretation—emphasizes that his major intent was to insist that the whole of united Germany must belong to the alliance, although the GDR territory might enjoy a separate status outside NATO's military structures. Ultimately, Genscher suggested, NATO and the Warsaw Pact might both work toward a cooperative relationship.[89]

Genscher, his collaborator said, "moved in those weeks with the caution of a giant insect who cautiously feels out the environment with his antennae, ready to move back if he detects resistance, and then immediately to try his feelers in another place."[90] Genscher's assistant Frank Elbe, who preceded his boss to Washington, felt that Baker's aides, Zoellick and Ross, responded positively to his explanation of the Tutzing formula; in return they urged the emerging six-power (two plus four) format for negotiation on the German question. As Elbe escorted his boss from Dulles airport for a half-day's conference first with Baker and then with Bush on February 2, Genscher agreed as long as it was to be two plus four and not four plus two. Since the foreign secretary stressed a united Germany's commitment to NATO, the two American leaders proved happy enough with this formula. Indeed Baker let pass the proposed special status that Genscher envisaged for the GDR without objection.[91] The White House staff remained wary, and so did its German counterparts in the chancellor's office. Kohl's personal adviser, Teltschik, was skeptical of two security regimes on one territory; nor did he want the FDP minister seizing the foreign policy initiative. The chancellory staff in Bonn, and the NSC staff in Washington each preferred a negotiation that tended to subordinate the other allies and alternative foreign-policy agencies at home. The State Department and the West German foreign minister, on the other hand, envisaged more European involvement, the elevation of CSCE, and the subordination of NATO; Mrs. Thatcher certainly cared about NATO and not CSCE but wanted Germany docile within it, and worried about the Anglo-American relationship. But this was idiosyncratic: the real question was whether the division of Europe would be overcome by an enlarged West Germany within NATO and patronized by the United States, or by a new somewhat vague and cross-bloc security arrangement. Only the Soviets could resolve this issue.

Wherein lay Russia's interest? Experts in the policy institutes envisaged great economic advantages from cooperation with a grateful united Germany.[92] Old-line Communists, appalled at the bleeding away of Soviet power, could not conceive that Moscow benefited from facilitating German unification. Shevardnadze certainly did not share their visceral reaction, but he still wanted to limit German options. As the Western leaders began a series of trips to Moscow in early February, the Soviet foreign minister told Baker on February 7, that a united Germany would be a potentially nationalist and dangerous country unless neutralized and disarmed. Baker responded that Germany's future was more calculable if it remained within a NATO where U.S. forces guaranteed stability. Two plus four would facilitate this upshot; and NATO jurisdiction, as Genscher had proposed, could remain out of the territory currently comprising the GDR. Most surprising, Gorbachev said he shared Baker's reasoning although he preferred four plus two, whereas Baker insisted that two plus four placed German self-determination, and not the old victors' alliance, at the center of the process. "We don't want to see a replay of Versailles, where the Germans were able to rearm themselves," the Russian leader told Baker, but he asked for time for decision.[93] Gorbachev had indicated the most flexible Soviet position to date, but Baker himself had to back off a bit. Rather than limit NATO's protective zone to the western portions of a unified Germany, his staff told him to include all Germany within the alliance sphere. What could be bargained for was to keep NATO troops from being based eastward in the territory of the current GDR—and German resources to pay for the downsizing of Russian power and hopefully the reconversion of a failing industrial base.

Ultimately Gorbachev must have thought there was little option on the German issue unless he was prepared to reverse glasnost and perestroika at home. The fate of Russian reform traditionally hung on its willingness or unwillingness to allow self-determination in its "near abroad." Consistency for perestroika hinged on self-determination for the Baltics and the satellites. Perhaps he felt all the heady freedom of a surfer on the crest of a rising wave: he could ride boldly and conspicuously or be churned under.

Wherein lay American interest? The European desk of the State Department remained closer to Shevardnadze or to the West Europeans' preference for gradualism and multilateral frameworks. The White House staff, however, wagered on Kohl and the record of German democracy. They believed that strong American support for unencumbered unification within NATO would assure a less disruptive united Germany than a neutralized uncommitted nation. Following their advice, Bush wrote Chancellor Kohl, as he and Genscher now made the flight to Moscow on February 10, that the United States would not let the Soviets use the four-power mechanism to neutralize or impede German unification. Go for it, the president wrote in effect, but make sure you remain in NATO. East Germany could enjoy, he wrote borrowing the phrase of Manfred Wörner, the German secretary-general of NATO, a special military status. Russian troops would go home; American ones would stay out.

Kohl exploited Washington's benevolence with alacrity. He told Gorbachev that united Germany would claim no eastern territory beyond the GDR and that he "could imagine" that NATO jurisdiction would not have to extend to GDR territory—a concept close to Genscher's Tutzing proposal of ten days earlier. The FRG was willing to assume East German economic obligations to the Soviet Union. To the delight of Kohl and Teltschik, Gorbachev apparently accepted the scenario and emphasized that the Soviets felt it was up to the Germans to decide on unification. Alliance status could be firmed up in negotiations to come, the Soviet leader said; he understood, though, that German neutrality was unacceptable to the chancellor. "This is the breakthrough!" recorded Teltschik in his diary. "What a meeting!"[94]

The Kohl-Gorbachev discussion indicated that the heads of government and their enthusiastic security advisers might outrace their painstaking and cautious foreign offices whether in the United States, the Soviet Union, or Germany. In each country diplomacy moved on parallel tracks, but more briskly in the executive offices: Teltschik and Kohl outlined a concept for unification more directly than Genscher; Gorbachev and Chernyayev more boldly than Kvitsinsky and certainly the hostile Falin, and for a time in late spring with greater ease than even the usually cooperative Shevardnadze; Bush and the NSC pressed unity with fewer preoccupations than the European desk of the State Department. On closer scrutiny, however, the generalization needs refinement. On the German side, Genscher remained too authoritative a diplomat to be simply eclipsed, and he was hardly constrained by excessive caution, although he wanted to expedite unification by Soviet agreement and had never expected how much Gorbachev was prepared to concede. Neither did Secretary of State Baker allow himself to be boxed in by State Department professionals; he consistently demonstrated a capacity to place himself slightly ahead of the curve, to exploit the opportunity to envisage formulations already in the works but which he might nail down as his own. With his intuitive capacity to run before the wind, Baker adopted the two-plus-four formulation, floated originally by French Foreign Minister Jobert and advanced in Washington by his staff assistants, Zoellick and Ross. "Two plus four" had the formulaic virtue of promising to serve either as a brake or accelerator: stress the "two" and it gave the Germans the initiative; stress the "four" and it allowed France or Russia to slow down the process. Indeed, when first floated by Baker's staff, the NSC advisers believed it was becoming a formula for slowing down the Germans, not encouraging them.[95]

Beyond all the chances for individual virtuosity and inventive formulation, one could perceive in these months the eclipse of policy-making apparatuses that had become the administrators of the cold war status quo. The foreign policy bureaucracies that had worked out all the mutual restraint that had made four decades of cold war bearable were being bypassed by a leadership that realized a burst of speed might yield decisive changes. This was the diplomacy of headiness; it partook of the same ebullience that had brought down the Wall. Did it have a danger? The German foreign minister believed it might. While Genscher demonstratively welcomed his chancellor's announcement in Moscow on February 10, that Gorbachev had just agreed that the Germans must and could decide for themselves when and how to become a united nation, he remained preoccupied about the surrounding conditions. Developments would reveal, Genscher has written—even as he has put the firmest possible emphasis on his NATO loyalties—that a cautious procedure which signaled to the Soviets a concern for their security interests would be more fruitful than the "objectively correct but naked demand that 'Germany must be a member of NATO.'" If that was what was desired, the Soviets must be reassured on the attendant issues they found so critical, including the exclusion of allied military forces from the territory of the former GDR. This last concession, which Baker himself had approved after his conversation with Genscher, was fraught with difficulty enough to produce the most serious rifts within the German government and potentially with the Americans. That my own government might create difficulties in the negotiations—so Genscher has claimed—"seemed impossible to me, but this bitter experience was not long in materializing."[96]

Resistance Again

CSCE foreign ministers assembled at Ottawa on February 11 to 13, ostensibly to talk about mutual troop reduction in Europe, but more urgently to confirm the two-plus-four procedure for negotiations. Ottawa, however, revealed the Allies' second thoughts as well as serious division between the Chancellery and the Foreign Office in Bonn. Teltschik hinted to Scowcroft in Washington that Kohl might not be in agreement with Genscher, and Bush asked Baker to have Genscher confirm his chancellor's support. Genscher was angry at what he deemed an effort to discredit him and derail the negotiations, and the situation had to be clarified with telephone calls to Kohl and then by Kohl to Washington. Was Genscher right to be suspicious? The NSC and presidential advisers believed that their German counterpart Teltschik had not behaved improperly, whereas Genscher was willing to make unnecessary concessions by excluding eastern Germany from NATO jurisdiction.[97] Genscher claims that his formulas allowed for the ambiguity needed to bring Moscow to agreement. The tension, rooted in diverse personal approaches, German political party rivalries, and the overlapping conduct of diplomacy, would persist, but never become disabling. Baker and Shevardnadze reached a compromise on Soviet forces outside

Russia and American forces in Central Europe. They would each have 195,000 in a central zone and the Americans could keep another 30,000 in Britain and Italy. Gorbachev could claim equality; Bush could claim he retained an American edge to compensate for the proximity of the Soviet troops based on Russian territory. Just as important Baker negotiated an announcement for a two-plus-four process: FRG and GDR foreign ministers would meet with the four powers to discuss the external aspects of unification and security. The lesser powers assembled at Ottawa were not happy but had little choice.

Nonetheless, the Ottawa decisions provoked a quick reaction as the Europeans above all worried how quickly they were being rushed along and as NATO allies asked for a widening of the discussions. Concerned with the unraveling of the two-plus-four agreement, Genscher refused to accommodate their concern: "'You are not part of the game,'" he insisted.[98] Bush himself publicly conceded that events had moved very quickly. The Soviets certainly felt uneasy about being pushed into a chess game, to cite Shevardnadze's metaphor, with five-minute time limits. Now they issued a Foreign Office pronouncement declaring that a united Germany could not claim NATO membership. The French, who had benevolently watched the unification process, reasserted their own importance but showed signs of doubt that they might continue their tutelary role with a powerful united Germany. Europe must take care of herself, Mitterrand said, but French officials were preoccupied that in fact France might have to do so without familiar American support. Mrs. Thatcher was happy to exploit French second thoughts and, warning that unified Germany would emerge more influential than Japan, she urged President Bush to make a deal that would let Russian troops stay in eastern Germany.

No onlookers were cheered by Chancellor Kohl's refusals in these weeks to endorse the East German–Polish border unconditionally as a frontier for united Germany. Kohl knew that he could not challenge the Oder-Neisse line, but he was not prepared to offend the conservative currents in the CDU and Bavarian CSU, which resented the loss of Silesia. He argued that only a united Germany could definitively confirm the new border, although East Germany had accepted its own frontier in a treaty with Poland in 1950, and Willy Brandt's 1970 treaty with Warsaw had ruled out any change by force of the East German border.

What role did American policy makers urge? They were preoccupied by both the NATO issue and the pitfalls that the two-plus-four process might entail. Our best documented account at this point is that left by Zelikow and

Rice, proud of their role in expediting unification that emerged and convinced all along that they might secure a Germany without restrictions on NATO participation.[99] In this respect, they agreed with the German chancellor's staff. Teltschik wanted to push his boss toward a stronger insistence on a united Germany's NATO role, and so too did the Ministry of Defense under Gerhard Stoltenberg of Schleswig-Holstein. Kohl, however, did not want a conspicuous disavowal of his foreign minister and he encouraged a joint ministerial declaration on February 19, which stipulated that neither NATO units nor non-NATO West German units would be moved into East German territory. The chancellor had his eyes on the upcoming East German elections. A public break with Genscher on which the Soviets would have to comment might well delay the momentum toward rapid unity and set back the CDU's electoral prospects as the advocates of quick unification and make the SPD's more neutralist stance appear more promising.

The White House and Chancellery staffs, however, both wanted to move beyond the halfway jurisdiction formula advanced by Genscher and never precisely amended by Baker. Press Kohl for a pledge, the NSC urged as the chancellor was about to come for talks to Camp David, to stay in NATO's military command and to include all German territory in the alliance's jurisdiction, even if some force restrictions in the East were conceded. Moscow might not like such a declaration, but Moscow was weak. So as not, moreover, to allow the Soviets more leverage, it was desirable to confine the writ of the "four" in the two-plus-four talks, while letting the German-German discussions forge ahead toward unity. The State Department agreed in part: two-plus-four, Zoellick and Baker advised the president should not be designed to take on substantive negotiations but to become a mechanism for finalizing the border and the end of residual four-power rights; the Germans themselves must decide their alliance and defense commitments. Still, State argued, the two-plus-four procedure must have enough jurisdiction so the Soviets do not make their own end run with Bonn.[100]

Kohl was riding high at Camp David on February 24–25. He enjoyed the woodsy informality and appreciated the baseball cap he received, even if after the lengthened day of his transatlantic flight and important conversations he could not remain awake through the president's late-night movie. "Everyone is confused but me," he told the Americans, referring to the contending voices at home. Calm down about the Oder-Neisse line, he advised; it was not a serious question, and do not accept Poland's call to be included as a member of a two-plus-five parley. Germany had paid a lot of reparations to Poland, Israel, and individuals. He agreed with the Americans—but it would have been hard to find a more pro-German partner!—to restrict the role of the four-power talks, which should get under way substantively only after the March 18 elections had demonstrated what Germans wanted and should wind up before the CSCE met in Paris in November. As for NATO, the chancellor understood NATO forces should not be moved forward into East German territory, but all of Germany would come under the NATO guarantee. Teltschik pressed for public clarification of this issue, and Baker agreed; Genscher was to be bypassed. The chancellor certainly wanted U.S. forces to remain in Europe, and the president wanted an end to the public musings about German neutrality. "We prevailed," he said, "and they didn't. We can't let the Soviets clutch victory from the jaws of defeat." Kohl agreed. "The time for games had passed." Let the Russians now name their real price tag for agreement.[101]

Germany's neighbors did not see the Polish border issue so cavalierly, but the issue was finally left behind. In his post–Camp David press conference, Kohl again refused to pledge acceptance of the frontier on behalf of the future united Germany, although Bush clearly stated he regarded the Oder-Neisse line as settled by mutual agreements. As international indignation heated up about the chancellor's reluctance to confirm what had long seemed to be FRG policy, Kohl tried to retreat, proposing to trade coordinated Bundestag and Volkskammer declarations in return for Polish renunciation of reparation claims against the Federal Republic and rights for the ethnic Germans still in Silesia (more of whom claimed this status all the time). The coupling of these issues seemed crude blackmail to most observers, including critics at home, and in a Bundestag declaration on March 8, Kohl did declare that Poland's right to live in secure borders would not be questioned by Germany now or in the future. As for the recent demand that Poland renounce any reparation claims, the Germans now accepted that the earlier Polish renunciation in its 1950 treaty with East Germany was binding for the future. When Polish premier Tadeusz Mazowiecki visited the White House on March 21 and 22, Bush promised to intervene privately with Kohl. Responding to the Polish premier's call for a border treaty to precede unification, the president explained that a treaty could not be written by a unified Germany that did not yet exist. But he did explain that the substance of a future recognition of the border might be inserted into West German and East German parliamentary declarations. Within a day Bush secured from Kohl agreement that the future treaty's confirmation of the German-Polish border would be cleared with Warsaw in advance. East German and West German legislatures formally declared their commitment to the current border; and at the two-plus-four negotiations on July 17, the status quo was confirmed anew.[102]

After a month of inflamed statements, the issue faded. Kohl and other Germans later claimed it was only an artifact of internal politics: faced with the multiple elections of 1990, the chancellor could not alienate the right wing of his coalition. Neither did he wish to give the nationalist Republikaner a talking point. For all his intense focus on achieving unification, the chancellor remained fundamentally attuned to German domestic politics. By the standards of Realpolitik his wager paid off; he could neutralize his own right wing without insuperably derailing the unification process. Despite the unease and temporary ill will, Bonn's hesitations on confirming the future frontier could have exerted a more serious impact only if Russia and Poland had been in closer alignment. But the Poles realized that, in terms of their economic future, it would be Germany that was critical.

Nonetheless, despite his self-professed interest in history, Kohl sometimes found it difficult to sense the echoes still resonating from the 1933–45 era. For him the Oder-Neisse border represented one of those postwar obligations that the Federal Republic must live with. He had no desire to alter the frontier and was prepared to consult with the Poles on any issue of relevance that arose out of unification. But he did not want to hold such discussions in Warsaw; "he had the impression," so he unburdened himself to Mitterrand on March 14, "that every people's feelings but the Germans' were being taken into consideration. . . . Not only the spirit of the Poles, but of the Germans had to be taken into account."[103] Having let out his anger, however, the chancellor could move on.

Modrow had returned to Moscow on March 5 and 6. The two governments resolved to intensify their economic collaboration and move toward trade based on world prices. Insofar as he trusted the Soviet leader, Modrow must have felt cheered by Soviet support. Gorbachev told Modrow that the West Germans could not simply stampede to unification. Reading the protocol of the meeting, one has the impression that the Soviet leader was not really measuring his words; there was a spontaneous reaction to his feeling foreclosed by the rush of events. Gorbachev had asked Bush—so he informed Modrow—that if a united Germany in NATO was no threat to peace, why might it not then join the Warsaw Pact. Moscow had also insisted that the process of unification proceed responsibly: "it could not be in the interests of the GDR, nor of the FRG, to let it become chaotic. The people of the GDR had their pride and dignity and the GDR's achievements were well known to everyone. The FRG had to think carefully, not play the bull in the china shop [Elefanten im Porzellanladen] and not become the hostage of political ambitions."[104] For all his excited objections to the rash pace of events, however, Gorbachev did not suggest to Modrow that German unification was avoidable. "The experiences that the GDR had gained," he said instead, "and the accomplishments of the Soviet-GDR relationship over the decades would have to be brought into and further developed in the relationship between united Germany and the Soviet Union. That could only happen in a process that proceded by stages." Again tempo was crucial. The East German leader came back from Moscow believing that Gorbachev meant well but was indecisive; in fact, Modrow's conviction that Gorbachev did not understand the GDR's economic plight, so Moscow's ambassador Kochemasov felt, was one reason Modrow accepted the Currency Union.[105]

Shevardnadze and then Gorbachev told the press that all-German membership in NATO would be unacceptable and that Kohl's aspirations to achieve unity by means of Article 23 rather than 146 was also out of bounds. Veteran Russian diplomats felt that this stiffened stand had come too late. The Soviets were pressing for an early beginning to the two-plus-four procedure at the same time that State and NSC officials were holding detailed talks designed to circumscribe the two-plus-four agenda. According to the Americans, four-power rights over Berlin (which would have to be surrendered), German borders (which were already deemed inviolable), and German forces inside the GDR might be discussed in the two-plus-four format. But Germany's NATO membership, the role of NATO nuclear weapons in the Federal Republic, the size of the Bundeswehr, and the recourse to article 23 were all decisions that were Germany's own. The Russians did not attempt to force a broad discussion at the first preparatory meeting on March 14; from Washington's point of view Paris and London were more troubling as London hoped a peace treaty might emerge from the negotiations.[106]

With so many second thoughts being aired, the chancellor's ebullient persona succumbed to doubt and pessimism. The tension of the electoral campaign was great. He enjoyed campaigning for his party's Alliance for Germany in the GDR, but the polls still suggested an SPD plurality would overwhelm his East German allies. Kohl reaffirmed his preference for article 23, and at Cottbus near the Saxon border on March 13, he announced that his monetary union would allow the East Germans a one-for-one exchange against East marks that had no real objective value. But to Teltschik he talked of having to go home rebuffed. The stunning electoral victory of March 18, however, reinfused his energy, and he now envisaged reaching agreement on unification by the fall, and completing the procedure in 1991. If every party was committed to the German right to self-determination, the elections suggested that it would be obstructive to block the outcome. Genscher now endorsed the chancellor's NATO position by dropping his earlier intimations that the East German territory might be partially exempted from NATO's security sphere, while Kohl moved to give the French a bon-bon by promising further collaboration on the political integration of the European community. The full-dress two-plus-four meeting was postponed to May 5.

As momentum resumed, the East Germans were to find themselves totally marginalized. For the first time they had a government that owed its existence to free elections, and it hardly accounted for anything. De Maizière's party had campaigned in effect for unification; the Soviets were hardly resisting. The key Foreign Ministry officials, now former parsons turned Social Democratic politicians, put what little political capital they still held behind pleas for the CSCE and sympathy with the emerging post-Communist neighbors. Markus Meckel, the Lutheran pastor of the SPD, who claimed the East German Foreign Ministry in the de Maizière Great Coalition, believed that he might make the GDR the champion of a strengthened CSCE that overcame the two alliances.[107] Genscher appreciated his contributions because they seconded his emphasis on reassuring the Russians. But the East German foreign policy of bridging East and West made little difference when they were no longer separated. Hans Miselwitz, another pastor from the peace movement, was named parliamentary state secretary, a position introduced as counterpart to the long-standing key official in FRG ministries. The Social Democratic pastors inherited a foreign service of 3,000 employees, 2,500 with diplomatic status, 500 or so adjunct staff. The West German foreign service had about 6,000, but only half the number of diplomats.[108] West German CDU circles envisaged their task to be that of winding up any East German foreign policy whatsoever. Soon the embassies were shutting down, and staff members at the cubic, modernist ministry on Marx-Engels Platz were taking up pensions or training for other jobs. Meanwhile an effort to work in common with Czech and Polish representatives to enhance the standing of the CSCE was vetoed in Washington. East German negotiators felt the standing of their state ebb daily by May and June as border-crossing formalities were given up. George Bush told de Maizière when he visited Washington at the beginning of June that the East Germans, or at least the SPD Foreign Office officials, were playing an obstructive role in the two-plus-four process. The East Germans felt that their contribution to the process was ignored when, to great fanfare, Checkpoint Charlie was opened up (and lifted off by crane) on June 22. The Czechs even asked their East German colleagues on July 10 whether it still was worthwhile to negotiate with the GDR. After Kohl met Gorbachev in mid-July, a British Foreign Office official told the president of the Volkskammer that her republic was no longer a player that could negotiate.[109] In effect, so the message was, she should lie back and think of Germany.

Striking a Bargain

Could the Soviets still demand neutrality? Returning home from his service as ambassador in Bonn, Kvitsinsky believed that Germany might earlier have been compelled to leave the military organization of NATO, much as de Gaulle had walked out years before. By April 1990, so he claims to have decided, neutrality was no longer an option, but perhaps membership in both alliances might still be sought; at the least Genscher's Tutzing formula should be retained. Gorbachev had responded positively to Baker's argument that a neutral Germany, potentially volatile and less anchored in the democratic West, was potentially more dangerous for Russia. But just to roll over and allow the United States and Germany to have unification on their terms seemed humiliating. Such a surrender offered a foothold for the enemies of perestroika as a whole, especially Yeagor Ligachev. Even Gorbachev thus found he could not go along and declared he was ready to risk all the arms control negotiations under way rather than let Germany in NATO. Let the Germans work toward their social and economic union; Soviet consent on security and international recognition, he insisted, was still crucial.

For the Russians their own status as a world power was in question. Gorbachev and Shevardnadze had argued that the Soviet Union could complete its reforms, federalize the Soviet Union, and move toward German unification without these changes representing "defeat." But as they debated, it was hard not to worry whether they were relinquishing the "greatness" that had been purchased with their country's immense wartime sacrifices. Were the Germans and Americans not rubbing their nose in their own weakness? How much unraveling could Moscow allow? After elections in Lithuania returned a majority for the national movement, Rukh, that Baltic republic had declared its independence from the Soviet Union in March 1990, while the Soviets sought to undermine Lithuanian resolve with economic sanctions and military pressure. Confronting the outright secession of the Baltics at the same time as German unification, Gorbachev himself bridled; he did not want to be reproached with the liquidation of the Soviet Union's great-power status.

Suppose the Russians did not yield? What would be the situation? De facto economic unification and confederation negotiated between the two Germanies, but the continued stationing of Soviet troops in Eastern Germany and an unresolved international status? The Soviet presentation at the May 5 two-plus-four meeting was hardly encouraging. For progress to continue, the Russians now seemed to insist, a treaty had to confirm four-power rights, rule out NATO membership, give the CSCE a voice on supervising the German military situation, and even have a role in overseeing German politics to avoid any neo-Nazi resurgence. These issues would doubtless take time; meanwhile the two Germanies might work on their internal unification. What on earth then might the two-plus-four communiqué, envisaging that unity would occur "in an orderly way and without delay," really mean? [110]

How should the West react? The American team pushing unification wanted speed because they were not sure that Gorbachev could remain influential long enough to sanction unification. The NSC staff members writing papers, advising Bush, Scowcroft, and Baker, were exhilarated by their opportunity to seal victory in the cold war. By April the early differences concerning tactics that had divided foreign service career officers, such as Raymond Seitz, James Baker's major advisers, Dennis Ross and Robert Zoellick, and White House NSC staffers led by Robert Blackwill, had largely been overcome: there was agreement on two plus four with four as circumscribed and delayed as possible. The position that Washington had defended since 1947 was now to be rewarded; history—to use the language of Bismarck—was rustling by and they could grab her hem. Perestroika was a precarious window of opportunity; the Baltic clashes showed it might close. Exploit the opening while one could. The NSC staffers argued that, if need be, the Soviets could be placed before a fait accompli by the Western allies, who should declare that they were renouncing their occupation rights and challenging the Soviets to do the same or run the costs of trying to hold on to their own.

On the West German side the rivalries were sharper but held in check. Kohl wanted unification quickly, completely, and with unrestricted NATO membership. Teltschik backed this approach, and added to it a competitive spirit: his boss and not the FDP foreign minister, too subtle and ambiguous, must remain the major player. Genscher played loyally but resented the

Chancellery's effort to marginalize his role, within the cabinet committee on unification and the working group on security policy. Genscher, seconded primarily by Dieter Kastrup, the political director of the Foreign Office, drew different conclusions from Gorbachev's mercurial views and precarious position than did Teltschik or the White House allies. Might not the speed to which the Americans aspired tend instead either to undermine Gorbachev within the Politburo or to make him bridle? Genscher believed that emphasizing the East-West CSCE and allowing the new territories to retain a special status would make it easier for the Soviet leader to sell unification within a Soviet foreign policy establishment that still mixed professional Germanists alongside perestroika enthusiasts. Genscher also lay greater emphasis on soothing Polish sensibilities.[111] Since he has written his memoirs in the knowledge that the West won big—unification under article 23, with unencumbered NATO membership for united Germany—Genscher has left us a narrative of these months that downplays any difference on fundamentals with the chancellor's advisers. But at the time the Americans and the chancellor's office feared Genscher was too responsive to Soviet hesitations, even though when he encountered resistance from by his chancellor and the Americans he backed away.[112] Neither Kohl nor Bush was in a mood to temporize. When the *Frankfurter Allgemeine Zeitung* ran a story on May 8 that Genscher agreed with the Soviets about the value of separating internal unification and international aspects, Kohl was apparently furious and dressed down his foreign minister.[113]

In fact the Russians were in a quandary. They might delay the four-power confirmation of unification, but the Germans would knit together their economic and soon their political institutions. The hard line that Moscow had advanced at the two plus four on May 5 yielded only an ambiguous communiqué. Chernyaev was scathing about those who resisted a deal on unification. The Soviet ambassador in Bonn, Kvitsinsky, returning home after the two plus four to become deputy foreign minister, was unhappy about the concessions that had been made but also aware that his government's confusions left little to rescue. Increasingly crucial was the financial calculation. Since earlier calculations of a profitable Soviet, FRG, and GDR "triangle" had been overtaken by events, West German economic assistance seemed increasingly necessary. Soviet military leaders were scornful of the compromises on Germany, but their pressure was countered by the acute financial realities. Just as it had constrained the GDR and Poland, indebtedness to the West now cut deeply into Soviet options. Moscow had accumulated foreign debts of about DM 24 billion or about $16 billion, a quarter of it owed to German sources. Shevardnadze had been delegated to plead for credits from Kohl on the eve of the two-plus-four meeting of May 5: perestroika could not be carried through if the ruble collapsed: might not the Germans therefore, so he had to plead, guarantee loans of DM 20 billion? Kvitsinsky had deep misgivings about undermining the foreign minister's leverage by making him play the role of mendicant—but the financial plight seemed determinative. "The Soviet Union stood on the edge of state bankruptcy. . . . Our government had simply no concept of how to lift the country out of the crisis or how even to develop exports and generate foreign currency. The request for a finance credit could thus just be the beginning of a long chain of similar requests that would lead to greater and greater humiliations and lead the western side to ever more unpleasant political counter demands."[114] Less than two weeks later, on May 16, Kohl proposed to Bush that the United States join him in economic credits, envisaging a German loan of DM 5 billion. But the president refused in view of the Lithuanian situation and congressional unhappiness with the Soviet pressure on that small emerging nation. Kohl warned Bush that this position might fatally undermine Gorbachev, but the president felt he could not yield. It was up to the Germans to become the Russians' bankers. It would not be easy, Bush pointed out, for the Russian supplicants to shut the door on German national aspirations if they hoped to open the purses of the Federal Republic.

Teltschik flew to Moscow with the president of the Dresdner Bank and the spokesman for the Deutsche Bank, weaving together financial and political talks. President of the Council of Ministers Ryzhkov told the delegation that it would be disastrous to go back to central planning but that in light of needed grain imports and falling oil prices as well as rising disposable incomes at home, new foreign credits were necessary. Teltschik responded that the chancellor wanted to be helpful: "he regarded the conversation in Moscow not only as a contribution to solving the problems of economic cooperation but as a significant component of an overall solution that had to be reached this year for the German question." But the Germans wanted to participate in a multilateral consortium; other lenders such as Italy, France, and Spain preferrred bilateral agreements. When Gorbachev received Teltschik and the bankers, he too stressed the precarious outlook for perestroika over the next few years. Teltschik said that Kohl wanted to follow unification with a general treaty with the Soviet Union that would establish the basis for a peaceful new Europe, and it was agreed that Kohl would visit the Russian leader in the Caucusus toward the middle of July.

Gorbachev understood that such a visit would have to result in a major agreement if popular hopes were not to be dashed.[115]

This did not mean, however, that the Soviet military and security establishment was prepared to cede major issues. When Baker came to Moscow on May 16–17, he found Shevardnadze "overwhelmed" and unable to cut through the issues. Hardly a surprise in light of the furious pace of the foreign minister's diplomacy: "Flights abroad and receptions in Moscow followed each other in uninterrupted sequence and had to be carefully prepared. Often I thought"—so Kvitsinsky recalls the pace of summer 1990— "for what end all this hecticness?"[116] The Americans came in part to negotiate the conventional force levels in Europe (CFE), but the Soviets had not yet resolved their own disagreements and wanted to address the limits on a German army in the two-plus-four format. Baker's aide Zoellick now offered a nine-point plan in an effort to persuade the Soviets to drop their veto on Germans in NATO. It promised talks on everything, guarantees about German weapons, forces, and borders, an enhanced role for the CSCE, and a pledge not to move NATO forces into former GDR territory for a finite period. But Kvitsinsky did not simply yield. The Soviet military leadership was digging in its own heels and not yet to be overriden, and the diplomat warned even the domestic aspects of unification would not be easy to arrange if the issue of military alignment remained unresolved. Gorbachev himself said that allowing Germany into NATO would be the end of perestroika. He repeated his request for $20 billion in loans and credits.[117]

Despite the apparent stalemate on unification, Soviet financial distress assured that difficulties were not insuperable. Genscher believed that ultimately the Soviets would concede and that Shevardnadze was prepared to negotiate calmly. In a long talk at Geneva on May 23, the Soviet foreign minister now said his government wanted a speedy resolution of the German problem. He emphasized the "simultaneity" of the international and the domestic aspects of unification, not to ransom the latter to the former as the Germans and Americans might fear, but to accelerate the whole process. Genscher suspected that the Russians were on the verge of conceding the issue of NATO membership, and as a sweetener he argued that Moscow would profit more from a united Germany than it had from two divided states. Germany—so Kohl had written Gorbachev the previous day—was prepared to offer DM 5 billion on its own and help secure more in a multinational effort. Shevardnadze's suggested German troop limit of a quarter million soldiers was unacceptably low, Genscher declared, but a united Germany's forces would remain less than the combined complement of the two current states. The key was not to impose limits on Germany alone but on every country's forces in the "central zone," including the Soviet Union's western military districts. Genscher refrained from citing figures; he argued that troop strength was an issue for the Vienna CFE negotiations, but was prepared ultimately to see the number resolved in the two-plus-four framework. The symbolic issue of maintaining Soviet war memorials in German territory could be satisfactorily resolved, Genscher reassured Shevardnadze, as could a limited transitional presence of Soviet troops in the eastern areas of the unified Germany.[118]

Was Gorbachev then prepared to strike a bargain? The Russian's alternatives were not happy. To renounce Germany was unpalatable and deeply threatening to Soviet conservatives; Poland and Hungary and Czechoslovakia were already lost to communism, even to reform communism. The Baltics would be emboldened to complete their secession—in Lithuania's case declared in March, but suspended pending negotiations. But to block a German settlement would shut off aid prospects from the West and preclude further reform as well. What advantages would the Soviets extract if domestic unification proceded and they insisted on blocking formal international ratification? Even if the SPD won the German elections scheduled for December, the Soviets would appear as a disgruntled spoiler, self-excluded from a German settlement as they had been from the treaty with Japan in 1951, and cut off from their major potential creditors for the sake of maintaining demoralized troops in East Germany.[119]

The Russian leader still basked in the admiration of Americans when he arrived for his second meeting of the year with Bush on May 30. Let Germany belong to both alliances or to neither, he first suggested to his White House hosts. But to their surprise he conceded that CSCE principles allowed countries to choose their own military alignments. Had he thought through the issue more legalistically, he need not have yielded such an admission. Germany, he might have parried, was to become a single sovereign country enjoying CSCE guarantees, if and only if the alliance question was settled as a precondition. But Gorbachev had already consented that a sovereign united Germany should emerge at the end of the process. The president telephoned Kohl to say that the Russian leader "kind of agreed" Germany could decide on joining NATO according to the Helsinki accords. Kohl did not seem to grasp the breakthrough. A vital concession granted halfheartedly, perhaps even without full awareness of its implications, thus hardly registered on the leader to whom it was of supreme importance. Of course it could be retracted, but the Americans nailed down the language for the public press announcement on June 3: Bush announced that he and Kohl agreed a united Germany should be part of NATO; Gorbachev did not, but he nonetheless recognized that alliance membership was a matter for the Germans to decide. In fact the Soviets had turned a corner. They moved on from the alliance question after May 30.[120]

German troop limits and the changing nature of NATO still remained to be worked out; the two-plus-four directors met again on June 9 to discuss the borders of a united Germany, which would include the territory of the FRG, the GDR, and all Berlin. Articles 146 and 23 of the Basic Law, which provided for incorporation of those German territories unable to join the FRG in 1949—already invoked for the Saar in 1955 and to be used for the East Germans in 1990—would thereafter be removed from the constitution. At Shevardnadze's request, Genscher journeyed to Brest, where the Soviet foreign minister's brother had fallen in summer 1941 during the early days of the German attack. The Soviet host expressed his concern that if Germany was to belong to NATO, the alliance must significantly evolve. Genscher again alluded rather vaguely to a new relationship with the Warsaw Pact. In fact, as both men understood, the East European alliance was rapidly dissolving. How then might Moscow balance an enhanced NATO; and how could the Soviet leadership persuade its population that a united Germany in NATO was not a real setback for Soviet security? "Give us time to convince our people," Shevardnadze pleaded; but Genscher insisted that the international aspects of unification must advance apace with the internal progress. The two men grew angry and Shevardnadze said that the Potsdam Agreement of 1945 would remain in force if there were no agreement. The essential, however, was that he be able to insist Russia still had imposed some limits on the power of a united Germany: how large an armed force did Germany insist on? Genscher estimated 350,000 to 400,000. "Transformation" of NATO and a troop ceiling, still to be agreed, were left as the possible bases of an agreement. The atmospherics of cordiality were restored a week later, when Shevardnadze received a warm welcome in Münster.[121]

But the two-plus-four discussions of June 22 did not go smoothly. The Soviets were anticipating a challenge from hard-liners at their upcoming Twenty-eighth Party Congress and did not want to appear compliant. The East Germans were annoyed because the Americans made a media event out of the removal of Checkpoint Charlie, which, they felt, ignored their people's role in opening the Wall.[122] Following "long and difficult internal debate," Soviet decision makers formulated a hard-line draft treaty text based

largely on Bondarenko's and Kvitsinsky's efforts to capitalize on the continuing Soviet troop strength in Germany. The tough document had the tone
of a peace treaty, such as it might have been imposed shortly after the war.
It provided a two-year probationary period for united Germany before ter-
minating four-power rights. Among the restrictions envisaged, for five years
the country would remain divided between the two alliances with troops of
all four powers remaining in place in their respective territories. The armed
forces of the to-be-merged FRG and GDR would remain based only in the
western and eastern edges of their halves of Germany and together would be
limited to 200,000 to 250,000, without offensive capacity or authorization.
Besides renouncing the development of atomic, biological, and chemical
weapons, Germany was not even to participate in NATO discussions of nuclear strategy. The Germans were to accept all prior denazification ordi-
nances, as well as prohibit any resurgence of neo-Nazi activity.[123]

East German Foreign Minister Meckel and Defense Minister Rainer Eppelmann, another parson, endorsed a similar scheme; let the East Germans
keep a special force under an independent command: a proposal that the
West Berlin *Tagesspiegel* derisively chalked up to either personal vanity or
the pipedream of two peacenik pastors.[124] For Meckel, the continuing, if
fading hope was to create an East Central European security zone: a CSCE
enclave where GDR authority might find its last vocation. Even the old
Communist hands at the East German Foreign Office began to develop the
concept as an innovative framework for Central European disarmament.
But it got nowhere: the potential Polish and Czech partners remained cool.
It was unclear even that the Soviets really agreed on fighting for an overlapping security condominium in Germany. Shevardnadze's planning chief,
Sergei Tarasenko, had confided to Genscher's aide Elbe in Münster that the
Germans could in effect disregard any Russian reversions to a hard stance,
and Shevardnadze and Baker had been far closer to agreement in Copen-
hagen, three weeks earlier. What did the Soviets really intend?

When Baker confronted Shevardnadze on the evening of June 22, his
Soviet counterpart agreed that the proposal was tough, but claimed that
there was tremendous domestic opposition to unification. If Germany were
to remain in the North Atlantic Treaty Organization, the Russian minister
desperately wanted a sign from the upcoming London NATO meeting that
there could be new security bridges across the alliances and strengthening
of the CSCE. Baker replied that he thought some transformation of NATO
would ensue but that ultimately America would concede a unified Germany
its sovereignty. The United States would retain its troops in Europe because

it had always been asked to. Americans thus had to prepare an innovative agenda for the London NATO summit in order to reassure Shevardnadze that NATO was transforming itself. As part of that assurance, Shevardnadze forwarded a proposed NATO–Warsaw Pact joint declaration whose provisions would still exclude the GDR territory from NATO protection, remove American nuclear forces from Europe, and all American forces as well as Soviet forces from Germany—all steps that would have essentially enfeebled the alliance and which European members of NATO as well as the United States had resisted for decades. To help strengthen Shevardnadze at home, Washington had to craft a response that seemed conciliatory but did not undermine the canons of security. The proposals worked out among State, Defense, and the NSC postponed a quantitative commitment on conventional disarmament, but did advocate a further round of cuts under CFE II (Conventional Forces in Europe) negotiations, removal of U.S. nuclear artillery, and new strategic doctrines that would replace flexible response and forward defense. The new proposals also stipulated permanent liaison missions for Warsaw Pact countries and NATO linkages with CSCE.

The essentials survived the various agency scrutinies, and the West Germans were delighted with Bush's initiative. Mrs. Thatcher clearly was not. What was the point of security if NATO brought the adversary of yesterday so close to the "innermost councils of our defense and preparedness?" Mitterand was also uneasy with weakening the reliance on a nuclear deterrent for the defense of Europe. The Germans agreed to a troop limit of 370,000 that might be cut down to 350,000. The summit endorsed much of the concept, including a move toward multinational corps. Bush presented the new resolutions to Gorbachev, who was also waiting to learn about economic aid. Bonn's DM 5 billion package was approved, but the Soviets were looking toward a total of $15 to 20 billion. This question was debated at the Houston meeting of G-7 leaders. Thatcher did not like the idea of unrestricted aid; Bush too was unwilling to support such a large infusion without pressing for economic reforms. For now the only agreement was for a special IMF study of Soviet economic needs.[125]

With Kohl's visit to Russia imminent, the time had come to settle. The Soviets had raised a hard line intermittently at the two plus four: in Bonn in early May and in Berlin in late June. But Shevardnadze had always seemed disconcerted by it, and Gorbachev had made decisive concessions on May 30. Both Soviet leaders preferred being adulated as liberal reformers in the West than opposed as hard-liners. They yearned for an easy transition to the new era, and they understood that they could forestall unification only by standing in the way of overwhelming German public opinion. Not prepared to use force, they would be excluded participants from a de facto national union, left only with delapidated barracks in the East and excluded from their creditors' largesse. Only their opponents at home really wanted the hard line they had flirted with on June 22; and the leadership managed to face down their bitter criticisms at the Twenty-eighth Party Congress in early July. "Why was the Soviet Union making concessions on every front? . . . the idea of a common European house was a phantom."[126] Gorbachev avoided foreign policy and prevailed on domestic issues. He endorsed his reformers' plans for a 500-day economic reform. The conservatives were hardly routed in the long run, but Gorbachev seemed to dominate.

The union treaty between the two halves of Germany went into effect on July 1 and the economically linked states were now hard at work on their political treaty. With the party congress behind him, Gorbachev was set to receive Kohl in the Caucasus on July 15–16. The West Germans hurried from Houston to Russia. In the late night telephone conversation that Gorbachev granted him, Falin desperately sought to reverse his leader's course: oppose article 23, oppose German membership in NATO, or at the very least ("minimum minorum") remove nuclear weapons from German territory. He got short shrift: "I fear the train has already left," responded Gorbachev as he hung up.[127] Under the brilliant sun and stars at Archys among the high peaks of the northern Caucasus—more remote and alpine than the Americans' wooded getaway at Camp David—Gorbachev told Kohl that he had been encouraged by the political transformation of NATO, which allowed a new situation. He gave the chancellor a position paper that would preclude the military structures of the alliance from being extended to the GDR so long as Soviet troops remained, and he wanted to keep troops in the GDR for three to four years, even while allowing united Germany full sovereignty and membership in NATO. In fact, the Germans could keep nonassigned troops in the East from the outset, affiliating them to NATO once the Soviets left. The Soviets, who earlier had envisaged a transitional renunciation of four-power rights, now announced their readiness to relinquish them immediately on a final settlement in the two-plus-four process. For the second time, Teltschik exulted to his diary: "The breakthrough is accomplished. What a sensation." Later Kohl told Gorbachev that he needed 370,000 men to prevent reversion to a professional army. The Soviets had preferred 350,000 but gave way. (The Germans and Soviets would sign a declaration of intent on August 30; the numbers would still have to be formally worked into the Vienna CFE negotiations.) The essential, so Gorbachev insisted, was that German unification be not an isolated phenomenon, but "part of our whole orientation toward a new Europe."[128] He was putting the best face possible on the agreement he could, but was correct nevertheless. The key to Germany's international role would remain the condition of European relations as a whole. German wealth and power, after all, had become imposing even before unification: it was the integration of Germany in stable international structures and the robustness of its democratic regime that alone could keep German power a force for cooperation and not crude hegemonic ambition.

The foreign ministers of the two-plus-four convened the next day in Paris—their remaining tasks cast somewhat in shadow by the dramatic agreements in the Caucusus. They took note of the German-Soviet agreement, added their collective assurance on the permanence of the western Polish border, and prepared to ready the accords of the six for a Moscow signing on September 12. Unification and the attribution of complete sovereignty would follow without a formal peace treaty. Shevardnadze told Bush that it was the assurances emanating from the London NATO conference and the July 2 party congress that had turned the situation around from June 22. Only the East Germans felt crestfallen; they had been left out in the cold. There was to be no scope for East German initatives. Meckel, who had tried to preserve an independent Central European initiative, later admitted that with respect to foreign policy, after June there was nothing to do but wind up (abwickeln) the GDR.[129] Criticized by the West German press for his efforts at an autonomous diplomacy, he was rather isolated. With his Foreign Office colleagues he bleakly surveyed the unachieved initiatives since April. Carl Christian von Braunmühl, seconded from the FRG Foreign Office to assist Meckel, criticized the GDR's foreign service officers who had not reacted sufficiently to the rapid progress of events. Unification had overtaken them, and Kohl had in effect negotiated directly with Russia, leaving them aside. The East German SPD hope for an atom-free Central European security zone would be unrealized. The effort to use the time until unification to conduct an independent foreign policy had failed; the government possessed no real authority. Press commentary pointed this out;[130] Yet, of course, it had been East Germans who in October and November and then the previous January had started this extraordinary chain of events. Then they had played catalytic roles, had really acted as agents of transformation. In the six months since, they had reverted once again to become if not mere objects of history, at best bystanders—a less oppressive history, to be sure, but little more heedful of their role than it had been before 1989.

On August 23, 1990, the Volkskammer set October 3 for its merger (or *Beitritt*) into the Federal Republic. The five former Länder of the GDR, dissolved by the regime in the 1960s, were to be reestablished legally and to hold new state elections on October 14. Each resurrected Land meanwhile also requested incorporation by virtue of article 23, following the procedure by which the Saar had reentered the Federal Republic in 1956. In the complex interlocking of treaty agreements, the two German states had agreed earlier in the year to regulate many of the outstanding issues with a Unification Treaty, slated for completion by the end of August. Negotiations for this pact were to follow completion of the "currency, economic and social union" confirmed by the first "State Treaty" in May. The diverse issues to be settled—claims to restitution of collectivized property, electoral procedures, extension of the federal-state tax-sharing arrangements—were highly complicated. On the West German side, Interior Minister Wolfgang Schäuble, assisted by an interministerial task force, was determined to achieve a comprehensive agreement in time for the CSCE meeting slated to wrap up the formalities of German unification on the international level. His East German counterpart, the industrious, young parliamentary state secretary, Günter Krause, and de Maizière, found themselves recapitulating the earlier humiliating experiences of Hans Modrow, as Schäuble announced at their first formal session in July: "We don't want to be coldhearted about your wishes and interests. But this is not the unification of two equal states."[131]

The weak East German government did not survive the negotiations without crises and division. De Maizière wanted to preserve a great coalition to take his country into the FRG, but the East German Social Democrats were restive. They threatened to walk out over tax issues, and their finance minister Walter Romberg was dismissed because he demanded that all East German receipts be kept within the territory of what would be the ex-GDR, while de Maizière held that the East would get more from West German fiscal subventions if it threw its taxes into the national pot. The eastern Social Democrats also objected to the emerging compromise for the first all-German elections that Schäuble wanted to hold before year's end. German parties had to reach a minimal threshold of votes to share in the proportional division of votes for parliamentary representatives: the East German "Bündnis 90" as well as the old PDS believed they would lose their representation if they had to collect 5 percent among both states' electorates, and the East German Social Democrats would not have mourned the disappearance of these competitors. Nevertheless, it was agreed that for the first unified election the 5 percent hurdle would be tallied separately in each half of reemerging Germany: the CDU was not averse to preserving the PDS rather than see its votes go to the SPD. The East Germans resisted the FRG's desire to take control of Stasi documents (and limit punishment of earlier informers); instead they established an independent authority to control access and sponsor scholarly evaluation. As divisive as the other issues, the differing access to abortion also endangered agreement, until it was agreed the day before scheduled signing of the treaty that the more liberal stipulations of the GDR (which allowed a woman to terminate pregnancy in the first trimester without restriction) could remain valid for East German women for at least two years after unification.[132]

The Germans finally had to produce a general treaty of friendship with the Soviets, which was easy, then a pact to settle East Germany's residual economic obligations, and finally a transition treaty that governed the conditions for the basing and later withdrawal of Soviet troops in Germany. This effort was where the Soviets hoped to extract as much hard cash as possible. They had sent a bill on September 5 up to DM 36 billion ($20 billion). Kohl offered DM 8 billion under various claims; Gorbachev demanded a minimum of DM 11 billion plus transportation and maintenance costs, and he threatened to hold up signature of the two-plus-four "Final Settlement." In a renewed weekend of haggling between finance ministers and then national leaders, an existing German offer of DM 12 billion plus a DM 3 billion credit was settled. This treaty was initialed on September 27.

Meanwhile the two-plus-four agreements—the treaty concerning the concluding regulations relating to Germany—had been completed by the foreign ministers in Moscow on September 12, but not without a last-minute crisis. Germany was to recover sovereignty; its borders included the current West, East, and Berlin. What rights might NATO claim in East Germany? Based on the Caucusus agreement, Kvitsinsky's language prohibited any NATO troops from being either stationed or deployed in eastern Germany before the Russians left in 1994, and would exclude non-German NATO forces or atomic weapons thereafter. The British, and indeed the American negotiators, were willing to live with the veto on U.K.-U.S. garrisons, but they did not wish to accept the restriction on deployment, which they interpreted as a veto on NATO maneuvers in the East. The Anglo-American objections irritated both the West Germans and de Maizière, who believed that the British stonewalling (they overlooked the U.S. difficulties with the text) represented a last-minute effort to postpone signature of the pact. After desperate midnight conferences, it was agreed that the restriction on deployment would remain, but to be interpreted when necessary by the Germans. The September 12 treaty culminated the two-plus-four process and announced the impending end of the four powers' residual occupation rights. At a CSCE meeting on September 26, the governments took official note of these agreements, including the renunciation of four powers' prerogative as of the date of unification: midnight October 2–3.[132]

World War II was over; so too was the cold war. Hard-liners in Moscow got another chance to ventilate their criticism of Soviet diplomacy as the Supreme Soviet formally debated the vacating of its friendship treaty with the East German state that had actually disappeared a day earlier. So too with the ratification of the new treaty of friendship with the FRG. But as Kvitsinsky—one of the tenacious fighters for as favorable a settlement as possible—wrote in a draft speech for his minister, it was not the treaties that had doomed East Germany. "The death sentence of the GDR was signed in the moment when it was decided to open the border. The treaties merely mirrored the changes, inevitable after that point and foreseeable. When the Berlin Wall fell no single voice in the Supreme Soviet of the USSR had been raised to preserve it. Why did one now seek to reach the impossible and to roll back history. There was no way back."[134]

Shevardnadze and Gorbachev, supported by Chernyaev and gradually by Kvitsinsky, had granted to the Germans the unity they wanted. But the disappearance of two Germanies, the reappearance of a unified national state, was not just the consequence of the fall of the Wall. It was also the result of the general disarray that overtook the Communist system: the decrepitude of its economics, the obsolescence of its military alliance, the firm support of the White House for an aspiration that many Germans and Americans had actually ceased to believe in, and the odd couple of Kohl and Genscher: the former understanding how to press for a maximal solution while reassuring his allies that he believed in Europe and promising the Soviets he would pay for their difficult transition; the latter assuaging the professional foreign services, who fretted about borders and security and the memories of history.

This author left a historians' conference in Berlin in mid-December 1990. With the withdrawal of residual Allied control over the city, Lufthansa was to recover the right to fly in and out of Berlin, which had been awarded to Pan American after World War II. In the interim decades, Lufthansa flights to and from the United States terminated or began in Frankfurt. I flew out on one of the last Pan-American flights—one of the little perquisites of conquest that disappeared only shortly before the airline itself. Three and a half years later I wandered through the halls of the American commandant on the Clay Allee, now being emptied by our final departing military units. A photographic exhibit traced the American presence from the ruins of 1945 and the airlift provisioning of 1948 to Kennedy's electrifying visit of 1963, and then to the present. Now, in summer 1994, the halls were emptying. Soviet troops too had been departing in the four years, abandoning their dilapidated barracks, selling their medals and caps for a bit of ready cash to American tourists, unloved in their period of transition. Their empty compounds stood desolate in Brandenburg and Potsdam, Jüterbog and elsewhere. An imperial era was closing, perhaps for Americans, certainly and far more bleakly for the Russians.

If not ending, at least being redefined. The Russians in the next five years would see their control even over Soviet space disintegrate. By 1991 the Soviet Union itself had fragmented, and it was far from clear whether Moscow would reconsolidate control or even economic leadership over the vast territories of its former state. After bipolarity, the governing structures of international politics became murky. Ethnic conflict flared even in Europe; liberals hoped that nongovernmental agencies might organize a transnational civil society; business and political leaders emphasized the potential of regional economic groups: the European Community, the North American Free Trade Area, East Asia, or the Pacific littorals. If development toward such regional markets continued, Germany might become the motor of European and East European development. But before the period in which it might exert the economic leadership in Europe and East Europe, it had to traverse a difficult transition at home.

Germany controlled its own territory and its own capital—or did it? Like all nominally sovereign countries, it was absorbing unwanted migrants who sought work or asylum, and witnessing periodic outbreaks of intolerant xenophobia. Germany had become a whole nation, even as nations appeared to be losing their grip on economic transformations that encroached on even the best organized of societies. The history that had climaxed on October 3, 1990, belonged irrevocably to a slowly disappearing world of organized alliances, of clear demarcations among states and systems and ideologies. That history was ending: not just the cold war, but the reassuring territorial organization of societies and nations. The Germans had recovered their 137,400 square miles (350,000 square kilometers) of national space, a tract the size of Montana; the United States had bested the Soviets—real achievements that might, however, quickly seem insubstantial as the agenda of world history began to transform itself, just as it had after the defeat of National Socialism in 1945. Indeed, the victories of both 1945 and 1989–90 had been major historical achievements; they made life far less oppressive for millions. But no such emancipation or constitutive moment ever removes the press of new problems.

Six

Anschluss and Melancholy

Souvenirs de l'est
Souvenirs qui me restent
Que me reste-t-il de mes souvenirs de l'est?
Un sourire, un geste . . .
Une chanson qui proteste
Que me reste-t-il de mes souvenirs de l'est?

—Patricia Kaas, French *chanteuse*

BETWEEN TWO BERLINS, 1990

One souvenir of the East that might remain was a piece of the Berlin Wall. Although it did not go up for sale officially until January 21, 1990, local entrepreneurs seized their opportunity and their chisels earlier. They hammered off fragments, added spikes of rusted barbed wire, then mounted each jagged miniature on a stained wood base and peddled them to tourists. West German public agencies embedded votive shards in plexiglass cubes to present to foreign dignitaries. And as early as Christmas 1989, the American shopper could buy a two-ounce chip of the Wall in Boston's Filene's Basement for $12.95. It was packed in a maroon velvet jewelry sack inside a special commemorative box and accompanied by an inspirational pamphlet:

"The Wall is Gone!" And from this rubble rose a new symbol for tomorrow, an icon for future generations; the Berlin Wall . . . dismantled. History is a look backward, a reconciliation of times and lives gone by. Now we are faced with the glowing view before us. It is the stuff of dreams. It is the blue sky that sails just out of view. Grip the artifact and in your hand is the past and future. Let your fingers wander slowly across its battered surface. You can tell the balance of our lives. You can feel the struggles and the triumphs, the grief and the joy, the hope and the fulfillment. You can feel the distant tremor of tomorrow's history gently unfolding in the palm of your hand.

But the visitor who returned to Berlin a year after buying his packaged artifact no longer felt the hope and the fulfillment or the distant tremor of tomorrow's history. What he sensed instead toward Christmas 1990 was an acute sense of dislocation. East Germans must have experienced it far more acutely. Germany was no longer two nations, but it certainly was not yet one. A regime had disappeared. With it a framework of inculcated collective values—cultivated by constraint to be sure, but nonetheless pervasive—had been abandoned, pronounced irrelevant, canceled. What East German party members and intellectuals referred to as "our republic," with its implicit distinction from "their republic," no longer existed. But the differences between East and West persisted. "I have lost my homeland, this gray, narrow, ugly land," lamented Konrad Weiss, a young filmmaker and Bündnis 90 intellectual, who despite his melancholy would make a good adjustment to postunification politics. "This beautiful land. In this land I grew up; it was the land of my first love, the land of my dreams, the land of my anger. It was the land of my children and it was to have been the land of my unborn grandchild. Now it is being taken away from under my feet. My hopes are withering and my dreams are dying. I am being made into an emigrant in my own land. I wanted to make a motherland out of my land. In a motherland weapons aren't necessary. . . . But now a raw, garish, shirt-sleeved fatherland is bursting in on us. It leaves us no way out, we can't defend ourselves against it."[1] The overwhelming presence of West Germany, which had originally beckoned as so redemptive, made it difficult for East Germans to take legitimate satisfaction in their own historical achievement. Their entry into the Federal Republic by virtue of article 23, that is, without any sacramental constitutional convocation, had allowed speed and convenience; but it also took a civic toll. How quickly the sense of euphoria had yielded to victimization!

At night the showy Kurfürstendamm was bright with Christmas lights. For over three decades it had glistened as the defiant easternmost outpost of Western consumerism as well as liberty, connecting half of the renewed capital city with threads of neon to market cultures that extended two-thirds of the way around the globe to Tokyo. The Kaufhaus des Westens or KaDeWe, Berlin's Harrod's, overflowing with opulence—its ground floor

crammed with ornate carved pine-tree candle holders ranging from orna-
ment to life-size—had an old Volkswagen in the middle into which shop-
pers could stuff money destined for Russian aid. Berliners and West Germans threw themselves into Russian charity with extraordinary enthusiasm.
The deeper the Soviet Union promised to slip into despair, the more ear-
nestly West Berliners responded. Even humble office workers moved by the
reports from the East were allegedly contributing up to DM 1,000 or $600
to ship food and supplies east. By the end of 1993, German private donors
had contributed $525 million (DM 735 million).

The fervor was revealing. Moscow, supposedly on the verge of starva-
tion and anarchy, was remote, its great collective people needy. As they had
periodically, before World War I and during the Weimar Republic, once
again the Russian people loomed as a distant and almost mystical mass.
No longer did they embody the brooding, menacing danger that was their
alternative collective persona. Now they stirred chords of German mission
as well as Christmas charity. Mediating Slavic needs with the West affirmed
a recurrent German role, characterized simultaneously by patronizing
concern, material self-confidence, and genuine sympathy. Between the end
of 1989 and June 1992, when Chancellor Kohl claimed that the country
had reached its limit, the German government would grant, lend, or indirectly guarantee more than $52 billion (aproximately DM 80 billion) to
the republics of the former Soviet Union and almost $20 billion (or DM 30
billion) more to the rest of Eastern Europe. By the end of 1994 the totals
had reached $71 billion (DM 100 billion) and over $36 billion (DM 51 billion) respectively.[2]

From the KaDeWe in December 1990, the Kremlin seemed hardly more
remote than the populated centers a few kilometers to the east. This Berlin
still remained dark at night. "Alex," or Alexanderplatz, the lively daytime
center of East Berlin life, shut down, the windows of its single large department store filled now with Japanese and Western electronic gadgets, but
otherwise devoid of cafés, pedestrians, people. No one walked the Karl Marx
Allee or Unter den Linden leading to the now open Brandenburg Tor. The
S-Bahn creaked over the fading scar where the Wall had been: the political
frontier had disappeared, the social frontier between affluence and shabbi-
ness remained.

Six months later the German Bundestag voted to confirm united Berlin as
the country's new seat of government.[3] The German Federal Republic had
selected Bonn only as a provisional seat of government. But after unification

many thought that Berlin's symbolic status might be preserved by an occasional Bundestag meeting and presidential visit; parliament and ministries should still be based in Bonn. This compromise would have been unacceptable for the East Germans, but their voice was hardly decisive. They seemed to be second-class citizens already without having the promise of the capital taken from them. Renewing the city as a capital would inject a tremendous economic boost; construction projects, new apartments, and hotels, would make Berlin hum into the new century and would counteract the depression settling over the old East Germany. Manfred Stolpe, the politically astute lay administrator of the Lutheran Church who had become minister-president of the Brandenburg state government, his reputation not yet tarnished by ambiguous revelations of Stasi collaboration, was a persuasive advocate. Federal President Weizsäcker and former Chancellor Brandt—the leaders with high moral profile—insisted on Berlin. Even the Bavarians were as willing to accept Berlin as Bonn. Within two to three years, East Berlin would brighten up at night and become smarter: West Berliners went to eat at Borchard's, the reopened landmark bistro around the corner from the bleak office building where the relaunched East German parties had established their makeshift electoral headquarters in March 1990. They would take late suppers in the cafés on the Kollwitzplatz, and lunches at the Jewish vegetarian restaurant next to the Oranienburgerstraße synagogue. Yuppie gentrification, regilding and restoration, all followed the flag. By the year 2000 it was likely that the "Kudam" would lose its commercial hegemony to the rebuilt Hotels Adlon and Bristol, and the crystal palace of the Galeries Lafayette on the refurbished Friedrichstraße.

As of 1990, however, West German public opinion in the West drew back from Berlin: who needed the expense? Who wanted another Megalopolis: a capital that would attract six million; would add the centripetal force of government employment to its theater, art scene, youth culture, and university attractions; would make the surroundings that East German backwardness had preserved in a charming rural state into dense suburbs? Would not Berlin reassert its Prussian military presence, or alternatively the anarchic traits of urban cynicism, punk, squatters, and youth culture? All these arguments preoccupied public opinion in the late spring of 1991; and after an eleven-hour Bundestag debate on June 20, which cut across party lines, deputies resolved to return to Berlin, 337 to 320. On August 16, 1991, the ashes of Frederick the Great were transferred from the ancestral family domain in Hohenzollern in southwestern Swabia and reburied in Potsdam. A small gesture, a renewal of tradition.

In effect the decision to reinvest Berlin as capital ratified what all the earlier developments had pointed toward. The new Germany was slated eventually to evolve as a different country. It would no longer comprise just a narrow hinterland behind a Rhenish and Bavarian axis; it might no longer play the role of a renewed *Rheinbund*, a cooperative state that seconded American policy and exported fine cars and machines. Its national bank in Frankfurt would dominate West European monetary policies. At the same time its diplomats and businessmen would look east as well as west, renew old interests and be petitioned by new clients in Budapest, Bratislava, and Zagreb. The international stucture in which united Germany was embedded would become far less constraining and limiting. The force field of the cold war no longer aligned the nations of Europe. The massive Soviet empire would fragment. An influence that seemed forever eradicated in 1945 would reconstitute itself in the middle of Europe, not necessarily by virtue of the Germans' own ambition, but the default of alternative actors.

How assertive and paramount a role the Germans would play by the end of the century and beyond was obviously unclear in the few years after unification. Certainly new questions about German power had to be resolved. Should the Germans participate in UN peace missions? How should they cooperate with the allies' military efforts outside Europe? Should they receive a permanent seat on the Security Council? But internal issues seemed far more preoccupying. For the Germans themselves, unification raised dilemmas at home, querulous complaints, and recriminations. In the aftermath of unity the economic breakdown in the East became even more burdensome than envisaged when the economic and currency union was instituted in the summer of 1990. Unification also embroiled Westerners and Easterners in the issue of responsibility for the former history of East Germany and its pervasive state security apparatus. Who was to be disqualified from public life? What constituted unacceptable collaboration with the old secret police? How large a role should the Westerners play in reconstructing the East German economy, its political institutions, and its research and educational establishment? "Ossies" wavered between resentment of the "Besser-Wessies," or know-it-alls, and a lack of confidence in their own capacity to reform. Bärbel Bohley, with her gift for pungent exaggeration, said privately that the West would not redeem the East, rather the rot in the East would infect the West. Tough-minded West Germans (or those who had earlier fled or had been expelled from the GDR) felt that former East Germans would never dismantle the old-boy networks of SED complicity (*alte Seilschaften*) unless pressured from without. West German academics decried the scholarly wasteland of the Academy of Sciences; writers in the old FRG grew angry about their Eastern colleagues unwillingness to "work through" the earlier conformism of the Writers Association. Demands for redress clashed with calls for reconciliation.

There was to be no final and clear-cut resolution of these confrontations. They continued to set the tone of public life in the half decade after unification, prolonging, in effect, the spectral presence of the German Democratic Republic. How were institutions to be meshed, how was new leadership to be generated, what productive role might a socialist rust belt play within Germany's fine-tuned corporate capitalism, what would happen to different marriage and child-rearing patterns—how should those who spent their lives negotiating with East German restrictions and its enthusiasms look back upon that long transaction, now pronounced a fool's errand by history? There can be no taking leave of the GDR without following some of these continuing issues. The effort to reconstruct a collapsing regional economy was the most agonizing practical concern. The project of reorienting the research and teaching establishment revealed how difficult inner unification was likely to prove. (It was also the issue this writer followed from closest hand.) The dilemma of rendering justice, coming to terms with the Communist past and its abuses of human rights, opened the most philosophical questions of national reconstruction. We will follow these three dimensions of unification in turn.

BETWEEN SOCIALISM AND CAPITALISM

Economic paradox prevailed. A productive machine that had seemed dynamic now appeared shabby and unrescuable. In 1991, the national product of the former East Germany had fallen around a third and industrial production around two-thirds. About four million East Germans were out of work or in make-work positions. Where jobs persisted they were based on the massive transfers from West to East. Once rated as perhaps the world's tenth or eleventh largest industrial producer, the former GDR now appeared just a junk heap of retrograde industry and pollutants. Many West German commentators declared that the economic situation was far worse than they had believed, as if they had been tricked into purchasing a defective product.[4] The claims of would-be property owners were multiplying. Who was heir to the run-down factories or to decaying houses that had been made state property in the last decades?[5] The effort to honor former owners' claims was probably counterproductive. It left many enterprises and pieces of real estate threatened with an ancient claim. It would probably have been better simply to wipe out most of the claims and offer compensation instead. A new class of profiteers promised to emerge. The switch to capitalism—everywhere in the former socialist bloc—threatened to reward not merely the energetic and entrepreneurial, but the speculator and the sharpy. American economists and those who did well at home implied that emergence of the new rich must be the price of rapid growth. But a population that had lived forty years under collectivism might well give equality a larger place in its value scheme. Angry at the privileges that party membership had bestowed, less agile East Europeans and Germans could also be resentful at the rewards of snapping up a factory in difficulty at a bargain price, or of taking over some residential property that the Treuhand or "trustee organization" was unloading. The market revealed its pathology as well as its promises. But were there alternatives?

Several major economic difficulties were hard to surmount. Elsewhere in Eastern Europe, economists argued whether "shock treatment" or gradual adjustment promised a more successful takeoff. Should the prices of basic goods be freed, credits curtailed, firms forced to liquidate and lay off workers, or should the transition be cushioned at the cost of perpetuating nonproductive firms?[6] By virtue of the GDR's absorption into the German economic currency system, some of these issues had been preemptively answered. The path to adjustment could not take place by a rapid depreciation of monetary assets. But how rapidly should wage rates converge between old and new Bundesländer? Given the rapid collapse of output and employment that ensued in 1991 and 1992, economic analysts searched for the crucial policy failures, blaming respectively the high conversion rate of the East German currency, the relatively rapid rise of East German wages and salaries, the dismantling of organized economic units, or the hesitations and difficulties of privatization. But could even a perfectly insightful policy package have averted the painful contraction as a down-at-heels plant was placed in competition with the oiled productive machinery of the Federal Republic? All the more daunting a challenge given the radical loss of markets in Eastern Europe.

Through the first two quarters of 1990, in fact, trade with the Soviet Union continued, and the former GDR's balance of payments actually strengthened. Exports to the Russians in 1990 slightly exceeded those of 1989. In 1991 the Berlin Kombinat still built 2,500 railroad cars for the Soviets with a price tag of DM 1.4 billion. The unification treaty stipulated that the Federal Republic assumed East Germany's contractual obligations toward the Soviet Union, and the Kohl government thus permitted East Germans to continue their trade until the end of 1990 in transferable rubles and then to claim DM 2.24 per ruble: in effect a policy of German credits to Moscow that were spent within the former GDR.[7] But as of 1991, the Russians would have to settle accounts in deutsche marks. East German consumers, moreover, now tended to shun Comecon goods; CMEA imports collapsed drastically. Although the fall in imports briefly created a surplus for the imputed Eastern German balance of payments vis-à-vis its East European partners, the resulting one-way trade could not be sustained. The political turmoil and fragmentation of the Soviet Union and the collapse of Russian and East European production further wiped out the traditional export markets for the East German exports in 1991. Revenues were thus plummeting in a period when the former Kombinate had to service deutsche mark indebtedness to the Bundesbank instead of its old and usually renewable Ostmark debts to the GDR Staatsbank. The currency union had halved the face value of East German company debt, but the real burden had become far higher. The very conversion of marks that had benefited East German households handicapped firms. Their goods, priced in deutsche marks from 1991 on, seemed radically more expensive for Polish or Russian importers with their drastically depreciated currencies. Now moreover, their products had to compete with the quality goods of the West. Robitron might be a premier computer firm for the Eastern bloc; its products were still noncompetitive with IBM or Siemens even as Eastern clients disappeared. The shipbuilding industry of the Baltic coast rapidly withered as Russian orders slowed and Western ones lagged.

Industrial production in 1991 was worth a third of the 1989 output. Baltic wharves and the coddled computer manufacturers, steel and machine tool producers, and the chemical heartland between Leipzig and Halle all furloughed their workers. The U.S. consulting firm McKinsey had estimated in May 1991 that only 3,000 of the 27,000 jobs in the Buna works could be saved. Similar conditions threatened in nearby Schkopau, Bitterfeld, Leuna, and the Wolfen film concern. West German investors had little appetite to recapitalize these firms, since they were ecological nightmares, contributing to the worst pollution in Europe. BASF went shopping instead at Schwarzheide in Brandenburg, and other Western corporations sought cleaner firms elsewhere. The East German steel industry, nurtured at the cost of immense subsidies in Eisenhüttenstadt in southeast Brandenburg, would drastically contract.[8]

In the very months that the run-down plants became redundant, they were all thrown on the market. The idea of placing the economic assets of the GDR into a form of "self-organization" was under discussion among participants in the civic movement at least since November 1989. Wolfgang Ullmann, the pastor and leader of Democracy Now, presented the idea on the part of one interested circle, the Freie Forschungsgemeinschaft Selbstorganisation (the Free Research Community for Self-Organization), to the Round Table on February 12.[9] East German Volkskammer delegates mooted vesting ownership of state firms either in their own work forces or in public mutual funds, as the Czech Republic would attempt. These forms, however, seemed unsuited to raise the infusions of West German capital that would be required to modernize the aging plant. Some decision seemed necessary: the Modrow government did not want to abandon the idea of social ownership but had to recognize how weak was its hold on power. Every one of the contending groups, including the new SPD and the reinvigorated CDU, felt they had to safeguard the GDR patrimony against a piecemeal sell-off to the West. Contending proposals were discussed but the regime issued its own Treuhand ordinance on March 1. The CDU wanted a more resolute privatization; the interim solution kept options open. The decree of March 1 (and constitution of the agency two weeks later) vested the administration of East German socialist assets in the hands of a Treuhand-Anstalt, a holding-company trust that provisionally became the largest nongovernmental accumulation of property in the world.[10]

The original Treuhand had the mandate to manage and restructure East German holdings for the state and to attract joint-venture capital from the West. Its holdings included 8,000 large and small enterprises and the land and plant of the GDR and employed two-thirds of the working population of the rapidly dissolving state. Originally it was granted DM 20 billion to keep firms afloat. In the first month alone the public firms applied for DM 17 billion, and rather than attempt to discriminate among claims, the Treuhand granted 41 percent of each applicant's request. On the basis of studies from American consulting firms, including Arthur D. Little and McKinsey, the Ministries of Finance and Economics estimated in May that about 30 percent of the property would be profitable, about a half might be brought to profitability, and about 20 percent was too obsolete and noncompetitive to rescue.

The original Treuhand mission, like many of Modrow's projects, was based on a somewhat blithe discounting of the obstacles that GDR indebtedness imposed. Advocates of a resolute privatization began to press for a more radical approach on the morrow of the March 18 elections. The Bonn government and other West German groups proposed new legislation; ideas for codetermination (*Mitbestimmung*) and the general distribution of vouchers or shares succumbed to the new promarket wind blowing out of the West. Following some intensive debate the Volkskammer approved a revised organization on June 17. Neither the Bündnis 90/Green delegates nor the SPD was happy with the new emphasis on privatization ("expropriation"), but the latter was committed to the East Berlin Great Coalition. Christa Luft, who had served as Modrow's economics minister, condemned the unseemly careerism of her former colleagues and the general deutsche mark intoxication.[11]

The redefined mission of the Treuhand, from the summer of 1990 on, stressed privatization, not fiduciary oversight. Detlev Rohwedder, director of the West German steel firm Hoesch, who had downsized but rescued that ailing steel giant, took over the chair of the board of directors until he was slain by Red Brigade terrorists nine months later. As of September only a few properties had attracted buyers; joint ventures had minimal appeal. In October 1990 the fifteen regional branches were entrusted to West German managers, and these branches were given more of the Kombinate to administer on a decentralized basis. Treuhand's role, Rohwedder emphasized, was to find purchasers: "it was almost heretical to speak about restructuring [*Sanierung*]," one of his staff admitted in early 1991. Rohwedder's own concept, "privatization is the best restructuring," set down in his so-called Easter letter of 1991, released after his slaying, gained force as a sort of political testament.[12]

But would there be purchasers without restructuring? Those who sought properties, many at seeming discounts, had to present concepts for making a go of the enterprise, large or small, that they were acquiring. Industrial firms were burdened with debt and would have to assume huge bills for environmental cleanup. The Treuhand ended up assuming the old debt and sanctioning the breakup of large units to allow for the sale of viable plants.[13] Critics pointed out how destructive this course of action seemed to be. East German Kombinate, after all, had been organized as mini-economies, often vertically and horizontally integrated. Within the framework dictated by the logic of public ownership, they had developed their own routines to minimize transaction costs. Now they would be pried apart, units shut down, others annexed to their West German corporations, while skilled labor teams would be dispersed: in the process the savings on transactions costs that had been achieved would be sacrificed, just as the once viable markets among East German producers was wrenched apart.[14] During late 1990 and early 1991, the Treuhand was becoming the symbol for a capitalist takeover that was at once rapacious and inefficient. After Rohwedder was killed in April, his successor as director, the doughty financial administrator, Birgit Breuel, tried to expedite Treuhand operations—but again emphasizing that her responsibility was to "create new gems from day to day" and find new owners as rapidly as possible.[15] Faced with growing dismay and protest over plant closures, the government had conceded by March 1991 that it would establish regional supervisory boards to consult on any shutdowns.[16] Still, until autumn 1991, the Treuhand administration argued that its task was preeminently to find new owners. At a speech in Hamburg on November 1, Breuel signaled the revised priorities: referring to the McKinsey and Goldman Sachs critiques of the deindustrialization of the chemical industry in Leipzig-Halle-Bitterfeld, she spoke of the need to preserve "industrial core regions." East German industry was no longer to be envisaged with so cavalier a regard to its regional embeddedness. The success story of Baden-Württemberg in the 1980s, where state government and enterprises had jointly worked to nurture an infrastructure of social capital, was to become a more explicit model for the post-1991 Treuhand.[17]

Treuhand pricing was based on asset value, including real estate, offset by allowances for the burden of old debt, future ecological costs, and severance pay that was likely to be incurred. It was no suprise that properties went begging, and that real-estate holdings became the major source of potential profit for the Treuhand. (The value of real estate after all was not dependent on the interrupted demand of Eastern Europe, nor did it suffer from the aging of capital.) Since, moreover, it had not been a source of private or public wealth in the GDR, the state had allocated large land allotments to enterprises. The Treuhand separated the holdings that were "unnecessary" for the industrial enterprise and established its own real-estate holding (TLG) that was especially active in East Berlin property and slated to remain in operation beyond the Treuhand dissolution at the end of 1994. The TLG, moreover, worked closely with public authorities in Berlin much to the annoyance of would-be purchasers of land in the capital. The relative profitability of the real estate operations and its similarity to a state enterprise led to internal conflicts in the organization.[18]

The operation grew more costly as, later in 1991, Breuel and her staff accepted the need for a more interventionist role in sustaining the companies they had privatized. They emphasized their efforts to create a new base of small and medium firms, reversing, in effect, the socialist concentration of industry in the 1970s. Flagship firms thus disappeared or shrank drastically, while their diverse productive units might end up tucked away as component parts of West German corporations. Nonetheless, Breuel's task was bound to be an ungrateful one. Whatever jobs might be rescued, the centers of industrial decision making would move to the West. And if East Germans commentators resented the Treuhand's fire sale of ex-GDR "gems" to West German firms, West German economists wanted rapid mass auctions of Treuhand holdings, not an effort to locate specific owners for particular enterprises.[19] When property could not be readily disposed of, complaints arose on the part of would-be entrepreneurs East and West that the agency was embroiled in unnecessary red tape and hobbled by former socialist administrators who resisted decisive action. And indeed, insofar as the Treuhand wanted to preserve jobs or industrial units, it rediscovered the logic of the state firms it was originally designed to liquidate.

The Treuhand could not have resisted the basic tendency toward deindustrialization. Unsellable and unrescuable plants were to be closed: the Pentacon camera works in Dresden, employing 3,000 workers, ceased production in October 1990, as did the Wartburg auto plant in Eisenach that employed 20,000 workers. The Trabi plant in Zwickau was next to be liquidated; Treuhand officials did not accept the director's arguments that supporting the unemployed would cost more than subsidizing the cars. Nonetheless, Opel, Daimler Benz, and Volkswagen did pledge to invest in the East: half of the 130,000 workers would be gone, but the basis of a modern industry would be consolidated. The venerable Carl Zeiss enterprise of Jena was likewise rescued after a catastrophic collapse of Soviet orders in 1991. Zeiss had divided in the postwar era; the Stuttgart branch proposed to take over the East German firm, if the Treuhand agreed to assume the existing debt. CDU Thuringian Minister-President Josef Duchac was not prepared to lose control of his state's premier industry; instead he recruited the former minister president of Baden-Württemberg, Lothar Späth, to rescue the Jena operation. Späth had been celebrated in Stuttgart for innovative industrial development strategies, but had fallen more recently under a cloud for alleged corruption. (His new townsfolk in Jena have paid bemused tribute to his ebullient entrepreneurship by referring to the large postmodern administrative headquarters he has built near the main square as the Empire Späth Building.) Späth split the Jena firm, allowing the Stuttgart branch to take a 51 percent share of "Carl Zeiss Jena," the optical core of the old firm that retained 20,000 workers. Ownership of the newly spun-off "Jenoptik," which was given the other 49 percent of Carl Zeiss shares, remained in the hands of the Thuringian state government with Späth as CEO.[20] Thuringia was to contribute DM 800 million toward restructuring costs and the Treuhand, DM 2.74 billion; 14,000 jobs were slated to disappear.

Wages comprised a second major difficulty. Along with a high currency conversion ratio, critics charged that the rapid rise in East German real wages played the principal role in the mass unemployment and fall in output. East German firms, so West German entrepreneurs estimated on the basis of productivity comparisons, might be competitive or break even if their workers earned 60 percent of the Western wages. But GDR labor demanded that wages soon be equalized; and the national trade-union federations took up the issue as they sought to recruit Eastern members. An I. G. Metall organizer explained that the unions were just keeping up with the workers. Not all businessmen were prepared to resist: the representative of the Northern Businessmen's Association signed a 1991 wage contract that envisaged working toward wage equality. This was denounced by Western colleagues. But the choice was a hard one. Industrial wages were negotiated by unions and employer federations on a national basis. To keep East Germany a low-wage island would also have been politically difficult given the commitment to national unity. Concern that East Germans would have migrated significantly to accelerate wage parity was probably mistaken, however. In any case, the 1991 contracts did not provide the Easterners the thirteenth month of salary and other benefits that their Western counterparts enjoyed.[21]

By the summer of 1991 the economic difficulties had taken much of the luster off Chancellor Kohl's achievement. On May 23, 1990, he had promised that "Tax increases that hurt productivity are not needed to finance aid to the GDR." "No one will be worse off," he had told the Bundestag on June 21, 1990, borrowing a phrase of de Maizière; "many will be better. . . . Germans in the Federal Republic shall not have to give up anything."[22] The first all-German elections in December 1990 gave Kohl a solid victory, ratifying, in effect the achievement of unification. Results in the East largely recapitulated those of the previous March. But by early 1991, the Christian Democratic Party suffered three setbacks in state elections, thus losing control of the upper house (Bundesrat) of the national legislature, which was chosen indirectly by state legislatures. By late spring it was clear that new taxes on the West were required. "How much more?" asked *Der Spiegel* in a cover article that showed a German taxpayer being wrung out.[23] Liberal commentators might accept the need for sacrifice.[24] After all, wasn't it a relatively small price for national unification? Would West Germans have renounced the accomplishments of the past two years to save an additional tithing? The difficulty was that the government had so soothingly promised that it could be costless to unite the country socially and economically.

By spring 1991 there was malaise on both sides. East German unemployment was climbing. Many former GDR citizens felt that their West German countrymen were arrogant and selfish, intent on securing university positions, vacation homes, or profitable business opportunities. They, the Ossies, would become a helot class, condemned to work at low-wages while the profitable parts of their industry were carved up for entrepreneurs from the West. Westerners complained that the East Germans were unused to rigorous work; they told jokes about how managers preferred the Poles, so long held in contempt for their alleged lack of industriousness, to East Germans on perpetual holiday. When BASF invested in a chemical plant in the East, it was willing to operate at a loss for several years, but did not expect the obstacles in terms of environmental costs, labor difficulties, and the like. It felt the experiment was unlikely to be repeated.[25] West Germans who went over to the East for work found the experience unnerving. Even those clearly social democratic in their sympathy, willing to make sacrifices for the new union, became depressed by the "colonial" mentality they encountered in Leipzig or elsewhere, as East Germans seemed grieved, passive-aggressive, both complaining of their treatment and convinced they were not up to the new competitive world. Indeed, they saw West Germans take over Treuhand properties, serve in the state governments: in effect teach administration and governance. Meanwhile over one million out of four million workers were without jobs and another million and a half on subsidized ABM (or Arbeitsbeschaffung Maßnahmen) make-work assignments. Industrial output fell sharply in the second half of 1990, and by 1991 was below a third of the 1989 level; industrial employment by mid 1992 was below a million, as compared with about 3.2 million in 1989. National product from the Eastern states fell by about a third in 1991 and more than another 10 percent in 1992; productivity was at 32 percent of the Western level. Nonetheless, because of welfare and make-work provisions as well as the rapid adjustment toward West German wage levels, household income rose 32 percent. Per capita income climbed to half the Western level, a jump of about 50 percent, although the price index also rose 21.4 percent. Still, East Germans remained in the unique condition among members of the former CMEA economies of earning more, even as they produced drastically less.[26] By 1995, they contributed perhaps 12 percent to the German national product and consumed 25 percent.

Table 6-1. Public-Sector Budget Deficits (DM billion)
(not including social security)

	1990	1991	1992	1993	1994	1995
Federal Government	−45	−52	−32	−61	−39.5	−50.5
Old Bundeslaender	−19.5	−16	−17.5	−26.5	−27	−34
New Bundeslaender	0	−9	−14	−16	−16.5	−13
German Unity Fund (also for eastern Germany)	−20	−31	−22	−13.5	−3	+2.5
Total	−90	−120	−106	−132	−105	−112

Source: Deutsche Bundesbank, "Table: Public Sector Finance," Annual Report 1991–1995.

Who then ended up paying for the wrenching restructuring of East Germany? The initial illusion was that the process of modernization would in effect be costless; the new Bundesländer would surge ahead without great infusions from the West. The de Maizière government set its hopes on joint ventures, which hardly materialized. Treuhand investment gradually constituted one source of transfers, but in return for restructuring funds, West German and foreign corporate purchasers received title to East German capital assets. By March 1991 the federal government passed an emergency investment program designed to invest $12 billion in infrastructure in each of the coming two years, to which would be added an extra $5 billion in 1991. This proved only a small portion of the transfer, which amounted to DM 140 billion in 1990 and more than DM 150 billion in 1991, or 70 percent of the GNP in the East: DM 9,600 per inhabitant. The following year saw an even greater transfer of almost DM 170 billion. Combined federal, *Land*, and local budgets went from a 1989 equilibrum to a DM 120 billion deficit, or over 4 percent of GNP. This public debt did not include the Treuhand's debt or the post office and railroad deficits.[27] Of course, Treuhand debt was not a real transfer to East German sources, but generally amounted to the loans extended to West German purchasers and rehabilitators of GDR property (see Table 6-1).

How were these deficits funded? The Federal Republic's hefty accumulated balance of payments covered the subsidies in 1990, and in 1991 the government introduced increases on tobacco, oil, and insurance excises, raised telephone fees, and imposed a temporary surcharge of 7.5 percent of income tax obligations. These levies still covered only about a quarter of the transfers. The recourse to deficit financing of the transfer—at least until autumn 1992—meant not only a large increase in Germany's national debt, but a drain on its European partners' resources as well. The Bundesbank raised interest rates three times in 1992, which required corresponding increases in the European currency partners. The controversial July increases from an 8 to 8.75 percent rediscount helped trigger a major crisis in September, in which Britain and Italy left the Exchange Rate Mechanism, and cast doubt on the feasibility of the currency union envisaged by the Maastricht Treaty.[28] In the very months that Bundesbank policy was provoking a crisis for the European monetary system, the chancellor seemed finally galvanized into a response that began to reveal the same creativity he had demonstrated in the diplomatic field almost three years earlier. "Two and a half years after the fall of the Wall, we've at last come to the point where government and opposition, chancellor and [SPD] chancellor-candidate are finally sitting at the same table. It's lasted a long time until Helmut Kohl recognized that the reunification exceeds his own formidable historical strength."[29] Over the course of the summer and fall he sought a compromise with unions and SPD on a "solidarity pact" that would place financing of the transfers on a tax basis. The Social Democrats, hoping for support from the sixty-four CDU deputies from the eastern states, asked for a forced loan; the chancellor opted instead for a resumption of the special tax surcharge of 7.5 percent, now labeled as a "solidarity contribution." In return for wage restraint and agreement on higher taxes, he suggested that Treuhand policy would change to allow for more active restructuring interventions, and not just plant closures and privatization. By the fall of 1992, after fencing between SPD and the CDU-FDP Coalition, the Bundestag agreed to renew the "solidarity contribution" on top of tax rates already owed. Indeed, by 1993 a small economic upswing was registered as the Bundesbank eased interest rates.[30]

By the time the loss of jobs began to slow in 1993 and 1994, Eastern employment (aside from public works jobs and job training) had fallen to 54 percent of those between 15 and 65 years of age, or 5.4 million jobs, whereas the GDR had employed 91 to 92 percent of employable population, or about 9.75 million. Even at the depths of the Depression, in the months before Hitler came to power, German unemployment had climbed no higher than 25 to 33 percent. The difference was that the jobless of sixty years later were sustained in artificially sustained employment or cushioned by pensions. By 1992 employment in agriculture and forestry had dropped from 976,000 to 282,000; in industry from about 8 million to 3.7 million; state and private employment from 2.3 to 1.6 million. Construction rose, trade and transport fell, but less drastically (1.51 to 1.16 million), and service enterprises likewise rose from 618,000 to 990,000.[31] With only half the workers, farm and forestry output remained relatively constant, mining and energy declined 30 percent, manufacturing (*verarbeitende*) industry more than 50 percent trade and transport about 30 percent; but services were up 26.7.[32]

Even with a more imaginative Treuhand approach, could the East German crisis really have been avoided? In effect, the anguish of the former GDR (like many of the difficulties elsewhere in Eastern Europe) derived from the vulnerabilities of both socialist and capitalist production. Afflictions inherited from the planned economies were reinforced by the new difficulties of Western industrial capitalism as it confronted the difficulties of what is loosely termed globalization. Analysts focused initially on the socialist liabilities. Arguing from the example of Hungary, Janos Kornai proposed that every postsocialist economy underwent a transitional recession that imposed sacrifices in production and employment deeper than in the Great Depression of the 1930s. A "sellers market" under the pervasive conditions of socialist scarcity changed brutally to the "buyers market" inherent in capitalist competition. Investment sources dried up; market instrumentalities were not sufficiently developed to replace bureaucratic coordination; uncertain property relationships discouraged rapid investment.[33] East Germany, of course, confronted a special set of problems. While Kornai did not ascribe a special role to the collapse of the CMEA trading system, the attrition of Soviet and other East European orders certainly had a major impact. The fact that GDR producers had to become competitive within a more technologically productive national economy also added to their woes. The new Bundesländer, moreover, became part of an economy where for two decades the service sector had been assuming an increasingly important role while heavy industry was shedding workers. No matter how productive and efficient the GDR's industrial organization might have been, it was now to be integrated into a national economy that employed far fewer workers in industry and far more in services. The result for the ex-GDR was an agonizing deindustrialization, but perhaps also the prelude to an economic reconstruction still under way. Nonetheless, the psychological costs of the layoffs were heavy. The legal and institutional framework that had defined the public world of East Germany disappeared in 1990; but much of the state's identity had derived from its role as industrial powerhouse for the CMEA. Now the traditional reassurance provided by the GDR's industrial vocation was vanishing as well.

By the mid 1990s the East's loss of jobs had become a part of the larger unemployment that afflicted capitalist economies as well. Even when growth resumed, workers were being shed, at all levels of the employment hierarchy. East Germany was in effect catching up with the West, compressing the structural change that had taken a generation in the capitalist economies—and not without its own painful redundancy—into a five-year bruising transition. As had Western Europe in the two decades after 1945, eastern Germany experienced a massive transfer of farmers from agricultural employment: half the GDR's farm population left their collectives (LPGs) by 1993, but with no fall of agricultural output, which revealed how redundant the large labor force had been to begin with. But whereas in postwar Western Europe, those leaving the land had helped drive the steady expansion of industry, East Germany was dismantling its mines and basic steel production and its manufacturing industries at the same time. By the end of 1993, Germany had 4 million unemployed with about 1.3 million out of work in the East and 1.3 million on reduced work week or retraining programs. Low wages in neighboring Eastern Europe, the new competition from East Asia, and the beginning of offshore production by German companies all played a role. Faced with this overwhelming difficulty, could the Treuhand really have made much of a difference? The very years in which political democratization seemed to be taking root, the industrial structure of the so-called market democracies was undergoing a buffeting as harsh as the later 1970s or even the 1930s. East Germany's industrial fate was as much that of a sacrificial vanguard as of a neglected region.

East German women felt that they had had to bear an especially hard burden. They, too, were hard hit by the prevailing unemployment—though whether harder than men is unclear. But the East German pattern had been for women to have children young, then work full-time. West Germany provided far less elaborate a structure of day care and it encouraged women to remain at home longer than in the East. East German women had reported sexism within the job and on the job, but they remembered the greater child-care facility.

As of this writing, unemployment persists in Germany and Western Europe. East Germany has been absorbed into a problematic European economy, subjected to long-term pressures by globalization, the challenges of an aging population and a strained welfare system, high wage costs, and overhanging debts. There are superficial similarities with the economy of the mid-1920s, when after another rupture between Eastern and Western Europe, the possibility of reconstruction and advance seemed at hand—only to exhaust its possibilities by the end of the decade and slip into catastrophic potectionism and depression. But the economic outcomes of the 1930s were not foreordained; they were aggravated by rigid and reactionary policies and the acceptance of central bankers' insistence on overcoming deficits and maintaining the gold exchange standard. Whether similar injunctions, now from Frankfurt, will again prevail has yet to be decided.

ABWICKLUNG: ACADEMIC PURGE AND RENEWAL

The economic glacis between West and East would diminish after a difficult transition, given the educated and motivated work force. But it was hardly the only barrier. The frontiers of intellectual life also remained harder to remove than the slabs of the Wall. Former East Germans were reconstructing their universities; and the united Germany was taking in hand the official institutes of the former GDR Academy of Sciences. Dozens of review committees, largely emanating from the West German Scientific Council (Wissenschaftsrat), augmented by some promising East Germans, were examining what was fit to keep and reorganize, which institutes would be simply dissolved, or—according to the neologism in the Unification Treaty—"wound up" or *abgewickelt*; or, in those cases where departments were preserved, how they were to be restructured and recruited anew. Individuals could be dismissed if their institute was dissolved, for insufficient qualifications, for transgressing basic norms, or for Stasi membership.

The academic review took place in several stages. The East German Länder were given until the end of 1990 to propose which institutions they wished to preserve or to close. Thereupon the Wissenschaftsrat set up ten working groups, predominantly West German in composition but with some GDR and non-German participation, to make on-site visits to institutions and report to the council by July 1991 its recommendations for preservation or restructuring. The working groups weighed staff size, scholarly output and reputation, and independence from ideologically imposed categories and functions. Their massive, but necessarily summary reports surveyed the whole research "landscape" of the GDR. A similar team of working groups (overlapping with those reviewing the nonuniversity institutes) visited university faculties and made recommendations for dissolution or reorganization. These went to the Länder who, guided by the recommendations of the Wissenschaftsrat committees, established state Structural Commissions and Appointment Commissions (Berufungskommissionen). The appointment commissions—constituted of local representatives and academics summoned from Western faculties—disqualified Stasi collaborators, egregious SED time-servers, or those who were notorious for dismissing dissenting students. They then readvertised the new positions and filled them from an applicant pool that included those who had been teaching as well as those, usually from the old FRG, enticed by the prospect of rebuilding the East German "academic landscape" or finding a better position. Those marginal academics who were not politically tainted by either Stasi activities or dismissal of students, but did not seem worth retaining, were usually given a year of grace, sometimes put into the "holding pattern" or *Warteschleife*. Reviewers insisted that the criteria imposed at each stage were not ideological, but were based on the individual's capacity for constructive research.

This was not an easy distinction to draw. Since the periodic waves of ideological mobilization, initially in the late 1940s, again in the 1950s, and at the beginning of the Honecker era, the universities had been repeatedly subject to party aspirations and control. Almost all faculty members (outside of theology) were expected to belong to the SED. Party stalwarts exerted special influence: the Stasi had collaborators in each department, while critical voices faced collective correction, and obstreperous students were subject to expulsion.[34] It was clear after 1989 that the departments devoted to Marxism-Leninism were to be liquidated; the difficulty was that many social science departments had been merged into "M-L" at the end of the 1960s. Historians were being weeded out collectively and individually: collectively, as when the sections for the history of the Soviet Union, the Soviet Communist Party, the GDR, and the SED were dissolved at Leipzig's Karl Marx University; individually in cases of Stasi activity or involvement in dismissing dissident students in the aftermath of Prague Spring and later. Others would remain jobless because their research was too sparse or ideologically clichéd to justify their rehiring when restructuring committees advertised for a reduced number of chairs. In some cases, such as that of Humboldt University historian Kurt Pätzold—one of the *Reisekader* or reliable academics whom the regime had favored with travel opportunities to meet Western colleagues but also one of the first East German historians to deal explicitly with the Holocaust—dismissal was justified on the grounds that the professor had been complicit in expelling politically troublesome students between 1968 and 1977.[35] Schools of journalism that were mere propaganda factories were also broken up, some of their hack faculty fired, a few placed in political science departments. Despite some obvious cases, the review committees had a delicate task.

Most of the older generation—forty-five and over—had made their peace with the party. The better ones had sought to enlarge the capacity for research and scholarship and debate; they had maintained contacts with established Western scholars. They might be termed accommodationists— but if freed from pervasive control, they might still have much to contribute. Those in the generation under thirty-five who had come of age in the 1980s found it rankling to abide the compromises, ideological and personal. They had organized outside the system in the last year and they wanted a more thorough purge. They saw older hacks protected and ensconced. In fact, by the end of the process those over fifty-five were hardest hit, almost certain to remain excluded if they failed to renew their position, pensioned off or trying to sell pharmaceuticals, real estate, or books. The younger ones might find the result to their advantage, if West Germans were not simply recruited.

If there was a triage by age, there was also a harrowing by rank. The East German universities and the academy had a larger stratum of academics in intermediate ranks who did not get promoted to full professorships or research appointments. This *Mittelbau* bore the brunt of the cuts. By November 1992, 20 percent of the professors and 60 percent of the *Mittelbau* had been dismissed. Again, the result was ambiguous: it had been honorable enough to remain in the *Mittelbau*, a relatively nontaxing if low-status academic position. In the university as in the economy, socialism accommodated the time-server—perhaps a humane solution, but unlikely to persist. And as in the industrial economy, so in the academy: East Germany experienced a compressed version of the "downsizing" that was to demoralize the academic and eventually the corporate sectors throughout the West in the early and mid–1990s.[36] The East German academic restructuring might eventually appear in effect as a special application of the general effort to slash the costs of white-collar labor throughout Western economies. Woe to the GDR's researchers who had joined the academic marketplace at the moment all markets sought to compress the cost of labor! Indeed, the very emphasis on reforming East German research and higher education obscured the need for a few years to address the old FRG's deficiencies. These were less those of productivity measured quantitatively (since student-faculty ratios were far higher than in the East) than of the quality of teaching.

What East Germans perceived as a result of the academic assizes that descended on their universities was the influx of Westerners. As one Heidelberg (and Berkeley) sociologist acutely observed, after having served on personnel committees for Halle and Frankfurt (Oder) and then assuming

the new deanship for sociology and political sience at Leipzig, the good
original intentions of creating a new and better East-West synthesis did not
come to pass. "Instead crisis-beset West German institutions" were introduced in the East. The Unification Treaty envisaged applying West German
research templates onto the new territories for better or worse. And, as the
author admitted, there was no great opportunity to reform the entire German structure of research and learning in 1990. East Germany had simply
joined the larger concern, its academic institutions had no autonomous tradition, and the revolution of 1989–90 had not struck an insitutional basis.
Thus the process sometimes envisaged as one of synthesis simply ended up
as one of "*Verwestlichung*" or Westernization.[37]

If East German academic institutions could not defend their own eroded
legitimacy, the structure of learning in the West was itself too brokered and
bureaucratized to encourage broader concepts of restructuring. The 1975
Research Promotion Convention had settled organizational rivalries over
research policy roles and budgets between federal and state governments
and the leading autonomous research foundations. The Deutsche For-
schungs Gemeinschaft (DFG), which served as federal funding agency, the
Max-Planck-Gesellschaft (MPG), which comprised the prestigious independent research organizations in the sciences and humanities, and, above all,
the Wissenschaftsrat (a council of scholarly advisers called on by the relevant ministries for evaluating priorities) all had their share of government
funds and institutional claims.[38] Such a dense network of prerogative—its
functions enhanced by the new mission awaiting in the East—was unlikely
to generate a program of all-German renewal.

Western academic colonization, Eastern academic wasteland: both im-
pressions had some validity and skewed the process of reform both parties
claimed to want. Regardless of intentions, any purge must strike erratically,
as had denazification four decades earlier. Over the course of 1990 the
purge atmosphere did intensify. One of the section heads at Leipzig, who
had been an accommodationist and had remained in the SED until the end
of 1989, might still serve as a force unifying his department through the
summer of 1990, protecting the work he felt was scientifically valid, weed-
ing out the hopelessly politicized. By December, however, he felt that "almost pogrom-like conditions" were prevailing. Even when the intellectual
assizes went well, the East Germans resented the paternalism of the review
committees. Jens Reich, biologist as well as New Forum leader, conceded
that just the excessive size of the research establishment required dismissals. Still, he called for understanding and solidarity from the West. There

was some justice, Reich admitted, in West German pronouncements (did he have Arnulf Baring in mind?) that the academic landscape of the GDR was a "desert." Still, Reich pleaded for collegiality. "Only those who have lost all sense of the history and entanglements of our generation of scholars can formulate the issue so snobbishly."[39] Often researchers felt disspirited and certain that their institute would be dissolved. Even when this threat did not loom, the review process could be humiliating. One research director, asked by his Western scholarly judges if his institute members could read the English scholarship in his field, answered ironically, "Look, it's not so simple. First we have to learn to eat with a knife and fork, then maybe we can start on English."

The Academy of Science could not have been rescued as a corporate entity since there was no counterpart in the West. West Germany did not have the large research establishment that the GDR, like the rest of Eastern Europe possessed, with its multiple institutes and sections. The academy had been singled out for change in the Unification Treaty; it was a GDR outgrowth of a venerable predecessor, and it was far larger than equivalent research organizations in the West. Some of this would have to be closed just on budgetary grounds. As a centralized group, which often mixed basic and applied research, it was not likely to fit into the West German structures. The relatively weak Federal Ministry of Research and Technology (BMFT) was not prepared to finance such a body, regarded with suspicion by academics with teaching duties or by the federal states or the MPG. Just as important though, the Round Table reformers were prepared to jettison the academy themselves. In the institutes and academy 31,000 were employed, of whom 12,000 were researchers; by mid 1994 the number was 13,500 or 43 percent, and East German research claimed 27 percent of the German funds devoted to scholarship outside the university. Nonetheless, of this amount only 5.5 percent of the funds went to humanities or social science institutes.[40] The science faculties were the easiest to safeguard or merge into universities. Overall a considerable amount of self-renewal did take place; two-thirds of the institute directors were removed according to Jens Reich, one to take a leading position in a Western pharmaceutical group; another, reproached by colleagues for special privileges (which he denied), ended up at Harvard. As for the social scientists, the Science Council set up nine new humanities centers in different fields to retain some of the more promising and untainted researchers: the history of science, the history of the Enlightenment, and for contemporary historical studies (GDR history) were among them. For three years these new institutes were supported quite generously by a special research-support society supervised by West Germany's research consortium, the Max-Planck-Gesellschaft. In 1995 they were tucked into the research budgets of the East German Länder and given loose affiliations with local universities.

Of these research institutes only the one for contemporary history generated much controversy, initiated primarily by the so-called Independent Historical Association, whose members denounced the official Institutes of History at the beginning of 1990, demanded a thoroughgoing cleansing of the profession, and resented any effort to give former Academy of Science researchers continuing public employment. Restructuring of the East German universities generated a far more turbulent phase of reorganization. The universities enjoyed a longer history; despite their intellectual subjugation by the SED, they still possessed an ancient corporate tradition; they were a source of local pride and they sometimes had quickly generated new partnerships with Western universities.

The pathos and difficulties of the new situation were encapsulated by the Fink affair. The new Humboldt University rector, Heinrich Fink, was one of the few professors who, as a theologian, had not been a member of the SED. A protagonist of the *Wende* with other reformist churchmen in autumn 1989, he claimed to want reform from within, but interpreted this as *Selbsterneuerung mit den vorhandenen Menschen,* self-renewal with the people at hand. Did not such a stance amount to no more than saving as many of the old faculty as possible? For Manfred Erhardt, the CDU senator for science and research, who supervised the Berlin universities, Fink's method meant just protecting the *Seilschaften,* or old-boy networks. Before Erhardt, when the SPD held the education portfolio, five faculties at Humboldt had already been shut down, a decision that would allow them to be reconstituted without going over every chairholder's qualifications individually. Fink had appealed to the Berlin administrative court and got the *Abwicklungs* process declared invalid. The senator responded with a law that would effectively deprive the rector of his powers and reconstitute new personnel and structure comittees on a basis of East-West parity, but under his and not the universities' oversight. By the end of November Erhardt sought to have Fink fired as professor (and thereby as rector) on the grounds that a check of his records with the Gauck commission revealed he had collaborated with the Stasi as an agent. Gauck had told Fink in February that according to information currently available he was not cited in Stasi files; but ten months later when Erhardt sought the information, new files allegedly revealed Fink as an IM or collaborator—more precisely, that an agent code-named

"Heiner" had had his file closed in 1989, and the number on the file matched the number on Fink's name card in Stasi files.[41] Students protested the charge. So did intellectuals such as Christa Wolf, Jens Reich, and Stefan Heym. The Gauck officials retreated from some of their claims; and Fink denied ever having signed a pledge to provide information—and the commission could not determine the truth. Here was a recurrent problem with the working of the Gauck commission, which announced only that it discovered certain names listed as Stasi informants, but did not reveal the extent or intent of collaboration—whether a circumspect report, say, on meetings as a condition for negotiation with the authorities, or a willing denunciation of unsuspecting comrades. (So too in Czechoslovakia the Lustration Commission revealed only the names, not the nature of collaboration.) Fink was criticized on several sides, having angered the SPD professors who wanted to purge the faculty as well as the CDU Senator Erhardt. Although the institute for Marxism-Leninism had been dissolved, SED activists sometimes found a berth in interdisciplinary faculties for social sciences or conflict research. Despite the charges, January elections for the academic council strengthened those who backed Fink's concept of self-renewal. His own fate lay in suspension until the exhaustion of his appeals in the spring of 1992. Was he the honorable defender of the university's integrity, a belated reformer who did not have resolution to get rid of the SED time-servers in the social sciences, or an opportunist exploiting the intellectuals' support for academic autonomy? A skilled rector or a "false populist"? For *Der Spiegel*, the Fink case testified to moral and political confusion: "United Germany in late autumn 1991—the world turned upside down. The victims are beaten up because they label the perpetrators as perpetrators. A strange alliance of utopians, exonerators, and political naifs has come together to defend the real no-longer-existing GDR." Admittedly Senator Erhardt, with the subtlety of an elephant, had acted with bureaucratic arrogance. Still, according to the weekly magazine, whether or not he had worked for the Stasi, Fink had helped the regime until the very end.[42]

Christian Meier, the Munich historian of antiquity who enjoyed widespread respect, expressed skepticism that self-renewal could really work in the East. Nonetheless, he called for less moralism. Students were proud of their university and reform imposed from the West would alienate them. "Change requires giving up the rigid positions of trench warfare." Innovation should take place on both sides of the former boundary: the East German universities had to strengthen their research capacity; the West German ones should create more coherent programs for undergraduate teaching and graduate research.[43] The West German universities, after all, should hardly serve as unquestioned models; they were overcrowded, relied on huge lectures, provided insufficient faculty contact with students, and had amorphous curricula. It was hardly likely, though, that a well-thought and badly needed reform concept for the Western universities could be instituted at the same time that a highly politicized review of Eastern universities was under way. Western scholars were not preoccupied by their own system's defects, just its evident superiority to the corrupted research of the East. And East German academics beheld a wholesale awarding of vacated chairs to Western professors and the replication of FRG academic politics in the new ministries of education in the eastern *Länder*. Were they not becoming just a great new trough for West German professors and their favored assistants? Controversy beset the nomination to a chair of political science at the University of Leipzig, where the Saxon minister in charge of higher education sought unsuccessfully to recruit a respected American-based German scholar in a manner felt to be more a pro-CDU than an academically justified procedure.

As the Fink case suggested, the Humboldt University in East Berlin was to be the arena for even more bitter feuds. In December 1990 the government of newly unified Berlin decided to dissolve and reconstitute (as provided for by the Unification Treaty) the departments of law, education, economics, philosophy, and history, with their 1,500 employees. The university contested the order in both the Berlin administrative court and the federal Constitutional Court at Karlsruhe. They lost in Berlin, but the federal court ruled that although the Unification Treaty gave the Berlin Senate the right to wind up the departments, what had taken place was not true *Abwicklung* but just a disguised maneuver to fire all the incumbent staff. The Humboldt administration thereupon used the Karlsruhe judgment to appeal the Berlin decision and had the personnel reinstated, at least temporarily. Meanwhile the university established its own Structure and Appointment Committees, which encouraged the departure of faculty near retirement age and made new appointments. The new historians summoned to the History Faculty included Heinrich Winkler, a preeminent scholar of the Weimar Republic and its Social Democratic Party, as well as nineteenth-century German nationalism. Winkler was a veteran of the internecine wars within the SPD from peace movement days, indeed remembered the Otto Suhr Institute in West Berlin after 1968, when professors had, he believed, cravenly passed any student half-educated in Marxist theory. Winkler (and other historians newly recruited) found the old department members unwilling to move out, appealing their dismissal in court and prolonging an ideological struggle in the corridors of the university. Meanwhile, Winkler nominated as his teaching and research assistants a trio of young East German scholars who had broken with the GDR academic establishment to constitute the Independent Historical Association. Two of them had quickly combed the archives after the transition in 1989 to publish the first important collection of Stasi documents, and bitterly condemned any compromises with the "accommodationists" among the old guard.

The battle over the history positions soon became in fact a struggle over the historical interpretation of the GDR, as the Independents claimed that the regime could be studied only in terms of occupation and repression, not processes of accommodation or consensus building. As noted already, the Independent Historians (or at least their most aggressive members) also moved to challenge the Potsdam Center for Contemporary History for employing colleagues they felt had been deeply collaborationist with the old regime. Jürgen Kocka defended his center's research team, but a continuing critique of their work and political pasts—diffused by skillful press polemics in the *Frankfurter Allgemeine Zeitung*—was designed to demoralize and undermine the enterprise. Kocka insisted that he would never retain a Stasi informant, but was embarrassed by the Independents' discovery that one of the older members had served the Stasi over twenty years earlier. Thus questions of personnel, ideology, and historical interpretation remained tense and intermingled. "Who should be allowed to write the history of the GDR?"[44] one of the critiques in the authoritative Frankfurt paper demanded. For at least some in the conservative camp, however, the underlying question was who should not be allowed, or at least not be employed, to write its history. It took a continuing public struggle to insist that there might be scope for historical interpretation and for the support of research approaches that did not presuppose either apologia or anathema.

STASI STAINS: THE OLD REGIME ON TRIAL

The process of academic *Abwicklung* constituted part of the more general question: how broad and profound a purge should take place? This was a problem faced by all the regimes that had moved from authoritarianism since the late 1970s. Among the Communist countries, Hungary was most clearly set against reexamination of judicial abuses by former Communist leaders. Victims and relatives of victims who had died in political prison camps wanted their former persecuters punished; they encountered the quiet and dogged resistance of bureaucrats, still-entrenched apparatchiks, the scattering and disappearance of files, finally a general feeling that silence about the past offered the best basis for national conciliation and the future functioning of democratic institutions. In Czechoslovakia, Vaclav Havel also urged a general de facto amnesty.[45] And in countries that had been ruled by the military, the situation was even more delicate, for too persistent an investigation into former army murders of opponents might trigger military reaction, as was feared in Argentina, Brazil, and Chile. For better or worse, a certain institutionalized amnesia seemed inevitable.

The German alternatives were different. East Germany was folded into the Federal Republic; Bonn placed the records of the Ministry of State Security in the hands of an independent authority mandated to "work through" the abuses of the GDR, the so-called Gauck commission, a sort of Treuhand for the historical record. Joachim Gauck, an East German pastor, had been instrumental in seeking open access for the Stasi archive; he would remain convinced that bringing complicity and secret machinations to light was a prerequisite for healing and overcoming the past. He impressed listeners, and angered critics, by his calm pietistic conviction as he defended the procedure by which he divulged the information under his control.[46] When asked whether a given name was included in Stasi records as an informant, his office responded yes or no. Individual petitioners could ask to see the files kept on them. One after another of the East Germans of the transition was revealed to have been, at least in Stasi eyes, an "unofficial collaborator": Wolfgang Schnur, Ibrahim Böhme, Lothar de Maizière, Heinrich Fink. But as denunciations increased, so too did the charges that the Stasi had set up "hit lists" of denunications to discredit the new politicans. Later came the revelations about Christa Wolf and, finally in the fall of 1995, news that Monika Maron, an acerbic critic of East Germany, had herself left Stasi tracks. The nature of the contacts was often vague. Gauck believed that those listed as unofficial collaborators had indeed performed that role; they were not being merely set up. Poland, he conceded as he looked back on five years of his work, had decided not to open the past for scrutiny, but Germany had a special burden to overcome. Germans had already experienced the belated trauma that arose when the past was suppressed or silenced. "We in East Germany did not want to take leave of a dictatorship for the second time with the implicit motto: 'Keep smiling,' but believed that with knowledge, rumination, and even sadness, we could succeed in becoming a democratic land."[47]

The records released did not always specify the extent of cooperation. In some cases Stasi collaborators had denounced damaging opinions confided in private, placing friends and even family in jeopardy of prosecution. In other cases the so-called agent might have fobbed off noncommittal lists of foreign contacts in order to facilitate travel arrangements; or explained away to the political police that one's colleague's remarks were a trivial outburst, not evidence of real opposition. Of course, collaboration soiled the informer, enmeshed him or her in a compromising relationship, cast suspicion on third parties. In the wake of continuing revelations about informers, postunification society became obsessed with secrecy, complicity, and betrayal. The Stasi files were deemed to contain the secret but essential history of the GDR. Angry intellectuals who had earlier quit the East demanded an unsparing reckoning with Stasi agents. Some who sought to trivialize the issue were themselves ultimately named as having played the collaborator's game. Stasi revelations threatened many politicians of the transition without really clarifying the nature of the transaction. But was it worth uncovering every collaborator if with each one the feeling of a soiled society increased? Should all levels of collaboration be prosecuted? Would the new East Germany be able to emerge from its sense of ethical twilight?

The fact that Germany had already lived through the aftermath of an evil regime after 1945 had a major impact on how citizens wanted to confront the GDR experience. "Ordinary" Germans after 1945 generally preferred to consign their Third Reich experience to historical oblivion. Many families had suffered greatly, sometimes expelled from their homeland or bombed out of their houses, their young men wasted in Russia. Doubtless many did feel ashamed of their support for a regime, so they were finally admitting, that had committed unspeakable brutality. But openly to echo the indignation of the victors took considerable moral initiative. Only gradually did a new generation of conscientious prosecutors push to extend the statute of limitations and try SS officers in long and arduous cases. Silence and stonewalling tended to prevail in the first two decades after the defeat. Except for the most conspicuous Nazis, the cadres of judges and teachers remained largely unpurged after 1945. After 1989 opinion divided more fundamentally. A newly mobilized cohort of post-Marxist intellectuals—most in the West but some in the East, some still social democratic, but many close to what in the United States would be labeled neoconservative—pressed for a harsh reckoning and a wholesale housecleaning of the professions. Those who had earlier made their peace with the system in the East—augmented by many, including students, who resented the annexationist thrust of the richer West—resisted. They were sometimes willing to rehabilitate intellectuals and political actors who had navigated in the gray zones of collaboration.

Contending moral attitudes entailed different historical judgments. In many ways the GDR regime had enforced uniformity and a party line more exhaustively than the Nazis had done. The climate of Marxism-Leninism at schools and in the youth groups, exemplified by the demands for orthodoxy as a key to advancement, was pervasive. More people were involved in informing; the number of "unofficial collaborators" serving the Stasi was far greater in proportional terms. It could thus be argued that the Stasi dictatorship was more thoroughgoing than even the Third Reich—hence, the need to purge its remnants more urgent. Such indices of dictatorship, however, focused on the pervasiveness of control, but neglected the mechanics of repression. By the 1960s the DDR rested on widespread manipulation: career advancement and travel required cooperation. But except for the show trials in the 1950s—and they were far less sanguinary than in Hungary or Czechoslovakia—"terror" was a rare recourse. Humiliation, expulsion from collegial gilds, or banishment while abroad had served to keep opinion docile—once the frontier was given lethal force. Neither did the SED refrain from imprisonment, pervasive spying, and routine denial of education and travel. But it achieved the intimidation it required with far lower levels of violence than did the National Socialists, who covered the land with concentration camps. Gestapo arrests without trial could be extended indefinitely, and within the camps cruel and brutal treatment was meted out as a matter of policy. The GDR had no genocidal project or agenda of conquest at its core, but even leaving out of account the National Socialist inhumanity organized against Jews, the level of violence was of a different order of magnitude. Beating, torture, semistarvation, and guillotining were recourses that the GDR did not employ but that the Nazis used without scruple. Finally, the Third Reich and the GDR had different developmental dynamics. During its relatively brief twelve years in power, the Nazi regime became increasingly radical and murderous, whereas over four decades, the East Germans progressively routinized their mechanisms of repression. This trajectory complicated issues of responsibilities with respect to those who played public roles only in the later phases of the state.

Comparison of the two German autoritarian states has become a major intellectual enterprise. Many serious analysts have sought to think through the analogues between the Third Reich and the GDR, to reflect on the continuities of the second and first German dictatorships, or, following important analytical studies, to meditate on the experience of twentieth-century totalitarianism as a whole. At the seventy-fifth and final session of the Enquete-Kommission in May 1994, leading historians discussed the comparability of the GDR and the Third Reich. The discussion brought out all the difficulties that might be expected: the more conservative academic Horst Möller grouped both regimes under the rubric of totalitarianism; Jürgen Kocka and Sigrid Meuschel stressed the differences (although Kocka has elsewhere sought to bring parallels and distinctions into one framework). Ultimately, said Meuschel, the SED claimed such a degree of total power that its aspirations for rationality led into irrationality. Kocka said that one could not simply contrast dictatorships as a category with democracies. The social scientists were careful and concerned for subtlety, but the abstractions tended to take on a life of their own. Commission members endorsed or contested their view as politics might predict.[48]

This author has always worked as a comparative historian, but in this case believes that the comparison drawn between the GDR and the Third Reich, even when suitably hedged with all sorts of sophisticated reservations, can only obscure the radically different regimes. Citizens in each regime might find non-political enclaves of everyday life. But those of the second dictatorship did not have to do so at the cost of looking away from the cruelty, fixation on conquest, and anti-Jewish obsession of the first. To bracket the two was often another strategy for normalizing the first.

The comparisons that Germans made between the two dictatorships, moreover, could not be divorced from current politics and were sometimes deployed to delegitimize East German public figures and set limits on political participation.[49] It was hardly surprising that after 1990, Germans resorted to comparison, not primarily in the context of academic debate, but in the compelling and divisive political trials after unification.

The first major case took place not in court but in the press and became a literary cause célèbre—the controversy surrounding Christa Wolf in 1990. Wolf had established a reputation as a critical novelist, never disavowing the regime but holding her distance. *Divided Heaven* had explored the human pathos imposed by German division; *A Model Childhood* had suggested parallels between the memories of the author's early years under Hitler and the practices of the SED regime. Wolf was one of the voices called on in the great rallies of November 1989; I heard her speak at a rally on "overcoming the past" in summer 1990. But she had avoided earlier overt resistance; her protagonists nursed the inner wounds of mindless political repression. Her sentimenal quietism was blood in the waters for more consistent critics once she published her memoir of Stasi surveillance, *What Remains*, in early June 1990. This brief book, written for the drawer in 1979, drew scornful reviews from young West German critics. "Now, that's something," wrote Ulrich Greiner; "the state poet of the GDR was apparently spied on by the state security service of the GDR." Greiner went on to attack the mawkish sentimentality of Wolf's narratives: "She is the painter of the idyll. She evokes nature with a sweet melancholy or undisturbed life or the bliss of a delicious breakfast." Danger gathers; she sings her familiar songs: "folk songs of all sorts, in the meadow, in the shower, in the garden. Fairy tales occur to her. . . . A sad case, a small chapter out of the long history: 'German poets and the powers that be.'"[50] *Frankfurter Allgemeine Zeitung* critic Frank Schirrmacher was equally critical, although less flippant; he recalled Wolf's 1987 admission that "many members of my generation have retained from their early formation the inclination to align and subordinate themselves . . . the fear of contradiction and resistance, of conflicts with the majority and of being excluded from the group." "Christa Wolf like other intellectuals of her generation constructed a familiar, almost intimate relation to her state and its institutions . . . she rejected the authentic, bourgeois family of her origins and replaced it through the state and its unconditional demands for loyalty." Her book was "sentimental and untrustworthy to the point of kitsch."[51]

But did West Germans, who had never had to face the pressures that their colleagues in the East had had to cope with, really have the right to sit in moralistic judgment? Günter Grass and Walter Jens attacked the critics' self-righteousness. Greiner responded that the intellectuals of the GDR had served, willingly or not, as legitimators of a murderous sysem and now refused to acknowledge their own responsibilities. On both sides of the Wall, Greiner wrote, there was a club of the like-minded: those labeled left, progressive, or committed to the Enlightenment. "I counted myself in the club. It was the club of those who wanted to count as being on the right side. The club excluded those who came from the East and wanted to tell the truth about the East that we didn't want to hear."[52] Further denunciations awaited Christa Wolf two and a half years later when it was revealed that she had consented to serve as a registered Stasi collaborator (albeit an innocuous interlocutor) from 1959 to 1962.[53] The controversy soiled both sides. Temporarily living in Santa Monica, Christa Wolf seemed damaged goods. But if every intellectual who had compromised with the regime was to be exposed and attacked, how would inner unification progress? Were justice and reconciliation at odds? "We wanted justice," said the 1989 New Forum leader, Bärbel Bohley, who usually condemned the compromises inherent in unification "and we got the *Rechtsstaat*." That was too clever by half; for the *Rechtsstaat* was a vast improvement. "I yearned many, many years for the *Rechtsstaat*," Joachim Gauck recalled five years later.[54] Nonetheless, the *Rechtsstaat* could serve political purposes, as the case of Manfred Stolpe abundantly demonstrated.

Stolpe had been a church administrator in Brandenburg; he was a negotiator, an arranger. He had sought to mediate in the 1989 transition as he had sought to negotiate an enclave for the "Church in Socialism" in the previous decade. I saw him preside in a small circle during July 1990, when he and Gottfried Forck, the Lutheran bishop of Brandenburg, brought together West German businessmen and East German local authorities to discuss economic ventures in the East. When the October 1990 elections returned an SPD plurality to the Brandenburg legislature, Stolpe became minister-president and constructed the only SPD-led cabinet in the East German Länder. As with other East German candidates for political leadership, charges of Stasi collaboration soon surfaced; their portent was ambiguous. Again, Gauck insisted, his mission was merely to confirm or deny whether a given individual was cited in Stasi records as an agent. In January 1992, Stolpe admitted that as the major administrator of the Brandenburg and East German Federation of Lutheran churches he met regularly with SED officials and Stasi officers from the mid 1960s until 1989. Was he negotiating on behalf of the church and colleagues who were under suspicion, helping to keep them from arrest or to assuage authorities about the growth of Lutheran political dissent? Stolpe's action was comparable to negotiating with terrorists, argued Richard Schröder, probably the most thoughtful of the East German SPD pastors. The role of the "Church in Socialism" and its relations with the Stasi, certainly required critical reexamination. "The standard, though, cannot be Western normality but that which was possible in the socialist era. GDR normality is unknown in the West and frightfully repressed in the East. The GDR threatens to become Terra Incognita."[55]

No matter how sympathetically one judged his role, Stolpe had tacked close to the wind. Had he in effect become an unofficial double agent? The Brandenburg legislature established an investigating committee in February 1992, which conducted investigations over two and a half years, then reported in May 1994 along party lines: SPD members essentially approving Stolpe's conduct, Greens on the left and Christian Democrats to the right condemning his behavior and his justification of events. When churchmen were summoned by the authorities, they normally kept each other informed about the upcoming meeting. By such preemptive disclosure they hoped to disqualify themselves as potential Stasi recruits. Stolpe did not so report. Bishop Forck, who was glad that his administrator could get churchmen out of trouble, also claimed that he never meant for the church as such to deal with the Stasi. Had Stolpe negotiated on behalf of the church, even if he had not always kept church colleagues informed? Well yes, so Forck and other churchmen agreed, insofar as he had negotiated for humanitarian causes; but he should not have discussed church matters in their own right. But was this distinction really possible to maintain in a conversation with political authorities?[56]

More damaging was the issue of whether Stolpe had accepted a formal obligation to inform the Stasi about church currents. Stolpe at first denied that he might be the agent that Stasi reports designated as "Secretary." (The "Secretary" dossier files had been destroyed, and the name appeared only in summary records.) "Secretary," so Stolpe originally maintained, must have been a designation used by the Stasi to indicate diverse sources of reports on church dissidence; he had never accepted such a code name. By the time he testified in mid-December 1992, however, Stolpe was forced to concede that he now realized he must have been the source the Stasi identified as "Secretary." Too many Stasi journal entries listing meetings with "Secretary" coincided with his own diary entries for talks with state security representatives. The CDU committee members found it hard to believe that Stolpe had not realized this earlier.[57] By the end of the investigation, Stolpe was insisting that to condemn his role amounted to attacking the stance of the Lutheran Church in the East. He should have proceeded more openly, he conceded, but still insisted that he had been right to negotiate with the regime. The SPD, FDP, and PDS committee members accepted his defense; minority reports by the CDU and the local civic movement delegates (Bündnis) condemned his conspiratorial behavior.

The ensuing parliamentary debate was highly charged. Stolpe refused to stake his tenure in office on ratification of the majority's acquittal. His critics on the left and right might indeed muster a preponderance of Landtag votes against him. But he was obliged to resign only in the unlikely case that they could join forces to pass a "constructive" vote of no confidence, that is, agree on a new minister-president. The bitter personal attack by the Bündnis delegate Günter Nooke made it easier for FDP Justice Minister (and former permanent representative of the FRG in East Berlin) Bräutigam to defend Stolpe, even though he had to admit that "The paths followed by Manfred Stolpe in the SED dictatorship appear to me in retrospect rather unique. I know no one who played a similar role."[58] But the case raised an issue that transcended the question of what Stolpe himself had intended: could one compromise at all with the Communist regime for any justifiable purpose, or was the only honorable and prudent stance a total refusal to cooperate? What degree of evil did the SED dictatorship represent? Conservatives said it was an authoritarian structure comparable with the Third Reich. The term *Unrechtsstaat* —a state of injustice—was easily applied to both regimes, but at the cost of any precision. Stolpe argued that despite its dictatorial nature much was possible. "We were confined, but we were no concentration camp."[59]

The Stolpe case was not fought out in a courtroom; the possible sanction was expulsion from public life, not a prison term. East Germany faced real trials as well: Politbüro leaders were indicted for human rights abuses, including the policy of shooting illegal border crossers and general persecution of political dissenters. The results seemed derisory at first. Erich Honecker, who had initially taken refuge in the Russian embassy, was placed on trial, and charged with responsibility for ordering acts against life and liberty. Proceedings were interrupted on humanitarian grounds in the spring of 1991 when he was allowed to fly to Moscow because he was allegedly dying of cancer; an awkward guest for the Russians, he departed for Chile, where he survived another four years. The aged Erich Mielke had served as head of the Ministry for State Security; but the government, concerned that organizational work alone might not be punishable, prosecuted him for the political murder of a policeman as a young Communist in 1931, almost sixty years earlier. The Honecker outcome was disappointing, but—so argued *Die Zeit* commentator Robert Leicht—no reason to drop plans for the trial of other GDR leaders. Only if Bonn politicians had fabricated the medical excuse would justice have become a travesty. "A Bonn pardon for Honecker would have meant de facto a total amnesty for the second German dictatorship. And total amnesty would soon have been followed by total amnesia."[60]

Leicht reflected a widespread demand when he urged pressing on with trials: bringing to justice the Wall shooters was not victors' justice, for East Berlin authorities had sought indictments even before unification. The Unification Treaty allowed trial for offenses that would have violated existing West German law, although punishment was to be precluded if governing East German law had not itself prescribed penalties. It might well be, Leicht thus wrote, that cases of criminal behavior would be demonstrated, but punishment would remain out of reach. Such a result would still be preferable to confirming the amoral legal positivism that one minister-president of Baden Württemberg had pleaded when arrested for brutal sentencing as a wartime judge: "What was law then cannot be against the law now." The point to establish was that it was always against the law.

The most compelling legal battles were the trials that arose from shootings at the Wall. Some 200 East Germans had been killed while trying to flee across the inner German border since 1961; 97 had died at the Berlin Wall, the last in February 1989. Where did responsibility lie? What retrospective justice should be sought? Approval of the order to shoot had been one of the charges against Honecker, and it was the major indictment against General Heinz Keßler, head of the National Defense Council. East German border guards had been instructed to prevent border flights since the closing of the demarcation line in the 1950s; firing on fugitives had been ordered since 1958. What became known as the *Schießbefehl* (command to shoot) included the service procedure III/2 issued on September 9, 1959, and then, following the army's assumption of border enforcement in October 1961, diverse regulations added subsequently. Border controls were discussed periodically by the National Defense Council; the session of May 3, 1974, in which Politbüro members charged with security affairs reviewed the border controls (the minutes and resolutions were later approved by Honecker), became a major piece of evidence in Keßler's trial. In spring 1982, the Volkskammer passed new border legislation that authorized firing on fugitives to prevent a crime—that is, unauthorized border crossing. The policy was openly announced and approved at the highest levels; the legislative text (Grenzgesetz 1982, clause 27) conformed to generally acceptable norms for the authorization of police fire to prevent an otherwise imminent criminal act. The potential human rights violation, of course, lay in the criminalization of efforts to leave the country.

The legal authorities sought to try both those who ordered the policy and those who carried it out. In addition to the Keßler trial, eighteen cases were opened against border guards for shooting at the Wall: fourteen in Berlin, of which four had been resolved by 1993, and four in other jurisdictions.[61] On January 20, 1992, a Berlin court convicted two of four border guards involved in the shooting death of Chris Gueffroy, who with a friend had tried to cross to the West on February 6, 1989, and sentenced the soldier who fired the fatal shots to three and a half years of prison. The judges drew on earlier postwar decisions asserting that no state had an unlimited right to decide what was just and unjust, and they cited Gustav Radbruch's classic

1946 pronouncement that positive law, that is, the law as written and applied, should prevail even if unjust, unless the degree of injustice reached an 'intolerable' degree. In the Gueffroy case, argued the judges, the "intolerable disproportionality" (*unerträgliches Mißverhältnis*) between the offense of unauthorized border crossing and the preventive execution of the fugitive voided the legal force of the order to shoot.[62] A second and decisive legal test involved two young soldiers, who on December 1, 1984, had shot the twenty-year-old Michael Schmidt after he had managed to carry a ladder across the border strip to the Wall and refused their command to stop climbing. The guards had fired some fifty-two shots, disabling the unsuccessful escapee, who was thereupon left to lie in the border strip for two hours before being taken to hospital where he died. In February 1992, the Berlin court sentenced the guards to eighteen and twenty-one months of confinement that it commuted to probation. The issue raised on appeal was not so much the justice of the sentences: certainly the judges seemed to have tried to reconcile contending concepts of law and responsibility for the death. The judicial question was whether the incident involved ordinary homicide or legally sanctioned law enforcement. The Berlin court had followed the provision of the Unification Treaty that stated that prosecution after unification required the act had to be punishable by East German courts when committed. Although it was recognized in the West as well as the East, that police could use weapons to deter the commitment of a crime, the Berlin court held that the duration of fire exceeded the statute's legitimation for employing what should be minimal force. Moreover, so the court argued, there had been no excuse for placing the would-be fugitive in danger of death since life was the highest good. While the GDR might have interpreted its law to allow potentially lethal fire, the judges decided that since the statute claimed to be based on the rule of law (*Rechtsstaatlichkeit*), it must be judged according to the norms of legality, which should have precluded shooting.

On appeal, the Federal Constitutional Court in Karlsruhe upheld the Berlin court's disposition of the case on November 3, 1992, but rejected its reasoning. By the authoritative interpretation and practice of East German jurisprudence, border flight was grave enough to warrant deterring by force. However, the Constitutional Court decided, the killing involved such an "extreme injustice" that it brought into play the appeal to higher law sanctioned by Radbruch. There were difficulties, however, in applying higher-law criteria to the case at hand. Instead, the Supreme Court argued, East

German adhesion to the 1966 international convention on civil and political rights rendered its own 1982 legislation invalid. Could the individual guards have been expected to recognize that they were committing an "extreme injustice" given the indoctrination inherent in their job? According to Karlsruhe, yes—although as the Supreme Court recognized, light sentences seemed appropriate.[63]

The upshot of the Wall-shooting cases left important issues open. Punishment, it was decided, was appropriate when excess force or departure from the GDR's own norms had taken place, when guards had shot without warning, or aimed lethally rather than at the legs, or the victim had been left to bleed. Punishment was not appropriate if the victim was evading pursuit for a common-law crime or shot back. But these judgments—so German commentators conceded—did not easily test whether the policy of enforcing the frontier by force was itself a criminal act. Perhaps their major legacy was precisely the one that the legal scholars had sought to avoid: by retroactive judgment they might have established limits on state policy for the future.

Other cases were opened as well: 1,300 on grounds of injury or attempted homicide at the border, several thousand for alleged perversions of justice (*Rechtsbeugung*), violation of post and telephone secrecy, deprivation of liberty, political inculpation, economic crime (large-scale misappropriation of public funds), *Landesverrat* or treason involving abuse of intelligence, and electoral fraud. A Dresden court convicted Modrow of this last charge but let him off with an admonition. The Berlin prosecutor established a task force on "governmental criminality" to prepare the cases against GDR leaders. By 1995 they were opening charges against the Politbüro chiefs. Krenz, Schabowski, and several others for their role in tacitly accepting the harsh border regime with its lethal enforcement—an indictment to which Schabowski admitted a moral complicity.

The trials sent an ambiguous message. East Germans had not been happy with their regime; many felt its officials deserved penalties for corruption or abuse of power, but the spectacle of public trials in courtrooms outside the ex-GDR conveyed a spectacle of victors' justice. The case against Markus Wolf, who had been sentenced in September 1993 to six years' imprisonment, seemed almost petty vindictiveness: a response to his often brilliant successes in recruiting agents for East German espionage. The judges in Karlsruhe finally decided 5–3 in May 1995 that citizens of the GDR who spied on West Germany could not be deemed criminal any more than West

German spies had been. The decision, which lifted the threat of prosecution against several hundred former GDR agents, arose not out of Wolf's own case, but conflicting judgments on Werner Großmann, last head of the central investigative office in the Stasi. A Berlin court had ruled out pursuing Großmann in July 1991 pending clarification by the Supreme Constitutional Court whether it would not be a violation of legal equality if West German intelligence agents were not also prosecuted. (In the Federal Republic the Constitutional Court is frequently asked for advance opinions on the validity of legislation or decisions.) The high court resolved that espionage was a normal activity for democratic as well as authoritarian states; it had not been illegal for GDR citizens nor were federal authorities moving to bring their own West German agents to be prosecuted. Former FRG spies who had spied against their own government remained subject to imprisonment; GDR agents who had settled in the West with the intent of spying might also be brought before the courts, but had they been blackmailed into espionage, mitigating circumstances might be cited. Eastern agents who had spied from a third country might under some circumstances be liable. Wolf was provisionally in the clear, although prosecutors threatened to pursue him for his activities outside Germany.[64]

United Germany was just one of many states that have had to confront the dilemma of coming to terms with the human rights abuses of earlier regimes. The fact that the new judicial unit was larger than the old one whose rulers were on trial made already difficult issues of retroactive justice even more complicated. In general, states have chosen one of several different alternatives: amnesty for the sake of reconciliation, as recommended by many and followed in Spain and Argentina; punishment of collaborators after individual trials—the method pursued against collaborators after World War II; collective denial of some political rights for those who had presumably participated in a certain group such as the secret police or the high ranks of the party (the procedure the Czechs termed lustration); or "truth commissions" charged with the task of evaluating records, publicizing what individual responsibilities had been, but not imposing any punishment.[65] This last recourse seemed a compromise, but for victims it provided no sort of compensatory penalties. Could there really be "justice" when retribution was excluded? On the other hand, lustration provided for penalties, but raised troubling issues of group justice. It imposed professional disqualification for previous membership in a specified group regardless of individual behavior. For the East German faculties and research institutes,

Stasi membership constituted grounds for a disqualification. Perhaps the broadest exclusion was that legislated by the 1992 Panev Law in Bulgaria, which stipulated the dismissal of university teachers who had listed courses in Marxism-Leninism, whether or not they taught them. The law was sustained 6–5 in February 1993, by the six non-Communist judges of the high court on the ground that merely "professional" criteria were being applied. Czech lustration was the most rigorously contested. Although the 1991 legislation, which established many categories for disqualification, was narrowed by the Federal Constitutional Court after eight months of hearing in 1992, it was still confirmed as a legitimate approach. An effort in Albania to disbar for five years lawyers who had been involved with the Communist Party or the uglier activities of the regime was overturned by the Constitutional Court in May 1993.[66]

The recourse to criminal trials and hearings presents its own difficulties. Trials establish a dramatically charged historical narrative in order to fix responsibility. Sometimes they establish justice, but often they reveal how many other potential defendants are evading justice. The West German trials of Auschwitz guards in the 1960s, more so than the Allies' tribunals at Nuremberg, allowed the Federal Republic to take judicial responsibility for some of the criminality of its predecessor regime, which was essential for its claim to represent German national continuity. But did the trials of the 1990s represent a society's self-interrogation, or just the triumph of the winners in a German-German war? It was not surprising that demands for a general amnesty found support, not just among old PDS activists, but some West Germans and foreigners as well. From late 1993 through spring 1994, calls for an amnesty multiplied. Ernst Goffried Mahrenholz, the vice-president of the Federal Constitutional Court argued that the "sharp sword of the criminal law" impeded the unification of East and West, while Roman Herzog, then seeking to emerge as a presidential candidate, and Wolfgang Thierse, one of the most prominent East German SPD parliamentary representatives, suggested concentrating investigations only on major offenses.[67] The case against the trials was a serious one: some of the indictments seemed vindictive since the state accused of sanctioning the injustices had been granted solemn recognition by the authorities now proposing to criminalize its policies.

If the FRG foreswore seeking criminal penalties, or if it was difficult to "try" the system for its collective abuses, was it still possible to have some sort of judicial reckoning? The concept of a truth commission, empowered to summon witnesses but not to impose punishment, developed often by private citizens who had no standing to hold a trial, appealed to many. Gauck had proposed such a forum in the last Volkskammer of the expiring GDR and Wolfgang Thierse and Wolfgang Ullmann suggested similar procedures. Friedrich Schorlemmer, the Wittenberg pastor and prominent spokesman for the citizens movements, urged the Bundestag's Committee of Internal Affairs to establish such a tribunal. Schorlemmer envisaged a massive body with representatives from all branches of government, academics, and major interest groups. The tribune would establish historical responsibilities and, so he suggested, lead to a healing catharsis; it would have no power to impose punishments. Thierse wanted to turn back the task of settling with the past to the East German citizens movement; Ullmann envisaged an international tribunal. Each proponent held that such a tribunal would help to overcome disillusion, bitterness, or in Ullmann's term "speechlessness." From September to December 1991, many intellectuals came out for such a forum.[68] The murderous attacks on German residents of foreign origin, such as the late 1991 assault in Hoyerswerda in the East, lent force to the argument that an open confrontation with the past was needed for the political health of the enlarged Federal Republic. But the new assaults also suggested that channeling "popular anger" might make the process hard to control.

Markus Meckel, the last SPD foreign minister in the de Maizière government, and his younger colleague Martin Gutzeit, both Sprachenkonvikt pastors, proposed as an alternative a parliamentary committe of inquiry, an Enquete-Kommission, that would work through the history of the GDR precisely to avoid a "self-selected quasi-judicial organ or a contested club of moralists who believe they can speak for everyone." The report found approval among all parties—it was no coincidence that on January 1, 1992, all Stasi files were to be opened—but it took until May 1992 to agree on terms of reference and composition. By then all parties, including the PDS, had signed on to the concept. Rainer Eppelmann, the pastor who had drafted with Havemann the Berlin Appeal for peace in 1982, then helped organize the Demokratischer Aufbruch as an alternative to New Forum, and was sitting as an East German Christian Democrat Bundestag member, was selected as chair.[69]

Eppelmann did not want the Enquete-Kommission to replace the judicial process, and he did insist on nonpartisan evaluation. But the Enquete, like any truth commission, faced an inherently difficult task. The trial, after all, seeks to establish individual responsibility against the backdrop of all the bureaucratic or structural issues that diffuse responsibility. The Enquete

Commission was intended to focus precisely on the structures and usages
that made it difficult to assess individual responsibility. To its credit it attempted a form of didactic public history. It heard witnesses and published
transcripts and summary reports.[70] Some of the testimony was graphic and
revealing, but too often it pitted contending narratives that had been organized along party lines. The historian experts included a relatively "soft"
Social Democrat, and two bitter critics of the GDR who insisted on its Stalinist essence. The report and materials generated no surprises, indeed left a
general sense of dissatisfaction. The political leaders from the different parties who had touchingly endorsed the commission sought from it a healing
and redemptive quality that the fractured accounts and contending evaluations could not provide. When discussed and scrutinized so exhaustively,
the *arcana imperii* lost their mystery.

The disappointment was instructive in its own right. It was natural
enough that the meaning of the GDR should be contested. Those who had
served it or those who had been connected with party aspirations would
emphasize its positive "achievements"—antifascism, above all, but also social welfare and economic security, its industrial output, or its success in
competitive athletics. Those who had suffered stressed its criminality or its
totalitarian qualities. The defenders argued for consensus and legitimacy;
the prosecutors focused on corruption and spying, and the GDR's continued
dependence on the Soviets. "What remains?" Christa Wolf had asked
rhetorically about her loyalties to the GDR. At the least, contested memories
and disputed history.

The difficulty with the public hearings though was precisely the failure to
make contestation central. The Enquete hearings were touchingly didactic.
For their proponents, they represented an earnest way to render justice, for
others a stratagem for finessing more painful and destabilizing judgments.
Many in East Germany and elsewhere came to feel that insisting on individual trials might undermine the creation of a democratic consensus. Might
not the success of the former West Germany in instituting democratic
habits have required integrating many ex-Nazis without scrutinizing their
past? Did not the examples of Spain, Argentina, and Poland show the wisdom of institutional amnesties? "Truth tribunals" elsewhere seemed at least
a worthy compromise, steering as they did between amnesia and retribution. But the compromise meant that victims and agents rehearsed the story
of East German repression with less catharsis than supporters of the procedure had promised. The Enquete established an indictment for a trial that
was not to take place. By assigning real consequences to the defendant, the

political trial forces an open contest between the excuses of the defendant or perpetrator and the remembered anguish of the victim. The historian, I think, must prefer the trial, not for its outcome, which will usually seem unjust to either the prosecutors or the defendant, but for its agonistic procedure. Of course, the trial is a stylized narrative, given a cohesion that events themselves do not possess. Nonetheless, only the contestation of truth, the simultaneous unfolding of rival perspectives, can assure an adequate history. No society or governing system has just one voice or, to use the fashionable locution, engages in just one conversation or agrees on a single discourse. At a minimum, rulers and ruled, those advantaged and disadvantaged, government and opposition, sometimes oppressors and victims, offer their own narratives. The historian can at best aspire to transcribe the counterpoint, not impose an artificial harmony.

By the mid 1990s, the German counterpoint included not only the antagonistic voices of former rulers and victims, but the discontents of East Germans within their new state. In 1989–90 most East Germans had no other wish than to be absorbed into a larger community of Germans and of economic success. But what had they achieved? Their experience suggested to many that they had not simply become full participants in a united Germany, but immigrants in their own territory, nursing selective memories of a past that comforted merely, and sometimes only, by virtue of its being shared. True, they benefited from vast income transfers and a sharp increase of real income as subsidies flowed East. But they perceived the rise in rents, erosion of a social net, and the disappearance of industrial jobs. Many had gone from the sites of badly rewarded work to the aimlessness of well-paid welfare. Older ones felt the young alone might reap the advantages. Their state governments relied on West German bureaucrats and ministers. Westerners claimed many of the university positions that were not simply abolished. They wanted a reckoning with their former masters, but were spectators at West German trials. They imagined a past of coziness and solidarity and forgot the rankling injustices they had earlier felt. They discovered that despite the antifascist founding myth, they harbored their own skinheads and violent youth. After days of exaltation came months of disillusion.

Any observer could find evidence enough to argue that disappointment or even resentment was likely to persist. Certainly intellectuals were prepared to lament the new "elbow" society or Wessi dominance. But gauging the popular mood is difficult and there were other indications that disorientation was being overcome.[71] More precisely, I believe, West Germans and

East Germans were converging toward a nuanced set of shared attitudes, which accommodated both enhanced national feeling and a new awareness of economic insecurity. Despite their melancholy, East Germans by the mid-1990s were becoming citizens of a large and wealthy nation-state. That larger community was often parochial, preoccupied with deciding who counted as German or how to impose monetary stability on its European associates. At the same time it accepted its nationhood more easily and comfortably, indeed in some cases with a bit of swagger, than it had when it was only two half republics. Even for social scientists who had continually emphasized the role of transnational developments—capitalism, modernization, Western liberal values—the nation beckoned warmly as a new unit of study. Historians who had earlier distrusted the narrative of the nation-state, who had sought to explain their country's development in terms of persisting premodern class formations or rapid economic change, redis-covered the significance of national identity, much as secular intellectuals might return to religious roots. By the summer of 1993 the nostalgia of nationhood suffused Berlin: Christof Stölzel, the director of the German Historical Museum in East Berlin, displayed Anton Werner's historical paintings, including the huge canvas that depicted the proclamation of the German Empire in 1871, while across the Linden advocates of rebuilding the razed Hohenzollern palace installed a fabric mock-up of the facade. Neo-imperial was in.

But what communal solidarity did this historicist nostalgia really offer at a moment when persistent unemployment, concern about loss of techno-logical leadership, or questioning of the Maastricht project made the future of German nationhood as much a source of anxiety as of encouragement? To raise this question is not to deny that Germans remain entitled to recon-struct a national narrative and identity. It is only in the name of national solidarity, after all, that the society accepted the massive financial transfers to the former East Germany, just as in the 1950s one accepted the costs of integrating refugees from the former territories of the East. Nonetheless, the national narrative that was being reinvented amounted to little more than an exhortation to historical pride. It remained too ill-defined to encompass the German past or guide the German future. Certainly it remained too simple to account for the end of East Germany.

The GDR, after all, had been a German regime, but not just a German enterprise. It had been German, first of all, less in any similarity to the Third Reich than to the earlier Central European *Polizeystaat*, whose bureaucrats maintained that they must discipline their subjects for their own collective good. But the GDR had also been not just German, but rather one constituent of the Communist system characterized by single-party rule and central planning. The dissolution of the GDR followed from the disabling difficulties that overtook that overarching system. Precisely because the dilemmas were systemwide, I believe that it advances our understanding to compare the problems of late communism with the contemporaneous difficulties faced by the advanced capitalist countries. This is an approach liable to arouse dissent from Anglo-American interpretors (as well as market enthusiasts in the ex-Communist countries) who insist on the unique flaws of state socialism. It is also likely to provoke disagreement from those Germans now transfixed by their national narrative, whether they approach it in a critical or a celebratory mode. Nevertheless, it yields a perspective that will seem increasingly justified. Both sides in the cold war had to cope for almost two decades with a set of fundamental transitions in the world economy and the ideologies that supported their respective ways of doing business. The harsh pressures of relative backwardness brought down the Soviet system in the 1980s and helped to liquidate the East German state that incorporated Russia's claim to have shared post-1945 leadership with the West. The pressures encroaching on the capitalist world from the 1970s to the 1990s led to the end of full employment, an acceptance of increasing inequality, and increasing dissension over economic integration. Thus the unease that East Germans brought to united Germany came to be increasingly matched by the malaise emerging in the wider society. In their post-1989 melancholy, the East Germans just threatened to lead their West German compatriots into a new epoch of vanished reassurance.

Epilogue

Wrapped Reichstag, 1995

DESPITE THE difficulties of unification, it would be wrong to close this history in a minor key. Germans had transformed their history, and for the better. They had demonstrated a rare solidarity and not just on the Leipzig Ring or at the Berlin Wall, but later to protest against crimes of hatred. The German Democratic Republic had dissolved in 1989 once crowds took over the streets. They were not menacing crowds then, save for the regime. They were often frightened, sometimes angry, gradually becoming aware of their own collective power. Almost six years after that mass mobilization, Berlin became the site of another remarkable crowd. From June 27 to July 6, 1995, the artist Christo and his wife and collaborator, Jeanne Claude, wrapped the Reichstag in specially woven nylon cloth, silverized, with blue ropes. The massive late Victorian building with its heavy neoclassical facade looked smaller and lighter in its silver shroud, even aethereal in the long summer dusk. Indeed it seemed almost possible that the building underneath might have somehow disappeared; the package created the sense of bulk without weight. For twenty-four years Christo and Jeanne Claude had nudged their project along against difficult odds; until 1989 the Reichstag backed on to the Berlin Wall and wrapping the back would have required clearance from the East German authorities. Although the artists financed the costs of the construction by the sale of preparatory drawings and evocative renderings, many West German political leaders had been skeptical. Might it not demean the once and future site of the German parliament? At best was it not frivolous? Certainly Chancellor Kohl did not like the idea—he knew art from a "PR" stunt, he said later when he arrived in Berlin during the wrapping, but still declined to visit the site. Nevertheless, he did agree to a nonparty Bundestag vote in February 1994, and a multiparty majority endorsed the project.

I came to Berlin for a last archival visit for this book during the fortnight the Reichstag was shrouded. It was a fitting moment to take leave of the GDR, which, for all its remembered aura in East Berlin and the provinces, was finally disappearing. The most remarkable aspect of Christo and Jeanne

Claude's work—could they have had any inkling how powerfully it would function?—was its suspension of the everyday. With its blue rope and silver fabric simplifying the surfaces underneath, the wrapped parliament building seemed almost a large mysterious gift deposited in its empty site by interplanetary visitors. The surrounding lawn and streets allowed a popular festival. Good-natured crowds milled round the site day and night. Until late 1989 the building had been enclosed in the West by the border that ran just behind it. Now crowds poured in from the former East Berlin, crossing the Spree or strolling north from Unter den Linden, as well as wandering from the Tiergarten to the West. Some gawked at the building, walked up to feel the fabric, or eagerly sought the sample patches that the Christos' young "monitors" distributed as relics. Others examined the wares of street merchants—silver jewelry, wooden toys, Turkish vests—and treated themselves to Bratwurst and beer. They watched the open-air performers: a classical basoonist, pop musicians, costumed human "statues" who struck poses. Those who passed the southwest corner examined the memorial to the almost one hundred Reichstag deputies that the Nazis had killed over the course of their regime. The monument consists of a set of parallel jagged gray slates, each about a meter high and inscribed on its edge with the name, party, and place of execution of a Reichstag victim.

The Reichstag—both the institution and the building—after all has not had a happy history. Although the Christos had often justified their selection of the Reichstag by referring to it as an important building in the history of democratic parliaments, it was hardly Westminster or the French National Assembly. Despite its pompous structure, with the pediment inscribed "To the German People," the Reichstag building had become home to a legislature that Bismarck had repeatedly cowed. Despite the proclamation of a German Republic from its balcony in 1918, the parliament had become paralyzed by bitter and often irresponsible partisan politics after World War I. After the famed fire of February 1933 gutted the interior, the building ceased to serve even the puppet assembly that Hitler periodically summoned to applaud his ranting. It was further ravaged as epicenter for the Soviet assault during the climactic battle for Berlin in spring 1945. As an outpost of the Federal Republic while Berlin was divided, the interior was reconstructed for historical exhibits and occasional ceremonial sessions of the West German Bundestag.

But this difficult past mattered little in July 1995. The wrapped Reichstag, in effect, took a holiday from this heavy legacy. The structure had already been designated as the site of united Germany's legislature (which in contrast to the building itself would remain titled Bundestag). For the strolling throngs who surrounded it, the artistic accomplishment absolved the Reichstag from its previous history. It liberated the buildings's parliamentary potential from the incubus of earlier failures of representative government. Unveiled, it might be born anew. The Christos' achievement in effect allowed millions of visitors and onlookers to forgive the building its uncertain past.

Normally historians regret the obscuring of memory. In this case, however, it was a healthy transformation. There was no deliberate forgetfulness, no concerted effort to invoke a statute of limitations. It was more that the wrapped Reichstag spontaneously worked as a site of expectation, not memory: a *lieu d'espoir*, not a *lieu de mémoire*. "The real forms of politics are not changed by a fascinating phenomenon," wrote Robert Leicht in *Die Zeit*. "But the possible forms, its greater potential for symbolic meaning, for the power of deeper ideas or creative imagination, can be happily presented on so visible a stage. The Germans might thus themselves emerge as cheerful and dreamy, not only martial and moralistic. The prose of politics has been transformed a bit into poetry."[1] "Afterward nothing is what it was," Monika Zimmermann commented in the Berlin *Tagespiegel*. Critics were right who warned about transforming a national edifice like the Berlin Reichstag into an artistic spectacle. But the opposite of what they feared came to pass: the symbol has been enhanced, not demeaned: "when the veils fall, everyone who saw the wrapped Reichstag will have another relationship to this building than he did before."[2]

Since this particular history has so involved crowds at decisive moments, it is fitting to end with the crowd at the Reichstag. German crowds are not easy constructions. Sometimes as at Carneval or in Bavarian beer halls with their lubricated and determined jollity, they can be vaguely intimidating. They have clear borders: those lonely remain outside; those within take on a collective persona that the spectator can find menacing. When Germany won the World Cup in July 1990, about a fortnight after the first unification treaty had come into force, crowds of youthful fans had also taken over the streets: wrapped in flags, rhythmically chanting Deutschland, Deutschland, singing even the old verse of *Deutschland über Alles*. The crowd, however, has rarely intervened in German history; when it has, it has often been combative and challenging. Cultural and national generalizations are risky. Still, the German crowd, I believe, has had its own character: perhaps its quasi-coercive determination reveals the other side of the disciplined loneliness of a Protestant morality. It reflects the difficulty of achieving political sociability as compared, say, with collective manifestations in France or Italy. The Christos' crowd—they deserve the credit—was different. It was not menacing. Families were there; people were enjoying themselves, without the continuous flow of beer or schnaps; without rhythmic oompah music or timeworn folk songs; enjoying themselves without the determination to have fun. The *Tagesspiegel* correspondent got it right when she wrote: "Never before, at least never in Berlin, have so may people gotten together so happily and peacefully. While the other great joyful event of the last years, the fall of the Wall, gave rise to a noisy euphoria [*lautstarkem Freudentaumel*] and cries of 'madness,' these visitors strolled happily around the work of art."[3] They mingled spontaneously; they were easy, in German terms *locker*, or to use an expression of the American sixties, mellow.

Five years after unification, the wrapped Reichstag seemed even to facilitate the ad hoc sociability, as contrasted with the commitment to formal organization, that has remained so relatively underdeveloped throughout recent German history. It allowed a relaxation, if only for a moment, of the continuous border drawing between Ossie and Wessie, German and Turk, young and old, us and them. They spilled over where once the Wall had been. Few seemed to recall the crowd of November 1989, although many had doubtless been present then. Germany had come a long way. For all the difficulties, despite the so-called wall in the head, by mid-1995 unification was no longer a wager, it was a fact. Of course there were many casualties and symptoms of resistance. Many of the late middle-aged who lost their jobs, whether as industrial dinosaurs were restructured or faculties were politically pruned, would never find more than occasional work and cushioning pensions. They would remain demoralized. A leftist subculture, sometimes brilliantly cynical about the blessings of capitalism, still exerted a strong presence in East Berlin theater and literary life. Its younger adherents sustained Frank Castorf's provocative stagings of reworked classics at the Volksbühne and the surrounding PDS cafés. Indeed, the functionaries of the old regime, concentrated in East Berlin, voted unrepentantly, if not for communism, nonetheless for a PDS that thrived on the dislocations brought by the new regime. The Party of Democratic Socialism could even cynically claim in the 1995 campaigns to include former resisters against SED persecution. The PDS emerged from the fall elections as the largest single party in East Berlin with over 30 percent of the vote: an ensconced cadre of resentment, grief, and chutzpah, which under Gregor Gysi's wiseacre leadership in Bonn especially vexed SPD politicians. These latter coveted PDS support in state and national legislatures, claimed that its voters should not be simply ostracized, but (restored party leader Lafontaine excepted) still hesitated to accept its unrepentant descent from the Communist regime.

In many institutions that Wessies had helped to reorganize, the East Germans sometimes conveyed the subaltern, vaguely hopeless manner of the colonized. Family formation seemed also to collapse, although what was most likely occurring was a rapid adaptation of the already stagnant West European birth rate.[4] But for all the difficulties the institutional settlement would stick. Those entering adulthood had spent their formative adolescence in a unified Germany, not in the republic remembered with misty memory. A *Spiegel* poll whose results were published even during the magical Reichstag wrapping supposedly revealed many indices of widespread nostalgia and the belief that GDR life had been less nerve-wracking and more nurturing. Respondents missed what Germans call *Geborgenheit*: a pleasantly circumscribed sense of security. But on the key question, whether respondents wished that unification had not taken place, only 15 percent said yes, 83 percent answered no.[5] Six years after November 1918, the first German Republic, despite its apparent stabilization, suffered from debilitating flaws. Six years after November 1989, the second German Republic, despite the flux into which its four-decade party alignment was probably slipping, was far more robust. Political life was not polarized; 1990 Germany was confident of its European role without being arrogant, but not dangerously humiliated; the middle classes were not pulverized and fragmented. For all the difficulties of restructing the economic basis of the new *Bundesländer*, the former GDR would not turn out to be a new Italian Mezzogiorno as some had feared. It would recover productivity, even if it clung under new circumstances to the somewhat confined and provincial society it had had under more repressive conditions.

Would this new sociability evoked by the wrapped Reichstag persevere, or must it remain ephemeral, like the political exaltation of November 1989? Was the Europe Union perhaps—its twelve-starred flag displayed alongside the German banner—going to make this sometimes uptight society in the heart of Europe more free and easy, or at least more friendly? Was German public life durably to become less poised between wary loneliness and spasmodic collective action, between bureaucratic rationality and decisionistic temptation? Did the mélange of visitors to the silver parliament prefigure an easier acceptance of ethnic diversity? The Haus der Geschichte, or museum of contemporary history, which Chancellor Kohl had had constructed in Bonn, brilliantly conveyed the progress of postwar democracy and material culture. But except for a small marginal exhibit, it neglected the themes of migration and ethnic pluralism. Moreover, a bitter sarcasm about "multiculturalism" was emerging as one of the major themes of a new intellectual right, some of whom did not hesitate to redeploy the anti-Western motifs that had characterized the antidemocratic radical conservativism of the Weimar era. The question of national identity, which had seemed so problematic an issue during the historians' controversy three years earlier, was now explored with far less reticence.

In effect some of the conservatives were using the debate over the history of the GDR to reopen the *Historikerstreit* of 1986–88. But then the right, which had argued that National Socialist genocide was comparable with, indeed partly a response to Soviet Communist terror, had provoked a vigorous response. The social philosopher Jürgen Habermas, followed by leading academic historians, had bitterly criticized these arguments; even President von Weizsäcker had intervened to cut off what he feared might be an attempt to exculpate the Nazis. By the early 1990s the wind was shifting. National narratives were becoming more attractive, defended by mainstream historians who would have earlier distrusted their political premises, and taken up in more extreme forms by a new right-wing intelligentsia.[6] The new right declared that the postwar era had ended, that the consequence of 1989 meant that 1945 no longer had to be viewed through the victors' perspective, but as a national defeat. Its exponents sometimes suggested that Hitler's attack on the Soviet Union was a preemptive defense, or they maintained that all wartime violence was morally equivalent, whether exercised by the SS, by partisans in northern Italy, Soviet troops in East Prussia, Czech reclaimants of the Sudetenland, or even allied airmen high over German cities. As for current politics, they denounced the alleged new German trend toward multiculturalism or the "null-identity of *Verfassungspatriotismus*."[7]

Granted, it would have been alarmist to exaggerate the importance of this new right. A handful of reactionary *feuilletonistes* did not adumbrate a new national revolution. But renewed concern with German identity was not just a theme for the far right. Even for social scientists who had continually emphasized the role of transnational developments—capitalism, modernization, Western liberal values—the nation beckoned warmly as a new unit of study. Historians who had earlier distrusted the narrative of the nation-state, who had sought to explain their country's development in terms of persisting premodern class formations or rapid economic change, rediscovered the significance of national identity, much as secular intellectuals might return to religious roots. Conservatives might celebrate this revival, even social democrats and liberals participated. National identity was normal, it was healthy. What this meant for the interpretation of the events of 1989–90, was an emphasis on the national narrative—the continuity of underlying German allegiances and the story of unification.

Nor was it only the right that indulged in bitter rhetoric. As the participants in the Christa Wolf debate had revealed, German intellectual debate relied on irony and imputations of bad faith or self-delusion. Weimar political life had amply demonstrated that brittle brilliance does not necessarily strengthen democratic resilience. The German public had confronted many serious issues since 1989, and indeed had taken on new domestic and international duties—although it did so usually by referring many of the challenging issues to its Supreme Court for resolution. German intellectual life had become transfixed by a series of disputes that mobilized writers: the *Historikerstreit* just before unification, the *Literaturstreit* just after, the dispute over the rights of political participation—all debates about who was morally fit to take part in a national community. So much of German political energy had gone into frustrated efforts at proscription. It might no longer be realistic to exclude Turks or Asian migrants, but in some quarters the dream of stigmatizing those who had believed in a socialist Germany still persisted. The energies of confessionalism still raged.

Perhaps the wrapped Reichstag was just a transient festive denial of a workaday difficulties, or a momentary lull between renewed anathemas. No one could answer this question in 1995. National habits are not quickly overcome, but perhaps they had been slowly changing. Again, one recalls Chancellor Kohl's pride that Germany was a normal country. Of course, this was an achievement: it had not been normal before 1945 to be preoccupied by race and conquest. It had not been normal before 1989, as Timothy Garton Ash had observed, to have a wall down the middle of one's capital. "Altogether, it was more normal for a nation that had once been united in a single state again to live in one."[8] But what was a normal country? The United States, which kept more than a million inhabitants in prison of whom hundreds waited for their lethal injections, and where the airwaves could be saturated with phone-in rage? Canada in perpetual quasi dissolution; a Russia in its fifth year of economic distress; a Britain ruled by a royal family that could never sustain its family relations? Was it an accomplishment to be a normal country? Much of German culture remained slightly offbeat in its traditional way: its theater featured music, nudity, blood, and heavy symbolism; its philosophers yearned for large categorical abstractions; its advertising was redolent with an overripe luxury; its youth sported pink, purple, and green hair. But none of these phemonema meant that Germany lived in expressionist anarchy. Its newspapers' hefty economic sections continually covered the well-crafted machines and autos that earned its prosperity. Its earnest well-meaning middle-class professionals were concerned about the environment and transgressions of human rights. And the wrapped Reichstag suggested that these diverse Germans could be friendly as well as challenging. Would they remain so? What would emerge from the Christos' chrysalis after the Reichstag was unwrapped, as it was on July 7? The same massive building—which had always housed a parliament either subordinate to a monarch or disastrously fractured—or perhaps a durably new spirit. Summer 1995 was promising. Was it illusory; or might it be that Germany was not just a normal country, but perhaps actually emerging as a more responsible and outward looking society?

Give the final word to the East Germans. Joachim Gauck, the stern guardian of the Stasi archives who had survived five years of controversy, urged maturity, not normalcy in the fall of 1995, when he was reappointed for another term as the publicizer of East Germany's complicitous and shameful past. He spoke in the same serious Protestant tones that had characterized those who had spilled from the churches into the streets six years earlier:

> I would like us to be an adult nation and to become an even more adult one. I see the fact that we can endure conflicts about the past, that we did not ordain any rapid peace from above, as a sign that the nation has become more adult. It needs no quick [closing of the books]. It can take controversy. It has become more democratic. . . . But I am not fixated with the past; rather I want to bid it farewell; I want to be really rid of it. We Germans have had to bear a terrible dictatorial burden twice in this century, and for which we are guilty. . . . We East Germans need time to bring those who for decades ruled us from above to say what they did with us below. And although we are only a third or a fourth of the population, I would plead in our enlarged Germany: give us time for this controversial debate. Five years beyond unification still hasn't given us time enough, still hasn't provided the occasion to close the books, for we are still in the middle of a controversial debate. We have to bear the conflict a bit longer. Out of the controversy will emerge the leave taking from what has burdened us.[9]

By 1995 Germany was taking leave, fitfully, imperfectly, of what had burdened it and divided it.

Notes

CHAPTER 1

1. Carola Stern, *In den Netzen der Erinnerung: Lebensgeschichten zweier Menschen* (Reinbek bei Hamburg: Rowohlt, 1989), pp. 13, 11.

2. Jörg Jüdersleben and Holger Hens Karlson, "'Es kommt keiner unterm Regen durch': Wie das Politbüro den Fall Biermann bereinigte," *Deutschland Archiv* 26, 7 (July 1993): 818–829, quotation from p. 827.

3. Reiner Kunze, *Die wunderbaren Jahre* (Frankfurt am Main: S. Fischer, 1976). My own story most in the spirit of Kunze's episodes dates from December 1964, when I proposed to drive with a DDR friend from Potsdam for a day trip to Dresden. The woman in charge of my small hotel decided to call the police to get help with my question whether we would pass control points in retraversing some of the Berlin Autobahn. They wished to know the name of my DDR passenger; I told the woman that it was none of their business; after all they might not approve that one of their citizens wished to travel so extensively with an American. "But, Herr Maier," she protested quite sincerely, "dann wäre unsere ganze Friedenspolitik ein Schwindel . . . [in that case our whole peace policy would be a fraud]."

4. See Wolfgang Leonhard, *Child of the Revolution*, trans. L. M. Woodhouse (New York: Pathfinder Press, 1979), for memories of this experience.

5. For this brief experience, see Lutz Niethammer, Ulrich Borsdorff, and Peter Brandt, eds., *Arbeiterinitiative 1945: Antifaschistische Ausschüsse und Reorganisation der Arbeiterbewegung in Deutschland* (Wuppertal: Hammer, 1976); also Stefan Heym's novelistic treatment of a Saxon border area that for a few weeks in May 1945 remained unoccupied by either Soviet or American forces: *Schwarzenberg: Roman* (Munich: Bertelsmann, 1984).

6. For the most recent general treatment see Norman Naimark, *The Russians in Germany: A History of the Soviet Zone of Occupation, 1945–1949* (Cambridge, MA: Harvard University Press, 1995). For the emphasis on the Oder-Neisse frontier and

the Wismut deliveries, see Alexei Filitov, "Soviet Policy and the Early Years of the Two German States, 1949–1961," paper presented at the conference organized by the Cold War International History Project of the Woodrow Wilson Center for Scholars, the Kulturwissenschaftliches Institut, Essen, and the Forschungsschwerpunkt Zeithistorische Studien, Potsdam: "The Soviet Union, Germany, and the Cold War, 1945–1962: New Evidence from Eastern Archives," Essen and Potsdam, June 28–July 3, 1994 (cited hereafter as CWIHP Conference).

7. This interpretation is based on my reading of the diplomatic record in the yearly and triennial volumes of the U.S. Department of State, *Foreign Relations of the United States* (Washington, DC: U.S. Government Printing Office, 1969–) and archival materials in Washington, London, Paris, and elsewhere. Naimark, *The Russians in Germany*, and David Pike, *The Politics of Culture in Soviet-Occupied Germany, 1945–1949* (Stanford, CA: Stanford University Press, 1992), provide the best documented discussion of evolving Soviet and German Communist goals. For an interpretation that Stalin came only unwillingly to establishment of the GDR, see Wilfried Loth, *Stalins ungeliebtes Kind. Warum Moskau die DDR nicht wollte* (Berlin: Rowohlt, 1994).

8. Similar Western concerns over Soviet intentions precluded economic cooperation. The Soviets justified their dismantling of industry in the eastern zone by pointing to Washington's alleged retreat from earlier commitments to sanction massive reparation removals from Germany as a whole. In turn, however, Soviet policy reinforced Anglo-American conviction that Moscow wanted to carry off so much that the U.S. and U.K. would indirectly subsidize the Soviets by supporting the Germans. See Alex Cairncross, *The Price of War: British Policy on German Reparations 1941–1949* (Oxford: Basil Blackwell, 1985), for a recent account. Both the conflicts over reparations and the future form of an all-German administration came to a head at the Moscow Foreign Ministers Conference of March–April 1947.

9. Public Record Office: FO371/55586 = C1480/131/18: Steel report, Feb. 7, 1946. Churchill had already resorted to the phrase in cables to Truman, and would make it famous in his Fulton, Missouri, address a month later; in February 1945, Goebbels had already predicted the possibility in case of a German defeat.

10. For the most complete recent account of the fusion, see Harold Hurwitz, *Die Anfänge des Widerstandes*, part 1, *Führungsanspruch und Isolation der Sozialdemokraten*, and part 2: *Zwischen Selbsttäuschung und Zivilcourage; Der Fusionskampf*, vol. 4 of *Demokratie und Antikommunismus in Berlin nach 1945* (Cologne: Wissenschaft und Politik, 1990). See also Henry Krisch, *German Politics under Soviet Occupation* (New York: Columbia University Press, 1974). Similar choices confronted

Social Democrats elsewhere. The Polish Socialists split and the majority voted to join the coalition led by the Communists in the elections of 1947; in Prague the wing of the Social Democrats led by Rudolf Fierlinger likewise opted for a similar collaboration.

11. Gert-Joachim Glaeßner, "Vom 'realen Sozialismus' zur Selbstbestimmung: Ursachen und Konsequenzen der Systemkrise in der DDR," *Aus Politik und Zeitgeschichte* B1–2/90 (Jan. 5, 1990): 3–20, citations from p. 9.

12. Dietrich Staritz, *Geschichte der DDR 1949–1995* (Frankfurt am Main: Suhrkamp, 1995), pp. 21–22. On the notion of "Ostorientierung," see Hurwitz, *Die Anfänge*.

13. David Childs, *The GDR: Moscow's German Ally*, 2nd ed. (London: Unwin Hyman, 1988), pp. 20–22.

14. For early GDR developments I have relied on Staritz, *Geschichte der DDR*; Hermann Weber, *Geschichte der DDR* (Munich: Deutscher Taschenbuch Verlag, 1985); and Childs, *The GDR: Moscow's German Ally*.

15. For the Slansky trials, in which the script was changed so that the 1950 bourgeois-nationalist conspiracies to assassinate General Secretary Slansky became the 1951–52 conspiracy by Slansky and his "Jewish-Trotskyite" clique to discredit socialism, see Karel Kaplan, *Report on the Murder of the General Secretary*, trans. Karel Kovana (Columbus: Ohio State University Press, 1990); also the memoir by defendant Artur London, *The Confession*, trans. Alastair Hamilton (New York: Ballantyne Books, 1971).

16. For the text of the note, see U.S. Department of State, *Foreign Relations of the United States, 1952–1954, VII: Germany and Austria*, pp. 169–172.

17. The West German controversy over the Stalin note played a somewhat analogous role to the revisionist controversy over cold war origins in the United States. The case for a genuine offer was made by Rolf Steininger, *Die Stalin Note. Eine vertane Chance: Die Stalin Note vom 10. März 1952 und die Wiedervereinigung* (Berlin: Dietz, 1985). For a dismissal of the offer as spurious, see Hermann Graml, "Nationalstaat oder deutscher Teilstaat: Die sowjetischen Noten vom Jahre 1952 und die öffentliche Meinung in der Bundesrepublik Deutschland," *Vierteljahrshefte für Zeitgeschichte* 25 (1977): 821–865, and Graml, *Die Märznote von 1952: Legende und Wirklichkeit* (Melle: Knoth, 1988); and Hans-Peter Schwarz, ed., *Die Legende von der verpaßten Gelegenheit* (Stuttgart: Belser, 1982). Those who have explored the question in recently opened Russian archives stress the lack of evidence for a meaningful offer. See Gerhard Wettig, "Deutschland-Note vom 10. März 1952 auf der Basis diplomatischer Akten des russischen Außenministeriums: Die Hypothese des Wiedervereinigungsangebots," *Deutschland Archiv* 26, 7 (July 1993); also Wettig, "Dis-

cussion Paper on the Policy Background of the Soviet 10 March 1952 Note," and the review of the literature in Rund van Dijk, "The Stalin-Note: Last Chance for Unification?" papers presented at the CWIHP Conference, 1994.

18. Rudolf Herrnstadt, *Das Herrnstadt-Dokument*, ed. Nadja Schulz-Herrnstadt (Reinbek bei Hamburg: Rowohlt, 1990), p. 74. This memoir drafted after Herrnstadt's disgrace presents his history of the crisis and intraparty tension.

19. See *Das Herrnstadt-Dokument* for the best inside history; also Arnulf Baring, *Der 17. Juni 1953*, rev. ed. (Stuttgart: Deutsche Verlags-Anstalt, 1983); Weber, *Geschichte der DDR*, pp. 232–245; and the essays in Ilko-Sascha Kowalczuk, Armin Mitter, and Stefan Wolle, eds., *Der Tag X - 17. Juni 1953: Die "innere Staatsgründung" der DDR als Ergebnis der Krise 1952/54* (Berlin: Ch. Links Verlag, 1995). On the confusion in West Berlin, especially at RIAS, the West Berlin radio station, see Manfred Rexin, "Der 16. und 17. Juni 1953 in West-Berlin," *Deutschland Archiv* 26, 8 (August 1993): 985–994. Wladimir S. Semjonow, *Von Stalin bis Gorbatschow: Ein halbes Jahrhundert in diplomatischer Mission 1939–1991*, trans. Hilde Ettinger and Helmut Ettinger (Berlin: Nicolai, 1995), pp. 290–300, discusses Soviet disarray over German policy in this period, but little about his relations with the East Germans. On the Beria-German interaction, see Gerhard Wettig, "Zum Stand der Forschung über Berijas Deutschland-Politik im Frühjahr 1953," and "Neue Erkentnisse über Berijas Deutschland-Politik," *Deutschland Archiv*, 26, 6 (June 1993): 674–682 and 26, 12 (Dec. 1993): 1412–1413.

20. For an account of the trials, purges, and opposition to Ulbricht, see Staritz, *Geschichte der DDR*, pp. 107–118. Other punishments were lighter than Harich's. By 1957 members of the opposition—and there were many—were compelled to undergo self-criticism, but then assigned to academic positions. See also John Christopher Torpey, "Between Anti-Fascism and Opposition: East German Intellectuals, Socialism, and the National Question, 1945–1990" (Ph.D. dissertation, University of California, 1992), chap. 3. On Harich, see the obituary by Manfred Jäger, "Zum Tod von Wolfgang Harich," *Deutschland Archiv*, 28, 4 (Apr. 1995): 339–341.

21. Besides the limited nature of the sanctions, there was another important difference in the role played by political assizes in the United States and Europe. In the United States cold war political justice became ugly in part because its most zealous advocates were not at the center of political power; they emerged at the margins of the established parties—preeminently but not exclusively among the Republicans— and exploited their demagogy to gain an influence far beyond their numbers or normal institutional power. In European cases, those in control used political trials as a method of enforcing their new rule.

22. I rely on Falco Werkentin's archivally based work, *Politische Strafjustiz in der Ära Ulbricht* (Berlin: Ch. Links Verlag, 1995), esp. pp. 21–35, 113–167; also Werk-

entin, "Zwischen Tauwetter und Nachtfrost (1955–1957): DDR-Justizfunktionäre auf Glatteis," *Deutschland Archiv*, 26, 3 (Mar. 1993): 341–349. For a resume of recent literature, see Annette Weinke, "Neue Veröffentlichungen zum Justizsystem in der SBZ/DDR," *Deutschland Archiv* 28, 2 (Feb. 1995): 203–206.

23. Walter Janka, *Schwierigkeiten mit der Wahrheit* (Reinbek bei Hamburg: Rowohlt, 1989), p. 16. For a discussion of post-1989 East German autobiographical strategies (including Janka's, Günter de Bruyn's, and Günter Schabowski's), see Manfred Jäger, "Die Autobiographie als Erfindung von Wahrheit: Beispiele literarischer Selbstdarstellung nach dem Ende der DDR," *Aus Politik und Zeitgeschichte* B41/92 (Oct. 2, 1992): 25–36.

24. Janka, *Schwierigkeiten mit der Wahrheit*, p. 41. For Becher see also Hans Mayer, *Der Turm von Babel: Erinnerung an eine Deutsche Demokratische Republik* (Frankfurt am Main: Suhrkamp, 1991), pp. 11–15, 100–115.

25. Günter Erbe, "Geschmack an der 'Dekadenz': Wandlungen im literarischen und kulturellen Traditionsverständnis," in Gert-Joachim Glaeßner, ed., *Die DDR in der Ära Honecker: Politik–Kultur–Gesellschaft* (Opladen: Westdeutscher Verlag, 1988), pp. 656–673. See also J. H. Reid, "Another Turn in the Road: Kafka in the GDR," *GDR Monitor*, 13 (summer 1985); Simone Barck, "Das Dekadenz-Verdikt. Zur Konjunktur eines kulturpolitischen 'Kampfkonzepts' Ende der 1950er bis Mitte der 1960er Jahre," in Jürgen Kocka, ed., *Historische DDR-Forschung. Aufsätze und Studien* (Berlin: Akademie Verlag, 1993), pp. 327–344. Also, Scott D. Denham, "Franz Kafka in the German Democratic Republic, 1949–1989," *Journal of the Kafka Society of America* 16, 1 (June 1992): 31–39.

26. See Gerhard Wettig, "All German Unity and East German Separation in Soviet Policy, 1947–1949," based on Soviet foreign policy archives and presented at the CWIHP Conference, 1994. Wettig holds that the Soviets believed at least as late as 1947 that they might eventually persuade West Germans to join a united Germany dominated by Communists.

27. Cited from the transcripts of the plenary session of the Central Committee of June 1957 by Vladislav M. Zubok, "Khrushchev's Motives and Soviet Diplomacy in the Berlin Crisis, 1958–1962," presented at CWIHP Conference, 1994.

28. See Hope Harrison, "Ulbricht and the Concrete 'Rose': New Archival Evidence on the Dynamics of Soviet-East German Relations and the Berlin Crisis, 1958–1961," CWIHP Working Paper No. 5 (Washington, DC: Woodrow Wilson Center, May 1993); also Hannes Adomeit, *Soviet Risk-Taking and Crisis Behavior: A Theoretical and Empirical Analysis* (Boston: George Allen and Unwin, 1982); Valentin Falin, *Politische Erinnerungen*, trans. Heddy Pross-Werth (Munich: Droemer-Knaur, 1993); the older Robert Slusser, *The Berlin Crisis of 1961: Soviet-American Relations and the Struggle for Power in the Kremlin* (Baltimore: Johns Hopkins University Press,

1973); Marc Trachtenberg, "The Berlin Crisis," in *History and Strategy* (Princeton: Princeton University Press, 1991), pp. 169–234.

29. See John Connelly, "Creating the Socialist Elite: Communist University Policies in East Germany, Poland, and the Czech Lands, 1945–1954" (Ph.D. dissertation, Harvard University, 1994). Also Connelly, "Zur 'Republikflucht' von DDR-Wissenschaftlern in den fünfziger Jahren," *Zeitschrift für Geschichtswissenschaft* 42, 4 (1994): 331–352.

30. Staritz, *Geschichte der DDR*, p. 139.

31. See Rüdiger Wenzke, *Die NVA und der Prager Frühling 1968. Die Rolle Ulbrichts und der DDR-Streitkräfte bei der Niederschlagung der tschechoslowakischen Reformbewegung* (Berlin: Ch. Links Verlag, 1995).

32. For the evolution, of Ostpolitik and the German question see Timothy Garton Ash, *In Europe's Name: Germany and the Divided Continent* (New York: Random House, 1993), esp. pp. 28–83. For a summary of the 1970–72 treaties, see Honore M. Catudal, Jr., *The Diplomacy of the Quadripartite Agreement on Berlin: A New Era in East-West Politics* (Berlin: Berlin Verlag, 1978).

33. See Garton Ash's evaluation in *In Europe's Name*, pp. 260–267.

34. See Sigrid Meuschel, "Auf der Suche nach Madame l'Identité? Zur Konzeption der Nation und Nationalgeschichte," in Glaeßner, *Die DDR in der Ära Honecker*, pp. 77–93.

35. For the biographer of Frederick the Great (Ingrid Mittenzwei) and the "tradition and heritage," debate, see, besides the large historiographical output, Hendrik Bussiek, *Die real existieriende DDR: Neue Notizen aus der unbekannten deutschen Republik* (Frankfurt am Main: Fischer, 1985), pp. 63–64.

36. Marlies Menge, *Mecklenburg: Reisebilder aus der DDR* (Cologne: Kiepenheuer und Witsch, 1989), pp. 43–44.

37. Bussiek, *Die real existierende DDR*, pp. 57–58.

38. Günter Gaus, *Wo Deutschland liegt. Eine Ortsbestimmung* (Munich: Deutscher Taschenbuch–Verlag, 1986), p. 126.

39. Gaus, *Wo Deutschland liegt*, p. 117. Gaus's book cannot be read just as a fine piece of reportage, which it is. It is conceived equally as a critique of West Germany through the image of the East (or, as he insists, "Middle Germany"). For a critique of concepts, see Volker Zastrow, "Die Legende von der 'Nischengesellschaft' im Sozialismus," *Frankfurter Allgemeine Zeitung*, July 12, 1990, p. 29.

40. See the commentary by Reinhard Koch, "Alltagswissen versus Ideologie? Theoretische und empirische Beiträge zu einer Alltagsphänomenologie der DDR," *Politische Vierteljahresschrift*, special issue 20/1989 *Politik und Gesellschaft in sozialistischer Ländern* (Opladen, 1989), 99–120.

41. Stefan Moses, "Farewell and Beginning: East German Portraits, 1989-1990," photographic exhibit organized by the German Historical Museum, Berlin, and exhibited at the Goethe Institute of Chicago, spring 1993.

42. Templin testimony to the twentieth session of the Bundestag's "Enquete-Kommission, 'Aufarbeitung von Geschichte und Folgen der SED-Diktatur in Deutschland,'" Protokolle 20, p. 65, now printed in Deutscher Bundestag, ed., *Materialien der Enquete-Kommission, "Aufarbeitung von Geschichte und Folgen der SED-Diktatur in Deutschland,"* 9 vols. in 18 (Frankfurt am Main: Suhrkamp, 1995), II, 1, pp. 122–131 and 146–150. Citation from p. 148.

43. For an "inside" account, see Peter Przybylski, *Tatort Politbüro: Die Akte Honecker* (Berlin: Rowohlt, 1991), pp. 101–116. Honecker's distress with ponytails recounted by Kurt Hager to James McAdams, Hoover Institution Oral History Project.

44. The act provoked a protest from thirteen leading authors, including Stephan Hermlin, Volker Braun, and Christa Wolf. Honecker himself monitored the massively orchestrated surveillance, demands for recantation, and exclusion from the Writers Union for those who refused to buckle. See Jüdersleben and Karlson, "'Es kommt keiner unterm Regen durch.'"

45. See his major address, "Hat Philosophie den modernen Naturwisssenschaften bei der Lösung ihrer Probleme geholfen?" in Robert Havemann, *Die Stimme des Gewissens* (Reinbek bei Hamburg: Rowohlt, 1990), pp. 45–46.

46. Christa Wolf, *Kindheitsmuster* (Berlin: Aufbau-Verlag, 1976), trans. Ursule Molinaro and Hedwig Rappolt as *A Model Childhood* (New York: Farrar, Straus, and Giroux, 1980); Günter de Bruyn, *Märkische Forschungen: Erzählung für Freunde der Literaturgeschichte* (Halle: Mitteldeutscher Verlag, 1978), and de Bruyn, *Neue Herrlichkeit: Roman* (Frankfurt am Main: Fischer, 1984); Christoph Hein, *Der fremde Freund* (Berlin-Weimar: Aufbau-Verlag, 1982), trans. Krishna Winston as *The Distant Lover* (New York: Pantheon, 1989).

47. See Timothy W. Ryback, *Rock around the Bloc: A History of Rock Music in Eastern Europe and the Soviet Union* (New York: Oxford University Press, 1990).

48. I am indebted to Raelynn Hillhouse for the story of FDJ discos. See also Egon Krenz's file on rock music in BA-SAPMO: IV 2/2.039/242.

49. For these controversies, see BA-SAPMO: Büro Kurt Hager, DY 30/39004: Ursula Ragwitz to Hager, May 29, 1984, on Olaf Leitner's book; the report of the Generaldirektion beim Komitee für Unterhaltungskunst, "Versuch einer Bestimmung der politischen Zielrichtungen des Buches 'Rockszene DDR' [Reinbeck bei Hamburg; Rowohlt Taschenbuch, Nov. 1983]," May 21, 1984. On the same committee's survey of GDR rock, see the confidential "Standpunkt zur Entwicklung der Rockmusik in der DDR"; and on the dispute over allowing foreign bands at the

scheduled New Year's Rock for Peace concert, see Peter Mayer to Hager, July 24, 1986; Ragwitz to Hager, cautiously supporting Mayer, Aug. 26: "All the participants feel themselves unable to change the current concept of the 'Rock for Peace' festival. . . .[But] in my opinion it would be good to reconsider whether we might correct the decision to make 'Rock for Peace' an exclusively national event." Finally, Kurt Hager to the Abteilung Kultur, Feb. 12, 1987: "Rock for Peace/accept proposal/ Condition: for 1987 Canada and Cuba/English group too [concerned with] internal politics."

50. On consumption patterns in the GDR and the effort to provide delicacies, see Gernot Schneider, *Wirtschaftswunder DDR. Anspruch und Realität*, 2nd ed. (Cologne: Bund-Verlag, 1990), pp. 117–141; also Bodo von Rüden, *Die Rolle der D-Mark in der DDR: Von der Nebenwährung zur Währungsunion* (Baden-Baden: Nomos-Verlag, 1991). I am aware that I move from a contrast of public and private to one of political and private; the regime would have conceded that the private realm was different from the political, but it would have found it more difficult to allow a public sphere that was outside the political.

51. For a survey, George C. Iggers, "New Directions in Historical Studies in the German Democratic Republic," *History and Theory* 28, 1 (Feb. 1989): 59–78.

52. Norbert Kapferer, "Die Psychologie der DDR im Spannungsfeld von politischer Functionalisierung und wissenschaftlicher Emanzipation," *Politische Vierteljahresschrift*, Special issue 20/1989, *Politik und Gesellschaft in sozialistischen Ländern* (Opladen, 1989): 77–98.

53. Ulrike Poppe, "Das kritische Potential der Gruppen in Kirche und Gesellschaft," in Detlef Pollack, ed., *Die Legitimität der Freiheit. Politisch alternative Gruppen in der DDR unter dem Dach der Kirchen* (Frankfurt am Main: Peter Lang, 1990), p. 63.

54. Glaeßner, "Von 'realen Sozialismus' zur Selbstbestimmung," p. 3.

55. For the concept of *Eigen-Sinn* and workplace autonomy see Alf Lüdtke, "'Helden der Arbeit'—Mühen beim Arbeiten. Zur mißmutigen Loyalität von Industriearbeitern in der DDR," in Hartmut Kaelble, Jürgen Kocka, and Hartmut Zwahr, eds., *Sozialgeschichte der DDR* (Stuttgart: Klett-Cotta, 1994), pp. 188–213. Cf. Mary Fulbrook, "Herrschaft, Gehorsam, Verweigerung—Die DDR als Diktatur," in Jürgen Kocka and Martin Sabrow, eds., *Die DDR als Geschichte: Fragen–Hypothesen–Perspektiven* (Berlin: Akademic Verlag, 1994), pp. 77–85; and Peter Hübner, *Konsens, Konflikt und Kompromiß: Soziale Arbeiterinteressen und Sozialpolitik in der SBZ/DDR 1945–1970* (Berlin: Akademie Verlag, 1995), pp. 239–43.

56. This pattern (as well as more outright informing) emerges from the huge documentation of Gerhard Besier and Stephan Wolf, eds., *"Pfarrer, Christen und Katholiken," Das Ministerium für Staatssicherheit der ehemaligen DDR und die Kirchen*, 2nd rev. ed. (Neukirchen-Vluyn: Neukirchener Verlag, 1992).

57. Ulrike Poppe, "Das kritische Potential der Gruppen in Kirche und Gesellschaft," p. 64.

58. Rudolf Bahro, *The Alternative in Eastern Europe*, trans. David Fernbach (London: New Left Books, 1978). Bahro was allowed to emigrate to the West after serving several months of a prison sentence imposed in 1978.

59. Torpey's dissertation, "Between Anti-Fascism and Opposition," explores this difference; cf. chapter 3, below, pp. 140ff.

60. BA-SAPMO: Büro Günter Mittag, DY 30/41797, Bd. 2: "Aktennotiz über ein Gespräch des Genossen Erich Honeckers mit Genossen Wadim Medwedjev . . . am 28.8.1988."

61. BA-SAPMO: Büro Egon Krenz, IV 2/2.039/70. Sitzung des Politbüros: "Bericht über den Besuch von . . . Jan Fojtik," Feb. 14, 1989.

62. Vaclav Havel, "The Power of the Powerless," in Havel et al., *The Power of the Powerless* (Armonk, NY: M. E. Sharpe, 1989), p. 27.

63. Fundamental for any discussion of the relation between state and society in the late GDR is Sigrid Meuschel, *Legitimation und Parteiherrschaft in der DDR. Zum Paradox von Stabilität und Revolution in der DDR 1945–1989* (Frankfurt am Main: Suhrkamp, 1992); section III, pp. 221–273, are of relevance for this discussion.

64. See Ehrhart Neubert's estimate that DDR citizens were organized 3.2 times over, i.e. that all mass organizations, parties, etc., claimed a membership of 50 million among a population of 16 million. *Enquete-Kommission, "Aufarbeitung von Geschichte und Folgen der SED-Diktatur in Deutschland,"* II, 1, pp. 115–122.

65. BA-SAPMO: Büro Günter Mittag, DY 30/41797, Bd. 2: "Aktennotiz über ein Gespräch mit Medwedjev. . .28.8.88."

66. Martin Diewald, " 'Kollektiv,' 'Vitamin B' und 'Nische': Stereotype persönliche Netzwerke in der DDR," in Johannes Huinink, Karl Ulrich Mayer et al., *Kollektiv und Eigensinn. Lebensverläufe in der DDR und danach* (Berlin: Akademie Verlag, 1995).

67. "Ein deutsches Familiendrama oder wie politisch ist das Private?" in Lutz Niethammer, Alexander von Plato, and Dorothee Wierling, *Die volkseigene Erfahrung* (Berlin: Rowohlt, 1991), pp. 529–530.

68. Manfred Jäger, "Das Wechselspiel von Selbstzensur und Literaturenkung in der DDR," in Ernest Wichner and Herbert Wiesner, eds., *"Literaturentwicklungsprozesse" Die Zensur der Literatur in der DDR* (Frankfurt am Main: Suhrkamp, 1993), pp. 18–49. The research of Siegfried Lokatis offers sophisticated insight into the actual functioning of the publication process. For the early period of the GDR, see Lokatis, "Verlagspolitik zwischen Plan und Zensur. Das 'Amt für Literatur und Verlagswesen' oder die schwere Geburt des Literaturapparates der DDR," in Kocka, *Historische DDR-Forschung*, pp. 303–326; also Lokatis "Dietz. Probleme der Ideolo-

giewirtschaft im zentralen Parteiverlag der SED," and "Wissenschaftler und Verleger in der DDR. Das Beispiel des Akademie Verlages," unpublished essays, Potsdam: Forschungsschwerpunkt für Zeithistorische Studien.

69. See Robert Darnton's revealing essay, "The Viewpoint of the Censor," *Berlin Journal, 1989–1990* (New York: Norton, 1991), pp. 202–217.

70. Christine Horn, "IRRGARTEN. Über Zensur und Staatssicherheit. Ein Gespräch mit Frauke Meyer-Gosau," *Text+Kritik*, no. 120 (October 1993): 36–47, citations from p. 39. For the interaction of the Stasi with the art and literary world, see Joachim Walther and Gesine von Rittwitz, "Mielke und die Musen: Die Organisation der Überwachung," in *Text+Kritik*, no. 120 (Oct. 1993): 74–88.

71. Cited by Jäger, in *Literaturentwicklungsprozesse*, p. 24. Cf. Manfred Jäger, *Kultur und Politik in der DDR: 1945–1990* (Cologne: Wissenschaft und Politik, 1995), pp. 167–169. See Jüdersleben and Karlson, " 'Es kommt keiner unterm Regen durch,' " for the 1976 admonitions of Wolf, Hermlin, and other authors.

72. See Joachim Walther et al., eds., *Protokoll eines Tribunals. Die Ausschlüsse aus dem DDR-Schriftstellerverband 1979* (Reinbek bei Hamburg: Rowohlt, 1991), for the extensive debate in the Writers Union as well as relevant correspondence (Heym quotation from p. 47).

73. Cited by Ulrike Poppe, "The Humiliated Elite of the Political System," paper for the conference on "The Responsibility of Intellectuals: State Security Services and Intellectual Life in the GDR: The Case of Sascha Anderson," organized by the Chicago Goethe Institute and the University of Chicago, Apr. 29–May 3, 1992. Publication forthcoming from the University of Chicago Press, Michael Geyer and Robert von Hallberg, eds. For the development of the Sascha Anderson case, which followed Wolf Biermann's harsh denunciation of the author as an informer (and which many of Anderson's friends initially found hard to credit), see the coverage in *Der Spiegel*: "Kulturnik 7423/91," in no. 43, Oct. 21, 1989, pp. 336–337; "Viehisches Gefecht," no. 44, Oct. 28, 1991, pp. 327–330; "Pegasus an der Stasi-Leine," no. 47, Nov. 18, 1991, pp. 276–280; the two-part essay by Jürgen Fuchs, "Landschaft der Lüge," in no. 47, Nov. 18, 1991, pp. 280–291 and in no. 48, Nov. 25, 1995, pp. 72–92; and "Der Verräter seiner Freunde," no. 50, Dec. 9. 1991, pp. 22–24. Also Wolf Biermann, "Tiefer als unter die Haut," no. 5, Jan. 27, 1992, pp. 180–185.

74. For this aspect, see the collection of testimonies by Wolf Biermann, Bärbel Bohley, Jürgen Fuchs, Lutz Rathenau, Vera Wollenberger, and others in Hans Joachim Schädlich, ed., *Aktenkundig* (Berlin: Rowohlt, 1992).

75. Karl Wilhelm Fricke, *MfS Intern. Macht, Strukturen, Auflösung der DDR-Staatssicherheit* (Cologne: Wissenschaft und Politik, 1991) pp. 21, 44. This is the best of the many general summaries of the Stasi.

76. This material is based on the papers and testimony to the University of Chicago conference, "The Responsibility of Intellectuals." Similar critical reflections and testimonies are collected in Peter Böthig and Klaus Michael, eds., *Macht-Spiele: Literatur und Staatssicherheit im Fokus Prenzlauer Berg* (Leipzig: Reklam Verlag, 1993). On the general issues concerning writers and the regime, see Manfred Jäger, *Literatur und Politik in der DDR*, 2nd ed. (Munich: Deutsche Verlags-Anstalt, 1995).

77. See the interview with Christa Wolf by Todd Gitlin, "'I Did Not Imagine That I Lived in Truth,'" *New York Times Book Review*, Apr. 4, 1993, p. 1. On Wolf and the Stasi, cf. the penetrating comments by Manfred Jäger, "Auskünfte: Heiner Müller und Christa Wolf zu Stasi-Kontakten," *Deutschland Archiv* 26, 2 (Feb. 1993): 142–146.

78. Marko Marin, "'Geschaffene Machwerke,' Die Sprache der Stasi," *Text+Kritik*, no. 120 (Oct. 1993): 48–56.

79. "Auch mir wird ja unterstellt, daß ich Morde geplant hätte . . ." [interview with Major Glewe, 43], in Olaf Georg Klein, *Plötzlich war alles ganz anders: Deutsche Lebenswege im Umbruch* (Cologne: Kippenheur & Witsch, 1994), p. 84.

80. See Frauke Meyer-Gosau, "Hinhaltender Gehorsam. DDR-Schriftseller über ihre Kooperation mit der Staatssicherheit," *Text+Kritik*, 120 (Oct. 1993): 103–115.

81. Klaus Michael, "'Die Stasi ist kein Thema mehr.' Strategien der unabhängingen Literatur im Umgang mit der Macht," University of Chicago Conference, "The Responsibility of Intellectuals." Cf. Klaus Michael, "Samisdat-Literatur in der DDR und der Einfluß der Staatssicherheit," *Deutschland Archiv*, vol. 26, 11 (Nov. 1993): 1255–1265.

82. Besier and Wolf, *Pfarrer, Christen und Katholiken*, pp. 56–60.

83. Havemann, *Die Stimme des Gewissens*, p. 149.

84. Seweryn Bialer explores these issues in *Stalin's Successors, Leadership, Stability, and Change in the Soviet Union* (Cambridge: Cambridge University Press, 1980), pp. 183–205.

85. Cf. Meuschel's contrast of the regime's claims for legitimacy—resting on economic innovation or antifascism—with a normative notion of legitimacy based on human rights, which she denies to one-party regimes: *Legitimation und Parteiherrschaft in der DDR*, pp. 22–29. Discussions of legitimacy usually go back to Weber; I have tried here just to sort out some of the overlapping criteria ordinary usage seems to presuppose.

86. J. P. Nettl, *The Eastern Zone and Soviet Policy in Germany, 1945–50* (London: Oxford University Press, 1951), pp. 304, 314.

87. Bertolt Brecht, *Briefe*, ed. Günter Glaeser, 2 vols. (Frankfurt am Main: Suhrkamp, 1981), 1: 693–694.

88. Lutz Niethammer has focused particularly on this strategic generation in his recent GDR oral history interviews (1987–88). See Niethammer et al., *Die Volkseigene Erfahrung*. For a rich sociological investigation of different generations' life experience in the GDR (and since), see Huinink, Mayer, et al., *Kollektiv und Eigensinn*.

89. On antifascism as ideology, see Werkentin, *Politische Strafjustiz in der Ära Ulbricht*, pp. 168–173; Meuschel, *Legitimation und Parteiherrschaft in der DDR*, pp. 29–41; also Wilfried Schubarth, Ronald Pschierer, and Thomas Schmidt, "Verordneter Antifaschismus und die Folgen: Das Dilemma antifaschistischer Erziehung am Ende der DDR," documenting the counter-productive effect by the end, and Hans Helmuth Knütter, "Antifaschismus und politische Kultur in Deutschland nach der Wiedervereinigung," both in *Aus Politik und Zeitgeschichte* B 9/91 (Feb. 22, 1991): 9–16 and 17–23. The ideology also prevented the regime from recognizing that by the 1980s it had a significant skinhead problem of its own.

90. Cf. Jon Elster, *Ulysses and the Sirens: Studies in Rationality and Irrationality*, rev. ed. (Cambridge: Cambridge University Press, 1984).

91. The generalization must be modified for the Soviet Union, where the regime also had a domestic revolutionary legacy (no matter how brutal) and the credit for victory in the Second World War.

92. See "Enquete-Kommission, 'Aufarbeitung von Geschichte und Folgen der SED-Diktatur in Deutschland,'" Protokolle 20, p. 17, now in the published edition, II, 1, p. 124. Cf. Erhart Norbert's analysis of "Adjustment or Refusal" (Anpassung oder Verweigerung) as a spectrum of GDR civic stances, presented in the same discussion of the Enquete-Kommission, pp. 115–122.

93. The extensive political science literature on "transitions to democracy" is better at analyzing the process of democratization than at proposing underlying causes. Until the recent upheavals in Eastern Europe, these studies all focused on Southern Europe and Latin America. Occasional comparisons were made with the dismantling of Italian fascism or the introduction of democracy in West Germany in the late 1940s. See Guillermo O'Donnell, Philippe C. Schmitter, and Laurence Whitehead, eds., *Transitions from Authoritarian Rule: Prospects for Democracy* (Washington: Woodrow Wilson Center for Scholars, and Baltimore: Johns Hopkins University Press, 1986).

94. The late Tim Mason made this point about the Nazis during the conference "Reevaluating the Third Reich," Philadelphia, April 1988. (Papers but not discussion are published in Thomas Childers and Jane Caplan, eds., *Reevaluating the Third Reich* [New York: Holmes and Meier, 1993].) Mason's point can be usefully generalized to Stalinist regimes as well.

CHAPTER 2

1. BA: Potsdam: DC 20 I/3/2861, Bl. 89: 112: Sitzung des Ministerrats vom 19. Okt. 1989, Anlage 3: "Niederschrift über die inhaltliche Wiedergabe der Diskussionsbeiträge der Mitglieder des Ministerrats."

2. BA: Potsdam/Berlin: Akten der Plankommission, DE 1/56320: "Analyse der Lage der DDR mit Schlußfolgerungen," Oct. 30, 1989. Also in Stiftung Archiv der Parteien und Massenorganisationen der DDR, Berlin (henceforth: BA-SAPMO): J IV 2/2/2356: Akten des Politbüros, Protokoll Nr. 47 der Sitzung des Politbüros des Zentralkomites der SED vom 31. Oktober 1989, Anlage Nr. 4. (Henceforth, abbreviated dating and citation will be used for archival documents.) Schürer presented a somewhat fuller version to the Central Committee Executive on November 10, BA-SAPMO: IV/2/1/709. For the background of the report, commissioned for the Politbüro by Egon Krenz on October 24 (supposedly to have the truth without "cosmetic"), see Hans-Hermann Hertle, "Staatsbankrott. Der ökonomische Untergang des SED-Staates," *Deutschland Archiv* 25, 10 (Oct. 1992): 1019–1030, and the accompanying interview with Schürer, pp. 1031–1039; Maria Haendke-Hoppe-Arndt, "Wer wußte was? Der ökonomische Niedergang der DDR," *Deutschland Archiv* 28, 5 (May 1995): 588–602. Assisting with the report were the trade minister, Gerhard Beil, the finance minister, Ernst Höfner, the director of the Central Statistical Administration, Arno Donda, and that éminence grise of special deals with the West, Alexander Schalck-Golodkowski, who served as director of the Division of Commercial Coordination in the Foreign Trade Ministry and as special commissioner for the Ministry of State Security. See also this group's estimate of the foreign debt burden to non-socialist creditors, "Prognose über die Bewegung und Beherrschbarkeit der DDR Schulden von 1989 bis 1995 . . .," in Peter Przybilski, *Tatort Politbüro Band 2: Honecker, Mittag, und Schalck-Golodkowski* (Berlin: Rowohlt, 1992), pp. 358–363. On the concept of a "valuta mark," see Ernst Höfner, "Zur Problematik: Was ist notwendig, damit die Mark der DDR auf dem Weltmarkt eine Valutamark wird?" Sept. 13, 1988, in BA: Potsdam/Berlin: DE 1/56318. At this time the valuta mark corresponded to a value of about 4.3 East German marks. An East German salary of 2,000 marks per month would have brought a purchasing power of approximately 500 deutsche marks in the West. At the beginning of May 1989 commercial payments were made at the rate of 1.88 valuta marks per dollar. See Vienna Institute for Comparative Economic Studies, ed., *COMECON Data, 1989* (London: Macmillan, 1990), p. 381. The figures for the current account deficit were provided by Krenz to Gorbachev on November 1. See BA: Potsdam/Berlin: DE1/

56320: Niederschrift des Gespräches des Gen[ossen]. Egon Krenz . . . mit Gen. Mikhail Gorbatschow . . . am 1.11.1989 in Moskau."

3. BA-SAPMO: IV 2/1/708: Ehrensperger statement in Ninth Meeting of the Central Committee, Nov. 9, 1989.

4. BA: Potsdam/Berlin: DE 1/56320. See also note 2 and Hans-Hermann Hertle, "Der Weg in den Bankrott der DDR-Wirtschaft. Das Scheitern der 'Einheit von Wirtschafts- und Sozialpolitik' am Beispiel der Schürer/Mittag-Kontroverse im Politbüro 1988," *Deutschland Archiv* 25, 2 (Feb. 1992): 127–131, the attached interview with Schürer by Hertle, pp. 131–142, and the television transcript of Schürer's interview with Fritz Schenk, Sept. 24, 1991, pp. 143–145.

5. BA: Potsdam/Berlin: DE 1/56320. "Warum wurde die Höhe unserer Verschuldung bisher nicht veröffentlicht?" Schürer differentiated among $20 billion of obligations: half of it had been used to import capital goods for the chemical, refining, furniture industries, etc., that would ultimately strengthen the DDR's export capacity, but half had gone for grain imports, which the West would not want to refinance. BA-SAPMO: Berlin: J IV/2/1/709.

6. The yield had not risen significantly during the latter half of the 1980s; at about 65–75 million valuta marks annually it did not significantly offset growing indebtedness. See the weekly figures collected by division HA XVIII of the Stasi, in Bundesbeauftragte für die Unterlagen des Staatssicherheitsdienstes der ehemaligen DDR [Gauck-Behörde]: MfS: ZAIG/3424, and ZAIG/3729.

7. BA: Potsdam/Berlin: DE 1/56346. Schürer to Modrow, Dec. 15, 1989, with memo to prepare him for talks with the Soviets: "Zur ökonomischen Lage der DDR und zur ökonomischen Zusammenarbeit mit der UdSSR." East German statistics included an overall "accumulation" rate, and a rate for "productive" investment (i.e., excluding housing and social investments).

8. Heinrich Potthof, *"Die Koalition der Vernunft": Deutschlandpolitik in den 80er Jahren* (Munich: Deutscher Taschenbuch Verlag, 1984), pp. 19–21.

9. For the two-thirds national income estimate, see Schürer to Modrow, Dec. 15, 1989, as cited, note 7. For the burden of the debt service in terms of exports see "Analyse der ökonomischen Lage der DDR mit Schlußfolgerungen," and for general background see the CIA study, "Eastern Europe Faces Up to the Debt Crisis," in Joint Economic Committee of the Congress of the United States, *East European Economics: Slow Growth in the 1980's* (Washington, D.C.: U.S. Government Printing Office, 1986), 2: 151–185.

10. See the warnings of Pal Ivanyi, the Hungarian delegate, against imposing compulsory decisions on individual members. BA-SAPMO: Büro Günter Mittag: DY 30/J NL23/19: "Stenographische Niederschrift der Beratung der Sekretäre für Wirtschaft der Zentralkomitees kommunistischer-und Arbeiterparteien der Mitglie-

derländer des RGW in Berlin," June 6, 1989 (RGW = Rat für Gegenwärtige Wirtschaftskooperation = CMEA).

11. For recent clear explanations, see Randall Warren Stone, "Pursuit of Interest: The Politics of Subsidized Trade in the Soviet Bloc" (Ph.D. dissertation, Harvard University, 1993), chap. 2 (a revised version of the dissertation, which is based on extraordinary documentation and interviews, has now been issued as *Satellites and Commissars: Strategy and Conflict in the Politics of Soviet-Bloc Trade* [Princeton: Princeton University Press, 1996]); also with respect to one Soviet partner: Gabor Oblath and David Tarr, "The Terms-of-Trade Effects from the Elimination of State Trading in Soviet-Hungarian Trade," *Journal of Comparative Economics* 16 (1992): 75–93. For a résumé of the controversies over size of the subsidy, see Vlad Sobell, *The CMEA in Crisis: Toward a New European Order?* (New York: Center for Strategic and International Studies, and Praeger Publishers, 1990), pp. 12–20. See also Michael Marrese and Jan Vanous, *Soviet Subsidization of Trade with Eastern Europe— A Soviet Perspective* (Berkeley: University of California Press, 1983), and Keith Crane, *The Soviet Economic Dilemma in Eastern Europe* (Santa Monica, CA: RAND, 1986); Raymond Dietz, "Advantages and Disadvantages in Soviet Trade with Eastern Europe: The Pricing Dimension," in Joint Economic Committee, *East European Economies: Slow Growth in the 1980's,* 2: 263–301. For an alternative view that sees East Europeans as facing real opportunity costs from rising Soviet oil prices after 1982, see Friedrich Levcik, "Hat die Wirtschaft Osteuropas Zukunft?" in Hans-Hermann Hohmann and Heinrich Vogel, eds., *Osteuropas Wirtschaftsprobleme und die Ost-West Beziehungen* (Baden-Baden: Nomos, 1984), pp. 45–50. For the terms of trade (export-import price indices: 1970 = 81, 1980 = 100, 1985 = 124, 1988 = 109), see *COMECON DATA, 1989,* p. 201.

12. Institute for the Economy of the World Socialist System, Moscow, briefing paper, cited by Stone, "Pursuit of Interest," pp. 306–307 and n. 1. The transferable ruble during the 1980s was assigned a dollar value that went from about $1.40 to $1.25.

13. Stone, "Pursuit of Interest," pp. 327–328.

14. Kleiber and Jozsepf Marjai both cited from the CMEA stenogram, June 4–5, 1987, by Stone, "Pursuit of Interest," pp. 320–322. As Stone explains, the East Germans were more preoccupied by the relaxation of trade quotas and the fear that the Soviets might import Western machinery than by the currency issue; they too looked toward approaching convertibility, provided they could continue to be the chief provider of machine tools.

15. BA-SAPMO: Büro Günter Mittag, DY 30/41796, Bd. 3: Ernst Höfner and Horst Kaminsky, "Stellungnahme zur inoffiziellen Material sowjetischer Experten zu Fragen der Weiterentwicklung und Neugestaltung der Valuta-, Finanz-, Kredit-, und Verrech-

nungsbeziehungen zwischen den Mitgliedsländern des RGWs," Berlin, Jan. 15, 1987. With this memo, Kaminsky sent Mittag a translation of materials that he had been given in Moscow by Borissov, deputy minister for finance, and Ivanov, president of the Foreign Trade Bank of the Soviet Union: "Die Vervollkommung des Kreditsystems des RGWs, einschließlich der Tätigkeit der kollektiven Banken des RGWs."

16. BA-SAPMO: Büro Günter Mittag. DY 30/41796, Bd. 2: "Vermerk über das Arbeitsgespräch des Vorsitzenden des Ministerrates der DDR, W. Stoph, mit dem Vorsitzenden des Ministerrates der UdSSR, N. Ryshkov am 28.5. 1987 im Palast-Hotel in Berlin," Berlin, May 29, 1987. The East Germans repeated their plea for restoration of the pre-1981 oil allocation a month later. See ibid., "Protokoll über die Beratungen der Partei- und Regierungsdelegation der DDR und der UdSSR," Moscow, June 22, 1987. For the 1981 oil cutback, see Haendke-Hoppe-Arndt, "Wer wußte was? Der ökonomische Niedergang der DDR," esp. pp. 592–593.

17. BA-SAPMO: Büro Günter Mittag, DY 30/41797, Bd. 2: Schürer, "Information über Gespräche mit dem Vorsitzenden des Staatlichen Planungskomitees der UdSSR, J. D. Masljukow," Prague, July 7, 1988. The statistics on the volume of Soviet-GDR trade and the value of gas and oil products to the nonsocialist world are from BA-Potsdam/Berlin: DE-1/56318: "Volkswirtschaftliche Berechnungen zum Warenaustausch DDR/UdSSR" and "Programm zur Ablösung von Heizöl zur tieferen Spaltung von Erdöl," undated.

18. COMECON Data, 1989, pp. 179–200, for overall and regional export totals in local currencies (or in the foreign exchange units used for international commercial transactions). This source, p. 382, provides the monthly dollar exchange rates, which I have averaged for 1988 as follows: 1.75 valuta marks, 50 forints, 5.2 crowns (kcs), and 475 złoty. To be sure the valuta mark was artificially high in terms of the dollar. Forints and złoty were quasi-convertible by 1988, so the East German trade probably lay between the Czech and the official total. Total East German exports in millions of valuta marks were as follows: 1985: 93.5; 1986: 91.5; 1987: 89.9; 1988: 90.2. On the Complex Program, see BA-SAPMO: Büro Günter Mittag, DY 30/41796, Bd. 1: Minister für Wissenschaft und Technik, Berlin,"Beratungsmaterial über die Durchführung des RGW-Komplexprogramms des wissenschaftlich-technischen Fortschritts," Dec. 29, 1987.

19. BA-SAPMO, Büro Günter Mittag, DY 30/41807, Bd. 2: unidentified essay on DDR social and economic policy and "Bilanz der engen Zusammenarbeit in Wissenschaft, Technik und Ökonomie zwischen der DDR und der UdSSR."

20. Jürgen Stehn and Holger Schmieding, "Spezialisierungsmuster und Wettbewerbsfähigkeit: Eine Bestandsaufnahme des DDR-Aussenhandels," Die Weltwirtschaft, no. 1 (1990): 71, and Harry Maier and Siegrid Maier, "Möglichkeiten einer Intensivierung des innerdeutschen Handels," Deutschland Archiv 22, 2 (Feb.

1989): 186–187, both cited in Ulrich Voskamp and Volker Wittke, "Industrial Restructuring in the Former German Democratic Republic (GDR): Barriers to Adaptive Reform Become Downward Development Spirals," *Politics and Society* 19, 3 (Sept. 1991): 341–371 (p. 351).

21. BA-SAPMO: Büro Egon Krenz, IV 2/2.039/291: "Bericht über die 44. Tagung des RGWs, Prag, 5.–7. Juli, 1987." First Ryzhkov speech, and Willi Stoph speech. (Two further Ryzhkov speeches are included in the file. The second called for eventual establishment of meaningful exchange rates between RGW currencies, the transferable ruble, and Western currencies. The third complained that the CMEA nations used 1.4 times as much energy per unit of national output as the European Community countries consumed about 1.6 times as much material and operated at about half the labor productivity.) The Complex Program was a five-year CMEA agreement for high-technology cooperation in microelectronics, automated production, nuclear energy, and biotechnology. See Ministerium für Wissenschaft und Technik, "Beratungsmaterial über die Durchführung des RGW-Komplexprogramms des wissenschaftlich-technischen Fortschritts," Dec. 29, 1987, included in BA-SAPMO: Büro Günter Mittag, DY 30/41796, Bd. 1. On the difficulties for Soviet-GDR economic cooperation, cf. Wjatscheslaw Kotschemassow, *Meine letzte Mission. Fakten, Erinnerungen, Überlegungen* (Berlin: Dietz Verlag, 1994), pp. 78–87.

22. BA-SAPMO: Büro Günter Mittag, DY 30/41807, Bd 1: "Zu den Ergebnissen der Gespräche mit Sljunkow," undated memo, filed along with the reports cited in note 23 below.

23. BA-SAPMO: Büro Günter Mittag, DY 30/41807, Bd. 1: "Interne Niederschrift über das Gespräch Günter Mittag mit Gen. Sljunkow am 25. Januar 1989." For the February discussions, see ibid., Abteilung Planung und Finanzen, Berlin 10. Feb. 1989. "Information über die Atmosphäre anläßlich der Beratung des Gen. Schürer mit . . . Gen. Masljukov." The pleas for secrecy came at the end of both discussions; the quotation is from January 25. See also "Information" for the "Kleiner Kreis," Jan. 25, 1989, with earlier undated material.

24. BA-SAPMO: Büro Egon Krenz, IV 2/2.039/70: Politbüro Sitzung, Feb. 21, 1989.

25. Stone, "Pursuit of Interest," pp. 314–315.

26. W. I. Shimko's intervention, in BA-SAPMO: Büro Günter Mittag, DY 30/J NL 23/19: "Stenographische Niederschrift der Beratung der Sekretäre für Wirtschaft der Zentralkomitees kommunistischer- und Arbeiterparteien der Mitgliederländer des RGWs in Berlin, 6. Juni 1989."

27. Schürer's figures on subsidies, which amounted to an average compounded increase of 7 percent per year vs. 3 to 4 percent for national income growth (he admitted that the published 4 percent average was too optimistic), in BA-SAPMO: IV

2/1/709: Stenographische Niederschrift der 10. Tagung des Zentralkomitees der SED, Nov. 10, 1989.

28. BA-SAPMO: IV 2/1/709: Schürer testimony. For the "small circle," see Hertle's interview with Schürer, "Der Weg in den Bankrott der DDR Wirtschaft," *Deutschland Archiv* 25, 2 (Feb. 1992): p. 133. Participants generally included Politbüro members with economic responsibilities, but the committee was advisory and not an official organ. The other critical but unofficial body was the committee on balance-of-payment questions.

29. BA-SAPMO: IV 2/1/709: Schürer testimony.

30. BA-SAPMO: IV 2/1/708: Ehrensperger testimony ("Wenn es so wäre, müßten wir aufhören").

31. BA: Potsdam/Berlin: DE 1/56319: Schürer to Honecker, Apr. 26, 1988. On the controversy, see Hertle, "Der Weg in den Bankrott der DDR-Wirtschaft," and the attached "Gespräch mit Gerhard Schürer." See also the corroborative testimony of Werner Krolikowski, Jan. 16, 1990, as well as earlier critical reports on the economy (for Soviet "friends") of Dec. 16, 1980, and Mar. 30, 1983, reproduced in Peter Przybilski, *Tatort Politbüro: Die Akte Honecker* (Berlin: Rowohlt, 1991), pp. 321–356. Krolikowski became an embittered critic of Honecker and Mittag.

32. BA: Potsdam/Berlin: DE 1/56319: Mittag "Vorlage für das Politbüro des Zentralkomitees der SED," Anlage, May 4, 1988.

33. BA-SAPMO: IV 2/1/709.

34. MfS: Berlin: ZAIG/5252: unsigned report for the Minister: "Hinweise zum Stand der Arbeit an der Staatlichen Aufgabe 1989 und einigen sich dabei abzeichnenden Problemen," June 7, 1988. Hauptabteilung (HA Division) XVIII of the MfS included over 600 agents, whose main task was industrial espionage and procurement of embargoed items. But it also reported on the currents of opinion among Kombinate leaders, monitored border-crossing statistics, and in general developed an independent capacity for evaluation of economic intelligence. Unit HA XVIII/4 was responsible for monitoring the central GDR economic organs, including the Plan Commission, Finance Ministry, and the State Bank. On the activities of HA XVIII, see Haendke-Hoppe-Arndt, "Wer wußte was? Der ökonomische Niedergang der DDR," pp. 594–601; see also the interview with Horst R[oigk], leader of HA XVIII/4 in Gisela Karau, *Stasiprotokolle. Gespräche mit ehemaligen Mitarbeitern des 'Ministerium für Staatssicherheit' der DDR* (Frankfurt am Main: dipa-Verlag, 1992), pp. 20–34.

35. BA: Potsdam/Berlin: DE 1/56318: "Arbeitsniederschrift über eine Beratung beim General Sekretär des Zentralkomitees der SED . . . 6.Sept.1988." Honecker's mind wandered; he also pointed out that the Leipzig Zoo had grown threefold in the 1970s while the price of entry remained the same. On the 1981 curtailment of Soviet oil supplies, see note 16.

36. BA-SAPMO: Büro Günter Mittag, DY 30/41797, Bd. 2: "Aktennotiz über ein Gespräch des Gen. Erich Honecker m. Gen. Wadim Medwedjew . . . am 28.8.88."

37. See note 2. The chief of the Stasi division that monitored state economic performance agreed. See the interview with Roigk in Karau, *Stasiprotokolle*, p. 27.

38. BA: Berlin: DE 1/56319: "Überlegungen zur weiteren Arbeit am Volkswirtschaftsplan 1989 und darüber hinaus," Apr. 26, 1988. According to Harry Maier, an economic expert who fled to the West in 1987, East Germany devoted about 35 percent of its industrial investments, or 14 billion marks, to the electronics sector in the 1980s and the efforts of 120,000 scientists, engineers, and workers—but with meager results. See "Die Innovationstragfähigkeit der Planwirtschaft in der DDR—Ursachen und Folgen," *Deutschland Archiv* 26, 7 (July 1993): 807–818.

39. BA: Berlin: DE 1/56346: Information über ein Gespräch mit dem Minister für Schwermaschinen und Anlagenbau, Gen. Dr. Lauck, Sept. 13, 1989. I am grateful to Jörg Roesler for information on the CAD sector.

40. Ibid, with Schürer's recommendation for the acceleration of microelectronic applications. Also BA: Potsdam/Berlin: DE 1/56319: "Überlegungen zur weiteren Arbeit am Volkswirtschaftsplan 1989 und darüber hinaus." Also DE 1/56343: Schürer to Mittag with "Einschätzung möglicher Auswirkungen aus Veränderungen der Preisbildung und der Zahlungsbedingungen . . ." Mar. 13, 1989.

41. BA: Potsdam: DC 20 I/4/6532: Minister für Wissenschaft und Technik und Minister der Staatlichen Plankommission, "Automisierung der Konstruktion im Maschinenbau," Nov. 2, 1989. For a relatively optimistic Western assessment of GDR computer capacities, which compared Robotron's freedom to act with a Western corporation, see Seymour E. Goodman, "The Partial Integration of the CEMA [sic] Computer Industries: An Overview," in Joint Economic Committee, *East European Economies: Slow Growth in the 1980's*, 2:329–354. For Schürer's defense of computers as the "key industry," BA: Potsdam: DC 20 I/3/2861, Anlage 3.

42. MfS: Berlin: ZAIG/5252, June 7, 1988.

43. Schürer's evaluation in BA: Potsdam DC 20 I/3/2861. "Niederschrift und die inhaltliche Wiedergabe der Diskussionsbeiträge der Mitlieder des Ministerrats," Sitzung 112, Oct. 19, 1989, p. 46. (This uncorrected protocol followed the official record of the meeting; except for the transcripts of Ministerpräsident Stoph provided in the protocols, it is the only verbatim transcript I have found.) For Jarowinski's analysis, see BA-SAPMO: IV 2/1/709.

44. BA-SAPMO: IV 2/1/709.

45. BA: Potsdam/Berlin: DE 1/56343: "Einschätzung möglicher Auswirkungen aus Veränderung der Preisbildung und der Zahlungsbedingungen im Handel mit der UdSSR in den Jahren 1991 bis 1995 gegenüber dem Fünfjahrplanansatz," Mar. 13, 1990.

46. For handicaps to the computer industry, see Voskamp and Wittke, "Industrial Restructuring in the Former German Democratic Republic (GDR)," which in turn draws upon the unpublished reports of the Zentralinstitut für Wirtschaftsforschung der Akademie der Wissenschaften in Berlin. In one respect, the authors' critique seems misplaced: the GDR did not develop its industry just for home needs, but to take advantage of intrabloc export possibilities. I am also not certain that the East German difficulty derived from its unwieldy *Kombinate* as compared with the now legendary flexibility of American software and hardware producers. Firms were linked with university centers of research; the results might have been less inflexible than conventionally depicted.

47. Discussion of the Walkman by Günter Kleiber in BA: Potsdam: DC 20 I/3: 2861: "Niederschrift und die inhaltliche Wiedergabe der Diskussionsbeiträge der Mitglieder des Ministerrats," Sitzung 112: Oct. 19, 1989, p. 56.

48. BA: Potsdam: DC 20 I/3/2661: 112. Sitzung des Ministerrats, 19. Oct. 1989, p. 22.

49. MfS: Berlin: ZAIG/5233.

50. BA: Potsdam: C 20 I/3/2874. VV b2–948/89, "Beschluß zur Information über die Bauindustrie," Nov. 30, 1989.

51. MfS: Berlin: ZAIG/3605: "Information über Reaktionen der Bevölkerung der DDR zu Problemen des Handels und der Versorgung," Sept. 14, 1987.

52. In general see Jörg Roesler, "The Rise and Fall of the Planned Economy in the German Democratic Republic, 1945–89," *German History* 9, 1 (1991): 46–51, citing K. C. Thalheim, *Die wirtschaftliche Entwicklung der beiden Staaten in Deutschland,* 3rd expanded ed. (Opladen: Leske + Budrich, 1988). Schürer's own estimate was that in the GDR labor productivity was about 60 percent of the FRG's.

53. BA: Potsdam/Berlin: DE 1/56346: "Information über ein Gespräch mit dem Minister für Schwermaschinen- und Anlagenbau, Genossen Dr. Lauch," Sept. 13, 1989.

54. BA: Potsdam: DC 20: I/3/2873. VV b2-b5–120/89: "Beschluß zur Information . . . über den Staatshaushaltplan 1990."

55. For a vivid and well-informed account of GDR economic decline that stresses Mittag's nefarious influence, see Prybylski, *Tatort Politbüro Band 2*; and for an excellent study that focuses on long-run institutional failings see Jeffrey Kopstein, *The Politics of Economic Decline in East Germany, 1945–1989* (Chapel Hill: University of North Carolina Press, 1996). For Günter Mittag's own memoir, see *Um jeden Preis: im Spannungsfeld zweier Systeme* (Berlin: Aufbau Verlag, 1991).

56. BA: Potsdam: DC 20 I/4/6530: Vertrauliche Verschlußsache V1199/89: "Kurzinformation zu Fragen der planmäßigen Versorgung der Bevölkerung." Of the

221,000 pairs of jeans most recently shipped from Hong Kong, 48,000 were defective and had to be replaced.

57. "In der Verteilung sind wir Spitze." BA: Potsdam/Berlin: DE 1/56318: "Arbeitsniederschrift über eine Beratung beim Generalsekretär des ZK der SED, Gen. Erich Honecker . . .," Sept. 6, 1988. What the regime designated as funds for consumption increased at the expense of funds for capital equipment. See BA-SAPMO: IV 2/1/709; Stenographische Niederschrift der 10. Tagung des Zentralkomitees der SED, Nov. 10, 1989.

58. *New York Times*, Jan. 15, 1990, p. A9.

59. BA-SAPMO: Büro Günter Mittag, DY 30/41713: "Information Nr. 14/89 des Komitees der ABI" (Arbeiter- und Bauerninspektion), Apr. 20, 1989.

60. BA-SAPMO: Büro Werner Jarowinsky, DY 30/41853, Bd. 1: "Bericht zur Arbeit mit den Warenbeständen im Konsumgüterbinnenhandel" (undated but reporting up to July 31, 1988); and Bd. 2: "Bericht über die Kontrolle zur Sicherung eines hohen Niveaus in der gastronomischen Versorgung der Bevölkerung," Aug. 8, 1989.

61. BA: Potsdam: DC 20 I/3/2861: "Niederschrift und die inhaltliche Wiedergabe der Diskussionsbeiträge der Mitglieder des Ministerrats," Sitzung 112, Oct. 19, 1989, p. 56–58.

62. BA-SAPMO: Büro Werner Jarowinski, DY 30/41853, Bd. 2: Komitee der ABI, Inspektion Aussenhandel: "Kontrollbericht zur Realisierung des Anlagenexportvertrages des AHB TAKRAF Export-Import . . .," June 28, 1988. The overall project was originally valued at DM 50.5 (about $20 million).

63. Janos Kornai, *The Socialist System: The Political Economy of Communism* (Princeton: Princeton University Press, 1992).

64. BA: Potsdam/Berlin: DE 1/56346: Schürer to Modrow, Dec. 15, 1989. Also DE 1/56320: "Analyse der Lage der DDR mit Schlußfolgerungen," Oct. 30, 1989. Harry Maier also dates the serious decline from the 1970s, and attributes the systemic crisis to the failure to keep up in the new high-tech and electronic sectors—and this despite R & D expenditure that was roughly equal in percentage terms to West Germany's. See Maier, "Die Innovationsträgheit der Planwirtschaft in der DDR," esp. p. 813.

65. For some of the many diagnoses: James M. Buchanan and Richard E. Wagner, *Democracy in Deficit: The Political Legacy of Lord Keynes* (New York: Academic Press, 1977); Samuel Brittan, *The Economic Consequences of Democracy* (London: Temple Smith, 1977); Assar Lindbeck, "Stabilization Policy in Open Economies with Endogenous Politicians," *American Economic Review* 66 (May 1976 [*Papers and Procedings* 1975]): 1–19; E. J. Mishan, "The New Inflation in Theory and Practice," *Encounter* 42 (May 1974): 12–24; William D. Nordhaus, "The Political Business

Cycle," *Review of Economic Studies* 42 (Apr. 1975): 169–90. For contemporary critiques of capitalism from a more "left" orientation, see Charles E. Lindblom, *Politics and Markets: The World's Political Economic Systems* (New York: Basic Books, 1977); also Fred Hirsch, *Social Limits to Growth* (Cambridge, MA: Harvard University Press, 1976).

66. Michael Marrese and Jan Vanous, *Soviet Subsidization of Trade with Eastern Europe* (Berkeley: University of California Institute of International Relations and University of California Press, 1983).

67. For the formidable problems, see Paul Marer, *Dollar GNPs of the U.S.S.R. and Eastern Europe* (Baltimore: Johns Hopkins University Press and World Bank, 1985).

68. Comparisons are difficult because of different national income conventions, but the UN statistics are adjusted to include services in the East European accounts. (Inclusion of the Soviet Union would have brought the East bloc to 7 percent per year.) For a discussion of the Czech performance and the problems of measurement, see Peter Havlik and Friedrich Levcik, *The Gross Domestic Product of Czechoslovakia, 1970–1980*, World Bank Staff Working Papers, no. 772 (Washington, DC: World Bank, 1985). The estimates of annual rates of growth for 1970–80 were 4.7 percent in official NMP terms, but only 1.0 to 1.7 percent in real GDP terms. See pp. 37, 76 (table 18).

69. Cf. W. Brus, "Postwar Reconstruction and Socio-Economic Transformation," in M. C. Kaser and E. A. Radice, eds., *The Economic History of Eastern Europe, 1919–1975*, vol. 2: *Interwar Policy, the War, and Reconstruction* (Oxford: Clarendon, 1986), pp. 564–643.

70. Irwin L. Collier, "Effective Purchasing Power in a Quantity Constrained Economy: An Estimate for the German Democratic Republic," *Review of Economics and Statistics* 68, 1 (Feb. 1986): 24–32. For the general problem, see Kornai, *Socialist System*, pp. 228–261.

71. Irwin L. Collier, "The Measurement and Interpretation of Real Consumption and Purchasing Power Parity for a Quantity Constrained Economy: The Case of East and West Germany," *Economica* 56 (Feb. 1989): 109–120; Kornai, *Socialist System*, pp. 229–240. Of course, neither Western nor Eastern statistics suggested the equally important disappointments produced in both systems by having to settle for undesired jobs. Classical economic theory implies most work has a homogeneous disutility (exceptions made for hazardous or physically exhausting employment) that wages must compensate, a vast oversimplification. The economic analysis of consumer frustration is more advanced than the economics of blighted career hopes.

72. Philip J. Bryson and Manfred Melzer, *The End of the East German Economy: From Honecker to Reunification* (New York: St. Martin's Press, 1991), pp. 87–88.

Fixed assets per worker were almost as high in the DDR as in the FRG, but the productivity of labor and capital were about half as high. Seventy-three percent of capital stock in mining, energy, and manufacturing sectors was over five years old. Cf. Kornai, *Socialist System*, pp. 292–301.

73. See Harriet Friedman, "Warsaw Pact Socialism and NATO Capitalism: Disintegrating Blocs, 1973–89," paper presented at the conference "Rethinking the Cold War," University of Wisconsin, Madison, Oct. 18–20, 1991.

74. For emphasis on human losses throughout the Soviet period, see Grigorii Khanin, "Economic Growth in the 1980s," in Michael Ellman and Vladimir Kontorovich, eds., *The Disintegration of the Soviet Economic System* (London: Routledge, 1992), esp. pp. 73–74.

75. Marvin R. Jackson, "Economic Development in the Balkans since 1945 compared to Southern and East-Central Europe," in *Eastern European Politics and Societies* (henceforth EEPS) 1, 3 (fall 1987): 395–455, concludes, however, that after forty years the Balkan lands are closer to other Communist countries in structural characteristics (e.g., sectoral distribution of the labor force) than to non-Communist countries at comparable development levels.

76. Western economists in the 1950s and 1960s, it should be recalled, also envisaged Third World development as a process of attaining industrial self-sufficiency. The possibility of exploiting world market forces and international trade to emerge as a technologically advanced society (as distinct from even a well-to-do commodity producer) seemed plausible only after the emergence of Japan and the East Asian exporters.

77. For a comprehensive account of policies during and after Stalinization, see Brus, "Postwar Reconstruction and Socio-Economic Transformation," and chapters 23–26 by W. Brus, in M. C. Kaser, ed., *The Economic History of Eastern Europe*, vol. 3: *Institutional Change within a Planned Economy* (Oxford: Clarendon Press, 1986), pp. 3–249; on the standard of living, 1950–53, see pp. 33–36.

78. See J. P. Nettl, *The Eastern Zone and Soviet Policy in Germany, 1945–50* (Oxford: Oxford University Press, 1951), pp. 239–241.

79. Wolfgang F. Stolper, with the assistance of Karl W. Roskamp, *The Structure of the East German Economy* (Cambridge, MA: Harvard University Press, 1960), pp. 415–417. Labor productivity increased substantially in the early 1950s, if somewhat less than in West Germany, but recovery also depended on raising employment levels from their low 1950 level. West Germany enjoyed a substantially more rapid growth but East German performance was creditable. By 1955 GNP in East Germany was about 110 to 113 percent of the 1936 level depending upon the indices chosen. In West Germany it was 180 percent of 1936. But there were even larger differences earlier: in 1950 East German output was still significantly lower than the 1936

levels; it grew 40.6 percent in the next five years to get just to the index of 110. In West Germany by 1950, the 1936 figure had been surpassed, and the economy grew 63.5 percent by 1955 to reach the index of 180.

80. I follow the chronology and analysis of Brus, chaps. 24–26, in *Economic History of Eastern Europe*, 3:40–249.

81. For the circumstances of the reform period, Šik's own views, and the economic prescriptions, see Jiri Kosta, *Abriss der sozialökonomischen Entwicklung der Tschechoslovakei 1945–1977* (Frankfurt am Main: Suhrkamp, 1978), pp. 90–104, 113–157; Vladimir Kusan, *The Intellectual Origins of the Prague Spring: The Development of the Reformist Ideas in Czechoslovakia, 1956–1967* (Cambridge: Cambridge University Press, 1971). For Ota Šik's ideas, see *Plan and Market under Socialism* (White Plains, NY: International Arts and Sciences Press, 1967); Šik, "Czechoslovakia's New System of Planning and Management," in *Economic Reforms in the Socialist Countries* (Prague: Peace and Socialism Publishers, 1967), pp. 27–47; and his 1972 ruminations after the crushing of Prague Spring: *The Third Way: Marxist-Leninist Theory and Modern Industrial Society*, trans. Marian Sling (London: Wildwood House, 1976). On Libermanism, see Emil Bej, "Some Aspects of Industrial Planning under Brezhnev-Kossygin Rule," *Jahrbuch der Wirtschaft Osteuropas* 13, 1 (1989): 176–197. For a contemporary evaluation of the innovations, see Gregory Grossman, "Economic Reforms: A Balance Sheet," *Problems of Communism* 15 (Nov.–Dec. 1966): 43–56. Cf. Brus, in *Economic History of Eastern Europe*, 3:40–69.

82. Ivan T. Berend, *The Hungarian Economic Reforms, 1953–1988* (Cambridge: Cambridge University Press, 1990), pp. 129–200.

83. Jörg Roesler, *Zwischen Plan und Markt. Die Wirtschaftsreform 1963–1970 in der DDR* (Freiburg and Berlin: Rudolf Haufe Verlag, 1990), provides an excellent, archivally based account of the New Ecomonic System. For a revealing account of the weaknesses of NÖS and its abandonment, see Michael Keren, "The Return of the Ancien Regime: The GDR in the 1970's" in Joint Economic Committee, *East European Economies Post-Helsinki* (Washington, DC: U.S. Government Printing Office, 1977), pp. 720–765.

84. Ibid., pp. 40–44, 60–68.

85. Marer, *Dollar GNPs*, tables A-10 and A-11, pp. 218–219. For a description of the East German reforms by an official spokesman, see Wolfgang Berger, "The New Economic System in the GDR—Its Essence and Problems," in *Economic Reforms in the Socialist Countries*, pp. 48–64; see also W. Brus in *Economic History of Eastern Europe*, 3:185–194.

86. See Grzegorz Ekiert, "Prospects and Dilemmas of the Transition to a Market Economy in East Central Europe" (Cambridge, MA: unpublished manuscript, 1990), n. 9.

87. See Gert-Joachim Glaeßner, *Die andere deutsche Republik: Gesellschaft und Politik in der DDR* (Opladen: Westdeutscher Verlag, 1989), pp. 19–23.

88. For an interesting discussion of the cycles of reform and repression see Valerie Bunce, "Domestic Reform and International Change: The Gorbachev Reforms in Historical Perspective," *International Organization* 47, no. 1 (winter 1993): 107–138. For the developments inside Czechoslovakia, see Gordon Skilling, *Czechoslovakia's Interrupted Revolution* (Princeton: Princeton University Press, 1976); and Zdenek Mlynař, *Nightfrost in Prague*, trans. Paul Wilson (New York: Karz Publishers, 1980) and Vladimir V. Kusin, *From Dubček to Charter 77: A Study of Normalization in Czechoslovakia 1968–1978* (New York: St. Martin's Press, 1978).

89. For accounts of the difficulties encountered in the 1970s, see Paul McCracken et al., *Towards Full Employment and Price Stability* (Paris: Organization for Economic Cooperation and Development, 1977); Lawrence B. Krause and Walter S. Salant, eds., *Worldwide Inflation: Theory and Recent Experience* (Washington, DC: Brookings Institution, 1977); Leon N. Lindberg and Charles S. Maier, eds., *The Politics of Inflation and Economic Stagnation* (Washington, DC: Brookings Institution, 1985).

90. Cited, Roesler, *Zwischen Plan und Markt*, p. 41.

91. David Granick, *Enterprise Guidance in Eastern Europe: A Comparison of Four Socialist Economies* (Princeton: Princeton University Press, 1975), pp. 161–164.

92. Roesler, *Zwischen Plan und Markt,* pp. 153–156; Brus, chap. 26, in *Economic History of Eastern Europe*, 3:190–194.

93. Interview with Mittag: "Es Reißt Mir das Herz Kaputt," *Der Spiegel* no. 37, Sept. 9, 1991, p. 96.

94. Statistisches Bundesamt, *DDR 1990: Zahlen und Fakten*, (Wiesbaden, 1990), table 8.1, p. 43. Enterprise here refers to an accountable firmlike unit with at least ten employees. See also Doris Cornelsen, "Die Wirtschaft der DDR in der Honecker-Ära," in Gert-Joachim Glaeßner, ed., *Die DDR in der Ära Honecker: Politik-Kultur-Gesellschaft* (Opladen: Westdeutscher Verlag, 1988), pp. 357–370. It is worth noting that whereas Soviet efforts at economic reform (including decentralized decision making) usually emphasized meeting consumer needs, even at the cost of military or investment goods, the East German NÖS of the 1960s had coupled reform with increased investment. In contrast, the recentralization of the 1970s stressed the provision of consumer goods. Cf. Keren, "The Return of the Ancien Regime," for post NÖS results.

95. Bryson and Melzer, *The End of the East German Economy*, pp. 5–7. See also for the overall problems, Manfred Melzer and Arthur A. Stahnke, "The GDR Faces the Economic Dilemmas of the 1980's: Caught between the Need for New Methods and Restricted Options," in Joint Economic Committee, *East European Economics: Slow Growth in the 1980's*, 3:131–168.

96. For a description, see David Stark, "Coexisting Organizational Forms in Hungary's Emerging Mixed Economy," in Victor Nee and David Stark, eds., *Remaking the Economic Institutions of Socialism* (Stanford, CA: Stanford University Press, 1989), pp. 137–169. Also Paul Marer, "Economic Reform in Hungary: From Central Planning to Regulated Market," in Joint Economic Committee, *East European Economics: Slow Growth in the 1980s*, 3:223–297; and for the earlier stages, Richard Portes, "The Tactics and Strategy of Economic Decentralization," *Soviet Studies* 23 (Apr. 1972): 629–658; David Granick, "The Hungarian Economic Reform," *World Politics* 25 (Apr. 1973): 414–429; and for the renewed reform, Berend, *Hungarian Eonomic Reforms*, pp. 232–245.

97. Karel Dyba, "Understanding Czechoslovak Economic Development: 1968–1988. Growth, Adjustment and Reform," *Jahrbuch der Wirtschaft Osteuropas* 13, 2 (1989): 141–166, esp. 143. See also Alice Teichova, *The Czechoslovak Economy, 1918–1980* (London: Routledge, 1988), pp. 150, 161–162. For the sharp Hungarian decline in performance, see Paul G. Hare, "Industrial Development of Hungary since World War II," *EEPS* 2, 1 (winter 1988): 115–151, esp. 123–124. Hare attributes the change to the end of "extensive growth" possibilities. (See the discussion by Gur Ofer cited in n. 106 below.) During the course of the decade East German, Czechoslovak, and Hungarian growth fell from its 5-to-6 percent pace to somewhat over 3 percent. Polish growth remained robust but largely a function of massive capital imports.

98. On the difficulties and contradictions of partial reform, see Granick, *Enterprise Guidance in Eastern Europe*; Janos Kornai, *Economics of Shortage* (Amsterdam: North Holland, 1986); and Ellen Comisso, "Market Failures and Market Socialism: Economic Problems of the Transition," *EEPS* 2, 3 (fall 1988): 433–465.

99. Marer, *Dollar GNPs*, table 1–2, p. 7.

100. Statistisches Bundesamt, *DDR 1990: Zahlen und Fakten*, table 8.8, p. 47.

101. Timothy Colton, *The Dilemma of Reform in the Soviet Union*, rev. ed. (New York: Council on Foreign Relations, 1986), pp. 24–25, 33–57. For the party's role in stagnation, see Peter Rutland, *The Politics of Economic Stagnation in the Soviet Union* (Cambridge: Cambridge University Press, 1993).

102. See Hans-Hermann Hohmann, "Die sowjetische Wirtschaft nach dem Wachstumstief. Stagnation, Zwischenhoch oder anhaltender Aufschwung," in Hohmann and Vogel, eds., *Osteuropas Wirtschaftsprobleme und die Ost-West-Beziehungen*, pp. 13–41; Friedrich Levic, "Hat die Wirtschaft Osteuropas Zukunft?" in ibid., pp. 43–59; and Eugene Zaleski, "Die polnische Wirtschaftskrise und ihre Auswirkungen auf den RGW," in ibid., 61–89, inc. table 1, pp. 62–63.

103. Jochen Bethkenhaben, "RGW und Weltwirtschaft: Konsequenzen zweier Wirtschaftskrisen," in ibid., pp. 91–113.

104. Ellman and Kontorovich, *Disintegration of the Soviet Economic System*, pp. 14–19. The volume as a whole is a harsh critique of the Gorbachev reforms, but it is not clear what alternative model the diverse authors propose. The monographic contributions on railroads, agriculture, technology, and regionalization remain valuable, however. For the mid-1980s recovery, see also Hohmann, "Die sowjetische Wirtschaft nach dem Wachstumstief," pp. 19–24.

105. See Vladimir Kontorovich, "Technological Progress and Research and Development," in Ellman and Kontorovich, *Disintegration of the Soviet Economic System*, pp. 217–238. See also Kazimierz Z. Poznanski, "Economic Determinants of Technological Performance in East European Industry," *EEPS* 2, 3 (fall 1988): 577–600.

106. See the discussion in Gur Ofer, "Soviet Economic Growth, 1928–1985," *Journal of Economic Literature* 25, 4 (Dec. 1987): 1767–1833; here p. 1806. Also Stanislaw Gomulka, *Growth, Innovation and Reform in Eastern Europe* (Brighton: Wheatsheaf, 1986).

107. Phillip Grossman, "Labor Supply Constraints and Responses," in Holland Hunter, ed., *The Future of the Soviet Economy: 1978–1985* (Boulder, CO: Westview, 1978).

108. On these difficulties and others, see Colton, *The Dilemma of Reform in the Soviet Union*, chap. 2; Gertrud E. Schroeder, *Consumption in the USSR: An International Comparison*, Joint Economic Committee, U.S. Congress (Washington, DC: U.S. Government Printing Office, 1981); also Schroeder, "Soviet Consumption in the 1980s: A Tale of Woe," in Ellman and Kontorovich, *Disintegration of the Soviet Economic System*, esp. p. 91, for decadal consumption increments; Herbert S. Levine, "Possible Causes of the Deterioration of Soviet Productivity Growth in the Period 1976–80," in Joint Economic Committee, *Soviet Economy in the 1980s: Problems and Prospects* (Washington, DC: U.S. Government Printing Office, 1983), Part 1, pp. 153–168. This strand of analysis retains some degree of causal indeterminacy. Did insufficient labor supply constrain the development of new economic activities, or did the failure of innovation (coupled with the reluctance to lay off workers) lead to the piling up of excess labor in older industries?

109. Bryson and Melzer, *End of the East German Economy*, pp. 32–47; see also my earlier discussion.

110. BA: Potsdam/Berlin: DE 1/56343: Staatliche Plankommission, "Analyse der Wirksamkeit der umfassenden Anwendung des Prinzips der Eigenwirtschaftung der Mittel in den ausgewählten 16 Kombinaten im Jahre 1988," Apr. 14, 1989, and "Bericht über 'Wirksamkeit der umfassenden Anwendung des Prinzips der Eigenwirtschaftung,'" Sept. 15, 1989.

111. BA: Potsdam/Berlin: DE 1/56321: Wolfgang Biermann to Günter Mittag, May 8, 1988.

112. Wolfgang Heinrichs, "Comments" (Symposium on the German Democratic Republic), *Comparative Economic Studies* 29, 2 (summer 1987): cited in Bryson and Melzer, *End of the East German Economy*, p. 19.

113. Cf. Voskamp and Wittke, "Industrial Restructuring in the Former German Democratic Republic," pp. 344–345.

114. Véronique Maurus, "A l'est, le declin du charbon," *Le Monde*, June 26, 1990, p. 27.

115. George Orwell, *The Road to Wigan Pier* (New York: Harcourt, Brace, Jovanovich, 1958), p. 35.

116. Allan M. Williams, *The Western European Economy: A Geography of Post-War Development* (London: Hutchinson, 1987), p. 296.

117. Kornai, *The Socialist System, pp. 140–145.*

118. Maurus, "A l'est, le declin du Charbon."

119. BA: Potsdam: DC 20, I-3/2905: Minister for Heavy Industry to Minister-President Modrow, Jan. 23, 1990, forwarding "Vorschlag zur Bildung der Regierungskommission zur komplexen Lösung der ökologischen und ökonomischen Probleme im Raum Bitterfeld/Wolfen."

120. Swedish experience suggested intensive job retraining as an alternative, but Sweden was small with a highly educated labor force and low unemployment.

121. Jeffrey Sachs, "Wages, Profits, and Macroeconomic Adjustment: A Comparative Study," *Brookings Papers on Economic Activities 2: 1979*, pp. 269–313. For the macroeconomic policies of the 1970s and their implications, see Lindberg and Maier, eds., *The Politics of Inflation and Economic Stagnation,* with extensive additional references.

122. Peter Hall, *Governing the Economy: The Politics of State Intervention in Britain and France* (Cambridge: Polity Press, 1986), pp. 93–107, 198–202.

123. Cf. E. Dirksen and M. Klopper, "Is There an Economic Crisis in the USSR?" *Comparative Economic Studies* 28, 1 (spring 1966).

124. Bethkenhagen, "RGW und Weltwirtschaft," table 3, p. 108, for trade shares; *COMECON Data, 1989*, table III/3/12, p. 261, for totals. The overall trade figures do not include intra-German trade.

125. See Franklyn D. Holzman, "Comecon: A 'Trade Destroying' Customs Union?" *Journal of Comparative Economics* 9, 4 (Dec. 1985): 419–423.

126. Colton, *Dilemma of Reform*, p. 203.

127. Friedman, "Disintegrating Blocs."

128. BA: Potsdam/Berlin: DE 1/56320: "Warum wurde die Höhe unserer Verschuldung bisher nicht veröffentlicht?"

129. Bej, "Some Aspects of Industrial Planning under Breshnev-Kossygin Rule," p. 191.

130. For different insights into the difficulties of the delayed efforts at reform in CMEA economies in which property was still largely socialist, see the essays collected in the special issue of *EEPS* 2, 3 (fall 1988); also the upbeat analysis of David Lipton and Jeffrey Sachs, "Creating a Market Economy in Eastern Europe: The Case of Poland," *Brookings Papers in Economic Activity 1: 1990*, pp. 75–133, with discussion, pp. 134–148; J. Winiecki, "Obstacles to Economic Reform of Socialism: A Property Rights Approach," *Annals of the American Academy of Political and Social Sciences* 507 (1990): 65–71; Grzegorz Ekiert, "Prospects and Dilemmas of the Transition to a Market Economy in East Central Europe" in Frederick D. Weil, ed., *Research on Democracy and Society: Democratization in Eastern and Western Europe* (Greenwich, CT: JAI Press, 1993), 1:51–82.

131. MfS: ZAIG/3605: "Information über Reaktionen der Bevölkerung der DDR zu Problemen des Handels und der Versorgung," Sept. 14, 1987.

CHAPTER 3

1. This sketch of *Vormärz* Germany takes into account the contrasting emphases of the two major recent efforts at historical synthesis: Thomas Nipperdey's *Deutsche Geschichte 1800–1860. Bürgerwelt und Starker Staat* (Munich: Beck, 1984), which stresses the potential for public participation in liberal nationalism, and Hans-Ulrich Wehler's *Deutsche Gesellschaftsgeschichte*, 4 vols. (Munich: Beck, 1987–), which emphasizes pervasive hierarchy. Benedict Anderson, *Imagined Communities* (London: Verso, 1983); and Jürgen Habermas, *Strukturwandel der Öffentlichkeit* (Neuwied: M. Luchterhand, 1962), both illuminate how the participants in print culture can form a proto-elite. For the actual events of 1848 the literature is enormous; but the recent stress on democratic mobilization exemplified, for instance, by Jonathan Sperber, *Rhineland Radicals: The Democratic Movement and the Revolution of 1848–1849* (Princeton: Princeton University Press, 1991), is a useful antidote to the highly structured explanations of why the revolution failed.

2. Johann Heinrich Gottlobs von Justi, *Grundsätze der Policeywissenschaft*, 3rd ed. (1782), pp. 4, 14, cited in Alf Lüdtke, *Police and State in Prussia, 1815–1850*, trans. Pete Burgess (Cambridge: Cambridge University Press and Editions de la Maison des Sciences de l'Homme, 1989), p. 205.

3. Helga Königsdorf, *Adieu DDR: Protokolle eines Abschieds* (Reinbek bei Hamburg: rororo aktuell, 1990), p. 64. The book comprises a series of anonymous interviews. For a confirmatory but dismaying testimony, see the radical right agitator

cited in *New York Times* ("German Attacks Rise As Foreigners Become Scapegoat," Nov. 2, 1992): "We want to build a monument to Erich Honecker. He was a Communist idiot, but his policies preserved an island of 17 million pure-race Germans with some vestige of Aryan consciousness."

4. Over a half-century ago Crane Brinton's *Anatomy of Revolution* (New York: W. W. Norton, 1938; rev. eds. 1952, 1965) most completely charted the parallels between British, American, French, and Russian revolutions. One sensitive historian of the French radicalization, who lived through the 1989 upheaval in West Berlin, was repeatedly impressed by parallels, but then had to accept that the revolution had ended. For his successive vignettes of the upheaval, see Robert Darnton, *Berlin Journal, 1989–1990* (New York: Norton, 1991).

5. This argument is not concerned primarily with the scope and forms of crowd protest. For analysis of the repertoires of protest and how they evolved through 1848 (after which protest allegedly crossed a modern threshold), the most notable literature concentrates on France. See Charles Tilly, *The Contentious French* (Cambridge, MA: Harvard University Press, 1986); William H. Sewell, Jr., "Collective Violence and Collective Loyalties in France: Why the French Revolution Made a Difference," *Politics and Society* 18, 4 (1990): 527–552; also Sewell, *Work and Revolution in France: The Language of Labor from the Old Regime to 1848* (Cambridge: Cambridge University Press, 1980); Sidney Tarrow, "Modular Collective Action and the Rise of the Social Movement: Why the French Revolution Was Not Enough," *Politics and Society* 21, 1 (March 1993): 69–90; also Tarrow's recent survey, *Power in Movement: Social Movements, Collective Action, and Politics* (Cambridge: Cambridge University Press, 1994). These analyses do not usually address the issue of "reflexivity" in recent collective action—that is, the feedback of media coverage and event that gave local crowds significant national impact and made the coverage of protests destabilizing in its own right. To a degree, Paris journalism might have provided some surrogate in earlier periods, but since 1968 at least television has enhanced the interaction among demonstrators, audience, and authorities.

6. Reinhard Schult, "Kirche von Unten," cited in Matthias Geis, *Tageszeitung* (henceforth *taz*), Aug. 15, 1989. (Reprinted in *taz: DDR Journal zur Novemberrevolution. August bis Dezember 1989*, 2nd enl. ed. (Berlin, 1990; henceforth *taz: DDR Journal*), p. 6.

7. Cited from Leopold Schönhoff, "Die Politik und die Strasse," *Über Land und Meer* 3 (1907–8): 19, in Bernd Lindner, "Die politische Kultur der Straße als Medium der Veränderung," *Aus Politik und Zeitgeschichte* B27/90 (June 29, 1990): 18.

8. For the history and application of the concept of civil society, see chapter 4, pp. 185–95. The most recent and comprehensive treatment is Jean L. Cohen and

Anthony Arato, Civil Society and Political Theory (Cambridge, MA: MIT Press, 1992). See also Zbigniew Rau, ed., The Emergence of Civil Society in Eastern Europe and the Soviet Union (Boulder, CO: Westview Press, 1991). By the 1980s the term referred to those associations and organizations that might form the basis for challenging the Communist regimes.

9. History is in this sense "overdetermined," and it is thus a misplaced effort to look for the "parsimony" so prized by political scientists. From another perspective, however, historical outcomes appear underdetermined; they might have turned out differently, and some events are of such a magnitude that the causes we adduce seem intuitively insufficient to account for them. It is only an apparent paradox that history remains both overdetermined and underdetermined: the first condition refers to the number of plausible explanations; the second condition refers to the difference in magnitude between causes and results.

10. This section raises the central issue of whether Germany had a deviant political trajectory or Sonderweg. Naturally every country has its own "exceptionalism." Critics of the Sonderweg argument have correctly emphasized how rich an associative life and how much political debate characterized Germany. (See preeminently David Blackbourn and Geoffrey Eley, The Peculiarities of German History: Bourgeois Society and Politics in Nineteenth-Century Germany [New York: Oxford University Press, 1984].) Nonetheless, office holding and policies remained less a function of parliamentary elections in Germany. Even in Britain, where great domains of collective life remained nondemocratic and nonmeritocratic, the policies of rival contenders for state office had to be tested in electoral decisions, as in most of the United States and in France.

11. "Parlament und Regierung im neugeordneten Deutschland" (May 1918), in Gesammelte politische Schriften, 3rd rev. ed. (Tübingen: J. C. B. Mohr, 1958), ed. Johannes Winckelmann, pp. 306–443, citation from pp. 395–396. Weber feared mass politics but sensed that, without continually struggling for majority support, governance must become ossified. See also "Wahlrecht und Demokratie in Deutschland" (Dec. 1917), in ibid., pp. 245–291.

12. Cf. Robert Darnton, "Did East Germany Have a Revolution?" New York Times, Dec. 3, 1989, p. A19.

13. Testimony of Gudula Ziemer and Holger Jackish, Dec. 17, 1989, cited in Neues Forum Leipzig, Jetzt oder Nie—Demokratie: Leipziger Herbst '89 (Leipzig: Forum Verlag, 1989; and Munich: C. Bertelsmann Verlag, 1990), pp. 26–27.

14. Rainer Eckert, "Staatssicherheit und DDR-Universitäten (am Beispiel politischer Verfolgungen an der Sektion Geschichte der Humboldt-Universität zu Berlin 1971/72," paper presented at the conference, "Deutsche Geschichte von innen und

aussen gesehen," Leipzig, May 21–23, 1992; now published as "Die Berliner Humboldt Humboldt–Universität und das Ministerium für Staatssicherheit," in *Deutschland Archiv* 26, 7 (July 1993): 770–785. The author was himself a young student who was pushed into the Academy of Sciences.

15. Königsdorf, *Adieu DDR*, p. 118. The citation is from a CDU member, but former SED activists have told me the same thing.

16. Theo Kühirt testimony, in Neues Forum Leipzig, *Jetzt oder Nie*, p. 92.

17. Hans-Hermann Hertle, "Der Weg in den Bankrott der DDR-Wirtschaft . . . Gespräch mit Gerhard Schürer," *Deutschland Archiv*, 25, 2 (Feb. 1992): 139.

18. BA-SAPMO: Büro Günter Mittag, DY 30/41797, Bd. 3: "Aktennotiz über ein Gespräch Erich Honeckers mit Wjatsceslaw Kotschemassow am 1. Februar 1988."

19. BA-SAPMO: Büro Egon Krenz, IV 2/2.039/73: Report of meeting of Honecker and Czech General Secretary Milos Jakeš, May 3, 1989.

20. BA-SAPMO: Büro Egon Krenz, IV 2/2.039/74: "Bericht über die Beratung . . . am 6–7.6 in Havana."

21. BA-SAPMO: Büro Egon Krenz, IV 2/2.039/290: "Problemspiegel," July 20, 1989, and attached stenographic protocol.

22. BA-SAPMO: Büro Egon Krenz, IV 2/2.039/76. Politbüro Session, Aug. 1, 1989: "Gedanken, die führende Funktionäre Nikaraguas in den Gesprächen äusserten . . ."

23. This author recalls seeking to change an exit visa at the Potsdam police headquarters in December 1964 so that he might cross the frontier at a different point from where he had entered it. At that time comment books were ubiquitous in the DDR; in the police presidium there was one poignantly labeled "Here the citizen has the word." Inside were fulsome thanks (and even some pressed flowers) for having been allowed to travel or extend the time abroad.

24. Königsdorf, *Adieu DDR*, p. 63.

25. BA-SAPMO: Büro Egon Krenz, IV 2/2.039/304.

26. Günter Schabowski, *Das Politbüro* (Reinbek bei Hamburg: Rowohlt Taschenbuch-Verlag, 1990), p. 63: "Da haben uns die Ungarn etwas eingebrockt."

27. BA-SAPMO: Büro Egon Krenz, IV 2/2.039/76. Krenz's papers include transcribed pages of the Politbüro's August 29 meeting.

28. BA-SAPMO: Büro Egon Krenz, IV 2/2.039/304: "Vermerk über das Gespräch . . . Oskar Fischer mit Gyula Horn am 31. Aug. 1989"; and "Vermerk über das Gespräch . . . Günter Mittag mit Gyula Horn am 31. Aug. 1989."

29. BA-SAPMO: Büro Egon Krenz, IV 2/2.039/77: Sitzung des Politbüros . . ., Sept. 5, 1989.

30. Ibid., Sept. 12, 1989.

31. Ibid. "Notizen," Sept. 17, 1989.

32. BA-SAPMO: Büro Egon Krenz, IV 2/2.039/304: "Niederschrift über das Gespräch des Generalsekr. des ZK der SED . . . Erich Honecker m. Rudolf Seiters am 4. Juli 1989."

33. BA-SAPMO: Büro Egon Krenz, IV 2/2.039/304: "Vermerk über des Gespräch des Stellvertretenden Ministers des Auswärtigen Amtes Kurt Nier, mit Klaus-Jürgen Duisberg, Leiter des Arbeitstabes 20 im BKA . . . 11 August 1989."

34. BA-SAPMO: Büro Egon Krenz, IV 2/2.039/304. "Vermerk über das Gespräch . . . Herbert Krolikowski mit . . . Rudolf Seiters am 18. Aug. 1989." In fact the chief of the FRG division of the East German Foreign Ministry, Hans Schindler, was a bit more forthcoming when he met with the head of the permanent mission of the FRG, Franz Bertele on August 30 and 31. He did not promise exit visas but did concede that those leaving the embassy could return to work and petition again immediately to emigrate. His further indication that Vogel's good offices would be used hinted that the regime would allow emigration, not as a fully legal recourse, but as a special circumstance. See the summary in ibid.: "Aktivitäten der DDR gegenüber der BRD im Zusammenhang mit dem widerrechtlichen Aufenthalt von DDR-Bürgern im diplomatischen Vertretungen der BRD." The memo identified the six conversations of August 11 (Nier-Duisberg), August 16 (Schindler-Bertele), August 18 (Krolikowski-Seiters), August 23 (Schindler-Seiters), and August 30 and August 31 (Schindler-Bertele).

35. Ibid., Honecker to Kohl, Aug. 30, 1989.

36. Ibid., Anlage to report by Günter Rettner to Honecker.

37. BA-SAPMO: IV 2/2A/3250: "Information über die Entwicklung und Lage auf den Gebieten des Reiseverkehrs, der ständigen Ausreisen und des ungesetzlichen Verlassens der DDR."

38. Gyula Horn, *Freiheit, die ich meine*, ed. Angelika Maté and Pieter Maté (Hamburg: Hoffman and Campe, 1991), pp. 311–322. Phillip Zelikow and Condoleezza Rice, who have reconstructed diplomatic events most thoroughly, have found no evidence of a formal FRG offer. See their book, *Germany Unified and Europe Transformed: A Study in Statecraft* (Cambridge, MA: Harvard University Press, 1995), pp. 67–68, 390 n.20. But cf. Timothy Garton Ash's citation of Németh testimony in *In Europe's Name: Germany and the Divided Continent* (New York: Random House, 1993), pp. 371, 600n.

39. Ibid. Translation of Shevardnadze to Oskar Fischer, Sept. 1, 1989.

40. Cf. Schabowski, *Das Politbüro*, pp. 68–69.

41. For West German diplomacy in this crisis see Zelikow and Rice, *Germany Unified and Europe Transformed*, pp. 75, 392; Hans-Dietrich Genscher, *Erinnerungen* (Berlin: Siedler Verlag, 1995), pp. 643–649.

42. "Information über erste Hinweise auf Reaktionen . . . ," Oct. 4, 1989,

in Armin Mitter and Stefan Wolle, eds., *"Ich liebe euch doch alle!" Befehle und Lageberichte des MfS Januar–November 1989* (Berlin: BasisDruck, 1990), pp. 192–194.

43. Hauke Brost, "Beginn der Flucht," in *Berliner Illustrirte*, special issue, Dec. (Berlin: Springer Verlag, 1990), p. 92.

44. Albert O. Hirschman, *Exit, Voice, and Loyalty: Response to Decline in Firms, Organizations and States* (Cambridge, MA: Harvard University Press, 1970). For the application of the argument to the GDR, see "Exit, Voice, and the Fate of the German Democratic Republic," *World Politics*, 45, 1 (Jan. 1993): 173–202, reprinted as chapter 1 of Hirschman, *A Propensity to Self-Subversion* (Cambridge, MA: Harvard University Press, 1995), pp. 9–44.

45. "Hinweise auf wesentliche motivbildende Faktoren im Zusammenhang mit Anträgen auf ständige Ausreise nach dem nichtsozialistischen Ausland und dem ungesetzlichen Verlassen der DDR," in Mitter and Wolle, *Ich liebe euch doch alle*, pp. 141–147.

46. "Der Exodus is nur ein Zeichen für angestaute gesellschaftliche Probleme in allen Bereichen der Gesellschaft." Cited in Rolf Henrich's foreword to Neues Forum Leipzig, *Jetzt oder Nie*, p. 12.

47. Ibid., p. 141.

48. "Hinweise zur Reaktion der Bevölkerung im Zusammenhang mit der Vorbereitung und Durchführung der Kommunalwahlen am 7. Mai 1989," in Mitter and Wolle, *Ich liebe euch doch alle*, p. 29.

49. ZAIG report, June 1989 (7.7.89), in Mitter and Wolle, *Ich liebe euch doch alle*, pp. 97–107.

50. Schabowski, *Das Politbüro*, p. 56.

51. Ulrike Breach et al., eds., *Oktober 1989: Wider den Schlaf der Vernunft* (Berlin West: Elefanten Press, and Berlin DDR: Neues Leben, 1989), p. 18. "In unserem Lande ist die Kommunikation zwischen Staat und Gesellschaft offensichtlich gestört." On the founding meeting September 9–10 see Reinhard Schult, "Offen für alle—das Neue Forum," in Hubertus Knabe, ed., *Aufbruch in eine andere DDR* (Reinbek bei Hamburg: Rowohlt, 1989), pp. 163–170.

52. "'Reformen in unserem Land sind dringend notwendig': Synode des DDR-Kirchenbundes fordert politische Rechte und wirtschaftliche Reformen," in *taz: DDR Journal*, p. 15. Other examples of Protestant sociology include the essays collected in Detlef Pollack, ed., *Die Legitimität der Freiheit. Politisch alternative Gruppen in der DDR unter dem Dach der Kirche* (Frankfurt am Main: Peter Lang, 1990), esp. Pollack, "Sozialethisch engagierte Gruppen in der DDR. Eine religionssoziologische Untersuchung," pp. 115–154; and Ehrhart Neubert, "Religion in der DDR-Gesellschaft. Zum Problem der sozialisierenden Gruppen und ihrer

Zuordnung zu den Kirchen," pp. 31–40, and Neubert, "Gesellschaftliche Kommunikation im sozialen Wandel. Auf dem Weg zu einer politischen Ökologie," pp. 155–202.

53. Manfred Loetsch, "Abschied von der Legitimationswissenschaft," in Knabe, *Aufbruch in eine andere DDR*, p. 196.

54. Sebastian Feydt, Christiane Heinze, and Martin Schanz, "Die Leipziger Friedensgebete," in Wolf-Jürgen Grabner, Christiane Heinze, and Detlev Pollack, eds., *Leipzig im Oktober. Kirchen und alternative Gruppen im Umbruch der DDR. Analysen zur Wende* (Berlin: Wichern-Verlag, 1990), p. 127; cf. Hans-Jürgen Sievers, *Vom Friedensgebet zur Demonstration: Die Kirche in Leipzig in den Tagen der Revolution 1989: Das Stundenbuch einer deutschen Revolution* (Zollicon: GZW-Verlag, 1990); alternative title for the West German publication: *Das Stundenbuch einer deutschen Revolution: Die Leipziger Kirchen im Oktober 1989* (Göttingen: Vandenhoeck & Ruprecht, 1990).

55. See Victor W. Turner, *The Ritual Process: Structure and Anti-Structure* (Chicago: Aldine Press, 1969); also Emile Durkheim's notion of collective effervescence in *The Elementary Forms of the Religious Life*, trans. Joseph W. Swain (London: George Allen and Unwin, and New York: Macmillan, 1915); similarly Francesco Alberoni's concept of the *stato nascente* in *Movement and Institution*, trans. Patricia C. Arden Delmore (New York: Columbia University Press, 1984).

56. Mielke to Honecker et al., Mar. 14, 1989, included in Mitter and Wolle, *Ich liebe euch doch alle*, p. 28.

57. Feydt et al. "Die Leipziger Friedensgebete," and Albrecht Doehnert and Paulus Rummel, "Die Leipziger Montagsdemonstrationen," both in Grabner et al., *Leipzig im Oktober*, esp. pp. 124–125, 148. Cf. Johannes Richter, "Wir sind Sachsen," in Gerhard Rein, ed., *Die Opposition in der DDR. Entwürfe für einen anderen Sozialismus* (West Berlin: Wichern-Verlag, 1989), pp. 182–187.

58. Petra Bornhöft, "Ausreiser und Bleiber marchieren getrennt," *taz*, Sept. 9, 1989, in *taz: DDR Journal*, pp. 8–9. It was this Monday prayer meeting of September 4 that produced the first countercry of "We are staying here." See Doehnert and Rummel, "Die Leipziger Montagsdemonstrationen," p. 149. For a careful reconstruction and evaluation of Leipzig events see the historical memoir by one of the university's leading historians: Hartmut Zwahr, *Ende einer Selbstzerstörung. Leipzig und die Revolution in der DDR* (Göttingen: Vandenhoeck & Ruprecht, 1993), esp. p. 19 for Sept. 4; also Sievers, *Stundenbuch*, pp. 29–30.

59. "Die Zeit ist reif," *taz*, Sept. 13, 1989. The manifesto is reproduced in several other sources, including *Oktober 1989: Wider den Schlaf der Vernunft* (Berlin [East]: Neues Leben, and West Berlin: Elefanten Press, 1989), pp. 18–19.

60. Doehnert and Rummel, "Die Leipziger Montagsdemonstrationen," p. 149.

61. Interview with Dirk Barthel, cited in Neues Forum Leipzig, *Jetzt oder Nie*, p. 45.

62. Pastor Ebeling proposed to his fellow Leipzig pastors that peace prayers be allowed only as a prelude to communion services; this was rejected as an attempt to exclude the many participants who were not confessed worshipers. Besides the Nikolaikirche the Reformed Church held peace services, as did St. Peter's and St. Michael's and the Roman Catholic Probsteikirche at the height of the movement. See Feydt et al., "Die Leipziger Friedensgebete," pp. 134–135.

63. BA-SAPMO: Büro Egon Krenz, IV 2/2.039/70. Politbüro session of Feb. 7, 1989.

64. Rainer Tetzner, *Leipziger Ring. Auszeichnungen eines Montagsdemonstranten Oktober 1989 bis 1. Mai 1990* (Frankfurt am Main: Luchterhand, 1990), p. 32.

65. Interview with Dr. Kurt Meyer, in Neues Forum Leipzig, *Jetzt oder Nie*, p. 282.

66. Michael Hofmann, "Die Kohlenarbeiter von Espenhaim. Versuch einer Milieubiographie," paper presented to conference on Deutsche Geschichte von innen und aussen gesehen, Leipzig, May 1992. See also Michael Hofmann and Dieter Rink, "Der Leipziger Aufbruch 1989: Zur Genesis einer Heldenstadt," in Grabner et al., *Leipzig im Oktober*, pp. 114–122, which stresses the environmental problems, urban overcrowding, and pollution (sulfur dioxide figures, p. 118) and the divergence of two streams of protest: the one emanating from dissident groups and the church-oriented; the other based on the region's smokestack-industry working class, fed up with urban overcrowding and material and ecological privation.

67. For the best coverage of the diverse and often ambivalent relations of the churches to the regime, see the massive documentation edited by Gerhard Besier and Stephan Wolf, *"Pfarrer, Christen und Katholiken," Das Ministerium für Staatssicherheit der ehemaligen DDR und die Kirchen*, 2nd rev. ed. (Neukirchen-Vluyn: Neukirchener Verlag, 1992).

68. Lothar Vogel, *Leipziger Volkszeitung*, Sept. 29, p. 2. Cited in Neues Forum Leipzig, *Jetzt oder Nie*, p. 41.

69. Worker of the VEP Leipzig wool fiber factory, cited from the *Leipziger Volkszeitung*, Sept. 30, in ibid., p. 42.

70. *Mitteldeutsche Neueste Nachrichten* Oct. 9, p. 2.

71. Christof Wielepp, "Montags abends in Leipzig," in Thomas Blanke und Rainer Erd, eds., *DDR-Ein Staat Vergeht* (Frankfurt am Main: Fischer Taschenbuch Verlag, 1990), pp. 71–78, esp. p. 74. For the Stasi's report on the October 2 "renewed provocative-demonstrative action in connection with the so-called Monday prayer," see Mitter and Wolle, *Ich liebe euch doch alle*, pp. 190–191. The security apparatus estimated 2,000 people inside the church and 3,000 in adjacent streets. "The situation came to physical attacks on Volkspolizei members and slanderous insults, especially on the part of groups of young people. These forces succeeded in

part in breaking through the ranks of the Volkspolizei." For a pictorial record of the Monday demonstrations, see Wolfgang Schneider, comp., *Leipziger Demontagebuch: Demo, Montag, Tagebuch, Demontage* (Leipzig: G. Kiepenheuer, 1990). The wordplay in the title combines "Demonstration, Monday, Diary, and Dismantling."

72. Gudula Ziemer and Holger Jackisch, cited in Neues Forum Leipzig, *Jetzt oder Nie*, p. 26.

73. Petra Bornhöft, "Ihr konnt abdanken, jetzt sind wir dran!" *taz*, Oct. 4, 1989, in *taz: DDR Journal*, pp. 22–24.

74. Testimonies of Thomas and Franz, cited in Neues Forum Leipzig, *Jetzt oder Nie*, p. 49.

75. In addition to the books cited already, see *Schnauze. Gedächtnisprotokolle 7. und 8. Oktober 1989, Berlin, Leipzig, Dresden*, with a foreword by Heinrich Fink, Rector of the Humboldt University (Berlin: Berliner Verlags-Anstalt Union, 1990).

76. Mielke to Diensteinheiten, Oct. 5 and Oct. 8, 1991, in Mitter and Wolle, *Ich liebe euch doch alle*, pp. 199, 201.

77. Report of Gabriella Schmidt, Oct. 28, in Neues Forum Leipzig, *Jetzt oder Nie*, pp. 66–69.

78. Ibid., pp. 69–70.

79. See Klaus Hartung, "Leipzig: Wut, Ironie und Angst," *taz*, Oct. 9, 1989, in *taz: DDR Journal*, pp. 36–38. For the demonstrations on October 7, see *Schnauze*, pp. 133–155.

80. Wielepp, "Montags abends in Leipzig," p. 75.

81. Steffen Alisch, "Die Gebetswand in der Leipziger Thomaskirche," in Grabner et al., *Leipzig im Oktober*, pp. 136–146, citation from p. 139 (an analysis of 1,300 written prayers including 250 Soviet ones, many Japanese, American, British, Czech, and Polish, and at least 100 West German).

82. Rummel, Fischer, and Freitag testimonies, Neues Forum Leipzig, *Jetzt oder Nie*, pp. 83–85. See also Vera Gaserow, "Demonstration in Leipzig: 'Wir sind das Volk!'" *taz*, Oct. 11, 1989, in *taz: DDR Journal*.

83. Wielepp, "Montags abends in Leipzig," p. 76.

84. For a cataloging of the slogans that demonstrators carried on placards or painted on bedsheets, many quite witty, see Zwahr, *Ende einer Selbstzerstörung*, esp. pp. 129–141.

85. Egon Krenz, *Wenn Mauern fallen. Die friedliche Revolution: Vorgeschichte-Ablauf-Auswirkungen*, with the assistence of Hartmut Koenig and Günter Rettner (Vienna: Paul Neff Verlag, 1990), pp. 136–138. Krenz did not dispute the efficacy of the Masur appeal, nor did he claim that he alone had pushed through a policy of restraint, but did argue that "the switches were set in Berlin." Kurt Masur disputed his emphasis: "We six began to defend ourselves only when we were depicted as having sought to influence the demonstration under remote control from Egon Krenz." See

Dec. 29, 1989, interview printed in Neues Forum Leizpig, *Jetzt oder Nie*, p. 275. See also the similar skeptical opinion by Leipzig SED secretary Woetzel: Werner Adam, "Verhinderte Krenz am 9. Oktober eine 'chinesiche Lösung'?" *Frankfurter Allgemeine Zeitung [FAZ]*, Nov. 21, 1989, p. 3. Schabowski argues that he and Krenz were agreed that the use of force, as in China, would have been a disaster; see *Das Politbüro*, p. 79.

86. "Hinweise über Reaktionen progressiver Kräfte auf die gegenwärtige innenpolitische Lage in der DDR," Oct. 8, 1989, in Mitter and Wolle, *Ich liebe euch doch alle*, pp. 204–207.

87. ("Bei vielen Genossen sind da Erkenntnisprozesse in Gang gesetzt worden. Auch aus der grossen Angst heraus . . .") Theo Kühirt, engineer and member of the Kampfgruppen, *Jetzt oder Nie*, pp. 90–92.

88. Ibid., p. 90. Helga Wagner, university teacher, testimony, in *Oktober 1989: Wider den Schlaf der Vernunft*, pp. 87–90.

89. Masur interview of Dec. 29, in ibid., pp. 273–277. See also Kurt Masur, "'Man darf nicht schon wieder verfälschen': Was dem 9. Oktober in Leipzig vorausging und was ihm folgte," *FAZ*, Nov. 29, 1989, p. 33.

90. Text of the appeal for a "peaceful solution," a "free exchange of ideas concerning the continuation of socialism in our country," and "reasonableness," in *Wider den Schlaf der Vernunft*, p. 105.

91. Interview by Grit Hartmann with Zimmermann, Dec. 14, 1989, reprinted in Neues Forum Leipzig, *Jetzt oder Nie*, p. 292.

92. Revealing interviews in *Oktober 1989: Wider den Schlaf der Vernunft*, pp. 62–64, 74–82. For the Stasi report on the October 9 demonstration, which estimated 70,000 participants, see "Information über eine Demonstration . . ." (no date) in Mitter and Wolle, *Ich liebe euch doch alle*, pp. 216–219. On the preparations for a clash see the well-informed account by Elizabeth Pond, *Beyond the Wall: Germany's Road to Unification* (Washington, DC: Brookings Institution, 1993), pp. 105, 111–115, and 304–306. Pond weighs the diverse hypotheses and leaves open the question of whether force was ordered. I agree with Pond that violence could have exploded, but it is important to stress how badly local authorities wanted to avoid a violent showdown. For the Krenz-Kochemasov conversation see Kotchemassow, *Meine letzte Mission* (Berlin: Dietz, 1994), pp. 168–169. Also Zelikow and Rice, *Germany Unified*, p. 84.

93. For reports of the police action in Dresden on October 7 and 8, see *Schnauze*, pp. 158–248. Cf. Hans Modrow, *Aufbruch und Ende* (Hamburg: Konkret Literatur Verlag, 1991), pp. 13–18, and Pond, *Beyond the Wall*, pp. 108–110.

94. John Connelly has provided a detailed report of the Plauen clashes in "Moment of Revolution: Plauen (Vogtland), October 7, 1989," *German Politics and Society* no. 20 (summer 1990): 71–89.

95. Marlies Menge, "Dialog statt Dreinschlagen. Tauwetter in Dresden—ein Vorbote?" *Die Zeit*, Oct. 13, 1989.

96. "Information über eine Demonstration," in Mitter and Wolle, *Ich liebe euch doch alle*, p. 217.

97. Interview of Liane Auerswald with Martin M., in *Oktober 1989: Wider den Schlaf der Vernunft*, p. 9.

98. "Ich Zeige An. Berichte von Betroffenen zu den Ereignissen am 7. und 8. Oktober 1989 in Berlin." Assembled by the Arbeitsgruppe "Materialsichtung" of the "Zeitweilige Kommission der Stadtverordnetenversammlung von Berlin," I have drawn on these reports in pulling together the account of October 7 and 8. For the circumstances in which the two committees were established and merged, see *Schnauze*, p. 9. The *Schnauze* volume also reprints many of the testimonies.

99. Author's interview with Hans-Dietrich Schmidt, July 1990; Schmidt had spent the prior Sunday afternoon at a citizens meeting at the East Berlin Sophienkirche; the future of the GDR and anxiety about the move toward unification was a dominant theme; so too was dissatisfaction with the fate of the investigation.

100. Mitter and Wolle, *Ich liebe euch doch alle*, pp. 11–13, 17–19.

101. One television journalist cited by the Stasi, Michael Schmitz, was my guide in March 1990, when he covered the meeting of the Round Table and the emerging political parties.

102. Mitter and Wolle, *Ich liebe euch doch alle*, pp. 46–71.

103. "Information über eine Veranstaltung in der Gethsemanekirche im Stadtbezirk Berlin-Prenzlauer Berg am 8. Juni 1989," in ibid., 76–77. The report concerning the behavior of the church officials suggested an informant quite knowledgeable of the attitudes within the Lutheran leadership, yet anxious to stress that churchmen were preeminently interested in channeling dissent and "correct" in their obligations to the regime. The two-sided briefing (passed along by Mielke to fellow Politbüro members) revealed the approach of many informants caught up in the Stasi network, but seeking simultaneously to limit the damage of their reports. On the churches, see Mary Fulbrook, *Anatomy of a Dictatorship: Inside the GDR, 1949–1989* (New York: Oxford University Press, 1995), pp. 89–125; also Robert F. Goeckel, *The Lutheran Church and the East German State: Political Conflict and Change under Ulbricht and Honecker* (Ithaca, NY: Cornell University Press, 1990); Basier and Wolf, eds., *Pfarrer, Christen und Katholiken*.

104. For the Stolpe controversy, see chapter 6. Pastor Zimmermann confessed quickly after 1989 that he had worked for the Stasi. The result—so I heard him charge in a painful outburst at a historical conference in Leipzig in May 1992—was to be ostracized like an AIDS patient.

105. "Information über die Lage und Entwicklungstendenzen der ständigen

Ausreise von Bürgern der DDR nach der BRD und Westberlin sowie des ungesetzlichen Verlassens der DDR in der Zeit vom 1. Januar bis 30. Juni 1989," and "Hinweise auf wesentliche motivbildende Faktoren im Zusammenhang mit Anträgen auf ständige Ausreise nach dem nichtsozialistischen Ausland und dem ungesetzlichen Verlassen der DDR," in Mitter and Wolle, *Ich liebe euch doch alle,* pp. 82–92, 141–147.

106. "Dienstbesprechung beim Minister für Staatssicherheit," Aug. 8, 1989, in Mitter and Wolle, *Ich liebe euch doch alle,* pp. 113–140. Gehlert's report from Gera, cited p. 135.

107. Ibid., pp. 116–117.

108. "Hinweise auf wesentliche motivbildende Faktoren im Zusammenhang mit Anträgen auf ständige Ausreise nach dem nichtsozialistischen Ausland und dem ungesetzlichen Verlassen der DDR," in ibid., p. 142.

109. Königsdorf, *Adieu DDR,* pp. 100–101.

110. "Dienstbesprechung," in Mitter and Wolle, *Ich liebe euch doch alle,* p. 125.

111. Ibid., p. 133.

112. Ibid., p. 127.

113. Ibid., p. 137.

114. Schabowski, *Das Politbüro,* p. 62.

115. Ibid.

116. "Hinweise über Reaktionen progressiver Kräfte auf die gegenwärtige innenpolitische Lage in der DDR," Oct. 8, 1989. This may have been the report whose suggestion of superannuation so enraged Honecker at the Politbüro meeting two days later, in Mitter and Wolle, *Ich liebe euch doch alle,* p. 204.

117. Ibid., pp. 62–66.

118. Iwan Kusmin, "Die Verschwörung gegen Honecker," *Deutschland Archiv,* 28, 3 (Mar. 1995): 286–290.

119. Daniel Küchenmeister, "Wann begann das Zerwürfnis zwischen Honecker und Gorbatschow? Erste Bermerkungen zu den Protokollen ihrer Vier-Augen-Gespräche," *Deutschland Archiv,* 26, 1 (Jan. 1993): 30–40. Also BA-SAPMO: DY 30/41797, Bd. 3: Aktennotiz über ein Gespräch von Erich Honecker mit Wjatscheslaw Kotschemassow am 1. Februar 1988. See also Wjatscheslaw Daschitschew, "Die sowjetische Deutschlandpolitik in den achtziger Jahren. Persönliche Erlebnisse und Erkentnisse," *Deutschland Archiv,* 28, 1 (Jan. 1995): 54–67, which stresses Gorbachev's reluctance in 1989 to take measures that might undermine the East German leadership. See also chapter 5.

120. BA: Potsdam/Berlin: Akten der Staatlichen Plankommission: DE 1/56320: "Niederschrift des Gesprächs des Genossen Egon Krenz . . . mit dem Generalsekretär des ZK der KPdSU und Vorsitzenden des Obersten Sowjets der UdSSR, am 1. 11. 89 in Moskau." For reports and Soviet assessments of the Honecker-Gorbachev

meetings, see Igor W. Maxymytschew and Hans-Hermann Hertle: "Die Maueröffnung: eine russisch-deutsche Trilogie," *Deutschland Archiv* 27, 11 (Nov. 1994):
1137–1158, esp. Teil I. Maximychev was second in charge at the Soviet embassy; he
kept notes of Ambassador Kochemasov's daily briefing of the embassy staff.

121. Igor W. Maximytschew and Hans-Hermann Hertle, "Die Naueröffnung.
Eine russisch-deutsche Trilogie," in *Deutschland Archiv*, 27, 11 (Nov. 1994): 1138–
39. Krenz, *Wenn Mauern Fallen*, p. 96, reports Gorbachev's injunction to act; Maximytschew and Hertle, "Die Naueröffnung," Teil I, emphasizes the instructions not
to intervene.

122. Wjatscheslaw Kotschemassow, *Meine letzte Mission* (Berlin: Dietz, 1994),
pp. 168–170; see also note 92, above.

123. Schabowski's memoir provides what seems the most credible report we have
of these events; see *Das Politbüro*, pp. 78–95, and, for further elaborations and general reflections, *Der Absturz* (Berlin: Rowohlt, 1991), pp. 243–273. Nonetheless, his
veracity about the role he played in events, especially the October 8 meeting, has
been challenged. Rector Fink charged later that Schabowski lied to the investigating
committee by denying he was instrumental in Berlin security measures and he
claimed that tape recordings show Schabowski wanted to limit the later inquiry into
police violence, *Schnauze*, pp. 11–13, 16. For Schabowski's slant on his alleged non-
involvement in enforcing Berlin security, which is the least convincing part of his
memoir, see *Das Politbüro*, pp. 78–79, 120–121. It is interesting that Schabowski's
"allies" in this period, including Krenz and Schürer, have effectively discontinued
personal contact.

124. Ibid., pp. 96–111.

125. BA-SAPMO: IV 2/1/701: Stenographische Niederschrift der 9. Tagung des
Zentralkomitees der SED, Oct. 18, 1989.

126. See Walter Süß, "Reformen a la Krenz," *taz*, Nov. 10, 1989, in *taz: DDR
Journal*, p. 93. Cf. Monika Zimmermann, "Es dialogisiert- doch was heißt Dialog in
der DDR? Leipziger Szenen," *FAZ*, Oct. 21, 1989, p. 3.

127. Accounts of the demonstrations in Georgia Tornow, "Berlin Alexanderplatz: Geschichte wird Gemacht," *taz*, Nov. 6, 1989 (with speeches by Christoph
Hein, Stefan Heym, and Christa Wolf reported on Nov. 9), and Klaus Hartung, "Die
Wut in Leipzig nimmt zu: Massenproteste gegen Reisegesetz. . . ." *taz*, Nov. 8, 1989,
both now in *taz: DDR Journal*, pp. 71–75, 88–89.

128. Hans-Hermann Hertle, *Chronik des Mauerfalls: die dramatischen Ereignisse
um den 9. November 1989* (Berlin: Ch. Links Verlag, 1996), p. 145. See Pond's reconstruction in *Beyond the Wall*, pp. 130–134, and notes on p. 309; Modrow's sketchy
account in *Aufbruch und Ende*, pp. 24–25; Krenz, *Wenn mauern Fallen*, pp. 165–190.
On the degree of consultation with the Soviets, which led apparently to some confusion between Moscow and its ambassador, see Zelikow and Rice, *Germany Unified*,

pp. 98–101, and notes on pp. 400–401. See also the Henrich Bortfeldt interviews with Hans Modrow, Hoover Institution Interviews with GDR leaders, esp. p. 15. For the debates of the Central Committee on November 8, 9, and 10, see BA-SAPMO: IV 2/1/705: Stenographische Niederschrift der 10. Tagung des Zentralkomitees der SED; and for an extended analysis of the debates see Gerd-Rüdiger Stephan, "Die letzten Tagungen des Zentralkomitees der SED 1988/89. Abläufe und Hintergründe," *Deutschland Archiv* 26, 3 (Mar. 1993): 296–325. See also the discussion of the November ZK debates in chapter 4.

129. On the confusion of what was intended and what resulted, see Maxymytschew and Hertle, "Die Maueröffnung," Teil II, pp. 1145–1158; M. E. Sarotte, "Elite Intransigence and the End of the Berlin Wall," *German Politics* 2, 2 (Aug. 1993): 270–287.

130. "What was possible?" Nationale Volksarmee General, Klaus Dieter Baumgarten, rhetorically asked in a later interview. "The situation was extremely complicated; it was dangerous and we had to be clear about what we would do at this time. Among other possibilities was the question: should the border troops be strengthened so that they could keep the whole thing under control? There was never an option, not even a military option, to shoot. . . . We weren't a band of dark people who had emerged from the underworld. We were an offical organization of the state and its political instrument so long as that state existed." See Hans-Hermann Hertle, "Der Fall der Mauer aus der Sicht der NVA und der Grenztruppen der DDR," *Deutschland Archiv* 28, 9 (Sept. 1995): 901–919 (citation, p. 914; Kochemasov's concern, p. 916), featuring NVA officers' comments on Hertle, "Anfang und Ende der Vorbereitung eines militärischen Einsatzes," *Deutschland Archiv* 27, 12 (Dec. 1994): 1241–1251. Hertle had proposed that the NVA contemplated closing the border by force; General Fritz Strelitz, chief of staff of the NVA, responded that troops were being readied only to keep order in the border-crossing district and that the Krenz government would never have acted to close the Wall without express Soviet approval. Interviews with Strelitz and Generals Baumgarten and Joachim Goldbach turned in part on what the order for "erhöhte Bereitschaft," or special alert, implied. It did allow greater authority for the use of force at the lower levels of command, but there was clearly no intent by the NVA to countermand or modify political decisions.

131. For full citations of Reinhold's internal party studies and the debate they aroused (Krenz and Modrow both belittled their reformist potential), see Stephan, "Die letzten Tagungen des ZK der SED," pp. 316–317.

132. BA-SAPMO: IV 2/1/708: Stenographische Niederschrift der 10. Tagung des Zentralkomitees der SED, Nov. 9, 1989. The speaker was Otto König. The reader should be aware that I have compressed, paraphrased, and consolidated from different places some of the extensive interventions in these impassioned Central Committee debates. But I have remained faithful to content and tone, and material in

direct quotes represents literal translations from the protocol, which itself, however, may involve some paraphrasing.

133. BA-SAPMO: IV 2/1/709: Stenographische Niederschrift der 10. Tagung des Zentralkomitees der SED, Nov. 10, 1989. Hager apparently saw no irony in echoing what had become an infamous byword for authoritarian governance in nineteenth-century Prussian history: the appeal of the Berlin commandant for public order after the army's disastrous defeat by Napoleon at Jena in December 1806.

134. Ibid.

135. BA-SAPMO: IV 2/1/714: Stenographische Niederschrift der 11. Tagung des Zentralkomitees der SED, Nov. 13, 1989.

136. Schabowski, *Das Politbüro*, p. 128.

137. I heard the reports from Jens Reich, but cf. Rosemarie Stein, ed., *Die Charité, 1945–1992: Ein Mythos von Innen* (Berlin: Argon, 1992).

138. Darnton, *Berlin Journal*, p. 260.

139. Ibid., p. 119.

140. I am grateful to my former student Stein Berre for the relevant citations.

141. See the *Report of the National Advisory Commission on Civil Disorders* [Kerner Commission] (Washington, DC: U.S. Government Printing Office, 1968) and related studies for interpretations of the 1960s urban demonstrations. For the American revolutionary era, Pauline Maier, "Popular Uprisings and Civil Authority in Eighteenth Century America," *William and Mary Quarterly* 27 (1970): 3–35.

142. I have tried to develop this argument further in "Democracy since the French Revolution," in John Dunn, ed., *Democracy: The Unfinished Journey, 508 B.C.–A.D. 1993* (Oxford: Oxford University Press, 1992), pp. 125–155. Zwahr's memoir and analysis of 1989 in Leipzig implies the same conclusion; see *Ende einer Selbstzerstörung*.

CHAPTER 4

1. Included in Gerhard Besier and Stephan Wolf, eds., *"Pfarrer, Christen und Katholiken," Das Ministerium für Staatssicherheit der ehemaligen DDR und die Kirchen*, 2nd rev. ed. (Neukirchen-Vluyn: Neukirchener Verlag, 1992), p. 533.

2. "Außerparlamentarische Opposition. Partei oder Platform mit politischem Arm," interview with Hans-Jochen Tschiche, spokesperson for the New Forum in Magdeburg by Klaus-Helge Donath, *taz*, Nov. 15, 1989, in *taz: DDR Journal*, pp. 135–136.

3. Hermann Rudolph, "Neues Forum für 'neue Einheit,'" *Süddeutsche Zeitung* (henceforth *SZ*), Jan. 29, 1990.

4. Interview at Palast der Republik (Volkskammer), July 12, 1990; and address at

Center for European Studies, Nov. 6, 1990. For an acute but sympathetic description of Reich's ambivalence toward politics, see Robert Leicht, "Als Bürger in die Politik geraten: Jens Reich vom Neuen Forum nimmt wahr, was er nicht verändern kann," *Die Zeit*, Feb. 9, 1990, p. 5.

5. For a good coverage of the dissident groupings ("Störversuche—Mißbrauch der Kirchen im Sinne des Gegners. Von Außen und von Innen") within the church, see the Stasi's own reports: "Informationsmaterial der ZAIG zu Kirchenfragen, Berlin Mai 1987," included in Besier and Wolf, *Pfarrer, Christen und Katholiken*, pp. 468–496. The report began with a didactic history of the church in Germany: "German history demonstrates that the official church was always allied with the exploiters of the people. This explains those contradictions [between idealistic and reactionary trends] that also mark the history of the churches still active in the DDR today" (p. 469). On the Berlin appeal of February 1982, see also ibid., pp. 325–327. For a non-Stasi history, see the environmentalist Wolfgang Rüddenklau, *Störenfried: DDR-opposition 1986–1989* (Berlin: BasisDruck, 1992). For the best general coverage of dissidence, see Mary Fulbrook, *Anatomy of a Dictatorship: Inside the GDR 1949–1989* (Oxford: Oxford University Press, 1995).

6. MfS: ZAIG, No. 150/89: "Information über beachtenswerte Aspekte . . . innerer feindlicher, oppositioneller und anderer negativer Kräfte in personellen Zusammenschlüßen," June 1, 1989, in Armin Mitter and Stefan Wolle, eds., *"Ich liebe euch doch alle!" Befehle und Lageberichte des MfS Januar–November 1989* (Berlin: BasisDruck, 1990), pp. 46–71.

7. Robert F. Goeckel, *The Lutheran Church and the East German State* (Ithaca, NY: Cornell University Press, 1990), pp. 56–85, 172–80, 255–60.

8. See, for instance, Heino Falcke, "Unsere Kirche und ihre Gruppen. Lebendiges Bekennen heute?" (1985), in Detlef Pollack, ed., *Die Legitimität der Freiheit. Politisch alternative Gruppen in der DDR unter dem Dach der Kirche* (Frankfurt am Main: Peter Lang, 1990), pp. 41–55.

9. Mitter and Wolle, *Ich liebe euch doch alle*, pp. 59–61. See also Ronald D. Asmus, "Is There a Peace Movement in the GDR?" *Orbis* 27 (summer 1983): 301–341; Joyce M. Mushaben, "Swords into Ploughshares," *Studies in Comparative Communism* 17 (summer 1984): 123–135; Goeckel, *Lutheran Church*, pp. 261–267.

10. For a comprehensive treatment of the Euromissile controversy of the early 1980s from this perspective, see Jeffrey Herf, *War by Other Means: Soviet Power, West German Resistance, and the Battle of the Euromissiles* (New York: Free Press, 1991); also David Gress, *Peace and Survival: West Germany, the Peace Movement and European Security* (Stanford, CA: Hoover Institution Press, 1985).

11. For "hysterically exaggerated" [hysterisch aufgebauschten. . .] see "Informationsmaterial der ZAIG zu Kirchenfragen," May 1987, in Besier and Wolf, *Pfarrer*,

Christen und Katholiken, p. 481. See also Jan Wielgohs and Marianne Schulz, "Von der 'friedlichen Revolution' in die politische Normalität," in Hans Joas and Martin Kohli, eds., *Der Zusammenbruch der DDR* (Frankfurt am Main: Suhrkamp, 1993), p. 225; also MfS: ZAIG, June 1, 1989: "Information" in Mitter and Wolle, *Ich liebe euch doch alle*, p. 66; and Günter Krusche, "Gemeinden in der DDR sind beunruhigt. Wie soll die Kirche sich zu den Gruppen stellen?" in Pollack, *Die Legitimität der Freiheit*, pp. 57–62.

12. MfS: ZAIG, No. 77/89, Feb. 14, 1989: "Information über das 'Grün-Ökologische Netzwerk Arche . . .," in Mitter and Wolle, *Ich liebe euch doch alle*, pp. 17–19. The new organization, "Network, Ark," emerged not only as a result of the crackdown on the old group, but from rivalries between eco-enthusiasts Wolfgang Rüddenklau and Carlo Jordan.

13. Some of this information was provided by Ulrike Poppe (conversation, Chicago, May 1992). See her essay "Das kritische Potential der Gruppen in Kirche und Gesellschaft," in Pollack, *Die Legitimität der Freiheit*, pp. 63–80. On Gerd Poppe and the founding of IFM and *Grenzfall*, see John Christopher Torpey, "Between Anti-Fascism and Opposition: East German Intellectuals, Socialism, and the National Question, 1945–1990," (Ph.D. dissertation, University of California, 1992), pp. 208–210. Torpey's work provides a useful guide to the protest scene.

14. See the contributions to Pollack, *Die Legitimität der Freiheit*, for the stress on groups; also Ehrhart Neubert, *Eine protestantische Revolution* (Osnabruck: Kontext, 1990), pp. 52–64ff.

15. Torpey, "Between Anti-Fascism and Opposition," pp. 231–240.

16. Wolf-Jürgen Grabner, "Zur Stellung der Kirchen in den gesellschaftlichen Veränderungen der DDR," and Ulrike Franke et al., "Der Pfarrer im Spannungsfeld von Kirche und Gesellschaft," both in Wolf-Jürgen Grabner, Christiane Heinze, and Detlef Pollack, eds., *Leipzig im Oktober: Kirchen und alternative Gruppen im Umbruch der DDR; Analysen zur Wende* (Berlin: Wichern Verlag, 1990), esp. pp. 32–62.

17. Besier and Wolf, *Pfarrer, Christen und Katholiken*, p. 481. The memo writer ascribed the failure of ecological causes to provide a real rallying point to the well-elaborated environmental guarantees afforded by the GDR—an assessment that the inhabitants of the industrial regions of Saxony would find ludicrous. For a measured assessment of the church role in 1989, see Detlef Pollack, "Religion und gesellschaftlicher Wandel. Zur Rolle der evangelischen Kirche im Prozess des gesellschaftlichen Umbruchs in der DDR," in Joas and Kohli, *Zusammenbruch der DDR*, pp. 246–266.

18. MfS:. ZAIG, No. 150/89: "Information," June 1, 1989, in Mitter and Wolle, *Ich liebe euch doch alle*, p. 51.

19. Ibid., pp. 47–48. See also Sigrid Meuschel, "Revolution in der DDR. Versuch einer sozialwissenschaftlichen Interpretation," in Joas and Kohli, *Zusammenbruch*

der DDR, p. 107; and Detlef Pollack, "Sozialethisch engagierte Gruppen in der DDR. Eine religionssoziologische Untersuchung," in Pollack, *Die Legitimität der Freiheit*, pp. 115–154. The centers of activity cited in this paragraph are from the Stasi "Information" of June 1, 1989, in Mitter and Wolle, *Ich liebe euch alle*, esp. pp. 49–59.

20. Founding manifesto of New Forum. For a critical analysis of this program see Uwe Klussmann, "A Whimper or a Bang," *Konkret*, Nov. 1989. For a more extended discussion by the major New Forum intellectual, see Rolf Heinrich, *Der vormundschaftliche Staat* (Reinbek bei Hamburg: rororo aktuell, 1989).

21. Klaus Hartung, "Die Wut in Leipzig nimmt zu," *taz*, Nov. 8, 1989, in *taz: DDR Journal*, pp. 88–89.

22. Cited in Christiane Kohl, "'Der wäre fast gelyncht worden,'" *Der Spiegel*, no. 48, Nov. 27, 1989, p. 55.

23. "Wenn wir nichts unternehmen arbeitet die Zeit gegen uns," Sept. 18, 1989, and "Reformen in unserem Land sind dringend notwendig," Sept. 19, 1989, both in *taz: DDR Journal*, pp. 14–15.

24. "Sozialistische Konkurrenz für Honecker," ibid., pp. 16–18.

25. Marlies Menge, "Anwalt der Bürgerbewegung," *Die Zeit*, Feb. 16, 1990, p. 6.

26. "Wir haben ein Recht," and "Demokratie ohne Wenn und Aber," both in *taz: DDR Journal*, pp. 45–46. (I have resorted to Democratic Breakthrough as the English title of the Demokraticher Aufbruch, although "Upsurge" would be a more literal equivalent.)

27. Matthias Geis, "'Reformen a la Hager sind uns zu Mager,' In der DDR beginnt die entscheidende Phase für die Formierung der Opposition," *taz*, Oct. 18, 1989, in *taz: DDR Journal*, pp. 47–49.

28. See Menge, "Anwalt der Bügerbewegung."

29. Cited in Bernd Lindner, "Die politische Kultur der Straße als Medium der Veränderung," *Aus Politik und Zeitgeschichte* B27/90 (June 29, 1990): 17. Also, "'Wir stellen uns der Diskussion': Erklärung des SED-Politbüros vom 11. Oktober in Auszügen," *taz*, Oct. 11, 1989, in *taz: DDR Journal*, p. 47.

30. Max Thomas Mehr, "Schlüsselläuten der Revolution," *taz*, Oct. 18, 1989, in *taz: DDR Journal*, p. 51.

31. For a detailed account of the origins, configuration, and activity of the Round Table, see Uwe Thaysen, *Der Runde Tisch. Oder: Wo blieb das Volk? Der Weg der DDR in die Demokratie* (Opladen: Westdeutscher Verlag, 1990). On the diverse groups as of 1989, Gerda Haufe and Karl Bruckmeier, eds., *Die Bürgerbewegungen in der DDR und in den Ostdeutschen Ländern* (Opladen: Westdeutscher Verlag, 1993).

32. For a useful summary of the rapid changes in party and state, see Gerd-Joachim Glaeßner, *Der schwierige Weg zur Demokratie: Vom Ende der DDR zur deutschen Einheit*, 2nd ed. (Opladen: Westdeutscher Verlag, 1992), pp. 66–94.

33. Summary of the Stasi developments in Thaysen, *Der Runde Tisch*, pp. 77–80. Newspaper coverage and comments on the growing controversy: "Neue Spannungen am 'runden Tisch,'" *Frankfurter Rundschau*, Jan. 4, 1990; "Regierung Hans Modrow nimmt den 'runden Tisch' nicht ernst," *Die Welt*, Jan. 4, 1990. "Einlenken der Opposition verhindert Scheitern der Gespräche am Runden Tisch," *SZ*, Jan. 9, 1990, p. 1; Monika Zimmermann, "Die Arbeiter vor der Volkskammer fühlen sich alleingelassen," *FAZ*, Jan. 11–13, 1990; also "Opposition mißtrauisch, Machthaber verstockt . . . ," *FAZ*, Jan. 9, 1990, p. 1; "Bricht Regierung auseinander?" *Die Welt*, Jan. 10, 1990; "Modrow verzichtet auf Verfassungsschutz," *Frankfurter Rundschau*, Jan. 13, 1990; "Modrow gibt vor der Volkskammer nach," *FAZ*, Jan. 13, 1990, p. 1; Hermann Rudolph, "Die SED spielt Ordnungsmacht," *SZ*, Jan. 13–14, 1990, p. 4; "Oppositionsparteien über Modrow empört," *SZ*, Jan. 15, 1990, p. 3; "Der 'Runde Tisch' stand auf der Kippe," *Frankfurter Rundschau*, Jan. 9, 1990. Modrow's version and his January 15 speech to the Round Table in *Aufbau und Ende* (Hamburg: Konkret, 1991), pp. 71–78, 163–168.

34. Joachim Nawrocki, "Unruhe wird zu Zorn," *Die Zeit*, Jan. 19, 1990, p. 7.

35. Development of the late January crisis in Thaysen, *Der runde Tisch*, pp. 82–87, with a critique of Modrow, pp. 163–172. For press coverage, Joachim Nawrocki, "Regieren auf Treibsand," *Die Zeit*, Jan. 26, 1992, p. 4; Olaf Ihlau, "Kurssuchen, während der Untergang droht," *SZ*, Jan. 29, 1992, p. 3; "Die Basis der Ost-CDU versteht ihre Führung nicht mehr," *Stuttgarter Zeitung*, Jan. 22, 1990; "DDR-Opposition zu Regierungsbeteiligung bereit," *SZ*, Jan. 23, 1990, p. 1; Olaf Ihlau, "De Maizière: Wir brauchen schnell eine grosse Koalition," *SZ*, Jan. 27–28, 1990, p. 2; Ihlau, "Kabinett Modrow kann weiter regieren," *SZ*, Jan. 27–28, 1990; "Vertreter der Opposition beraten mit Modrow über Regierungsbildung," *SZ*, Jan. 29, 1990. On the SED-PDS internal debate, "Gysi lehnt Auflösung der SED ab," *SZ*, Jan. 29, 1990, and for Modrow's view of expanding the cabinet see "Bilanz nach 150 Tagen: Rückblick auf meine Regierungszeit (I)—Ein Dokument zur Zeitgeschichte," *Die Zeit*, Apr. 13, 1990. See also *taz: Journal Nr. 2: Die Wende der Wende. Januar bis März 1990: Von der Öffnung der Mauer des Brandenburger Tores zur Öffnung der Wahlurnen* (Berlin, 1990), p. 63 (hereafter, *taz: Journal Nr. 2*).

36. "Eine 'Regierung der nationalen Verantwortung' bis zur vorgezogenen Wahl am 18. März in der DDR," *FAZ*, Jan. 30, 1990; Joachim Nawrocki, "Wo alles ins Schwanken gerät," *Die Zeit*, Feb. 2, 1990; "DDR-Opposition regiert jetzt mit," *Frankfurter Rundschau*, Feb. 6, 1990.

37. See Janine P. Holc, "Solidarity and the Polish State: Competing Discursive Strategies on the Road to Power," *EEPS* 6, 2 (spring 1992): 121–140. I follow Holc's exposition in discussing the Geremek, Kuron, and Hall notions of civil society.

38. "Die Zeiger der Uhr stehen auf fünf nach zwölf," Petra Bornhöft interview with Pastor Michael Turek and bridge construction engineer Ernst Demele, in *taz*, Oct. 18, 1989, in *taz: DDR Journal*, p. 52.

39. Jadwiga Stanizkis, *Poland's Self-Limiting Revolution* (Princeton: Princeton University Press, 1984).

40. Ullmann cited in Thaysen, *Der Runde Tisch*, p. 210.

41. Vaclav Havel et al., *The Power of the Powerless* (Armonk, NY: M. E. Sharpe, 1989), pp. 64–67. For the lineage of the idea, see Jean Cohen and Andrew Arato, *Civil Society and Political Theory* (Cambridge, MA: MIT Press, 1992). For a report on the contemporary political uses. see Timothy Garton Ash, *The Uses of Adversity* (New York: Random House, 1989), pp. 193–95, 270–74. See also Bronisław Geremek, "Between Hope and Despair," *Daedalus* (winter 1990): 104–105: "The birth of Solidarity . . . was understood to be a self-organization of civil society."

42. Jacques Rupnik, "Dissent in Poland, 1968–78: The End of Revisionism and the Rebirth of Civil Society in Poland," in Rudolf Tokes, ed., *Opposition in Eastern Europe* (Baltimore: Johns Hopkins University Press, 1979); also Z. A. Pelczynski, "Solidarity and 'the Rebirth of Civil Society' in Poland, 1976–81," in John Keane, ed., *Civil Society and the State: New European Perspectives* (London: Verso, 1988), pp. 361–380. Pelczynski separates the private concern of interest groups as "civil society" from their public aspirations, which, following Tocqueville's *Democracy in America* [1835], he calls "political society." See also Andrew Arato, "Civil Society against the State: Poland, 1980–81," *Telos* 47 (1981): 23–47; and Arato, "Empire vs Civil Society: Poland, 1981–82," *Telos* 50 (1981–82): 19–48. Havel citation from "Power of the Powerless," p. 91.

43. Ehrhart Neubert, "Religion in der DDR Gesellschaft . . .," in Pollack, *Die Legitimität der Freiheit*, p. 35.

44. Friedrich Schorlemmer, "Macht und Ohnmacht kleiner Gruppen . . .," in ibid., p. 17.

45. Poppe, "Das kritische Potential der Gruppen in Kirche und Gesellschaft," in ibid., p. 70.

46. Havel, *The Power of the Powerless*, p. 95.

47. Ibid., pp. 78–81. See also in Havel, *The Power of the Powerless*, Petr Uhl, "The Alternative Community as Revolutionary Avant-Garde," pp. 188–197, and Vaclav Benda, "Catholicism and Politics," pp. 110–124. Benda differentiated between the relatively intellectual Czech Catholic approach and the more populist or national-church oriented traditions of Slovakia and Poland.

48. Günter Gaus, *Wo Deutschland liegt. Eine Ortsbestimmung* (Munich: Deutscher Taschenbuch-Verlag, 1986), esp. pp. 115–125; see also chapter 3. For the earlier fate

of clubs, see Czesław Miłosz, *The Captive Mind*, trans. Jane Zielonko (New York: Vintage, 1990), pp. 197–198.

49. The Whigs entrusted national development to economic and mercantile interests; Tories looked to the church and the squires. Neither really denied the capacity of civil society; they had competing visions of what it incorporated or should incorporate. For the respective analyses, see Isaac Kramnick, *Bolingbroke and His Circle: The Politics of Nostalgia in the Age of Walpole* (Cambridge, MA: Harvard University Press, 1968); and J. G. A. Pocock, *The Machiavellian Moment: Florentine Political Thought and the Atlantic Republican Tradition* (Princeton: Princeton University Press, 1975). See also John Keane, "Despotism and Democracy: The Origins and Development of the Distinction between Civil Society and the State, 1750–1850," in Keane, *Civil Society and the State*, pp. 35–71; also Adam Ferguson, *An Essay on the History of Civil Society* (1767).

50. Laurence W. Dickey, *Hegel: Religion, Economics, and the Politics of Spirit, 1770–1807* (Cambridge: Cambridge University Press, 1987); G. W. F. Hegel, *Grundlinien der Philosophie des Rechts*, 20 vols. (Frankfurt am Main: Suhrkamp, 1970), vol. 7, paragraphs 182–256.

51. Antonio Gramsci, *Selections from the Prison Notebooks*, ed. Quintin Hoare and Geoffrey Nowell Smith (New York: International Publishers, 1971), p. 235; Norberto Bobbio, "Gramsci and the Concept of Civil Society," in Keane, *Civil Society and the State*, pp. 73–127.

52. Andrew Arato stresses this aspect in "Revolution, Civil Society, and Democracy," in Zbigniew Rau, ed., *The Reemergence of Civil Society in Eastern Europe and the Soviet Union* (Boulder, CO: Westview Press, 1991), pp. 161–181; cf. also Timothy Garten Ash's concept of "refolution," in *The Uses of Adversity: Essays on the Fate of Central Europe* (New York: Random House, 1989), pp. 309–324; also Adam Michnik, "The New Evolutionism," in *Letters from Prison and Other Essays* (Berkeley: University of California Press, 1986); and Lawrence Goodwyn, *Breaking the Barrier: The Rise of Solidarity in Poland* (New York: Oxford University Press, 1991), pp. 255–260.

53. Geremek's offer was perhaps designed to let the party sanction a renewed pluralism, and indeed characterized the settlement reached by the Polish Round Table in the fall of 1988, which provided that 65 percent of the seats in the lower house of the Sejm would be reserved for the Communist Party and its longtime coalition partners. This party prerogative lasted only a year, however. Even had it not quickly provoked tensions, in the long run such divided domains as Geremek proposed could not have lasted. Just debating a national budget hopelessly mingles social and political issues.

54. Holc, "Competing Discursive Strategies." For the difficulties of early Solidarity in both representing workers and seeking to be a more inclusive party, see David

Ost, *Solidarity and the Politics of Anti-Politics: Opposition and Reform since 1968* (Philadelphia: Temple University Press, 1990); for its difficulties in the late 1980s, see Jadwiga Stanizkis, "The Obsolescence of Solidarity," *Telos* 80 (summer 1989): 37–50; and Bronislaw Misztal, ed., *Poland after Solidarity: Social Movements versus the State* (New Brunswick, NJ: Transaction, 1985). For later controversies over the role of intellectuals versus workers in the movement, see note 55.

55. Charles E. Lindblom, *Politics and Markets: The World's Political Economic Systems* (New York: Basic Books, 1977); Alexis de Tocqueville, *Democracy in America*, trans. Henry Reeve, ed. Francis Bowen and Phillips Bradley, 2 vols. (New York: Vintage, 1990) vol. 2, part 2, chap. 7.

56. Labor movements could be strong even when markets were weak, as in Poland and under Peronism. They too put pressure on authoritarian governments (indeed their original pressure was often the motive for *pronunciamentos* as in Argentina in 1955 and Brazil in 1964, and Poland in 1981). But the structures that derived from a union-government standoff were usually more corporatist than those that derived from market pressure. On these issues, see Guillermo O'Donnell, Philippe C. Schmitter, and Laurence Whitehead, eds. *Transitions from Authoritarian Rule: Comparative Perspectives* (Washington, DC: Woodrow Wilson International Center for Scholars, and Baltimore: Johns Hopkins University Press, 1986); and most recently Juan J. Linz and Alfred Stepan, eds., *Problems of Democratic Transition and Consolidation: Southern Europe, South America, and Post-Communist Europe* (Baltimore: Johns Hopkins University Press, 1996); also Grzegorz Eckiert, "Prospects and Dilemmas of the Transition to a Market Economy in East Central Europe," paper presented at the American Political Science Association meeting, Aug. 31, 1990, and Eckiert, "Democratic Processes in East Central Europe: A Theoretical Reconsideration," *British Journal of Political Science* 21, 3 (July 1991): 285–313; Samuel Valenzuela, "Labor Movements in Transitions to Democracy: A Framework for Analysis," *Comparative Politics* 21, 4 (July 1989): 445–472; and on the corporatist outcome, Stanizkis, *Poland's Self-Limiting Revolution*.

57. For a revealing set of interviews with opposition intellectuals (though heavily structured and interpreted), see Dirk Philipsen, *We Were the People: Voices from East Germany's Revolutionary Autumn of 1989* (Durham, NC: Duke University Press, 1993), pp. 292–327; 351–381.

58. For a critique of the intellectuals and insistence on the workers' autonomous contribution to Solidarity, see Goodwyn, *Breaking the Barrier*, and Roman Laba, *The Roots of Solidarity* (Princeton: Princeton University Press, 1991). For an alarmed diagnosis of the populist revival, see Irena Grudzinska Gross, "Post-Communist Resentment, or the Rewriting of Polish History," *EEPS* 6, 2 (spring 1992): 141–151.

Anti-Semitism as such remained limited in its political impact, even in Russia. Voters turned to former communists, not anti-Semites in Hungary. No responsible political leaders exploited the theme in united Germany; rather, an effort to "recover" aspects of the German Jewish past was undertaken East and West.

59. Cf. Jirina Siklova, "The Solidarity of the Culpable," *Social Research*, 58, 4 (winter 1991): 765–773.

60. Sandro Setta, *L'uomo Qualunque 1944–1948* (Bari: Laterza, 1975).

61. See Charles S. Maier, *The Unmasterable Past: History, Holocaust and German National Identity* (Cambridge, MA: Harvard University Press, 1988).

62. For ideas of liminality and antistructure, see citations in chapter 3, n. 55; also Ari Zolberg, "Moments of Madness," *Politics and Society* 2, 2 (1972): 183–207.

63. As Andrew Arato has written in Rau, *Reemergence of Civil Society*, p. 162: "The new Eastern European regimes have increasingly turned their attention to two projects: the establishment of elite-pluralistic systems of party competition and of liberal market economies. The first of these projects actually tends to the demobilization of civil society—either directly or indirectly (that is, by reducing its influence to the narrowest possible channels). The second, quite compatibly, tends to reduce civil society to economic society."

64. Rolf Schneider, "Die Einheit wird kommen," *Der Spiegel*, no. 48, Nov. 27, 1989, p. 45.

65. "Der Streit der Ideologien und die gemeinsame Sicherheit: Gemeinsame Erklärung der Grundwertekommission der SPD und der Akademie für Gesellschaftswissenschaften beim ZK der SED vom 27. August 1987," in Erhard Eppler et al., eds., *Kultur des Streits: Die gemeinsame Erklärung von SPD und SED. Stellungnahmen und Dokumenten* (Cologne: Pahl-Rugenstein, 1988). For a critique of SPD policies, see preeminently Timothy Garton Ash, *In Europe's Name: Germany and the Divided Continent* (New York: Random House, 1993), pp. 324–342.

66. See the portrait by Gerhard Spörl, "Außenseiter im Inneren der Macht," *Die Zeit*, Oct. 6, 1989, p. 8. See also Dieter Bohl's interview with Modrow in *Die Zeit*, Nov. 17, 1989 ("'Wir müssen aus der Hektik herauskommen'"). Also: Modrow's own three-part series, "Bilanz nach 150 Tagen," *Die Zeit*, Apr. 13, 20, 27, 1990, and his memoir of 1989–90, *Aufbruch und Ende*. For Lutz Niethammer's discussion of generational politics, see "Erfahrungen und Strukturen. Prolegomena zu einer Geschichte der Gesellschaft der DDR," in Hartmut Kaelble, Jürgen Kocka, and Hartmut Zwahr, eds., *Sozialgeschichte der DDR* (Stuttgart: Klett-Cotta, 1994), pp. 95–115, esp. 104–105.

67. "Markt zwischen den Zeilen," *Die Zeit*, Nov. 24, 1989. See also Modrow, "Bilanz nach 150 Tagen (I)," *Die Zeit*, Apr. 13, 1990.

68. "Die Mauer ist gefallen. Das Neue Forum über die Konsequenzen der Reisefreiheit," *taz*, Nov. 12, 1989, in *taz: DDR Journal*, p. 132. For Bärbel Bohley's alleged reaction, ibid., p. 118: "The regime has showed its incompetence, and free elections under these conditions would be a catastrophe."

69. "Gegen die Herrschaft des Geldes. Gespräch mit Pfarrer Schorlemmer," interview with Klaus-Helge Donath, *taz*, Nov. 14, 1989, in *taz: DDR Journal*, p.133.

70. Monika Zimmermann, "Bei aller Freude Unsicherheit und Ratlosigkeit," *FAZ*, Nov. 17, 1989, p. 3.

71. "Ausserparlamentarische Opposition, Partei oder Platform mit politischem Arm?" Hans-Jochen Tschiche," interview, Nov. 15, 1989, in *taz: DDR Journal*, pp. 135–136. See also Peter Thomas Krüger, "'Demokratie braucht Initiative und Phantasie,'" *Das Parlament*, Feb. 16, 1990, p. 8.

72. Vera Gaserow, "Mein Platz ist in der Opposition," *taz*, Feb. 26, 1990, in *taz: Journal II*, pp. 60–62.

73. Marlies Menge, "Plädoyer für andere Kräfte," *Die Zeit*, Apr. 20, 1990.

74. Stefan Heym, "Aschermittwoch in der DDR," *Der Spiegel*, no. 49, Dec. 4, 1989, p. 58.

75. Matthias Geis, "Neues Forum: Keine Einheit für die Einheit," *taz*, Jan. 29, 1990, in *taz: Journal Nr. 2*, pp. 54–56. "In a painful process of shedding illusions, under pressure from the change of public opinion, the New Forum bids farewell to its original idea of a society that diverges in its new democratic quality, not only from that of the last 40 years, but from the model of the Federal Republic."

76. See "Der Schalck Skandal," *Der Spiegel*, no. 19, May 6, 1991, pp. 36–56.

77. Quotations from "Unerträgliche Selbstgerechtigkeit: Der Aufstand der SED-Basis gegen ihre eigenen Funktionäre," *Der Spiegel*, 46, Nov. 13, 1989, p. 40.

78. Christianne Kohl, "Der wäre fast gelyncht worden."

79. Peter Jochen Winters. "Das grosse Stühlerücken in den Bezirken," *FAZ*, Nov. 17, 1989, p. 3. Cf. Joachim Nawrocki, "Angst vor der Abrechnung," *Die Zeit*, Nov. 17, 1989; and "Heut' gehn wir ins ZK," *Der Spiegel*, no. 48, Nov. 27, 1989, pp. 47–53.

80. Landolf Scherzer, "Das letzte Gefecht," *Die Zeit*, Jan. 5, 1990, pp. 9–11. Scherzer's report on SED party conditions in December 1989 were a sequel to his book *Der Erste* (Cologne: Kiepenheuer & Witsch, 1989)—which detailed the day-to-day work of SED *Kreis* (county) leader Hans-Dieter Fritschler, who emerged not unlike a benevolent political boss in any party stronghold, be it Chicago, South Boston, or Palermo.

81. Fritz Ulrich Fack, "Die alten Kräfte sind noch mächtig," *FAZ*, Jan. 9, 1990, p. 1; cf. the concerned editorial in the left-wing *Frankfurter Rundschau*: Hans-Herbert Gaebel, "Kampf um die Macht," Jan. 9, 1990, p. 3.

82. "Kohl sagt Bonner Treffen mit Modrow nicht ab," *SZ*, Jan. 11, 1990, and "'In zwei Schritten vollziehen': Der Kanzler enttäuscht über Modrows Reformzusagen," *SZ*, Jan. 13–14, 1990, p. 5. Cf. the warnings in "Schädliche Gespräche," *FAZ*, Jan. 9, 1990, p. 1.

83. "Erst Mitleid, dann zuschlagen," *Der Spiegel*, no. 3, Jan. 15, 1990, pp. 19–28; also report in *Frankfurter Rundschau*, Jan. 9, 1990, p. 2. The rhymes in German were: "Lügen haben kurze Beine—Gysi zeig uns doch mal deine"; "SED- und Stasi-Macht, haben noch nicht Schluß gemacht."

84. "Die alte SED hat die DDR ruiniert: Austrittserklärung von 40 Mitgliedern in Wortlaut"; and Albrecht Hinze, "Wolfgang Berghofer. Ehemaliger stellvertretender SED-Vorsitzender," both in *SZ*, Jan. 23, 1990, p. 5.

85. Cited in Hans Holzhaider, "Eine Klausur mit vielen Unbekannten," *SZ*, Jan. 15, 1990, p. 3. On the CSU effort in the East, "CSU findet programmatische Übereinstimmung," in the same issue.

86. "Union: Ost-CDU soll sich von der SED distanzieren," and "Waigel: Unser Partner in der DDR ist die DSU," *SZ*, Jan. 23, 1990, p. 2. See also the report on the Leipzig party conference by Christian Wernicke, "Harmonie im konservativen Dreiklang," *Die Zeit*, Feb. 23, 1990, p. 2; and Brigitte Fehrle, "Die CSU spielt Geburtshilfer in Sachsen," *taz*, Jan. 15, 1990, in *taz: Journal Nr.* 2, p. 24.

87. Rüdiger Rosenthal, "Auf dem Wege zur Macht? Startbedingungen der größten Oppositionspartei," *Das Parlament*, Feb. 16, 1990, p. 8.

88. Also "Aufbruch zu neuen alten Ufern," *SZ*, Jan. 15, 1990, p. 3. The vote at the East Berlin Delegates Congress to resume the old name was 440 to 24.

89. For a report on foundations of independent unions, see Ralf Boerger's discussion of the "reform-Union," *Der Spiegel*, no. 44, Oct. 31, 1989. But as Boerger noted, the situation was reversed from that of Solidariność: the union appeared after the movement in the country; it did not lead the movement.

90. See also the portrait by Matthias Naß, "Im Grundvertrauen zu den Menschen," *Die Zeit*, Mar. 16, 1990, p. 5. See also for the SPD in the campaign two articles from *taz*: Matthias Geis, "Der SPD fehlte die Lust an der Debatte," Feb. 26, 1990, and Petra Bornhöft, "Ibrahim Boehme für Präsident?" Feb. 19, 1990, both included in *taz: Journal Nr.* 2, pp. 117–121.

91. See note 87 above; also "Das Geschäft erleichtert: Die neuen Sozialdemokraten in der DDR—viel Papier und wenig Organisation," *Der Spiegel*, no. 46, Nov. 13, 1989, pp. 50–53, which emphasized the role of the twenty-nine-year-old pastor Stefan Reiche. On Meckel, see Christian Wernicke, "Der Moralist und die Macht," *Die Zeit*, Mar. 2, 1990, p. 5.

92. Rosenthal, "Auf dem Wege zur Macht?"

93. Joachim Nawrocki, "Die Saat geht auf: Schon Minister: Rainer Eppelmann

vom Demokratischen Aufbruch," *Die Zeit*, Mar. 2, 1990, p. 5. Ulrich von Hutten was the imperial knight who fought as a Protestant and German national champion in the early Reformation.

94. Cf. J. Leithäuser, "Die Konkurrenz ist unter den Parteien noch lebendig," *FAZ*, Mar. 8, 1990.

95. Udo Bergdoll, "Der Nachlaßverwalter zeigt Statur," *SZ*, Feb. 14, 1990, p. 3; Karl Feldmeyer, "Zwei Jahre nach Honeckers Besuch ist alles anders. Modrows Visite in Bonn," *FAZ*, Feb. 14, 1990, p. 3. See also chapter 5.

96. See "Es war wie eine Ohrfeige," and the interview with Wolfgang Ullmann in *Der Spiegel*, no. 8, Feb. 19, 1990, pp. 19–26.

97. Joachim Nawrocki, "Die Saat geht auf," *Die Zeit*, Mar. 2, 1990, p. 5.

98. Ibid.

99. "PDS drängt Modrow zu Spitzenkandidatur," *SZ*, Feb. 24–25, 1990, p. 1.

100. Marlies Menge, "Glück mit Hans?" *Die Zeit*, Mar. 2, 1990, p. 6.

101. "DDR-SPD strebt marktwirtschaftliche Ordnung an," *SZ*, Feb. 14, 1990.

102. See Elisabeth Noelle-Neumann, "Ein demokratischer Wahlkampf gab den Ausschlag. Wie es zur überraschenden Veränderung der Wahlabsichten in der DDR kam," *FAZ*, Mar. 23, 1990, p. 9; and the detailed analysis by electoral sociologists Manfred Berger, Wolfgang Gibowski, and Dieter Roth, "Ein Votum für die Einheit," *Die Zeit*, Mar. 23, 1990, p. 5; also Dieter Roth, "Die Wahlen zur Volkskammer in der DDR: Der Versuch einer Erklärung," *Politische Vierteljahresschrift* 31, 3 (Sept. 1990): 69–93; also Roth, "Die Volkskammerwahl in der DDR am 18. März 1990. Rationales Wahlverhalten beim ersten demokratischen Urnengang," in Ulrike Liebert and Wolfgang Merkel, eds., *Die Politik der deutschen Einheit* (Opladen: Leske + Budrich, 1991), pp. 115–138; and Matthias Jung, "Parteiensystem und Wahlen in der DDR: Eine Analyse der Volkskammerwahl vom 18. März 1990 und der Kommunalwahlen vom 6. Mai 1990," *Aus Politik und Zeitgeschichte* B27/90 (June 29, 1990): 3–15.

CHAPTER 5

1. BA: Potsdam: DC 20 I/3/2891. V 10/90, "Staatshymne der DDR," Jan. 4, 1990 ("Auferstanden aus Ruinen / und der Zukunft zugewandt / lass uns dir zum Guten dienen / Deutschland, einig Vaterland.")

2. Becher was a fascinating figure. He became a sort of commissar for poetry for the regime, dedicating servile lyrics to Stalin. On the other hand Marxist intellectuals who retained some independence never saw him merely as a hack, no matter how much they regretted his forswearing independence. See Hans Mayer, *Der Turm von Babel* (Frankfurt am Main: Suhrkamp, 1993).

3. See Hans-Hermann Hertle's discussion with Schürer of Schalck-Golodkowski's ideas, "'Das reale Bild war eben katastrophal,' Gespräch mit Gerhard Schürer," *Deutschland Archiv*. 25.10 (Oct. 1992): 1035.

4. See chapter 1. Most likely the concept was designed just to throw Western security plans into disarray.

5. For the best-documented study of American policy, see Philip Zelikow and Condoleezza Rice, *Germany Unified and Europe Transformed: A Study in Statecraft* (Cambridge, MA: Harvard University Press, 1995), which I draw upon extensively here. Elizabeth Pond, *Beyond the Wall: Germany's Road to Unification* (New York: Twentieth Century Fund, 1993), had access to fewer documents but provides a highly informed and shrewd narrative based in large part on interviews. Michael R. Beschloss and Strobe Talbott, *At the Highest Levels: The Inside Story of the End of the Cold War* (Boston: Little Brown, 1993), is a well-informed study of the making of Soviet-American foreign policy through 1989–90. Jeffrey Gedmin, *The Hidden Hand: Gorbachev and the Collapse of East Germany* (Washington, DC: AEI Press, 1992), is attentive to the indicators of shifting Soviet policy. Two fundamental contributions to FRG policy are at hand: Timothy Garton Ash, *In Europe's Name: Germany and the Divided Continent* (New York: Random House, 1993), which focuses on the years from 1968 to the mid-1980s, and criticizes the tendency of Social Democratic Ost-politik to lend legitimacy to the SED. For a response, see the massive documentary collection based on West German and East German sources published with a schol-arly introduction by Heinrich Potthoff, *Die "Koalition der Vernunft": Deutschland-politik in den 80er Jahren* (Munich: Deutscher Taschenbuch-Verlag, 1995), which defends the collaborative approach with the DDR as a rational and bipartisan West German effort.

6. Julij A. Kwizinskij, *Vor dem Sturm. Erinnerungen eines Diplomaten* (Berlin: Siedler Verlag, 1993), p. 421.

7. His memoir strikes a curiously apologetic note (which he italicizes): "In the concrete situation then prevailing we did the best possible with respect both to the maintenance of our own interests and the preservation of peace in Europe." Michail Gorbatschow, *Erinnerungen*, trans. Igor Petrowitsch Gorodetzki (Berlin: Siedler Verlag, 1995), p. 700.

8. For the Euromissiles debate and its impact, see, among other sources, Jon-athan Haslam, *The Soviet Union and the Politics of Nuclear Weapons in Europe, 1969–1987: The Problem of the SS-20* (London: Macmillan, 1989); Michael Sodaro, *Moscow, Germany, and the West: From Khrushchev to Gorbachev* (Ithaca, NY: Cornell University Press, 1990); Jeffrey Herf, *War by Other Means: Soviet Power, West German Resistance, and the Battle of the Euromissiles* (New York: Free Press, 1991); David Gress, *Peace and Survival: West Germany, the Peace Movement and European Security* (Stanford, CA: Hoover Institution, 1985).

9. Hannes Adomeit, "Gorbachev, German Unification and the Collapse of Empire," *Post-Soviet Affairs* 10, 3 (Aug.–Sept. 1994): 197–230. Adomeit has drawn on East German Politbüro records and interviews with Soviet participants; I have relied on him for a description of the Soviet policy establishment.

10. For the Honecker-Kohl meetings see the protocols in Potthoff, *Koalition der Vernunft*, pp. 237–241, 305–310.

11. Adomeit, "Gorbachev, German Unification and the Collapse of Empire."

12. Wjatscheslaw Kotschemassow, *Meine letzte Mission. Fakten, Erinnerungen, Überlegungen*, trans. Klaus J. Herrmann (Berlin: Dietz, 1994), pp. 66–67, 72–73.

13. Adomeit, "Gorbachev, German Unification, and the Collapse of Empire," cf. Garton Ash, *In Europe's Name*.

14. Daniel Küchenmeister, "Wann begann das Zerwürfnis zwischen Honecker und Gorbatschow? Erste Bemerkungen zu den Protokollen ihrer Vier-Augen-Gespräche," *Deutschland Archiv* 26, 1 (Jan. 1993): 30–40; Gorbatschow, *Erinnerungen*, pp. 930–31. Gorbachev felt that some easing of the tension occurred briefly in 1987 when Honecker arrived to celebrate the seventieth anniversary of the October Revolution in Moscow. He also claimed to take into account Honecker's service in helping to reconcile Germans and Russians after the National Socialist war, (p. 938).

15. Kotschemassow, *Meine letzte Mission*, pp. 51–55.

16. Witnesses diverge over whether Gorbachev's deferral to history should have been read as a positive concession, or just a polite way to dismiss the issue of unification. See, for the hopeful "spin," Garton Ash, *In Europe's Name*, p. 108; Potthof, *Koalition der Vernunft*, p. 37; and above all Hans-Dietrich Genscher, *Erinnerungen* (Berlin: Siedler Verlag, 1995), pp. 633, 723. But Genscher and Kohl (as recorded by Teltschik) consistently emphasize what they regard as one breakthrough after another on the way to unification; statesmen shape world events in congenial musings along the Rhine (June 1989) or, a year later, in the crisp air of the Caucusus. There is a patterned structure to the memoirs: great men manage to escape from bureaucratic settings and make history as they bond. For a more guarded interpretation of the July conversations, see Kwizinskij, *Vor dem Sturm*, p. 421. At this time, concluded Kvitsinsky, Gorbachev neither regarded German reunification as inevitable, nor did he seek it. Cf. Gorbatchow, *Erinnerungen*, p. 701: "In other words, I didn't exclude the reunification of the German nation in principle, but considered discussion of the question premature and harmful." Cf. Anatoli Tschernajew, *Die letzten Jahre einer Weltmacht: Der Kreml von Innen*, trans. Friederike Börner, Norbert Juraschitz, and Ulrich Mihr (Stuttgart: Deutsche Verlags-Anstalt, 1993), pp. 144–154.

17. Tschernajew, *Die letzten Jahre einer Weltmacht*, p. 130. On the origin of the phrase "common European home," see the wry tracing of conflicting sources in Garton Ash, *In Europe's Name*, pp. 2–3, 429.

18. For the evolution of policy including the contributions of Portugalov and Dashichev, see Gedmin, *The Hidden Hand*, pp. 40–53; Garton Ash, *In Europe's Name*, pp. 107–110, and the notes on pp. 494–495, in which the author communicates much of the subtlety of policy evolution; also Sodaro, *Moscow, Germany and the West*, p. 354. For Chernyaev's advice to Gorbachev, see *Die letzten Jahre einer Weltmacht*, pp. 57–58, 131, 450. I had the chance to ask Shevardnadze, at a dinner for Harvard honorary degree candidates in June 1992, when German policy had changed, and received the same answer he provided to Timothy Garton Ash four months earlier.

19. Gorbatchow, *Erinnerungen*, p. 701; cf. the critique in Igor Maximychev and Pyotr Menshikov, "One German Fatherland?" *International Affairs*, July 1990, p. 33 ("Socialist nation: . . . an armchair catchword which nobody could spell out with reasonable clarity"). The authors were second and third in charge of the Soviet embassy in the GDR in the period they analyze.

20. BA-SAPMO: Büro Günter Mittag, D 30/41797, Bd 3: "Aktennotiz über ein Gespräch Gen. Erich Honecker mit Wjatsceslaw Kotschemassow am 1. Februar 1988." (Cf. Kotschemassow, *Meine letzte Mission*, p. 84, which stresses the unfavorable consequences of GDR indebtedness and dependency vis-à-vis the FRG.) Gorbachev spoke similarly to Lothar Späth, minister of Baden-Württemberg and an advocate of advanced industrial development, a few days later (*Izvestia*, Feb. 11, 1988, cited by Adomeit, "Gorbachev, German Unification, and the Collapse of Empire"), so the theme was probably a current one in Soviet policy discussions and position papers.

21. Tchernajew, *Die letzten Jahre einer Weltmacht*, pp. 228–230, 259. On Kohl's euphoric reading of the meeting: Garton Ash, *In Europe's Name*, p. 118; and for Genscher's equally optimistic interpretation of his concurrent talks with Shevardnadze: Genscher, *Erinnerungen*, pp. 627–628.

22. BA-SAPMO: Büro Egon Krenz, IV 2/2.039/290: "Problemspiegel": Reden führender Representanten auf der Tagung des politischen beratenden Ausschusses des Warschauer Vertrages in Bukarest, 7.–8. Juli 1989.

23. Potthoff, *Koalition der Vernunft*, p. 37.

24. Cf. Adomeit, "Gorbachev, German Unification, and the Collapse of Empire," and the Krenz-Gorbachev talks cited in note 26.

25. Richard Kiessler and Frank Elbe, *Ein runder Tisch mit scharfen Ecken: Der diplomatische Weg zur deutschen Einheit* (Baden-Baden: Nomos, 1993), p. 47. Gorbachev's November 10 message summarized in Zelikow and Rice, *Germany Unified*, p. 107.

26. BA: Potsdam/Berlin: DE 1 /56320; "Niederschrift des Gespräches des Genossen Egon Krenz, Generalsekretär des ZK der SED und Vorsitzender des Staatsrates der DDR, mit Genossen Michail Gorbatschow, Generalsekretär des ZK der KPdSU

und Vorsitzender des Obersten Sowjets der UdSSR, am 1. 11. 1989 in Moskau." The memorandum is written in the subjunctive, which means that although the points of the respective speakers are attributed closely, they are not intended as direct quotation.

27. Tyll Necker, president of the Bundesverband der Deutschen Industrie: "'Es geht nicht schnell genug': Symposium: DDR Wirtschaft" *Die Zeit*, Feb. 9, 1990, pp. 38–44. Cf., in a similar vein, Karl-Heinz Paqué, "Die Schimäre aus dem Nirgendwo . . . Zur Reformdebatte in der DDR," *FAZ*, Jan. 13, 1990, p. 13; but for a different perspective: Uwe Jens (economic spokesman in the SPD Bundestag delegation), "Staatskapital zum Volkskapital umwidmen," *FAZ*, Jan. 11, 1990, p. 13. As for the so-called "third way," so easily dismissed as utopian, actual outcomes do not prove might-have-beens impossible; they demonstrate only that they were not tried or became difficult to stabilize. One can neither discredit nor show the value of a counterfactual possibility by its hypothetical status alone. Social observers and historians all too easily dismiss the potential of roads not taken. This is not to assert the potential of a "third way" but to insist that substantive grounds be adduced for asserting its infeasibility. The simple reason was that if the Soviet Union was casting the GDR loose, and it had to parachute into the capitalist world economy, it would have to play by capitalist rules.

28. This summary and subsequent citations from the February meeting are taken from BA: Potsdam: DC 20 I/3/2912: "Bericht über den Besuch des Vorsitzenden des Ministerrates der DDR und seiner Regierungsdelegation am 13. und 14. Februar in Bonn." Two parallel sets of negotiations were held: between Modrow and Kohl and their advisers Karl Seidel and Hans Teltschik, and between the two general delegations. Positions were repeated in both, though with slight changes of wording; I have cited both without differentiation.

29. BA: Potsdam: DC I/3/2887: "Beschluß über die Einschätzung zur Stabilität der Währung der DDR," Jan. 4, 1990. Exchange rates went from 2.50 East marks per deutsche mark in 1980 to 4.4 in 1988 (= 4.75 to 8.14/$).

30. BA: Potsdam: DC 20 I/3/2867. Beschluß zur Information über die Erfüllung des Staatshaushaltsplanes 1989 bis zum 30. Sept.

31. Both speech and resolution, in BA: Potsdam: DC 20 I/3/2872.

32. BA: Potsdam: DC 20 I/3/2873: Interior Minister Ahrendt to Modrow, Nov. 19, 1989.

33. BA: Potsdam: DC 20 I/3/2873: Beschluß zur Information . . . des Staatshaushaltsplanes, 1990.

34. Harry Maier comment in "'Es geht nicht schnell genug,'" *Die Zeit* (Wirtschafts Symposium), Feb. 9, 1990. For Luft's own slight memoir see *Zwischen Wende und Ende* (Berlin: Aufbau Taschenbuch Verlag, 1991).

35. Cited in Gorbatchow, *Erinnerungen*, p. 720.

36. "'Es geht nicht schnell genug,'" *Die Zeit*, Feb. 9, 1990.

37. The phrase appears in what is in fact a sober analysis of GDR difficulties and potential by Henz Warzecha, then general director of the East Berlin machine-tool Kombinat "7. Oktober." See Nikolaus Piper, "'Eine Art sozialistische Schweiz,'" *Die Zeit*, Dec. 1, 1989, p. 25. For some of the other mixed reactions, see the chastened tone of one West German entrepreneur trying to invest in the still-standing DDR, "'Es geht langsamer als erhofft,'" *Die Zeit*, Nov. 17, 1989, p. 27; Carl-Christian Kaiser, "Der Preis der Freizügigkeit," *Die Zeit*, Nov. 24, 1989, p. 4.

38. *SZ*, Jan. 24, 1990, p. 18. Granted, the statistics were misleading.

39. BA: Potsdam/Berlin: DE 1/56350. Wolfgang Pagel of the Institut für angewandte Wirtschaftsforschung, "Vom Wert der Mark des Bürgers der DDR—ein Plädoyer für die soziale Verträglichkeit einer Währungsunion," Feb. 23, 1990, citing in part: Bundesministerium für innerdeutsche Beziehungen, "Zahlenspiegel: Bundesrepublik Deutschland/Deutsche Demokratische Republik: ein Vergleich" (1988). The net subsidy equaled 58 billion marks of gross subsidies less 29 billion collected in indirect taxes.

40. BA: Potsdam: DC 20 1/3/2903. V 117/90, Jan. 25, 1990. Also on specific conditions: BA: Potsdam: DC 20 1/3/2932. V412/90, "Einschätzung der Lage in den Bezirken für den Zeitraum vom 7.3. bis 13.3.1990."

41. Statistics from BA: Potsdam: DC 20 1/3 /2932. V412/90, "Einschätzung der Lage 7.3 bis 13.3.1990."

42. The reports became more alarming in April. See Renate Filip-Kohn and Udo Ludwig, "Kaufkraft umschichten," *Wirtschaftswoche*, 15, Apr. 6, 1990, p. 128, which argued that productivity was lower than heretofore recognized and recommended an initial capital injection for industrial modernization of DM 200 billion; also Andreas Mauksch, "Verschlissen, veraltet und verkommen: Die Lage in der DDR am Beispiel des Bezirks Dresden," *FAZ*, Apr. 21, 1990, p. 15.

43. BA: Potsdam/Berlin: Plankommission: DE 1/5350: Institut für angewandte Wirtschaftsforschung, "Expertise zur Notwendigkeit und den Modalitäten eines Strukturanpassungsprogrammes . . .," Mar. 1, 1990.

44. BA: Potsdam/Berlin: Plankommission: DE 1/5350: "Expertise: Einschätzung von Hauptrichtungen der Veränderung der Struktur unter den Bedingungen einer Währungsunion und Wirtsschaftsgemeinschaft mit der BRD," Feb. 23, 1990.

45. For the Modrow-Seiters conversation, see BA: Potsdam: DC 20 1/3/2904, Bl. 67–100. "Who is Europe?" Bismarck had retorted when the British ambassador warned that Europe would not tolerate Prussia's helping the Russians to suppress the Polish insurrection in 1863. "Several great nations" was the response. Cited in F. H. Hinsley, *Power and the Pursuit of Peace: Theory and Practice in the History*

of Relations between States (Cambridge: Cambridge University Press, 1963), p. 251. But in 1990, except for the British, the great nations supported Kohl's agenda. The positive connection between German and European aspirations (pan-European, not just West European) is one of the underlying themes of Garton Ash's study, *In Europe's Name*.

46. Jonathan R. Zatlin, "Hard Marks and Soft Revolutionaries: The Economics of Entitlement and the Debate on German Monetary Union, November 5, 1989–March 18, 1990," *German Politics and Society* 33 (fall 1994): 57–84. Zatlin is completing a dissertation on the currency union.

47. Chronology of events and Waigel and Pohl citations from Peter Christ and Ralf Neubauer, *Kolonie im eigenen Land. Die Treuhand, Bonn und die Wirtschaftskatastrophe der fünf neuen Länder* (Berlin: Rowohlt, 1991), pp. 74–76. Cf. Andreas Busch, "Die deutsch-deutsche Währungsunion: Politisches Votum trotz ökonomischer Bedenken," in Ulrike Liebert and Wolfgang Merkel, eds., *Die Politik zur deutschen Einheit* (Opladen: Leske & Budrich, 1991), pp. 185–207, esp. 194–195.

48. *Der Spiegel*, no. 8, Feb. 19, 1990, p. 119.

49. BA: Potsdam/Berlin: DE 1/56350: Institut für Angewandte Wirtschaftsforschung, "Expertise" Feb. 23 and Mar. 1, 1990, cited in notes 43 and 44.

50. BA: Potsdam: DC 20 I/3/2926: "Besuch einer Regierungsdelegation der DDR unter Leitung des Vorsitzenden des Ministerrates, Hans Modrow, in der UdSSR am 5./6. März 1990." Cf. Hans Modrow, *Aufbruch und Ende*, 2nd ed. (Hamburg: Konkret, 1991), pp. 120–125.

51. BA: Potsdam: DC 20 I/3/2926. V 363/90: "Einschätzung der Lage in den Bezirken für den Zeitraum 28.2 bis 6.3. 1990," Berlin, Mar. 7, 1990. And ibid., "7.3 bis 13.3.90," on political meetings and rightist activity.

52. Gerhard Hennemann, "Der Preis des kurzen Wegs," *SZ*, Apr. 6, 1990, p. 4.

53. Jürgen Habermas, "Der DM-Nationalismus," *Die Zeit*, Mar. 30, 1990, p. 62.

54. *Report of the Deutsche Bundesbank for the Year 1990* (Frankfurt am Main, April 1991), p. 46. About 10 percent of the East German money stock headed West in the second half of 1990 (reducing M3 in the new Länder from DM 180 billion to DM 163 billion). By and large, the technical aspects of the conversion were well executed. As the bank indicated, however, the "real economic problems were far harder to handle than the monetary integration. The scale of the competitive weakness of East German enterprises, as compared with their western competitors on national and international markets, was underestimated in some quarters" (p. 1). East German bank accounts were overwhelmingly savings accounts. Life insurance face values also had to be converted, but they represented only a small percentage of the whole.

55. For these debates within the government, see the well-informed *Der Spiegel* article, "'Ohne 1:1 werden wir nicht eins,'" Apr. 9, 1990, pp. 16–23.

56. Ibid. Helmut Schlesinger, second in charge at the Bundesbank, and the industrialist Otto Wolf von Amerongen also warned against the one-to-one rate. See reports in SZ, Apr. 17, 19; Lambsdorff views in ibid., Feb. 14, 1990. The bankers' critiques were seconded within the SPD by Lafontaine, who was happy to watch Kohl squirm under the criticism.

57. For the calculation of valuta mark ratios to the internal value of the East mark (calculated in this case on factory prices less subventions and taxes), see BA: Potsdam/Berlin: DE 1/56318: "Eine Bemerkung zu der Frage, warum 1 Mark der DDR im Ausweis des Devisenerlöses nur 25 Valutapfennige wert ist," Aug. 30, 1988, and also my chapter. 2. See also in DE 1/56318: Ernst Höfner, "Zur Problematik: Was ist notwendig, damit die Mark der DDR auf dem Weltmarkt eine Valutamark wird." In fact the statistics provided by Höfner ("Aufwand der DDR im Export in Mark zur Erwirtschaftung eines Dollar," Sept. 19, 1988) suggested that 4:1 was too optimistic a ratio. In 1980 it required 4.85 marks spent at home to earn a dollar in the West; by 1984 that was 6.74; by 1985, 9.10; and in both 1986 and 1987 approximately 10.85. For the forces driving down the East mark in the weeks after freedom of travel was permitted, see "Ostmark zum Willkür-Kurs," Der Spiegel, no. 48, Nov. 27, 1989, pp. 112–113. The discussion of plans and projected exchange rates is summarized in Erik Gawel, Die deutsch-deutsche Währungsunion: Verlauf und geldpolitische Konsequenzen (Baden-Baden: Nomos, 1994), pp. 147–171.

58. See table in "'Ohne 1:1 werden wir nicht eins,'" p. 22. In the case of the appliances the local price in the East might be 2.5 times that of the deutsche mark price; but the Western wage in deutsche marks was already almost three times the East wage in East marks. For many necessities the price in the East was lower in East marks than it was in deutsche marks in the West.

59. Die Zeit "Symposium," Feb. 9, 1990. According to Knop in the same discussion, East German private savings accounts totaled 177 billion marks as of the end of 1989; most were held by upper-income professionals and workers. The sum amounted to about 10,000 per capita. If 30 billion represented currency overhang— that is, forced savings that arose because nominal income exceeded available national product—that would mean roughly one-sixth of the savings accounts corresponded to frustrated consumption, five-sixths, though, expressed savers' preferences. Monetary "overhang" was thus a containable problem; it alone would not have required a drastic write-down of savings accounts.

60. "Umtausch von eins zu eins birgt Inflationsrisiko," SZ, Apr. 21, 1990. But cf. Genscher, Erinnerungen, p. 764, for a critique of similar petty, bookkeeper-like calculations within the FDP: the conversion ratio was an issue "of destinies, of men for whom in a society hostile to property a slightly more than modest pension and a

small savings account were the only material accomplishment of a long and hard working life."

61. See different selections from the speech in *FAZ*, p. 8, and the *SZ*, p. 11, both Apr. 20, 1990.

62. Gawel, *Die deutsch-deutsche Währungsunion*, pp. 190–191. For the text and commentary, see Klaus Stern and Bruno Schmidt-Bleibtreu, eds., *Staatsvertrag zur Währungs-, Wirtschafts-, und Sozialunion. Verträge und Rechtsakte zur deutschen Einheit*, vol. 3 (Munich: Beck, 1990); also the useful summary by Peter E. Quint, "The Constitutional Law of German Unification," *Maryland Law Review* 50, 3 (1991): 475–631.

63. Horst Teltschik, *329 Tage: Innenansichten der Einigung* (Berlin: Goldman Verlag, 1993), p. 74.

64. Hartmut Zwahr, *Ende einer Selbstzerstörung: Leipzig und die Revolution in der DDR* (Göttingen: Vandenhoeck + Ruprecht, 1993), p. 155. For the data on the Leipzig Crowds, ibid., pp. 142–152. Cf. Konrad H. Jarausch, *Die unverhoffte Einheit 1989–1990* (Frankfurt am Main: Suhrkamp, 1995), pp. 137–147, for this national turn or "Wende in der Wende."

65. Rolf Schneider, "Die Einheit wird kommen," *Der Spiegel*, no. 48, Nov. 27, 1989, 44–45. "Die deutsche Einheit wird kommen, früher, als alle mutmaßten. Sie wird kommen und auf das berechtigte, historisch begründete Unbehagen selbst vieler Deutscher stoßen."

66. On Momper's earlier gradualism, Gedmin, *The Hidden Hand: Gorbachev and the Collapse of East Germany*, p. 114. For the Kohl-Gorbachev interchanges, via Ambassador Kochemasov on November 9 and directly on November 11, see Tschernajew, *Die letzten Jahre einer Weltmacht*, p. 266; Teltschik, *329 Tage*, pp. 27–28; Gorbatschow, *Erinnerungen*, p. 713.

67. November 10 speeches in Bundesministerium für innerdeutsche Beziehungen, *Texte zur Deutschlandpolitik*, ser. 3, vol. 7 (Bonn: Deutscher Bundes-Verlag, 1990), pp. 399–407; November 11 press conference, in Teltschik, *329 Tage*, p. 29; for the Bundestag speech, November 8, see Karl Kaiser, *Deutschlands Vereinigung. Die internationalen Aspekte* (Bergisch Gladbach: Gustav Lübbe Verlag, 1991), pp. 155–156.

68. Zelikow and Rice, *Germany Unified*, pp. 31–32.

69. Ibid., p. 26.

70. This includes Jews. Despite the careless or malicious remarks later made, Jewish organizations and representatives did not align against unification. Not forgetting the experiences of the Third Reich was not tantamount to opposing the unification of a democratic Germany forty-five years later.

71. Bush's comments cited seriatim in Zelikow and Rice, *Germany Unified*, pp. 31, 81, 94.

72. Ibid., p. 26.

73. "Together Again?" *Economist*, June 17, 1989.

74. Margaret Thatcher, *The Downing Street Years*, (London: HarperCollins, 1993), pp. 792–799; also Zelikow and Rice, *Germany Unified*, pp. 114–116. For a sampler of foreign opinion, see Harold James and Marla Stone, *When the Wall Came Down* (London: Routledge, 1992).

75. For Mitterrand's attitudes, see Jacques Attali, *Verbatim. Tome 3: Chronique des Années 1988–1991* (Paris: Fayard 1995), esp. pp. 331 (Nov. 3, 1989), 364–366 (conversation with Gorbachev, Dec. 6, 1989), 422–429 (conversation with Kohl, Feb. 15, 1990), 495–501 (conversation with Gorbachev, May 25, 1990).

76. Zelikow and Rice, *Germany Unified*, pp. 111–118, and notes, pp. 406–407, provide well-documented details of the different position papers worked up in the State Department, the range of U.S. editorial opinion, and the reaction of Thatcher and Mitterrand, as well as the various Genscher interviews during the visit of November 20–21. The quotation from Genscher appears in an earlier draft of the Zelikow and Rice volume.

77. On these events, including the Portugalov interview, and the calculations about party policy, and the drafting of the ten-point speech, see Teltschik, *329 Tage*, Nov. 21, 23–27, pp. 42–54. On what Portugalov really intended, Zelikow and Rice, *Germany Unified*, p. 118.

78. Teltschik, *329 Tage*, pp. 54–58.

79. Attali, *Verbatim, Tome 3*, p. 350 (Nov. 28, 1989). Teltschik gave the British, French, and U.S. ambassadors a masterly and reassuring exegesis of the speech on the afternoon of the speech. See ibid., p. 351.

80. Zelikow and Rice, *Germany Unified*, pp. 125–134; Teltschik, *329 Tage*, pp. 62–66. On Gorbachev's apparent complaisance at his Malta meeting with Bush, see Tchernajew, *Die letzten Jahre einer Weltmacht*, p. 268: the Allies "underestimated Gorbachev's capacity . . . to come to terms with the facts."

81. Gorbatchow, *Erinnerungen*, pp. 713–714; Kiessler and Elbe, *Ein runder Tisch mit scharfen Ecken*, p. 70; Ralf Georg Reuth and Andreas Bönte, *Das Komplott: Wie es wirklich zur deutschen Einheit kam* (Munich: Piper, 1993), p. 177; Zelikow and Rice, *Germany Unified*, pp. 134–136, 147–148. Teltschik, *329 Tage*, pp. 73–81.

82. Full discussion of the ambiguous speech and its preparation, see Zelikow and Rice, *Germany Unified*, pp. 149–152.

83. Thatcher on Mitterrand, December 8, *Downing Street Years*, p. 796; Mitterrand at St. Martin, and NSC hesitations in mid-December, Zelikow and Rice, *Ger-*

many Unified, pp. 139, 154–55. On French invocation of the Polish border issue and German reaction, see Teltschik, *329 Tage*, p. 76.

84. Zelikow and Rice, *Germany Unified*, pp. 139–141; Genscher, *Erinnerungen* p. 696; Kiessler and Elbe, *Runder Tisch mit scharfen Ecken*, pp. 73–76. Kotchemassow, *Meine letzte Mission*, pp. 196–198, defends the meeting as a response to a genuine need.

85. Zelikow and Rice, *Germany Unified*, pp. 159–160, 167–173; Pond, *Beyond the Wall*, pp. 176–182.

86. Tschernajew, *Die letzten Jahre einer Weltmacht*, pp. 296–297; Gorbatchow, *Erinnerungen*, pp. 714–716; Valentin Falin, *Politische Erinnerungen*, trans. Heddy Pross-Werth (Munich: Doremer-Knauer, 1993), pp. 489–490; Falin's account has been sharply criticized by Chernayev and others; see Adomeit's discussion of the bureaucratic factors in "Gorbachev, German Unification and the Collapse of Empire," pp. 217–222.

87. Modrow's admission cited in Gorbatchow, *Erinnerungen*, p. 714; see also for the Modrow plan and Moscow trip, Kotchemassow, *Meine letzte Mission*, pp. 212–218, and Modrow, *Aufbruch und Ende*, pp. 118–127.

88. Tschernajew, *Die letzten Jahre einer Weltmacht*, pp. 289–291.

89. Genscher at Halle, *Erinnerungen*, p. 700, for the NATO issue and the Tutzing speech, pp. 710–714. Cf. Zelikow and Rice, *Germany Unified*, pp. 174–176, 420–421. Genscher has contested the Zelikow and Rice emphasis in private correspondence, and his own memoir version may represent an implicit response to this account.

90. Kiessler and Elbe, *Runder Tisch mit scharfen Ecken*, pp. 78–79.

91. Ibid., 86–89; Genscher, *Erinnerungen*, p. 716; Zelikow and Rice, *Germany Unified*, pp. 177–178. The Americans allegedly welcomed the foreign minister's adhesion to the formula precisely because it was supposedly contested by the NSC. In fact, it was contested at least initially from the European desk within State.

92. Cf. the January 1990 internal memo cited by Garton Ash, *In Europe's Name*, pp. 364–365; also see my discussion, pp. 220–224, 226.

93. Zelikow and Rice, *Germany Unified*, pp. 182–184.

94. Teltschik, *329 Tage*, pp. 139–141.

95. Zelikow and Rice, *Germany Unified*, pp. 168, 193.

96. See Genscher, *Erinnerungen*, pp. 722–723. The misunderstandings, according to Zelikow and Rice, emerged at the Ottawa conference in mid-February, *Germany Unified*, pp. 194–195. "This episode was by far the most serious example of internal disagreement within the United States government during the process of German unification. [The statement echoes Pond, *Beyond the Wall*, p. 180.] It appears to have turned largely on misunderstandings between State and the White House on how far

the concept of the two plus four had progressed. . . . neither Scowcroft nor Baker fully understood each other's concerns at the time. Ironically, officials in both camps shared the objective of accelerating German unification and thought the other side had the opposite desire." Nonetheless, Zelikow maintains, personal relationships did not rupture and the disagreement was overcome.

97. There are conflicting accounts of this contretemps. Genscher and his assistant Elbe felt that Teltschik was seeking to undercut their authority at Ottawa. Zelikow and Rice argue that Genscher misconstrued the purpose of Teltschik's call to Scowcroft, which was simply to seek information. The real source of hesitation on the two-plus-four procedure, the American authors argue, arose not from Bonn but from within the American government—specifically the NSC staff, who feared it would make unification hostage to Moscow's delaying tactics. Still Teltschik never lost sight of the CDU-FDP political balance, and a call to Washington, even ostensibly just for information, could also signal the chancellor's desire to retain the key negotiations in his own hands and to sideline the Foreign Office, which obviously Genscher felt was at stake. See Genscher, *Erinnerungen*, p. 726; Stephen F. Szabo, *The Diplomacy of German Unification*, (New York: St. Martin's, 1992), p. 64; Kiessler and Elbe, *Runder Tisch mit scharfen Ecken*, pp. 101–102. Beschloss and Talbot, *At the Highest Levels*; and Zelikow and Rice, *Germany Unified*, pp. 191–195, and notes, pp. 424–445.

98. Genscher, *Erinnerungen*, p. 729.

99. Zelikow and Rice, *Germany Unified*, p. 203, and sources listed on pp. 427–428, again with a critique of Kiessler and Elbe's interpretation of Genscher's wish to exclude NATO (and non-NATO German forces) from the GDR territory. Cf. Kiessler and Elbe, *Runder Tisch mit scharfen Ecken*, pp. 81–85; Genscher, *Erinnerungen*, p. 731, says little over the disagreement. The FRG had created a cabinet committee on German unity to supervise the negotiations.

100. Zelikow and Rice, *Germany Unified*, pp. 209–210, for the different concepts of what the two-plus-four negotiations should yield. The wider its writ, the more potential for disruptive Soviet negotiations, but if restricted greatly (as the State Department's European Bureau desired according to Zelikow and Rice), the danger existed that the Germans might become impatient and deal directly with the Soviets.

101. Zelikow and Rice, *Germany Unified*, pp. 212–216; Teltschik, *329 Tage*, pp. 158–162. Sources disagree as to what film was screened: Teltschik claims to have watched *Schatzinsel* (Treasure Island); Beschloss and Talbott (p. 191) report more plausibly that it was *Internal Affairs*.

102. Zelikow and Rice, *Germany Unified*, pp. 220–222. As the authors point out, the claim that the FRG could make no commitment on behalf of the future united

Germany would have had validity only if the two states merged under article 146 (a new constitutional convention). Kohl's March 8 declaration that envisaged unification on the basis of article 23 (which provided for the GDR's merger into the continuing FRG) meant the Federal Republic's commitments would continue in force after enlargement.

103. Teltschik, *329 Tage*, p. 174.

104. BA: Potsdam: DC 20 I/3/2926: "Besuch einer Regierungsdelegation der DDR unter Leitung des Vorsitzenden des Ministerrates, Hans Modrow, in der UdSSR am 5./6. März 1990." Cf. Modrow, *Aufbruch und Ende*, pp. 120–123. Zelikow and Rice, *Germany Unified*, p. 225.

105. Kochemassow, *Meine letzte Mission*, pp. 215–217.

106. Zelikow and Rice, *Germany Unified*, pp. 223–227, for Soviet and American preparations as well as the March 14 meeting.

107. Ulrich Albrecht, *Die Abwicklung der DDR. Die "2+4-Verhandlungen": Ein Insiderbericht* (Opladen: Westdeutscher Verlag, 1992), pp. 18–20. Albrecht, a West Berlin political scientist, served as an adviser to Meckel in this period and became head of a planning staff at the East German Foreign Ministry.

108. Albrecht, *Die Abwicklung der DDR*, p. 192, n. 19.

109. Albrecht, *Die Abwicklung der DDR*, pp. 48–49; on Bush to de Maizière, Zelikow and Rice, *Germany Unified*, pp. 289–290.

110. Kwizinskij, *Vor dem Sturm*, pp. 18–24; Tschernajew, *Die letzten Jahre einer Weltmacht*, p. 297, for the Politbüro arguments of May 3 and his own critique of the "pseudopatriotism of the masses" (Gorbachev cites the date, *Erinnerungen*, p. 721, but no details); Zelikow and Rice, *Germany Unified*, base their account on copies of Soviet position papers, pp. 243–250, and notes, pp. 444–445.

111. On the politics of gestures toward Poland and the mutual sensitivities of Bundeskanzleramt and Foreign Office, see Teltschik's reflections on his conversation with Genscher on June 13, 1990, *329 Tage*, pp. 272–773: both men agreed on what was a correct symbolic move but were convinced that a partisan press would attack them respectively for clumsiness or appeasement. For Genscher's concerns about Shevardnadze's sensibility and Gorbachev's domestic difficulties, see his *Erinnerungen*, pp. 768–786, concentrating on the two-plus-four meetings of May 5.

112. Kiessler and Elbe, *Runder Tisch mit scharfen Ecken*, pp. 126–129; Pond, *Beyond the Wall*, pp. 213–214; Zelikow and Rice, *Germany Unified*, pp. 251–254, and n. 5, p. 447. For a useful summary of the distinctions among policy actors in each of the major powers, see Szabo, *Diplomacy of German Unification*, pp. 17–30.

113. Claus Gennrich, "Genscher begrüßt Moskaus Bereitschaft zur Trennung der inneren und äusseren Aspekte der Vereinigung," *FAZ*, May 8, 1990. See Teltschik, *329 Tage*, p. 226, for a sparse account, and Genscher's rejection of the

substance of the charge in *Erinnerungen*, pp. 781–782. Genscher's assistant Elbe, was convinced that Teltschik had planted the story; see Kiessler and Elbe, *Runder Tisch mit scharfen Ecken*, pp. 126–129; Pond, *Beyond the Wall*, pp. 213–214; and Zelikow and Rice, *Germany Unified*, pp. 252–253, and n. 5, p. 447, for efforts to get behind the story.

114. Kwizinskij, *Vor dem Sturm*, pp. 24–25.

115. Ibid., pp. 26–31; Teltschik, *329 Tage*, pp. 226–228, 230–235.

116. Kwizinskij, *Vor dem Sturm*, p. 39.

117. Zelikow and Rice, *Germany Unified*, pp. 262–266. Cf. Kwizinskij, *Vor dem Sturm*, p. 40, on the limits of the military trump that remained.

118. I base this account on Genscher, *Erinnerungen*, pp. 786–796, and it is not certain that these particular conversations played the crucial role in the subsequent Soviet concessions that the author believes. See also Zelikow and Rice, *Germany Unified*, pp. 267–271 (and p. 455, n. 59, concerning the numbers cited on May 23), which emphasizes the Americans' preoccupation with the troop limitation issue and their effort, evidently successful (or not in fact needed), to dissuade Genscher from specific negotiations. The Germans wanted troop limits discussed at the Vienna CFE parleys, but this threatened to make unification dependent on resolving the whole complex of issues at Vienna. A CSCE summit was supposed to ratify the process of uniting Germany, but the CSCE summit was also supposed to wait on a CFE agreement. On the other hand, to negotiate limits within the two plus four threatened to delay this forum as well. Ultimately Baker and Shevardnadze agreed in early June that if Germany declared a satisfactory limit it would later accept at the CFE, the logjam could be broken. At Brest on June 11 and Münster on June 18, Genscher and Shevardnadze made progress on this issue (Zelikow and Rice, pp. 284–285).

119. Kwizinskij, *Vor dem Sturm*, p. 40, on the limits of the military "trump" that remained.

120. Zelikow and Rice, *Germany Unified*, pp. 277–283; Adomeit, "Gorbachev, German Unification and the Collapse of Empire," 197, 229; Gorbatchow, *Erinnerungen*, pp. 721–722, provides a memorandum of the conversation of May 30, but no real comment. Shevardnadze confirmed the May 30 agreement at the Copenhagen CSCE meeting on June 15. See Genscher, *Erinnerungen*, pp. 815–818; and Beschloss and Talbott, *At the Highest Levels*, p. 230. The Russians, and later Genscher, would argue that NATO's willingness to transform the alliance and contemplate common security structures provided the crucial reassurance to the Soviets. In this regard, the so-called Message of Turnberry, issued by the North Atlantic Council on June 8, has been endowed with an almost sacramental role. For its brief text, see Kaiser, *Deutschlands Vereinigung*, pp. 225–226; cf. Genscher, pp. 801–805, on the meeting.

121. Genscher, *Erinnerungen*, pp. 805–823; also Kiessler and Elbe, *Runder Tisch mit scharfen Ecken*, pp. 154–159. The historian must, in effect, choose between or reconcile two different versions of the negotiation process. Genscher's memoirs emphasize the contribution of his own meetings with Shevardnadze in Geneva and Brest (and to a lesser extent in Münster) as critical steps in reaching agreement. Gorbachev's concession on NATO on May 30 was important but not conclusive; indeed, Genscher's lieutenants Kiessler and Elbe claim that Zoellick told them he was not originally certain whether Gorbachev had really conceded the point (*Runder Tisch mit scharfen Ecken*, p. 151). Conversely, in the Genscher scenario, Shevardnadze's reversion to a tough line on June 22 was also not a serious disavowal of what he had promised to the German foreign minister. Genscher claimed that immediately afterward he extracted Shevardnadze's jocular if implicit confirmation that he was just posturing to mollify Soviet resistance at home. So too, in the perspective of Genscher's memoirs, Kohl's visit to the Caucusus in July likewise just tended to formalize what the two foreign secretaries had worked out. Indeed, Raisa Gorbachev appealed to Genscher in the Caucusus to reciprocate her husband's heroic concessions. In contrast to the Genscherite scenario must be set the Teltschik version in *329 Tage*, which emphasizes the chancellor's achievement and Gorbachev's concessions, thereby tending to marginalize the foreign minister, and the similar perspective that informs the White House centered on the Zelikow and Rice volume.

122. Albrecht, *Die Abwicklung der DDR*, pp. 73–74.

123. The text is reproduced in Kwizinskij, *Vor dem Sturm*, pp. 41–46, (quote from p. 40), who notes that it was presented on the fiftieth (sic: June 22, 1990, was the forty-ninth) anniversary of the German attack on the Soviet Union. Cf. Zelikow and Rice, *Germany Unified*, pp. 296–297.

124. "Meckels Armee," in *Tagesspiegel*, July 19, 1990, cited in Albrecht, *Die Abwicklung der DDR*, p. 63. For the self-perceived weakness of the East German delegation, see also Barbara Munske, *The Two Plus Four Negotiations from a German-German Perspective: An Analysis of Perception* (Münster and Hamburg: Lit Verlag, 1994).

125. Zelikow and Rice, *Germany Unified*, pp. 299–327; Kiessler and Elbe, *Runder Tisch mit scharfen Ecken*, pp. 157–159, for Tarasenko's assurance.

126. See Kwizinskij, *Vor dem Sturm*, p. 37.

127. Falin, *Politische Erinnerungen*, p. 494.

128. Gorbatchow, *Erinnerungen*, pp. 724–725, emphasizes that he satisfied Soviet priorities by assuring that a security threat would never emanate from Germany, even after the withdrawal of Soviet troops. Cf. Genscher's summary, which stresses his role in assuring that NATO-assigned German troops could be stationed in the East immediately after Soviet troop withdrawals. See *Erinnerungen*, pp. 836–841.

129. Reports from London and Meckel interview cited by Albrecht, *Die Abwicklung der DDR*, p. 50.

130. Cf. Christian Wernicke, "Ein Regieren zum Ende hin," *Die Zeit*, July 27, 1990, p. 3; Albrecht, *Abwicklung der DDR*, pp. 119–122, 157–158. The East German Social Democrats were disappointed that they had no room for maneuver. Even had they been more skilled—and many initiatives were launched prematurely—they could not have prevailed against the United States–Soviet and West German–Soviet thrust to agreement. It was considered a special mistake to insist on a continuing East German army after the Caucusus meeting (see Albrecht, p. 161).

131. Cited by Jarausch, *Die unverhoffte Einheit*, p. 265; see also Wolfgang Schäuble, *Der Vertrag: Wie ich über die deutsche Einheit verhandelte* (Munich: Knaur, 1993).

132. Daniel Hamilton's interview with Lothar de Maizière, Nov. 12, 1991, Hoover Institution Oral History Project, devotes relatively little attention to these issues. For chronologies of the coalition crises in July and August see Presse- und Informations amt der Bundesregierung, *Deutschland 1990: Dokumentation zu der Berichterstattung über die Ereignisse in der DDR und die deutsche politische Entwicklung*, vol. 14 (Bonn, 1993). Among other articles reprinted: Peter Christ, "Lust an die Konfrontation," *Die Zeit*, Aug. 24, 1990, provides a resumé.

133. For these final negotiations, see Zelikow and Rice, *Germany Unified*, pp. 342–363; Szabo, *Diplomacy of German Unification*, pp. 109–112; Genscher, *Erinnerungen*, pp. 854–876; Tschernajew, *Die letzten Jahre einer Weltmacht*, p. 312. Germans and Russians also settled the issue of compensation for expropriation carried out by the Soviets in their zone of occupation by a June 15 declaration that declared 1945–49 expropriations could not be reversed (although they might perhaps be compensated for); the declaration was taken note of in the German state treaty.

134. Kwizinskij, *Vor dem Sturm*, p. 69.

CHAPTER 6

1. Konrad Weiss, "Der Heimat Verlust schmertzt," *Der Spiegel*, no. 8, Feb. 19, 1990, p. 27. For an effort—also in a minor key—to measure public mood before and after unification see Lawrence H. McFalls, *Communism's Collapse, Democracy's Demise? The Cultural Context and Consequences of the East German Revolution* (New York: New York University Press, 1995).

2. "German Support for the Transition to Democracy and Market Economy in the Former Soviet Union," position paper of the German Embassy, Washington, DC, distributed by German Information Center, New York, June 1992; also Helmut Kohl

to American Newspaper Publishers Association, May 5, 1992, reported in "The Week in Germany," German Information Center, May 8, 1992. For the 1994 totals, see the German Information Center's "Focus on German Support for the Reform Process in the Former Soviet Union and the Countries of Central, Southeastern and Eastern Europe," March 1995. Aid to the former Soviet Union included the sum negotiated in 1990 to pay for Soviet troop withdrawals and to fulfill preexisting GDR commitments. Aid to the countries of Eastern and Southeastern Europe included Germany's share of European Community assistance.

3. See Robert Leicht, "Bonn adieu! Berlin also Symbol, aber wofür?" and Günter Hofmann, "Das Wagnis eines späten Neuanfangs. Wird aus der Bonner Republik eine Berliner Republik—und was würde dies bedeuten?" Die Zeit, July 5, 1991, pp. 1, 3. "Hilflos vor dem Showdown," "Eine wunderbare Katastrophe," and "Das Pendel schlägt zurück," Der Spiegel, no. 25, June 17, 1991, pp. 18–24; no. 26, June 24, 1991, pp. 18–30; no. 27, July 1, 1991, pp. 36–37.

4. For example, Ferdinand Protzman, "East Germany's Economy Far Sicker Than Expected," New York Times, Sept. 20, 1990, sec. A, pp. 1–2. Cf. for a withering (and tendentious) dismissal: "One short visit is enough to make one aware of the current malaise: nearly half a century of socialism was a phase of incredible wealth destruction. Neither in the area of public infrastructure nor in the sector of state-owned firms did any positive net investment take place; the leading position of the GDR within the socialist hemisphere was due to a comparatively favourable initial endowment with infrastructure and capital resources and continuous subsidies from the West German budget." Michael Hüther and Hans-Georg Petersen, "Taxes and Transfers: Financing German Unification," in A. Ghanie Ghaussy and Wolf Schäfer, eds., The Economics of German Unification (London: Routledge, 1993), p. 73.

5. Cf., on this theme, Daniela Dahn, Wir bleiben hier oder Wem gehört der Osten: Vom Kampf um Häuser und Wohnungen in den neuen Bundesländern (Reinbek bei Hamburg: Rowohlt, 1994). Also Hans Willgerodt, "Wiedereinsetzung der Alteigentümer (Reprivatisierung)," in Wolfram Fischer, Herbert Hax, and Hans Karl Schneider, eds., Treuhandanstalt. Das Unmögliche wagen (Berlin: Akademie Verlag, 1993), pp. 241–262. As of 1989, 41 percent of dwellings remained in private hands and as of 1990, 71 percent of agricultural land was likewise privately held. By June 30, 1993, 1,360 of 9,916 enterprises or almost 14 percent passed back to earlier owners. Of the quarter of the requests for recovery of real estate that had been processed, one-third had been awarded to the petitioners. For the story from the viewpoint of a family recovering property (in this case the Wallich residence in Potsdam), see Katie Hafner, The House at the Bridge: A Story of Modern Germany (New York: Scribner, 1995).

6. See on these issues Rudiger Dornbusch, "Priorities of Economic Reform in Eastern Europe and the Soviet Union," Centre for Economic Policy Research, Lon-

don, Occasional Paper No. 5 (no date); also Olivier Blanchard et al., *Reform in Eastern Europe* (Cambridge, MA: MIT Press, 1991).

7. Peter Christ and Ralf Neubauer, *Kolonie im eigenen Land. Die Treuhand, Bonn und die Wirtschaftskatastrophe der fünf neuen Länder* (Berlin: Rowohlt, 1991), pp. 193–194. As of 1994 the transferable ruble balance paid to East German exporters amounted to almost $15 million (DM 20.6 million). (See German Information Center, "Focus on German Support.") The old GDR Staatsbank had credited East German exporters with 4.5 East marks per transferable ruble, but the GDR's mark would in turn have been credited (if at all) as a fourth of the deutsche mark. Hence the 1990 arrangements were still highly favorable.

8. Christ and Neubauer, *Kolonie im eigenen Land*, pp. 157–164. Cf. Peter Christ, "Der Fortschritt ist eine Schnecke. Zwischen Ost und West hat sich die Kluft vertieft," *Die Zeit*, July 5, 1991, p. 9.

9. For an exhaustive account of the origins of the Treuhand, see Wolfram Fischer and Harm Schröter, "Die Entstehung der Treuhandanstalt," in Fischer et al., *Treuhandanstalt*, pp. 17–40.

10. Besides Fischer et al., *Treuhandanstalt*, see Wolfgang Seibel (also with a chapter in Fischer et al.), "Zur Entwicklungslogik der Treuhandanstalt, 1990–1993," *Politische Vierteljahresschrift*, 35, 1 (1994): 3–39. For an early critique of the Treuhand, see Peter Christ, "Wie auf dem Bazar," *Die Zeit*, Aug. 31, 1990.

11. Fischer and Schröter, "Entstehung der Treuhandanstalt," in Fischer et al., *Treuhandanstalt*, pp. 32–39; cf. Christa Luft, *Treuhandreport. Werden und Vergehen einer deutschen Behörde* (Berlin: Aufbau, 1992). Agricultural collectives were left outside the THA purview until 1991.

12. Fischer and Schröter, "Entstehung der Treuhandanstalt." Also Seibel, "Zur Entwicklungslogik," pp. 11–12. This line changed by November 1991 when the Treuhand leadership accepted the need for restructuring under the slogan of "preservation of the industrial core regions" (Seibel, p. 23). There is now a huge literature on the diverse approaches to privatization in Eastern Europe; Treuhand presupposed that investors would come from West Germany to capitalize restructured productive units. In Poland, Hungary, and Czechoslovakia nonnational investment had to be sought. See the contributions by David Stark, Laszlo Bruszt, and David Bartlett in "Transforming the Economies of East Central Europe," a special issue of *East European Politics and Society* 6, 1 (winter 1992). Also, Janusz M. Dabrowski, Michal Federowicz, and Anthony Levitas, "Polish State Enterprises and the Properties of Performance: Stabilization, Marketization, Privatization," unpublished paper of the Labor Market and Firm Adjustment Group of the Gdansk Institute of Economics, May 1991; Herbert Matis and Dieter Stiefel, eds., *Der Weg aus der Knechtschaft: Probleme des Übergangs von der Planwirtschaft zur Marktwirtschaft* (Vienna: Ueberreuter, 1992); "Privatization and Emerging Market Econo-

mies: Lessons and Opportunities for Business and Government," résumé of a conference held by the Harvard University Center for International Affairs, Cambridge, MA, Jan. 28–30, 1992.

13. On privatization see Joachim Schwalbach with the assistance of Sven E-Gless, "Begleitung sanierungsfähiger Unternehmen auf dem Weg zur Privatisierung," and Klaus-Dieter Schmidt with the assitance of Uwe Siegmund, "Strategien der Privatisierung," both in Fischer et al., *Treuhandanstalt*, pp. 177–210, 211–240. For the dissolution of unviable firms, Eckhard Wandel with the assistance of Marcus W. Mosen, "Abwicklung nicht sanierungsfähiger Unternehmen durch die Treuhandanstalt," in ibid., pp. 283–314.

14. As a countermeasure to this trend, see the experiment with the ATLAS model of Treuhand enterprises (outlined in cooperation with the Saxon state government in September 1992) for combining regional development goals as represented by the Landtag, with trade union and entrepreneurial consultation. See Seibel, "Zur Entwicklungslogik," pp. 30–33; also Horst Kern and Charles Sabel, "Die Treuhandanstalt: Experimentierfeld zur Entwicklung neuer Unternehmensformen," in Fischer et al., *Treuhandanstalt*, pp. 481–504.

15. *Die Zeit*, Aug. 2, 1991. For an alternative Treuhand concept based on active managerial restructuring, see the article by SPD managing director Karl-Heinz Blessing: "Wer alte Industriestandorte aufgibt, hat die Region abgeschrieben," *Frankfurter Rundschau*, Mar. 30, 1992.

16. Kern and Sabel, "Treuhandanstalt," in Fischer et al., *Treuhandanstalt*, pp. 481–504; and Christ and Neubauer, *Kolonie im eigenen Land*, pp. 129–132.

17. Seibel, "Zur Entwicklungslogik," pp. 22–23. For a discussion of the evolving restructuring approaches before and after fall 1991, see Jürgen Müller with the assistance of Georg Merdian and Donat von Müller, "Strukturelle Auswirkungen der Privatisierung durch die Treuhandanstalt," and esp. Kern and Sabel, "Die Treuhandanstalt," citing the Saxon ATLAS and Brandenburg EKO-Stahl projects, both in Fischer et al., *Treuhandanstalt*, pp. 374–408, 481–504.

18. On the TLG and the issues it raises, see Seibel, "Zur Entwicklungslogik"; for a balanced evaluation of the Treuhand at the moment of its dissolution, see "Abschied eines Buhmanns," *Der Spiegel*, no. 51, Dec. 19, 1994, pp. 78–82.

19. See the extensive discussion between Breuel and diverse commentators—the economists Olivier Blanchard and Rudiger Dornbusch, sociologists Charles Sabel and Horst Kern, and Klaus von Dohnanyi, former mayor of Hamburg and new director of TAKRAF—at the Center for European Studies on November 16, 1991. With some caveats almost all commentators praised the Treuhand approach. Center for European Studies, Program for the Study of Germany and Europe, "Treuhandanstalt: A One-Day Workshop, Rapporteur's Report," Cambridge, MA.

20. Christ and Neubauer, *Kolonie im eigenen Land*, pp. 172–182.

21. For the controversies over excess real wages as a cause of the industrial collapse, see Helmar Drost, "The Great Depression in East Germany: The Effects of Unification on East Germany's Economy," *East European Politics and Societies* 7, 3 (fall 1993): 471–475; also George A. Akerlof et al., "East Germany in from the Cold: The Economic Aftermath of Currency Union," *Brookings Papers on Economic Activity* 1 (1991), p. 46. For productivity estimates as of 1991, see D. M. W. N. Hitchens, K. Wagner, and J. E. Birnie, *East German Productivity and the Transition to the Market Economy* (Aldershot: Avebury, 1993). This study (designed to compare selected East German industries with those of Northern Ireland) suggested that the 60 percent productivity level of 1991 already represented a 50 percent improvement over a year earlier. (At the same time it gave the GDR productivity percentages preunification as 50 percent in manufacturing and 40 percent for the economy as a whole.)

22. Cited in Christ and Neubauer, *Kolonie im eigenen Land*, pp. 101–102.

23. *Der Spiegel*, "Die Steuerrechnung für die Einheit: Ein Staat in Geldrausch," no. 27, July 1, 1991, pp. 21–26.

24. Wilfried Herz, "Die Mühsal des Teilens," *Die Zeit*, Aug. 2, 1991, p. 1.

25. Kurt Bock comments on BASF at the Harvard Center for European Studies Workshop, "The Economic Impact of German Unification," Cambridge, MA, April 6–7, 1991.

26. Bureau of Statistics report, Sept. 1992, summarized in "The Week in Germany," Sept. 11, 1992, German Information Center. For the statistics of industrial production, see Drost, "The Great Depression in East Germany," pp. 452–481; also Gerlinde Sinn and Hans-Werner Sinn, *Jumpstart: The Economic Unification of Germany*, trans. Juli Irving-Lessmann (Cambridge, MA: MIT Press, 1992), pp. 29–30; the German statistical publication, *Wirtschaft und Statistik*, publishes monthly statistical tables of cumulative performance as well.

27. Christ and Neubauer, *Kolonie im eigenen Lande*, pp. 206–207; *Deutsche Bank Research*, "Government Finances Being Put to the Test" (Frankfurt am Main, May 15, 1992). The deficits listed in the table for 1992 were estimated transfers. Cf. "Die wirtschaftliche Einheit droht zu scheitern," *Der Spiegel* no. 13, March 23, 1992, pp. 22–29; and "Das Teilen für den Aufbau im Osten fällt schwer," *Der Spiegel*, no. 18, Apr. 27, 1992, pp. 18–27.

28. The Bundesbank blamed speculators for the currency turmoil; but even in Germany criticism finally came into the open: see the remarks of the Deutsche Bank Board's economic spokesman, Ulrich Cartellieri on December 8, as reported in the *Financial Times*, Dec. 9, 1992, p. 14 ("Bank Blamed for Currency Crisis"). Spain and Portugal devalued by late November. For a useful narrative of the crisis, see the case

study prepared by the John F. Kennedy School of Government, "Black Wednesday: The Bundesbank Connection," Harvard University, Cambridge, MA, 1995.

29. Robert Leicht, "Wenn schon teilen, dann solidarisch," *Die Zeit*, May 29, 1992, p. 1.

30. On the Solidarity Pact and taxes see: "Es muß Masse in den Topf," *Der Spiegel*, no. 46, Nov. 9, 1992, pp. 16–20; also Quentin Peel, "Forced to Find Common Ground," *Financial Times*, Dec. 8, 1992, p. 14.

31. Jürgen Boje and Doris Gladisch, "Arbeitsmarkt und Beschäftigung in Ostdeutschland," in Institut für Wirtschaftsforschung Halle, ed., *Wirtschaft im Systemschock. Die schwierige Realität der ostdeutschen Transformation* (Halle: Analytica, 1994), pp. 41–68.

32. Robert Skopp, "Sektoraler Strukturwandel in den neuen Bundesländern," in ibid., 55–68.

33. Janos Kornai, "Transformational Recession. A General Phenomenon Examined through the Example of Hungary's Development," Harvard Institute of Economic Research, Discussion Paper No. 1648, July 1993. Cf. Hubert Gabrisch, "Stabilisierungspolitik in post-sozialistischen Ländern: eine Synopse aus empirischer und theoretischer Sicht," in *Wirtschaft im Systemschock*, pp. 185–199.

34. For an account of the formative period, see the dissertation by John F. Connelly, "Creating the Socialist Elite: Communist Higher Education Policies in the Czech Lands, East Germany, and Poland, 1945–1954," Ph.D. dissertation, Harvard University, 1994, and for a brief but impressive description of party control, Wolfgang Schuller, "Zwei Nationen—Zwei Wissenschaften? Eindrücke vom Wiederaufbau der Wissenschaftsorganisationen in den neuen Bundesländern," *Deutschland Archiv* 27, 5 (May 1994): 470–477.

35. For the Pätzold case see the *FAZ*, Nov. 12, 1990, the *Tagespiegel*, Nov. 13, 1990, and Pätzold's reply in *Neues Deutschland*, Dec. 30, 1990, as cited by Georg G. Iggers, "L'histoire sociale et l'historiographie Est-Allemande des années 1980," *Vingtième Siècle*, no. 34, special issue (Apr.–June 1992), pp. 5–24. Pätzold's appeal was rejected by the Berlin labor court on Jan. 29, 1993. More generally, see Rainer Eckert, Wolfgang Küttler, and Gustav Seeber, *Krise-Umbruch-Neubeginn. Eine kritische und selbstkritische Dokumentation der DDR-Geschichtswissenschaft 1989/90* (Stuttgart: Klett-Cotta, 1992), with contributions on the failings and crisis of GDR historiography.

36. Dieter E. Zimmer, "Einstürzende Mittelbauten," *Die Zeit*, Nov. 27, 1992, p. 41.

37. Wolfgang Schluchter, "Die Hochschulen in Ostdeutschland vor und nach der Einigung," *Aus Politik und Zeitgeschichte* B25/94 (June 24, 1994): 12–22. Also Schluchter, "Der Um- und Neubau der Hochschulen in Ostdeutschland. Ein Er-

fahrungsbericht am Beispiel der Universität Leipzig," *Berliner Journal für Soziologie* 1 (1994): 89ff. And Andreas Fischer, *Das Bildungssystem der DDR. Entwicklung, Umbruch und Neugestaltung seit 1989* (Darmstadt 1992).

38. Cf. Dieter Simon, "Der Wissenschaftsrat in den neuen Bundesländern. Eine vorwärtsgewandte Rückschau," *Aus Politik und Zeitgeschichte* B51/92 (Dec. 1992): 9ff.

39. Jens Reich, "Wissenschaft und Politik im deutschen Einigungsprozeß," *Aus Politik und Zeitgeschichte* B9/91 (Feb. 22, 1991): 34.

40. For a shrewd analysis of the disappearing options in 1990 for the Academy of Sciences, see Renate Mayntz, "Multi-organizational and Multi-level Interactions in the Restructuring of a National Research System," Lecture at the Max Planck Gesellschaft, September 1991. And for a general summary of results, Gerhard Neuweiler, "Das gesamtdeutsche Haus für Forschung und Lehre," *Aus Politik und Zeitgeschichte* B25/94 (June 24, 1994): 3–11. Neuweiler, a zoologist, had become chair of the Wissenschaftsrat in 1993. For early support of the Geisteswissenschaftliche Zentren, see Dieter Henrich, "Nur ein mattes Abbild des Westens? Der Umbau der Geisteswissenschaften im Osten," *FAZ*, Oct. 28 1991, p. 35. Early stages of the review process are described in Peter Marcuse, "Abwicklung in East Germany: Renewal, Destalinization, Suppression," Working Papers of the Institute on East Central Europe, Columbia University, 1 (August 1991). Marcuse cites somewhat different figures for the academies: 57 institutes and 23,000 employees in the Academy of Sciences, plus another 63 institutes with about 18,000 employees including the Academy of Social Sciences attached to the Central Committee of the SED, and specialized academies for pedagogy, agronomy, building, and higher education. As he points out, the largest independent Western research establishment, the French CNRS, had about 10,000 researchers for a country three times as large.

41. See on the Humboldt, Uwe Wesel, "Geisterstunde," *Die Zeit*, June 21, 1991, p. 16; and on the Gauck charges of Stasi collaboration: "Humboldt-Rektor Fink fristlos entlassen," *taz*, Nov. 28, 1991, p. 6; Christoph Dieckmann and Norbert Kostede, "Ein Leben halb und halb. Der Fall Fink, der Fall Gauck—Streit an der Humboldt-Universität: An ihren Akten sollt Ihr sie erkennen?" *Die Zeit*, Dec. 13, 1991, p. 3. They cite Ruth Misselwitz, a reformist pastor active in 1989, who charged that Fink connected the future of the university "too exclusively with his own personal fate. See also Matthias Geis, "Makabre Konsequenz," *taz*, Dec. 4, 1991.

42. "Die DDR in uns," *Der Spiegel*, no. 50, Dec. 9, 1991, pp. 18–24. For a critique of Fink as a university rector, including the charge of phony populism, Manfred Bierwisch, "'Identitätsbewahrung' behindert die Erneuerung," *Tagesspiegel*, Jan. 5, 1992. For the results of the late January rectorial campaign: Mechtild Küpfer, "'Pro

Humboldt' siegt," *Tagesspiegel*, Jan. 26, 1992, p. 27; the Berlin administrative court upheld the possibility of firing Fink on January 28, but said that the university, not Senator Erhardt, could relieve him of his post. "Entlassung Finks nicht unrechtmäßig," *FAZ*, Jan. 29, 1992, p. 5. Testimonials issued on behalf of Fink as well as other materials on the case have been printed in *UTOPIEkreativ: Dokumentation* (special issue: January 1992).

43. Christian Meier, "Den Grabenkrieg überwinden," *Die Zeit*, Dec. 6, 1991, p. 3; Meier, who had been active in the earlier Historikerstreit as Chair of the German Historians Association, was a member of the Berlin state university structure commission (Landeshochschulstrukturkommission). I also draw on the Center for European Studies' workshop on German Unification and the Universities, Cambridge, MA, March 13–15, 1992.

44. "Inquisitoren auf der Faultierfarm," *Frankfurter Allgemeine Zeitung*, 9.9. 1993. For the conflicts at the Humboldt up to mid-1991, see Marcuse, "Abwicklung in East Germany"; see also Hermann Weber, "Werden DDR-Geschichtswissenschaft und Marxismus plattgewalzt und ausgemerzt?" *Deutschland Archiv* 24, 3 (Mar. 1991): 246–273. The three "independents" connected with Winkler's chair included Rainer Eckert, Stefan Wolle, and Armin Mitter. The last two published the documentary collection *"Ich liebe euch doch, alle!" Befehle und Lageberichte des MfS Januar–November 1989* (Berlin: BasisDruck, 1990) and then *Untergang auf Raten: Unbekannte Kapitel der DDR-Geschichte* (Munich: Bertelsmann, 1993). A word about my own role: I served as a board member of the Potsdam Center from 1992 through 1995; Winkler and Kocka have been long-term personal friends; I reviewed favorably Mitte and Wolle's documentary collection, but have disagreed with their overall interpretation of GDR history. See Charles S. Maier, "Geschichtswissenschaft und 'Ansteckungsstaat,'" *Geschichte und Gesellschaft* 20 (1994): 617–625.

45. Celestine Bohlen, "Victims of Hungary's Past Press for an Accounting but with Little Success," *New York Times*, Aug. 3, 1991, p. 3.

46. For insight into Gauck's views, see Johannes Paulmann's resumé of his speech and of his answers to critics at the symposium of the London German Historical Institute, "Vergangenheitsbewältigung: The Aftermath of Dictatorship (1945/ 1990)," June 19, 1992, published in *Bulletin of the German Historical Institute London* 16, 3 (Nov. 1992): 34–38. And among many interviews, "Ich werde kein Zensor sein," *taz*, Nov. 12, 1991, p. 12; and his broadcast conversation of Oct. 1, 1995, printed as "Interview mit Joachim Gauck," *Deutschland Archiv*, 28, 11 (Nov. 1995): 1228–1232 (citation from p. 1229). When the interviewer asked Gauck whether the Spanish decision not to open the past might not be healthier, he responded that Spain had had a bloody civil war and it seemed better not to reopen these wounds; the post-Communist situation was different.

47. "Interview mit Joachim Gauck."

48. Enquete-Kommission, *Aufarbeitung von Geschichte und Folgen der SED-Dik-tatur in Deutschland*, vol. 9, *Zwei Diktaturen in Deutschland* (Frankfurt am Main: Suhrkamp, 1995), pp. 575–643.

49. See on this general theme "Recht oder Rache: Die Last deutscher Vergangen-heit," including Eberhard Jäckel, "Die doppelte Vergangenheit," *Der Spiegel*, no. 52, Dec. 23, 1991, pp. 30–43.

50. Ulrich Greiner, "Mangel an Feingefühl," *Die Zeit*, June 1, 1990, cited in Thomas Anz, ed., *"Es geht nicht nur um Christa Wolf" Der Literaturstreit im vereinten Deutschland* (Munich: Spangenberg, 1991), pp. 66–70. Marcel Reich-Ranicki with his renowned sarcasm had already savaged Wolf in *FAZ* (Nov. 12, 1987), repro-duced in Anz, pp. 35–40; as had Hans Noll in the conservative *Welt* of July 4, 1987, "The big life-lie of Christa Wolf is that she placed herself at the disposition of a political system whose immorality she was well aware of" (cited in the introduction by Anz, p. 30). The title of this edited collection comes from Wolf Biermann's sum-mary of the conflict.

51. " 'Dem Druck des härteren, strengeren Lebens standhalten': Auch eine Studie über den autoritären Charakter: Christa Wolfs Aufsätze, Reden und ihre jüngste Erzählung 'Was Bleibt,' " *FAZ*, June 2, 1990, pp. 77–89; citations from pp. 86, 80, 87, respectively.

52. Cited, Anz, *Es geht nicht um Christa Wolf,* pp. 244–247. Cf. Ulrich Greiner, "Die Falle des Entweder-Oder. In der Stasi-Debatte wird altes Unrecht durch neues Unrecht ersetzt," *Die Zeit*, Jan. 31, 1992, p. 1. The trap of the either-or, Greiner said, was the unwillingness to break with socialism because capitalism was allegedly not much better, just as once it had been thought better not to criticize Stalin for fear of helping Hitler.

53. Fritz J. Raddatz, "Von der Beschädigung der Literatur durch ihre Urheber," *Die Zeit*, Feb. 5, 1993; cf. John Connelly, "Christa Wolf, Round Two," April 15, 1993, unpublished manuscript.

54. "Interview mit Joachim Gauck," p. 1231.

55. See Schroeder's judgement, and "Die Wahrheit soll ans Licht," in *Der Spiegel*, no. 9, Feb. 24, 1992, pp. 24–35. For a defense of Stolpe, see Klaus von Dohnanyi, "Pakt mit dem Teufel," and other articles in *Der Spiegel*, no. 5, Jan. 27, 1992; for critiques, Gerhard Besier, "Der Mann für grobe Falle," *Der Spiegel*, no. 20, May 11, 1992, pp. 38–48, and Klaus Hartung, "Die Macht und der Schmutz," *Die Zeit*, Feb. 7, 1992, p. 4. For analysis of the Stolpe case I draw also on Anne M. Sa'adah, "Justice and Democracy in United Germany: Reflections on the Stolpe Case," now revised as chapter 5 of *Germany's Second Chance: Trust, Justice and Democratization* (Cam-bridge, MA: Harvard University Press, 1998).

56. *Abschlußbericht des Stolpe-Untersuchungsausschusses des Landtags Brandenburg*, edited, abridged, and arranged thematically by Ehrhart Neubert (Cologne: Heinrich-Böll-Stiftung e.V., 1994), pp. 78–79.

57. *Abschlußbericht*, p. 155. Cf. Stolpe's declaration before the Landtag of Sept. 3, 1992, in Manfred Stolpe, *Demokratie wagen: Aufbruch in Brandenburg* (Berlin and Marburg: Schüren, 1994), pp. 65–66.

58. *Abschlußbericht*, pp. 268–272 (Stolpe's speech), 279–283 (Nooke), 285–286 (Bräutigam).

59. Manfred Stolpe, "Wer hierblieb, wollte das Land verbessern" (June 1990), now in Stolpe, *Den Menschen Hoffnung geben: Reden, Aufsätze, Interviews aus zwölf Jahren* (Berlin: Wichern, 1991), pp. 249–255 (p. 254). Cf. "Spiegel-Gespräch mit Ministerpräsident Manfred Stolpe," *Der Spiegel*, no. 21, May 18, 1992, pp. 32–36, where he repeated that he did not realize he was "Sekretär" until February 12, and also maintained that the general public was sick of the whole controversy.

60. Robert Leicht, "Keine Flucht vor der Vergangenheit. Mit oder ohne Erich Honecker: Die Gerechtigkeit muß ihren Lauf nehmen," *Die Zeit*, Dec. 20, 1991, p. 1.

61. For accounts of the Wall shootings, " 'Sie wirft schatten bei Nacht,' " *Der Spiegel*, no. 22, May 27, 1991, pp. 18–22; and " 'Wir machen alles gründlich': Die Todesgrenze der Deutschen (I): Schreibtischtäter aus Wandlitz," ibid., no. 26, June 24, 1991, pp. 58–83; also " 'Taktisch klug und richtig': Die Todesgrenze der Deutschen (II): Protokolle über Schießbefehl und Republikflucht," ibid., no. 27, July 1, 1991, pp. 52–71. The *Spiegel* series accompanied the first Mauerschützen trials. For coverage of the Gueffroy trial, see Gisela Friedrichsen, "Wer so auf Menschen schießt," *Der Spiegel* no. 5, Jan. 27, 1992, pp. 40–43. A television report based on archival material of the border troop command also appeared at this time and was then issued as a book: Werner Filmer and Herbert Schwan, *Die Opfer der Mauer— Protokolle des Todes* (Munich: Bertelsmann, 1991). For a general overview of the legal situation as of 1993, see Herwig Roggemann, *Systemunrecht und Strafrecht am Beispiel der Mauerschützen in der ehemaligen DDR* (Berlin: Berlin Verlag Arno Spitz, 1993). For a list of the regulations comprising the Schießbefehl, see p. 54, n. 102. For a journalist's account of the issues in the context of other issues of repression, complicity, and postcommunist justice in Eastern Europe, see Tina Rosenberg's impressive *The Haunted Land: Facing Europe's Ghosts after Communism* (New York: Vintage, 1996), pp. 261–305.

62. Opinion partially reprinted in *Frankfurter Rundschau*, April 11, 1992, p. 11. Before 1933 Radbruch had been a staunch legal positivist, which was what made his 1946 concession to natural law or higher-law principles more authoritative. On the general conflict between legal positivism and natural law appeals in the post-1989 jurisprudence, see Andrew Tauber, "Tyranny on Trial: Natural Law and Legal Posi-

tivism in the Federal Republic of Germany" (Ph.D. dissertation, Massachusetts Institute of Technology, 1996). Cf. also Hans Schueler's comment at the opening of the Gueffroy trial, "Im Namen des geplagten Volkes. Zum zweiten Mal muß mit einer deutschen Diktatur ins Gericht gegangen werden," *Die Zeit,* July 26, 1991, p. 1.

63. See Roggemann, *Systemunrecht und Strafrecht,* pp. 59–60. I have also relied on Robert Alexy, *Mauerschützen. Zum Verhältnis von Recht, Moral, und Strafbarkeit. Berichte aus den Sitzungen der Joachim-Junius-Gesellschaft der Wissenschaften e.v. Hamburg* 11, 2 (Göttingen: Vandenhoeck und Ruprecht, 1993). By citing the human rights convention, the court avoided the difficulties of imposing ex post facto legal criteria. Nonetheless, both Alexy (pp. 15–20, 25–30) and Roggemann (pp. 65–68) believe that there were problems with the court's reasoning and that it was not clear the 1966 convention bound the GDR. Instead, Alexy argues, the formula of "extreme injustice" could have stood on its own and in fact set limits to GDR legislation at the time. Alexy provides a guide to the voluminous legal literature; he also feels that the guards should not have been expected to recognize the "extreme injustice" of their action in light of the general approval that the regime enjoyed at home from intellectuals and the church as well as from aboad. The Radbruch formula cannot "cognitively overburden" those on trial if they are to be held responsible. For the Schmidt case opinion (and two others: the Gueffroy case and the Sievert case), see Roggeman, *Systemunrecht und Strafrecht,* pp. 80–160.

64. *General-Anzeiger,* Bonn, May 24, 1995, p. 4, including background of the spy cases and selections from the court opinion.

65. Luc Hoyse, "Justice after Transition: On the Choices Successor Elites Make in Dealing with the Past," *Law and Social Inquiry* 20, 1 (winter 1995): 51–78. For a related discussion of judicial treatment of genocidal crime, see Mark J. Osiel, "Ever Again: Legal Remembrance of Administrative Massacre," *University of Pennsylvania Law Review* 144, 2 (Dec. 1995): 463–704, an exemplary discussion.

66. On the Czech and other East European cases, see Herman Schwartz, "The Lustration Decisions of the New Central European Constitutional Courts," speech at Constitutional Court Conference, Warsaw, Sept. 10, 1994. Also Schwartz, "Lustration in Eastern Europe," *Parker School Journal of East European Law* 1, 2 (1994): 141–171, and Rosenberg, *The Haunted Land,* pp. 67–121.

67. Rudolf Wassermann, "Dritte Schuld der Deutschen? Die neue Amnestiedebatte belastet die Strafverfolgung," *Recht und Politik* 30, 3 (Sept. 1994): 138–142. For a report on trial results as of spring 1994, see Christof Schaefgen (leader of the task force on government criminality at the Berlin prosecutor's office), "Die Strafverfolgung von Regierungskriminalität der DDR—Probleme, Ergebnisse, Perspektiven," ibid., pp. 150–160. He cited 1,162 cases settled in Berlin since unification, and 52 cases of violence at the frontier, still to be settled.

68. Collected in Albrecht Schönhofer, ed., *Ein Volk am Pranger? Die Deutschen auf der Suche nach einer neuen politischen Kultur* (Halle: Aufbau Taschenbuch Verlag, 1991).

69. Petra Bock, "Von der Tribunal-Idee zur Enquete-Kommission," *Deutschland Archiv* 28, 11 (Nov. 1995): 1171–1183. Also, Schorlemmer, "Gerichte reichen nicht. Ein Tribunal ist vonnöten," *Tagesspiegel*, Sept. 13, 1991; the similar proposal for a "tribunal" to deal with the past by Wolfgang Thierse of the SPD, "Schuld sind immer die Anderen. Ein Plädoyer für die selbstkritische Bewältigung der eigenen Geschichte," *Die Zeit*, Sept. 6, 1991, p. 13; and Thierse, "Weder Rechthaberei noch Selbstmitleid," *taz*, Nov. 26, 1991, p. 11. But cf. Richard Schröder, "Gesinnungs-Justiz ist Unrecht," *Die Zeit*, Dec. 13, 1991, p. 5, and interview with Eppelmann, *Der Spiegel*, no. 10, Mar. 10, 1992, pp. 29–37.

70. The materials of the first Enquete-Kommission were published under Bundestag auspices as *Materialien der Enquete-Kommission, "Aufarbeitung von Geschichte und Folgen der SED-Diktatur in Deutschland,"* in both a thirty-volume hardcover edition by Nomos Verlag (Baden-Baden, 1995) and an 18-volume paperback series by Suhrkamp Verlag (Frankfurt am Main, 1995). A second Enquete-Kommission concerned with "Überwindung der Folgen des SED-Diktatur im Prozess der deutschen Einheit" was established in 1995.

71. See the indices and thoughtful comments by M. Rainer Lepsius, "The Legacy of Two Dictatorships and Democratic Culture in United Germany," *Schweizerische Zeitschrift für Soziologie / Revue suisse de sociologie* 21, 3 (1995): 765–776. Questioned in 1992, 1993, and 1994, up to 54 percent of East Germans continued to believe that the overall situation had improved; the number believing that the economic situation was bad declined from 60 percent to 30 percent, and the number believing their own economic situation was good rose from 30 percent to 55 percent. Lepsius cautions that political passivity and a sense of collective inferiority still persisted as deficits of a democratic political culture.

EPILOGUE

1. Robert Leicht, "Aufbruch zur neuen Republik," *Die Zeit*, July 7, 1995, p. 1.

2. Monika Zimmermann, "Ende einer Andacht," *Der Tagesspiegel*, July 7, 1995, p. 1.

3. Ibid.

4. Christof Conrad, Michael Lechner, and Welf Werner, "East German Fertility after Unification: Crisis or Adaptation," *Population and Development Review* 22, 2 (June 1996).

5. "Stolz aufs eigene Leben," *Der Spiegel*, no. 27, July 3, 1995, pp. 40–52.

6. Cf. Stefan Berger, "Viewpoint: Historians and Nation-Building in Germany after Unification," *Past & Present*, no. 148 (Aug. 1995): 187–222.

7. For a collection of the new right intellectuals: Heimo Schwilk and Ulrich Schacht, eds., *Die Selbstbewusste Nation* (Berlin and Frankfurt am Main: Ullstein, 1994); phrases cited are used by Reinhard Maurer, "Schuld und Wohlstand: Über die westlich-deutsche Generallinie," pp. 77, 83, and Klaus Rainer-Rohl, "Morgenthau und Antifa: Über den Selbsthaß der Deutschen," pp. 97–98.

8. Timothy Garton Ash, *In Europe's Name: Germany and the Divided Continent* (New York: Random House, 1993), p. 385. In fact, it may be becoming almost normal for many states, like many marriages, to come apart.

9. "Interview mit Joachim Gauck," *Deutschland Archiv* 28, 11 (Nov. 1995): 1228–1232, citation from p. 1232.

A Note on Sources

ARCHIVAL SOURCES AND ABBREVIATIONS

Bundesarchiv Potsdam (BA: Potsdam; formerly Deutsches Staatsarchiv)

Akten des Ministerrats der DDR
  Sitzungen des Ministerrats der DDR: Series DC 20 I/3
  Sitzungen des Ministerrats der DDR: Series DC 20 I/4

DC 20 I/3 extends through the end of the state; DC 20 I/4 carries through November 1989. Footnote references include the sequential file numbers of the archival folders. These documents include agendas, discussion transcripts, recorded decisions, and the reports and planning papers that formed the basis of deliberation. Although the Ministerrat, or Council of Ministers, presided over by Willi Stoph and grouping "ministers" who headed each important industrial sector, was not formally a party body and had little power, its deliberations during the terminal crisis of the GDR were often frank and revealing. The prefix "D" was to be assigned by the Bundesarchiv for all documents of the German Democratic Republic; however, individual archival folders are usually labeled without the "D," that is, as series C20.

Bundesarchiv Potsdam/Berlin (BA: Potsdam/Berlin)

Akten der Staatlichen Plankommission der DDR = DE 1.
When I consulted them, these files were in provisional storage at the former Stasi headquarters in East Berlin, and cataloged under the signature E 1. The collection is massive and essential for the economic history of the GDR. I researched only those documents culled for the use, or recording the activity, of long-term director Gerhard Schürer.

Bundesarchiv-Stiftung Archiv der Parteien und Massenorganisationen der DDR (BA-SAPMO)

This branch of the Bundesarchiv includes the records that were formerly housed in the PDS Archive in East Berlin. The PDS Archive originated in turn as the archive of the Institut für Marxismus-Leninismus of the SED, that is, the ruling party, before 1989. In the autumn of 1995 the documents were moved to a new depository in Berlin-Lichterfelde; I consulted them in the original site. BA-SAPMO records cited here include:

SITZUNGEN DES POLITBÜROS (FULL TITLE: PROTOKOLLE DER SITZUNGEN DES POLITBÜROS DES ZENTRALKOMITEES DER SOZIALISTISCHEN EINHEITSPARTEI DEUTSCHLANDS)

Reinprotokolle (J IV 2/ 2/volume number)
Arbeitsprotokolle (J IV 2/2A/volume number)
These records only rarely include discussion transcripts; they comprise agendas and documents and reports presented for discussion. The Arbeitsprotokolle include reports and other materials circulated for discussion at the respective meetings; the Reinprotokolle generally, but not always, contain less supporting material. The two series run in parallel, with volume numbers keyed to meeting dates. The Politbüro of the Central Committee of the SED was the most important decision-making body of the GDR.

TAGUNGEN DES VORSTANDES DES ZENTRALKOMITEES DER SED (IV 2/1/VOLUME NUMBER)

The Central Committee was nominally the supreme organ of the party for the stretches between party congresses. Its large Vorstand or Executive functioned as a sort of legislative organ, with its Politbüro serving as a collective executive. The records include extensive stenographic transcripts of Central Committee debates.

INDIVIDUAL OFFICE FILES

Büro Kurt Hager
Büro Werner Jarowinsky
Büro Egon Krenz
Büro Günter Mittag
The office files are now being renumbered under one continuous archival signature: DY 30/five-digit volume number. Büro Egon Krenz remains cited as IV 2/2.039/ volume number.

Documents of the Ministry for State Security (MfS), Economic Branch or Division HA XVIII

These were consulted at the offices of the historical section of the Gauck Behörde (Bundesbeauftragte für die Unterlagen des Staatssicherheitsdienstes der ehemaligen DDR), directed by Klaus Henke. These are classified as ZAIG (Zentrale Auswertungs- und Informationsgruppe) plus volume number.

PUBLISHED PRIMARY SOURCE MATERIAL

Several collections of Stasi records were published shortly after the MfS documents were taken over by the citizens movement in early 1990. A sample of Stasi situation reports and memos appeared as *"Ich liebe euch doch alle . . .": Befehle und Lageberichte des MfS. Januar–November 1989*, ed. Armin Mitter and Stefan Wolle (Berlin: Basis-Druck, 1989). Stasi penetration of the church emerges from Gerhard Besier and Stephan Wolf, eds., *"Pfarrer, Christen und Katholiken." Das Ministerium für Staatssicherheit der ehemaligen DDR und die Kirchen*, 2nd rev. ed. (Neukirchen-Vluyn: Neukirchener Verlag, 1992). Many collections of manifestos and reports of meetings were issued by participants in the protests after 1989: *Oktober 1989: Wider den Schlaf der Vernunft* (Berlin DDR: Neues Leben, and Berlin West: Elefanten Press, 1989); also Neues Forum Leipzig, *Jetzt oder Nie—Demokratie: Leipziger Herbst 1989* (Leipzig: Forum Verlag, 1989, and Munich: C. Bertelsmann Verlag, 1990); for reports by those arrested: *Schnauze. Gedächtnisprotokolle 7. und 8. Oktober 1989. Berlin, Leipzig, Dresden* (Berlin: Berliner Verlags-Anstalt Union, 1990); and the photo-reproduced "Ich zeige an, Berichte von Betroffenen zu den Ereignissen am 7. und 8. Oktober 1989 in Berlin," assembled by the "Arbeitsgruppe 'Materialsichtung' of the Zeitweilige Kommission der Stadtverordnetenversammlung von Berlin." For a good English-language set of interviews with opposition leaders, consult Dirk Philipsen, *We Were the People: Voices from East Germany's Revolutionary Autumn of 1989* (Durham, NC: Duke University Press, 1993).

For continued publication of East German primary source material and well-informed interviews with East German political actors the *Deutschland Archiv* is indispensable. Through 1995 it appeared as a monthly; since early 1996 it has switched to a bimonthly format.

I relied on the following newspapers: the centrist and sometimes conservative *Frankfurter Allgemeine Zeitung* (*FAZ*) as the paper of record; the Munich *Süddeutsche Zeitung* for liberal, well-informed daily coverage; *Die Zeit*, as the weekly paper of opinion, specializing in editorial reflection usually by liberal and social democratic columnists; the *Berliner Tagesspiegel* for coverage especially of Berlin and cultural or educational developments; and, perhaps most useful, the *Berliner Tageszeitung*, known familiarly as the *taz*, which enjoyed its glory days during 1989–1990 as an irreverent journal with fresh inside coverage of East German events. The *Tageszeitung* collected its reports and commentary in several chronological anthologies issued as *taz: DDR Journal zur Novemberrevolution*, 2 vols. (Frankfurt am Main: Tageszeitungsverlagsgesellschaft, 1990). Some items of interest appeared also in the SPD-oriented *Frankfurter Rundschau* and the conservative *Die Welt*. The weekly news magazine *Der Spiegel* is indispensable for its roundup articles, usually well informed but with pronounced editorial slants. Surveying the press was facilitated by the massive compendia of newspaper and magazine articles published by the government's information office: *Deutschland 1989* and *Deutschland 1990: Dokumente zu der Berichterstattung über die Ereignisse in der DDR und die deutschlandpolitische Entwicklung* (Bonn: Presse- und Informationsamt der Bundesregierung, 1993) for 1989 and 1990.

Extensive testimony as well as written evaluations of conditions in the former GDR was presented to the Bundestag's Enquete-Kommission and has been published as *Materialien der Enquete-Kommission "Aufarbeitung von Geschichte und Folgen der SED-Diktatur in Deutschland" (12. Wahlperiode des Deutschen Bundestages), Herausgegeben vom Deutschen Bundestag*, 9 volumes in 18 partial volumes (Baden-Baden: Nomos, and Frankfurt am Main: Suhrkamp, 1995), simultaneous hardback and softback editions. For the origins of this Enquete-Kommission, see chapter 6. Given the recent date of publication, I have been able to use this source only sketchily; however, many of the experts' reports included recapitulate separately published articles.

Memoir material was important and full citations will be found in the endnotes to the various chapters. Thus, memoirs concerned with the earlier German Democratic Republic are cited in chapter 1; those treating the political crisis of the GDR are cited in chapter 3; Soviet and other memoirs dealing with the diplomacy of unification in chapter 5, and so forth. The GDR Oral History Project of the Hoover Institution, A. James McAdams principal investigator, has been conducting and transcribing an extensive series of interviews with GDR leaders and dissenters; those consulted are listed in the notes.

SECONDARY SOURCES

Books and articles are cited only in the endnotes. For works dealing with the GDR and its longer history, see the notes for chapter 1. For material on the economy of East Germany and the CMEA (or Comecon), including statistical compendia, consult the notes to chapter 2, to chapter 5 (2 = 1 or 1 = 1? The Economics of Unification), and to chapter 6 (Industrial Receivership). For treatments of new political groupings, including the Citizens Movements and New Forum, and their programs, chapters 3 and 4 are relevant. Books and articles on the Stasi are noted in chapter 1 again (Privilege, Secrecy, and Complicity), at different points in chapter 3, and again in chapter 6 (The Old Regime on Trial). The international framework is based on work cited in chapters 1 and 5. Reflections on the nature of the regime and totalitarianism more generally are found in chapters 1, 4, and 6.

Index